FORTY YEARS OF
LANDSCAPE ARCHITECTURE:
CENTRAL PARK

Frederick Law Olmsted
About 1860

FORTY YEARS OF LANDSCAPE ARCHITECTURE: CENTRAL PARK

FREDERICK LAW OLMSTED, SR.

EDITED BY

FREDERICK LAW OLMSTED, JR.

AND

THEODORA KIMBALL

THE MIT PRESS
CAMBRIDGE, MASSACHUSETTS, AND
LONDON, ENGLAND

This edition is reproduced from Volume 2 of *Frederick Law Olmsted, Landscape Architect, 1822–1903: Forty Years of Landscape Architecture; Being the Professional Papers of Frederick Law Olmsted, Senior.*
The original publisher was G. P. Putman's Sons, New York and London, and it was copyrighted in 1928 by Frederick Law Olmsted.

First MIT Press Paperback Edition, October 1973
ISBN 0 262 15009 3 (hardbound)
ISBN 0 262 65006 1 (paperback)
Library of Congress catalog card number: 73–14121

Printed in the United States of America

PREFACE

In Volume One of *Forty Years of Landscape Architecture* the Editors presented some brief notes on the life of Frederick Law Olmsted, Senior, together with a few selections from his early letters and writings, to serve as a background for a projected series of volumes containing his most important professional papers. Central Park, designed in collaboration with Calvert Vaux, was chosen as the subject of Volume Two, both because it was Mr. Olmsted's first great work of landscape architecture and because it offered the most connected sequence of papers dealing with park design and management.

Furthermore, as the Editors stated in the preface to Volume One, the history of Central Park was "considered of such importance in the development of the City of New York that the Russell Sage Foundation," in connection with the surveys undertaken by the Regional Plan of New York and Its Environs, "made a special grant to enable the Editors of the Olmsted Papers to produce a monograph on Central Park which shall not only present the Park from the standpoint of design, but shall also give a connected history of its conception, design, construction, and management up to the time of its fullest development before its principal designers lost touch with it in the 80's. The volume will therefore offer not merely, or even primarily, Mr. Olmsted's personal contribution as a designer, but rather the conception of the Park as he always regarded it,—as a great collaborative effort in and for a democratic community."

In view of the movement on the part of the citizens of New York to save Central Park from the deteriorating effects of neglect and misuse which it has suffered during the last few decades, and to restore it for the enjoyment of present and future generations, this volume devoted to the Park is full of significance. Here Park defenders may find clear and convincing statements, by the designers, of the reasons underlying the development of the Park's design and opinions as to its possibilities for deep-rooted usefulness in the

life of the City of New York. Those who would find "a solid
ground of resistance to dangers" threatening the integrity of
Central Park, can take as a text the words to be found on page
248: *"The Park throughout is a single work of art, and as such,
subject to the primary law of every work of art, namely, that it shall be
framed upon a single, noble motive to which the design of all its parts,
in some more or less subtle way, shall be confluent and helpful."*

Moreover, in the long series of papers occasioned by the problems
of a single great park, its designers set forth principles of park
design in general, and of parks in relation to the city plan, which
have enduring value and inspiration for the landscape architect,
the student, the park official, and all those who would more intelligently use and appreciate the many landscape parks to the formation of which the early success of Central Park gave the initial
impetus. To the student of the history of the landscape art in
America the definitions of landscape architecture and of the nature
of parks which may be found in hitherto unpublished correspondence
of Mr. Olmsted and Mr. Vaux,—as, for instance, on pages 74 and
212,—are vastly illuminating, and show that certain perplexing
problems in matters of terminology and scope are not so much
nearer solution in our present day.

The Olmsted and Vaux papers relating to Central Park comprise
numerous reports published in official documents or as pamphlets
—most of which have long been out of circulation—and in addition
many unpublished letters, notes, and drafts—most of these latter
from Mr. Olmsted's hand—written with greater frankness and freedom than the papers which were prepared with a view to publication
at the time. All these Central Park papers, which form Part Two
of the present Volume, have been grouped by subject (as the Table
of Contents will show) in order to give a more logical and consistent
presentation of the designers' conception of the general design,
of planting, of architectural features, and of the use and "keeping"
of the Park. The most important of the papers have been given
in full, many of the lesser have been abbreviated. Preceding each
group will be found a little editorial introduction, which sets the
papers somewhat in relation to each other and to the history of the
Park.

The connected narrative account which forms Part One of the
volume is intended to lay before the reader first the historical background of the park movement in Europe and America, and then the
evolution of a great landscape park for the City of New York, in its

political, administrative, and cultural aspects, using as many quotations as possible from contemporary discussions which throw light on the developing influence of the Park. Chapters I through XII (with the exception of X which is a reprinting of Mr. Olmsted's *Spoils of the Park*) have been written by Mrs. Theodora Kimball Hubbard with the invaluable advice and criticism of the present Mr. Frederick Law Olmsted, who has himself written Chapter XIII, which rounds out the review of the Park's evolution. This concluding chapter is intended not only as an interpretation of the immediate situation of Central Park but also as a direct contribution to the objects for which the Regional Plan of New York sponsored the grant of assistance for producing this monograph.

Since at the close of the series of Olmsted Papers a compiled index is projected, an index to Volume Two has not been deemed necessary, especially as the fullest possible footnote cross-references and an analytical table of contents have been here given. Furthermore, in order to offer a convenient summary for reference purposes, there have been given in the form of appendices: a chronological table of important events in the history of the Park; a digest of the Acts of Legislature under which the Park was developed and administered; a record of those official documents of the Central Park which relate specifically to Central Park during the period of Mr. Olmsted's connection with it; and a brief bibliography of the most important other sources of information. Of these last, the authoritative account of Central Park by Dr. Edward Hagaman Hall in the Sixteenth Annual Report of the American Scenic and Historic Preservation Society (1911) should be mentioned as giving early historical and topographical facts as well as detailed recent history, together with a table of the names and dates of all Park Commissioners, which this present volume has not attempted to duplicate. Similarly, in the illustrations selected for this present volume, the Editors have tried to add to those already available in various publications,—such as, for instance, the original "Greensward" plan reproduced in I. N. P. Stokes's *Iconography* and the portraits in Samuel Parson's *Memories*,—rather than to repeat the latter merely for the sake of completeness.

It would be impossible either by picture, or by words in the brief space of this preface, to give an adequate appreciation of the many personalities connected with the development of Central Park. Mr. Olmsted, Senior, has paid his own tribute to the talents of Mr. Vaux, especially in the letters on pages 78 and 160 of this volume; and Mr. Olmsted and Mr. Vaux together have elsewhere in these pages recorded the names of Waring, Pilat, and Fischer for the engineering and planting skill which helped to realize their general design. To Andrew H. Green, the administrator and watch-dog of the Park funds, there are many references; and of subsequent defenders Samuel Parsons and William A. Stiles are conspicuous in later chapters. No acknowledgment, however incomplete, of the debt which the literary heirs of Frederick Law Olmsted, Senior, owe to the writings of several of these figures in Park history should omit a tribute to William Cullen Bryant and Andrew Jackson Downing, who fired the imagination of the citizens of New York to the novel enterprise of park-making.

Any acknowledgments to those who have materially assisted the Editors in the production of the present volume must necessarily be quite inadequate: to Mr. Bowyer Vaux, for his generous permission to use freely selections from his Father's papers; to the Regional Plan of New York, especially to the Director, Mr. Thomas Adams, for information kindly furnished in response to many requests, and to the legal staff, Messrs. Edward M. Bassett and Frank B. Williams, for advice and criticisms; to the Central Park Association, for its permission to use material from the present Mr. Frederick Law Olmsted's report of 1926; to the New York Public Library, especially the Local History, Prints, and Economics Divisions, and the Photostat Desk for constant courtesies, and to the Municipal Reference Library for substantial help in identifying documents; to the New York Historical Society Library, the Library of Harvard University and the Special Library of the Harvard School of Landscape Architecture, for the use of valuable material; to the Park Department of the City of New York for numerous courtesies, especially in connection with the original "Greensward" drawings; to Mr. Robert W. De Forest, Mr. I. N. Phelps Stokes, Miss Mabel Parsons, Dr. Edward Hagaman Hall, Mr. Harold A. Caparn, and Mr. Charles Downing Lay, for encouragement and assistance in various stages of the work; to Mr. W. B. Van Ingen, for his constant interest and help, and his kind preparation of the "Greensward" sketches for publication; to the members of the staff of Olmsted Brothers, who have been concerned with matters of proof and of illustrations, but especially Mr. Gordon J. Culham who has contributed liberally of his time in preparing the key map; to Mr. Henry V. Hubbard for criticisms on the manuscript of Part One; and, not least, to Major George Haven Putnam,

—cousin of Frederick Law Olmsted and one time subforeman on the Central Park during the summer vacation of 1859, as one may find from his delightful *Memories of My Youth*,—for his never-failing interest and wise guidance during his publication of this work.

T. K. H.

BROOKLINE, MASSACHUSETTS,
December 1, 1927.

CONTENTS

CENTRAL PARK, NEW YORK

AS A WORK OF ART AND AS A GREAT MUNICIPAL ENTERPRISE

PART I

A REVIEW OF THE HISTORY AND EVOLUTION OF THE PARK

CHAPTER I

PAGE

ORIGINS OF THE MUNICIPAL PARK MOVEMENT . . . 3

Meaning of the word Park—Public parks in England—Parks on the Continent—Public open spaces in the American Colonies.

CHAPTER II

THE BEGINNINGS OF A PARK FOR NEW YORK . . 18

The Letter of 1785—Open spaces provided in the Plan of the Commissioners of 1807—Pleasure gardens and park-like cemeteries— William Cullen Bryant's advocacy of a public park—Andrew Jackson Downing's appeals—Mayor Kingsland's Message, 1851 —The Park: How large and where?—The Act for a Central Park.

CHAPTER III

THE CENTRAL PARK CHOSEN 30

Its acquirement, uncurtailed, 1856—Temporary government of the Park —The Board of Commissioners of the Central Park created by the Legislature, 1857—Party politics—F. L. Olmsted a candidate for Superintendent — Appointment — Introduction to the duties of superintendence.

CHAPTER IV

THE WINNING DESIGN BY OLMSTED AND VAUX . . 41

Announcement and terms of the competition for a design—Entry of Olmsted and Vaux—"Greensward" plan awarded first prize—The conception of the winning plan explained by its authors—Changes proposed—Appointment of Mr. Olmsted as Architect-in-Chief, 1858.

Contents

CHAPTER V

PAGE

EARLY DEVELOPMENT AND USE OF THE PARK .   .   .   51

The great construction force—Enlargement of the Park to 110th Street; cost of the Park—The Park in the light of contemporary European pleasure grounds — Guidance of public enjoyment — State Senate vindication of Park management—Immediate influence of the Park on public taste.

CHAPTER VI

THE PARK DURING THE CIVIL WAR AND AFTER .   .   .   68

Work on the Park not discontinued—Resignation of the Landscape Architects; their relation to Andrew H. Green—The Park to 1865; the work of Ignaz I. Pilat—Return of Olmsted and Vaux; their relation to each other and to the Park plan—The development of the Upper Park—Museums—The location of the Zoo.

CHAPTER VII

THE TWEED RING AND THE PARK   86

The Ring in power—The Department of Public Parks—Discharge of Olmsted and Vaux—Damaging alterations in the Park—Public awakening.

CHAPTER VIII

A PERIOD OF REHABILITATION, 1871–1873   .   .   .   92

A new Board—Reappointment of Olmsted and Vaux; Mr. Olmsted's Presidency of the Park Board—A general stock-taking of the Park, 1872–1873—Park keeping—Administrative difficulties.

CHAPTER IX

THE PARK UNDERMINED BY POLITICS   104

Harassing years—The politicians unleashed—Dismissal of Mr. Olmsted—Public protests—The Park in 1880 and 1881.

CHAPTER X

"THE SPOILS OF THE PARK"   117

A reprinting of Mr. Olmsted's pamphlet of 1882.

CHAPTER XI

THE PARK IN THE LAST FOUR DECADES   156

The essential cause of the Park's decline—Ups and downs in the early eighties; the work of Samuel Parsons—Advice officially sought from the Park's designers—Continual threats at the integrity of the Park and its protection by public opinion—Attempts at rehabilitation.

Contents

CHAPTER XII

PAGE

THE INFLUENCE OF CENTRAL PARK ON AMERICAN LIFE   169

Central Park as a successful municipal enterprise—The impetus to outdoor recreation—The effect of the Park on the landscape art—The
inception of the American park movement in Central Park—The
influence of parks on other public improvements; city planning.

CHAPTER XIII

THE PARK IN RELATION TO THE CITY PLAN   .   .   .   187

The designers' conception of the functions of Central Park as a part of the
city plan—Relation to growth of city and to other park facilities—
Relation to general street traffic—Relation to zoning—The kinds of
scenic qualities held important for the dominant function of the Park
—Secondary recreational functions of the Park recognized by the
designers—Success in realizing the designers' conception—Failures
in the realization of the designers' conception—The test of time
applied to the soundness of the designers' conception—The future of
Central Park.

PART II

SELECTED PAPERS OF FREDERICK LAW OLMSTED AND CALVERT VAUX RELATING TO CENTRAL PARK

CHAPTER I

THE GENERAL DESIGN   211

Description of a Plan for the Improvement of the Central Park, by "Greensward" (F. L. O. and C. V.), 1858—Report of Special Committee
on Plan, Board of Commissioners, 1858—Report as to Proposed
Modifications in the Plan, from F. L. O. and C. V., 1858—A Review
of Recent Changes, by the Landscape Architects (F. L. O. and C. V.),
1872—Two letters to President of the Department of Public Parks,
from F. L. O., 1886.

CHAPTER II

CONSIDERATIONS OF CONSTRUCTION AND COST .   .   .   281

Particulars of Construction and Estimate for a Plan of the Central Park
(F. L. O. and C. V.), 1858—Report on Construction by Contract, by
Superintendent (F. L. O.), 1858—Report upon Changes made in
Original Plan and Their Cost, by Architect-in-Chief (F. L. O.), 1859—
Letter regarding classification of work for estimates, to Mr. Grant
from F. L. O., 1861—Letter regarding costliness of political interference in construction of the Park, from F. L. O., 1861—Letter
regarding results of undue reduction of appropriations for Park
maintenance, from F. L. O., 1875.

Contents

CHAPTER III

PAGE

PROFESSIONAL DUTIES OF DESIGN AND SUPERINTENDENCE .   305

Selection from Report on European Visit, by F. L. O., 1859—Letter offering F. L. O.'s resignation as Architect-in-Chief and Superintendent, 1861—Letter analyzing difficulties in current executive system, from F. L. O., 1872—Letter offering F. L. O.'s resignation on ground of his untenable position as executive officer, 1873— Explanation of main divisions of responsibility in the Park organization, memorandum by F. L. O., 1874.

CHAPTER IV

THE CHOICE AND CARE OF PLANTATIONS   .   .   .   330

Report from Superintendent (F. L. O.) relative to Trees, 1857—Descriptive Guide to the Arboretum, "Greensward" Plan, 1858—Letter regarding inspiration from tropical scenery for park planting, to Mr. Pilat from F. L. O., 1863—Letter regarding improvement of planting details, from O., V. & Co., 1870—Letter regarding progress work, and planting instructions, from F. L. O., 1872—"Superintendent of Central Park to Gardeners," draft of circular by F. L. O., 1873—Two letters on "Gardener Organization," from F. L. O., 1875—Letter regarding false economy in maintenance of plantations, from F. L. O., 1877— Observations on the Treatment of Public Plantations, by F. L. O. and J. B. Harrison, 1889.

CHAPTER V

ROADS, WALKS, AND RIDES   376

Letter regarding the System of Walks and Rides, from F. L. O., 1858— Report on Communication between the Terrace and the Reservoirs, and on the deficiency of shade, by F. L. O., 1872—Report on the Proposed New System of Walks in the Southeast Quarter of the Central Park, by F. L. O., 1872—Report on a Promenade, by F. L. O., 1875.

CHAPTER VI

BOUNDARIES AND ENTRANCES   391

Letter regarding boundary treatment of the Park, from F. L. O., 1860— Report (abridged) on Nomenclature of the Gates of the Park, by Standing Committee on Statuary, Fountains, and Architectural Structures of the Board, 1862—Letter submitting Study for Sixth and Seventh Avenue Entrances at Fifty-ninth Street, from O., V. & Co., 1869.

CHAPTER VII

THE USE AND ABUSE OF THE PARK BY THE PUBLIC   .   406

Letter regarding the posting of Park rules, to A. H. Green from F. L. O., 1860—Letter suggesting music from the water, to A. H. Green from F. L. O., 1861—Circular of inquiry regarding Park lighting, 1872—

Contents x

PAGE

Hand-bill, "To those having the care of Young Children," 1872—
Communication on concessions in the Park, from F. L. O., 1875—
Report on Applications for Appropriation of Ground in the Central
Park for special purposes, by F. L. O., Landscape Architect, 1874—
Papers regarding the difficulties of preserving green turf, by F. L. O.,
1874 and 1875—Report on Damage to Park by Crowds at unveiling of
Halleck Statue, by F. L. O., 1877.

CHAPTER VIII

THE PARK KEEPERS' FORCE: MANAGING THE PUBLIC . 437

Letter as to policing of Park, from F. L. O., 1860—Report relative to the
Police Force of the Department, by F. L. O., 1872—Instructions to
Keepers of the Central Park, 1873 (by F. L. O.)—Report on Changes
recently made in the Management of the Keepers' Force, by F. L. O.,
1873.

CHAPTER IX

BUILDINGS IN THE PARK 472

Report from O., V. & Co. relative to works in progress on their designs, 1870
—Report on Boat and Refreshment Houses on the Lake of the Park,
by F. L. O., 1873.

CHAPTER X

THE PROPER FUNCTION OF STATUARY IN THE PARK . . 486

Report of Committee of the Board on the subject of Statuary on the
Central Park, 1873—Communication on a Proposition to place a
Colossal Statue at the South end of the Mall, from F. L. O. and C. V.,
1874.

CHAPTER XI

THE ZOO 499

Report on Provision for Zoological Collections in Manhattan Square, by
O. & V., 1866—Circular letter against location of Zoo in Central Park
Meadows, signed by F. L. O. and C. V., 1870—Report on Disposition
of the Zoological Collection of the Department, by F. L. O. (and C. V.,
consulting), 1873—Report as to possibility of combined Zoological
and Botanical Garden in the Park, by F. L. O., 1878—Letter as to
the purpose and site of the Zoo, from F. L. O., 1890.

CHAPTER XII

VARIOUS ENCROACHMENTS PROPOSED AND WARDED OFF . 518

Letter regarding real purpose of Park in relation to subversive new projects
to C. V. from F. L. O., 1883—Letter giving reasons against Speeding
Track in Central Park, to Paul Dana from F. L. O., 1890—"The
Justifying Value of a Public Park" (Selections), paper by F. L. O., 1880.

Contents

APPENDICES

PAGE

I.—CHRONOLOGICAL TABLE 533
    Including important dates in the history of Central Park.

II.—LAWS RELATING TO CENTRAL PARK . . . 538
    Table of Laws, with Digests, 1853–1892.
    Central Park Arsenal Decision, 1920.

III.—THE FACTS IN THE VIELE CASE 554

IV.—BIBLIOGRAPHY 563
    A.   LIST OF DOCUMENTS RELATING TO CENTRAL PARK,
        1857–1878 564

    B.   SELECTED LIST OF BOOKS, ARTICLES, ETC.. . 571

ILLUSTRATIONS

PART I

FACING
PAGE

FREDERICK LAW OLMSTED, ABOUT 1860 . . *Frontispiece*

PARK LANDSCAPE 4

THE LAKE, CENTRAL PARK 24

CENTRAL PARK COMPETITION ADVERTISEMENT . *on page* 40

PARK LAND, BEFORE 1858 (OLD PHOTOGRAPH OF LAKE SITE),
AND "GREENSWARD" SKETCH ("NO. 5") OF LAKE . 44

MIXED TRAFFIC ON A TRANSVERSE ROAD IN 1859 . . 48

SKATING IN CENTRAL PARK AT NIGHT 66

THE PARK IN 1863 (OLD BIRD'S-EYE VIEW, LOOKING NORTH) 76

CENTRAL PARK IN SUMMER, 1865 (OLD BIRD'S-EYE VIEW,
LOOKING SOUTH) 80

A NAST CARTOON OF 1870 90

ACROSS THE BRIDLE PATH AND POND 96

A LANDING ON THE LAKE 120

FREDERICK LAW OLMSTED IN THE LATE 1880's . . 142

THE MALL IN ITS PRIME, 1906 168

COASTING IN 1924 174

CENTRAL PARK TO-DAY (AERIAL VIEW) 200

PART II

FACING
PAGE

THE OLMSTED AND VAUX DESIGN (PLANS 1858 AND 1868)   214

"GREENSWARD" SKETCH ("NO. 1") FOR THE LAKE IN LOWER
PARK   224

"GREENSWARD" SKETCH ("NO. 7") FOR MEADOW IN UPPER
PARK   232

WINTER SCENE, 1924   278

THE GORGE AT THE POOL   310

FACSIMILE OF OLMSTED LETTER, 1863   .   .   .   346

SKETCH SHOWING SCHEME OF GRADE SEPARATIONS   .   .   378

ROWING ON THE LAKE   416

A RUSTIC SHELTER ON A ROCKY LEDGE   .   .   .   478

BETHESDA FOUNTAIN ON THE TERRACE   .   .   .   492

DIAGRAM FOR ZOOLOGICAL BUILDING   .   .   *on page*   502

CARTOON SHOWING PROPOSED INVASIONS OF THE PARK *on page*   517

THE VIELE MAP AND PLAN, 1856   556

KEY MAP OF CENTRAL PARK (OVERLAY)   .   } *Inserted in*

AERIAL MAP OF THE PARK, 1925   .   .   .   } *back cover*

CENTRAL PARK

PART I. A REVIEW OF THE HISTORY AND EVOLUTION OF THE PARK

CHAPTER I

ORIGINS OF THE MUNICIPAL PARK MOVEMENT

Meaning of the word Park.

Whatever the various meanings of the word *park*,—to the cottager of Chaucer's time watching the deer over the paling of the manor woods, to the courtier of Louis XIV philandering through the broad allées at Versailles, to Mr. Humphrey Repton and Prince von Pückler-Muskau, to the East side urchin of today grasping his chance for play in Seward Park,—it always suggests to us some kind of a green open space with turf and trees. The best accepted derivation finds the source of the word in the *enclosure* of a place and another less common one in the preservation of game or trees within. When Mr. Olmsted used the term in his address "The Justifying Value of a Public Park" in 1870, he considered that he was entitled to restrict the meaning to a large tract of land set apart by the public for the enjoyment of rural landscape, as distinguished from a public square, a public garden, or a promenade, fit only for more urbanized pleasures.[1]

At the period just before the birth of the movement for municipal parks in Europe in the early nineteenth century, landscape parks were the property of nobility or royalty, and the public enjoyed the right to walk therein only in certain cases where royal graciousness had so provided. As the population of London had grown, St. James's Park, Green Park, Hyde Park and Kensington Gardens had been allowed to become public grounds and the French Revolution had opened the royal gardens of Paris. But there had not yet been established the responsibility of the municipality to provide for its citizens the restful sight of green landscapes and the opportunity for free exercise in the open air as the city slowly engulfed the country and made rural pleasures more and more inaccessible to the poorer population.

While the park was at first and long remained the peculiar possession of the nobility, the public place or square has been for cen-

[1] Cf. Part II, Chapter I, p. 212.

turies the ground of the people, be it as market, forum, or shaded walk; and the common, "a tract of ground, for pleasure or pasturage, etc., the use of which belongs to the public" (Webster), is also theirs by ancient rights.

An interesting recognition of the character of plaza and common may be found in the Royal Ordinances concerning the laying out of New Towns, issued by King Philip II from the Escorial in 1573 for the guidance of settlers in the New World.[1] Minute directions are given as to the size and proportions of the main square which is required to form the center of each town, and there is a provision that "A common shall be assigned to each town, of adequate size so that even though it should grow greatly there would always be sufficient space for its inhabitants to find recreation and for cattle to pasture without encroaching upon private property." Such an enlightened proprietor as William Penn, laying out his settlement of Philadelphia in North America, reserved a number of blocks in his plan as public squares more for future than for present benefit.

The history of the transference of responsibility for providing public breathing spaces, small and large, from kings and benevolent proprietors to the municipality itself may be well traced not only in England but also in Germany, both of which countries offer precedents for the action of New York in 1851 in setting about the establishment of a great public pleasure ground.

PUBLIC PARKS IN ENGLAND.

The early parks in England were private enclosures made by nobles and the Crown for the preserving of deer. During the middle of the sixteenth century contemporary accounts bitterly complain of the deer and of the enclosing of common lands for their use. Each park was an occasion of heartburning to the poor of the neighborhood who thus lost their commons.[2] Parliament generally upheld these parks, as well as extensive enclosures for sheep raising, but in 1592 an act was passed, which was liberal in spirit although in practice useless against the nobles who did not hesitate to violate it: "no person shall inclose or take in any part of the commons or waste grounds within 3 miles of the gates of the City

---

[1] Discovered in 1912 by Mrs. Zelia Nuttall, in the National Archives in Madrid and published in Spanish and English translation in the *Hispanic American Historical Review*, Vol. 4, No. 4, and Vol. 5, No. 2, Nov., 1921 and May, 1922.
[2] T. E. Scrutton. *Commons and Common Fields*, Cambridge University Press, 1887.

1926

Park Landscape

Looking across the Ball Field, Central Park

Photograph by Edward Heim

of London, nor sever nor divide by any hedges, ditches, pales or otherwise any of the said fields lying within 3 miles etc., to the hindrance of the training or mustering of soldiers, or *of walking for recreation, comfort and health of her Majesty's people.*" In several of the enclosure laws enacted during the long struggle between the large property owners and the small holders, all village greens are specifically reserved from enclosure.

At the time of the Commonwealth, there is an interesting and isolated example of royal property becoming a municipal park by resolution of Parliament. In 1649 Parliament passed an act presenting to the City of London the Richmond Great Park, formerly a possession of King Charles. And in 1650,—doubtless to settle questions which must have arisen as to the use of this property by the city,—Parliament passed a resolution, "That it was the intention of Parliament in passing the Act for settling the new Park at *Richmond* on the Mayor and Commonalty of the City of *London*, that the same should be preserved as a Park still, without Destruction; and to remain as an Ornament to the City, and a Mark of Favour from the Parliament unto the said City."[1] While this was not a municipal "Park" in our modern sense of the word, it was a large public open space belonging to the City which could scarcely fail to become a ground for public recreation; and it was ultimately opened to public use by the royal owners to whom the park was given back by the City after the Restoration. Downing describes its charms as a place for popular enjoyment in one of his letters to the *Horticulturist* in 1851.

Gradually from the days of the Plantagenets the public had been allowed the privilege of walking in the great royal hunting parks of London. Even before they were declared the property of the Commonwealth in 1649, hunting had gradually diminished and the parks had become fashionable resorts. By the latter part of the eighteenth century in St. James's Park, Green Park, Hyde Park, and Kensington Gardens, this privilege had become practically a public right.[2] The parks had been laid out by the Crown with a

---

[1] Quoted in *Richmond Park*, by Sir T. J. Nelson, 1883.
[2] Mr. Chubb of the Commons Preservation Society, who furnished to the editors valuable information on the London parks, states: "It is on record that Queen Caroline was debarred from taking in for her private use more of Hyde Park than the Kensington Palace Gardens enclosure. Walpole is recorded to have told her Majesty that the cost of any further enclosure would be 'Three Crowns.'" Mr. Chubb adds that since the Restoration "public access would seem to have been enjoyed subject to rules made from time to time 'for the better keeping of Hyde Park in order.'"

view to this public use, and travelers were wont to exclaim with admiration at the beauties thus made free to all.

At about the same period it became evident that there was advantage to be gained by the creation of parks and gardens in connection with land speculations. In this way Regent's Park was created out of Crown land, at the official instance of the Treasury, ultimately according to a design by Mr. Nash, Architect of the Commissioners of Woods and Forests. Actual work did not begin until 1812. In the center of the lands developed for building was reserved a park area, but this came only slowly into general public use.[1] Similarly in Liverpool, much later, the Prince's Park was laid out by private enterprise as a land speculation including "villas for the wealthy and promenades for the poor."[2]

It is fortunate that we have a very full and interesting record of the condition of England in regard to public open spaces through the work of a Select Committee appointed by Parliament in February, 1833, "to consider the best means of securing Open Spaces in the vicinity of populous Towns, as Public Walks and Places of Exercise, calculated to promote the Health and Comfort of the Inhabitants."[3]

This committee, after hearing a large amount of testimony from reliable witnesses representing rapidly-growing manufacturing towns all over England agreed to the following points:

1st. That during the last half century a very great increase has taken place in the population of large towns, more especially as regards those classes who are, with many of their children,

[1] Cf. the testimony in the Report of the Select Committee of 1833. Also in the British Museum may be seen two editions of a pamphlet: "Some Account of the Proposed Improvements of the Western Part of London by the formation of the Regent's Park, [etc.]," 1814 and 1815, which give the history of the enterprise, which apparently started purely as means of improving the Royal Revenues. However, in the very important Government Document describing the enterprise, First Report of The Commissioners of His Majesty's Woods, Forests, and Land Revenues, 1812, we read: "But His Majesty's Government having thought that, besides considering how the Annual Value of this Property might be best improved, it was incumbent on them to keep equally in view other purposes of a public nature, as well as to secure abundant means of free Air and Exercise, for the preservation of the Health of the inhabitants, Mr. Nash was directed after an interview with the Chancellor of the Exchequer, to reconsider the subject, and alter his Design, in the Contemplation of fewer Buildings and a greater extent of open Ground."

[2] Fraser's Guide to Liverpool, in 1858, gives the notice to the public set up on the grass: "If you carefully avoid walking on the grass it will remain green and beautiful for you."

[3] Report of the Select Committee, in British Parliamentary Papers, Vol. 15 of 1833.

almost continually engaged in manufacturing and mechanical employments.

2nd. That during the same period, from the increased value of property and extension of buildings many inclosures of open spaces in the vicinity of towns have taken place, and little or no provision has been made for public walks or open spaces fitted to afford means of exercise or amusement to the middle or humbler classes.

3rd. That any such provision of public walks and open places would much conduce to the comfort, health and content of the classes in question.

The Committee felt that there had been a "neglect of what would appear to be a duty of the government (as conducing to the health and content of the people)," in that "no adequate provision has been made for public walks, or any reservations of open spaces, giving facilities for future improvement"; and the Committee's "duty is to submit suggestions how this omission may be in some measure supplied."

Aside from London with its royal parks open free to the public, the only towns mentioned as having "some open space in their immediate vicinity yet preserved as a Public Walk" were: Liverpool, Bristol, Norwich, Nottingham, and Shrewsbury. At Manchester there was a society or committee for the preservation of public foot paths which had been "effectual in preventing many foot paths which would otherwise have been stopped up from the public." At Liverpool the St. James's Walk formed by the Corporation of Liverpool and kept up by them, part having been planted to form a garden and formerly much used, had been damaged by smoke and was no longer popular in 1833. A witness from London remarks that outdoor pleasures had diminished by the disuse of the tea gardens by upper laboring classes, "for some reason or other" not understood. Another witness from London complains that Moorfields,[1] a nice promenade with fine elms where he used to play as a boy, the property of the City, had been let by the City on building leases and "now the public are entirely excluded." The general lack of place for active recreation—"play-grounds"—and also of places for public bathing is constantly reiterated by witnesses in answer to the skillful questioning of the Committee.

Some of the suggestions made by the Committee to meet the situation thus universally apparent are: that a grant from the gov-

---

[1] Cf. William Penn's reference to this, p. 15, and the mention by *Veritas*, p. 18, *post*.

ernment should be made to towns to help finance the creation of public walks; that some of the money should be raised by local subscription; that a small rate should be assessed on property-holders; that proprietors of land developments should dedicate a certain amount of land for public walks; that recreation grounds should be operated, possibly with a nominal admission fee, and possibly by private companies; that a bill should be introduced into Parliament reserving land at least 100 yards wide along any new turnpike road or canal from or to any town above a certain population; that other legislation should be passed to simplify the exchange of entailed or corporate property and thus facilitate the acquisition of land for public grounds, and also to enable persons to bequeath or dedicate property for such purposes.[1] The Committee looked with some favor on the suggestion of a witness that there should be two classes of grounds; gardens, and play-places, in which latter only there should be the trifling admission fee. Public bathing places, also operated with a small fee, are recommended for all towns having available waters. Public walks along the banks of the Thames are especially recommended, London being classed as inferior to Paris, Lyons, and Florence in this respect. More large public grounds for London, especially the reservation of Kennington Common and Battersea Fields, are specified. The whole matter is left to the earnest and early consideration of the House of Commons as one touching the welfare of a large number of the population of England.

That little more hope lay in immediate action by Parliament than from city initiative may be gathered from an article in *Blackwood's Edinburgh Magazine* in 1839[2] called "The Lungs of London," in which an anonymous writer makes the following animated remarks *à propos* of St. James's Park:

> When I enter this park, my notions of government, let me tell you, become highly monarchical. I touch my hat to the memory of our kings who devised and confirmed to us these places of harmless recreation, and am more and more established in my contempt for your close-fisted, shabby, commercial republicans, . . . Let us never forget that the legislature treated Mr. Buckingham's bill for the establishment of public walks near great towns with almost silent contempt; and although they pass I know not

---

[1] In 1840 a wealthy silk manufacturer of Derby laid out and presented a public pleasure garden, the Derby Arboretum, to the inhabitants of the town. See the description by Mr. Downing in the *Horticulturist* for 1850.

[2] Aug., 1839, Vol. 46, pp. 212–227.

how many enclosure bills every session, it was not without much unseemly debate that they were prevailed upon to grant for the recreation of the commoners, thus dispossessed without compensation of their immemorial inheritance, as much of the land to be enclosed as you would whip a cat in. The necessity of public walks—when we say public, we *mean* public, not gentility-mongering places, but spaces thrown open freely and altogether to the lowest class of our labouring and manufacturing population, who need all the rational recreation we can afford them—is but too apparent. Genteel people are abundantly provided for already: they can afford to go down the Thames and up the Thames—to the suburbs, the parks, the country. . . . The poor artisan or labouring man . . . cannot afford time or means to set out with his wife and children on a Sunday voyage of discovery—and to find the shades of night, perhaps, falling around him just as he has succeeded in refreshing his eyes with a bit of any thing green. . . .

Let us hope that the Commissioners of Metropolitan Improvements will bestir themselves, and that in the east end of London—in Southwark and in Lambeth—something may be done. . . .

A very valuable illustration of enlightened sentiment in regard to public open spaces—doubtless stimulated by the discussions arising during the Parliamentary investigation and the subsequent much-debated bills—appears in the instructions to the Surveyors-General for South Australia and New Zealand, which recall the Royal Spanish Ordinances of 1573 already referred to.

The Letter of Instructions[1] by the Colonization Commissioners for South Australia to Colonel William Light, Surveyor-General for the Colony of South Australia, contains the following section: "When you have determined the site of the first town, you will proceed to lay it out in accordance with the 'Regulations for the preliminary sales of colonial lands in this country' (acre town lots). You will make the streets of ample width and arrange them with reference to the convenience of the inhabitants and the beauty and salubrity of the town; and you will make the necessary reserves for squares, public walks and quays." The town thus laid out by Colonel Light in 1836 was named Adelaide, and the "Park Lands" have remained a distinctive feature to the present day.

Three years later the Directors of the New Zealand Land Company issued even more liberal instructions for the reservation of

[1] British Parliamentary Papers for 1836, Vol. 36, Colonization of South Australia, Appendix No. 9.

open spaces, in their first town, afterward named Wellington, and, indeed, proved themselves precursors of the "Garden City" movement. The Surveyor-General, Captain Smith, was instructed as follows:[1]

> The Directors wish that, in forming the plan of the town, you should make ample reserves for all public purposes, such as a cemetery, a market-place, wharfage, and probable public buildings, a botanical garden, a park and extensive boulevards. It is, indeed, desirable that the whole outside of the town, inland, should be separated from the country sections by a broad belt of land which you will declare that the Company intends to be public property, on condition that no buildings be ever erected upon it.
> The form of the town must necessarily be left to your own judgment and taste. Upon this subject the Directors will only remark that you have to provide for the future rather than the present, and that they wish the public convenience to be consulted, and the beautiful appearance of the future city to be secured, so far as these objects can be accomplished by the original plan,—rather than the immediate profit of the Company.

Still a few years later we find a landmark in the park movement in England when the municipality of Birkenhead, having acquired land for a park, gave it to Mr. Paxton for design in 1844 and laid out the grounds in 1845. A description of this Park and the impression it made on Mr. Olmsted in 1850 have been given in Volume One.[2]

Mr. Downing's descriptions in 1851 of the older London parks, of Hyde Park, and Kensington Gardens, of St. James's and Green Parks, show how thoroughly popular these had become through long tradition; and his comments on the new Regent's Park and the newer municipal enterprise, Victoria Park, and his delight in Kew Gardens, Hampton Court, and Richmond Park, show how adequate the open spaces of London seemed to him in comparison with their paucity in New York.

Parks on the Continent.

The conscious movement for municipal parks in Germany dates from a decade or so earlier than the agitation in England. We find[3]

---

[1] These instructions are given in a little book by the secretary of the Company, John Ward, *Information relative to New Zealand compiled for the use of Colonists,* 2nd edition, 1840.

[2] Pp. 95–101.

[3] Hoffman, *Hygienische und sociale Betätigung deutscher Städte auf den Gebieten Gartenbaus,* 1904.

that in 1815 the *Stadtbaumeister* Harte of Magdeburg wrote a letter to the City Council calling attention to the fact that the various public gardens around Magdeburg had been destroyed during the late wars and that soon hardly a tree would be seen in the neighborhood. He pointed out that the town would be a sad place for those who loved rural pleasures, and that it was an obligation for the general good on the part of the authorities to do something about it. Although at this date Herrenkrug, an old city property already used somewhat as a recreation ground, was proposed as a public park, troublous times caused any action to be postponed until 1818 when the *Oberburgermeister* Franke declared publicly the need of a park provided by the municipality and went ahead with the proposed Herrenkrug park, out of which he hoped to make something worth while. This park, however, was not finished until 1845. In 1824 he undertook a more ambitious scheme, the Friedrich-Wilhelmsgarten, said to be the first municipal park in Germany actually laid out for that purpose as a new creation. The well-known garden-artist Peter Joseph Lenné was intrusted by the City Council of Magdeburg with the design of the new park. The letter[1] which Lenné wrote on this occasion to the *Oberburgermeister* of the city is of great interest:

It is not new to me that princes and rich private individuals should spend large sums on works of the finer garden art (*schönen Gartenkunst*). But an undertaking of this sort which from preliminary estimates, exclusive of buildings will cost not less than 18,000 Taler, on the part of a City Council, is the first example that has been tendered to me in my career as an artist.

It is undoubtedly true that the damage caused by the Napoleonic wars acted as the special stimulus in the case of Magdeburg, but the more general movement for municipal parks arose a little later from the spread of industrialism in Germany and the inadequacy of the tree-planted city walls and royal parks as places for popular recreation. Herr Bertram of Dresden[2] sees also a conscious wish on the part of municipalities to make up for the ravages of industrial growth by the improvements in appearance which parks and gardens bring.

The Friedrichshain in Berlin was set off by the municipality as a public park in 1840, and Munich and Frankfort, Dresden and

---

[1] Wüttke, editor, *Die deutschen Städte*, 1903, Vol. 1, Chapter 7.
[2] Who contributed the chapter in Wüttke already referred to.

Leipzig followed just before and during the years when Central Park in New York was first being thrown open to the public.

The impression which a traveler's account of the parks of Germany and the Continent made on Andrew Jackson Downing in 1848 has been recorded in the well-known dialogue printed in his *Horticulturist* for October of that year.

Traveler. I dare say you will be surprised to hear me say that the French and Germans—difficult as they find it to be republican, in a political sense—are practically far more so, in many of the customs of *social* life, than Americans.

Editor. Such as what, pray?

Trav. Public enjoyments, open to all classes of people, provided at public cost, maintained at public expense, and enjoyed daily and hourly, by all classes of persons.

Ed. Picture galleries, libraries, and the like, I suppose you allude to?

Trav. Yes; but more especially at the present moment, I am thinking of public parks and gardens—those salubrious and wholesome breathing places, provided in the midst of, or upon the suburbs of so many towns on the continent—full of really grand and beautiful trees, fresh grass, fountains, and, in many cases, rare plants, shrubs and flowers. Public picture galleries, and even libraries, are intellectual luxuries; and though we must and will have them, as wealth accumulates, yet I look upon public parks and gardens, which are great social enjoyments, as naturally coming first. Man's social nature stands before his intellectual one in the order of cultivation.

Ed. But these great public parks are mostly the appendages of royalty, and have been created for purposes of show and magnificence, quite incompatible with our ideas of republican simplicity.

Trav. Not at all. In many places these parks were made for royal enjoyment; but even in these they are, on the continent, no longer held for royal use, but are the pleasure grounds of the public, generally. Look, for example, at the Garden of the Tuileries—spacious, full of flowers, green lawns, orange trees and rare plants, in the very heart of Paris, and all open to the public, without charge. Even in third rate towns like the Hague, there is a royal park of 200 acres, filled with superb trees, rich turf, and broad pieces of water,—the whole exquisitely kept, and absolutely and entirely at the enjoyment of every well disposed person that chooses to enter.

Ed. Still, these are not parks or gardens made for the public; but are the result, originally, of princely taste, and afterwards given up to the public.

Trav. But Germany, which is in many respects a most instructive country to Americans, affords many examples of public gardens, in the neighborhood of the principal towns, of

extraordinary size and beauty, originally made and laid out
solely for the general use. The public garden at Munich, for
example, contains above 500 acres, originally laid out by the
celebrated Count Rumford, with five miles of roads and walks,
and a collection of all the trees and shrubs that will thrive in
that country. It combines the beauty of a park and a garden.

Ed. And Frankfort?

Trav. Yes, I was coming to that, for it is quite a model of this
kind of civilization. The public garden of Frankfort is, to my
mind, one of the most delightful sights in the world. Frankfort
deserves, indeed, in this respect, to be called a "free town"; for
I doubt if we are yet ready to evince the same capacity for self-
government and non-imposition of restraint as is shown daily
by the good citizens of that place, in the enjoyment of this beautiful public garden. Think of a broad belt, about *two miles long*,
surrounding the city on all sides but one (being built upon the
site of the old ramparts), converted into the most lovely pleasure
grounds, intersected with all manner of shady walks and picturesque glades, planted not only with all manner of fine trees
and shrubs, but beds of the choicest flowers, roses, carnations,
dahlias, verbenas, tuberoses, violets, etc., etc.

Ed. And well guarded, I suppose, by *gen-d'armes*, or the police!

Trav. By no means. On the contrary, it is open to every man,
woman and child in the city; there are even no gates at the various entrances. Only at these entrances are put up notices, stating that as the garden was made for the public, and is kept up
at its expense, the town authorities commit it to the protection
of all good citizens. 50,000 souls have the right to enter and
enjoy these beautiful grounds; and yet, though they are most
thoroughly enjoyed, you will no more see a bed trampled upon,
or a tree injured, than in your own private garden here at home.

Ed. There is truly a democracy in that, worth imitating in
our more professedly democratic country.

The character of these German parks was recognized by Downing as something new and distinct from that of the older type of
public garden or promenade such as, for instance, the Prater at
Vienna, the Alameda at Madrid, the Chiaga at Naples, and the
promenade at Berne, both mentioned with respect by Loudon in
his review of gardens and parks in the 1826 edition of his *Encyclo-
pædia of Gardening.*

Mr. Olmsted, who visited England about the same time as Mr.
Downing and the Continent several years after, dates the real rise
of public parks somewhat later. Recalling these origins, Mr. Olmsted said in his address before the American Social Science Association in 1880:

Allow me to use the term *park movement*, with reference to what has thus recently occurred on both continents. With us, it dates from Mr. Downing's writings on the subject in 1849.[1] But these could not have obtained the public attention they did, nor have proved the seed of so large a harvest, but for their timeliness, and a condition of expectancy in the soil upon which they fell.

Our first act of park legislation was in 1851. In 1853, the first Commissioners for the Central Park entered upon their duties. It was only in the latter year that some ill-considered steps were taken toward supplying Paris with its first public park. It was not until 1855 that Mr. Alphand came from Bordeaux, and gave the work (Bois de Boulogne) its final form and impetus. A little earlier, three small park undertakings had been entered upon in England. The leading one under the direction of Paxton, afterward Sir Joseph. I know of none in Germany,[2] Italy, or Belgium; but a few years afterward, I saw in each of these countries evidence that, about the same time, planting and gardening for the public benefit had taken new life.

Parks have plainly not come as the direct result of any of the great inventions or discoveries of the country. They are not, with us, simply an improvement on what we had before, growing out of a general advance of the arts applicable to them. It is not evident that the movement was taken up in any country from any other, however it may have been influenced or accelerated. It did not run like a fashion. It would seem rather to have been a common spontaneous movement of that sort which we conveniently refer to the "Genius of Civilization."

PUBLIC OPEN SPACES IN THE AMERICAN COLONIES.

In America, as abroad, the municipal park was a late development. In the New England colonies the traditional largely utilitarian type of public ground known in the old country appeared again spontaneously in the new. Boston set aside a common as early as 1634, and in 1640 protected it from future diminution. In 1728 its improvement began in recognition of its long use as a recreation ground.[3] The Lower Green at Newburyport is drawn out on the most ancient plat of the Old Town. Rowley Common was acquired about 1670 (by exchange of land) as a training field. All through Massachusetts, Connecticut and New Hampshire

---

[1] Cf. p. 22, *post*.

[2] He had evidently forgotten Downing's descriptions of Munich and Frankfort.

[3] The Public Garden in Boston, originally a marshy part of the common lands and illegally sold, was not repurchased until 1823. Another post-colonial enterprise commented on in *Boston Common or Rural Walks*, 1838, was what is now the Eastern Promenade at Portland, Maine.

numerous examples still exist of more or less beautiful village greens, of various origins, and in various states of preservation or retrogression from their original sizes and forms. But these commons were probably seldom, if ever, set aside by the colonists as any part of a conscious town planning scheme or predominantly for recreation.

In two of the English proprietary colonies, however, we find the same intelligent attention to the town of the future which the Spanish King and his advisers had shown in regard to their settlements in the New World. William Penn assigned five open squares in the plan for Philadelphia, drafted in 1682 by his Surveyor-General, Thomas Holme. The following description is said to be an extract from Mr. Holme's own account of his plan.[1]

> The city, as the model shews, consists of a large *Front-street* on each river, and a *High-street*, near the middle, from river to river, of one hundred feet broad; and a *Broad-street*, in the middle of the city from side to side, of the like breadth. In the center of the city, is *a square of ten acres*; at each angle to build houses for public affairs. There is also in each quarter of the city, *a square of eight acres*, to be for the like uses, as *Moorfields*, in *London.* . . .

The early historian of Pennsylvania regrets that these beneficial regulations "whose future great importance to the city, having since not been sufficiently considered and attended to, some of them have either been neglected, or violated."

General James Oglethorpe went much further in his plans for the principal city of his ideal colony of Georgia in 1733. Mr. Robert Wright[1] thus describes the settlement of Savannah[2]

> Although the first settlers were but 120 in number, Oglethorpe thought of those who were to come after them, and their descendants. Acting on the motto of the Trustees, "Not for themselves, but for others," his imagination depicted a populous city, with a large square for markets and other public purposes in every quarter, wide and regular streets crossing each other at right angles and shaded by rows of noble trees. . . . Even in his own lifetime, his expectations were in a great degree realized, but not so completely as afterwards.
>
> Knowing that man cannot live by bread alone, he made provision for future luxuries, and laid out a public garden which he

---

[1] Printed in Robert Proud's *History of Pennsylvania*, 1797, Vol. I, p. 244.
[2] In *A Memoir of General James Oglethorpe*, London, 1867, based on historical documents.

designed as a nursery to supply the colonists with white mulberry trees, vines, oranges, olives and other fruits for their several plantations, and appointed a gardener to take care of it.

Gen. Oglethorpe also had many of the fine forest trees spared when the site for the town was cleared.

When the proprietor re-visited his colony in 1736 he found substantial progress made in the carrying out of his plan: the streets were wide, the squares had been left, and each freeholder, besides his own town plot, had five acres outside the Common, to serve as garden and orchard. Oglethorpe was greatly pleased by the Public Gardens, which comprised ten acres of undulating ground in a delightful situation near the river. There is a charming description of this garden as he saw it in 1736 contained in Mr. Wright's *Memoir*.[1]

A facsimile of the original plan for Savannah shows no less than twenty-four of the small squares and open spaces in addition to the Public Garden and Common. So generous a provision for future needs has hardly a parallel in the early history of town planning. It is greatly to the credit of Savannah that a hundred and fifty years later when many cities were conspicuously lacking in public grounds, she had thirty-three acres in twenty-three public places, besides a ten-acre park and a twenty-acre parade ground.[2]

When Major L'Enfant drew up the plan for the Federal City under the guidance of Washington and Jefferson, in 1791, again there was a vision of a future city with stately parks and pleasure gardens. The plan shows fifteen squares, intended to be developed by the fifteen states, a grand cascade, a public walk, grand avenues, a President's park, and so on. In the bustle and haste of a young democracy's superabounding growth, many features of this generous plan for Washington were forgotten; and although some little attempt at park development was made in Downing's day, it was not until 1900 that the plan was rescued and given new life.

The Dutch colony of New Amsterdam was not unlike the New England colonies in their unthinking neglect of the future. The houses in old New York were built close together, the streets were narrow, and scarcely any open space was left in the oldest part of the town. One small place called the Bowling Green was kept free

[1] P. 109.
[2] Charles Eliot comments on this in his article "Parks and Squares of United States Cities" in *Garden and Forest*, Oct. 24, 1888.

of buildings, its use having been granted since 1732 to various specified persons in consideration of its upkeep; and in the upper part of the settlement a rather extensive waste of land called "The Fields" (of which a part is now City Hall Park) had been used as a common from early days. No attempt had been made to improve this land or the pond it contained and various encroachments gradually decreased its size.

Such was the situation in New York at the beginning of the Republican period. If parks were ever to be provided for the people of a future great metropolis, it would not be through the preservation of legacies from early colonial days but by some conscious effort of a democratic body of citizens to meet a proven need. How this came about will be traced in the next chapter.

CHAPTER II

THE BEGINNINGS OF A PARK FOR NEW YORK

THE LETTER OF 1785.[1]

TO THE MAYOR AND ALDERMEN OF THE CITY OF NEW-YORK.

I hope it will not be deemed presumption in an individual, to point out in a public address to you, any measure which relates to the advantage or convenience of the citizens over whom you preside. . . .

It is a very general complaint that there is not in this great city, nor in its environs, any one proper spot, where its numerous inhabitants can enjoy, with convenience, the exercise that is necessary for health and amusement.

Those whose affluence supplies the means, fly in their carriages to enjoy the refreshing breezes of the evening, during the sultry months of summer, thro' the different tours that our little island affords; . . .

In all cities of this magnitude, older countries have been ever attentive to contrive certain places, where the bulk of the citizens can enjoy the benefits of exercise and wholesome air. In London, the inhabitants have, at one end of the town, three extensive parks, the most convenient of which is St. James's, and at the other end of the city they have Moorfields. These places are laid out in walks, regularly planted with trees, and furnished throughout with garden benches; the walks are rolled, kept clean from grass; and the benches under the shade of venerable trees, afford a charming resting place. . . . Paris has her *Tuileries*, and the different gardens of the *Palais Royales*. And Dublin her squares, one of which (St. Stephen's green) is perhaps the largest in Europe, with a gravel walk all round, planted with full-grown elms; this green is an exact square of a mile in circumference. These places are all resorted to after the fatigues of the day. . . .

The size and consequence that this town must one day arrive at, ought strongly to impress the necessity of attending to this object, as well from a desire to contribute to the comfort and health of the inhabitants, as from the propriety of adding to the public ornaments of the city.

[1] Printed in the *New York Packet*, August 15, 1785.

In this view the Battery naturally presents itself as a subject capable of vast improvement; were the margin of this ground laid out with judgment, planted with a row of trees, and furnished with seats, from whence, after being jaded with the heats of August, we could enjoy the cool breezes of the evening, and admire the beauties of one of the finest harbours in the world—what an ornament would this city derive from it!

There is also another space of ground, which calls loudly for the hand of improvement—now a public nuisance, from whence the inhabitants of the neighbourhood are infested, during the summer season, with continual clouds of stinking dust, if not as pestiferous as the heated sands of the desert Arabia, yet sufficiently obnoxious, to demand immediate attention from those, who have the means of remedying the evil in their power. The ground I mean is the place commonly called the Fields.[1]—This place laid out with judgment and taste, would become a blessing to the inhabitants of New-York, and an elegant ornament to a fine city.

For the purpose of reaping advantage from the judgment of men where taste leads them to matters of this kind, I would take the liberty to suggest the mode by which the best plans are procured for public improvements in Great-Britain and Ireland; both from artists whose provence it immediately is, and from persons who amuse themselves by gratifying a passion for the arts.

When a public improvement is intended, an exact survey is made of the ground, with all the avenues leading to it. This ground survey is hung up on Change and other places of public resort, and a reward is offered for the three best plans that shall be produced on a certain day.[2] The best plan receives a reward (for instance) of one hundred dollars; the next but a compliment of fifty, and the third an acknowledgement of twenty-five. By this means a proper plan is adopted in the first instance, and in the next, the public have the satisfaction of seeing their money judiciously disposed of.

I would therefore take the liberty to observe, that it would be highly proper in the improvements I have mentioned, to have a survey of the grounds made on a large scale, and hung up in the Coffee-House; there will, no doubt, be many candidates for the honor of pre-eminence; and after the most eligible plan is fixed on, an estimate of the expense can easily be procured from workmen knowing in the business; which I would most sanguinely wish, may be found not incompatible, with the funds or resources of the Corporation.

.   .   .   .

VERITAS.

[1] Cf. p. 17.
[2] Cf. the competition instituted for the design of Central Park in 1857.

The suggestion for the improvement of the Fields contained in this letter was apparently brought further to public notice, for in the same year it was definitely proposed to enclose the ground "commonly called the Fields." In 1787 the improvements were actually begun by having paupers in the Alms House collect dirt and prepare the ground for seeding. In 1792, by public act, part of the land was enclosed by a fence and trees were planted. In 1821[1] the iron railing was continued all around what had then come to be called "the Park."

The land now Battery Park was made by filling in around the old Fort Clinton. Beginning in 1723, the area was gradually enlarged. In 1794 a license was granted for the sale of small drinks on the grounds, but not until 1826, after the Fort was given up, and the place leased for amusement as Castle Garden, was the Battery enclosed by an iron railing in recognition of its character as a park.

OPEN SPACES PROVIDED IN THE PLAN OF THE COMMISSIONERS OF 1807.

When the Commissioners of Streets and Roads appointed in 1807 to lay out Manhattan Island submitted their plan in 1811, they showed several spaces left open in the gridiron of streets, comprising seven "squares" or "places" and a Parade Ground extending from 23rd Street to 34th Street, and from Third Avenue to Seventh Avenue, these eight pieces of ground totalling about 450 acres. In their report, they stated:

It may, to many, be a matter of surprise that so few vacant spaces have been left, and those so small, for the benefit of fresh air, and consequent preservation of health. Certainly if the City of New York were destined to stand on the side of a small stream such as the Seine or the Thames, a great number of ample places might be needful; but those large arms of the sea which embrace Manhattan Island render its situation, in regard to health and pleasure, as well as to the convenience of commerce, peculiarly felicitous; when therefore, from the same causes the price of land is so uncommonly great, it seemed proper to admit the principles of economy to greater influence than might, under circumstances of a different kind, have consisted with the dictates of prudence and the sense of duty.

[1] The dates are from articles on the Park, with excerpts from old records, in *Valentine's Manual* for 1855 and 1856.

The idea of a Parade Ground was subsequently abandoned, and in 1838 the area of the remaining squares had been reduced to less than 120 acres.[1] The Park (City Hall) and the Battery added twenty acres to this, and Washington Square and the small downtown triangles and enclosed residential parks brought the total up to 170 acres.

By 1853, when the Act was passed authorizing the acquirement of the Central Park, this total had been reduced to 117 acres.

PLEASURE GARDENS AND PARK-LIKE CEMETERIES.

In New York of the early nineteenth century there were a number of popular pleasure gardens of which Vauxhall, Niblo's, and Contoit's are perhaps the best known. Vauxhall, at Astor Place, flourished until the late forties, on fine afternoons and holidays, its trim walks being crowded with women and children. Niblo's on Broadway was made over from Columbia Gardens[2] about 1828,— almost at the same time that Vauxhall Garden was cut in halves,— and remained for some time a green space, before it became merely a name attached to the theater which had come to form its principal attraction. Contoit's New York Garden, transferred to a successful location on Broadway in 1809, was also popular through the forties. But the spread of city buildings gradually destroyed the original rural character of these gardens, and their planted area suffered one encroachment after another, until in 1855 there remained only the memory of their pleasures.

Other places of outdoor resort were the rural cemeteries rapidly springing up, following the tremendous popularity of Mt. Auburn near Boston, the first rural cemetery (1831) to be provided in America.[3] Greenwood Cemetery had been laid out in New York, described by Downing in 1849 as "grand, dignified, and park-like." He estimated that something like sixty thousand people must have visited it in a season, many of these for the pleasures of its foliage

---

[1] There is a map of this date "Public Squares, Parks and places in the City of New York," surveyed by Francis Nicholson, City Surveyor, reproduced in *Valentine's Manual* for 1850. In the 3rd Annual Report of the Central Park Commissioners, for 1859, there is a table of areas and values of parks and squares in the City of New York, in 1856.

[2] For a description see article by Sarah Lewis Pattee, "American Parks a Century Ago," in *Landscape Architecture*, Oct., 1926, as well as references to other early pleasure gardens.

[3] There is an interesting volume of engravings by James Smillie, entitled *The Rural Cemeteries of America*, containing descriptive text: "Greenwood in 1846" and "Mount Auburn," published in New York by R. Martin, 1847.

and lawns. Lacking public gardens,—he even went on to suggest,—privately managed gardens might be laid out on the same plan as rural cemeteries, the proceeds of admission fees providing for their upkeep.

Another writer has ingeniously advanced the theory that when the new park-like cemeteries began to be filled up with monuments, the people looked for rural parks which should be free of mournful suggestion. However this may have been, the time was becoming ripe for the cause of public parks to be actively championed and before 1850 both Bryant and Downing had brought the issue squarely to public attention.

WILLIAM CULLEN BRYANT'S ADVOCACY OF A PUBLIC PARK.

It is singular that Mr. Olmsted should not have been familiar with Bryant's editorials in the New York *Evening Post* advocating a large public park more than four years before Downing's first letter in the *Horticulturist* touching this subject.[1] Indeed Mr. Olmsted and the authors of early histories of the Central Park seem to have been unanimous in ascribing the original proposal to Downing, and it is only very recently that the prior credit due to Bryant has been made clear.[2]

Although the first editorial "A New Park" in the *Evening Post* is dated July 3, 1844, as early as 1836 Bryant expressed the opinion to his family that the city of New York should reserve as a park the finest area of Woodland remaining there, before it should be too late. In 1844 he traversed the island and fixed upon the tract known as Jones' Wood as one suitable for park purposes. After suggesting that "If the public authorities, who expend so much of our money in laying out the city, would do what is in their power, they might give our vast population an extensive pleasure ground for shade and recreation," his Editorial points out the beauties and possibilities of Jones' Wood, and the charms of existing European pleasure grounds. He regrets the loss of the "Parade" provided for New York by the plan of the Commissioners of 1807, and justly complained that, while at the beginning of the century any one had been able to walk in a half hour from his home to the open fields, soon all Manhattan would be covered with brick and mortar.

[1] Cf. Chronological Table of the Park in Statistical Report of the Landscape Architect, 1873, in which 1849 is the first date given.

[2] The history of the *Evening Post* by Allan Nevins, published 1922, contains a chapter "New York becomes a Metropolis; Central Park," giving full references to Bryant's editorial leadership of the movement.

A year later, writing from London in glowing terms of the parks he was enjoying there, Bryant suggested a "central" reservation in New York:

> The population of your city, increasing with such prodigious rapidity; your sultry summers, and the corrupt atmosphere generated in hot and crowded streets, make it a cause of regret that in laying out New York, no preparation was made, while it was yet practicable, for a range of parks and public gardens along the central part of the island or elsewhere, to remain perpetually for the refreshment and recreation of the citizens during the torrid heats of the warm season. There are yet unoccupied lands on the island which might, I suppose, be procured for the purpose, and which, on account of their rocky and uneven surfaces, might be laid out into surpassingly beautiful pleasure-grounds; but while we are discussing the subject the advancing population of the city is sweeping over them and covering them from our reach.

Bryant and the *Evening Post* repeatedly brought the park project before the public. "Its editors had the more faith in it, they said, because while New Yorkers were somewhat slow in adopting plain and homely reforms, they were likely to engage eagerly in any scheme which wore an air of magnificence."[1]

ANDREW JACKSON DOWNING'S APPEALS.

Bryant's editorials thus made the public ear the more receptive to the arguments for parks set forth by Downing in his dialogue in the *Horticulturist* for October, 1848, called "A Talk about Public Parks and Gardens."[2] Again in July, 1849, he developed an idea previously suggested as to public cemeteries and public gardens.[3]

During his visit to England in 1850, he—like Bryant in 1845— used the London Parks[4] as a model and a reproach to the New Yorkers over-proud of their commercial metropolis. He wrote in August, 1850:[5]

> I will merely say, . . . that every American who visits London, whether for the first or the fiftieth time, feels mortified that no city in the United States has a public *park*—here so justly considered both the highest luxury and necessity in a great city.

---

[1] Nevins, *The Evening Post*, p. 196.
[2] Cf. *ante*, p. 12.
[3] Cf. *ante*, p. 21–22.
[4] Cf. *ante*, p. 10.
[5] Published in *Horticulturist* for Oct., 1850.

What are called parks in New-York, are not even apologies for the thing; they are only squares or paddocks.

Writing somewhat later, he closes his enthusiastic letter on the London parks[1] with the following paragraph:

We fancy, not without reason, in New-York, that we have a great city, and that the introduction of Croton water, is so marvelous a luxury in the way of health, that nothing more need be done for the comfort of half a million of people. In crossing the Atlantic, a young New-Yorker, who was rabidly patriotic and who boasted daily of the superiority of our beloved commercial metropolis over every city on the globe, was our most amusing companion. I chanced to meet him one afternoon a few days after we landed, in one of the great Parks in London, in the midst of all the sylvan beauty and human enjoyment I have attempted to describe to you. He threw up his arms as he recognized me, and exclaimed—"good heavens! what a scene, and I took some Londoners to the steps of the City Hall last summer, to show them *the Park* of New-York!" I consoled him with the advice to be less conceited thereafter in his cockneyism, and to show foreigners the Hudson and Niagara, instead of the City Hall and Bowling Green. But the question may well be asked, is New-York really not rich enough, or is there absolutely not land enough in America, to give our citizens public parks of more than ten acres?

Mayor Kingsland's Message, 1851.

The subject of a park for New York, due chiefly—it may be inferred—to·the publicity given the project by the *Evening Post*, became in 1850 a matter of politics. Both candidates for Mayor, Fernando Wood who was defeated and Ambrose C. Kingsland who (supported by the *Evening Post*) was elected, favored the establishment of a park.[2]

On April 5, 1851, Mayor Kingsland sent the following historic message to the Common Council of the City of New York:

TO THE HONORABLE THE COMMON COUNCIL:

Gentlemen:—The rapid augmentation of our population, and the great increase in the value of property in the lower part of the city, justify me in calling the attention of your Honorable

---

[1] In *Horticulturist*, June, 1851.

[2] A very graphic account of the fight for and against a park by the press of New York covering several years may be found in Mr. Nevin's book already referred to.

Photograph by Edward Heim   1926

The Lake, Central Park

Body, to the necessity of making some suitable provision for the
wants of our citizens, who are thronging into the upper wards.
which but a few years since were considered as entirely out of
the city.   It seems obvious to me that the entire tongue of land
south of the line drawn across the [City Hall] Park, is destined
to be devoted, entirely and solely, to commercial purposes; and
the Park and Battery, which were formerly favorite places of
resort for pleasure and recreation, for citizens, whose residences
were below that line, are now deserted.   The tide of population
is rapidly flowing to the northern section of the island, and it is
here that provision should be made for the thousands whose
dwellings will, ere long, fill up the vacant streets and avenues
north of Union Park.   [Union Square at 14th Street].

The public places of New York[1] are not in keeping with the
character of our city; nor do they in any wise subserve the purpose for which such places should be set apart.   Each year will
witness a certain increase in the value of real estate, out of the
city proper, and I do not know that any period will be more
suitable than the present one, for the purchase and laying out
of a park, on a scale which will be worthy of the city.

There are places on the island easily accessible, and possessing
all the advantages of wood, lawn and water, which might, at a
comparatively small expense, be converted into a park, which
would be at once the pride and ornament of the city.   Such a
park, well laid out, would become the favorite resort of all classes.
There are thousands who pass the day of rest among the idle and
dissolute, in porter-houses, or in places more objectionable, who
would rejoice in being enabled to breathe the pure air in such a
place, while the ride and drive through its avenues, free from
the noise, dust and confusion inseparable from all thoroughfares,
would hold out strong inducements for the affluent to make it a
place of resort.

There is no park on the island deserving the name, and while
I cannot believe that any one can be found to advance an objection against the expediency of having such a one in our midst, I
think that the expenditure of a sum necessary to procure and lay
out a park of sufficient magnitude to answer the purposes above
noted, would be well and wisely appropriated, and would be
returned to us four fold, in the health, happiness and comfort of
those whose interest[s] are specially intrusted to our keeping—
the poorer classes.

The establishment of such a park would prove a lasting monument to the wisdom, sagacity and forethought of its founders,
and would secure the gratitude of thousands yet unborn, for the
blessings of pure air, and the opportunity for innocent, healthful
enjoyment.

I commend this subject to your consideration, in the convic-

[1] See footnote on p. 21, *ante.*

tion that its importance will insure your careful attention and prompt action.

A. C. KINGSLAND, MAYOR.

The Committee on Lands and Places to whom this message was referred, reported favorably[1] on the idea of a park and recommended as the most suitable site Jones' Wood, the land first proposed by Bryant for this purpose in 1844.

On July 11, 1851, the Legislature of the State of New York passed an act[2] authorizing the taking of the desired land for a public park.

THE PARK: HOW LARGE AND WHERE?

Opposition to the taking of Jones' Wood immediately developed. Some wanted no park at all and some felt that an area of 160 acres was too small for the only large park in a great and growing city, like New York. Among the latter were Downing and Bryant.

In the *Horticulturist* for August, 1851, Downing's leading article, "The New-York Park," points this out, giving his conception of what the proposed park should hold in store.

Looking at the present government of the city as about to provide, in the People's Park, a breathing zone, and healthful

---

[1] The Committee's resolutions read:

Resolved, That it is highly desirable that a plot of land, lying between Sixty-sixth and Seventy-fifth streets, and Third avenue and the East river, and also, that portion of the Schermerhorn estate, lying adjacent to said plot, between Sixty-fourth and Sixty-sixth streets, and Third avenue and the East river, be procured for a public park, for the free use of all the citizens of the city of New York.

Resolved, That the Counsel to the Corporation be directed to make application to the legislature of this state, at its next special session, for the passage of an act for the appointment of commissioners to take the property mentioned in the preceding resolution, for public use, and that the Finance Committees of the two Boards, together with the Comptroller and his Honor the Mayor, be authorized to purchase the same, at any time, before the actual appointment of said commissioners.

Resolved, That the Counsel to the Corporation be also instructed to make application to the legislature at its next special session, for authority to fund the amount to be paid for said plot of land or public park, the sum of fifty thousand dollars annually, to be paid by tax alone, with the interest thereon, not to exceed five per cent, until the whole sum be paid.

WM. A. DOOLEY,   } Committee
JAMES R. BALL,   } on Lands
JACOB F. OAKLEY, } and Places.

This report was adopted by a vote of fourteen to four, and sent to the Board of Assistants for concurrence.

[2] For reference to the text of the Act, see Appendix II.

place for exercise for a city of half a million of souls, we trust they will not be content with the limited number of acres already proposed. *Five hundred acres* is the smallest area that should be reserved for the future wants of such a city, *now*, while it may be obtained. Five hundred acres may be selected between 39th street and the Harlem river, including a varied surface of land, a good deal of which is yet waste area, so that the whole may be purchased at something like a million of dollars. In that area there would be space enough to have broad reaches of park and pleasure-grounds, with a real feeling of the breadth and beauty of green fields, the perfume and freshness of nature. In its midst would be located the great distributing reservoirs of the Croton aqueduct, formed into lovely lakes of limpid water, covering many acres, and heightening the charm of the sylvan accessories by the finest natural contrast. In such a park, the citizens who would take excursions in carriages, or on horseback, could have the substantial delights of country roads and country scenery, and forget for a time the rattle of the pavements and the glare of brick walls. Pedestrians would find quiet and secluded walks when they wished to be solitary, and broad alleys filled with thousands of happy faces, when they would be gay. The thoughtful denizen of the town would go out there in the morning to hold converse with the whispering trees, and the wearied tradesmen in the evening, to enjoy an hour of happiness by mingling in the open spaces with "all the world."

The many beauties and utilities which would gradually grow out of a great park like this in a great city like New York, suggest themselves immediately and forcibly. Where would be found so fitting a position for noble works of art, the statues, monuments and buildings[1] commemorative at once of the great men of the nation, of the history of the age and country, and the genius of our highest artists? In the broad area of such a verdant zone would gradually grow up, as the wealth of the city increases winter gardens of glass, like the great Crystal Palace, where the whole people could luxuriate in groves of the palms and spice trees of the tropics, at the same moment that sleighing parties glided swiftly and noiselessly over the snow covered surface of the country-like avenues of the wintry park without. Zoological Gardens like those of London and Paris, would gradually be formed, by private subscription or public funds, where thousands of old and young would find daily pleasure in studying natural history, illustrated by all the wildest and strangest animals of the globe, almost as much at home in their paddocks and jungles, as if in their native forests; and Horticultural and Industrial Societies would hold their annual shows there, and great expositions of the arts would take place in spacious

[1] For comment on the change of public opinion in regard to buildings in the Park, see Part II, Chapter IX, pp. 472 ff.

buildings within the park, far more fittingly than in the noise and din of the crowded streets of the city.

The *Evening Post* was for taking both Jones' Wood and a central site,—"the range of parks and public gardens along the central part of the island" suggested by Bryant in 1845. "'There is now ample room and verge enough upon the island for two parks,' wrote Bryant, 'whereas if the matter is delayed for a few years, there will hardly be space left for one.' Having again and again expressed its hopes with regard to Jones' Wood, it [the *Evening Post*] now published glowing descriptions of the Central Park area."[1]

THE ACT FOR A CENTRAL PARK.

The Board of Aldermen, in view of public opinion, appointed a committee on August 5, 1851, to report on the advantages and disadvantages of the land designated in the Act of July 11, and to see if there were not some other site more fitted for a public park.

This committee consisting of Daniel Dodge and Joseph Britton reported strongly in favor of a central site. The Board of Aldermen adopted the report on January 2, 1852,[2] and secured the passage of an Act by the Legislature, July 21, 1853, authorizing the city to acquire the land now Central Park.[3] At the same time the Legislature passed again the Act for taking Jones' Wood, the Act of 1851 having been held up because of alleged errors in the bill. The opposition to two parks was so great that the Jones' Wood Act was repealed in April, 1854, and New York lost what would have been a splendid waterfront recreation ground.[4] The

---

[1] Nevins, p. 198. It should be remembered that there were fine views from parts of the Central Park lands at that time, now shut off by the surrounding wall of high buildings. See p. 42 of Doc. No. 5 referred to later.

[2] The report is printed in full in the first report of the Commissioners of Central Park, being Doc. No. 5 of the Board of Aldermen, 1857, pp. 139 ff.

[3] For reference to text of the Act, see Appendix II. The land from 106th Street to 110th Street was not added until Apr., 1859.

[4] Mr. Olmsted in later years often called attention to the fact that the land which had been selected for Central Park was topographically very ill adapted for its purpose as well as obstructive of the street system, and it appears to have been his mature opinion that a mistake was made in shifting to that site from the original Jones' Wood proposition instead of enlarging the latter. Looking back from today, seventy-five years later,—in view of the very minor commercial use of the upper East River waterfront and the enormous advantage for park purposes of the outlook over the river from that region, and in view of the conflict between the northward development of the central business district of Manhattan and the permanent conservation of the full park values of Central Park,—it seems clear that it would have been wiser to select two large parks, one on the East River and one on the Hudson rather than the Central Park, even though this was later supplemented by the narrow Riverside Park and a very small local park on the East River.—F. L. O.

narrow commercial point of view that defeated that project may
be judged by a memorial sent to the Legislature in 1853 signed by
Mayor Westervelt, Peter Cooper, and other prominent citizens.

Your memorialists, inhabitants, freeholders, and taxpayers of
the city of New York, respectfully represent:—That they have
heard with regret that great efforts are being made to procure
from your honorable body the passage of a law conferring upon
the Corporation the power to take the grounds known as Jones'
Woods for a public park. Your memorialists admit "the propriety and necessity of an additional park of adequate dimensions to meet the wants of our rapidly increasing population,"
but they object to the proposed measure, for the following, among
other reasons:—1st. The ground spoken of is on one side of the
island, and too remote for what must ever remain the centre of
population, to be generally available to the masses as a place of
recreation and healthful exercise. 2nd. It occupies some thousands of feet of the margin of the East river none of which ought
ever to be taken from the purposes of commerce, as the whole
will eventually be required, including, as your memorialists
believe, the ground now known as the "Battery."

On November 17, 1853, the Supreme Court appointed five
Commissioners[1] of Estimate and Assessment to take the land for
the Central Park, all men in whom wide confidence was felt. In
spite of the opposition to be looked for in the long process of acquiring the land and the hostility of Mayor Westervelt, the Park
project was at last actually under way.

[1] William Kent, Michael Ulshoeffer, Luther Bradish, Warren Brady, and
Jeremiah Towle.

CHAPTER III

THE CENTRAL PARK CHOSEN

ITS ACQUIREMENT, UNCURTAILED.

For the next three years—from 1853 to 1856—the Commissioners of Estimate and Assessment were at work taking the land for the Park. In addition to the claims of the owners of some seven thousand five hundred city lots comprised within the Park area, the owners of adjacent property had to be heard in relation to the assessments for benefit placed upon them.

Meanwhile the opponents of the Park were enlisting support for a proposed act to reduce its size. In 1854 the Committee on Public Lands of the Common Council recommended a measure to cut off the lower portion of the Park and, out of the area remaining, to reserve a strip of land 400 feet wide along both Fifth and Eighth avenues for sale as villa sites. After some delay, in 1855 the Board of Aldermen also passed this measure. Fortunately, however, it was vetoed in no uncertain terms by Mayor Wood, who, whatever his political misdeeds, had early espoused the park project. Of the curtailment measure he said, "though it proposes, only to take from the Central Park a portion of the area agreed upon, still, it will be in effect, a blow at the whole. . . . To admit the necessity of a great park, and to assert that this will be too large, is, in my opinion, an exceedingly limited view of the question, and entirely unworthy of even the present position of this metropolis, to say nothing of a destiny now opening so brilliantly before us." The measure was vetoed on March 23, 1855.[1]

On February 5, 1856, the Supreme Court confirmed the report of the Commissioners of Estimate and Assessment. The amount awarded to owners of the land taken was $5,069,693 of which sum $1,657,590 was payable by owners of adjacent lands assessed for benefit.[2] To pay for the land of the park, an ordinance was passed

---

[1] The minority and majority reports for the reduction of the park area and the text of Mayor Wood's veto may be found in the first Central Park report (Doc. No. 5 of Board of Aldermen, 1857). [2] Cf. p. 54, *post.*

forthwith creating "The Central Park Fund," the shares bearing interest at five per cent, for which the lands of the Park were pledged.

Temporary Government of the Park.

Since the Legislature had as yet been unable to pass any provision for the government of the Park, an ordinance was adopted by the Common Council on May 19, 1856 (approved by the Mayor on May 21) giving the control and management to a Board of Commissioners consisting of the Mayor and Street Commissioner, to be termed "Commissioners of the Central Park."[1] They were to have full power to determine upon the plan for improvement of the Park, to lay out and regulate the grounds, and to employ a force of "such gardeners, engineers, surveyors, clerks and laborers as may be necessary." To secure public confidence the new Board extended invitations to certain well known citizens[2] to attend its meeting and form a Consulting Board for determining on the plan to be pursued. The Consulting Board organized on May 29, 1856, by electing Washington Irving as President.

A few days later,[3] various projects having been considered, the Commissioners appointed Mr. (formerly Lieut.) Egbert L. Viele[4] Chief Engineer at a salary of $2500 a year. At odd times since 1853 Mr. Viele had been preparing on his own initiative and at his own expense, a preliminary topographical survey of the Park lands and a general plan for their development based on this survey,

---

[1] For reference to the ordinance, see Appendix II, p. 539. Control of the Park was very necessary, as we find from an item in the *Evening Post* of May 31, 1856 (also *Tribune*, June 2) that trees and plants were being stolen and the place was "a rendez-vous of villains." The Commissioners immediately formed a force called the "Central Park Police," consisting of a captain, three sergeants, and fifteen men.

[2] Washington Irving, George Bancroft, James E. Cooley, Charles F. Briggs, James Phalen, C. A. Dana, and Stewart Brown. (1st Report, Central Park.)

[3] The exact date is uncertain.

[4] Egbert L. Viele (born Waterford, N. Y., 1825) was graduated at West Point in 1847. After serving in Mexico, he resigned in 1850 and settled in New York City, entering the practice of civil engineering. From 1854 to 1856 he was state engineer of New Jersey. From 1856 until his dismissal in 1858 he was Chief Engineer of the Central Park. He was captain of engineers and later Brigadier-General of volunteers in the Civil War, resigning in 1863 to resume his engineering practice. He was concerned more especially with sanitary and municipal improvements, including various rapid transit schemes for New York and several land development projects. He published a number of papers and reports on all of these subjects. In 1883 he was appointed a Commissioner of the New York Park Board and was elected its President for 1884, resigning at the end of the year. He was elected to Congress as a Democrat in 1884, but defeated in 1886. He died in 1902. For the claims made on his behalf in relation to the design of Central Park, see Appendix III.

trusting, as he later testified, to the "chance" that he could secure from the city authorities "compensation suitable to the time and skill . . . expended on the work."

This plan was published in the first report of the Commissioners, 1857, with the superscription "Adopted June 3, 1856," having been either tacitly or expressly accepted at the time of Mr. Viele's appointment.[1] This plan governed such work as was done on the Park for the next year or more. However, only a small amount having been appropriated by the Common Council[2] for the improvement of the Park, active operations were confined to clearing the ground and little was done in carrying out Mr. Viele's design.[3] On June 16, 1857, Mr. Viele was re-appointed Chief Engineer by the new Board of Commissioners recently created by Act of Legislature. But at the same meeting, a resolution was introduced that the Board advertise for plans for the laying out of the Central Park, offering premiums for the four best, thus showing no commitment to the Viele plan.

The Board of Commissioners of the Central Park Created by the Legislature

The political situation underlying the creation of the new Board of eleven Commissioners is suggested in the autobiographical fragment of Mr. Olmsted's about to be quoted. When no substantial progress on the Park had been made during almost a year under the Mayor's administration, many friends of the Park were fearful lest it be bungled if responsibility for its design and improvement were left in the hands of a political group which they believed to be corrupt and inefficient. And professed partisan opponents of the Wood régime naturally looked with disfavor upon turning over to it the patronage and perquisites of so large an undertaking. There was secured from the Legislature "An Act for the Regulation and Government of the Central Park in the City of New York," passed April 17, 1857,[4] taking control of the park away from the Mayor and city government and vesting it in a (theoretically) non-partisan and wholly independent commission. The eleven

[1] Cf. Appendix III.
[2] On July 18, 1856, $100,000 was appropriated for the use of the Commissioners of the Central Park, in addition to the proceeds from rent or sale of buildings existing on the Park appropriated by the ordinance of May 21.
[3] The report of the Senate Committee of the New York State Legislature to investigate Park affairs stated (1860) in regard to Mayor Wood's Board: "Not being able to obtain the funds applicable, no progress was made."
[4] For the substance of this Act, see Appendix II.

Commissioners[1] were named in the act, and held their first meeting on April 30, 1857, all being present. Mr. Cooley was elected President and Mr. Elliott, Secretary. On June 9, Mr. Green was elected Treasurer.[2] Their initial difficulties were considerable. The area of the park was in a condition of chaos,[3] much of it was deep in mire, rubbish lay everywhere, squatters' huts had scarcely been vacated, and the whole place was infested with goats,[4] not dislodged like their former squatter owners. The political difficulties were even greater.

PARTY POLITICS.[5]

Wood being a democrat, the republicans who held the majority of the state legislature took advantage of the momentary popular disgust with him and his associates to take the regulation of certain parts of the city business from the elected government of the city, and to give it to a series of professedly nonpartisan commissioners. One of these, composed of eleven members, part republicans, part Wood democrats, part "reform" democrats, part nondescript, was appointed to supersede Wood and Taylor in the special government of the Central Park. It had to go to the Common Council of the city for its supplies, and a majority of the members of the Common Council, siding with the Mayor, were disposed not to honor its requisitions. Eventually they would be obliged to do so unless indeed a decision of court could be obtained, as they professed to expect, declaring the act of the legislature unconstitutional. But supplies could be delayed and, when yielded, given in driblets, and various difficulties and obstructions could be put in the way of the Commission.

Two considerable influences were working in favor of the Commission: first, a desire with many that some progress should be made in turning to use the property in the land appropriated to the park which had cost the city five million dollars; second, the

[1] Robert J. Dillon, James E. Cooley, Charles H. Russell, John F. Butterworth, John A. C. Gray, Waldo Hutchins, Thomas C. Fields, Andrew H. Green, Charles W. Elliott, William K. Strong, and James Hogg.

[2] The administrative history of the Commission and Mr. Green's part in keeping the Park out of politics for almost twenty years except for a brief period during the zenith of the Tweed Ring are recorded in *The Life and Public Services of Andrew Haswell Green*, by John Foord, 1913.

[3] Cf. description, "Topography of the Site" given on p. 214.

[4] Goats must still have been rampant as late as Aug., 1858, for we find the following amusing passage in a document of the Park Commissioners, urging an amendment: "The ordinance of the Common Council providing for the impounding of animals at large in the streets is incomplete in so far that it does not include goats . . . the trees in the Park have already suffered much from these animals; they are very numerous in the neighborhood of the Park, and unless some measures are immediately taken, their depredations will be great and not easily reparable."

[5] This and the succeeding autobiographical fragment, given under "Introduction to the Duties of Superintendence," with some more general observations on municipal government, were published in *Landscape Architecture*, July, 1912.

desire of the laboring population to obtain the employment which the construction of the Park was expected to give.[1] This latter influence was strongest in those parts of the city where Wood and his supporters in the Common Council had hitherto obtained the most votes, and on their popularity in which they depended for reëlection.

To counteract it, the Act of the Legislature was denounced as a tyrannical usurpation of power, by which the Black Republicans and Abolitionists were to put themselves in office and plunder the city against the will of the local majority.

But these denunciations had to be uttered in the face of the fact that the Commissioners were to receive no pay; that they had elected a democrat as their President, another democrat as their Treasurer, and had reappointed Wood's whole Engineer corps. They had gone so far in this respect that a clamor was beginning to rise from the republican side that the Commission was wholly given over to the democrats.

At this period in its history, one of the Commissioners came to spend a Sunday at a seaside inn where I had been finishing the manuscript of my *Journey in the Back Country*. Sitting next him at the tea-table he told me what I have just recited of the history of the Commission, and added that they were now taking on a force of laborers. Having no money as yet at their command, each of the men employed was required to sign an agreement releasing the Commissioners from personal liability on account of the wages he might earn, and, in lieu of wages, due bills against the city were to be issued, which would be payable when the Common Council should make the appropriation, in favor of which an additional element of popular interest would thus be established. He added that at their next meeting they intended to elect a Superintendent, and it was thought necessary that he should be a republican. There were several candidates, but no republican had appeared with whom he was much pleased, and he asked if I knew of a suitable man. I inquired what would be the duties of the Superintendent?

"He would be the executive officer of the Engineer with respect to the labor force, and would have charge of the police and see that proper regulations were enforced in regard to the public use of the Park."

"Must he be a politician?"

"No, a republican but not a politician; much better he should not be a practical politician. The republicans can do little without the coöperation of the reform democrats, and are ready to compromise on the understanding that the park shall be managed independently of politics."

---

[1] Although the Act of Legislature creating the Commission had authorized the issue of corporate stock to provide funds for building the Park, the financial crisis of 1857 made the marketing of bonds difficult; and the Common Council, applied to for money on June 2, did not comply until Sept. 29.

"I am delighted to hear it," I said. "There's no limit to the good influence a park rightly managed would have in New York, and that seems to be the first necessity of good management."

"I wish we had you on the Commission, but, as we have not, why not take the superintendency yourself? Come now."

Till he asked the question, the possibility of my doing so had never occurred to me, though he probably suspected I was thinking of it. I at once answered, however, smiling:

"I take it? I'm not sure that I wouldn't if it were offered me. Nothing interested me in London like the parks, and yet I thought a great deal more might be made of them."

"Well, it will not be offered you; that's not the way we do business; but if you'll go to work I believe you may get it. I wish that you would!"

"You are serious?"

"Yes; but there's no time to lose."

"What is to be done?"

"Go to New York and file an application; see the Commissioners and get your friends to back you."

"I'll take the boat tonight and think it out as I go. If no serious objection occurs to me before morning, I'll do it."

F. L. OLMSTED A CANDIDATE FOR SUPERINTENDENT.

Accordingly, the next day I was looking for my friends in New York. At that season they were much scattered, but one I found who took up the matter warmly, and my application was in a few days fortified by a number of weighty signatures. I shall presently refer to the fact that among them was that of Washington Irving.

The President of the Commission being out of town on my arrival in New York, I first called on the Vice-President, bearing a letter to him from my friend in New Haven.

The Vice-President, who was a republican, repeated that it was desirable that the Superintendent should not be a democrat, yet that he should be as little objectionable as possible to the democrats. He seemed to think that my prospects in this respect were good. He offered to introduce me to one of the democratic Commissioners who was a very practical man, and also to the Engineer, whom again he described as a very practical man; if their judgment should be favorable, I might count on his support.

The practical democratic Commissioner having ascertained that I had had no experience in practical politics even no personal acquaintance with the republican leaders in the city, that my backing would be from unpractical men, and that I responded warmly to virtuous sentiments with regard to corruption in both parties, after a long conversation, gave me to understand that I might hope that, if the republicans brought me forward, he should be less inclined to oppose me than a possible republican who had been deep in the mire and who disapproved of the practice of virtue in politics.

The Engineer I found at a house on the Park about which was a crowd of laboring men, each bearing a letter addressed to him. On the ground that my letter was from a Commissioner, I was allowed to precede those who had stood waiting outside the door before me. The room in which the Engineer sat at a desk was crowded with applicants for employment, whose letters were collected in batches by men wearing a golden star on the breast of a very dirty and seedy jacket, and handed to the Engineer. These letters were chiefly from members of the Common Council. As each was opened and its writer's name recognized, the bearer was either abruptly told that there was no work for him at present, or his name was taken and looked for on a list furnished by the writer of his letter, in which it appeared that a limited number had been named whom he wished to have preferred among all those to whom he gave letters. If found there, the applicant was, without further examination, given a ticket, and told to call again on a given day.

At the first opportunity, I presented my letter and card. Reading a few lines the Engineer glanced at me, dropped the letter and went on with his canvass of the laborers. I stood among them half an hour, and then, pointing to my card, asked if I might hope to find him less engaged later in the day. As he seemed to assent, I walked out a little way, looking at the ground for the park. I returned and withdrew again three times before I found the enlisting business ended. As I came in the last time, the Engineer was about leaving. I walked with him, and took a seat by his side in the street car running to the city.

I then had an opportunity to state on what grounds I had ventured to think that he would find me useful as an assistant in his work. He replied that he would rather have a practical man. I did not learn why I could not be regarded as a possibly practical man, but it was only too evident that the gate of hope was closed to me in that direction.

Calling, by appointment, on the Vice-President, the next day, I was not surprised to find that doubts had been growing, over night, in his mind, as to whether the office of Superintendent should not be filled by a practical man.

Some time after my election, which occurred at the first subsequent meeting of the Park Board, another of the Commissioners told me that this objection would have defeated me had it not been for the autograph of Washington Irving on my papers.[1] That turned the balance.

---

[1] A facsimile of the signatures of Washington Irving, Peter Cooper, and others on one of these petitions for Mr. Olmsted's appointment will be found in Vol. I, *ante*, opposite p. 120.

APPOINTMENT.

The details of Mr. Olmsted's appointment he tells in a letter to his brother John, written September 11, 1857.

I have moved to town and done nothing else since I last wrote but canvass for the Superintendent's office: I am now awaiting the result, the Board being in session below a few doors. In the Committee on Offices and Salaries night before last I got the nomination by one vote, that of a member who unexpectedly came in town that evening, but at the same meeting the salary was fixed at $1500 instead of $3000. This was a sort of compromise, one party wanting that the Superintendent's office should be equal in rank with that of Engineer, the other that it should be distinctly subordinate and that of a mere overseer of laborers. I am favored as a gentleman able to take the place of the Engineer, in case of his removal or death by the first party. But one of these being a politician on the "retrenchment" tack, a compromise game was played by which the office was given to me but with the other sort of man's salary.

The office of Engineer and Superintendent are thus (at the last meeting) defined—"The Chief Engineer shall have the entire control, direction, and responsibility of all persons employed on the park, under the supervision and instruction of the Board. He shall execute such plans as may be decided upon by the Commission, and lay out and direct all operations, both preparatory and final, which the Commission shall direct.

"The Superintendent, during the progress of active operations, shall personally attend to the force employed in the Park, see that all give due attention to their duty and report to the Engineer any neglect or dereliction therefrom, which he may discover. He shall co-operate with the Engineer in the execution of the details of the work which may be laid out and when any portion or portions of the plans agreed upon have been carried out, attend to its proper preservation as completed. He shall have charge of the general police of the Park to see that the ordinances of the Board are respected and obeyed. He shall report to the Board upon matters not pertaining to the construction of the work, monthly."

P.S. After a very long session and much debate, I am elected: on the final vote, 8 of those present voting for me, one against me,[1] Elliott and Green (Pres. Bd. Education) being my determined advocates. The strongest objection to me, that I am a literary man, not active: yet if I had not been a "literary man" so far, I certainly should not have stood a chance. My strongest competitor was a Professor Nott, son of President Nott—but after the report of the Committee in my favor, he said he was

[1] Thomas C. Fields.

willing to take the office of Deputy Superintendent, and he was not voted for. Another candidate who was dropped entirely was a son of Audubon—one of the brothers who are authors of the great Mammalia. The "practical men" were Smith, formerly a city surveyor, and Chambers, a builder of Fifth Avenue houses. There were several other applicants. Green and Elliott made a strong effort to get the salary raised, but they would not vote against the Committee's Report.

Introduction to the Duties of Superintendence.

It is hardly necessary to say that even after my election I did not quite feel myself out of the woods. Had it been concluded that it was, after all, just as well not to have a practical man? Or had they been convinced that, after all, I was a practical man?

These gentlemen, most of whom had themselves made large fortunes in business, would hardly defer to Washington Irving on such a point. No, I owed my election to something else than their estimate of my value as a practical man, and to what I did not understand.

When I next came to the office on the park, my first experience was repeated until I said to the Engineer: "I was instructed to report to you for orders, Sir." Upon this, he called to one of the starred men: "Tell Hawkin to come here." Then to me: "I have given my orders to Mr. Hawkin; he is what I call a practical man, and I will tell him to show you what you have to do."

Mr. Hawkin, a cautious, close-mouthed, sensible-looking gentleman, wearing no coat, and with trousers tucked in the legs of a heavy and dirty pair of boots, here opened the door and said, "Want me?"

"Yes; this is Mr. Olmsted, the new Superintendent; take him round the park and show him what work is going on, and tell the foremen they will take their orders from him after this."

"Now?"

The Engineer looked at me.

"I am quite ready, Sir."

"Yes, now."

In truth, as I had intended this to be rather a call of ceremony or preliminary report to my superior officer, I was not quite so well prepared as I could have wished to be for what followed.

Striking across the hill into what is now the Ramble, we came first upon a number of men with bill-hooks and forks collecting and burning brushwood. Under a tree near-by a man sat smoking. He rose as we approached.

"Smith; this is Mr. Olmsted, your new Superintendent; you'll take orders from him after this."

All the men within hearing dropped their tools and looked at me. Smith said, "Oh! that's the man is it? Expect we shall be pushed up, now." He laughed, and the men grinned.

"What is Smith doing?" I asked.

"He's grubbing round here, and burning up what he can get together," and Mr. Hawkin moved on.

"See you again, I suppose," said Smith still laughing.

"Yes, Sir; good-day for the present."

And this process was repeated with little variation, as we passed from gang to gang to the number of perhaps fifteen, there being at this time about 500 men at work. As they were nearly all democrats, and all appointed by a democrat, and a democrat who had himself been appointed first by Wood, and as they were mostly introduced to him by democratic members of the Common Council, the presumption that the Commission was to be managed exclusively in the interests of the republicans and as a means of defeating Wood was considerably weakened.

As I stood in the office, I had not been able to observe that the slightest consideration was given to the apparent strength or activity of the laborers. Each man undoubtedly supposed that he owed the fact of his preference over others, often much abler than himself to do a good day's work, to the fact that a member of the Common Council had asked his appointment. He also knew that the request of his patron was made, not because of his supposed special fitness to serve the city on the park, but because of service that he was expected to render at primary meetings and otherwise with a view to the approaching election. He knew too that he was for an indefinite period to receive no pay for his work, but only a promise to pay which he must turn to account by selling it at a discount.

Under all the circumstances, it was plain enough that when Foreman Smith pleasantly remarked that he supposed that they would be pushed up now, and the men laughed with him at the suggestion, it was because the idea that I might expect a day's work from them for each day's due-bill was thought a good joke.

Neither Foreman Smith nor any other that day said anything aloud to me about my not being a practical man, but I saw it in their eyes and their smile, and felt it deeply. In fact, for other reasons I could have wished, long before our round was finished, that I had worn a pair of high-legged boots and left my coat behind me, for it was a sultry afternoon in the height of dog-days, and my conductor exhibited his practical ability by leading me through the midst of a number of vile sloughs, in the black and unctuous slime of which I sometimes sank nearly half-leg deep.

He said but one word to me during the afternoon beyond what his commission strictly required. As I stopped for an instant to kick the mire off my legs against a stump, as we came out of the last bog, he turned and remarked:

"Suppose you are used to this sort of business."

I believe that he was some years my junior, and it is probable that I had been through fifty miles of swamp to his one. There was not one operation in progress in the park in which I had not considerable personal experience, and he spoke with apparent gravity; nevertheless I felt very deeply that he was laughing in his sleeve, and that I was still a very young man. So I avoided a direct reply by saying that I had not been aware that the park was such a very nasty place. In fact, the low grounds were steeped in the overflow and mush of pig-sties, slaughter-houses, and bone-boiling works, and the stench was sickening.

For several days there continued to be something that stimulated good humor in my appearance, and in the inquiries and suggestions which I made as I walked from gang to gang, feeling my way to an intelligent command of the business. It was as if we were all engaged in playing a practical joke. The most striking illustration of this good fellowship that I remember occurred, I think, on the third day, when a foreman who was reading a newspaper as I came suddenly upon him exclaimed "Hello, Fred; get round pretty often, don't you?"

Having no power to discharge or secure the discharge of a man, I found it was better to give every offender the benefit of the largest possible assumption of ignorance, forgetfulness and accident and urge him to give more attention to his duties and use more care.

CHAPTER IV

THE WINNING DESIGN BY OLMSTED AND VAUX

ANNOUNCEMENT AND TERMS OF THE COMPETITION FOR A DESIGN.

At the same meeting of the Board of Commissioners at which Mr. Olmsted was appointed Superintendent, the report of the Special Committee on advertising and preparing specifications for plans for laying out the Park was received and ordered printed.[1]

The Committee to whom was referred the matter of advertising for designs, beg leave to report the following form of advertizements for circulation:—

The Board of Commissioners of the Central Park offer the following sums for the four designs for laying out the grounds of the Central Park, which may be chosen by the Board:—

> For the first..........$2000
> For the second.......$1000
> For the third........$ 750
> For the fourth........$ 500

The designs chosen are to become the property of this Board.

The grounds for the Central Park are bounded by Fifty-ninth street on the south, and one hundred and sixth street on the north, by the Fifth avenue on the east, and the Eighth avenue on the west, forming a parallelogram of some 770 acres, of which about 150 acres are reserved for the Reservoirs for the Croton Water. The whole space is about 2½ miles long, and one-half a mile broad.

In the designs to be accepted, the following details should be provided for:

First.—Reference should be had to the whole amount of expenditure allowed by the Legislature, viz., about $1,500,000.

Second.—Four or more crossings from east to west must be made between Fifty-ninth and one Hundred and Sixth street.

Third.—A parade ground of from twenty to forty acres, should be designated, with proper arrangements for the convenience for spectators.

[1] Printed as Doc. No. 8 of the Commissioners for the year ending Apr. 30, 1858. The offer of premiums was publicly announced on Oct. 13, 1857.

Fourth.—Three playgrounds, of from three to ten acres each, should be designated.

Fifth.—A site for a future hall for exhibitions, concerts, etc., should be reserved:—

Sixth.—Also a site for one principal fountain and one prospect tower.

Seventh.—Grounds should be reserved for a flower garden of some two or three acres in extent, and a design be given for the same.

Eighth.—Space should be reserved for flowing with water to form a winter skating ground.

Designs offered should conform to the following scale, viz.: 100 feet to 1 inch, being 10 feet 2 inches in length, by 2 feet 3 inches in breadth.

Designs should be finished up with indian ink and sepia, not with colors.

Designs should be accompanied with a well digested written description, with a sealed envelope containing the designer's name.

Designs should be handed in before first day of . . . [1] 1858, to the rooms of the Board.

Topographical maps may be consulted at the rooms of the Board; and a list of buildings to be reserved obtained.

ENTRY OF OLMSTED AND VAUX.

Mr. Olmsted had no intention of going into the competition. When he was asked by Calvert Vaux to collaborate in the preparation of a plan, he declined, on the ground that for him to enter the competition would savor of discourtesy to his official superior, Mr. Viele, whose first plan was set aside, and who was going into the competition himself. But when Mr. Viele took occasion to express, rather contemptuously, complete indifference as to whether Mr. Olmsted entered the competition or not, he accepted Mr. Vaux's proposal.

His routine duties as superintendent kept him busy all day and his work on the plan with Mr. Vaux was done mostly at night and on Sundays, although he was of course constantly thinking of it as he went about his daily executive work on the ground. Mr. Vaux and he often went out together by moonlight to discuss features of the plan, with the land before them and free from interruption and listeners. They doubtless then entered upon the first of those long, searching, exhaustive and exhausting arguments that

---

[1] March 1st, afterwards extended to April 1st,

were characteristic of their collaboration for years. Both were argumentative, very much in earnest and interminably persistent until fully convinced.

On January 14, 1858, Mr. Olmsted wrote to his father:

> I have got the park into a capital discipline, a perfect system, working like a machine 1000 men now at work.[1] The confidence of the Commission in me has constantly increased and my salary raised to $2000.
>
> I am greatly interested in planning the park with Vaux. If successful, I should not only get my share of $2000 offered for the best, but no doubt the whole control of the matter would be given me and my salary increased to $2500.

In connection with the joint preparation of the competition plan, there is an amusing reminiscence by Mr. Vaux's son Downing. "When the drawing of the plan of Central Park to go in the competition was being made at my father's house in 18th Street, in conjunction with Mr. Frederick Law Olmsted, there was a great deal of grass to be put in by the usual small dots and dashes, and it became the friendly thing for callers to help on the work by joining in and 'adding some grass to Central Park.'"[2]

A few weeks later Mr. Olmsted again wrote to his father:

> My circumstances are peculiar. I have in fact started in a new business, and a most important one, not only without capital, but badly hampered with debt.[3] To have my time and mind for my business I have had to constantly throw back old debts by making new ones. And I must continue to do so. The plan of the park, which I have decided to present, will cost some hundred dollars. It is certainly worth while for me to go into the competition, the reward of success being so large. Yet the chances are much the largest against succeeding, there being 50 competitors. While attending to the park and to the plan, I have also, if possible, to complete my book[4] for publication, the labor already expended in it, being too much to let slide. Unquestionably I am undertaking too much.

However, the park plan was finished under the signature "Greensward" and delivered on the very last day of the competition.

[1] Cf. Chapter V, p. 51.
[2] "Historical Notes," in *Transactions of the American Society of Landscape Architects*, 1899–1908, p. 81.
[3] From his earlier publishing venture. See Biographical Sketch by F. L. Olmsted, Jr., introductory to the 1904 edition of *A Journey in the Seaboard Slave States*.
[4] *A Journey in Texas*.

"Greensward" Plan Awarded First Prize.

There proved to be thirty-five sets of drawings submitted to the Board, of which two were not in competition. These were all hung in a room secured for the purpose, and the accompanying reports printed for study by the Commissioners.[1] On April 28, 1858, after long and careful consideration, the Board voted to award the first prize to Plan No. 33 signed "Greensward," seven commissioners out of eleven voting in its favor.

The second prize was awarded to Mr. Samuel I. Gustin, the superintendent of planting at the Park, the third to Messrs. Miller and McIntosh, two employees in the office of the Superintendent (Mr. Olmsted), and the fourth to an architect, Mr. Howard Daniels.[2]

The discussion before the Board leaves no doubt that the "Greensward" plan was by far the most promising of those submitted, and the press immediately acclaimed the design as worthy of the prize. The plan comprised a variety of desirable features not specifically called for by the terms of the competition, and although some misrepresentations of the plan were circulated, these did not prevent its popular acceptance.

Thus in spite of preliminary fears, publicly expressed, that the park would cater only to one class of people,—the rich or the poor, according to the politics of the doubter,—the winning design gave no reasonable ground for further complaint. It bore out the fact subsequently stated in the first official description of the plan that "the primary purpose of the Park is to provide the best practicable means of healthful recreation for the inhabitants of all classes."[3] Its character as a democratic enterprise is unquestionable.

That Mr. Olmsted was fully cognizant of this appears in a letter of his about the Park written to Parke Godwin on the first of August following:

It is a matter of very great public interest as is evident from the fact that already visitors come here from distant parts of the

[1] A copy of the complete catalogue of these and the reports as printed for the use of the Commissioners, with annotations as to the supposed authorship of the various plans, may be seen at the New York Public Library.
[2] See comment on the competition and the state of landscape gardening at that date in Vol. I, *ante*, pp. 123–124.
[3] 2nd Annual Report, C. P. C., Jan. 1, 1859. The point is worth making because of a current erroneous belief that the American park movement was in its origin directed towards providing ornamental pleasure grounds mainly for the enjoyment of the so-called "upper classes."

"GREENSWARD" SKETCH NO. 5

(Map showed this view was taken from "Point E," southwest corner, Old Reservoir.)

" PRESENT OUTLINES "

" EFFECT PROPOSED "

Park Land Before 1858.   Lake Site
(See page 232)

country to study it.   It is of great importance as the first real
park made in this country—a democratic development of the
highest significance and on the success of which, in my opinion,
much of the progress of art and esthetic culture in this country
is dependent.

The Conception of the Winning Plan Explained by its Authors.

The descriptive report submitted by Olmsted and Vaux with
their design will be found in full in Part II.   This rather explains
the features of the plan than interprets its spirit, so that some
passages in two later reports, both in defense of the main outlines of
the original conception, are necessary supplements.

The Park throughout is a single work of art, and as such subject to the primary law of every work of art, namely, that it shall
be framed upon a single, noble motive, to which the design of all
its parts, in some more or less subtle way, shall be confluent
and helpful.

To find such a general motive of design for the Central Park,
it will be necessary to go back to the beginning and ask, for what
worthy purpose could the city be required to take out and keep
excluded from the field of ordinary urban improvements, a body
of land in what was looked forward to as its very centre, so large
as that assigned for the Park?   For what such object of great
prospective importance would a smaller body of land not have
been adequate?

To these questions a sufficient answer can, we believe, be found
in the expectation that the whole of the island of New York
would, but for such a reservation, before many years be occupied
by buildings and paved streets; that millions upon millions of
men were to live their lives upon this island, millions more to go
out from it, or its immediate densely populated suburbs, only
occasionally and at long intervals, and that all its inhabitants
would assuredly suffer, in greater or less degree, according to
their occupations and the degree of their confinement to it, from
influences engendered by these conditions.

Provisions for the improvement of the ground, however,
pointed to something more than mere exemption from urban
conditions, namely, to the formation of an opposite class of
conditions; conditions remedial of the influences of urban
conditions.

Two classes of improvements were to be planned for this purpose; one directed to secure pure and wholesome air, to act
through the lungs; the other to secure an antithesis of objects of
vision to those of the streets and houses, which should act

remedially by impressions on the mind and suggestions to the imagination.[1]

It is one great purpose of the Park to supply to the hundreds of thousands of tired workers, who have no opportunity to spend their summers in the country, a specimen of God's handiwork that shall be to them, inexpensively, what a month or two in the White Mountains or the Adirondacks is, at great cost, to those in easier circumstances. The time will come when New York will be built up, when all the grading and filling will be done, and when the picturesquely-varied, rocky formations of the Island will have been converted into formations for rows of monotonous straight streets, and piles of erect buildings. There will be no suggestion left of its present varied surface, with the single exception of the few acres contained in the Park. Then the priceless value of the present picturesque outlines of the ground will be more distinctly perceived, and its adaptability for its purpose more fully recognized. It therefore seems desirable to interfere with its easy, undulating outlines, and picturesque, rocky scenery as little as possible, and, on the other hand, to endeavor rapidly, and by every legitimate means, to increase and judiciously develop these particularly individual and characteristic sources of landscape effects.[2]

Considering that large classes of rural objects and many types of natural scenery are not practicable to be introduced on the site of the Park,—mountain, ocean, desert and prairie scenery for example,—it will be found that the most valuable form that could have been prescribed is that which may be distinguished from all others as pastoral. But the site of the Park having had a very heterogeneous surface, which was largely formed of solid rock, it was not desirable that the attempt should be made to reduce it all to the simplicity of pastoral scenery. What would the central motive of design require of the rest? Clearly that it should be given such a character as, while affording contrast and variety of scene, would as much as possible be confluent to the same end, namely, the constant suggestion to the imagination of an unlimited range of rural conditions.

The question of localizing or adjusting these two classes of landscape elements to the various elements of the natural topography of the Park next occurs, the study of which must begin with the consideration that the Park is to be surrounded by an artificial wall, twice as high as the Great Wall of China, composed of urban buildings. Wherever this should appear across the meadow-view, the imagination would be checked abruptly, at short range. Natural objects were thus required to be interposed, which while excluding the buildings as much as possible from view, would leave an uncertainty as to the occupation of the

---

[1] From the Landscape Architects' "Review of Recent Changes," 1872, given in full in Part II, pp. 240–270.
[2] From Doc. No. 5 of 1858, C. P. C.

space beyond, and establish a horizon line, composed, as much as possible, of verdure.[1]

It was, then, first of all, required that such parts of the site as were available and necessary to the purpose should be assigned to the occupation of elements which would compose a wood-side, screening incongruous objects without the Park as much as possible from the view of observers within it.

Secondly, of the remaining ground, it was required to assign as much as was available to the occupation of elements which would compose tranquil, open, pastoral scenes.

Thirdly, it was required to assign all of the yet remaining ground to elements which would tend to form passages of scenery contrasting in depth of obscurity and picturesque character of detail with the softness and simplicity of the open landscape.

By far the most extensive and important of the constructed accommodations of the Central Park are those for convenience of locomotion. How to obtain simply the required amount of room for this purpose, without making this class of its constructions everywhere disagreeably conspicuous, harshly disruptive of all relations of composition between natural landscape elements on their opposite borders, and without the absolute destruction of many valuable topographical features, was the most difficult problem of the design.

Observations of . . . . . [traffic difficulties] both in our own streets and in European parks, led to the planning of a system of independent ways; 1st, for carriages; 2d, for horsemen wishing to gallop; 3d, for footmen; and 4th, for common street traffic requiring to cross the Park. By this means it was made possible, even for the most timid and nervous, to go on foot to any district of the Park designed to be visited, without crossing a line of wheels on the same level, and consequently, without occasion for anxiety or hesitation.

Incidentally, the system provided, in its arched ways, substantial shelters scattered through the Park, which would be rarely seen above the general plane of the landscape, and which would be made as inconspicuous as possible, but to be readily found when required in sudden showers.

Without taking the present occasion to argue the point, we may simply refer to another incidental advantage of the system which, so far as we have observed, has not been publicly recognized, but which, we are confident, may be justly claimed to exist, in the fact that to the visitor, carried by occasional defiles from one field of landscape to another, in which a wholly different series of details is presented, the extent of the Park is practically much greater than it would otherwise be.[2]

[1] See discussion in Part I, Chapter XIII, of the changed condition due to the far greater height.
[2] The foregoing paragraphs have also been selected from the Landscape Architects' "Review" of 1872.

A full perusal of the various reports and letters in which Mr. Olmsted and Mr. Vaux discussed their design for the park brings out clearly how important they felt to be the subordination of architectural and engineering features to the predominant rural character,—so fine a feeling for unity of effect distinguishes the artistry of their plan from the commonplace points of view embodied in most of the others. The idea of the sunken transverse roads (said to have been suggested to Mr. Olmsted and Mr. Vaux by the traffic difficulties in Hyde Park and Regent's Park[1], London) was unique among all the plans submitted. While some other competitors stated that the cross-roads (for general street traffic) would not be a serious detriment to the park, Olmsted and Vaux felt that on their elimination from the park landscape depended the continuity of rural atmosphere.[2] No feature more thoroughly justified itself than this and by none is the originality of the plan more marked.

CHANGES PROPOSED.

At the time of awarding the prizes an unsuccessful attempt was made to pass a resolution that the Board was not committed by the award to the carrying out of the winning plan, but that good ideas from all plans should be used for selection. Fortunately the majority of the Board were more single-minded, and instead appointed a committee to confer with the Superintendent to report on the prosecution of work and "what, if any modification," should be "advisable in Plan No. 33, adopted by the Board." This committee reported on May 10 (see page 233) preserving the integrity of the Olmsted and Vaux plan against the subversive changes urged by one of the Commissioners (Mr. Dillon).

The Committee's report was accepted and resolutions passed "that the Superintendent be required to proceed forthwith to form working plans for the construction of the Park, and to stake out the principal features upon the ground," and "be authorized to call in the service of his associate (in design No. 33), and such other assistants, not exceeding six in number, as may be necessary to expedite the purpose of the first resolution."

A few days later Mr. Olmsted himself presented a report as to desirable changes in the "Greensward" plan.

---

[1] See Part II, Chapter I, p. 217. It is interesting to know that the first underpass in the Regent's Park Zoo was constructed before 1850 so that both Mr. Vaux and Mr. Olmsted may have been familiar with this, although they do not mention it in the "Greensward" report.

[2] See Appendix III, p. 560. Cf. p. 275.

Mixed Traffic on a Transverse Road in 1859

SUPERINTENDENT'S OFFICE, CENTRAL PARK,
14th May, 1858.

TO THE BOARD OF COMMISSIONERS, OF THE CENTRAL PARK.

A resolution of your body of the 13th instant requests me to report what modifications of plan 33, suggested by the other plans exhibited, or my own reflections, I should recommend to be adopted.

A careful examination of the plans referred to, has not at present suggested any changes which it would be desirable to make in plan 33, other than such as were recommended in the report of a Committee made to the Board May 10th after a conference between the Committee and myself. In the recommendations of that report, I concur.

Many very interesting and artistic conceptions that are not introduced in plan 33, are, without doubt, to be found in the other plans exhibited, but they do not, it is believed, contain any desirable feature of prominent importance that is not already provided for in plan 33.

The above remarks are intended to apply only to the skeleton or general idea of the plan for the Park. In detail, it is to be presumed that a more accurate study of the ground, as the construction of the Park proceeds, together with a careful consideration of the criticisms and suggestions of individual Commissioners, founded upon a personal examination of the plans, would lead to various modifications and improvements in the working out of the ideas presented in the plan and report. At present, the reasons given for the introduction of the various features still appear to hold good in all important particulars.

Respectfully,

FRED. LAW OLMSTED,
Superintendent.

APPOINTMENT OF MR. OLMSTED AS ARCHITECT-IN-CHIEF.

On May 17, 1858, the Commissioners amended the By-Laws of the Park to provide instead of a Superintendent a "Chief executive officer who shall be styled the Architect in Chief of the Central Park"; and a resolution was adopted: "That Mr. Frederick Law Olmsted, the present Superintendent, be appointed to the office." . . . (at a salary of $2500 per annum). It was also resolved "that the duties heretofore imposed on the Chief Engineer[1] and Superintendent be and the same are hereby devolved on the Architect in Chief. He shall be the chief executive officer of this Board, by or through whom all work on the Park shall be executed, and shall have the government and supervision of all employees at the Park. He

---

[1] Mr. Viele's office was thus abolished. Cf. Appendix III.

shall attend every meeting of the Board, but shall have no vote." At the meeting of May 27, 1858, the following communication was received from Mr. Olmsted:

CENTRAL PARK, May 20, 1858.

TO THE BOARD OF COMMISSIONERS OF THE CENTRAL PARK:

Gentlemen: I wish to acknowledge the honor I have received in your appointment to the office of Architect-in-Chief. You will allow me to assure you with what personal feeling and purposes it is accepted. On the first occasion in my life in which I ventured to address the public, I used the words, 'What artist so noble as he who, with far reaching conception of beauty and designing power, sketches the outlines, arranges the colors, and directs the shadows of a picture upon which nature shall be employed for generations before the work he has prepared for her hand shall realize his intentions'.[1] I had not, until within a few weeks, expected to be called to such a duty. I need not say with what diffidence and with what serious intention I undertake it, or how highly I value the judgment upon the preliminary study of Mr. Vaux and myself, which has induced you to select me for it.

In the first and highest responsibility of the office, I shall steadfastly regard the distant future, when alone it can be fully seen how far I am worthy of it.

As the Chief Executive Officer of the Board I shall aim to effect the realization of the plan of the Park, modified as a matured study of the needs of the public may seem to you desirable, in the most energetic and economical manner.

I hold myself responsible to the Board as an undivided body. I have asked favors of no party and of no man, and I acknowledge obligations in which the Park can be concerned to no party and to no man.

I am aware of the difficulties of the position. I meet them confidently, because if an honest and direct method of pursuing the purpose of my office cannot be successful, it will serve no ambition of mine.

Respectfully,
FRED. LAW OLMSTED,
Architect-in-Chief.

[1] The quotation is from Mr. Olmsted's first book, *Walks and Talks of an American Farmer in England.*

CHAPTER V

EARLY DEVELOPMENT AND USE OF THE PARK

THE GREAT CONSTRUCTION FORCE.

On June 17, 1858—just a month after his appointment as chief executive officer—Mr. Olmsted reported to the Board in regard to the organization and progress of work on the Park:

> A few short of one thousand men, on an average, have been at work during the week past. It is not possible to give an exact return of their employment, the excessive duty imposed upon the clerks having prevented the usual record during the last three weeks. Between four and five hundred men are engaged in excavation and filling for the entrance-drive and the promenade, about four hundred in draining and pond excavation, and seventy in grubbing and tillage of the nursery. The work is organized in divisions; Mr. Fielder, with two general foremen, directing the first; and Mr. Waring, also with two general foremen, the draining and pond excavation; Mr. Pilat, general foreman, has charge of the grubbing and nurserywork; Mr. Grant, is employed as my principal assistant over all.

In September, there were 2300 men employed on the Park. In October, a daily average of 2500 was authorized by the Board.

It is interesting to read[1] what this large force accomplished in the five months before winter weather set in.

> The thorough drainage of the part of the Park below the old Reservoir is nearly completed; the Drive is for the most part graded not only within the same area, but also extending to the north above the New Reservoir. Portions of the Drive intended as examples have been constructed in different methods, with their superstructure, in order to test the relative cost and efficiency of each. The Ride for equestrians is in progress. Several miles of

---

[1] 2nd Annual Report, C. P. C., for 1858.

the walks are graded, drained and gravelled, and in a condition for use.

Three bridges or viaducts over which the carriage road is carried and under which the horseback ride is to pass, are in a state of forwardness and promise to be structures of beauty as well as of utility; the Promenade, a prominent feature of the Park, is nearly complete with its broad walk and rows of transplanted trees of twenty years' growth.[1] The planting of the Park with a great variety of shrubs and trees was rapidly progressing when the cold weather suspended operations. A Lake of about twenty acres above Seventy-sixth street is so far completed as to admit of filling it with water during the winter, and has afforded healthful amusement and recreation for thousands in skating; the lower lake at Fifty-ninth street near the Fifth avenue is also well advanced.

The public demand for the pushing of construction work increased as the attractions of the partially finished portions were unfolded. The largest number of persons employed in construction on the Park at one time is recorded in 1859, amounting to 3666. By 1861, the Senate Investigation Committee reported that the number of men employed "was not over twenty-six hundred during any one time in the year 1860, and the work has so far progressed that it is not probable that so large a number will be again employed."

ENLARGEMENT OF THE PARK TO 110TH STREET; COST OF THE PARK.

As early as January, 1858, it had been recognized in the Board that the land above the original northern boundary of the Park at 106th Street, up to 110th Street, was logically a part of the Park and should be added to the area already acquired.

On January 6, Mr. Russell introduced a resolution providing for a Committee to report on the expediency of securing this additional land and to memorialize the Legislature.[2] On August 5,

[1] Cook's *Description of The New York Central Park*, 1869, comments on the lack of success with these large trees, so that the experiment was abandoned.

[2] The memorial (signed by Mr. Green as President of the Board) presented in January, 1859, (Doc. No. 16) argued as follows:

"[The Park's] present boundary on the north follows the line of the southerly side of One Hundred and Sixth street, crosswise the island, without respect to the natural topography of the land, and without reference to those features of the immediate neighborhood that so clearly indicate a natural boundary for the Park at One Hundred and Tenth street.

"The piece of land between One Hundred and Sixth and One Hundred and Tenth streets is mainly a ledge of rocks, the surface of which rising from the former towards the latter street, there abruptly terminates by a descent of about forty

1858, Mr. Olmsted, then recently appointed Architect-in-Chief of the Park, was directed to prepare a plan for the proposed addition, including the necessary adjustments in the "Greensward" design.

On April 2, 1859, the Legislature passed an act authorizing the extension of the Park north to 110th Street and the appointment of commissioners to take the land. The first Commissioners of Estimate and Assessment appointed in July, 1859, by the Supreme Court reported in November, 1860, giving the valuation of the additional sixty-five acres as $1,499,430 and also presenting an unduly large bill of expenses, later reduced by litigation. The Commissioners of the Central Park by resolution of December 26, 1860, discontinued proceedings to acquire the property, on the ground that the valuation was excessive. On June 27, 1861, they set about securing a different appraisal, and on February 28, 1862, proceedings for the extension of the Park were reopened by the appointment of three new Commissioners of Estimate and Assessment,[1] two of whom had served on the board to take the land of the original park. On March 31, 1863, their report was presented to the court, and confirmed April 21st. This second appraisal placed the value of the land at $1,179,590 with costs amounting to only one-fourth of the amount claimed by the former appraisers.

The Central Park Board was obliged to content itself with the necessity of paying this price for the land of which the value had been many times enhanced by the success of the original park in the five years consumed by the actual acquirement of the extension. How rapidly land values had been enhanced is recorded in Dr. Edward Hagaman Hall's account of Central Park (American Scenic and Historic Preservation Society, 16th Annual Report), which notes that the assessed valuation of this land in 1860 was only $183,850. Dr. Hall also gives a table covering the total cost of acquiring land for Central Park, which it is interesting at this point to review.

---

feet to the plain that extends over a mile and a half to the Harlem river. If it is permitted to owners of property to build houses on the north side of One Hundred and Sixth street at the present level, it must be at the exclusion of the most extended view commanded from the Park, including the High Bridge, the lower part of Westchester county, the Highlands of the Hudson, the East River and its islands, the Bay, Staten and Long Islands, and the shores of New Jersey.

"To lay and grade streets through this piece of land would be at very great cost, requiring a cutting of forty feet through solid rock. The cost of this to the city would form a very large portion of the value of the property.

"Your Memorialists believe that this piece of land should be added to the Park, and in this they are sustained by an almost unanimous public opinion."

[1] Samuel B. Ruggles, Luther Bradish, and Michael Ulshoeffer.

9½ acres purchased in 1838 for old reservoir site	$	22,000.00
27½ acres of common lands for old reservoir site		. . . . . .
106¾ acres for new reservoir site, award of April 14, 1856, including $342,695 to city for common lands..................................		729,964.50
10 acres in 1856, arsenal building and grounds.....		275,000.00
624¼ acres between 59th and 106th streets, award of Feb. 5, 1856.............................		5,069,693.70
Error and additional cost of same.............		3,749.85
Expenses and compensation of commissioners for same...................................		54,345.10
Incidental expenses of same..................		6,653.15
65 acres between 106th and 110th streets, award of Apr. 21, 1863...........................		1,179,590.00
Cost of first appraisal of same................		30,316.43
Cost of second appraisal of same..............		18,415.23
843 acres		$7,389,727.96 [1]

Of the total expenses of acquiring the land for the park, $1,657,-590[2] was assessed on property owners for the original area, and $171,075 for the extension. The net cost of land acquirement to the City can thus be placed at something like $3,850,000 for the original area, and $1,000,000 for the extension (these figures again varying in the various documents giving costs).

Apparently taking more or less these figures, Dr. Hall follows his table just quoted with the following observation: "It is interesting to note the rise in the price of land as improvements progressed in that [Central Park] region. The first nine and one-half acres bought in 1838 for the old reservoir cost about $2,316 an acre. In 1856, the new reservoir site cost about $6,838 an acre and the rest of the land south of One Hundred and Sixth street (not counting the Arsenal grounds) cost about $8,121 an acre. In 1863, the sixty-five acres north of One Hundred and Sixth street cost about $18,147 an acre."[3]

[1] As is not surprising where so many detailed items entered into the final result, the above figures vary somewhat from those given in the analysis of park costs by Commissioner Martin in Dept. of Public Parks Doc. No. 64 (Mar. 5, 1875), and these again from figures in earlier Central Park Reports (see 1863, p. 8). Cf. also pp. 95, 163, and 173-4, and the amount of early appropriations, mentioned in footnote on p. 65 *post*.

[2] Figures from Doc. No. 64.

[3] Ed. Note: At the time of the original taking the average market value of the land which was subsequently included in the second taking was undoubtedly much less than that of the land originally taken, because of its greater distance from the center of population. The extra cost to the city of making two bites of the cherry, due directly to the effect of the original park-taking in raising the value of adjoining land, was doubtless considerably greater than the actual difference in cost per acre as shown by the table. Part of this increase in price is of course attributable to a general rapid upward trend of land values in central and upper Manhattan irrespective of the Park, but it is questionable how much, if any, that increase alone would have exceeded the saving in compound interest and plus taxes during the seven-year period between the two takings. The transaction is a

In the Fall of 1859, Mr. Olmsted, worn out by the arduous duties and political harassments involved in organizing the park work, was granted leave of absence by the Commissioners[1] for a European study tour, and the sum of five hundred dollars was appropriated for his expenses. As the accredited representative of a great municipal enterprise in the new world which had already attracted much attention in the older countries,[2] Mr. Olmsted was enabled to make a comparison between park progress abroad and the accomplishments and possibilities of Central Park. His letter to the Commissioners reporting on his tour gives us an idea of contemporary objects of interest in Europe and doubtless the sources of some details in the later development of the Olmsted and Vaux designs.

CENTRAL PARK, DECEMBER 28TH, 1859.[3]

TO THE BOARD OF COMMISSIONERS OF CENTRAL PARK:

Gentlemen:—In accordance with your resolution requesting me to visit parks in Europe, I left New York on the 28th day of September, and arrived in Liverpool on Saturday the 11th of October. The same day I visited Birkenhead Park,[4] and obtained full particulars of its construction, maintenance, and management. On Monday, the 13th, I visited the Birmingham Sewerage and Filtering Works, in company with the Engineer, who subsequently furnished me with details of construction and working drawings. They are intended to relieve a park in the vicinity from a nuisance which had occasioned legal proceedings against the town, are ingenious and effective, and furnish valuable suggestions for the Central Park.

The same day I visited Aston Park, and called on the Secretary in charge, who supplied me with all desirable information. Some points in its management being peculiar, I subsequently called on the Mayor of Birmingham, who gave me his judgment with regard to them, and furnished me with police statistics by which

---

notable example of the extravagance of piecemeal successive acquirements in forming a park as opposed to the sound policy of determining the logical boundaries at the start and taking all the land at one and the same time so as to avoid paying for increments in value caused by the earlier park acquirements.—F. L. O.

[1] Resolution of Sept. 23, 1859.

[2] It is interesting to know that in 1860 the City of Hamburg made a gift of twelve swans for the Central Park, and also the Worshipful Company of Vintners and the Worshipful Company of Dyers of London, a gift of fifty swans.

[3] Doc. No. 4, C. P. C., for the year ending Apr. 30, 1860.

[4] Cf. description by Mr. Olmsted in 1850 quoted in Vol. I, *ante*, pp. 95 ff.

he considered them justified. The following day, the 14th, I visited the Park and Gardens of Chatsworth, including the private grounds of Sir Joseph Paxton, whom I regretted to find absent from home.

The next day I visited the Derby Arboretum, on the 16th the Botanic Garden of Birmingham, on the 17th the Royal Park and Forest of Windsor; on the 18th I reached London, early, and spent the day in the West-end parks.

The following day I was engaged in delivering letters and in correspondence, but, finding none of the gentlemen in town, to whom I had been especially accredited for the purposes of the Commission, on Monday I introduced myself at the office of Works of Her Majesty's Palaces and Parks. I was received with the most frank and generous kindness, and the same day orders were given to the Superintendents of all the public parks in the vicinity of London, respectively, to hold themselves at my disposal whenever I should visit their grounds, and to give me information on every point, without any reserve. I was also offered the use of documents and plans at the office, and, indeed, all assistance which I could desire was at once given to my purpose.

During the following fortnight, I was engaged every day upon the parks of London, some of which required several visits. I then proceeded to Paris, being detained one day on my way thither by a violent gale which prevented the boats from crossing the channel. At Paris I met Mr. Phalen, formerly a Commissioner of the Central Park, and yet retaining undiminished interest in the work. By him I was presented to M. Alphand, head of the government department of Roads and Bridges, under which the suburban improvements of Paris are carried on, who kindly supplied me with such information as I required, and directed an Engineer to attend me in my visit to the Bois de Boulogne. I remained a fortnight in Paris, examining as carefully as practicable in that time, all its pleasure-grounds and promenades, also visiting the parks of Versailles, of St. Cloud, and the wood of Vincennes, the improvement of which is now being prosecuted under the general direction of M. Alphand. To the Bois de Boulogne I made eight visits, four of them in company with either Mr. Phalen or Mr. Bigelow, of New York, whose previous observations upon the customs of the ground were of value to me.

On the 11th of November, I proceeded to Brussels, in the park and gardens of which capital a single day was most profitably occupied, owing to the great kindness of Dr. Linden, the director of the horticultural department of the Horticultural and Zoological Garden, and of Dr. Funck, the director of the zoological department, and chief editor of the *Royal Belgium* [sic] *Horticultural Journal,* both of whom evinced great interest in the Central Park

On the 12th, I visited the gardens, parade-ground, and promenade of Lille, and proceeded the same night to London. I remained again a week in the vicinity of London, visiting the Royal Botanic Gardens of Kew, the superintendent of which, Sir William Hooker, I found extremely interested in the Central Park, expecting my visit, and ready to furnish me with most valuable advice; the Crystal Palace Grounds at Sydenham, recently completed under the direction of Sir Joseph Paxton, the Secretary of the Company furnishing me with important information; the Royal Botanic Garden, and the Garden of the Zoological Society in Regent's Park, to the kindness of the Secretary of which I am also much indebted; and several public and private grounds of minor importance in and near London.

During this week, I was also engaged with Mr. Parsons in selecting a valuable collection of trees and shrubs to be shipped for the Central Park next spring; in examining the police department, and in obtaining plans, drawings, and photographs of English parks.

The following week, I visited the park at Elvaston Castle, which has the finest plantations of Evergreens in Europe; Trentham, the seat of the Duke of Sutherland, which I believe to be the best private garden in England; Biddulph Grange, a private place, remarkable for its rock-work; Stoneleigh Abbey, a very ancient park; Peel Park, and the Botanic Garden at Manchester, and other less noted parks and gardens in the Midland counties.

On the second of December, I crossed to Ireland, and on the third, visited Phoenix Park and the Zoological Garden of Dublin. On the fourth, I went to Cork, from whence, on the fifth, I took the Cunard steamer for America.

.   .   .   .

I am indebted to the liberality of Sir Richard Mayne, the commissioner and commanding officer of the Metropolitan Police of London, for an opportunity of studying the whole management of that admirable body, and to the Superintendent of the division patrolling the West-end parks, and the instructor of recruits, for very detailed information, which I trust will be of value on the Central Park, and well compensate the time employed in obtaining it.

Meeting Mr. Parsons before he had executed orders sent him some time before my journey was contemplated, to purchase trees for the Central Park, I thought it right to spend a short time in assisting him, and incidentally in more fully informing myself of the value and the cost of the varieties of trees and shrubs recently introduced.

I return with greatly improved health, and with a satisfaction in my duty increased by a contemplation of the finished work abroad. I am much impressed with the value of a close study, and the constant superintendence of details by a cultivated eye, in a work of the kind placed under my charge.[1]

    .   .   .   .

In my journey in Europe, the whole amount[2] authorized by the Board was expended. A collection of plans, drawings, photographs, documents, and books, purchased for the use of the Park, will be received from the Custom-House this week.

I recommend that an expenditure of one hundred dollars be authorized for mounting the plans, and arranging the collection in a safe and convenient form for reference.

Respectfully,

FRED. LAW OLMSTED,
Archt. and Supt.

GUIDANCE OF PUBLIC ENJOYMENT.

Only a month after Mr. Olmsted began his connection with Central Park as superintendent in 1857, he reported to the Commissioners[3] in regard to the training of the public in the use of its newly acquired pleasure ground.[4]

It is desirable that visitors to the Park, should be led to feel as soon as possible, that wide distinction exists between it and the general suburban country, in which it is the prevalent impression of a certain class that all trees, shrubs, fruit and flowers, are common property. So strong is this conviction with our gamin that the teachers of our ragged schools, when taking their pupils for a holiday into the country, have found it quite impossible to prevail upon them to refrain from completely ravishing the private gardens of the benevolent gentlemen who have offered them entertainment. This suggests what will probably be found a most delicate and difficult duty of the Commission and its officers. A large part of the people of New York are ignorant of a park, properly so-called. They will need to be trained to the proper use of it, to be restrained in the abuse of it, and this

---

[1] There follow some suggestions for the relief of the Superintendent from unimportant details connected with employment of common labor on the Park to leave time for the important duties of design. See text on p. 307 of Part. II.

[2] On Sept. 27, 1859, the Board had passed a resolution authorizing the sum of one hundred pounds sterling "for the use of the Architect-in-chief (F. L. Olmsted), to enable him to procure drawings and designs for entrances, and manner of irrigation, and the system adopted for the government and keeping of the various parks he may visit in Europe, and in supplying himself with such other information as he may deem useful in the future progress to completion of the Central Park." These drawings, etc., although delivered to the Board in 1859, cannot now be found in the archives of the Park Department.

[3] Monthly report read Oct. 13, 1857. An extract was printed in the *New York Tribune* the next day.

[4] See also Part II, Chapter VII.

can be best done gradually, even while the Park is yet in process of construction, and before it shall be thronged with crowds of unmanageable multitudes of visitors. So long as the Park remains uninclosed it will be difficult to draw a distinction between it and the adjoining commons. The attempt to do so will be calculated to foster malicious feeling with which it is said to be regarded by some persons, and which it must be the policy of the Commission, by every means consistent with its dignity, to allay, since it will always be in the power of individuals to do deplorable damage to the Park, with small danger of detection.

The Commissioners at the same meeting requested the Chief Engineer (Viele) and the Superintendent (Olmsted) to report what regulations would be necessary "for the proper preservation of order in the Park, and for the efficient prosecution of the work." A committee of the Board was appointed also to confer with the Police Commissioners as to the appointment of a police force for the Park.

The Police Commissioners did not wish to appoint and pay a special police force for the protection of Central Park but signified their willingness to empower any number of men as special policemen if nominated and paid by the Park Board. That the Board was content appears in a statement in its Report for 1859: "The training of the Park is essentially different from that of the general police force of the city, and the Board for this reason, has deemed it better that this full force should be of its own appointment and subject to its control." On February 9, 1858, the Park Commissioners authorized the nomination by the Superintendent (Olmsted) of twenty-four men "as keepers on the Central Park, at a compensation of $1.50 per day, the men to be sworn and empowered as special policemen and to be under the immediate direction of the Superintendent, and subject to removal by him." On February 3, 1859, the Board provided for keepers' uniforms and increased the size of the force to thirty-two. The importance of this larger force had been implied by the Board's statement in the Second Annual Report, January, 1859:

> The desire for healthful recreation and exercise, and the taste for the natural beauties of the Park, whether in its similitude to the garden, the forest or the field, develop and increase with the opportunity for their gratification. The Board at this early period, amid the bustle and business of forming the structure, clearly perceive that the high expectations of its beauty, as well as of its beneficent influence, must be disappointed unless *order and propriety* are maintained *supreme* over every foot of its surface, and within all of its Departments.

Mr. Olmsted's observations on park management abroad and his keen initial appreciation of the importance to the Park's popularity of specially-trained, courteous park police caused him to devote much thought and energy to the creation of an adequate force.[1] The following notice posted in the Keepers' Room in 1860 suggests his ideas of keepers' duties beyond those of merely preventing and arresting transgressions of the law.

I propose soon to make an examination of the Keepers to ascertain how well each is informed with regard to his duty, especially as to his ability to direct strangers to different parts of the park, to instruct them as to distances, size, purposes, cost, etc., of different objects in the park, as to his knowledge of the proper method of proceeding under certain circumstances, etc.

On all points where information, likely to be inquired for by visitors, is lacking, I propose to supply it, and shall be glad to answer any inquiries with regard to park matters, which may be proper subjects of public interest.

FRED. LAW OLMSTED.

In 1860 also, the Senate Investigation Committee commended the

well organized force of fifty men . . . styled "park-keepers"; allowing eight hours of active service per day to each man, this provides, on an average, but one man to guard each forty acres. The keepers are in the prime of life, and have been taken mainly from among the foremen and mechanics employed in the construction of the Park. They are neatly uniformed, are subject to military drills and discipline; and their well established efficiency and popularity evince the discrimination with which they have been selected, and the care with which they are trained for this duty.

By vote of March 16, 1858, the Commissioners had published their first ordinances for the government of the Park, and these were enlarged by vote of September 23, 1859.[2] The regulations were intended to secure to the public the enjoyment of riding or driving or walking free from the solicitations of pedlers or the noises of commercial traffic with as few limitations as were compatible with the rights of all and the preservation of the park scenery. From time to time these rules were added to, as experience proved necessary, until the ordinances posted about the park in 1860 were not far different from those in many parks of today.

[1] See Part II, Chapter VIII.
[2] For the full text of these regulations, see p. 409, and Minutes of the Board, Nov. 1, 1860, Dec. 8, 1864, etc.

The Commissioners wrote in their Annual Report for 1861:

> When it is considered that the establishment and successful conduct of a park of great extent has not yet been accomplished under any except those forms of government where absolute and peremptory authority is maintained, it becomes an interesting problem whether the rules requisite for the maintenance of the Park in a condition such as will gratify a cultivated taste, and operate as an educator of the people, will meet with cheerful acquiescence.

That the original organization of Park Keepers was a success and that the public soon became accustomed to the reasonable restraint of the rules and regulations are attested by the Board's statistics of arrests accompanied by the following comment in the Annual Report for 1863.

> Of the great numbers that visit the Park, but a very small portion require the hand of authority to check mischievous practices.
> The quietude of the grounds, the natural beauties, and the order that prevails, are invitations to enjoyment, and are all, by the mere eloquence of their silent teachings effectual appeals to sustain, rather than transgress, the necessary regulations for their preservation.

A year later the same general disposition prevailed "to conform to the prescribed regulations—The larger portion of arrests are for fast driving." As late as 1868 the Board could report: "Nothing has occurred during the year to disturb good order. The number of arrests is less than the previous year." The early orderliness is well to remember in the light of the later attempts to restore it after the demoralizing influences of the Tweed administration.

State Senate Vindication of Park Management.

In April, 1860, the New York State Senate "having expressed its confidence in the management of the Board by passing without a dissenting voice a bill placing the sum of two and one-half millions of dollars at its disposal for the completion of the Park, constituted Senators Murphy, Munroe, and Rotch,[1] a committee to examine into its affairs, condition, and progress."[2]

[1] The members of the committee are further characterized in the 5th Annual Report, C. P. C., for 1861: Hon. John McLeod Murphy, widely known as an engineer of skill and experience; Hon. Allen Munroe, experienced merchant and banker; Hon. Francis M. Rotch, a Vice-Pres. of the New York State Agricultural Society.
[2] From 4th Annual Report, C. P. C., for 1860.

From this committee's report presented January 25, 1861,[1] we find that "The foundation for the resolution by which your committee was raised is believed to have been certain rumors first set in motion by the disappointments of ex-members of the commission and discharged employees. The failure to fix any malpractice or want of integrity on the commissioners, is complete and thorough."

The entire satisfaction of the committee is expressed at the conclusion of the report:

The committee, with the view of a more thorough and detailed examination of the various departments of work at the Park, the strength and sufficiency of the architecture, its drainage, both above and below ground, and its water system, engaged the services of Julius Kellersberger, Esq., a skillful and competent architect and engineer. Mr. Kellersberger occupied twenty-one days in the examination; his opinion, which is herewith submitted, furnishes the highest testimony as to the character, efficiency, economy, and management of the work.

In the selection of officers and agents, for carrying out the design, the commissioners have been singularly fortunate, as the results of their operations thus far clearly show—the work standing already foremost and conspicuous among those of its kind in Europe.

From the commencement of operations at the Park the Commissioners seem to have been guided by a desire to complete the work acceptably to that portion of the public who appreciate the benefits of good management, and the advantages and ultimate economy of a substantial structure, over one superficial, though perhaps less expensive and durable.

The plan is harmonious;[2] it is an entire design for the whole ground, contrived with a knowledge of the capacities of the land, and of the wants of a great city. It is obvious that the same minds that have thus far carried out the work, should continue it without interruption.

---

[1] Printed in full as a State Senate Document and also in the 4th Annual Report, C. P. C., for 1860.

[2] Earlier in the report the committee had stated:

"The plan adopted was that of Messrs. Olmsted & Vaux, upon which, with some alterations, the Park is now being constructed. Its merits are peculiar, presenting in the proposed mode of developing the ground, an extraordinary combination of beauties, with accommodation for the throngs of a great city both novel and useful."

"The few witnesses offered for the purpose of showing a deficiency of taste in the laying out of the Park, of course differed, in some respects, from the authors of the plan adopted by the Board. It would be singular if differences of opinion did not exist in such matters. In this respect, the Park is its own justification; it is open to public examination; it has received the approbation of the public, with an almost unprecedented unanimity, and meets fresh enconiums as it daily develops its attractions."

The enterprise is of such a nature that it will continue to require, for its present conduct and subsequent care, a highly cultivated taste, combined with integrity in its pecuniary affairs.

Whenever its management becomes subject to the changes attending the success of one political party or the other, the highest results of this beneficent work will be lost, and it will pass into the control of persons who keep their position only while they maintain themselves in the turbid pool of the politics of the city. In order, therefore, to obviate this contingent source of embarrassment, and not to imperil the progress and early completion of the Park, the committee are of opinion that the Board of Commissioners should be separate and distinct, in their control and management of the work entrusted to them, from the municipal government.

The committee, after a careful examination into the subjects referred to them, do not hesitate to say, that the Commissioners have now among them the elements required for the completion and control of their work, superadded to a comprehension acquired by nearly four years of experience.

It would be unwise, and in contravention of the dictates of good judgment, to relinquish the services of those who have so far successfully carried on, without remuneration, this important undertaking.

The committee concur in what they believe to be the general judgment of the commissioners, that as the duties have now become executive, they would be more conveniently performed by a less number, and they would respectfully recommend to the Legislature the reduction of the Board, so that it shall not exceed six members,[1] and that the arrangement be effected in such way as will best preserve to it the experience and judgment of the most efficient of its present members.

All of which is respectfully submitted.

> JNO. McLEOD MURPHY,
> ALLEN MUNROE,
> FRANCIS M. ROTCH,
> *Committee.*

It was just at the time when the findings of the Albany investigators were being made known that Mr. Olmsted made the following comments on the Park in a letter to Charles Brace (December 8, 1860):

> It is not yet time to fully estimate the merit of the Park as a work of art. There were great difficulties both essential and political (or social). The former consisted in the heterogeneous, barren and immobile qualities of the ground to be dealt

---

[1] The Board was reduced to eight members in Feb., 1862, by a resolution of the Board itself declaring three offices vacant.

with. I believe that they have been overcome very successfully and that the park will not only be more convenient for exercise than any existing Metropolitan pleasure-ground, its details more studied, more varied and substantial in character, but subordinate to general effects, than in any other. In anything you say of the design, remember that Vaux is to be associated. There were 34 plans in competition before the Commissioners, some of them coming from Europe. As to the organization and management of the work, I think it more creditable to me than anything I have done publicly. It was within a fortnight of a most exciting election (when Wood was defeated) and during the prevalence of bread-riots, a larger number of men being out of employment than at [any] previous period of the city's history, that the Common Council voted money to go on with the work and I was unexpectedly ordered to organize a large force for the purpose. It was a general impression that the pretence of work was merely a form of distributing the public money to the poor and my office was for several days regularly surrounded by an organized mob carrying a banner inscribed "Bread and Blood." This mob sent in to me a list of 10,000 names of men alleged to have starving families demanding that they should be immediately put at work. I had almost no assistance, but within a week I had a thousand men economically employed and rigidly discharged any man who failed to work industriously and to behave in a quiet orderly manner. Since the plan was adopted from two to four thousand men have been generally at work besides those employed by contractors, but with a single exception, when a thousand workmen on an adjoining work struck for higher wages and two gangs on the park joined them and were immediately discharged, there has been the most perfect order, peace and good feeling preserved, notwithstanding the fact that the laborers are mainly from the poorest, and what is generally considered the most dangerous class of the great city's population. Mr. Kellersberger, an experienced Swiss engineer, appointed by the Senate Investigating Committee last spring to make a detailed inspection of the work, and who made his inspection very faithfully, without communicating with me at all and as respects the management without consulting any of us, reported the other day that the organization and superintendence were most excellent and much better than on any other public work in the United States.

I think it important to me that the public should know this and that I should have the credit of it. I am anxious to remain superintendent of the Park, that is.

Only a few weeks later, however, Mr. Olmsted, harassed by the restrictions imposed by the Board through Mr. Green as comptroller, attempted to resign from his position at the Park.[1] The circum-

[1] See Part II, Chapter III, pp. 309 ff.

stances of his continuance in the work, he explains to his father in a letter dated March 22, 1861:

> I presented my resignation in January. It was read in the Board and they agreed to take no notice of it in their minutes and consider it as not read. After a long talk with a majority I was induced to withdraw it, but with a clear understanding that my authority on the park should be placed on a different footing this spring or that I should quit. We have been working hard at estimates all winter. The rate of cost must be reduced 20 percent or we are likely to fail of completing the park within the sum assigned.[1] As I should be held responsible, I refuse to go on unless I can manage it my own way. All this has been carefully kept mum, so as not to embarrass the proceedings at Albany.

IMMEDIATE INFLUENCE OF THE PARK ON PUBLIC TASTE.[2]

In spite of the difficulties which beset Mr. Olmsted in the management of the Park, he could not fail to derive satisfaction from its great popularity and the immediate benefits which it conferred upon the people of New York.

As early as December 29, 1858, the first skating was permitted on the Park,—a sport then little practiced by the citizens. In reviewing the tremendous growth of skating as a popular diversion, the Commissioners reported in 1866:

> During the first season a scanty supply of commonplace American skates, with a few old-fashioned pairs of English manufacture, were all that could be discovered in the shop-windows. This matter of skating and the necessary implements had been fairly left to private enterprise from time immemorial, and the results showed that the varieties of skates were few and poor and the varieties of skaters still fewer and poorer.
>
> A single year, however, developed a marked improvement. Ice there had always been; but ice preserved day after day in good order and order preserved day after day on good ice were attractive novelties, and the tide . . . was fairly set in the direction of this health-giving winter amusement.
>
> On the whole it may be said, that up to this time the influence of

---

[1] In the Act of 1857 (see p. 541) the Legislature set $100,000 as the maximum annual interest on the sum for which stock could be issued for the construction of the Park. This sum was increased by act of 1859 (see p. 542) to bear an annual interest of $125,000. Reckoned with interest at six percent the revised capital sum was thus $2,083,333. In March, 1860, an additional capital sum to bear an annual interest of $150,000 (Cf. p. 543) was voted for construction; or a total appropriation of $4,583,333. For a discussion of the difficulties of keeping the cost of the Park down in the face of political pressure, see p. 299.

[2] Cf. Part I, Chapter XII.

the Park on the amusement of skating has been beneficial, for it has directly encouraged habits of active winter exercise in both old and young, and, indirectly, has stimulated invention and assisted in the development of a new branch of home manufacture.

Although throughout the country a great impulse was given to skating by the opening of the lakes of the Central Park, nowhere was the sport more celebrated.   There is a description in one of the reports of the Central Park Commissioners (1863) that quite transcends the usual prosy style of official documents:

The movements of a throng of skaters, on a clear day, chasing each other in gleeful mood over the crystal ceiling of the imprisoned lake, the fur-clad inmates of a thousand gay vehicles coursing along the silver snow to the music of bells, the dusky foliage of the fir and pine on the adjacent heights, wrapped with wreaths of fleecy white; leafless branches strung with a fairy network of icy pearls, frail but gorgeous as it glistens and flashes with a thousand hues in every glance of the sunlight, form in our midst a winter scene unmatched by that of any capital or country of modern times, because it is obtainable only in a climate, amid an extent of population of wealth and liberality, such as peculiarly characterizes this Queen City of the Western Hemisphere.

To match this gay winter's scene, the same report has a picture drawn on an equally popular summer occasion,—one of the regular Saturday band concerts instituted in July, 1859, and thereafter given weekly during long summer seasons.

Few landscapes present more attractive features than that of the Park on a music day.   Thousands of brilliant equipages throng the drives.   The waters of the Lake are studded with gaily-colored pleasure boats, appearing now and then in striking contrast with the green foliage that fringes its banks; the waterfowl float proudly over its surface; children play on the lawns; throngs of visitors from divers climes move among the trees, whose leaves, fanned with the soft lays of the music, wave silent approval; all seems full of life and enjoyment; and as some familiar strain breathes a sweet influence around, the whole appears like some enchanted scene.

Every effort was made by the Commissioners to keep abreast of foreign progress by introducing new band instruments and to elevate the popular taste by the variety and excellence of the

Courtesy of New York Public Library

Published by Edmund Foerster & Co.   John Bachmann, Del.

Skating in Central Park at Night, 1865

compositions performed. The official reports[1] mention the Commission's gratification at popular approval of the classical music which formed an important part of the concert programs. Although the early concerts were financed wholly by contributions from the street-railroads which profited by the transportation of crowds, it was not long before the major burden was borne from municipal coffers, and public demand could be satisfied only by concerts on both Wednesdays and Saturdays.

The recreations of driving and riding were almost immediately stimulated by the opening of the Park roads. No such good pavements had been known before and comparatively few carriages had been kept for pleasure driving, and still fewer horses for town riding. The excellent surface of the drives in the Park which the Commissioners threw open as fast as a section was completed met with instant patronage. The same remark could have been made about Central Park as about Prospect Park some years later:

As the park has come more and more into use, new habits and customs, and with them new tastes, have been developed. There is already many times as much pleasure driving as there was five years ago.

Although there was a delay in securing the tan-bark ordered for the rides, as soon as these could be thrown into use, they shared the same popularity as other features.

The first real park in America was a success, and whatever obstacles to its completion were to be met during the troublous days of the Civil War and its aftermath had little effect on its increasing enjoyment by the public.

[1] A very interesting discussion of outdoor music abroad and on the Central Park will be found in the 11th Annual Report of the Commissioners for 1867.

CHAPTER VI

THE PARK DURING THE CIVIL WAR AND AFTER

WORK ON THE PARK NOT DISCONTINUED.

On April 24, 1861, almost immediately after the outbreak of the Civil War, the Board of Supervisors of the County of New York adopted a resolution to the effect that the Commissioners of the Central Park and other Boards deriving money from the County treasury "be requested to suspend the work under their control, so far as may be warranted by a proper regard for the public interest."

In reply to this, the following communication was addressed to the Supervisors:

> The Commissioners of the Central Park respectfully suggest, that the discontinuance of work at the Park at this time, when employment is with difficulty obtained, will be peculiarly onerous. . . . [Also] it would be expensive and uneconomical. Many structures on the Park are unfinished and will sustain damage if not protected and completed. . . . While the Commissioners of the Central Park believe that a sound public sentiment coincides with the views as to the propriety of limiting public expenditure, . . . yet they do not deem this a time for public bodies to manifest a greater degree of timorousness and apprehension than has yet been shown by business men in their affairs, nor do they believe that they would be justified in a suspension of their work.[1]

To this policy the Board of Supervisors agreed on July 9th, by rescinding its earlier resolution.

Although the development of the Park was to proceed without interruption, its designers were obliged to modify their connection with it. In June of 1861, Mr. Olmsted had secured leave of absence to accept appointment as secretary of the "Commission of Inquiry and Advice in respect of the United States Forces," later the Sanitary Commission, from which sprang the American Red Cross. Mr. Vaux, whose health at the time forbade his engaging in the Union Service, generously undertook to carry on Mr. Olmsted's

[1] 5th Annual Report, C. P. C., for 1861.

duties at the Park, as far as possible freeing him to remove to Washington for active executive work. Mr. Green's wielding of the Park Comptrollership made the designers' advice less sought than before.

At intervals Mr. Olmsted returned to New York, in the first four months of his leave of absence managing to spend some six weeks on the Park.

On January 6, 1862, we find in the Minutes of the Central Park Board:

> Whereas, for the last half year or more this Board have not required the services of Mr. Olmsted, for the greater part of the time; and,
>
> Whereas, since the month of June last the Board has yielded the services of Mr. Olmsted, as Architect-in-Chief and Superintendent, to his other public engagements on the Sanitary Commission, and it being represented that he desires to continue to devote a further portion of his time to the service of such Commission, therefore,
>
> Resolved, that his salary be reduced one half, from July 12, 1861, at which rate Mr. Olmsted shall be paid for his services, from and after that date.[1]

In the arduous days of the Fall of 1862 Mr. Olmsted still did what he could for Central Park. He wrote of himself from Washington to his wife, in reply to the suggestion of a vacation:

> I think you may calculate thus: Fred will come to New York in a few days, *to work on the park*. That is his object and his only justification for being away from Washington. He will need to give the greater part of every day to the park and of every night to the Sanitary Commission, which holds regular meetings two evenings in the week at about Madison Square and four times a week after three o'clock at 498 Broadway. He will come short of this only from very constraining and important demand elsewhere or from fatigue amounting to illness. That is simply his duty as a man. Local and special family duties must rightly be arranged when they can on this stem, because if *the men* don't as a rule, at this time so arrange their special family duties in relation to the larger communal-part of their family duties, there is the greatest possible danger of such an upsetting of the very frame of society, that it would have been better that our children had never been born. A rather dark prospect, but not as dark as most other folks' that I meet now-a-days—and whether it is dark or not is simply a question of heroism. It is a day for heroes and we must be heroes along with the rest.

[1] Mr. Olmsted shared the salary with Mr. Vaux, who by the summer of 1862 felt that both should resign, if the latter's health warranted volunteering.

As we have seen from the descriptions in Chapter V, the results on the Park justified the great effort which Mr. Olmsted made not to take his hand from guiding the fulfillment of the "Greensward" design. Writing in a retrospective letter,[1] Mr. Olmsted said of this period to the conclusion of 1862:

> The construction of roads and walks, arches and bridges, the formation of lakes, greens and lawns, the changes of surface and the preparation and distribution of soil on the rocky parts to be planted, was principally executed. The main bodies of foliage were brought to a high state of provisional finish; the nucleus of a keepers force was formed and instructed and certain customs of public use were established, the rude fundamental work needed for the realization of the design was thus in a great measure done and some little more.

Resignation of the Landscape Architects; Their Relation to Andrew H. Green.

The friction between the landscape architects and the Park Commissioners, whose authority was represented by the Comptroller of the Park, Mr. Green, was caused not only by the actual political circumstances but largely by fundamental differences of temperament between Mr. Green on the one hand and Mr. Olmsted and Mr. Vaux on the other.

No one was perhaps more thoroughly aware than Mr. Green of the rotten politics of the City of New York at that period, or more thoroughly determined to keep the Park from becoming a prey to the political harpies ready to pounce on it at the slightest relaxation of vigilance. Mr. Green's ability and integrity being well known to the Commissioners, on September 15, 1859, they had entrusted the full control of the Park to him with the title of Comptroller. He was watchdog of the Treasury and guardian of the development of the park in the interest of all the citizenry of New York, as opposed to its use as a vehicle for the enrichment of politicians or the gratification of individual whims. His temperament appears to have been that of an honest, active-minded, self-confident, masterful man, intolerant of opposition, perhaps rather lacking in sense of humor, apt to carry his vigilance in the city's behalf roughshod over the beliefs of others equally honest and sincere and sometimes no less intelligent. Apparently he was not free from what is perhaps the most besetting limitation of executives of great personal

[1] F. L. O. to the Hon. Philip Bissinger, 1873.

energy,—unwillingness or inability to delegate plenary powers to subordinates in their designated fields and refrain from dictatorial interference in the details of their work. He was a sort of practical idealist, perhaps a little obstinate in his methods of realizing the ideals he so constantly had to defend.

Mr. Olmsted and Mr. Vaux were equally idealists, but there was about them something less Spartan and more human. They were artists, with the sensitiveness and delicacy of touch natural to their genius. More than Mr. Vaux, Mr. Olmsted was, like Mr. Green, an organizer and director of men. From 1858 to 1859, the management of Park affairs had been largely in his hands as Architect-in-Chief and Superintendent, responsible directly and solely to the Board as a whole.

To a man of Mr. Olmsted's sensibilities the exasperation caused by the political machinations to secure patronage in the Park had been great and disturbing. He was physically and mentally worn out at the time of his European trip late in 1859. He felt the responsibility for the attainment of results of priceless value to the public, which he clearly envisaged as implications of the "Greensward" design, but many of which others had to take on faith until he worked them out. He thus became more and more chafed at the tying of his hands by the Comptroller in matters which he considered vital to the fullest success obtainable under the recognized limitations, financial and otherwise;[1] and fettered as he was from the start by these difficulties, especially of securing tolerable efficiency of labor, it is indeed small wonder that the additional restrictions imposed by Mr. Green as the overlord of the Park strained their relations almost to the breaking point.

We can quite imagine on one side Mr. Green,—who was one of the staunch advocates of the "Greensward" design,—determined as an experienced administrator to put it through within the appropriation allowed by the Legislature, distrustful of the practical judgment of a man as little experienced in New York politics as Mr. Olmsted and as recently embarked on the new profession of park making; and on the other side, Mr. Olmsted and Mr. Vaux, tremendously imbued with certain still invisible ideals of the Park as they intended to create it, cognizant of details necessary to this end and of means calculated to produce the desired results, unused to a strong hand above them, and feeling themselves thwarted or overridden arbitrarily, even though with the most worthy motives.

---

[1] See his own statement of these vexing limitations given in Part II, pp. 309 ff.

Was it not inevitable that sparks should fly, that slow friction should wear away the less resistant surface?

In the light of this understanding of their characters, it is possible to reconcile both the picture of Mr. Green resolutely guiding the Park in safety for over ten years, as drawn by his biographer Mr. John Foord,[1] and the almost amusing letter written by Mr. Olmsted to one of the Commissioners attempting to explain and mitigate remarks which he had made about Mr. Green in an explosion of accumulated irritation.

CENTRAL PARK, NOVEMBER 12TH, 1861.

My dear Sir:—I think it right to state to you the conviction which led me to use certain expressions, in our conversation today, which you heard with surprise. I do not like to have said that of a man in his absence which I might avoid saying in his presence, or which I might prefer not to have repeated to him, without giving a reason for it. Nor do I like to seem to deal in innuendo.

My conviction is—and it certainly has been acquired with reluctance and deliberation enough—that the limits within which it might have been possible for me to effectively serve the Central Park Commission, have been gradually, skilfully, carefully and circumspectly curtailed. From the day when Mr. Green received the first instalment of a salary larger than that of the Architect-in-Chief and Superintendent, there has been a constant effort not only to assume more important responsibilities and more valuable duties, but to include all other duties and responsibilities within his own, and to make those of the inferior office not only completely and servilely subordinate but to make them appear of a temporary value only and unimportant even temporarily. How successful this policy has been, the fact that I could be absent from the park four months, without giving occasion for the slightest action on the part of the Commission, demonstrates, as possibly it has been intended that it should, very effectually. What part, may I ask, have you, my dear sir, supposed that I bore in the economy of the park when (yourself the only arboriculturist of the Commission) you drove through the park in the heart of the planting season without ascertaining my presence and without inquiring how, supposing me absent, the responsibility to the Board, for the planting could be assumed by anyone else? Since I first went to Washington, I have in fact been six weeks on the park. But I have never had reason to think that I was wanted there by the Commission or its representative. My advice has not been asked when present, any more than it has by letter when absent. When in New York, I have never been asked how long I should stay, nor when I should come again. I have no reason to believe and I do not believe

[1] See Chapters V and VI in the *Life and Public Services of Andrew H. Green.*

that my taste, judgment and skill in the laying out and management of the work, was any more wanted, *or was of any more use,* last year than this. For the means of performing what duties were then yet nominally allowed me I was made so absolutely and to the last detail dependent on Mr. Green's pleasure . . . that I feel, though relieved of an immense weight of anxiety and humiliation, I have no less impressed my own taste on the work this year, than the last.

Mr. Green's services as a politician have been perhaps essential to the Commission. The power he has may be the proper price of these services. Cooperation with Mr. Green, while he thus controls the park, so far as I can hope to yet influence it, is essential. I cannot counterplot him. To charge upon him individually that for which the Commission is finally responsible is unnecessary. To do so, to his face, would be to stimulate enmity and to establish a quarrel. To quarrel with him, while I am his official subordinate, would be undignified and impolitic, and would be playing into the hands of the enemies of the park. I said to you once before, "I will not remain on the park to quarrel with Mr. Green." I will not, if I can avoid it, quarrel, or give occasion for quarrel with him while I remain in the service of the park. But, conscious that my devotion to the park has forced me to patience, he has continued to pursue a course toward me, of which no honest man could know himself to be subject without occasionally giving more or less articulate vent to his feelings such as I was so unfortunate as to betray to you.

Yours very respectfully,

FRED. LAW OLMSTED.

Each man was devoted to the Park, and each believed in his own judgment as to different methods for making the Park of the utmost service to the people of New York. It is pleasant to record that Mr. Green appears to have later appreciated the importance of supplementing his own abilities to serve the Park by recalling Olmsted and Vaux in 1865; and that Mr. Olmsted was finally harried off the Park by the politicians in 1878 only after Mr. Green's steadfast official support of the Olmsted and Vaux ideals was withdrawn by the termination of his service as Comptroller of the City and County of New York, for which office he had relinquished his seat on the Park Board in 1873.

In the stress of war-time the progress and arrangements of the Park became increasingly unsatisfactory to the landscape architects; and on May 22, 1863, Mr. Olmsted wrote to his father:

Vaux has been finally badgered off the park and my relations with it are finally closed. We couldn't bear it even as consulting

architects. They wound it up with a very innocent compli-
mentary resolution.

At the meeting of the Board of Commissioners on May 14, 1863,
the Olmsted and Vaux letter of resignation had been read:

NEW YORK, MAY 12TH, 1863.

TO THE PRESIDENT OF THE BOARD OF PARK COMMISSIONERS

Dear Sir,—As we now find that it will be impracticable for
either of us to give a continuous personal attention to the Park
operations during the ensuing summer, we feel called on with
much regret to give up the appointment we at present hold
under the Commissioners, so soon as in their estimation our
resignation may be acted on without inconvenience to the work.[1]

We remain, dear sir,
Yours faithfully,
OLMSTED AND VAUX,
Landscape Architects.[2]

[1] On motion of Mr. Green,
Resolved, that the resignation of Messrs. Olmsted and Vaux, Landscape
Architects, to the Board, be accepted and that their letter of resignation be
entered in full upon the minutes.
Resolved, that on this the termination of official relations with Messrs. Olmsted
and Vaux, the Board takes pleasure in expressing its high esteem for them personally, and its unabated confidence in their high artistic taste, and in their
superior professional abilities.
[2] The official use of the term "landscape architect," perhaps adopted by Mr.
Vaux, appears to have arisen between Jan. 1862 and Jan. 1863 during Mr. Olmsted's absence in Washington. The map in the annual report presented on the
former date is signed: "Fred. Law Olmsted, Archt. in chief; Calvert Vaux, Consulting Architect," while the signature on the map of the latter date is Olmsted
and Vaux, Landscape Architects. Mr. Vaux speaks of the term in a retrospective
letter written to Mr. Olmsted in 1865: "I felt that the L. A. must be the title
I must fight under if I fought at all, and fight I feel I must some day; and yet as
you know, it nearly made you feel that I had deserted you and taken advantage
of your absence." Of the term, Mr. Olmsted wrote shortly afterwards to Mr.
Vaux:
"I am all the time bothered with the miserable nomenclature of L. A. *Landscape* is not a good word, *Architecture* is not; the combination is not—*Gardening*
is worse. I want English names for *ferme* and *village ornée, street* &c. *ornée*—but
ornée or decorated is not the idea,—it is artified and rural artified, which is not
decorated merely. The art is not gardening nor is it architecture. What I am
doing here in California especially is neither. It is sylvan art, fine art in distinction from Horticulture, Agriculture, or sylvan *useful* art. We want a distinction between a nurseryman or a market gardener or an orchardist, and an
artist; the planting of a street or road, the arrangement of village streets, is neither
Landscape Art, nor *Architectural* Art, nor is it both together in my mind,—of
course it is not, and it will never be in the popular mind. Then neither park nor
garden, nor street, road, avenue, or drive, nor boulevard, apply to a sylvan
bordered and artistically arranged system of roads, side walks and public places,—
playgrounds, parades, etc. There is nothing of park, garden, architecture, or
landscape (ED. NOTE: Landscape is evidently here used in a much narrower sense
than that which Mr. Olmsted later came to use it.) in a parade ground—not

THE PARK TO 1865; THE WORK OF IGNAZ I. PILAT.

Two years after the official severance of relations between the Landscape Architects and the Park Board, Mr. Vaux had occasion to come to the rescue of the Park, then threatened in its southern portion by the proposed enlargement of the Fifth Avenue entrance.[1] He took this occasion to explain publicly the status of the Park's development by printing in the New York *Evening Post* a copy of his letter of May 1, 1865, to the President of the Park Commissioners, containing the following statement:

> For the first five years the improvements were made in accordance with our plans and under our general direction and supervision. In the spring of 1863, feeling that we were placed by the action of the Board in an impracticable position, we resigned the appointment we then held as Landscape Architects to the Commission, and have, since that time, ceased to exercise any recognized control over the work. No appointment has, however, been made to fill the vacancy caused by our resignation, and all that has been done during the last two years is, as you are aware, based on plans that were prepared by us and approved by your Board prior to the termination of our engagement. During these two years I have cheerfully responded to such inquiries in regard to the plan as have been made to me from time to time by Mr. Green, the Commissioner to whom the management of the affairs of the Park has been chiefly intrusted, and on some few occasions I have visited the work with him for the purpose of making suggestions in regard to points of special interest. The Commissioners have not, to be sure, thought it incumbent on them to recognize our authorship of the design they are using, and with somewhat questionable taste have erased our names from the plan that accompanies their annual report; they have also considered it unnecessary to offer us any compensation for our services either in the preparation of the plan adopted for the extension of the Park to One Hundred and Tenth Street, (in itself a costly public improvement,) or for the time occupied in consultations with their representative; but my aim throughout has been simply to secure, if possible, a virtual carrying out of the leading ideas of our scheme, and I now have the satisfaction of knowing that at this time the Park, although a mere outline, incomplete in a thousand ways even where it seems most finished, and only a crude suggestion of what we intended to make it, is

---

necessarily, though there may be a little of any or each or all. If you are bound to establish this new art, you don't want an old name for it. And for clearness, for convenience, for distinctness, you do need half a dozen technical words at least."

[1] For a discussion of Mr. Hunt's gateway design and proposed rearrangement of adjoining park features, see Part II, Chapter VI.

still an accomplished fact, a whole, and is in such a stage of forwardness that it exhibits clearly to every transient visitor the
special characteristics intended to be given it when we set to work
to solve the somewhat intricate municipal problem involved in its
arrangement, and the general intention we had in view when
first intrusted with its development as a work of landscape
architecture.

The really park-like impression created by Central Park in
1864–5 found expression also in the Commissioners' report of that
date.[1]

Citizens and strangers appreciate the ample and increasing
attractions of this common pleasure ground.
The foliage, becoming dense with the lapse of time, constantly
presents new and more striking effects.   The planting has been
done in areas as the ground was prepared; upon some portions,
consequently, the growth gives evidence of more maturity than
upon others.   Already in some parts of the Park, there is sufficient
development to readily lead the imagination to realize, in some
measure, beauties which the hand of nature will perfect in her own
good time.

How much credit for the success of the planting effects was due
to the work of Mr. Ignaz I. Pilat,[2] then Head Gardener of the Park,
appears pleasantly in a letter from Olmsted & Vaux to Mr. Pilat
written in July, 1865.

DEAR MR. PILAT,
You will we know be glad to learn that we have accepted a
re-appointment and are again Landscape Architects to the
Central Park.
Although our general plan, as approved by the Board has been
pursued during the suspension of our engagement, and the
vacancy caused by our resignation has remained unfilled, we are
well aware that very much has depended on you in the interval
and that if our design has been virtually carried out, it is your
persistent adhesion to its letter, and to its spirit when that would
not suffice, that has ensured this result under circumstances of
peculiar embarrassment.   It is unnecessary to pursue this subject
farther now, but before going on to the work again, we desire, as
artists, to express our thanks to you, a brother artist, for the help
you have so freely rendered to the design in our absence, and we
have no hesitation in asking your acceptance of the enclosed
cheque for $500, feeling assured that you will not for a moment

---

[1] 8th Annual.
[2] Cf. letter from Mr. Olmsted to Mr. Pilat, 1863, pp. 343 ff, *post.*

Published by John Bachmann

The Park in 1863

Looking north.   Compare the view of the Park to-day given opposite page 200

suppose that we have any idea of thus cancelling our obligation which is not of a character to have a money value set on it.

We remain Dear Mr. Pilat, Your friends,
OLMSTED & VAUX, *Landscape Arcts.*

During 1864 and 1865 when Mr. Olmsted in California kept in close touch with park matters in New York, Mr. Pilat had written to him:

> The work on the Park is going on as usual, the main force being engaged at the north end in building drives and excavating for the proposed lake. The planting is now nearly completed South of 104th Street, 8th Avenue, and of 97th Street, 5th Avenue. I am at present engaged in writing a descriptive catalogue of plants cultivated on the C. P. up to 1864 which I am informed is to be printed in connection with the annual report of the Commissioners.[1]

By this time, the numerous gates to the Park had all received names in accordance with a very interesting report on nomenclature submitted to the Commission in 1862.[2] The first map bearing the gate names appeared in the Annual Report for 1865, the year of their official adoption, but a list had been printed in the report for 1864.

This map of 1865 shows graphically the progress described in Mr. Vaux's and Mr. Pilat's letters just quoted, and suggests, too, the need for the designers to return for carrying out the development of the upper park in conformity with their adopted plan.

THE RETURN OF OLMSTED AND VAUX: THEIR RELATION TO EACH OTHER AND TO THE PARK PLAN.

Late in 1863 Mr. Olmsted, worn out by his labors on the Sanitary Commission, had removed to California as Superintendent of the Mariposa Company's mining estates. Although his interest in Central Park did not diminish, he was inclined to be hopeless of an improvement in the attitude of the Park Commissioners, and he was by no means certain of his own continuance in the profession of Landscape Architecture. Many of the friendly letters addressed by Mr. Vaux to Mr. Olmsted at this period were devoted to persuading him of his superior fitness for the work and of his clear duty to return to the Central Park.

[1] See 7th Annual, 1863, Supplemental Catalogue in 9th Annual Report for 1865. Mr. Pilat's original catalogue of Plants in the Park, compiled in collaboration with Charles Rawolle, was published as a brochure in 1857.
[2] See Part II, Chapter VI, pp. 398 ff.

At the time of the trial of the Viele suit,[1] Mr. Vaux had taken occasion to secure from Mr. Olmsted a definition of their mutual relations in the design of the Park which he might use with more confidence than the general "power of attorney" contained in a letter written by Mr. Olmsted soon after his arrival in California:—

"I make you my attorney and authorize you to use my name for any purpose to which you are willing to give your own, with reference to the park, or our affairs. Express your own view as the view of the designers whenever it is desirable."

This considered definition Mr. Vaux communicated to Dr. Henry W. Bellows, who was a warm friend and defender of the "Greensward" designers:

N. Y. FEBRY. 25TH, 1864.

My dear Sir: My connection with Olmsted having been of a somewhat delicate character in the Central Park matter from first to last, and my personal relation towards him being close and fraternal, I found when he had left for California, that I might at any time be called on to act as agent for both, and that I hardly felt myself in a position to do so with the necessary ease and confidence unless a somewhat more precise definition of our intellectual relation to the C. P. work was arrived at than there had hitherto been any necessity for. I therefore obtained from him the following, which is an extract from a letter dated Campo Del Aso, Nov. 26th, 1863: "There are several properties in the Park held or properly belonging to us; 1st, the general Design in which our property is mutual, equal, and indivisible; 2nd, Detail of general design, from which cannot be separated something of superintendence and in which there is also equality of property between us; 3rd, Architectural design and superintendence, in which I have no appreciable property, which is wholly yours[2]; 4th, Organization and management of construction force, in which you have very little property though more than I have in the last; 5th, Administration and management of the public introduction to and use of the park, in which you have very little property and which I hold to be my most valuable property in it.[3]

"The relation of the last to the first is vague, but intimate; dependent upon the fittingness of the design for an easy, safe, and convenient habituation of the public to the customs desirable to be established in it and especially to gaining the public regard

[1] See Appendix III.
[2] Mr. Vaux noted here: "I consider that although in a technical sense Olmsted has no property in this item his advice was valuable and that his knowledge of agriculture in its finer sense (to which he does not refer) balanced my technical knowledge in this special respect."
[3] Cf. Vol. I, *ante*, p. 119.

and respect for it, and for that which was necessary to its permanent good use and maintenance.

"Therefore in one sense this belongs to you equally with me, but so far as this can be disregarded, I mean that you have had little to do with this last division of our service and I have taken more interest in it, given more thought to it, had greater satisfaction in it than in all else together. It was in this too that without any exertion or labor, but by fact of natural gift, I have been worth most to the park and have equitably acquired consequently the most of my share of whatever property there is between us resulting from it."

I send you this extract before doing anything in the Viele matter so that you may be in full possession of Olmsted's ideas with regard to our relation to the C. P. work.

I have replied to this letter accepting his definition as the one by which I shall be guided in my future action with regard to the park, both in the letter and in the spirit.

Yours respectfully,

CALVERT VAUX.

In the Spring of 1865 the opportunity was opening for Mr. Vaux to undertake the design of a large park for the neighboring city of Brooklyn. Referring to their collaboration on Central Park and to this new undertaking Mr. Vaux wrote to Mr. Olmsted:

If you had been disheartened there very likely might have been no park to chatter about today, for I alone was wholly incompetent to take it up. I approached the work first by arranging the terms of the competition just before you came on the Park or saw me, but I had no idea of competing because I felt my incapacity;—I feel it no less—I will not say *no* less, but very little less;— now, and enter on Brooklyn alone with hesitation and distrust, not on the roads and walks or even planting which Pilat would have to attend to, but in regard to the main point,—the translation of the republican art idea in its highest form into the acres we want to control.

From May until July of 1865 the Central Park Commissioners, largely through Mr. Green, were attempting to induce Mr. Vaux in association with Mr. Olmsted to resume professional services under conditions acceptable to all parties. On May 22 Mr. Vaux wrote to Mr. Olmsted:

If you were here today my scheme would be to make the Board cry *peccavi*, make what conditions we chose, go in as artists and keep the art *management* in the shade for a week or month or year or two till we had the whole thing done, and then we or you, if it turned out that that was the logical result, could control the matter in its entirety.

Again on June 3 Mr. Vaux wrote:

The Central Park progresses . . . Green is under the impression that his very life depends on it, I should think by the way he is working—He has been a main prop in one sense and I cannot reconcile myself to the idea of any man who has stood by the plan being left in the lurch, so we must try and make his mind easy as to his Comptroller-ship—just the proper name for his work—and proceed by judicious means to get the power over the vital management of the park by proper reports and influence with the Board and public.

On July 21 Mr. Vaux wrote:

DEAR OLMSTED:

O & V. were reappointed yesterday L. A. to the C. P. with the understanding that they are to be called on to advise and report on arch. designs that may be submitted to the Board, etc. (this forms part of the resolution of which I have as yet recd. no official copy). Salary $5000—$5000 for past services.

The latter might have been in full if you had been here, I have little doubt.

I should be satisfied with the result if I felt well assured of your real cooperation. As I said before my main perplexity all through has been in this direction.

You are, and I am, and several other people are necessary to this work, and it can be successfully carried through in an artistic spirit to a real end, that is to a point that is beyond much chance of harm, both as a constructed work and as a vital organism; but it depends on you—and the spirit in which you now approach it— whether this result is to be arrived at or not. I am willing to contribute all I can. Are you content to do the same?

The telegraph is out of order.

Please reply, if it is in order, as soon as you receive this letter. Do not delay your return if possible.

Yours Aff'ly,

CALVERT VAUX.

It was on July 19 that the Executive Committee of the Central Park Board was authorized to appoint Olmsted & Vaux as "landscape architects to the Board," but Mr. Olmsted in California did not receive his partner's letter of notification until the 30th of August, when he was prepared to accept the offer, after he should

Courtesy of New York Public Library

Published by Edmund Foerster & Co. John Bachmann, Del.

Central Park in Summer, 1865

Looking south

have closed up his affairs in California. In November, 1865, he reached New York and plunged into the new work with Mr. Vaux on the Park for Brooklyn in addition to the renewed activities on the Central Park.

THE DEVELOPMENT OF THE UPPER PARK.

On the day of their resignation in 1863, the plan by Olmsted & Vaux for the Park addition had been "essentially approved. . . . subject to such modifications as the Board may from time to time, in the progress of the work, deem it expedient to make." During 1864 there were various inconclusive discussions before the Board as to modifications, but the work went forward apace, especially the drive in the Upper Park. The Annual Report of the Commissioners covering the work of 1864 notes:

> With the exception of the expenditure upon the enclosing wall, the main outlay of the year has been upon that portion of the Park lying above One Hundred and Sixth Street, upon which the Board could not properly commence work until the protracted legal proceedings for its acquisition were complete. The addition of this land to the Park can scarcely fail to be a continuing source of satisfaction.

By the 31st day of December, 1865, the Commissioners were able to report:

> The completion of the walks and drive in the northerly portion of the Park, the bridges over or under which they are carried, the shaping of the surface of the ground, and the variety of work comprehended in the treatment of the deep valley that is a peculiarly marked feature of this part of the Park, and the waters that pass through it, "the Loch," its rustic stone dam and waterfall, the formation of its varied shore of bays and promontories, the excavation of the basin for the larger sheet of water, known as the Harlem Lake, the construction of its banks and dam, and the preparation of the ground to retain the water.

The map showing progress to the end of 1866 indicated the Upper Park as almost completed, the white spaces of 1865 for unfinished ground having given way to the green wash for turf, and the dotted lines for path and shore line being filled except in a few minor places. The onward sweep of the work from year to year appears nowhere more vividly than in these colored maps found folded in the annual report for each year up to this period of the approximately complete fixing of the whole plan upon the ground.

Descriptions of the Park in 1869 such as those in Mr. Clarence C. Cook's delightful book *The New York Central Park*[1] remind us, however, that even at that date the whole northern half of the Park appeared to the visitor far from being finished and that "every year, for some years to come the Commissioners will be adding to the attractions and to the variety of this neighborhood . . . a region much more capable of picturesque treatment than the lower park. . . . A profusion of scattered boulders beside a great quantity of fixed rock . . . gives opportunity to . . . open new paths, almost every season, in and out between these clefts and among these craggy irregularities." The opportunities for artistry in planting detail were endless, and it was fortunate that the Tweed régime, soon to come, did not last long enough to wreck completely the rural charms sketched by the designers, during their five years in office before the catastrophe.[2]

MUSEUMS.

Although in later years the designers of Central Park expressed regret that any large public building had ever been permitted within its area,[3] nevertheless in the beginning the inclusion of some museum or shelter for educational collections formed part of the original conception of a park for New York.[4] The old Arsenal building purchased with the Park lands had been almost immediately designated for that use by the Commissioners; and applications entertained from the Lyceum of Natural History and the New York Historical Society to display their treasures under its roof. The State Legislature had finally passed an act in 1862 authorizing the use of the Arsenal building by the New York Historical Society "for the purposes of establishing and maintaining therein by the said Society a Museum of Antiquities and Science and a Gallery of Art " and also authorizing the Park Commissioners to set aside adjoining grounds necessary for the fulfillment of these purposes.

By resolution of April 19, 1864, premises were set aside on which the Historical Society should erect a building subject to the approval of the Commissioners, this site comprising the area along Fifth Avenue from Sixty-third Street to Sixty-fifth Street, extending two hundred and twenty-five feet westerly into the Park. The object

[1] Published 1869.
[2] Cf. pp. 266 f. in the "Review of Recent Changes," 1872, given in Part II.
[3] For a fuller discussion of buildings in the Central Park plan, see Part II, Chapter IX. See also references to museums, etc., in Appendix II.
[4] The Act of 1859 for the government of the Park permitted bequests for the establishments of Museums within the limits of Central Park.

of the resolution was stated as "being to assure within the boundaries aforesaid to the New York Historical Society ample room to construct the buildings for the purposes contemplated in the said Act of the Legislature, and at the same time to retain in the exclusive keeping, control, and management of the said Commissioners of the Park all grounds within said boundaries not actually covered by such buildings. The buildings and their interior managements to devolve upon said Society." It was further stipulated that the Society was to provide in the buildings ample space for the offices of the Park Commissioners.

Negotiations as to the building continued between the two interested parties, and, as it became clear that an inadequate site had been provided for such an undertaking in a great metropolis like New York, in 1868 the Legislature passed a new act permitting the use of a strip of Central Park lying along Fifth Avenue between Eighty-first and Eighty-fourth streets, not over three hundred feet wide.

When in 1869 no progress appeared to have been made by the New York Historical Society towards establishing a museum on the allotted site, an act was secured from the Legislature authorizing the Board of Commissioners of Central Park to "erect, establish, conduct and maintain" not only a Gallery of Art, but also an Observatory and Museum of Natural History, the money being raised in the same way as for the construction of the Park itself. No definite site had been assigned to the Museum of Natural History, but its location on the Park was approved by resolution of the Board, and the making of plans for this as well as for the Gallery of Art placed under the direction of the Comptroller. Excavations for one department of the Park Museum to house a collection of American fossil animals had actually been begun near Eighth Avenue.

Thus in 1870, when the Board of Commissioners of Central Park was abolished by the Tweed Charter, the authorization stood for two museums to be included within the Park's boundaries, and still other land was already withdrawn from landscape purposes by the growing demands of the zoological collections.

THE LOCATION OF THE ZOO.

The Zoo in Central Park threatened almost literally to be a case of the camel that got his head under the Arab's tent. Zoological

and botanical specimens as educational features of the Park were
contemplated by the Park Commissioners from the first, but no
specific provision was made in the "Greensward" plan for grounds
actually designated for these purposes. While the designers' competition report of 1858 does not mention a Zoological Garden,
their first official description of the Plan (in Annual Report prepared
in January, 1859) states that ground is reserved for this and several
other "incidents." In March of 1860 the Commissioners adopted a
resolution to oppose the allotment of sixty acres to a Zoological
Garden in the Park made in a bill there before the State Legislature.
Nevertheless in 1860 the Legislature chartered the American
Zoological and Botanical Society and gave the Commissioners of the
Park authority to set apart a portion of it, not exceeding sixty acres,
for the use and the establishment of a Zoological and Botanical
Garden. The Society, however, manifested no immediate desire
for an allotment of ground, although in the opinion of the Park
Commissioners such an establishment would meet a popular
demand. Their Annual Report for 1862 discusses at some length
the advantages and difficulties of the undertaking either as a public
or semi-public enterprise. Meanwhile the Board was continually
forced to provide adequate facilities, in the vicinity of the Arsenal,
for preserving the numerous animals donated every year to the
Park. It was soon felt that to fence off a part of the Park for a
botanical or zoological garden,—so that perhaps a small admission
fee might make it self-maintaining,—would be likely to injure the
Park's landscape effect.

At the period of the return of Olmsted and Vaux to the Park
after the Civil War, it was suggested that the Zoo might be located
in Manhattan Square, a piece of land across Eighth Avenue under
the jurisdiction of the Central Park Commissioners but not forming
any integral part of the Park's plan. Olmsted and Vaux were
instructed to prepare a plan, which encompassed the housing on
this ground of the zoological collections not suitably accommodated
in shelters congruous with the park landscape.[1] Olmsted and Vaux
at that time felt that it was "eminently proper" for the Commission to provide, "a collection representative of the animal
kingdom so liberally arranged that it will afford ample gratification
and entertainment to the public generally and at the same time be
especially valuable as an adjunct to the Common School system
of Education."

[1] For the text of the Olmsted and Vaux report on this and later proposals, see
Part II, Chapter XI.

Manhattan Square was officially adopted as the location of the Zoological Gardens, but the difficulty of proper drainage dependent on sewer work beyond the control of the Commissioners occasioned a considerable delay. In 1869 preparatory excavations for some of the larger houses had been made, and designs and models of the proposed structures were in course of preparation.

It was a radical change from this already adopted and apparently reasonable plan, discarded suddenly by the Tweed Commissioners in 1870 without consulting Olmsted and Vaux, that was brought to public attention as one of the most flagrant subversions of the "Greensward" plan (see page 88); and thenceforth on and off for more than twenty years the Zoo continued to be a major point of attack on the integrity of the park landscape.

CHAPTER VII

THE TWEED RING AND THE PARK

THE RING IN POWER.

From about the year 1860, corrupt elements in the forces of Tammany[1] had been gathering strength and infiltrating the government of the City of New York with even more rotten politics and jobbery than in the days of Fernando Wood. With the election of November, 1868, these elements reached the zenith of their power by the election of John T. Hoffman as Governor of the State and A. Oakey Hall as Mayor of the City. The Comptrollership was already in their hands in the person of Richard B. Connolly, and William M. Tweed had become the guiding spirit of the Board of Supervisors. With control of the State Legislature and of the City Treasury, the stage was set for the stupendous frauds of the Tweed Ring.

The Democratic party of New York State was pledged to the restoration of local government to the voters of New York City, but the Ring had no desire to have its control of the city government jeopardized at each succeeding election. "What was known as the Tweed Charter was, therefore, a thoroughly delusive substitute for the promised scheme of local self-government,"[2] but nevertheless by corruption and bribery it passed the State Legislature on April 5, 1870, as an act "to reorganize the local government of the City of New York." Under the new Charter Mayor Hall was able to appoint Tweed head of the New Department of Public Works and Peter B. Sweeny president of the Department of Public Parks.

THE DEPARTMENT OF PUBLIC PARKS.

The Tweed Charter abolished the Board of Commissioners of the Central Park created by the Legislature in 1857 and substituted a new board of five commissioners called the Department of Public

---

[1] A reliable account of the rise and fall of the Tweed Ring and the relation of its bosses to Central Park may be found in Mr. Foord's *Life and Public Services of Andrew Haswell Green*, already referred to.   [2] Foord.

Parks,[1] having in charge the management of all parks above Canal Street. When the bill for the Tweed Charter was still before the Legislature and it became evident to the old Board that its days were numbered, it proceeded to wind up its affairs as best it could on short notice and entrusted to Mr. Green, whom the Mayor dared not oust, its accounts and papers. A public address was prepared by a committee of three commissioners reviewing the substantial achievements of the Board in the thirteen years of its existence; and to this address was appended a tribute to Andrew H. Green, signed by six of his fellow-commissioners.[2]

In the first organization of the new Board under the Tweed Charter in April, 1870, an executive committee of two (Hilton and Fields),with the newly elected president (Peter B. Sweeny) secured power over all appointments and over the execution of all orders. Mr. Green was soon obliged to resign the treasurership (succeeded by Mr. Hilton) and was literally frozen out of any participation in park management. All during the early part of 1871, stated meeting after stated meeting of the Board was adjourned because only Mr. Green was present. The real work of the Department was being done by the ingeniously devised executive committee, meeting and acting at their own pleasure.[3]

[1] See summary of text of acts, Appendix II.

[2] "Having presented the above address as the official act of the Board, there remains to be performed by the undersigned an act of justice and of duty in a full recognition of the obligations of the Commissioners of the Park and of the community to Mr. Andrew H. Green, their late associate in the Commission and Comptroller of the Park, with whom their official relations are now severed.

"At an early day Mr. Green exhibited those characteristics that justified the Commissioners in committing to him a large discretion and important responsibilities.

"His calm and reliable judgment and vigorous execution and his cultivated taste, added to a patient forbearance, and singleness of purpose, rendered him an administrative officer fully adequate to the duties and responsibilities of his executive position and it gives the retiring Commissioners unqualified pleasure to pay this parting tribute to his abilities, his efficiency, and his integrity.

HENRY G. STEBBINS,
R. M. BLATCHFORD,
J. F. BUTTERWORTH,
CHARLES H. RUSSELL,
M. H. GRINNELL,
WALDO HUTCHINS."

It should also be said that the Board itself deserved a tribute for the serious way in which most of its members had taken their duties. Questions had been studied into by special committees who considered both general expediency and technical details with minute attention.

[3] It should be remembered that the Department of Public Parks had under its charge not only Central Park and the smaller parks and squares, but the extensive boulevard and street improvements of the West Side and Upper Island, initiated under the old Board of the Central Park Commissioners. The opportunities for patronage and plunder were therefore immense.

Mr. Green's position was publicly defined in a letter prefacing the Park Department report for 1870 published late in 1871:

This volume, the First Annual Report of that Department, evinces a singular want of comprehension of the methods, purposes and designs of the original Commission; it makes concessions respecting the public proprietorship of the lands of the Park, which are not to be accepted, and contains numerous statements and implications which are to be received with caution.

As the name of the undersigned appears on its title page, he deems it due to the public, to his colleagues of the earlier Board and to himself, to submit this brief disavowal of responsibility for this Report, which he never saw till it was in print, as well as for the administration that it records.

Discharge of Olmsted and Vaux.

Doubtless as a sop to public opinion, the new Board had almost immediately passed a resolution recognizing Olmsted & Vaux "as chief Landscape Architects, as such, advisers to the Board," and continuing "their employment under the resolution of the late Board adopted in January, 1865." That this reappointment was a complete farce became evident when not the slightest attention was paid to the advice of the Landscape Architects,[1] offered from time to time as pressing questions arose. A draft of a letter dated November, 1870, regarding important and necessary revisions in the Park planting is marked in Mr. Olmsted's hand, "Not acknowledged or noticed." It is not surprising, therefore, that before the end of the year we find in the minutes of the Board the resolution "that the existing arrangement for the services of Messrs. Olmsted & Vaux shall terminate on the first of December next (1870) and that it be referred to the Executive Committee to make such new and other engagement with them as may seem desirable."

On November 25, while still nominally connected with the Department, Olmsted & Vaux learned "by the public prints" that the Department had under discussion and had resolved upon "a proposition to transform the open ground of the north division of the Central Park into a Zoological Garden." Although they had no official knowledge of the contemplated revisions, Olmsted &

[1] Cf. Part II, Ch. I, p. 241. Also see the letter from the Landscape Architects prefacing the first report of the Department of Public Parks, for 1870, disclaiming any participation in the changes proposed in the Park. "At the close of our relations with the Department, in November, 1870, no opportunity had been offered us of meeting either the Board or its Executive Committee, and the suggestions contained in our written communications had been entirely neglected."

Vaux nevertheless immediately addressed a letter to the President of the Department of Public Parks (Sweeny), containing the following request:

> When we accepted the office of Chief Landscape Architects Advisory to your Department, the terms of the resolution secured to us an opportunity to report on the effect on the general design of the Park of all propositions involving the introduction of new structures upon it.
>
> As the location now proposed for the Zoological Garden buildings would seem to involve a neutralization of features which have hitherto been deemed important elements of the executed design of the Park, we should be glad of an opportunity to carefully examine the scheme and to submit a report thereon before the termination of our present relations with the Department.

Although this communication was acknowledged, two sessions of the Board passed without attention to the matter; thereupon in January, 1871, Olmsted & Vaux proceeded to lay the matter before the public through the newspapers.[1] Little could be done, however, at that time, when the ring was still pursuing its own pleasure in a riot of power. The Landscape Architects could only hope to do their share in gradually awakening public opinion to the real political situation of the City of New York.

DAMAGING ALTERATIONS IN THE PARK.

The Central Park Board in its farewell report on the Park work had pointed out:

> In some branches of the work much has been entirely completed and only requires skilful maintenance; much more is in that far advanced stage that needs daily attention and adjustment to insure the best artistic success; portions of the design are still in skeleton on the ground; some features have been adopted by the Commissioners but not yet executed, and much is still in the stage of preliminary study.
>
> Very little of the routine of public works is applicable to the work of the Park development. The greater portion of what is done is more or less artistic in character, requiring special study and arrangement, and the agencies through which it can be accomplished are not readily to be found and made available.

Whatever the limitations felt during the sixties by the Landscape Architects in Mr. Green's method of controlling the develop-

[1] See Part II, Chapter XI, p. 503.

ment of the Park, he had been a staunch advocate and defender
of the Olmsted and Vaux ideals of design. His helpless situation
on the new Board made it impossible for him to prevent "the
routine of public works," from swamping any "special study and
arrangement" in the Park. The open lands and unfinished projects
were therefore a paradise for exploitation by the Tweed
administration.

An account of the damaging alterations in the Park is given in
the "Review of Recent Changes" prepared by the reinstated Landscape Architects in 1872 (see Part II).

The "cleaning up" of the planting was one of the most violent
subversions of the original conception of the Park landscape, undertaken by the Ring Board to remedy the previous alleged "neglect,"
and purporting to secure "circulation of air,"[1] "opening beautiful
views of lawn and scenery," and "clearing the Park of 'tangled
weeds.'"

> In parts of the Park in which intricacy and low growth and
> picturesque obscurity had been required by the design, the
> natural underwood has been grubbed up, the original admirably
> rugged surface made as smooth and meadow-like as ledge-rock
> would allow, and the trees, to a height of from ten to fifteen feet,
> trimmed to bare poles. . . No shrubbery or low growth seems to
> have been valued unless it could be seen within a clean-edged
> dug border.[2]

A large number of structures were projected by Ring Commissioners, and others under way in 1870 were recast, all with little
or no regard for their proper place in the landscape of the Park.
The extensive series of buildings begun on the largest meadow in the
Park, with their attendant yards and rows of trees were intended to
obliterate the meadow completely; and in the defense of this scheme
in its first annual report the administration did not consider "the
landscape value of this opening worth mentioning."

A Nast cartoon (see opposite) of this period shows how Central
Park might actually have looked had the control of the Ring not
been shortly overthrown by its own excesses.

PUBLIC AWAKENING.

How completely the respectable element of the community had
been bamboozled for over a year by the fair promises of Mr. Tweed

---

[1] See Minutes, Dept. of Public Parks, Dec. 6, 1870, for resolutions of Ring
Board as to revisions of Park planting. Cf. p. 266, *post*.
[2] From Landscape Architects' "Review."

Courtesy of *Harper's Weekly*

A Nast Cartoon of 1870

At the bottom, Central Park is scarcely recognizable. Compare the cartoon on page 517

may be judged by the fact that there was little suspicion of the gigantic frauds perpetrated by the Ring until the finances of the municipality approached actual disaster. Even then the group of highly-respected bankers on whom the City Treasury relied could be convinced only by the public exposure of the books of the Finance Department. To avert bankruptcy and the consequent suffering of hundreds of innocent claimants, public sentiment forced the appointment of Mr. Green as Deputy-Comptroller of the Finance Department on September 16, 1871. The history of his appointment and of his successful efforts to rehabilitate the city's finances, —the history of the exposure and fall of the Tweed Ring,—is told in Mr. Foord's biography. It is significant that the public blindness which made the city completely the financial dupe of the Ring must have been accompanied by an equally stupid blindness in the toleration of the Ring's activities threatening the beauty and enduring value of the Central Park. Fortunately the exposures were soon followed by a reorganization of the Department of Public Parks.

CHAPTER VIII

A PERIOD OF REHABILITATION, 1871–1873

A New Board.

On November 23, 1871, coincidently with the resignation of Messrs. Peter B. Sweeny and Henry Hilton, two new commissioners were appointed: Mr. Henry G. Stebbins, formerly President of the old Board of Commissioners of the Central Park who was immediately elected President and also Treasurer, and Mr. Frederick E. Church, the artist. On November 24, Mr. Olmsted wrote to a friend:

> Church's name was first suggested by Vaux, and we both did what we could to secure his appointment, which was made on Col. Stebbins' nomination. There is, I think, a peculiar propriety & significance in it. A quiet, retired man, a model of rank and file citizenship, but who in his special calling has earned the respect and regard of the Community—called at last to serve the public in an office where his special training will be of value, in place of a professional politician, is the more significant that the particular politician is one so much the opposite in his qualifications,—Sweeny. (His appointment reads "in place of Peter B. Sweeny.") The appointment of Stebbins as President, of Green as Treasurer (which he declines), and of Olmsted & Vaux as Landscape Architects, Advisory, is the public vindication of the Old Board. The appointment of Church signifies more,—that offices (for the present) are not for sale to those who want them, but are to seek and draw in the best men, and that they are to be expected to serve whether convenient or not.
>
> We were anxious as a matter of propriety that the art element should be recognized—that the public utility of devotion to art & the study of Nature in a public service of this kind should be recognized & Church seemed on the whole the most appropriate and respectable man to express this.

The majority of the new Board were now sympathetic with the aims of the original Central Park Commissioners and the way was clear to undo as far as possible the unhappy results of the Ring administration. Besides an order of investigation into the "present condition of the affairs of the Department," the new Board promptly passed an order directing the suspension of work on some "expensive enterprises not essential to the main purposes of Central Park." A press report of the Board's reorganization goes on to say: "It is very evident that the present Commissioners will continue the same general policy as that which was so successfully carried out by the old Commission that was displaced by the Ring about a year ago. We are of the opinion that the people will hail this restoration with universal satisfaction."

REAPPOINTMENT OF OLMSTED AND VAUX; MR. OLMSTED'S PRESI-
  DENCY OF THE PARK BOARD.

Almost a year after the termination of their official connection with the Park, Olmsted & Vaux became Landscape Architects Advisory to the Board (November 23, 1871) with the proviso in the resolution of appointment "that no structure be placed on Central Park until after they have first seen a plan of the same, and reported thereon to this Board." Referring to the circumstances of their reappointment, Mr. Olmsted wrote: "I solicited the position of Superintendent of the Central Park, stating in answer to questions from two Commissioners that I desire no appointment in which I could not have the Superintendence, under orders of the Board, of the planting and keeping of the Park." For a time, his old relation to the work seemed to be assured. Almost immediately, however, he was asked to assume new duties.

On the 28th May, 1872, the President of the Board, Mr. Henry G. Stebbins, having occasion to temporarily leave the country, resigned from the Commission. His place was filled by Mr. Frederick Law Olmsted, who was elected President of the Board. On the 23rd October, 1872, Mr. Olmsted resigned, and Mr. Stebbins was reappointed as Commissioner and reelected as President of the Board.[1]

In order that Mr. Olmsted might accept the Presidency (and also the Treasurership) of the Board, Olmsted & Vaux resigned as Landscape Architects and General Superintendents, and Mr. Vaux was appointed Landscape Architect and Superintendent (at the same salary, $6000).

On the return of Mr. Stebbins, Mr. Vaux resigned, to be immediately appointed Consulting Landscape Architect, and Mr.

[1] 3rd Report, Dept. of Public Parks (May 1, 1872, to Dec. 31, 1873).

Olmsted was reappointed Landscape Architect (November 24).
The differentiation in title between Mr. Olmsted and Mr. Vaux was
occasioned by the dissolution of their partnership, which, for reasons
of mutual convenience, had been formally agreed upon scarcely a
week before.[1]

During Mr. Olmsted's brief presidency of the Park Board in
1872, he prepared its second annual report, which set forth the
Department's financial situation and discussed especially the use
of Central Park by the public. Earlier in 1872 Mr. Olmsted and
Mr. Vaux had made a "Review of Recent Changes, and changes
which have been projected, in the plans of the Central Park,"[2]
summarizing the esthetic condition of the Park and the damage
wrought by the Ring schemes. In 1873 Mr. Olmsted as landscape
architect and superintendent presented a complete historical and
statistical survey of the Park enterprise to that date.[3]

A GENERAL STOCK-TAKING OF THE PARK, 1872–1873.

In November, 1872, when the Tweed administration lost control
of Central Park, the liabilities of the Park Department amounted
to upwards of $1,620,000, overdue bills constituting nearly a third
of this, and the Department bank account was overdrawn $109,-
353.74. The greater part of the funds from 1872 which became
available to the new Board had therefore to be applied to liquidating
previous indebtedness. The accounts of the Department also were
found to be much involved, since funds intended by law for a
specific purpose, raised and deposited with the Department, had
been applied without authority to other works. It took the new
Board some time to rectify these irregularities. Moreover the
problem of cutting down the cost of maintaining Central Park
had to be faced. During the first six months of 1871 at the height
of the Tweed administration this had cost over $250,000. The
new Board was able to reduce the amount for the corresponding
period in 1872 to $170,000 largely by elimination from the pay-rolls.

As soon as the financial affairs of Central Park were sufficiently

110 BROADWAY, N. Y., Oct. 18th, '72.

[1] It is hereby mutually agreed between Fredk. Law Olmsted and Calvert Vaux
that the partnership heretofore existing under the name of Olmsted and Vaux
Landscape Architects (which has for some months been inoperative in reference
to Central Park) shall now close so far as new work is concerned, and that all outstanding engagements on joint account shall as soon as practicable be adjusted to
this date.   CALVERT VAUX.
[2] See p. 240. Published as an appendix in the 2nd Annual Report. Reprinted
in Part II, Chapter I, of this present volume.
[3] Published as an appendix in the 3rd Annual Report.

rehabilitated, the Commissioners were able to proceed with new construction,[1] expending for this purpose almost a million and a half between May 1, 1872, and the close of the year 1873. To the latter date the Central Park had cost the city $13,902,515.60, of which $5,028,844.10 was for the land and $8,873,671.50 for its improvement.[2] It was estimated that the annual increase of taxes directly resulting from the development of the Park exceeded the annual interest on the cost of Park land and improvements by over four million dollars.[3] Looked at purely from a commercial standpoint, therefore, the Park was a success beyond all expectation.

From the point of view of usefulness to the public, the Park had also exceeded expectations. During 1871 the number of visits to the Park was over ten millions, an average of about thirty thousand per day. Actually the average number of visitors on days other than Sundays, holidays, and concert days, was about twenty-three thousand, of which about nine thousand came on foot and fourteen thousand in carriages or on horseback. The number of women and girls was estimated to have been in fair weather about forty per cent of all; of children of both sexes when the schools were closed in summer, about forty per cent.

On Sundays and concert days the number of foot visitors was found to be very much higher, almost fifty thousand on three of the finest days of the season. As one would expect, the weather greatly affected the attendance,—for instance causing it to vary from about a thousand total visitors on an inclement day in winter to one hundred and nine thousand on a fine day in September. It was

---

[1] In the Appendix to 3rd Annual Report, D. P. P., we find the following interesting *Statement of the Quantity of certain Classes of Work done and of the Materials used in the Construction of the Central Park, exclusive of Operations on the General Water Works of the City* (The Reservoirs): "The quantity of material handled in grading, fertilizing, and building has been 4,825,000 cubic yards, or nearly ten millions of ordinary city one-horse cart-loads, which, in single file, would make a procession 30,000 miles in length. Of the above amount 4,140,000 cubic yards were of the original ground material of the Park, and the change in place of this has been equal to the lifting and rearrangement of all the ground to a depth of 3¾ feet; 476,000 cubic yards of rock (besides small boulders) have been excavated, removed and reset. . . . 272,000 cubic yards of masonry have been laid, chiefly of first-class building stone, one-third of it in curved work. More than half the stone has been quarried on the Park. All the masonry laid is equal to 27 miles in length of ordinary four-story house front, sixteen inches thick. The larger part of it is either under ground or below the level of the eye and concealed from observation.

"114 miles of subterranean channels [pipes and tile drains] have been laid in the Park. . . . Over ten miles of curbing has been set on curves . . . In the study of the plans and for the guidance of the operations 14,000 drawings (maps, tracings, and copies included) have been prepared, and a million and a half stakes set."

[2] Cf. p. 54.   [3] See also Chapter XII, p. 173.

remarked that in spite of the attractions of the Saturday concerts, of which there were twenty-five in 1872, the attendance on a fine Sunday was much greater. This could apparently be accounted for by the fact that the working population, although largely free on Saturday afternoons, devoted this time to the purchase of family supplies and to regular social meetings, and therefore took the air "together with their families and female friends" on Sunday afternoons.

On fine winter days the ice increased attendance records by attracting throngs of skaters, as it had in the earliest days of the Park,—the winter of 1872-73 being exceptionally favorable to the sport with fifty-nine skating days. In summer the boats continued to be popular, and as high as a hundred thousand passengers had been served during one year.

The preponderance of carriage visitors on ordinary days indicated that the majority of persons who frequented the Park were people in comfortable circumstances, usually families the heads of which were either retired from business or able to leave it early in the day. The distance from the lower part of the city was so great and the street cars so crowded at the end of the working day that the pleasure of a short visit to the Park after hours for the laboring man would scarcely compensate him for the fatigue and discomfort involved. To the great body of citizens the Park was thus yet too difficult of access to be of use except on special occasions; and for visits of short daily recreation, it was of use mainly to those able to afford pleasure carriages or saddle horses, or from whose homes the walk to the Park was easy and agreeable.

It was not until 1874 that the center of population of the City of New York reached Union Square, from which point it is two and seven-tenths miles to Central Park. From Central Park to City Hall is four and three-tenths miles, from the Park to the Harlem River at the North of the Island, two and a quarter miles.

In a letter written in May, 1872, to Mr. William Robinson, editor of the English magazine *The Garden*, Mr. Olmsted discussed the use of Central Park in comparison with that of foreign parks and with its own probable future.

You assume that the attendance at the Central Park will be much less than that at the London and Paris parks. This is natural when you see it as at present situated four miles from the centre of population of a town of less than a million inhabitants with very inconvenient means of access to it. The consideration

1924

Photograph by Edward Heim

View Across the Bridle Path and Pond

I wish to present to you is that it was designed as a park to be situated at the precise centre of population of a city of two millions, that population cut off from all rural suburbs and this its only park; whether with good judgment or not the designers made their calculation upon a much larger attendance than they had been accustomed to see in the London and Paris parks. Up to the present time the attendance fully equals their anticipations; in ten years more there is every reason to believe that the park will be enclosed by the compact town, the borders of which were a mile away when it was laid out. As yet the streets which bound the park are incompletely graded. At present we rarely have over 100,000 at a time on the park. But as commerce drives the people northward for their homes and means of communication are improved, if this number should not often be several times multiplied, it can only be because the attractions of the park are counterweighed by the dangers, discomforts and annoyances which will arise from its crowded condition.

It may be owing to its peculiar form, and the disposition of the people after having travelled so far to reach it not to walk two or three miles to enjoy its further parts, but I have never seen the parks of London or Paris appear to be as much used as the lower division of the Central Park is already every fine Saturday and Sunday. Last Sunday the count of those entering the gates on foot was over 70,000 and a large number were taken in in omnibusses—special park vehicles carrying ten or twelve each—and the most of them must have travelled at least three miles to reach the lower end of the park.

The park is so far away that of course working people can not yet get to it after the work of the day is over and have only holiday use of it but I think that we ordinarily in fair weather have an attendance of ten to twenty thousand a day.

I have no statistics of the London parks but of course a larger number than this would be likely to saunter through some of them on their way from one point outside them to another—a kind of use of the Central Park which has not yet begun.

It will be seen, therefore, that considered in relation to its distance from the center of population, the designers felt that the use of the Park by the public was satisfactory and, with the upward sweep of the city, the prospect of its increased popularity still more promising. To quote from the Report for 1872:

But little vacant space remains south of the Park, and any notable further enlargement of population will be accommodated by building on its flanks. As the Park takes up one-third of the breadth of this part of the island for a distance of two and a half miles, the centre of population will be brought rapidly nearer to it, and hundreds will find a walk to it rewarded where one does so now.

The Boulevard and other spacious driving ways now preparing near and beyond the Park, being far better adapted for display and for the recognition of acquaintances than the Park roads, will, when finished, have the effect of reducing the number of carriages relatively to that of persons on foot visiting the Park. What is chiefly to be apprehended in the future of the Park is, first, the inconsiderate introduction of elements unfavorable to its rural and natural character, and consequently to its advantages for offsetting the special wear of the town, and, second, the impatience of visitors with regulations, and laxity of discipline in enforcing them, which are essential to the development and maintenance of this character, and of good order and harmony in its use.

In the public prints of the day it was frequently stated that the new Brooklyn Park was in some respects more attractive than the Central Park. Olmsted and Vaux attributed this largely to the greater expanse of ground available for pastoral effect as against the broken and rugged character of the Central Park lands. Repairing the inroads made by the Ring Board on the Central Park meadows was therefore one of the first cares of the designers after their return to office. By 1873, the meadow ground had at considerable expense been restored to practically its original condition. Another blow to the rural beauties of Central Park had been the disaster to the trees which occurred in the winter of 1871–72. Nearly eight thousand were killed, including almost every individual tree of certain conifers usually considered hardy and of several deciduous varieties. Since similar losses occurred in other parts of the Northeastern United States, the disaster could be accounted for by unusual winter weather conditions of open ground and deep frost.

During 1872 and 1873 the principal new construction on the Park was a system of walks and archways in the popular southeast portion,[1] and an enlargement of the accommodations near the music-stand on the Mall, necessitated by the increasing number of visitors at concerts and the destruction of turf caused by the crowd.

In the general esthetic stock-taking of the Park, the designers and the Board realized the menace of unregulated gifts of statuary. Early in the spring of 1873, therefore,

In view of the increasingly numerous propositions to place sculptural works on the Park and of applications in advance for an assignment of special sites for them, the Board . . . gave full consideration to the subject, the result of which was the

[1] See Part II, Chapter V, pp. 384 f.

adoption of a series of rules[1] governing the question of the acceptance and disposition of statues which may hereafter be offered to it. These rules were established with the purpose of guarding against the acceptance of works of inferior quality and also to secure the subordination of such as should be accepted to the motives of the general design.

PARK KEEPING.

The beauty and value of the Park were threatened not only by sculptural invasions but more immediately by the increasing carelessness of the public in its use. The force of park keepers, demoralized under the Ring rule, contained many men physically unfit and indifferent to duty. As an important move in the rehabilitation of the Park, Mr. Olmsted obtained permission from the Board to reorganize the keepers' force.

To understand how vital to the Park's success was and is an adequate system of park keeping, one must read Mr. Olmsted's statements in the series of documents[2] prepared in connection with his scheme of reorganization, from which the following paragraphs have been selected.

The Park Commissioners[3] are trustees and managers for the whole body of owners of a large amount of public property. Their business with it is of two kinds, first, that of forming parks; second, that of keeping them.

The first of these duties employs many the more men, costs much the more money, and makes greatly the larger show to the eye, but the second is the graver responsibility, and the Commissioners are to be holden to a stricter account if the arrangements they make for it are ill-judged, or if they delegate it to faithless or inefficient agents.

What is here meant by the keeping of the parks in distinction from the forming of them, and why it has so much more importance than the comparative extent of business would indicate may be suggested by an illustration:

A man may buy and fit up a costly house, but if, after he has done so, he finds coal and ashes scattered over his carpets, if decorated ceilings are stained and marred, if pictures are defaced, if books and dishes are piled on his chairs, windows and doors kept open during storms, beds used as tables and tables as beds, and so on, all that he has obtained for his expenditure will be of little value to him for the time being, and the possibility of its ever again being made of much value will lessen with every

[1] See Part II, Chapter X.   [2] See Part II, Chapter VIII.
[3] This selection is from "Instructions to Keepers," 1873, in which Mr. Olmsted explains the underlying principles of the work which the men have undertaken. See p. 444.

day that such misuse is suffered, through *inefficiency of house-keeping*, to prevail.

In the same way a park, as in the case of the Central Park, having been formed and furnished with a great variety of appliances, each, like chairs, and tables, and beds, and dishes, and carpets, and pictures in a house, designed to be used in a different way and for different ends, though all for the one general end of the comfort of the occupants, whatever value the owners are to enjoy for the twelve million dollars or more they have laid out upon the park will depend on the prevention of misuse, which again is a question of the efficiency of the park-keeping.

For example, rock has been removed, drains laid, deep soil formed and fine, short greensward gradually established upon the soil in certain places in order to secure that particular form of gratification which may be produced by a rich color and texture of turf, and by the contrast of this color and texture with that of other associated objects. To a limited extent and under certain conditions, the turf may be trodden upon without injury, but if walking upon it were generally allowed the particular object for which much labor during many years has been thus expended would be wholly lost. Hence it is an imperative part of the business of the Commissioners to prevent this misuse of it. . . .

Similar illustrations might be multiplied by the hundred, and keepers must realize that every foot of the Park's surface, every tree and bush, as well as every arch, roadway and walk has been fixed where it is *with a purpose*, and upon its being so used that it may continue to serve that purpose to the best advantage, and upon its *not being otherwise used*, depends its value. . . .

. . . The administration of this most important part of the Department's business does not turn simply upon the question, by what means can the misuse of the park be prevented? but . . . it must also be considered how the agencies employed for this purpose may best aid the proper use of the park, and especially how trustfulness in the means of prevention and confidence in the use of the aid to be provided may best be inspired.

· · · · · · ·

The designers of the Central Park[1] aimed to provide, or rather to retain and develop, in it certain elements of interest and attraction which, if they were successful, would be almost peculiar to itself. They saw, from the beginning, that the danger of failure lay chiefly in the liability of misunderstanding, misuse and misappropriation of these elements of the design by the public. They saw also quite as distinctly sixteen years ago as now, that in this respect the practicability and value of their plan turned upon the question, whether a keepers' service *adequate to its special requirements* could be maintained upon it. . . .

[1] This selection is from Doc. No. 47, D. P. P., "Report on Changes," July, 1873. See p. 466.

This park is, in many respects, an experiment, by the results of which the welfare of vast numbers of people in other great cities than New York cannot fail to be affected. . . . That it is worth while for civilized communities to use their wealth in this way; that humanity and patriotism and religion require that every community which occupies territory in which it is reasonably certain that a great city is to grow, should, if necessary, at some sacrifice of immediate convenience and comfort and prosperity, begin the formation of a park of this comprehensive and artistically complete character, is a conclusion that no intelligent man who will carefully study the effect on the people of the existing few and almost chance-formed city parks of the world, can resist.

Yet the demonstration of experience is lacking, and if the design of the Central Park is ever realized, will be first found in its realization. If, then, there is ground for the conviction held and stated by the designers, that the practicability and value of their plan is to turn upon the question whether a keeper's service can be maintained upon it adequate to its special requirements, neglect to secure this one condition involves much more than a waste of resources and a calamity to the people of New York. It must necessarily cause discouragement to enterprise in the same direction everywhere, and is a wrong and misfortune to the civilized world. . . .

Few persons fully comprehend the purposes of a park, and still fewer, especially of city-bred persons, fully appreciate the conditions upon which the real value of the various elements of a park depend. It requires some little reflection to understand that nearly all that is agreeable and refreshing at present on the Central Park would speedily disappear if practices, harmless elsewhere, were to be continued in it; if the multitude of visitors were to move through it, for example, as freely and inconsiderately as visitors at a watering place are allowed to move through the neighboring woods and fields. . . .

It is with reference to the prevention of ignorant and inconsiderate misuse of the park that the keepers' force chiefly needs to be organized, instructed, trained and disciplined. If it is sufficient for the part required of it, in the design of the park, in this respect, it will certainly be sufficient for protection against crime. And if its members are trained or allowed to hold the notion that their chief duty is to bring criminals to punishment, they will never serve the purpose of their organization effectively.

ADMINISTRATIVE DIFFICULTIES.

Every step which Mr. Olmsted made towards efficiency met with a storm of protest from politicians and press.[1] So violent the

---

[1] See the examples given by Mr. Olmsted in *Spoils of the Park*, reprinted as Part I, Chapter X, of this volume, pp. 117–155.

storm became that the Board bowed before it, all except the President, and Mr. Olmsted was "relieved of responsibility for the police of the park." As he considered this responsibility an essential part of park management, and included in the terms under which he had accepted office, he immediately sent in his resignation with the following explanation[1]:

Mr. Vaux and myself were appointed Landscape Architects and Superintendents with the distinct understanding, as we supposed, that the business was to be so arranged as to meet our views in this respect.

We were disappointed, but as the organization of the Department was regarded then as temporary and as by indirect and inefficient methods and agencies I was able to make some way in my purpose, I was induced to remain and for various reasons though much dissatisfied, have been induced to remain until the present time.

Within the last year there is almost no important duty of the Department that has not been put upon me excepting only those for which alone I have offered it my services. I have acted as Commissioner, as the President of the Board, as Treasurer of the Department, I have represented it in the Board of Audit and Apportionment, I have reorganized its executive service. I have prepared its memorials, reports and estimates. I have had responsibilities thrust upon me foreign to my profession and to my office and against my expressed wishes. I have met them promptly to the best of my ability and, as the minutes of the Board bear record, to its satisfaction.

You know by your own observation during the last month what multifarious and complex duties have been laid on me.

I was yesterday informed that in the reorganization now preparing by your Committee I should be relieved of certain of the duties of my office.

I think it proper therefore at this time to advise you, and I desire through you to advise the Committee, that I must decline to hold any executive office with reference to the Central Park in which I shall not have the Superintendence, under orders of the Board, of the plantations and keeping of the Park.

If your Committee should see fit to recommend and the Board to establish an office limited to the two duties on which my interest in the Department centres, I shall wish to be considered a candidate for it. I shall not, however, accept it unless it is the unanimous wish of the Commission that I should do so.

Although the Board could not be brought to meet Mr. Olmsted's views, nevertheless he was persuaded by the President "to resume

[1] From a letter to President Bissinger, dated July 15, 1873.

service under the Commission upon a modified arrangement," vindicating his professional standing and apparently securing him against another similar experience.[1]

Meanwhile the Board itself was undergoing reorganization under the new Charter of 1873 which went into effect on April 30, and resulted in new appointments by the Mayor confirmed by the Board of Aldermen. Mr. Stebbins had continued as President but resigned on June 27, 1873, to be succeeded by Mr. Bissinger. The threat of Tammany power was even in 1873 again hanging over the operations of the reform administration; and the obstacles encountered by Mr. Olmsted in his attempt to regain the former discipline and order on the Park were merely an earnest of the greater difficulties which gradually engulfed Park affairs from 1874 to his removal in 1878.

[1] See p. 305, *post*.

CHAPTER IX

THE PARK UNDERMINED BY POLITICS

HARASSING YEARS.

A note in Mr. Olmsted's own hand attached to a New York *Times* Editorial on "The City Government,"[1] records the general disappointment in the "Reform" administration as it developed during 1873–74:

> The Mayor and Common Council elected as though reformers gave themselves up entirely to political huckstering and bargaining. Every department except Health has been shown to be chiefly ruled by regard for patronage. The Department of Parks is no exception although probably better. The evil results of this are that work costs much more than twice what it would under good government.

How unfortunate it was that the Park should be thus deprived of the money's worth expended for labor was brought to public attention by the observations of Colonel George E. Waring, Jr., formerly Agricultural Engineer of Central Park,[2] who revisited the Park after an absence of fourteen years. His letter, published in the *Evening Post* in June, 1875, contained the following paragraphs:

> When the war broke out, in 1861, I left the Park, and I have never had an opportunity until now to fairly review it. Going carefully over its roads and walks at the end of these fourteen years, I am delighted with the total result to a degree that can perhaps hardly be understood by those who did not know the unpromising material out of which the Park was created, and who cannot recall the absence of every element of rural beauty that characterized the hideous ground which had been selected for its site.
> On the other hand, however, having known the details of the *modus operandi*, and watched the manner in which the early finished portions of the Park were treated, and the system by

---

[1] Apr. 24, 1874.   [2] See p. 51, *ante.*

which an ignorant public was educated to accept its pleasure ground in a proper spirit and to treat it with proper respect, I see perhaps more clearly than residents of the city do some serious shortcomings. In the old days the chief criticism of the management was suggested in the terms "red tape" and "martinet." Every border, every grass plot, every piece of shrubbery had been formed and was cherished with a degree of studious care whose importance only those having a practical experience in such matters could appreciate. The force of park keepers—that buffer that stood between the shock of an untrained public and this destructible work of art—was controlled, trained and minutely instructed, with a fidelity that grew out of a realization on the part of its chief (Mr. Olmsted) of the fact that only with ideally good service in this respect would heedless and untrained visitors be kept from falling into habits of using the Park in ways which would ultimately be ruinous to it.

At that day, when only parts of the Park were completed, these completed parts were almost perfectly well kept, and there could have been no better evidence of the civilizing influence of such a pleasure ground, managed as this one then was, than that shown in the conduct of the whole large community that visited it.

Today, although nature seems to have lost no single day of all her time in clothing the Park with a beauty that fifteen years ago seemed promised only for the next generation, no one who formed his ideal of the ultimate condition of what had been accomplished at the end of the first four years of work can fail to be sadly disappointed in many details—details which may not be obvious to the unprofessional visitor, but which, if left uncorrected, suggest very serious ultimate injury; nor will he be less disappointed in the change that has obviously come over the spirit of the public.

It is not necessary to speak of the barbarism of the Tweed dynasty and its results. The practical destruction of the beauty of acres of wood by the lopping away of lower branches; gross improprieties in planting, and the vast incidental demoralization of the mass of visitors, all of which is irremediable except by time and care. It is, however, worth while to say that even your reformers, from motives of false economy and through ignorance of the real character of their trust, have builded up a gigantic sin of omission, for which atonement cannot begin too early. For instance, in our climate good turf is hard to get and almost harder to keep. Not to argue a point which all experts concede, it is enough to say that, however it has come about, the turf of the Park is today in a condition that no one with knowledge of such matters can consider less than alarming. The grass borders, which from their accumulations of dust over-ride the curbstones at the very gates of the Park, would discredit a mechanic's dooryard. The most charming evergreens are slaughtering each other's beauty for the want of timely thinning, and much permanent injury is occurring for the lack of such ordinary good management as should be a matter of course after all these years of experience.

Much of this shortcoming is now due, as formerly, I do not doubt, to the well-meant interference of enthusiastic citizens who lack a knowledge of the true purport of their protests against necessary restrictions and essential prunings; but much more to the lack of sufficient labor to do the real work required. It is not to be expected that any public institution in New York shall fail to suffer from the spirit of political jobbery and favoritism that so generally pervades its departments; but it is really monstrous, with so much left undone, that, while good workmen are eagerly seeking work at fifteen cents per hour, the Park Commission is paying its laborers twenty-five cents per hour. In other words the Park only gets fifteen days' work when it sadly needs the twenty-five days that the same outlay might secure; and, as an added shame, when thousands are suffering for the want of employment, an amount of wages that would be a godsend to one hundred men working ten hours per day is given to seventy-five men working only eight hours per day. It would be rude to call this robbery, but how would the Commissioners themselves characterize such an expenditure of their own money by agents whom they had appointed to do their private work?

The force of keepers, who should be the custodians of the landscape-gardening details, seem to confine themselves chiefly to the more showy service of the drives, leaving the public to relapse elsewhere, as an unguarded public always will, into that condition of semi-barbarism that disregards obligations to public property.

These suggestions of criticism are more important than they may seem. The great things of the Park have been done. Its future value is now chiefly a question of nature's rule, and of protecting what has been and what may be secured. This can be accomplished only by an intelligent attention to minutiae. New York has today in its Central Park a greater treasure than the most enthusiastic of its original advocates promised. It has been secured for about the cost of the wretched Court House on Chambers street. Invaluable though this possession is, it is a possession that may easily be lost. There is hardly an item in the roads, the lawns, the trees or the architectural work (and especially in the archways) that can be secured in even its present condition without incessant care, and intelligent and studious care.

From 1874 to 1876, Mr. Olmsted never relinquished hope of securing an adequate gardening force to give the Park just the sort of care that Colonel Waring, if not the Commissioners, recognized as necessary. Although in 1875 the Board adopted a resolution reorganizing the force of gardeners in accordance with Mr. Olmsted's ideas,[1] actually little resulted from this, and in 1876 the force was still totally inadequate. In 1875 although construction work was suspended for a time owing to lack of funds, a certain amount of maintenance proceeded as usual. As the *Post* pointed out somewhat bitterly in an editorial accompanying Colonel Waring's letter, there was plenty of money for Museums and "buildings which are not necessary to the Park, even if they properly belong there at all," but little for preserving and beautifying landscape features. The difficulties of making headway with the laboring force responsible to a Park Superintendent himself unaware of the true objects to be sought in the care of park plantations chafed Mr. Olmsted constantly.

The public was greatly agitated in the latter part of 1875 by rumors that malaria was being fostered by the bad drainage of the Park. At that date the real source of malaria in the mosquito was still undiscovered, and the public alarm was the greater because of the vagueness of its causes. Mr. Olmsted made a thorough personal investigation of all circumstances on the Park which might give color to such statements and was able to assure the Board and the public that their fears were without foundation. He learned that the Park police, who were most exposed, had an unusually good health record in this regard, and that none of the laborers who had cleaned out the lakes—alleged to be a proceeding highly dangerous to the public health—had contracted the disease. In his reports to the Board, he recommended for its consideration a review of the entire drainage system of the Park. This system had been installed by Colonel Waring, whose comments on the Park have just been quoted, and was undoubtedly one of the most thorough and extensive pieces of work that had been done in the country, comprising ninety-five miles of buried pipe and tile. In the years since its installation, under various park managements and without any adequate method of current inspection, there could scarcely have failed to be stoppages and breaks. The first step towards bringing the system into full working order was to reassemble or replace the scattered set of drainage maps originally prepared by Colonel Waring. Mr. Olmsted suggested that Colonel Waring's services should be secured to examine the drainage system, to give information needed for the replacement of certain sheets of the drainage map, and to determine what repairs were then necessary. There

---

[1] The papers relating to the reorganization of the gardening force are given in Part II, Chapter IV.

is no record that Colonel Waring was given any opportunity of rendering these services.

Meanwhile the politicians were making a concerted effort at Albany to legislate Mr. Green out of the Comptroller's office. So long as he remained in that position, the newly elected Tammany government of the City of New York (1874) was handicapped in its schemes for power.

The Laws of 1874 had reduced the number of Park Commissioners to four, two Republicans and two Democrats. While aided by Mr. Green as Comptroller, two of the Board, Colonel Stebbins and Mr. Williamson, were still able to resist political attacks, two of the Commissioners were supposed to be taking their instructions directly from Mayor Wickham who foresaw—to quote the *Times* of April 28, 1875—"that the Park Department might be made very useful to his dear Tammany in future elections." The same Editorial says, "The Park is still a prize which Tammany— 'reconstructed' Tammany—yearns to get into its possession. It will always be the coveted booty of the Democratic organization, and we are sometimes inclined to think that the success of the designs upon it is only a question of time."

THE POLITICIANS UNLEASHED.

In November, 1876, at the expiration of five years as Comptroller, Mr. Green was removed by Mayor Wickham, in spite of Mr. Green's attempts to resist the removal on legal grounds.[1] Shortly before this a political attempt to get rid of Mr. Olmsted had been unsuccessful. His acceptance of an unpaid office as a Commissioner of the New York State Survey on May 31, 1876, was made a pretext for declaring vacant his office as Landscape Architect to the Park Department of the City of New York. The Counsel to the Corporation having given his opinion that it was doubtful whether Mr. Olmsted's acceptance of this office did not vacate his office held from the City, Mr. Olmsted resigned from the State Survey and was "reinstated and continued" Landscape Architect to the Park Board by a resolution of July 26th.[2] The same resolution recited that since Mr. Olmsted had during

[1] The Mayor claimed that five years was the term allowed under the Tweed charter and this provision remained unchanged in the subsequent charter. Mr. Green claimed that the Mayor had no power of appointment and that he (Mr. Green) held over until the Legislature made provision for the appointment of his successor.
[2] Minutes, Aug. 4, 1876, Resolution laid over from July 26.

the whole period since May 31st rendered his usual services to the Department, payment should be made to him at the rate of $6000 for that time. This resolution was successful over one introduced on the same date to secure his permanent removal.[1]

In spite of the resolution of reinstatement, Mr. Olmsted was obliged to bring suit against the City for the payment of his salary for the months of June, July, and August, 1876. The suit was finally decided in favor of Mr. Olmsted by Judge Spier of the Superior Court of the City of New York, May, 1877.

Selections from the Judge's decision are of particular interest as defining the legal status of a landscape architect employed by a municipal park department. The Judge found that a landscape architect was not an "officer" in the legal sense.

> The plantiff received no certificate of appointment, took no oath for the faithful performance of duties, had no term or tenure of office, discharged no duties and exercised no powers depending directly upon the authority of law.
>
> He was simply the servant of the Commissioners of the Park and responsible only to them. His responsibility was limited to them and is in no way distinguishable from that of the carpenter and the mason who are employed to build the bridges or erect the buildings designed by the architect. The nature and dignity of the duties confided to the employes by the Commissioners do not determine the character of the position. It is in no proper sense official according to any sense in which the term is used in the Statute above recited.

He was therefore not guilty of holding two offices and was entitled to the amount claimed with costs.

During 1877 various articles abusive of Mr. Green and Mr. Olmsted appeared in Tammany organs. Typical of these was a most violent article entitled "The Central Park: its Early History —The Beginning of Greensward and Grab etc." which appeared in the *Evening Express*. There were bandied about such characterizations as "the Greensward Ring, whose babble in the papers and in Society Circles, about æsthetics and architecture, vistas and landscapes, the quiver of a leaf and the proper blendings of light and shade bamboozled the citizens of that day. These were the Miss Nancies of Central Park art, the foes of nature, and the aids to money-making." These insidious witticisms were launched from the secure position which the friends of Mayor Wickham and of his

---

[1] Strangely enough the resolution for the discontinuance of Mr. Olmsted's services on grounds of economy was introduced by Commissioner Stebbins.

Park Commissioners Messrs. Wetmore and Wenman had now attained.

Dismissal of Mr. Olmsted.

Although the Tammany politicians had been unsuccessful in their first pretext for the removal of Mr. Olmsted, they soon found others. On December 12, 1877, the Park Commissioners received a statement from the Comptroller of the city that:

> He had withheld for the present, the salary of Mr. F. L. Olmsted, Landscape Architect, for the reasons that he has been informed Mr. Olmsted renders little or no service in that capacity; that his duties outside of the City of New York render his absence necessary and frequent, that he had been absent from his duties for twenty-six days during the month of October, and that the parks are in that state of completion that the services of an architect can be dispensed with; and asking to be informed whether the employment of Mr. Olmsted is continuous, or whether as is alleged, his absences from his duties are frequent and prolonged.

While this matter hung in abeyance, Mr. Olmsted was forced by his Doctor's orders (December 26th) to request a leave of absence for three months on account of the state of his health. The Board immediately granted him leave of absence for three months, without pay, from January 1st, 1878. The opportunity had now presented itself for Mr. Olmsted's opponents to strike the final blow. On January 9th he was to sail for Europe to secure much-needed rest. On January 5th, the Board of Commissioners passed the following high-sounding resolution, Commissioner Martin (to his credit) only dissenting:

> *Whereas,* The Board must discontinue the work of design, except where absolutely necessary; while the duties of superintendence must be concentrated in the officer designated for that special purpose; and
> *Whereas,* The distinguished head of that Bureau the Hon. F. Law Olmsted, so long identified with the Central Park and its improvements, enjoying the confidence of the community and the respect of every administration, since the formation of the work, should be placed in a position where the commissioners can still avail themselves of his extended experience and intimate knowledge of the designs and objects of the work;
> *It is therefore Resolved,* That the Bureau of Design and Superintendence . . . is hereby discontinued, and the offices connected therewith are abolished; and it is further

Resolved, That the Hon. F. Law Olmsted . . . is hereby appointed "Consulting Landscape Architect" to the Commission, his services to be paid for out of the appropriate fund from time to time, as they are availed of.

Various dates in successive postponements were assigned to the members of the Bureau of Design and Superintendence for "making an explanation in regard to their proposed removals," but since Mr. Olmsted was already crossing the ocean, this was a mere farce.

Before he sailed he addressed a letter to the Board:

Gentlemen: I am this evening informed of the proposition before your Board for abolishing the office of Design and Superintendence and advised that on Wednesday next I shall be allowed an opportunity to appear before you upon the question of my removal from my position in the Department . . .[1]

The notification comes to me on the eve of my departure for Europe under the leave of absence which you lately gave me.

In view of this leave of absence, I cannot doubt that you will think proper to defer the contemplated action, as far as concerns my position, until my return.

As, however, the abolition of the office of Design and Superintendence is intended, as I understand, to carry with it the immediate displacement of my Chief Clerk, Mr. H. A. Martin, I may be permitted to say that Mr. Martin having had for six years an intimate knowledge of all the business which I have had the honor to supervise, I had looked with confidence to the carrying on in my absence of the principles and aims which have been embodied in my plans and instructions . . . and I desire to bear testimony to [his] faithful, laborious, intelligent and honorable service.

Mr. Olmsted's letter had no effect upon the actions of the Commissioners, the removals proceeded, and the Park was left without sympathetic guidance.

PUBLIC PROTESTS.

So flagrant a piece of politics could scarcely fail to arouse a storm of public indignation.

As a counterpart to the petitions signed in 1857 by many noted New Yorkers to secure Mr. Olmsted's original appointment as

---

[1] Mr. Olmsted explains: "By my position is meant, as I understand, that which I hold under your resolutions of 5th Nov. 1875, giving me the duty of preparing plans for laying out the New Wards as well as that which I hold under the By-Laws of the Department placing me in supervision of the office of Design and Superintendence."

Superintendent of the Central Park,[1] there is a letter in the New York *World* of January 22, 1878, protesting against his removal:

MR. FRED. LAW OLMSTED

A STRONG PROTEST AGAINST HIS REMOVAL SIGNED BY MANY
PROMINENT CITIZENS

The following letter will be presented to the Park Commissioners today:

To the Commissioners of the Central Park.

Gentlemen: The undersigned, tax-payers and residents in the city of New York, have heard with deep regret and apprehension of the proposed abolition of the Office of Design and Superintendence in the Central Park, and dismissal of Mr. F. L. Olmsted from the position of Architect-in-Chief. Of his capacity as a landscape gardener the Park itself, as well as the Prospect Park in Brooklyn, of both of which he was in the main the designer, is sufficient proof. His reputation is even more fully recognized in Europe, where the art has been long cultivated, than in this country, where it is comparatively new. His continued professional superintendence of his work we cannot help considering highly desirable, if not absolutely necessary, in view of the well-known fact that the completion of a design in landscape gardening must wait on the slow work of nature, and is constantly exposed to unlooked-for modification through her action, and requires a long term of years where, as in this case, it has been begun on a bare and barren tract of land.

In addition to this, however, it is not unnatural that we, as taxpayers, should ascribe the successful management of the Park for the last twenty years largely to Mr. Olmsted's connection with it during the greater part of that period. No other enterprise in which the city has engaged and on which the municipal funds have been spent since 1860 has been equally satisfactory. The composition of the commission has been frequently changed, but its members have never felt themselves warranted in dispensing with Mr. Olmsted's supervision, a fact which has given the public a feeling of security about the Park which it is on all grounds desirable to strengthen and perpetuate. We mean no disrespect therefore to the present members of your honorable body when we say that considering the uncertainty with which the conditions of city politics surround their tenure of office, they would be assuming a serious responsibility in depriving the city of Mr. Olmsted's services, or leaving it to any one who had not himself considerable knowledge or experience of landscape gardening to decide when professional advice was needed.

[1] See Vol. I, *ante*, opp. p. 120.

We are all the bolder in urging these considerations, because the present condition of the city finances and of the city trade satisfies us that nothing which is likely to attract population or wealth to our streets can safely be neglected. Whatever New York loses in commerce or manufactures by the competition of other places it must make up by the inducements which it offers as a place of residence, and of these its parks are among the greatest. Anything which threatens them, therefore, with neglect, deterioration or mismanagement would be a fresh and serious aggravation of its recent misfortunes. We cannot help, therefore, protesting most earnestly against the notion that the saving of $4,500 a year by Mr. Olmsted's dismissal would be a real or wise economy, and we would earnestly and respectfully suggest to your board the consideration of other means of lessening your expenses by this amount.

JOHN A. STEWART,	W. C. BRYANT & CO.,
AUGUST BELMONT,	HORACE S. ELY,
BROWN BROS. & CO.,	HARPER & BROS.,
JOHN J. CISCO,	SCRIBNER, ARMSTRONG & CO.,
HENRY HAVEMEYER,	WILLIAMS & GUION,
GEO. W. BLUNT,	ROOSEVELT & SONS,
D. WILLIS JAMES,	C. C. BEAMAN, JR.,
MORRIS K. JESUP,	D. APPLETON & CO.,
JONATHAN EDWARDS,	GEO. K. SISTARE,
GEORGE A. ROBBINS,	ANTHONY LANE,
MORTON, BLISS & CO.,	WM. L. JENKINS,
JOHN K. PORTER,	JNO. A. GRAHAM,
WM. ORTON,	HENRY HOLT,
E. D. MORGAN,	WHITELAW REID,
WM. WALTER PHELPS,	J. G. BARNARD,
H. B. LAIDLAW,	WM. E. DODGE, JR.,
SAMUEL D. BABCOCK,	CLARENCE KING,
F. D. TAPPAN,	JOHN TAYLOR JOHNSTON,
BENJ. B. SHERMAN,	FREDERICK C. WITHERS,
JOHN MONROE & CO.,	WILLARD PARKER,
E. RALPH ROBINSON,	W. D. MORGAN,
ED. L. BURLINGAME,	BRAYTON IVES,
BAYARD TAYLOR,	JOHN JAY,
ALEX. HAMILTON,	J. LAWRENCE LEE,
GEO. CABOT WARD,	and many others
A. BIERSTADT,	

Various friends, including Dr. Bellows, Mr. Godkin, and Mr. Vaux, began a campaign for Mr. Olmsted's defense and reinstatement, but from abroad Mr. Olmsted wrote to his wife not to have people stirring about in his behalf. He was heartily sick of the results of New York politics. All the four months he remained away, he avoided looking at a New York newspaper.[1]

---

[1] The collection of newspaper clippings, and personal notes and papers, relating to park politics in New York which Mr. Olmsted saved during his twenty years' experience with the Parks of New York occupies many bundles of formidable size.

THE PARK IN 1880 AND 1881.

In 1880, Mr. J. Wrey Mould, an architect associated for some years with the Park Department and a collaborator with Mr. Vaux on the elaborate architectural details of the terrace in Central Park, was appointed Architect of the Department. He at once sought Mr. Olmsted's advice, in the most urgent personal letters, as to plans of development. Mr. Olmsted replied:

WASHINGTON,[1] 27TH OCT. 1880.

MY DEAR MOULD:

I would do what you want gladly and gratefully if it were only your affair. But you know that it would be the Department consulting me through you upon the business of the city and I must acknowledge that I don't like to put myself in that position. I don't know that I could fully explain why, but there is one circumstance of which you may not be advised that comes into it. The Department some time ago formally notified me that I should be officially called upon whenever I could be of any use in its business. Naturally I don't want to be advising indirectly when I am officially told [this] is not wanted. There is no reason I should not be asked officially.

Yours sincerely,

FRED[K]. LAW OLMSTED.

Mr. Vaux refers to the situation in a letter to Mr. Olmsted, January 7, 1881:

In regard to Park matters I have said that I understood that you were nominally consulting Landscape Architect now and that it could hardly be in good form for no recognition of this to be made by Mr. Wales and other unprejudiced Commissioners when so decided an expression of dissent was publicly made when you were turned out by Tammany.

That Mr. Olmsted's opinion was privately sought in regard to projects connected with Central Park is shown in a letter of January 15, 1881, addressed by Mr. Olmsted to The Honorable W. W. Astor:

Sir: I have just received a copy of the bill introduced by you to guard against the perversion of the Central Park to the pur-

---

[1] At this period Mr. Olmsted was occupied mainly with the Capitol grounds at Washington, Boston Parks, and Niagara Reservation. In 1883 he finally removed his residence from New York to Boston (Brookline).

poses of a Fair-ground.[1] I do not think that the danger which suggested it is wholly past and I hope that the bill may become law.

But I take leave to ask you to consider whether a more comprehensive measure may not be desirable.

There is but one purpose which justifies the permanent setting apart of large bodies of land in the midst of cities and the large outlays which the legislature has provided to be made upon them as "parks." Yet there has hardly been a year in the last twenty that projects have not been urged for appropriating park lands and diverting park funds to other purposes. The last brought to my attention not a month ago would have destroyed for its proper use at least a hundred acres of the Central Park and the gentleman who confidently sought to obtain my approval of the plan could not see that such destruction was not legitimate provided it would serve a purpose which might be thought of greater importance to the city even though foreign to that for which the legislature authorized the land to be purchased, money for its improvement to be raised by taxation and in view of which the entire property has been pledged as security for debts of the City.

I submit the suggestion that a declaratory act might be framed adapted to guard all lands held by cities under acts of state legislation and defined therein as "parks" from being used for purposes the pursuit of which would tend to seriously injure their value as places for the enjoyment of sylvan scenery and quiet open-air recreation.

There could be a section to prevent the act from interfering with plans already adopted in the case of our two museums,

---

[1] Plans for the proposed World's Fair for New York, finally set for 1883, fell through after a great deal of agitation as to possible locations in the Park. Cf. Appendix II, p. 548. It is also of interest to note that Senator Astor introduced into the Legislature of 1881, a bill which was never reported by the Committee on Cities, and therefore never passed as follows: *an Act to define and limit the uses of Public Parks:*

Sec. 1. It is hereby declared that all public parks in this State which have an area of over 100 acres, except as other special uses are provided for the same under the laws of this State, are intended and shall be appropriated for the recreation of the people by means of their rural, sylvan, and natural scenery and character.

Sec. 2. Hereafter the construction, maintenance and uses of said parks shall be in conformity with the declaration of the foregoing section and ground in said parks shall not be appropriated or used in such a manner as to lessen their value and advantages for such recreation.

Sec. 3. Nothing in this Act shall be construed to prevent the construction and enlargement of buildings in said parks for which plans have been heretofore adopted or the prosecution of works now in progress; nor the construction and erection of roads, walks, bridges, shelters, lodges, statues, works of art, horticultural buildings or other constructions designed and adapted to further the use of said parks as declared in Section 1. (*From a pencil copy, in Mr. Olmsted's own handwriting.*)

and its application might be limited to parks of more than fifty acres.

I am, sir,

Your obedient servant,

F. L. O.

Somewhat later than this Mr. Howard Potter wrote indignantly to Mr. Olmsted: "Effects which it has cost hundreds of dollars to produce, and which are essential to the rural features of the original design, are being destroyed, and the existence of what is left endangered."

Mr. Olmsted did not give up the idea of some public vindication of his work in New York. In 1881, he wrote to his friend Mr. Wales, President of the Department of Public Parks, a letter intended as a very private hint to produce spontaneous action and in no way as an application for the position mentioned:

> It occurs to me to say that if you are disposed and find it practicable to carry a resolution offering me either my old position or that of General Superintendent, which I do not need, I should rather like the vindication. There is no doubt that many regarded my removal as a reproach, though Mr. Lane at least did not so intend it, and it was carefully phrased to avoid that significance. It must of course be understood that though I make the suggestion to you, I should be at liberty to decline the appointment.

In the confusion of conflicting intrigues and debates,[1] no official action was taken in the matter until many years afterwards.

It was, however, reserved for Mr. Olmsted himself to issue the best brief in behalf of his ideals for the Park, when his permanent change of residence from New York to Brookline, Mass., had enabled him to regard the affair with a delightful humor that illuminates all the more clearly the essential pathos in such struggles of sound ideals and clear thinking against indirection and selfishness. In *Spoils of the Park*, to which the next chapter is devoted, one incident after another builds up a telling picture of the rotten politics which have balked the people of New York in their great democratic undertaking of Central Park.

---

[1] In 1881 there was an acrimonious exchange of letters in the *Tribune* between Commissioners Lane and Wales as to a resolution for the re-engagement of Mr. Olmsted. Mr. Lane, who had voted for his dismissal in 1878, introduced what Mr. Wales called a "buncombe resolution," against which Mr. Wales voted.

CHAPTER X

THE
SPOILS OF THE PARK.[1]

WITH A FEW LEAVES FROM THE
DEEP-LADEN NOTE-BOOKS OF "A WHOLLY UNPRACTICAL MAN."

They that have done this deed are practical;
What private griefs they have I know not
That made them do it; they are wise and practical,
And will with reasons answer you.

By FREDERICK LAW OLMSTED,

ONE OF THE DESIGNERS OF THE PARK; SEVERAL YEARS ITS SUPERINTENDENT; AND SOMETIME
PRESIDENT AND TREASURER OF THE DEPARTMENT.

FEBRUARY, 1882.

The demand for a change in the management of the parks has taken a more distinct form, even since I left the last of this pamphlet in the printers' hands. If I had been seeking office, it would have been a most foolish thing to write it: yet it may be best to refer to the fact that the frequent appearance of my name, either as a candidate or otherwise, in the debates of the Park Board, has in every case been against my repeatedly expressed wishes; that, whenever privately consulted, I have advised the immediate employment of men who could give the assurances of *efficiency with reference to the proper ends* of park management, which are only to be found in professional standing and in arrangements for this purpose, which left my own employment out of the question. I was more immediately moved to write by the opinion of a shrewd observer that Mr. Vaux's employment was the last thing that a *majority* of the Board had ever intended, and by seeing Mr. Wales blamed for "wrangling." I had in view, at starting, only to point out

---

[1] A reprinting of Mr. Olmsted's pamphlet.

117

good-naturedly that Mr. Wales's view of his Board's course was not that of a too contentious, so much as that of a too lenient man. Having taken up the case from this point of view, I found a more thorough treatment of it necessary. Though it is the first time[1] I have written critically of the business of the Department, except officially and with official sanction, it must be well known to my friends that the views expressed are of very old standing. In their more important points they are not even original with me, and are as far as possible from having been developed for the occasion. Though often urged to write on the subject, I have done so now without conference with any one, and, except in closing, without reference to any plans of legislation.

F. L. O.

Detroit, Mich., Feb. 23, 1882.

I

"This disorganized body has been masquerading before the public, a headless trunk, without policy, without order, without well-defined purpose."

THE words of my text were of late given to the WORLD by one of the members of the body they depict, sometime, withal, its president, worthy Master Salem Wales,—a man-of-peace, across whose shapely bows my yet more peaceful shallop could never hold her course but with the falling topsail of deferential salutation. Occasion cometh now in this wise:—

Having been kept much from home, seeing the Board and its works only through the eyes of the Press, and thus taking, if a less perspicuous, yet a more distant and therefore more comprehensive, view of its proceedings than Mr. Wales can have done, I fancy that I recognize a general drift in them of which he seems unconscious. I am the more moved to show the difference between his perspective point and mine, because I have observed, that, whereas till lately the meetings of the Board have been regarded by the Press as a sort of brawling farce, and as such, for amusement's sake, liberally reported, now for some little time back, through a growing wariness

---

[1] Ed. Note: He had, however, in 1879, prepared a vindication of his work, more especially in connection with Riverside Park, which he did not publish. In this we find the following significant passage:

"Perhaps I should admit, however, that I am unwilling that the public should wholly overlook a matter of some moment to my craft.

"I will not claim that my craft has as yet a perfectly firm and well-defined place among the callings by which the mark and measure of every people's civilization is so largely determined; but that there is a field of public as well as of private work which engineers as such cannot be expected to fully occupy, and in which thorough devotion of life is to be desired, I feel sure that no intelligent man, certainly no man of moderately liberal knowledge, will be disposed to question; and possibly the very conditions which make such a vocation as yet a comparatively inconspicuous one among the professions should rather commend a great city to be cautious of treating it with contempt than be regarded as a justification for its doing so."

of them as it is made to appear, an entire performance often gets no other notice than a single contemptuous paragraph. Thus I see a gaining tendency to look upon the Commissioners as an incapable and harmless set of witlings, with whose doings no sensible man can be expected to much concern himself. Such an impression is clearly unjust to Mr. Wales himself, else why should he be able to do so little with them as he tells us that he is? Yet the brief characterization of the Board which I have quoted, and with which much else that he has written tallies, tends to confirm the impression that it is pursuing a heedless, aimless, and essentially a harmless course.

Comparing his accounts with those of the newspapers, and judging both in the light of my experience in affairs of the Department, I am strongly drawn to think that there is more of tragedy than of farce in what is going on; and were the integrity, frankness, and manly straight-forwardness of all his colleagues at all less assured than it is, I should be disposed to think, that so far from being without policy, order, or purpose, the Board's proceedings had been all along nicely directed by the most wary gauging of the city's patience and credulity, and with a most craftily-formed and long-ripening purpose,—a purpose, I should add that would seem to me in direct conflict with that which the Commissioners are sworn to pursue.

Without ambition to appear as an advocate of such a view, I think it may subserve the city's interests, if, rather as a witness than an advocate, I state how it is that I can be at all tempted toward conclusions so different from those of the better-informed Mr. Wales. In the end, having on my way there shown my right to do so, I expect to testify as an expert witness. For the sake of compactness I shall confine my purpose to a review of some aspects of the Board's business with Central Park. As introductory to this, I wish to bring a few considerations to mind, upon which so much will hang of what is to follow, that I beg those in haste to get to the point, that they will not, because of the apparent self-evident character of my persuasions, leap them over. Their lack of self-evidence to many minds has cost the city millions of dollars.

1. After an investment of some fifteen millions in the Park, now in the twenty-fourth year of its growth, what is the proper business of the Commissioners with it? It is my experience that the answer given by men, in their conduct toward and in their comments upon the business as actually conducted, varies greatly with special points of view: that, for example, of a man who visits the Park on foot only, differing from that of one who sees it habitually from a carriage; and this again from the view of riders; and this yet again from that taken by those who would, but cannot, see it from "the silent steed." There are various real-estate points of view. There is a view from behind a trotter; there is the view of an employment broker; and there is the remote view of statesmen, to whom the paltry interest of the mere local community of New York, in its vacant lots called "parks," is of consequence only as it may at a

pinch be turned efficiently to account in affairs of great national and international concern.

Some more or less distorted reflections of these and of a hundred other special views may often be detected in the newspaper reports of the Commissioners' familiar discords. Putting them all aside as inadequate, and regarding the business as a trusteeship, my experience further is, that, asking what is the essence of the trust, not many business-men are to be found in Wall Street, nor yet in Water, who have ready upon it a business-like opinion. It is simpler to determine what it is not; and, by knocking off a few answers that may be suggested, we may converge toward a satisfactory conclusion.

For example: the Commissioners have elected, if I have reckoned aright, five several principal architects, one after another, to their business-staff; not one and four coadjutors, but five masters, each to a separate duty, dismissing none to make room for another. It is true that two are not appointed directly for building-duties (one being chief-of-staff, and another chief executive officer), and also that the last election was made with conditions that rendered its acceptance impossible; but as it was intended to supersede none of the previous building-strength at the Commissioners' command, sufficient, as it already was, for taking in hand all at once four great cathedrals, it strengthens the occasion for asking, At this stage, is building the distinctive and essential business of the commission? And no man can, upon reflection, fail to see that it is not.

The very "reason for being" of the Park is the importance to the city's prosperity of offering to its population, as it enlarges and becomes more cramped for room, opportunity of pleasurable and soothing relief from building, without going too far from its future centre. What else than this purpose justifies the reservation from commercial enterprise of more than a hundred blocks of good building-land right in the line of the greatest demand? Building can be brought within the business of the Park proper only as it will aid escape from buildings. Where building for other purposes begins, there the Park ends. The reservoirs and the museum are not a part of the Park proper: they are deductions from it. The sub-ways are not deductions, because their effect, on the whole, is to enlarge, not lessen, the opportunities of escape from buildings. Were they placed above the general surface, and made intentionally conspicuous; had they been built—as for a time it was difficult to convince people, even intelligent critics, that they were not—as decorative objects, it would have been in contravention, not in furtherance, of the essential business of the Park. Of late years they have, in the summer, almost disappeared from general view; and, by their action in facilitating passage clear of the drives and rides, much less apparent construction serves the general public purpose of the Park. If through ignorance and mismanagement their present seclusion is destroyed (as the Commissioners have promised that it shall be, as far as their means go), it must tend not to further, but to obstruct, the proper course of the Commissioners'

A Landing on the Lake

Before 1907

business. It must be concluded, then, that the Commissioners'
trust is essentially the reverse of that which the affluence of architectural force at its headquarters might be thought to imply.

If the essence of the Commissioners' business is not to be found
in building, neither is it in engineering, nor in inn-keeping, nor in
the decorative art of gardening, nor in a display of nurserymen's
samples, nor in forestry. All these callings may have their place;
but it is at best a subordinate and incidental or auxiliary place, as
calendar-printing in insurance business, as astronomy and pastry-
cooking in steamship business.

2. A man may be strong for any other business commonly
pursued in the city, yet unfamiliar with and inapt to acquire a sound
understanding of the ends, to grasp the principles and to seize the
critical points of management in the business of the Park.

3. By changes made for the purpose in the laws every few
years, and by the rotation of new men into office as often as practicable, the composition of the Commission is never long the same.
Its members, receiving no pay for the study they give the park
business, abandon no other to take it up, and rarely make any
change in their habits on account of it. Most of them deal with it,
as reports of their proceedings exemplify, more in the habit of mind
with which prosperous gentlemen take up their diversions, as of
whist or euchre, yachting, or trotting horses, than in that with
which they earn their living.

It is as unbusiness-like for the city to assume them masters
of the business, in an executive or an expert sense, or to allow them
to assume themselves so, as for the stock owners of a great railway
to allow a constantly changing board of directors to take upon themselves the duties of its Chief Engineer.

4. The view which has been thus suggested of what the Commissioners' trust is not, and of what the business-like method of
dealing with it for a board constituted as theirs is cannot be, is set
forth more at length and more forcibly in a communication
addressed to their predecessors in office four years ago, to which are
attached such names as MORGAN, BROWN, BELMONT, STEWART,
WARD, CISCO, COOPER, HAVEMEYER, POTTER, PHELPS, DODGE,
MORTON, JAY, JESSUP, SISTARE, HAMILTON, SCHUYLER, LIVING-
STON, ROOSEVELT, SHERMAN, MARSHALL, GRISWOLD, JOHNSTONE,
BABCOCK, GUYON, ROBBINS, LAIDLAW, WALLACH, JAFFRAY, COL-
GATE, THURBER, CLAFLIN, HARPER, APPLETON, CARTER, SCRIBNER,
PUTNAM, WESTERMANN, HOLT, CRAVEN, and of leading merchants,
artists, physicians, and barristers, each master in his own business,
ranging with these on the roll of the city's worthies to the number
of more than ninescore.[1]

If Mr. Wales's name is not among them, it is probably from
motives of delicacy, in view of his former connection with the
Commission which the paper in question calls to account; but

---

[1] ED. NOTE: Cf. p. 113, *ante*. The spelling of the names is *sic* in each case.

if otherwise, as Mr. Wales has of late been a commissioner of a public hospital as well as a commissioner of parks, he might ask himself whether, if his colleagues of the hospital trust had undertaken to manage it without aid of doctors, or with that only of doctors of divinity, he would have thought it implied but a weakness of purpose? Is it not such weakness that fills our prisons?

II

FOR years there was an office of the Board which at different times had different sorts of duty given it, and was designated by different titles, as the fancies of succeeding commissioners varied. It was once officially described as "the Chief Executive office by or through which all orders for the work should be executed and all employees supervised and governed;" at another and the latest period it could give no one an order—could govern nothing, only advise. But through all, one duty it held constantly, and that was to keep the Park under professional landscape-gardening supervision, with a view to the furtherance of consistency of purpose in the business of the Commissioners with it; to which end the occupant of the office had a seat with the Board, and was free to take part in its debates, though without a vote. When slighted as to this responsibility, the occupant offered his resignation, and the office was temporarily suspended.

In 1859, when it was working upon Central Park near upon four thousand men, and the records of the time say with extraordinary efficiency, the Board numbered eleven members. On the ground that it was too large for efficient *executive* management, it was gradually reduced. In January, 1879,[1] when it was working less than two hundred men, and the records say inefficiently, it numbered four members. In this month, unexpectedly to those interested in the Park otherwise than as a field of statesmanship, an element in the real-estate business, or some other specialty, the Commissioners concluded to extinguish such little (advisory) life as had till then been suffered to remain in the office. Since the day they did so, there has been no office under the Commission looking to landscape considerations; and the only man in its employment competent to advise or direct in matters of landscape-gardening has been degraded to an almost menial position, and this by methods and with manners implying a perfectly definite purpose to prevent him from exercising professional discretion, and to bring his art into contempt.

Reference is here more particularly made to occurrences imperfectly brought to public attention by reporters of the press two years ago or more; but Commissioner Wales has lately shown, to his honor expostulatingly, that the same policy is still pursued by the same methods, and with the same manners; the unfortunate repre-

[1] ED. NOTE: Mr. Olmsted must have meant 1878. Cf. p. 110, *ante*.

sentative of landscape art having been changed, and the tools of the ignoble work being new, and expressly adapted to it.

No plea will here be made that Landscape-Gardening is an art having due place side by side with the fair sisters, Poetry, Architecture, Music, Acting, Painting, and Sculpture. For nearly two centuries our greatest and our most popular teachers —as Sir Walter Scott, for example—have given it that rank; and I know not one man of accepted authority who has made bold to differ with them. Who are they that do so now? Is there an artist in any field who is with them? Is there a friend of art whose friendship is not the cloak of a hopeless snob? I am assured not one. Standing, then, for the youngest and modestest of the serene sisterhood, I know that not only every artist under every name of art, but every gentleman and every gentlewoman of New York, stands with me in challenging the Board to reconcile its course in casting out the profession of landscape art from the Park with faithfulness to its most sacred trust.

Where shall one be found more sacred?—a trust for all who, from our time onward, from generation to generation, are to be debarred, except as they shall find it in the Park, from what one of old aptly styled "the greatest refreshment of man;" from what our own Lowell calls "the wine and the oil for the smarts of the mind;" what our Emerson says "yet soothes and sympathizes in all our toils and weariness;" and again our Longfellow,—

> "If thou art worn and hard beset
> With sorrows that thou wouldst forget;
> If thou wouldst read a lesson that will keep
> Thy heart from fainting, and thy soul from sleep,
> Go"—

Where shall the poor man go when the Park has become what persistence in such management will make it?

III

FOR a few days after the determination of the Commissioners to leave the office of landscape out of their business was publicly reported, there was much interest to know their motives; and, in the absence of a satisfactory explanation, disapproval of their course was generally expressed. I had been holding the position in question, with the title, under the last shift, of Landscape Architect Advisory; and a friend had the kindness to make for me a collection of more than seventy cuttings from the journals of the time, bearing on the matter, which are now before me. Looking them over, I find, that, however differing in terms, they bear uniform testimony on a few points, which at this distance I would wish to have recalled: as, first, that to that time the people of New York had, notwithstanding some grumblings, on the whole, been proud of the

Park, and especially proud of its landscape promise; second, that the business-view set forth in the previous chapter in regard to the landscape office had been generally accepted; third, that there was a general, though not generally a very definite, perception of danger involved in its abolition.

So strong was the feeling for the moment, that a Park Defence Association was organized, and at least one older organization joined with it in urging the common conviction upon the Commissioners. It may be thought strange that it should have led to no debate or remark in the Board; but is it stranger than that, against constant outcry for fifty years, New York streets should have continued till now to be found the dirtiest to be found in all the large towns of Christendom?

One of the Commissioners is reported to have said, in the midst of the stir, "It will soon blow over." He appears to have been right; but, if I mistake not, a little silent breeze is even now perceptible, and if, after the revelations of the last four years, it once more gets up, it may not prove so easy to ride it gayly out.

May I refer to one thing more that appears all through these leaves?—such kind feeling toward me personally, as I have no words to acknowledge, but to which I can hardly avoid the poor response of drifting, as I write, into more personal narration than might otherwise befit my purpose.

IV

I HAVE shown what the highest authorities in the commercial business of the city hold to be the essence of the Commissioners' business with the Park, and what is essential to their success in it. But it must be known that a strong party has always stood opposed to this view, and from the start has been incessantly laboring, and never without some measure of success, to compel a disregard for it. The counter view is commonly termed by those urging it the *practical* view; and, if this seems strange, it must be considered that a given course is called practical or otherwise, according to the object had in view at the moment by the speaker. To relieve the charity of friends of the support of a half-blind and half-witted man by employing him at the public expense as an inspector of cement may not be practical with reference to the permanent firmness of a wall, while it is perfectly so with reference to the triumph of sound doctrine at an election. It will be important, in what follows, to keep in mind this relativeness of meaning in the word.

First and last, there have been some pretty dark rams in the Park Commission; but on the whole it has been the worthiest and best intentioned body having any important responsibility under the city administration in our time, and it has, till lately, had rightly more of public respect and confidence than any other, its distinction in this respect being not always pleasing to some other constitutents of the government. Yet with all the advantage their high standing might seem to give them, the Commissioners have rarely been able, when agreed among themselves, to move at all straight-forwardly upon the course, which, left to themselves, they would have marked out. Commissioner Wales has more than once, of late, referred to what he calls the "embarrassments" of the department, and has been careful to state, that, so far from these being new, he had in former years, when the public confidence in the Commissioners was much greater than at present, matched his strength with them till the breaking-point was reached, when he was compelled to resign, and go abroad to recruit his vigor in preparation for the renewed struggle in which he is now engaged.

He will excuse me for thinking that he has left the nature of these embarrassments in some obscurity, and for wishing to throw a little light upon it. I am going further on to mention circumstances connected with the dissociation of landscape-gardening from the business of the Park, which, if I had been in New York when the Commissioners' action for the purpose was taken, and had been disposed to make them public, would have added to the distrust and apprehension so generally expressed. They will even now cause surprise, even tax the credulity of many; and partly to lay a foundation for them, partly to give a clew to their significance, partly to reveal what Mr. Wales probably means by the embarrassments of the Board, I will, in this chapter, relate a few incidents of my earlier experience. My object being to throw light on methods and manners, for which we, citizens of New York, are every man responsible, and not to assail parties or persons, I shall aim to avoid names and dates.

My first narration will be of a commonplace character, and be given only to supply a starting-point.

1. The mayor once wanted to nominate me for the office of Street Commissioner. After some persuasion, perfectly aware that I was taking part in a play, though the mayor solemnly assured me otherwise, I assented, with the distinct understanding, that, if the office came to me, it should be free from political obligations; that I should be allowed to choose my own assistants, and, keeping within the law, my own method of administration. "Which," said the mayor, "is just what I want. It is because I felt sure that you would insist on that, that I sent for you." I smiled. The mayor preserved his gravity, and I took my leave. Within half an hour I received a call from a gentleman whom I had held in much esteem, to whom I had had reason to be grateful; who had once been a member of Congress,—a man of wealth and social position, but at the time holding no public office, and not conspicuous in politics. He congratulated me warmly, hoping that at last New York would be able to enjoy the luxury of clean streets. Conversation turned upon the character of the Board of Aldermen. The gentleman thought there need be no difficulty in getting their confirmation, but

suggested that it might be better for me to let him give a few confidential assurances to some who did not know me as well as he did, as to my more important appointments. He soon afterwards left, regretting plaintively to have found me so "unpractical" in my ideas. It was his opinion that half a loaf of reform was better than no bread. It was mine, that a man could not rightly undertake to clean the streets of New York with his hands tied confidentially.[1]

Soon another, also not holding an office, but president of a ward club, and as such having a certain familiarity with practical politics, called to advise me that —— wanted an understanding that I would give him fifteen per cent of my patronage. Not having it, he feared that——would throw his weight against me. I need not go on. When one of the mayor's friends in the city-hall understood that I seriously meant to be my own master, or defeated, he exclaimed, "Why, the man must be a fool!"

2. At one time, in a temporary emergency, I had the honor to be called to the quarter-deck, having been appointed a commissioner, and elected by the board of the period to be its president. In the few months that I held the position, I had some wonderful experiences, of which, for the present purpose, I will relate, because of their bearing on what follows, but five. That unpractical men may realize the wonder of them, it must be remembered that I was riding on the very crest of the glorious reform wave.

(1) A "delegation" from a great political organization called on me by appointment. After introductions and hand-shakings, a circle was formed, and a gentleman stepped before me, and said, "We know how much pressed you must be, Mr. President, and we don't want to be obtrusive, sir, nor exacting; but at your convenience our association would like to have you determine what share of your patronage we can expect, and make suitable arrangements for our using it. We will take the liberty to suggest, sir, that there could be no more convenient way than that you should send us our due quota of tickets, if you please, sir, in this form, *leaving us to fill in the name.*" Here a pack of printed tickets was produced, from which I took one at random. It was a blank appointment, and bore the signature of Mr. Tweed. "That," continued the spokesman, "was the way we arranged it last year, and we don't think there can be any thing better."

(2) Four gentlemen called by appointment on "important business." Three were official servants of the city: the fourth stated that he came from and was authorized to represent a statesman of national importance. Their business was to present a request, or rather a demand, so nearly naked that it would have been decenter if there had been no pretense of clothing it, for the removal of some of the minor officers of the Park, in order to make places for new men, whose names they were ready to give me. They said nothing to recommend their candidates, except that they were

---

[1] The word "unpractical" is not found in common dictionaries, but is so useful in our mandarin dialect, that I shall make bold for this occasion to adopt it.

reformers. The fact that the men whose removal they called for had been long enough employed to understand their duties, and to have proved their faithfulness and unpracticalness, was a sufficient reason that they should go. They had had their "suck." After a little conversation, which I made as pleasant as I could, I said smiling, "But excuse me, gentlemen, if I ask if you consider this to be reform?" There was no responsive smile (rather the contrary), and the representative of statesmanship said sharply, "What's the use of being a reformer, if it isn't?" And seriously, to these efficient public servants, this was the high-water mark of reform.

(3) Calling at this period upon another department head, and finding his lobby packed as mine was, when, after half an hour's waiting, I was admitted to a private interview,—of which the head took advantage to eat a cold lunch that had been waiting for him,— I said, "Is it possible that you are as hard beset by these gentlemen as I am?"—"Oh! more so, I think."—"Then, when do you get time for the proper business of your office?"—"Only before and after office-hours, when they think I am gone."

(4) Among those calling on me was one official of the city, who came regularly once a week, and, having been admitted, remained sometimes two hours, saying plainly that he did not mean to go until I had given him at least one appointment. At length I remonstrated with him somewhat severely. "Well, Mr. President," he replied, "you must excuse me. You know this is my business now, and I must attend to it. If I didn't, where should I be? But I'll let you off for to-day, and go round to ——'s office, and see what I can do with him."

(5) Twice it occurred to me, after passing through a large public office with many deputies and clerks, that the Chief remarked to me, "Among them all, there is but one man who is here by my own free choice, or in whose faithfulness I have confidence."

3. It has occurred five times in succession that I have been at the headquarters of the Department of Parks on the first visit of a new commissioner, and when, after a few passages of introductory courtesy, he has, as his first official movement in the business of the parks, asked to be furnished with a list showing the places at its disposal, the value of each, and the vacancies at the time existing. I believe that each of these gentlemen had been certified to the reporters to be entirely free from political obligations, and to owe his appointment solely to his eminent qualifications for the particular post of a park commissioner; but it will not be surprising, that, in view of my experience, I doubted the accuracy of the certificate.

4. A commissioner once said in my presence, "I don't get any salary for being here; it would be a pretty business if I couldn't oblige a friend now and then:" this being his reason for urging a most unfit appointment.

5. Writing of unfit appointments, nothing could be more ludicrous, if the anxiety they gave me had left room for a humorous view of them, than many most strenuously urged. A young man

was pressed for my nomination as a topographical draughtsman. I asked to see some of his work, and, after explanations, was answered, "I don't know that he ever made any maps or drawings on paper."—"How could you think he was qualified as a draughtsman?" To which the reluctant reply was this: "The fact is, he was a little wild a few years ago, and ran away to sea on a whaler, and when he came back he brought a whale's tooth, on which he had made a picture of his ship as natural as life. Now I think that a boy who could do that, you could do most any thing with in the drawing way." The very man who said this, and, incredible as it will be thought, said it seriously, was nominated by the mayor for a park commissioner. Can the reader say, that, if the favorite remedy for the moment, and that advocated by Mr. Wales, for all the evils of the present park mismanagement, shall be adopted, this same good business-man may not next year be chosen to exemplify the efficiency of a single-headed administration?

6. I once expressed to a gentleman surprise at the accuracy of certain information of which I found him possessed. "Oh! that's nothing," he said. "There is not a workingman living in my district, or who comes into it, or goes out of it, that I have not got him down on my books, with the name and ages of his wife and all his children, what house they are in, what rooms they occupy, what his work is, who employs him, who is to look after his vote, and so on. I have it all tabulated, and posted up. I have to make a business of it, you know. If a man means to succeed in politics, he must. It is not a business you can play with."

7. Another illustration of practical business-methods was given by a president of the Department as follows:—

"I want you to know," he said, after opening the door, looking out, closing and locking it, "of some things going on here. Yesterday a man applied for a certain position, bringing a letter dated at Albany the day before, in which the writer stated that he understood that the late holder of the position had been discharged. I told the applicant that he was mistaken; but he insisted that he was not, and I could hardly get rid of him. Here is a report coming this morning from the Park, making charges against the man in question, and advising his discharge. Information of a prospective opportunity of an appointment had gone to Albany and back, before it came to me here. You see how closely they watch us. But here is another example of it. I signed today an appointment which I had not determined to make five minutes before. I sent the appointee directly up to the Park, starting myself, at the same moment, for the city-hall. When I reached there, reference was made to the appointment by the first man who spoke to me, showing that not a moment had been lost in reporting it. But who made the report, and how, so quickly? I confess I hardly dare inquire. But there is something yet more inscrutable. I suspected the lock of my private drawer to have been tampered with. Last night I placed a bit of paper where it would be dislodged if the drawer was opened, and another in my memorandum-book of vacancies, applications and intended appointments. This morning I found both displaced."

8. There was an intrigue to remove a valuable officer by destroying his character, in order to make an opening for the advancement of a subordinate strongly backed with "influence." I asked and obtained a committee of the Board to try the case. The subordinate made oath to a statement which was proved to be false; and for the perjury he was dismissed. Shortly afterwards he met me on the Park, offered me his hand, and, with much flourish, thanked me for having brought about his removal, as it had compelled his friends to make proper exertions, and he now held a position much more to his taste than any on the Park could have been.

9. At a dignified public ceremony on the Park, I saw, while listening to the oration of the day, a roughly-dressed man approach the point where the Commissioners were arrayed, all in proper black, and facing a great crowd. As the man neared their position from the rear, he reached out a walking-stick, and punched one of them. The commissioner turned; and the man threw his head back, as if to say, "Come here, I want a word with you." The commissioner fell out, and there was a whispered conversation. "Now, what does that mean?" I asked. "Don't you know? Why, that is one of our new foremen; and he and the commissioner are both members of the same district committee. He is laying in with him to make a place for some fellow whose help they need in the primaries."

10. I suspended a man because of evidence of gross disobedience of a standing rule. He told a very improbable story; and I gave him a fortnight to produce corroborative evidence of it. Instead of doing so, he set a number of his "friends" after me. His special patron was a man in office, and proprietor of a weekly newspaper. A copy of it was sent me, with a marked article containing absurd and scurrilous abuse of me, and of the Commission for employing me. As this official had shortly before called at my house, and been profuse in compliments and professions of regard, I went to see him. Referring to the article, I said, "It would have given you but the slightest trouble to ascertain that you had been imposed upon in the statements to which you have given currency." He smiled, and asked, "Would you like to see an article I intend to publish tomorrow?" handing a galley-proof to me. I read it, and said, "I have marked and numbered with my pencil seven statements in this article, which, I give you my word, can be ascertained, by any one coming to the Park, to be quite untrue." The next day a copy of the paper was sent me containing the article without the change of a word. The suspended man at last confessed, hoping to be pardoned, but was dismissed. The paper continued to be sent me every week for perhaps a year, and I was told that every number had some attack on the Park. At another period another paper pursued a similar course. One day the editor, finding the president of

the Department on a railway-train going to Albany, gayly saluted him in terms of friendship. "I am surprised, sir," said the president, "that, after what you have been saying of our Board in your paper, you can offer me your hand."—"Oh!" replied the editor, "but that was business."

11. During all my park work it was a common thing to receive newspapers, addressed by unknown hands, containing matter designed to injure me; sometimes, also, anonymous threats and filthy caricatures. The object I take to have been to impress me with the insecurity of my position, and the folly of the unpractical view of its duties.

12. A foreman of laborers, discharged from the Park against strong political influence, was, at the next election, a candidate for the Legislature.

13. At one time, shortly after the police of the Park had a second time been put under my superintendence, I undertook an improvement of it. Asking the officer in charge to account for his own failure to secure the conviction and removal of some whom he described as "regular dead-beats," who had "never performed one honest tour of duty since they were taken on," he answered, "Why, damn 'em, they are every man laying wires to go to the Legislature, and they carry too many guns for me."

14. As my first step, I wrote an order to the surgeon, directing a medical survey of the force. The surgeon called on me, and said, "I am under your orders, sir, and if you insist I shall act on them to the letter; but perhaps you do not realize, as I do, what the consequences will be to me."—"What will they be?"—"Only that I shall have to eat my bread without butter for a while."—"I understand; but I must do my duty, and you must do yours." He did, reporting a quarter part of the entire force physically incapacitated for any active duty, and indicating that it had been used as an asylum for aggravated cases of hernia, varicose veins, rheumatism, partial blindness, and other infirmities compelling sedentary occupations. The surgeon was supported by the highest authorities of his profession, and had established on the Park an excellent character, professionally and otherwise. He had gained the affection and confidence of the force, but, in obeying orders without consulting its friends, had proved himself an unpractical man, and, as he had anticipated, was soon afterwards dismissed by order of the Board.

15. I asked an officer before me on a grave charge what he had to say. With a laugh, and a wink to his comrades, he answered, "You want to know what I have to say? Well, that's what I have to say," handing me a crumpled note which read, "If there is any thing against officer ——, please remember that he is my man, and charge it to account of Yours Truly, —— ——." He was dismissed.

16. I set a watch upon the night-watch; and five men, receiving three dollars a night for patrol-duty on beats of which two were a

mile and a half apart, were found together in the middle of their watch in a necessary building, which they had entered with false keys. They had made a fire, taken off their boots, and, using their rolled-up coats for pillows, were fast asleep; and this had doubtless been long their habit. With the sanction of the Board I changed the system, much reducing its cost, and employed mechanical detectors on the principle of those used for the night-watch of great mills. They were broken from their fastenings, and carried away. I devised a stronger and simpler apparatus. In several instances, within a week it was broken, as if by sledges, a great force being necessary.

17. The eldest of the watchmen had been originally employed for several years in the Park as a land-surveyor. He had received a good education, and, after his discharge as a surveyor, had suffered grievous domestic afflictions, and been left very poor. He was a religious man, had been active in church charities; and it was in part upon a letter from his pastor setting forth his trustworthiness that I had obtained his appointment as watchman. He had refused to join the others in their conspiracy, and was looked upon as a spy—wrongly, for he had given me no information. He was waylaid at night, murderously struck down, and left for dead. It was several weeks before he was able to leave his bed, and when he did so he was scarred for life.

18. Several other measures were adopted, all with the knowledge and sanction of the Board, and believed at the time, by the excellent gentlemen composing it, to be perfectly business-like. But they were all very unpractical in the view taken by many of the force and their friends, who consequently united in measures designed to convince the Commissioners of their mistake, and for self-protection against my cruelty. A fund was raised, and a "literary gentleman" regularly employed to write me down. At this time I received confidential warnings indirectly from high quarters outside the Commission, that I would not be allowed to succeed in what I was attempting, and had better drop it. I did not drop it, but worked on with all my might; and presently the literary gentleman got also to his work, first in some of the Sunday papers. At length, by one of those accidents that seem liable to occur in any great newspaper establishment, he managed to get a powerful article prominently displayed in a leading daily, in which, after referring to the reputation of the force with the public, gained by its alleged uniform activity, efficiency, civility; its high state of discipline and *esprit du corps*, it was represented, that, through some unaccountable freak of the Board, it had recently been placed under the orders of a silly, heartless, upstart, sophomorical theorist, through whose boyish experiments it was being driven into complete and rebellious demoralization. One of the Commissioners told me that he was asked a day or two afterwards, "Who is this young chap that you have put in charge of the police? How could you have been stuck with such an unpractical fellow?"

Now it happened that I was one of the few men then in America who had made it a business to be well informed on the subject of police organization and management. I had made some examination of the French system; had when in London known Sir Richard Mayne, the organizer of the Metropolitan force, upon the model of which our New York Metropolitan force is formed; had been favored by him with a long personal discourse on the principles of its management, and been given the best opportunities for seeing them in operation, both in the park service and in all other departments. I had made a similar study of the Irish constabulary. I had originally organized, instructed, and disciplined, and under infinite difficulties secured the reputation of this same Central Park force. Finally, by a singular coincidence, I had nearly twenty years before, when my defamer was himself a school-boy, been an occasional editorial writer for the journal which he thus turned upon my work and had contributed to it much of the matter, which, collected in a volume, had been later twice reprinted in London, and in translations in Paris and Leipsic.

I was asked by the president of the Department to make a public reply, and was allowed by the editor to do so in the same columns. I must gratefully add that the editor afterwards made all reparation in his power consistently with the ordinary rules of newspaper business. Nevertheless, the article served its purpose, was largely circulated among practical men, and I had reason to believe that even some of my friends thought there must be something in its ridiculous falsifications. The end was, that I was relieved of responsibility for the police of the Park. My duty was mainly assumed by a committee a majority of whom were new to the business; and the only two men who, besides the surgeon, had been conspicuously resolute in carrying out my orders, and sincere and faithful in efforts to enforce them, were dismissed— neither honorably nor dishonorably discharged, but simply notified that their services were no longer required. I am sure that the commissioners whose votes frustrated my efforts had been thoroughly convinced by the advice of friends that they were acting for the best interests of the city; that my intentions were good but impractical; and that in every thing they were doing God's service. The president to the last sustained me. Because he did so, and asked it as a personal favor and act of friendship, I consented, after having resigned my office, to resume service under the Commission upon a modified arrangement, vindicating my professional standing and securing me against another similar experience.

19. Within two years the rules which the Board had been persuaded to adopt to prevent unsuitable men from being recruited, and to secure advancement by proved merit, had become a dead-letter; and the force was left to drift into the condition in which one of the Commissioners lately stated in a Board meeting that he had found it, and which led to a beautifully drawn resolution that hereafter no man who could not read and write should be taken for

it. How soon to become in its turn a dead-letter, who can say? Some time after my defeat, a gentleman told me that he had walked, in a fine day, through the interior of the Park from end to end without seeing an officer. There was no lack of them on the fashionable drives; but in the most secluded and sylvan districts prostitutes were seeking their prey without hindrance, and it was no place for a decent poor woman to bring her children. I myself, since I left the Park, have seen an officer within a hundred yards of a carriage when it stopped, and when the coachman bent down an overhanging lilac-bush loaded with bloom, from which the occupants broke large branches, afterwards driving off without interruption or reproof. The officer, doubtless, thought it an unpractical thing to have lilac-bushes in the Park, as the present Commissioners think any thing like sylvan seclusion unsanitary.

At another time I met seven small boys coming from the Park, all carrying baskets. They were showing one another the contents of these as I came upon them; and I found that they were each filled with beautiful rock-moss, which they were going to sell for the decoration of hanging-baskets. The Park has always been very deficient in this lovely accompaniment of rocks, and it is difficult to secure it. I asked the boys if the police allowed them to strip it off. "No," said one: "we waits till their heads is turned." "No," said another: "they don't care; they just minds the carriages, they does." Nor are these incidents by any means the most alarming that I might report.

Do the owners of houses building near the Park fancy that its vicinity will be a more agreeable place of residence because of this practical style of management? I have seen a newspaper report that already last summer great numbers of tramps and gypsies regularly lodged in the Park. When the police was under unpractical direction, I have repeatedly walked through its entire length after midnight, finding every officer in his place, and not one straggling visitor. Hyde Park is closed at nightfall, as are all other city parks in Europe; but one surface road is kept open across Hyde Park, and the superintendent of the Metropolitan Police told me that a man's chances of being garroted or robbed were, because of the facilities for concealment to be found in the Park, greater in passing at night along this road than anywhere else in London.

If these incidents give little idea of the number, weight, and constancy of the embarrassments with which the Park Board has to struggle, they may have made plainer the nature of them, and the soil on which they grow.

But I must add a few more, that may, in some degree, remove misapprehensions as to the responsibility for various matters which are occasionally referred to in the interest of practical park management, as if they were the result of the ignorance or perversity of which the Commissioners intended to rid the Park in abolishing the landscape office.

For several years before that event, the management of the

parks had, as before stated, not been under my direction. I had only to advise about it. But even before this, there was, for some time, a standing order in force, forbidding me to have a single tree felled without a specific order, to be obtained by a majority vote of the Board. Before this order was passed, men seen cutting trees under my directions have been interrupted and indignantly rebuked by individual commissioners, and even by the "friends" of commissioners, having no more right to do so than they would for like action on a man-of-war. I have had men beg me, from fear of dismissal, to excuse them from cutting trees, and, to relieve them, have taken the axe from them, and felled the trees myself. I have been denounced to commissioners by their friends as "a Vandal" and a "public robber," because nurse-trees were cut from the plantations of the Park under my directions. It may have been noticed, that, notwithstanding much talk of the necessity of thinning plantations, Mr. Wales, in a triumphant way, announced lately that not a single live tree had been cut this winter. Why not? Nothing had been cut but bushes, the removal of which, one by one, would pass with little notice from the vigilant friends of the Commissioners. Who is there, with any authority on the Park, competent to judge what trees should and what should not be cut, with a view to the purpose for which the Park has been formed?

Rocky passages of the Park, which had been furnished under my direction with a natural growth of characteristic rocky hillside perennials, have been more than once "cleaned up," and so thoroughly that the leaf-mould, with which the crevices of the ledge had been carefully filled for the sustenance of the plants, was swept out with house-brooms in the interest of that good taste which delights in a house painted white with green blinds, whitewashed cherry-trees, plaster statuettes on stumps; and patty-cakes of bedding-plants set between rocks scraped of their dirty old lichens and mosses,—and all in the heart of an Appalachian glen. Whereupon Mr. Robinson, in that invaluable addition to the literature of landscape art, ALPINE FLOWERS, writes (I quote from a copy kindly sent me by my good friend the author, 2d London edition, p. 8),—

"In the Central Park of New York are scores of noble and picturesque breaks of rock, which have not been adorned with a single Alpine plant or rock-bush." He might have said, from which not only all such adornments, but even all the natural growth of rock-bushes, vines, perennials, and mosses, has again and again been cleaned away as exhibiting a low, depraved, and unpractical taste. The work is going on, I am assured, at this moment; and when it is finished, and August comes round again, and all the yellow turf and the dead, half-covered outcrops of smooth-faced, gray and brown ledge are fully exposed to view, God help the poor man who can find no better place of escape from the town!

20. The landscape office had been twice dispensed with for a time before its last abolition in 1879.[1] During one of these inter-

---

[1] Cf. footnote on p. 122, *ante.*

vals a much boasted improvement in the plan of the Park had been put through with the energy and efficiency characteristic of a bull earning his passage through a China shop. Later, something was found defective in the drainage of the adjoining region. After tedious and costly exploration, it was ascertained that a large main drain had been cut through at a critical point, and that the tile had been so broken and deranged as to make a complete dam, after which the excavation had been filled up, and built over. This led me to look at the drainage-maps, several sheets of which proved to have been lost. I begged to have a survey made for their renewal; and a man was employed for it who had been previously engaged in the work. While he was still occupied with the duty, what passes for economy in practical park management came and dismissed him. I doubt if complete drainage-maps will be found in the Department today. I will undertake to satisfy a fair jury of respectable sanitarians, that, if there is reason to believe that a single case of malarial disease has originated in the Park in twenty years, it has been due to conditions which have been established or maintained against the advice of the landscape office. The reverse has been asserted or implied in scores of publications, for which no commissioner, as such, has ever been responsible.

21. The more "practical" Commissioners have often given me advice received by them from friends having no official responsibility for the parks, and which betrayed exceptional ignorance, even for city-bred men, on matters which had been my life-study; which ran also directly counter to the practice of every respectable member of my profession; the folly of which I have often seen exposed in our agricultural journals, and the agricultural columns of our newspapers, but which they regarded, and expected me to regard, as of controlling weight. Some such advice I have, since I left the Park, seen carried out in practice.

22. The president once notified me that a friend of his was to come before the Board as spokesman for a "delegation" of citizens, to advocate the introduction of a running-course on the Park. He would ask me to explain some of the objections to the project, but hoped that I would do so in a way as little likely to provoke the gentleman as possible, as he had great weight in politics, and it would be in his power to much embarrass the Department. I followed these instructions as I best could; but it was impossible for me not to refer to the landscape considerations. At the first mention of the word the gentleman exclaimed, and by no means "aside," "Oh, damn the landscape!" then, rising, he addressed the president to this effect: "We came here, sir, as practical men, to discuss with your Board a simple, practical, common-sense question. We don't know any thing about your landscape, and we don't know what landscape has to do with the matter before us."

23. It will have been asked by many, as they have been reading, Why did you not appeal to public opinion? Why did not the Commissioners, who were superior to the courses through which

your professional judgment was overruled, if they could not other-wise overcome these embarrassments, lay them frankly before us, and see what we could do? Might not a corresponding question be asked in regard to what everybody knows is going on at this moment, and has been for years going on, of the highest officer of the nation?

If the reference seems presumptuous in one respect, let me show that it hardly can be so in another; I mean in respect to the absorption of time and energy of public servants, through the pressure of "practical advice." As superintendent of the Park, I once received in six days more than seven thousand letters of advice as to appointments, nearly all from men in office, and the greater part in legislative offices upon which the Commissioners have been much dependent for the means of accomplishing anything they might wish to do,—either written by them directly, or by Commissioners at their request.   I have heard a candidate for a magisterial office in the city addressing from my doorsteps a crowd of such advice-bearers, telling them that I was bound to give them employment, and suggesting plainly, that, if I was slow about it, a rope round my neck might serve to lessen my reluctance to take good counsel.   I have had a dozen men force their way into my house before I had risen from bed on a Sunday morning, and some break in to my drawing-room in their eagerness to deliver letters of advice. I have seen a president of the Park Board surrounded by a mob of similar bearers of advice, in Union Square, carried hither and thither by them, perfectly helpless; have seen policemen make their way in to him with clubs, drag him out, force him into a passing carriage, and lash the horses to a gallop, to secure his temporary relief from "embarrassments," the nature of which I trust that I have now sufficiently illustrated.

I do not remember ever to have seen the office of the Board with-out a poster, reading, "No laborers wanted;" and I do not believe that there has in twenty years been a time when nine-tenths of the intellectual force and nervous energy of the Board has not been given to recruiting duty.

V

DURING all of the summer before the Commissioners agreed to "damn landscape," I was aware that the practical view was getting the upper hand of them.   It would take too much space to tell how I became conscious of it.   There were symptoms such as this: that, while observing great ceremony of politeness with me, there were three of them whom I was never able to get to meet me on the Park (nor on any park).   In the case of two, I was careful not to let a month go by without separately asking the favor of an appointment for the purpose, and in reply was always assured of a desire and intention to make it soon.   Twice an appointment was actually made; and each time the commissioner failed to keep it, afterwards courteously apologizing. Thus and otherwise, there was no doubt left in my mind, that, with respect to my part of the business of the parks, these amiable gentlemen cared only how not to do it. If there had been, occurrences which have followed the abolition of my office would have removed it.

But it was not simply from observation of mere symptoms that I knew that the embarrassments affecting them were of an unusual character. I myself received from without the Board several warnings, both direct and indirect. By indirect, I mean threats made in such a manner as to leave me in no doubt that it was intended to guard against a public accountability for them. By direct, I mean not only friendly, confidential hints, but such as were given me, for example, in my own house, by a man who brought a line of introduction from a high public officer. After he had called three times (on each occasion while I was at dinner), I informed the introducer that his bearing had been such, that, if he called again, I should ask the protection of the police. I knew that my movements were being furtively dogged, and I presumed that they were so with a view to obtaining pretexts upon which to urge my removal.

Let it be understood what this meant to me,—the frustration of purposes to which I had for years given all my heart, to which I had devoted my life; the degradation of works in which my pride was centred; the breaking of promises to the future which had been to me as churchly vows. However I was able to carry myself by day, it will not be thought surprising that I should have had sleepless nights, or that at last I could not keep myself from over-wearing irritation and worry. The resulting depression, acting with an extraordinary prostration from the great heat of the summer, and the recurrence of an old malarial trouble, brought me, late in the season, to a condition comparable to that often produced by a sun-stroke, perhaps of the same nature. It has taken me four years to recover the strength which I then lost within a week. In view of this loss, I was advised by three well-known physicians to seek at once a change of air, scene, and mental occupation. I knew that any prolonged absence from New York would give an opportunity to the plotters against my work that might be fatal to it; and while I hesitated an incident occurred which made my retirement for a time impossible. A newspaper was sent to my house with a marked passage stating that disgraceful charges were pending against me. The president of the Department knew nothing of them at the time; but within two days he informed me that the report was authentic.

The charter, so called, of the city, provides, that, when any one in its service stands accused of official misdoings, there shall be a form of trial open to him before his dismissal. I determined to take no notice of the charges until I had the opportunity, thus supposed to be secured to me, of looking my accusers in the face. But it never came. On the strength of the charges,—deliberate and circumstantial lies, invented, as I imagine, by spies to cover their ill success from their employers,—my name had been struck from the pay-roll. A month afterwards I found it restored; and the instalment of salary, which had been due when the charges were made, and payment of which had been stopped on account of them, was silently sent me. Thus, though no word of retraction or explanation, of vindication or apology, followed, I was left to infer that the attempt to cast me out as a culprit had been abandoned.

Of many incidents emphasizing the character of this occurrence, I will make room for but one. I have shown that the charges were given to the press before they were officially known to the Board or to me. I have to add that this which I now make more than four years afterwards is the first public mention, to my knowledge, of their falsity or abandonment.

It is not to be supposed that I was gaining ground upon my nervous disorder during this month. At its end winter was setting in, and the principal work on the parks had stopped for the season. As soon as I was released from arrest, so to speak, I presented the medical certificate I had been holding back, showing my need of temporary relief from duty; and upon it leave of absence, with suspension of salary, was given me till spring. It was while this act was fresh and operating, and I was yet on the sea, that my office was abolished.

The general mistrust of the press, that the determination to do away with it had had other motives than those officially recorded, led to some "interviewing" of the Commissioners, under the torture of which one of them admitted that I had been suspected of having had "a pretty fat thing" in supplying the parks with trees. It happens that I had been anxious to obtain a few comparatively rare and costly trees for the Park. But I knew that the Commissioners were averse to authorizing purchases which might be taken as illustrations of extravagance. Moreover, the Park was in great need of another elephant; it actually did not possess a single rhinoceros; the gilding on the weathercocks was much tarnished; and the bronze nymph at Mount St. Vincent was almost as black as before she had, by the order of an older commissioner, been cleaned up, and painted white. Therefore I had, with the aid of friends, procured the trees I specially wanted without expense to the city. The value of the gift was, I believe, less than two hundred dollars; but that any such thing could be done from interest in the scenery of the Park had not probably occurred to the sufferer, and a confused recollection of something inexplicable about it led him, when squeezed, as I little doubt, to blunder upon the expression caught by the reporter. Still, in view of my absence from the country, to have been betrayed into such an innuendo is not characteristic of a lofty soul; and this may explain why it was also said that the Commissioners had had enough of "high tone."

But not too much importance should be given to these hasty expressions. I do not doubt that the Commissioners were quite sincere in stating that they abrogated the landscape office because they found it "of no practical use." That they really had the completest confidence in my integrity, esteem for my professional ability, and held me to have deserved well of my fellow-citizens in all official duty, they were forward to testify by placing a series of resolutions to that effect on their minutes, and also by giving me an appointment that the public has been often advised, through the published proceedings of the present Board, remains uncancelled; that, namely, of Consulting Landscape-Architect (without salary). Considering the form of this appointment,[1] it is significant, that, while I have been holding it, the Board has permitted designs prepared under its orders in my office, long discussed, laid before the public, and, after most mature deliberation, adopted by unanimous vote, to be, in some cases, strangely mutilated by men not of my profession, and of no public standing in any profession; in others, to be superseded by wholly new and radically different designs. The main object of the changes in these cases had been before most carefully considered with the aid of comparative drawings, models, and other demonstrations, and the Board satisfied that objections of a conclusive character applied to them. In the reconsideration, partly or wholly by new commissioners, no thought of these objections appears to have been had. I have been allowed no opportunity to point them out, or to defend, in any manner, the work for which I had been made publicly responsible; and they are now to be established by slow, provoking, and expensive public experience. Why was I appointed? and how is it that I still hold the office of Consulting Landscape-Architect to the Board? In the four years since it was made, there has been no communication between the Board and me.

In Victor Hugo's story, the practical M. Nortier says,—

"In politics we do not kill a man: we only remove an embarrassment; that is all."

VI

When Mr. Vaux and I first put our heads together in study of the design for the Central Park, we agreed to treat nothing as of essential consequence, except with reference to results which might be looked for, at nearest, forty years ahead. And with an outlook at least that far along, all our work and our advice has since been given. In this has consisted a large part of its unpracticality.

If a park be got up mainly with the use of money borrowed in long loans; if the ground upon which it is formed be mortgaged as security for the ultimate payment of the loans; if the conduct of the business be placed in the hands of men who accept the trust without salary, as a consolation for the loss of a paid commissioner-

---

[1] "Whereas Mr. Frederick Law Olmsted, long identified with the Central Park and its improvements, and enjoying the confidence of the community and the respect of this Department since its organization, should be placed in a position where this Department can avail itself of his large experience and intimate knowledge of the designs and objects of the work on the different parks," etc.

ship in a business of a very different character, or a place on a party committee, or a nomination for alderman, and who are far too knowing to accept advice except from practical men and of an instantly practical character:—if the business of these men be conducted with a view, first, to aid the cause of honest government at the next election; second, to suit the convenience of political contractors with notes coming due next month; and, lastly, to secure immediate satisfaction from one election to another of the public, it would not be surprising if even this *immediate* public satisfaction was not all they could wish.

It would be going further than is necessary to my purpose, to say that just this has occurred; but it may be well to ask if facts do not suggest methods of business which correspond nearly with what might be expected if it had. Let us see.

The Park Board, stimulated by the stings of the press and the public, and by the formal remonstrances of the leading business men of the city, has now had full four years in which to prove how well its business can be managed under the practical view, by practical men, and free from the embarrassment of professional advice and professional superintendence; and with what result?

Unless every newspaper that I have been in the way of seeing has been bearing false witness, and every thing that comes to me verbally is deceptive, no branch of the city government has ever failed so completely and humiliatingly to earn public respect and confidence. As supplying the only available pleasure-roads, the Park is yet, perhaps, with an increasing driving and riding population, increasingly resorted to in the fashionable driving and riding season; that is to say, by that part of the population who least need to have opportunities of rural recreation brought nearer to them. But spite of all that should have been gained after twenty years, by four years' growing together of trees planted with the design of securing broad, quiet, massing effects, the Park is reported to have been steadily losing attraction, and, relatively to the entire population of the city, to be made less use of, and less valuable use of, than before.

Notwithstanding the obvious fact that the motive of the management has been favorable to what may be termed the uniformly smug and smart suburban door-yard style, in distinction from a more varied treatment admitting here and there of at least a subdued picturesqueness, the verdict appears to be, that the Park has even taken on a slovenly and neglected aspect. This is not by any means the worst of the story; but, for the present, stopping here, if an explanation is needed, may it not be given in the one word "IGNORANCE"?—not ignorance of practical politics; of the stock, cotton, or iron markets; of Greek, physics, or botany; of horticulture, floriculture, or garden decoration, but ignorance—complete, blind ignorance—of the principles, even of the motives and objects, of an art to which many men of great wisdom and venerated character have thought it right to give as long and arduous study as is often

given to any other form of art, or to any learned profession,—an art
to which it is no more reasonable to suppose that a man can turn
at middle life, and in a few months be prepared to assume the
responsibility of a great public work, than that he can, in like
manner, qualify himself to take command of an army, to serve as
corporation counsel, superintending physician of Bellevue Hospital;
as a sculptor, chemist, or lapidary.

VII

WHAT has just been declared impossible many have been led
to believe to be just what Mr. Vaux and I attempted, and with
the result of leading the city, by our unfitness for the duties we
accepted, into disasters such as the present commissioners have
been seeking to mitigate. I have little doubt that many commissioners before the present, have, one after another, given a
certain degree, at least, of credence, to statements made with this
object, and I know that not a few estimable citizens must have done
so.   It is a matter of some moment to the city; it is of considerable
interest to my profession; and I believe it to be due to the cause not
alone of my art, but of all art, that the true state of the case should
be known.   The delusion so common and so melancholy, that because a boy has, or thinks he has, a natural gift for sketching, or
modelling, or mimicry, he may hope to mount to distinction as a
painter, sculptor, or actor, without far greater labor than is required
for learning a trade, has its full counterpart in respect to landscape
gardening.   I cannot say with what pity I have seen young men
advertising themselves as landscape-engineers, etc., on the strength
of having chanced to be employed as assistant surveyors for a few
months in the ruder preparatory processes of park-making.   Nay,
I have seen even greater effrontery than that.
     Mr. Vaux had, years before he took up the work of the Park,
been the chosen co-operator of the greatest master in America
of landscape-gardening, and had been associated with him in the
most important and best public work that had been done in the
country. He was personally familiar with the most useful of
European parks through having shared from childhood in their
popular use. He had made, in company with other artists, long
sketching-tours on foot, both in the old country and in the new;
had more than ordinary amateur skill in landscape-painting, and
had had thorough professional training in architecture.
     I myself began my study of the art of parks in childhood.
I had read, before I was fifteen, the great works upon the art,
—works greater than any of the last half-century,—and had
been under the instruction of older and more observant students of
scenery, under the most favorable circumstances for a sound education.   And there had been no year of the twenty that followed
before I entered the service of the Park Board, that I had not pursued the study with ardor, affection, and industry.

I had twice travelled in Europe with that object in view; had more than a hundred times visited the parks of London and Paris and once or oftener those of Dublin, Liverpool, Brussels, The Hague, Berlin, Vienna, Florence, Rome, and other old cities. I had travelled five thousand miles on foot or in the saddle, and more than that by other private or public conveyance, in study of the natural scenery of this continent. I had been three years the pupil of a topographical engineer, and had studied in what were then the best schools, and under the best masters in the country, of agricultural science and practice. I had planted with my own hands five thousand trees, and, on my own farm and in my own groves, had practised for ten years every essential horticultural operation of a park. I had made the management of labor in rural works a special study, and had written upon it acceptably to the public. I had been for several years the honorary secretary of two organizations, and a member of four, formed for the discussion of rural themes and the advancement of rural arts. I had by invitation written for the leading journal of landscape-gardening, and had been in correspondence with and honored by the friendship of leading men in its science on both sides of the Atlantic.

And essentially what I have thus said of myself had been known to the Commissioners, if not otherwise, then through those who introduced me to them, among whom were Mr. Irving, Mr. Bryant, Professor Gray, Mr. Greely, Mr. Raymond, Mr. Godwin, General Hamilton, Peter Cooper, Russell Sturgis, Charles II. Marshall, Edmund Blunt, Cornelius Grinnell, and David Dudley Field.

It is notoriously too easy to get the use of names, one following another: therefore I add, that most of these well-known men had been either my hosts or my guests; all had met me socially, and testified of my training not without some personal knowledge.

Since then, the work of Mr. Vaux and myself speaks for itself; and judgment upon it has been given, not by New York alone, which in natural landscape art, at least, might easily for a time be misled, but by the highest authority living. On what more worthy works rests the authority of those who tell the people of New York that we were quacks and knaves, and that our designs require such recasting of competent park-makers as it is now with all possible energy receiving?

If I seem tending to their level in thus speaking for myself, let it be considered that I have yet something more to say, and that I wish it to have all the weight that my rightful good name should entitle it to; let it be considered, also, that I have twenty times seen the assertion in print, made by some of the practical hounds, to whom this is my first reply in twenty years, that Mr. Vaux and I were brought upon the Park unknown, ignorant, incompetent pretenders, to serve a knavish scheme of base politicians; and that I happen to know that inquiries have been lately making in the vain hope to find ground of support for reiteration of the stupid fabrication.

Frederick Law Olmsted

In the late 1880's

And yet, in what has been spread abroad of this sort, there is just that yarn of truth that is usually to be found in the work of practised falsifiers. It is true that I had not set up to be a landscape-gardener before I came upon the Park. I had not thought myself one, and had been surprised and delighted when I was asked if I would accept even a journeyman's position in the intended work. Why? Simply because I held the art in such reverence, that, to that time, it had never occurred to me that I might rightly take upon myself the responsibilities of a principal in its public practice. My study of it had been wholly a study of love, without a thought of its bringing me pecuniary reward or repute: in many matters of detail, therefore, it was defective (it is still very defective); and it is perfectly true, for this reason, if no other, that the task which was ultimately given me in the Central Park would have been an impossible one, had I not been so fortunate as to enjoy, for a time, the ardent and most loyal aid of men better qualified in some important respects than myself. But I am more inclined to question now than I was when I accepted my first unsought and most unexpected appointment, whether, if I had been more elaborately fitted than I happened to be, I should have been more strenuously or more intelligently bent on serving, with all such skill as I could command, the highest ends of the art, or better fitted to escape beguilements from them through the pedantries or the meretricious puerilities which hang on all its skirts. Let me illustrate my meaning.

During the last twenty years Europe has been swept by a mania for sacrificing natural scenery to coarse manufactures of brilliant and gaudy decoration under the name of specimen gardening; bedding, carpet, embroidery, and ribbon gardening, or other terms suitable to the house-furnishing and millinery trades. It was a far madder contagion than the tulip-mania, or the morus-multi-caulis fever of our youth.

It ran into all park management, the only limit often being that fixed by annual appropriations. Long ago, for example, it seized Hyde Park, and put completely out of countenance the single charm of broad homely sylvan and pastoral simplicity which the fogs and smoke of London, and its weary miles of iron hurdles, had left to it. Why? I asked the old superintendent. "Well, you know the fashion must have its run, and it just tickles the nursery-maids." I take some credit for my schooling, then, that so far as Central Park has been under my guardianship, it has been perfectly quarantined; not a dollar having been spent, nor a rood of good turf spoiled, for garishness, under my superintendence, nor at any time, except against my protest.

Thirty years ago, before the Park was dreamed of, as a farmer, and with no more idea that I should ever be a professional landscape-designer than that I should command a fleet, I had printed these thoroughly unpractical words:—

"What artist so noble as he, who, with far-reaching conception of beauty and designing-power, sketches the outlines, writes the colors, and directs the shadows, of a picture so great that Nature shall be employed upon it for generations, before the work he has arranged for her shall realize his intentions!"[1]

VIII

IN the last chapter I observed that a loss of popular favor through slovenliness and neglect was not the worst misfortune that had befallen the Park. If it had been, I should have been still constrained to hold my peace. Neglect for considerable periods may do no serious permanent harm. Hence, while in the service of the Commission, I yielded much in that way to the practical policy. Neglect, if it continues not too long, may even have its advantages. The landscape-architect André, formerly in charge of the suburban plantations of Paris, was walking with me through the Buttes-Chaumont Park, of which he was the designer, when I said of a certain passage of it, "That, to my mind, is the best piece of artificial planting, of its age, I have ever seen." He smiled, and said, "Shall I confess that it is the result of neglect? I had planted this place most elaborately, with a view to some striking immediate effects which I had conceived, and others, to be ultimately obtained by thinnings. I had just worked out my plan, when the war came; and for two years I did not again see the ground. It was occupied as a camp; horses were pastured in it; it was cut up by artillery; fires were made in it. As a park, it was everywhere subjected to the most complete neglect. When, at length, I came back to it, expecting to begin my work over again at all points, Nature had had one summer in which, as well as she could, to repair damages; and I declare to you, that, on arriving at just this point, I threw up my hands with delight, for, spite of some yet unhealed wounds, I saw at once that in general aspect there was a better work than I had been able to imagine. That which was weak and unsuitable in my planting had, by natural selection, disappeared; and in the struggle for existence nearly all that remained had taken a wild character, such as in an art we may aim at, but can hardly hope to attain." (But see how the true artist at once bowed himself before his tutor, and recognized and seized the opportunity.)

Hence, were ignorant neglect and feeble-minded slovenliness the worst qualities of the Board's management, I should yet have had nothing to say. The reason I must now speak is, that the Park is at last, avowedly, boastfully, and with much brag of energy, managed in distinct contemptuous repudiation of the leading mo-

[1] From Mr. Olmsted's first book, *Walks and Talks.* See Vol. I, *ante*, p. 102, also Vol. II, p. 50, *ante*.

tives with which it was laid out.   This means, not, as Mr. Wales says, with no well-defined purpose, but with a purpose defined with perfect distinctness to undo, as far as practicable, what at least six million dollars of the city's debt have been heretofore spent to do. And of these six, two millions may be safely reckoned to be represented in structural works, which are to be found under the present policy simply obstructive to what is designed; so obstructive, that the results of this policy can at best be but botch-work.   Hereafter it will always be open to say of these results, I mean, that they would have been vastly better but for the obstructions which the original purpose had placed in the way of those responsible for them.[1]

[1] It is to be hoped that this will be denied.   I should be glad to submit the grounds of the assertion to a jury of experts; to any number, for example, of the following gentlemen, to whom the principles of landscape-gardening must have been a serious study: Adolph Strauch, Cincinnati; Henry Winthrop Sargent of Woodenethe; H. W. S. Cleveland, Chicago; H. H. Hunnewell of Wellesley; H. Hammond Hall, Sacramento, Cal.; William McMillan, Buffalo; Col. F. L. Lee, Albany; Professor Robinson, Harvard Arboretum; E. W. Bowditch, Boston; John Sturgis, Brookline, Mass.; F. J. Scott, Toledo; Professor C. E. Norton, Harvard College.   There are others whom I should include, as Mr. Weidenmann, but that I happen to be informed of their views.   Several of these named are personally unknown to me, and with none have I had any conversation on the subject. (ED. NOTE: Mr. Olmsted did actually draft such a circular in 1881, but it was not issued.   It began as follows:

CENTRAL PARK

Draft of Circular proposed to be sent to experts in matters of landscape gardening inviting their opinion on the design and management of Central Park. —Date probably 1881.

This circular will be addressed to a number of men who may be presumed to have had their minds for considerable periods directed to questions of a corresponding character to those which occur in public parks.   It is designed to submit to their consideration without concert, a few simple propositions applicable to the management of a park under the circumstances of the Central Park.   The object is to ascertain whether those who have given the subject studious attention free from political biases agree in holding such propositions to have been established and to be so far authoritative and binding that disregard of them implies culpable ignorance, negligence, or perversity.

The circumstances in question to be first more particularly considered are these:

The first proposition is that by no other treatment of such a property consistent with its designation as a park can it be given as much value to the people of a great city, as that which will make available to them upon it the enjoyment of beauty in natural scenery, or in scenery designed to affect the imagination and sensibilities of men by a semblance to natural scenery such as may be accomplished through the art of landscape gardening as its objects, principles, and processes have been defined by Gilpin, Repton, Price, Loudon, Downing, and other standard authorities on the subject.

It is hoped that questions growing directly from actual practice may be presented with this object in view, the answers to which will show that a certain footing has been firmly established for landscape gardening among the arts of design and that it is only ignorance which assumes to conduct a public undertaking involving outlays and affecting the value of property to amounts of many millions of dollars in denial of such laws as may thus be recognized as fixed for that art.)

The end will be that the park to be substituted for the original Central Park, without change of name, will be one better adapted to practical management; in which, for example, every operation can be directed and performed by men who have been unable to earn living wages in sewer and pavement work, in railroad and house-building work; who have broken down from incompetency in the hat-making and in the painting and glazing lines; and the services of whose sons and grandsons in carrying torch-lights, and stocking the primaries, must in some way be suitably acknowledged. The whole story is not told in this explanation; but, if it is considered how a constant gravitation in a general direction finally operates through many thousand channels of influence, it will be found to tell a good part of it.

I will later testify that the pretended landscape-gardening cloak under which this proclivity is disguised is a poor, tawdry piece of motley; but for the present let it be supposed that it is what it is claimed to be,—a much better-considered, wiser, and completer design than the old one; that it represents a higher culture and a nobler art, and as such is entitled to all possible respect. Then, I want to ask, was this respect paid to it, and did it mark a high sense of the Commissioners' responsibilities, and was it studiously deferential to the intelligence of the people of New York, that it should have been adopted, and work energetically begun upon it in the manner that it has been? With, so far as can be judged from the newspaper reports, absolutely no debate in the Board upon it, even apparently upon informal orders or verbal permits of Commissioners acting individually; with no public discussion, no opportunity for asking explanations, none for hearing remonstrances; without the publication of a single drawing, map, or plan, to aid an understanding of the great undertaking? (I will soon show more fully the contrasting methods in which the first Park Commissioners proceeded, but may mention here, that, in the first four years in which their design was developing, they issued over thirty maps and drawings, several thousand of which were distributed gratuitously, and that in some cases electrotype copies of them were supplied for newspaper publication.)

How many of those who read this paper will not, for the first time, know from it that an entirely new motive of design has been lately adopted, and vigorous work in pursuing it entered upon?

It is due to the enterprise of a single newspaper reporter, moved, it would appear, rather by a sense of the ludicrous than the grave aspect of the matter, that the completest exposition of the new policy has come before the public at all. Were it a question of the refurnishing and decorating of their board-room, the Commissioners could not have observed less formality, given less evidence of deliberation, forecast, and study, or used fewer of the commonest business precautions against foolhardy blundering, than they have in all this proceeding.

IX

THE points of identity between such of the purposes and motives of the present attempt to reform the Park as have been drawn out by the reporters, and those of that which was made at the cost of a million or more in 1871, are so many and so marked, that what is deficient in our information may be fairly taken to be supplied from what is of record as to what was then in view. The difference is only in the present lack of boldness, and a disposition to generalize rather than come to definite particulars. With this additional light upon it, the character of the scheme can be made comprehensible; and it is plain, that, if there had been knowledge and skill enough at the Commissioners' command, it would have been asserted for it that a new school of landscape-gardening had arisen, adapted especially to urban parks; that it had for them great advantages; and Mr. Robinson might have been quoted, and the experience of thousands of New York visitors to Paris cited, in confirmation of this statement. It would have had the value, too, for purposes of deception, of being true; and it is apparent that a dull sense of this truth has been mixed with another dull sense of the ideal of cockney villa-gardens in determining what should be said to reconcile the public to the destruction of the original Central Park. Let us see what the new school, thus clumsily serving as a decoy, really is.

It is in fact that of which M. Barillet-Deschamps is by repute the father, and M. André the most judicious and successful practitioner. It had its origin in the revision of the small interior public grounds of Paris, undertaken by Napoleon the Third; became very popular, largely because of the striking and spectacular effects rapidly obtained by profuse use of certain novel, exotic, and sickly forms of vegetation; and was allowed to have a certain degree of influence, always unfortunate, in the detailed management of much more important works. Meaning no disrespect to it, holding it in admiration in its proper place, I should say that it bears a relation to natural landscape-gardening, like that which the Swiss peasants of Mrs. Leo Hunter's costume lawn-party bear to the healthy cow-girls of Alpine pastures. As a fashion, it has had its run in Europe; and of those who have taken and carried it on as a fashion, and the results they have obtained, it is M. André himself who gives his opinion thus: "They did not see that this new art was in great part conventional." Then, after describing the mis-application of it upon works of larger scale, and in connection with genuine rural conditions, he continues, "Under the false pretext that lawns, trees, waters, and flowers are always pleasant, they have substituted for the old geometrical garden a still more artificial style. The former, at least, avowed its aim to show the hand of man, and master nature. The latter borrows the elements of nature, and, under pretence of imitating it, makes it play a ridiculous—I was going to say an effeminate—part." "It is not this—we say it emphatically—it is not this that constitutes landscape art.

If art seeks means of action in nature, it is in order to turn them to account in a simple and noble way." (*L'Art des Jardins*, chap. V.)

The best that can be claimed for the new design of the Central Park is, that it is in part an attempt to reclothe its rocky frame with second-hand garments of the fashion thus truthfully characterized by the master to whose ability the fashion itself is a tribute of ignorant reverence.

Further, I will not attempt to characterize it, certainly not to criticize it; but I will ask any who have been induced to suppose there is a real landscape purpose in it to reflect in what respect such conception as they have been led to form of it differs in its ideals of landscape from such as might be appropriately adopted on a site like that of Union Square, and then to ask themselves whether the ends and motives suitable to the area and topography of the one city property are probably at all such as should be had in view in business with the other; whether, with no intrinsically different purpose, it is justifiable—pardonable—to close from all ordinary use, from all commercial occupation, for all the future of the city, a hundred and fifty ordinary blocks, with the avenues and streets between them, in one continuous body, and that at the point where it will cause the most inconvenience,—the very centre of the city that is to be? Could a theory of the use and value of the Park be propounded better adapted to open it continually to schemes of subdivision, intrigues of "real-estate sharps," and to all manner of official corruption?

Can Commissioner Wales be right in basing his opposition to it on the ground that this means only indecision of purpose? Is not what he calls "no definite purpose" as distinctly a default of trust as a purposeless leaving-open the vaults and the outer doors of a bank? What is "no definite purpose" under such circumstances? What would be thought of a jury that would acquit the cashier or night-porter responsible for it?

I will further ask those who may suppose that the plan of the Park needs such general revision as is now promised, in the interest of what is called "utility," if they suppose that the only utility which can be held to excuse the attempt to form a park of such dimensions, on such ground, in such a situation, has heretofore been wholly disregarded in its design?

Yet another question for these gentlemen to put to themselves. If a direct cut is to be offered between every two points where a manifest utility is to be served by permitting it, fifteen millions more may easily be spent to accomplish the result, and in the end the Park will have been obliterated. A dozen projects have already been urged for opening additional roads through the Park, and more than that for entrances and walks through parts of it. There is not one of them, which, if the process of cutting up the Park could stop with it, would not, for the time being, tell to the advantage of somebody's real estate. But how will it be in the end, if the bars are once taken down?

Are there any who suppose that those are sincere who seek to create an impression that considerations of public utility and convenience in this respect had no weight in the old design of the Park? If so, I would ask them simply to recall the fact that that design had for its starting-point the necessity of provisions for carrying the ordinary traffic of the city across it in such a manner as not to interfere with its recreative use; that it was the only one of more than thirty plans submitted by different persons and associations in which this necessity had been so much as thought of; and that the chief opposition to the accepted design rested on the assertion that such provision was unnecessary, and, in the manner proposed to be used, absurdly impracticable. It has now been in use twenty years precisely as proposed; and not one of the objections said to have been made to it by "eminent engineers" has been heard of in all that time.

Are those who used this forecast likely to have been otherwise indifferent to motives of utility?

A very different objection to this arrangement will soon appear, if the aims lately announced in behalf of the Park Board are sustained, and if the work now said to be in energetic progress shall be long pursued. By a most careful disposition of plantations and underwood the sub-roads have been so obscured (as have with equal care most of the more finished architectural structures originally so disconcertingly conspicuous), that they make no impression upon those passing through it. I have known visitors to make the tour of the Park several times without being aware of their existence. How will it be when "a free circulation of air and light" beneath every bush and brooding conifer has been secured; when the way of the lawn-mower has at all points been made plain, and the face of nature shall everywhere have become as natty as a new silk hat?

X

But one poor apology can be contrived for the course the Commissioners have been following. That apology they have not as yet put forward,—those responsible for recent barbarities have not yet begun to think of apologizing,—but attempts to supply a base for it have been often seen; and some of the younger generation may have been led to suppose them to have substance. They are of precisely the same character, and they have the same origin, and the same motives and purposes, with those I have already cleared up in respect to Mr. Vaux and myself; and to assist the truth, a slight repetition of what I believe to be the facts may be necessary.

In 1857, twenty-five years ago, eleven citizens of New York were asked to take upon themselves, as a Board of Commissioners for the purpose, the extraordinary and gravely difficult duty of preparing for the transformation of a broken, rocky, sterile, and intractable body of land, more than a mile square in extent, into a public ground, to stand in the heart of a great commercial city. The project was without precedent, and remains without parallel. There were political motives in the determination of the arrangement, and governing the choice of the Commissioners selected. Among them, most prominent, was the desire of the leaders of the Republican party to reconcile the Democratic party, largely in majority in the city, to a relinquishment of the spoils of office in the proposed work. For this purpose they provided that no one of the Commissioners should, under any pretext, be entitled to pecuniary compensation for his services. They selected for Commissioners several men unknown in politics, but of high standing in liberal, benevolent, and unpartisan patriotic movements; others, who, if known in politics, were unknown as office-seekers, or, as the term is commonly used, as politicians. In a Board of eleven the Republicans were supposed to have a majority of one; but the first President elected was a Democrat; and seldom if ever (I remember not one case) from the first, in any important matter, did a division occur on party lines. When, near the first city election after the organization, an attempt was made to obtain a party advantage on the work, under orders given by one of the Commissioners, I as superintendent at once arrested it, suspended the foreman, who had acted upon the order, and was sustained in doing so by the vote of every other Republican in the Board.

It was obvious that such a ground as has been described, of very broken topography; rocky, sterile and intractable, in the situation contemplated; to be enclosed by a compact busy city, would, under any possible treatment, entail many and great public inconveniences, and that it could only be kept in suitable order at constant great expense. Whatever its treatment, it was to be anticipated that the land would in time come to have enormous value for purposes other than those to be at first had in view, and that crafty attempts would be made to obtain advantages from it for various selfish ends. It was plain that varied and competing purposes and interests, tastes and dispositions, would be concerned in its management; and that there would always be those, who, however it might be managed, would believe that it should have been very differently treated, and that certain elements of value should have been more amply or less lavishly provided.

From considerations such as these, it followed that the foremost, paramount, and sternest duty of the Commissioners was to be cautious in determining the ends and motives with reference to which the ground should be laid out and treated; to act only upon the most thorough study, and under the most carefully digested advice attainable.

That this duty was recognized, accepted, and deliberately and laboriously met, is a matter of plain, circumstantial, and irrefutable record. This record will also show that different theories of what the circumstances would call for, different opinions, ideals, tastes, and dispositions, were given patient consideration; that views widely different from those finally adopted were ably and warmly represented in the Commission itself; and that the problem had prolonged, earnest, and elaborate discussion.

It is to be added, in view of the very different way in which the undertaking to reverse, as far as practicable, the results of this deliberation, has come to the knowledge of the public, that no body of men charged with a like public trust has ever taken more pains to invite and give opportunity for general public discussion of what it was debating, and review of what it determined; and that discussion and review were prolonged and earnest. There were great differences of opinion; but, in the judgment of those responsible, public opinion steadily moved to a more and more intelligent acceptance of the conclusions adopted in the earlier management, as wisely foresighted.

The Commissioners entered upon their duty under a cloud of jealousy and distrust, and every device of what in city politics passes for statesmanship was employed to keep them there. There were desperate men using desperate means for the purpose; there were misled honest and worthy men who labored to the same end. Nevertheless, as public discussion proceeded, the Commission steadily advanced into the sunshine of public confidence, gained the good will of the more respectable of all parties; and from that day to this no man or party has appealed fairly to public opinion against their conclusions with any degree of success.

There have been strong alliances and combinations to do so. A most energetic attempt was made, as I have before said, in 1871; but it met with decided popular reprobation, and those responsible for it retreated in very bad order, two of them going abroad to escape criminal prosecution.

Essentially, the work now being energetically pushed in the Central Park is a revival of that then defeated: it has the same avowed objects; it has the same obscured ends; it is supported by the same sophistries; it calls for a like popular rebuke.

XI

Is the honest and business-like management of the city's park business to be always "embarrassed," as it has hitherto always been, and must a dead stop and reversion of its true course be come to every ten years, in the future as in the past? If not, how is it to be avoided?

His Honor the mayor has given the more important part of the answer in his message to the aldermen on the occasion of the assassination of President Garfield.

Beyond that, possibly the time may come when the management of the parks may be overlooked, and their business audited by a body of men, among whom there shall be representatives of those to whom the wholesome charm of simple natural scenery has been, as with most of the members of the National Academy of Design, for example, a matter of business-like study, and to whom the permanent reconcilation of a certain practicable degree of such charm, with the necessary conveniences of rest and movement of a vast multitude of people of all classes of the population of a great city, would not be felt a contemptible matter, even in comparison with the immediate practical requirements, from day to day, of republican government.

I cannot see, though it is so apparent to some true friends of the Park, what is to be gained of permanent value by saying to any one man, "Go work your sweet will there, till we find that we have had enough of you;" taking no security, making no official provision for watching, against that man's personal hobbies and freaks, ambitions and weaknesses. The concentration of executive functions in one man's hands is of too obvious advantage to ever need debate; but beyond and above this, in my judgment, it would be far better to return to something like the original arrangement, in which all questions of general administration, or of sub-legislation for the Park, and especially all determinations affecting its general design, ends, and aims, should be subject to review, discussion, and at least to veto, by an unpaid board of citizens, so large, and of such established reputation because of interest otherwise evinced in affairs allied to those of the proper business of the Park, that there could be some rational confidence that they would exercise conservative control. The labor of such a board need not be great,—a quarterly meeting would probably be sufficient for the auditing of accounts, the passing upon projects, and a review of operations upon previously prepared official reports. An annual report to the mayor would present the entire business satisfactorily to the public.

POSTSCRIPT.

This pamphlet had been so far written, and in part printed, before I knew that a practical proposition had been prepared— the first of the present session, and introduced in the form of a bill before the Legislature had organized—to amend the city charter in such a way as to provide for the abolition of the Park Board, and the substitution for it of a Superintendent, responsible directly to the mayor. Assuming, as I must, from the favor with which it is instantly received by friends of the Park, that there are no private, or party, or local interests moving the proposition; that there is no understanding as to who the superintendent is to be, whom he is to appoint, and what work he is to prosecute,—I can only recur to what I was just saying. If the man shall be qualified by the special study and training required for his duty, and shall have given proofs of it, and shall take up his duty with an earnest and serious purpose, he cannot but desire the moral weight which would be gained by such an arrangement as I have above been suggesting.

Considerations against the plan as I have seen it set forth are these:—

The results to which good management of the Park will be directed are not to be brought about quickly, by strokes, but gradually, by courses extending through several years. Good courses, consequently, require time for their vindication. A man cannot reasonably hope to be allowed to steadily pursue any courses looking solely to good results in the Park. He will be constantly pressed with advice from men who are neither competent nor disposed to give sound advice with reference to results of such limited scope,—men who will be not at all accountable for his failure to reach vindicating results; men who will never be known to the public to have had any thing to do with the matter; men who, nevertheless, will make a business, if he fails to be ruled by their advice, of obstructing his way upon any desirable course, and who, by one shameful means or another, will so accumulate embarrassments for him, that he will be fortunate if he succeeds in escaping a mortifying and apparently disgraceful failure.

Again: with whatever confidence we may look to the present mayor's intentions and shrewdness, it is not to be forgotten that no arrangement for the guardianship of the park property could be more tempting to a sly, smooth, and double-faced schemer, than that proposed; and that such an one, unscrupulous in making bargains for the purpose, ready to resort to falsehood and all manner of vile intrigues, would have unlimited advantages in contending with an honest man.

To come to a point, no well-matured scheme for the government of Central Park will fail to recognize that it is an essentially different form of city property,—on the one hand, from ordinary urban squares and places; on the other, from the great suburban parks of other cities,—nor will it fail to embody features nearly equivalent to the following:—

First, A definition of the trust, giving some fixed idea of what may and what may not be legally aimed at in its management.

Second, Provision for a board of directors with the ordinary duties of a commercial board of directors, in which board there will be, by some ex-officio appointment, representatives of the art of landscape-painting, of standing previously fixed by their fellow-artists.

Third, Provision for an executive office, with the executive duties of which the directors will be restrained from interfering.

Fourth, Provision for a professional adviser, qualified by study and practice in the art of landscape-gardening, with such prescribed duties and rights as will make him responsible for an intelligent and consistent pursuit of the main landscape-design of the Park; this office to be combined, or not, as may be found best by the directors, with the executive office.

Fifth, All such provision as legislators will think practicable for restraining, with reference to the park-service, that form of tyranny known as advice or influence, and that form of bribery known as patronage.

ED. NOTE: A few letters, taken from many occasioned by *Spoils of the Park*, are of particular interest: one from Theodore Roosevelt relating to Mr. Olmsted's suggested scheme for the government of the Park; one from Charles Eliot Norton touching the deep significance of the Park situation; and one from Mr. Olmsted himself.

ASSEMBLY CHAMBER, ALBANY, N. Y.
March 19th, 1882.

My Dear Sir:

Although personally unacquainted with you, I take the liberty of writing to you on account of my desire to do something to prevent the ruin of the New York parks. I read your pamphlet with intense interest; I could check off every statement with corresponding experiences of my own.

I should like to make an effort to get through some bill to save the park (I forgot to say that I am a member of the Legislature), though I do not believe there is much hope of success. Working on the plan you suggest, I have thought of naming, as a Board of Directors, Cornelius Vanderbilt (the younger), D. Willis James, Charles Marshall, Henry E. Pellew, Wm. E. Dodge Jr., Salem H. Wales, Frederic Church, Calvert Vaux and yourself; I should be obliged for any alterations that you would suggest. The Board should have power to choose, from their own number if they thought fit, a superintendent and Advisory Architect, who would appoint their own subordinates, absolutely free from any outside pressure. Everyone, of no matter what party, would most earnestly desire you to fill the office of superintendent. The Directors should be unsalaried; What salary should you suggest for the other offices? Could you kindly write me what you consider should be the respective duties of the directors, etc.; and any suggestions you see fit to make. There is not much hope of getting good legislation through; but it is worth while to try; and so, knowing the interest you take in the subject, I have ventured to write you. The bill abolishing the present board and substituting one man appointed by the mayor does not seem to me to meet the case—though better than the present system.

Very truly yours,

THEODORE ROOSEVELT.

A fortnight earlier, Mr. Olmsted had heard from his friend CHARLES ELIOT NORTON in regard to the *Spoils* pamphlet, as follows:

My dear Olmsted:

I have read your pamphlet with deep and painful interest. The story is worse than I knew. I am very glad you have told it. I wish you had put it into a more direct narrative form, for I fear lest the lightly sarcastic tone in which the pamphlet opens may prevent some readers from recognizing its deep and serious significance, and from reflecting that the essential question which it treats is neither the preservation of a great and beneficent public work of art, nor the vindication of an honorable reputation, but the very existence of popular, civic institutions and administration.

I trust you will take the steps necessary to have the pamphlet widely read.

In response to a similar letter from CHARLES LORING BRACE, Mr. Olmsted wrote on Mar. 7, 1882:

I am receiving many letters from strangers asking copies of the *Spoils of the Park*, but yours is the second letter commenting upon it and I think it singular that the Press takes so little notice of it.   I have seen the three references to it in New York and those all turning it to some partisan account, not looking to the rescue of the park, which, of course, is a disappointment to me.   But no doubt the fact is it hits hard on all sides and disturbs all manner of plans.   Few men of influence in New York are not interested directly or by regard for friends in some scheme which would cause good management of the park for its proper ends to fail.   I fear that its ruin is inevitable and it is very depressing to me.   But my mind is pretty well made up to it, and this probably is my last blow.   Of course, you understand that but for wounding the feelings of well-intentioned men, I could have given more effective and disgusting illustrations, and also that entente between Vaux, Parsons, Green and Tilden, regard for the memory of Col. Stebbins, and consideration of the responsibility of several men of good standing for some of the more atrocious bargains obliged me to steer as delicately as possible.   I consider it as bread thrown on the waters.

CHAPTER XI

THE PARK IN THE LAST FOUR DECADES

The Essential Cause of the Park's Decline.

The history of Central Park from the early eighties—when Mr. Olmsted's connection with it was entirely severed and Mr. Vaux's became tenuous and unsatisfactory—is explainable mainly on the basis of three shortcomings, sadly familiar in other political affairs, on the part of those responsible for the Park's administration, whether in the legislative and appropriating bodies, in the Board of Commissioners, or in their administrative staff: *First*, failure to understand clearly that adherence to some self-consistent controlling purpose and policy is essential to good results in the management of any long-term investment of a sort readily subject to depreciation like the Park, and failure to live up to such an understanding with courage and energy. *Second*, inability to comprehend the special justifying purposes and values appropriate to the Park, and failure to appreciate the technical means necessary for preserving these in the face of greatly increased use. *Third*, subordination, whether conscious or unconscious, of the motive of effective management of the Park as an instrument of public service to other motives such as the following: a desire to divert funds needed for the proper service of the Park to serve other more appealing ends, public or private; a complacent desire to please individual friends and political associates in disregard of the public interests; a desire to pursue hobbies or prejudices or even to wreak personal spites; and pervasively the shifting elusive motives of the game of petty personal and party politics.

While the Park was managed in sympathy with the designers' ideals—which became fundamentally the ideals adopted by the early Central Park Commissioners—the intended recreative and inspirational purposes and values came to be generally accepted by the public. But when these had been subordinated to other purposes, when there had been a long-continued failure to make adequate and well-directed expenditure on prosaic maintenance details,—on soil improvement, on care of plantations, on control of the public in its use and abuse of the Park,—when the public by this laxity of guardianship had lost its respect for the restraint of liberty that was necessary to preserve the intended quality of landscape beauty, it is not surprising that an atmosphere of shabbiness grew and, in growing, engendered a public carelessness that in turn engendered ever more shabbiness. In other words, the administrative difficulties of maintaining the Park and of managing the public proved too great for the administrative organization which had to face them, and the Park in consequence suffered a progressive decline. There is space to mention here only a few more important aspects of this decline and of various public and private attempts to rescue the Park, culminating in the determined and more promising undertaking of the present administration.

Ups and Downs in the Early Eighties; The Work of Samuel Parsons.

More than three years after the dismissal of Mr. Olmsted as landscape architect, Mr. Vaux was persuaded, late in 1881, to accept appointment as Superintending Architect of the Department of Public Parks. In April, 1882, his younger partner, Samuel Parsons, Jr.,[1] was appointed Superintendent of Planting. From this time on, the life of Mr. Parsons was bound up with the development and preservation of Central Park—in his official capacities as Superintendent of Parks (1885–1897), as Landscape Architect (1898–1911), for two brief intervening periods (1905–1907) as Park Commissioner, and after his retirement in 1911, until his death in 1923, as one of the staunch defenders of the Park against encroachments and as a leader in directing public opinion towards the urgent necessity for arresting the Park's decline. In spite of the ups and downs of politics in the early eighties and subsequently, Mr. Parsons maintained his incorruptible political independence and his avowed loyalty to the ideals of the Olmsted and Vaux design.

Shortly after the return of Mr. Vaux to the parks, the appointment of General Viele as a commissioner made the situation of the Park's designers the more difficult. Of this, Mr. Olmsted wrote to Mr. Vaux (Jan. 11, 1883): "I had thought myself prepared for

---

[1] For a full account of the long and honorable connection of Mr. Parsons with the parks of New York, the reader is referred to the autobiographical volume: *Memories of Samuel Parsons, Landscape Architect of the Department of Public Parks, New York*, edited by Mabel Parsons, 1926.

it but am really much shocked by Viele's appointment.[1] And it is bewildering to find no public comments recognizing the unquestionable fact that it has for twenty-five years been his principal public business to mutilate and damn the park."

In December, 1882, Mr. Vaux felt that his position had become entirely untenable and therefore resigned. Mr. Parsons remained, however, until the late summer of 1883, when his position also was made untenable and he was obliged temporarily to suspend his earnest efforts to save something of the original planting design. The point of which Mr. Vaux made public issue was the disposition of the Zoo in the Park as proposed by the Park Board, feeling that if he brought some tangible danger, such as the ruination of passages of Park scenery, to public attention, there would be greater likelihood of public action against the then Board. Mr. Parsons, meanwhile, with the aid of Mr. William A. Stiles, editorial writer for the *New York Tribune*, and a life-long defender of the Park, laid before the public the follies committed on the plantations in the name of artistic improvement. With the termination of General Viele's service on the Park Board—of which he was President in 1884— and with a new political group in office, the way was opened for Mr. Parsons to begin his long career as Superintendent, and ultimately for the resumption of the official relation of Mr. Vaux to the Park, with some consulting advice from Mr. Olmsted.

ADVICE OFFICALLY SOUGHT FROM THE PARK'S DESIGNERS.

In June, 1886, the designers were approached in the following letter:

MESSRS. FREDERICK LAW OLMSTED,
    CALVERT VAUX.

Gentlemen:—Many years have elapsed since Central Park was laid out and constructed according to your plans and under your direction. The time has now come when it will be of special value to the City that your work shall be reviewed by yourselves and such suggestions made and plans prepared for the completion of the Park and such alterations therein as, in your opinion, it would be of advantage to make.

[1] Cf. Appendix III. Mr. Olmsted was open to the accusation of prejudice about General Viele, as are the present editors, but we believe that a careful examination such as we have made of the mass of documents relative to the Viele controversy will convince any unprejudiced historian that General Viele was moved by a very natural but very persistent pique to oppose, to belittle, and to bring into contempt, any ideas and aims that had come to be particularly associated with the two men who superseded him in the original design and construction of the Park.

Experience has demonstrated to the Commissioners that various changes are desirable looking to the further development of the Park, and that something should be done to increase the area of the drives, foot paths and bridle paths in order to meet the present demand from the public for enlarged facilities in their use.[1]

The constant pressure for the construction of Riverside and Morningside Parks renders it necessary that a careful study of both Park areas should be made. . . .

The Park Commissioners consider it a fortunate circumstance that they are enabled to apply to you for the benefit of your professional experience in these matters, especially in view of your intimate knowledge of the topography of these parks and the ideas which have been so successfully realized in the Central Park, a spot unrivalled in its beauty.

On behalf of this Department I desire to ask whether you will undertake the office of examining and reporting upon the condition of these parks and preparing plans for their construction and completion, and upon what terms.

Trusting that your reply will be favorable, I am

Yours truly,

HENRY K. BEEKMAN,
President, Department of Public Parks.

Apparently this first official vindication of Mr. Olmsted's services to the Park, more than eight years after his dismissal, did not result in any continuing arrangment, although he made six brief visits to New York—"each one on the official request of the President for the time being of the Park Department . . . my opinion [having] been sought upon particular questions of design and management." We find Mr. Olmsted, after receiving official notification that he (alone) had been appointed Landscape Architect Advisory to the Department of Public Parks on April 20, 1887, stating publicly in the *Tribune*,[2] evidently in response to misrepresentations, that he had not accepted the appointment, since he had made association with Mr. Vaux in any plan for re-employment an essential consideration.

Shortly before this (July 2nd), Mr. Olmsted had addressed a letter to Commissioner Crimmins explaining the situation, and paying tribute to Mr. Vaux in terms calculated to impress on the Board the practical advantages of restoring a joint relationship.

MY DEAR MR. CRIMMINS: It was evident the other day that I had been asked to meet the Commissioners with expectations that I

[1] Cf. Mr. Olmsted's later discussion of this point, Part II, Chapter I, pp. 271 ff.
[2] Letter to the Editor of the *Tribune*, dated July 14, 1887.

was unable to sustain. I may possibly have been to blame that they should have had these expectations and I am sorry for it. To guard as far as I can against further loss of time on a matter that must be growing urgent, through any possible doubt remaining in your mind as to my position, I think it better to say that at no time since I left the service of the Department ten years ago have I been willing to take upon myself any obligations with regard to the Central Park unless they applied to the park as a whole, nor unless Mr. Vaux was to be associated with me. I have repeatedly said this to the Commissioners and others, successively inquiring year after year, and had supposed that it was well known to you. The reasons for it are derived from experience and the arguments you offer for a change of my mind do not apply to them.

With regard to the plans of Riverside and Morningside, Mr. Vaux's responsibility and mine are not identical. But there are problems to be solved in the revised plans for these works of much difficulty and no plans can be offered with regard to which there will not be heated differences of opinion. Mr. Vaux's judgment upon them would be of great value, greater than that of any other man in the country; it would be more convenient for me to work at them and I should reach conclusions sooner, with confidence to present them, if proceeding in conference with him than if studying the subject independently. I have no doubt that you would obtain better plans, that that they would stand fire better, and be more likely to be carried out.

On the latter point it is to be considered that no plans can be had, if a hundred men were engaged to make them, which would not be thought by a section of intelligent men of weighty influence to be unfortunate in essential particulars. The whole plan of the Central Park was shaped with regard to what the designers thought to be the necessity of sunken transverse roads. Take these out or essentially modify them and the plan in all its parts would be worthless. To the best of my information and judgment that necessity is today clearer and more obvious to the public than ever before, though its completest demonstration is yet to come. Yet you heard how differently Commissioner Hutchins looked upon the question the other day. He cannot yet see that the objections that he first felt to them, theoretically, are ever to be compensated by the advantages to be secured by them. Now, whatever arrangements you make, you will never get a plan for Riverside Park to some important points of which there will not be a similar fixed, intelligent and respectable antagonism. . . . Thus, whatever your plan, it must stand fire and you should not subject it, unnecessarily, to mean, malicious and pettifogging attacks, appealing to ignorance, jealousy and the lower sort of political prejudices. On this ground you will find it unfortunate if your professional adviser, respect for whose trained judgment upon matters of his training, would be your stronghold with the community in general against such attacks, were a man who had not lived in New York for ten years and whose attention was divided between parks in New York and parks in Boston and other cities. You would find it much better that it should be recognized that you were employing the same Olmsted & Vaux under whom, as designers and superintendents, the Central Park had been formed up to the time that it attained the highest and most undivided popularity, and one of whom had never ceased to be a citizen of New York, never lost his hold of New York life, nor allowed his attention to be withdrawn for a moment from the park system of New York.

Considerations of this class are secondary, of course, but they are not unimportant, even considered with reference to the statesmanship of a large city in these days.

And finally, if you are not to be influenced by them directly, yet think it desirable to secure my services, you should be influenced by the fact that they are important to me and to my doing satisfactorily what you want of me.

Yours respectfully,

･　FRED^k. LAW OLMSTED.

Although apparently Mr. Olmsted withdrew definitely from his expected connection with the Department in July of 1887, since his letter to the Commissioners stipulating the employment of Mr. Vaux in cooperation with him had not produced the result he desired, it was not until December that Mr. Vaux was appointed Landscape Architect to the Department to take effect the first of January, 1888. Mr. Olmsted thereafter remained in a loose consultative relationship to the Board, and on this basis answered various communications addressed to him from 1888 to 1890.[1] Mr. Vaux retained his office as Landscape Architect until his death in November, 1895.

Continual Threats at the Integrity of the Park and its Protection by Public Opinion.

It was during the period after Mr. Olmsted had removed to Brookline and was much engaged with the Boston parks that his perspective on the situation in New York enabled him to review the threats on Central Park[2] for the benefit of the Boston park commissioners, in the following penetrating statement:[3]

[A] most instructive circumstance in [the] history [of Central Park] is the gradual advance of public opinion toward a correct un-

[1] See Part II.　　　　　　　　[2] Cf. Part II, Chapter XII.
[3] From "Notes on the Plan of Franklin Park," Boston, 1886.

derstanding of the conditions of the park's value. Such an understanding has not yet, after twenty-nine years, been universally attained. The papers of the city are at this moment denouncing a proposition,[1] made in good faith and urged with elaborate arguments, for introducing an important new feature into the plan of the park. An interview is publicly reported (in the *Sun*, January 15) with a prominent citizen, who urges in counter-argument not the waste that would be involved in the value of the park as a place prepared at great expense for the ready enjoyment of rural scenery, but what is assumed to be the more practical objection of the contraction of areas available for games, a use of the park in which with the present area available for it when the park is in largest use, but one in several hundred of its visitors takes part.

Twice in the history of this park, after enormous expenditures had been made upon it with the stated purpose of excluding urban and securing rural scenery, this purpose has been distinctly and publicly repudiated; in one case, the Superintendent for the time being, explaining to a reporter of the press that his leading object was a display of architectural and urban elegance, and that he had removed certain trees because they prevented visitors passing through the park from seeing the stately buildings growing up outside of it.

But although these incidents may seem to argue otherwise, no one can have long been a reader of New York newspapers without knowing that the public opinion of the city has of late years been often aroused to prevent various proceedings upon the park, running counter to the purpose of rural recreation, that earlier would have been permitted to pass without objection. For example, when the trees of the park were yet saplings, and its designed rural scenery wholly undeveloped, the suggestion that the most central and important position upon it should be given to a public building was received with no apparent disfavor, and one of the Commissioners of the Park declared that any ground the promoters of the undertaking might desire would be gladly assigned to it. Fortunately, because of hard times, the scheme fell through. Ten years later, a monumental building was actually given a site upon the park, but it was one in which the structure would not interfere with any extended view, or be seen from a distance, and even this concession did not pass without much remonstrance. When the next scheme of the class was disclosed, though coupled with many most attractive incidental propositions, skilfully presented, and supported by eminent citizens, so much popular indignation was soon manifested that in response to petitions a bill was rapidly advanced in the legislature to make it illegal for the Commissioners to entertain the

[1] Mr. Olmsted in a footnote made a quotation from a leading article in the *New York Tribune* of Jan. 10, 1886, which classes the proposition with a thousand others urged one after another on the Park Commissioners. See p. 520.

proposition, and would have passed had not the head of the movement publicly and apologetically announced the abandonment of the idea. At the present time, a proposition similar to that once accepted in the case of the Museum of Art, no matter how highly its objects were valued, and no matter how worthy a body of public-spirited citizens were backing it, would be less agreeable to the public opinion of New York than would a proposition to build a public hospital in the middle of the Common to that of Boston.

As Mr. Olmsted frequently pointed out, the immense capital investment[1] by the public in Central Park in itself demanded, on fiscal grounds alone, a more intelligently self-consistent management than it often received. Yet in 1888 and 1889 a strong movement was set on foot, by a group of men in New York, renewing the effort of 1881, to have the World's Columbian Exposition located in Central Park.[2] Mr. Olmsted's aid was enlisted in creating public opinion against the proposition, but his often-stated arguments unfortunately made no lasting impression either on the public or on the Board, as appeared not long after in the Speedway proposals of 1890.

Mr. Olmsted's expression of opinion against the introduction of a Speedway into Central Park, replying to a request of Mr. Paul Dana of the *Sun* in December, 1890, may be found in the concluding chapter of Part II.[3] Although a law authorizing a Speedway was finally enacted in 1892, public indignation was so intense that serious trouble was feared from the menacing crowds which gathered at the Park when work on the Speedway was about to begin. Thirty-nine days after the passage of the law, it was repealed, and the Park was again saved from unintelligent mutilation.

The letter from Mr. Olmsted to Mr. Dana just referred to is of particular interest as being Mr. Olmsted's last brief in his long

---

[1] In a letter replying to inquiries concerning the cost of the New York parks, Mr. Olmsted gave the following summary to Dec., 1887: "The cost of the land of the Central Park has been $5,028,140. There has been paid out for the improvement and maintenance (1857–1887) $10,547,451, or an average yearly for thirty years (including the period of the war) of $351,581. In his report to the Central Park Association Mr. Olmsted, Jr., stated that in 1926 the land held for the Park was valued on the books of the Tax Department at $580,000,000. An experienced real estate operator, Mr. August Heckscher, gave it as his opinion that a fair market value of the land was more nearly in the neighborhood of $3,000,000,000. On the most conservative basis the fixed charges on the capital investment were well up into millions of dollars per annum, while the public value received was wholly dependent on the success of the annual maintenance and operation, which was then being starved to a figure of about $350,000 per annum.

[2] Cf. footnote on p. 115, *ante*.　　　　　　　　[3] See p. 524.

defense of the Park against encroachments.[1] There was one encroachment on the rural character of the Park which Mr. Olmsted had not foreseen and which he greatly lamented in his latter days, —the piercing of the air with skyscrapers, which no plantations could shut out and which could invade without redress many of the most carefully studied natural scenes.[2]

The attempts of one of the park superintendents in the early eighties to clear away trees obstructing the vistas of the new tall buildings of that day,[3] were doubtless in the minds of those who, in the late eighties after Mr. Vaux had rejoined Mr. Parsons on the Park, opposed all tree cutting, even where necessary to the health and beauty of the Park plantations. The indignation of the press in 1889 against tree cutting[4] moved the West Side Improvement Association to engage Mr. Olmsted and Mr. J. B. Harrison, Secretary of the American Forestry Congress, to report on the true merits of the case. Their findings may be read in the illuminating report *Treatment of Public Plantations* given in Part II, Chapter IV. A letter of Mr. Olmsted's in May, 1889, says:

> The substance of our report will be that we found no evidence of recent operations in the Park that had not been consistent with good tree husbandry and with respect for its landscape design. At points where decided gaps in the plantations seemed to have been made, caused by the removal of a number of contiguous trees, we saw no reason to doubt that all of them had been ruined for any lasting good end by previous neglect of timely thinning or that the course taken was on the whole the most judicious that remained available.

The revival of public interest in the preservation of the Park, in contrast to the indifference of the press which Mr. Olmsted noted in his letter of 1882,[5] showed how firmly its advantages had been

---

[1] Cf. Part II, Ch. XII. A history of these encroachments may be found in an article in *Landscape Architecture* (Oct., 1910), by Robert Wheelwright entitled "The Attacks on Central Park." Another article in *Landscape Architecture* (July, 1912) which should be read at the same time is entitled "Central Park, New York: A Work of Art" by Harold A. Caparn (see quotation on p. 198). The account of the Park by Mr. Samuel Parsons in the *Transactions of The American Society of Landscape Architects 1899–1908* is of interest; and also especially valuable is the section, "Proposed Mutilations, Intrusions and Perversions" in Dr. Edward Hagaman Hall's account of Central Park (American Scenic and Historic Preservation Society, 1911).

[2] Cf. Part I. Chapter XIII, pp. 200 and 205.

[3] Cf. pp. 47 and 90, *ante*.

[4] Cf. Mr. Olmsted's letter to Mr. Pinchot, p. 166.

[5] See p. 158.

woven into the life of the citizens of New York, and how the happy sleighing parties depicted in contemporary prints, the companies of horsemen, the picnic parties, the playing children, were all potential defenders of a treasure which they could enjoy even if they did not understand the means of conserving its higher values.

ATTEMPTS AT REHABILITATION.

Mr. Olmsted himself in his Franklin Park report, already mentioned, restates "briefly the lesson in conservatism most important" to be learned from the park-making experience of American cities.

That those in charge of a park work may proceed economically and with profit they must be able to proceed with confidence, method and system, steadily, step after step, to carry to completion a well-matured design. Until the point of completion is reached the work of each year must be the carrying out of work prepared for in the previous year, and the preparation of work to be done the following year. Plans laid with an economical purpose in this respect must not be held subject at any moment to be nullified, or hastily and radically modified, even under worthy impulses of economy.

Six years earlier Mr. Olmsted had said:[1]

Changes in the fundamental laws of our parks, in the boards governing them, or in the bodies governing these boards, occur annually. A certain weakness of human nature, usually exhibited in some degree after such changes, is expressed in the proverb, "New brooms sweep clean." There is generally a disposition with each new man in office to find an *ex post facto* reason for his being there. . . . It has happened more than once that plans have been adopted, work advanced under them, then thrown aside by new men, new plans adopted, and, after some years, these in their turn abandoned and the original plans resumed. The change of purpose in such cases will have been deliberate and intentional. But changes as great and as wasteful are more likely to occur through the passing of park works under the control, direct or indirect, of men who, through simple ignorance, forgetfulness, or indifference to such aims as have before time been had in view, let a large share of the value that has been once secured slip through their fingers.

The character and intelligence of many of the original Central Park commissioners were unfortunately seldom duplicated in subsequent appointments. However, from time to time, some keen

[1] "The Justifying Value of a Public Park."

supporter of the Park ideals came into office, as Mayor Strong's appointee William A. Stiles, an able writer whose pen had always been intelligently at the service of the Park, both in the *Tribune* and later in *Garden and Forest*,[1] and who held the appointment from 1895 until his death in 1897.

In Mr. Olmsted's last letter concerning the New York parks, not long before his retirement from professional practice, he touched on the heart of successful park administration,—a real appreciation on the part of the Park Commissioners of the ends to be held in view.

When Mr. Gifford Pinchot[2] wrote to him in January, 1895, for advice in regard to accepting or declining an appointment as park commissioner, Mr. Olmsted pointed out that although popular error might confuse the planting and management of trees with reference to timber on one hand and to scenery on the other, nevertheless a forester's knowledge of trees and his appreciation of this distinction between the use of trees in forestry and in the landscape art is far more than the equipment for the office of park commissioner of the citizen who would probably be appointed if Mr. Pinchot declined. Mr. Olmsted's letter continues:

The average respectable citizen, according to my experience, knows nothing of any such distinction. And, as business is commonly transacted in the Park Board, it is extremely difficult to get him to pay any intelligent regard to it. He habitually thinks of a tree as a tree; a piece of public property like a wall, a building, a bridge. He does not see a tree as an element of a future landscape any more than he sees it as an element of a forest. It is a piece of goods. It has cost public money. It represents public money. To fell it is a waste of so much public money. He cannot resist any ignorant public clamor against the destruction of it.

Once, as a result of such ignorant public clamor, the Park Board of New York passed an order forbidding me to have a single tree felled without a special order of the Board for that particular tree. There were at the time many thousands of poor, cheap rapid-growing trees scattered over the Park that had been planted to serve as nurses, and which were then, because of previous neglect when I was absent, over-growing, crowding and making wholly unfit for their purpose the trees which had been planted with a view to ultimate landscape effect.

[1] See the account of Mr. Stiles' services to the Park in *Memories of Samuel Parsons*, and the resolution on his death in Minutes of The Board, D. P. P., special meeting, Oct. 7, 1897.

[2] Mr. Pinchot as forester had been associated with Mr. Olmsted in the Biltmore, N. C. work.

You would have understood what I was after when I began systematically to thin out these nurses. The public, the Commissioners, could not . . .

I am inclined, for the reason thus illustrated, to advise you to take the position. . . . I am inclined to think that it would be an advantage to you professionally. Particularly so if you should be able to make it manifest that you recognize clearly that the proper management of public parks differs radically, on the one hand, from the proper management of *gardens*, and on the other hand from the proper management of *forests*. You can hardly believe how mischievous; how disastrous to good results and sound economy in obtaining them, is the inability of most intelligent men to make this differentiation. You would be able to make it. You do habitually make it, as I have seen at Biltmore. And in making it and keeping it, as you would, clearly before your associates of the Park Commission, you would render the City valuable service. And, confidentially, I will say that no one in the service of the Park Commission is nearly as much inclined to make this distinction as, in my opinion, is desirable. I think Central Park is, for this reason, a much less valuable property than it might have been, or than, even now, it might be made. . . .

It is of immense importance to New York of the future that its greater parks should at this period of their formation be intelligently administered. You, while a young man, are fully able to see that the policy of management cannot wisely, prudently, honestly be directed simply to producing a pleasing impression upon the ignorant visitor this year or next. The average commissioner cannot look further ahead at most than next year.

It is to be regretted that Mr. Pinchot felt obliged after all, because of expected absence from the city on professional duties, to decline the proffered appointment.

The deterioration of Central Park with respect to soil and trees became so marked in 1900, that the American Scenic and Historic Preservation Society secured the services of Professor Charles Sprague Sargent of the Arnold Arboretum, Professor L. H. Bailey of Cornell University, and Hon. William M. Canby of the Park Commission of Wilmington, Del., to make a critical examination of the Park.[1] In 1902, Park Commissioner Willcox had a similar examination made by Mr. N. L. Britton, Director of the New York Botanical Garden, Professer B. E. Fernow of Toronto University, Mr. J. A. Pettigrew, Superintendent of the Boston parks, together with Mr. Samuel Parsons.

These were forerunners of various examinations official and un-

---

[1] Again see Dr. Hall's account, cited *ante.*

official, made from time to time.   In 1910 while a study was in progress under the auspices of the Parks and Playgrounds Association of New York,—the Association which bestirred itself constantly in defense of the Park through this difficult period before the present revival of interest,—Park Commissioner Stover, under the guidance of Mr. Parsons, applied for $250,000 a year for five years for resoiling; but controversies as to its desirability terminated in 1911 not only the attempt but also Mr. Parson's long connection with the New York parks.

In recent years the Fifth Avenue Association has warmly espoused the cause of Park rehabilitation, and together with the Merchants Association and especially the Central Park Association, has had a large share in successfully convincing the Board of Estimate and Apportionment of the precarious state of the Park. The objects of the expenditure of the $1,000,000 announced as appropriated are at the present time being sympathetically studied. In the work of the Central Park Association[1] formed in 1926 for the defence of the Park "as a step towards public cooperation with city officials," and particularly in the studies of the Regional Plan of New York,[2] the present park administration has sources of information and support that augur well for the intelligent rehabilitation of this outstanding enterprise in public landscape art.

[1] See p. 537.   Mr. Olmsted, Jr.'s report to this Association has been drawn upon in the concluding chapter of Part I of this Volume.
[2] See Preface.

1906

Photograph by Harold A. Caparn

The Mall in its Prime

CHAPTER XII

THE INFLUENCE OF CENTRAL PARK ON AMERICAN LIFE

CENTRAL PARK AS A SUCCESSFUL MUNICIPAL ENTERPRISE.

The early recognition of the financial and administrative success of Central Park[1]—especially in the period prior to the ascendency of the Tweed Ring—is nowhere more strikingly stated than in Mr. Olmsted's own words in a paper before the American Social Science Association in 1870, "Public Parks and the Enlargement of Towns." He refers first to the headshakings which accompanied the acquisition of land by the City for a large park, and then to the present and future economic, hygienic, and social benefits which a scant dozen years of use had made manifest.

It was frequently alleged, and with truth, that the use made of the existing public grounds was such as to develop riotous and licentious habits. A large park, it was argued, would inevitably present larger opportunities, and would be likely to exhibit an aggravated form of the same tendencies, consequently anything like refinement of treatment would be entirely wasted.

A few passages from a leading article of the *Herald* newspaper, in the seventh year of the enterprise (1858), will indicate what estimate its astute editor had then formed of the prevailing convictions of the public on the subject:—

"It is all folly to expect in this country to have parks like those in old aristocratic countries. When we open a public park Sam will air himself in it. He will take his friends whether from Church street, or elsewhere. He will knock down any better dressed man who remonstrates with him. He will talk and sing, and fill his share of the bench, and flirt with the nursery-maids in his own coarse way. Now we ask what chance have William B. Astor and Edward Everett against this fellow-citizen of theirs? Can they and he enjoy the same place? Is it not obvious that he will turn them out, and that the great Central Park will be nothing but a great bear-garden for the lowest denizens of the city, of which we shall yet pray litanies to be delivered?"

[1] See especially Chapters V and VIII, *ante.*

In the same article it was argued that the effect of the construction of the Park would be unfavorable to the value of property in its neighborhood, except as, to a limited extent, it might be taken up by Irish and German liquor dealers as sites for dram-shops and lager-bier gardens.

There were many eminent citizens, who to my personal knowledge, in the sixth, seventh, and eighth year after the passage of the act, entertained similar views to those I have quoted.

I have been asked if I supposed that "gentlemen" would ever resort to the Park, or would allow their wives and daughters to visit it? I heard a renowned lawyer argue that it was preposterous to suppose that a police force would do anything toward preserving order and decency in any broad piece of ground open to the general public of New York.

. . . .

And what has become of the great Bugaboo? This is what the *Herald* of later date answers:

"When one is inclined to despair of the country, let him go to the Central Park on a Saturday, and spend a few hours there in looking at the people, not at those who come in gorgeous carriages, but at those who arrive on foot, or in those exceedingly democratic conveyances, the street-cars; and if, when the sun begins to sink behind the trees, he does not arise and go homeward with a happy swelling heart," and so on, the effusion winding up thus: "We regret to say that the more brilliant becomes the display of vehicles and toilettes, the more shameful is the display of bad manners on the part of the ―― extremely fine-looking people who ride in carriages and wear the fine dresses. We must add that the pedestrians always behave well."

Here we touch a fact of more value to social science than any other in the history of the Park. . . . The difficulty of preventing ruffianism and disorder in a park to be frequented indiscriminately by such a population as that of New York, was from the first regarded as the greatest of all those which the commission had to meet and the means of overcoming it cost more study than all other things.

It is, perhaps, too soon [1870] to judge of the value of the expedients resorted to, but there are as yet a great many parents who are willing to trust their school-girl daughters to ramble without special protection in the Park, as they would almost nowhere else in New York. One is no more likely to see ruffianism or indecencies in the Park than in the churches, and the arrests for offenses of all classes, including the most venial, which arise simply from the ignorance of country people, have amounted to but twenty in the million of the number of visitors; and of these, an exceedingly small proportion have been of that class which was so confidently expected to take possession of the Park and make it a place unsafe and unfit for decent people.

.   .   .   .

Jeremy Bentham, in treating of "The Means of Preventing Crimes," remarks that any innocent amusement that the human heart can invent is useful under a double point of view: first, for the pleasure itself which results from it; second, from its tendency to weaken the dangerous inclinations which man derives from his nature.

No one who has closely observed the conduct of the people who visit the Park can doubt that it exercises a distinctly harmonizing and refining influence upon the most unfortunate and most lawless classes of the city—an influence favorable to courtesy, self-control, and temperance.

At three or four points in the midst of the Park, beer, wine, and cider are sold with other refreshments to visitors, not at bars, but served at tables where men sit in company with women. Whatever harm may have resulted, it has apparently had the good effect of preventing the establishment of drinking-places on the borders of the Park, these not having increased in number since it was opened, as it was originally supposed they would.

I have never seen or heard of a man or woman the worse for liquor taken at the Park, except in a few instances where visitors had brought it with them. . . .

Every Sunday in summer from thirty to forty thousand persons, on an average, enter the Park on foot, the number on a very fine day being sometimes nearly a hundred thousand. While most of the grog-shops of the city were effectually closed by the police under the excise law on Sunday, the number of visitors to the Park was considerably larger than before. There was no similar increase at the churches.

Shortly after the Park first became attractive, and before any serious attempt was made to interfere with the Sunday liquor trade, the head-keeper told me that he saw among the visitors the proprietor of one of the largest "saloons" in the city. He accosted him and expressed some surprise; the man replied, "I came to see what the devil you'd got here that took off so many of my Sunday customers."

.   .   .   .

To fully understand the significance of the result so far, it must be considered that the Park is to this day, at some points, incomplete; that from the center of population to the midst of the Park the distance is still four miles . . .

It must be remembered, also, that the Park is not planned for such use as is now made of it, but with regard to the future use, when it will be in the center of a population of two millions hemmed in by water at a short distance on all sides; and that much of the work done upon it is, for this reason, as yet quite barren of results.

The question of the relative value of what is called off-hand common sense, and of special, deliberate, business-like study, must be settled, in the case of the Central Park, by a comparison of benefit with cost. During the last four years over thirty million visits have been made to the Park by actual count, and many have passed uncounted. From fifty to eighty thousand persons on foot, thirty thousand in carriages, and four to five thousand on horseback, have often entered it in a day.

Among the frequent visitors, I have found all those who, a few years ago, believed it impossible that there should ever be a park in this republican country,—and especially in New York, of all places in this country,—which would be a suitable place of resort, for "gentlemen." They, their wives and daughters, frequent the Park more than they do the opera or the church.

There are many men of wealth who resort to the Park habitually and regularly, as much so as business men to their places of business. Of course, there is a reason for it, and a reason based upon their experience.

As to the effect on public health, there is no question that it is already great. The testimony of the older physicians of the city will be found unanimous on this point. Says one: "Where I formerly ordered patients of a certain class to give up their business altogether and go out of town, I now often advise simply moderation, and prescribe a ride in the Park before going to their offices, and again a drive with their families before dinner. By simply adopting this course as a habit, men who have been breaking down frequently recover tone rapidly, and are able to retain an active and controlling influence in an important business, from which they would have otherwise been forced to retire. I direct school girls, under certain circumstances, to be taken wholly, or in part, from their studies, and sent to spend several hours a day rambling on foot in the Park."

The lives of women and children too poor to be sent to the country can now be saved in thousands of instances, by making them go to the Park. During a hot day in July last, I counted at one time in the Park eighteen separate groups, consisting of mothers with their children, most of whom were under school age, taking picnic dinners which they had brought from home with them. The practice is increasing under medical advice, especially when summer complaint is rife.

The much greater rapidity with which patients convalesce, and may be returned with safety to their ordinary occupations after severe illness, when they can be sent to the Park for a few hours a day, is beginning to be understood. The addition thus made to the productive labor of the city is not unimportant.

The Park, moreover, has had a very marked effect in making the city attractive to visitors, and in thus increasing its trade, and causing many who have made fortunes elsewhere to take up their residence and become tax-payers in it,—a much greater effect in this way, beyond all question, than all the colleges, schools, libraries, museums, and art-galleries which the city possesses. It has also induced many foreigners who have grown rich in the country, and who would otherwise have gone to Europe to enjoy their wealth, to settle permanently in the city.

As early as 1861, in the report of the special committee appointed by the State Senate to investigate the Central Park,[1] the direct financial advantage to the City was acknowledged:

> Although the committee do not think it proper for municipal corporations to purchase lands on speculation, yet it cannot be concealed—that the Central Park has been, and will be, in a merely pecuniary point of view, one of the wisest and most fortunate measures ever undertaken by the City of New York. It has already more than quadrupled the value of a large extent of property in its vicinity.

In the general stock taking of the Park after the breaking up of the Tweed Ring, it was estimated that some four million dollars were accruing annually to the city in excess of the taxes collected *as a direct result of the development of the Park* over the annual interest on the cost of park land and improvements.[2]

Less than ten years after the first law was passed authorizing a park and only three years after the beginning of construction, the Commissioners could declare:[3]—

> If the Park is regarded in a pecuniary point of view only, it is the most profitable enterprise ever undertaken by the city, and in the higher aspect of its moral advantages, its sanitary benefits, its features of attraction and interest to large numbers of people who seek amusement, the Central Park, with its annually developing beauties, will remain, if its management is such as it should be, through successive seasons and centuries an ever changing and yet enduring testimony to the wisdom of its projectors.

In 1884 when the enlargement of the park area of the City of New York was being considered, an open letter[4] on the subject

---

[1] See p. 61, *ante.*
[2] See Chapter V, p. 54, and Chapter VIII, p. 95, *ante.* Doc. No. 64 of 1874–75, D. P. P., gives detailed figures showing the investment of the City and returns in taxes on excess increased valuation over and above normal valuation.
[3] Annual Report, C. P. C., for 1860.
[4] A copy of this pamphlet may be seen in the New York Public Library. The names of the signers represent such well-known families as the Astors, Belmonts,

signed by some of the most substantial men of the city was addressed
to the Mayor. The financial success of the Central Park enterprise
was cited as the precedent for embarking on the needed new parks:

> We consider the enlargement of our Park area so important a
> matter that we beg respectfully to call your especial attention
> to a few of the salient points in the very able Report of the
> Commission appointed by yourself, which Report we most fully
> approve and endorse.

1st.	The Central Park cost the city...........	$ 6,666,381
	Construction account and maintenance....	16,378,844
	Interest at 7 per cent. during 25 years.....	20,755,925
	Total..............................	$ 43,794,150[1]

> Taxes collected during this period in the
>   wards in which the Park is situated..... $110,000,000

Estimating fifty millions of this as an increase from ordinary
causes, there remain sixty millions, leaving a balance to the credit
of the city of seventeen millions.
The city thus has this magnificent domain for nothing, with the
enormous increase of tax income from the district in its neighborhood besides.

The Impetus to Outdoor Recreation.

The public desire for participation in the newly available pleasures of winter as well as of summer in the Park has already been
commented on in Chapter V, and the fashion of skating, promoted
by the success of the Central Park lakes, spread throughout the
country.

While in 1857, town riding was so little practiced that "not half
a dozen citizens of New York kept riding horses and among innumerable suggestions offered . . . for . . . the park, there was
not one from any quarter for a bridle road,"[2] it was not long before
hundreds of horsemen made daily use of the Park rides.

Whereas in 1861 the Annual Report of the Central Park Commissioners set forth arguments for outdoor exercise and recreation
for school children, with testimony as to the then evil effects of their
lack, and urged the formation of a feasible plan for both boys and

---

Jays, Livingstons, Putnams, and many others.   After the long list of signatures,
the names are classified under headings: Bankers, Owners of Real Estate and
Taxpayers, Lawyers, etc.
    [1] The sum of the above figures should read $43,801,150.   There is no means of
checking whether the total or one of the three figures composing this was an error.
These figures are higher than those given by Mr. Olmsted (see p. 163, *ante*).
    [2] See Part II, Chapter I, p. 276.

Coasting on a Slope of the North Meadow

1924

girls to be "instructed and practiced in harmless, athletic, out-of-door sports," in 1868 "Notes on the Educational Department of the Park,"[1] states that "The value of the Central Park to the citizens of New York . . . and its salutary effects upon the community are already well known, and the facilities it affords to the children of the Common Schools for varied and healthful exercise are appreciated."

It was a matter of record that "the attractions of the Park appear to have increased very much, among all classes, the disposition for out-of-door exercise."

In addition to stimulating active sports, the Park gave a general impetus to spending time out-of-doors, not only to citizens of New York but to those of other cities following her example in undertaking the development of a park. The Commissioners remark in 1866:

> The Park, as a whole, is undoubtedly expected to afford to the citizens of the metropolis, day after day and year after year, a succession of views of a rural character so real and genuine as to convey very positive ideas in regard to natural scenery, even to a person who might never see anything more country-like than will ultimately be contained within its limits; and this, in connection with the opportunity it offers for a social enjoyment of fresh air and exercise, is perhaps the most important service that it is calculated to perform in a direct way. Hill and dale, wood and water, grass and green leaves, are the natural food and refreshment of the human eye—an organ of sense [that is] so delicately adjusted as to require something more than dull and uninteresting forms, and is but little ministered to, in a pleasant way, in the portion of the city devoted to plain, straight-forward business or even domestic routine.
>
> Indirectly, however, the influence of the Central Park as an educator of the popular taste,[2] in regard to natural scenes, works in the same way as it has been shown to do in reference to the more easily defined amusement of skating, and as it may doubtless be made to do in other matters, such as music, playgrounds, zoological gardens, museums, &c.
>
> The almost undeveloped capacity for enjoyment of broad, simple, natural lines, forms and colors, being gradually fostered by habitual visits to the city Park, the taste grows by what it

---

[1] Mr. Green from his long connections with the Board of Education and with the Park Board was able to see opportunities for correlation.

[2] In the Olmsted & Vaux preliminary report on the Buffalo park in 1868, this point is emphasized:

"It must be observed, also, that a really fine, large and convenient park exercises an immediate and very striking educational influence, which soon manifests itself in certain changes of taste and of habits, and consequently in the requirements of the people."

feeds on, and ere long demands something fresh that shall be more broad, more simple, and more natural; the result of all this being that thousands of residents of this city acquire the habit of going into the country every now and then, in search of interesting scenery.

During the last few years the change in this respect, so far as New Yorkers are concerned, has been very easily traceable. Quiet localities that used to be almost wholly neglected, are now visited by hundreds every summer; and there is in every direction the same evidence that an increased proportion of the population manages to spend some time every year in this way.

The Effect of the Park on the Landscape Art.

That the Commissioners felt that the indirect benefits of Central Park had been conferred on a wider public than the citizens of New York appears in the report for 1863, where we read:

> It is no exaggeration to say that this work is doing much towards elevating the general public taste of the country, not only in the more extended and spacious public and private dwellings and gardens, but in the adornment of the more numerous and less pretentious habitations of our rural population.

In an unissued circular letter drafted by Mr. Olmsted in 1881 when he was preparing *Spoils of the Park*[1] he showed himself thoroughly aware of the widespread significance of the success or failure of the ideals embodied in the Central Park design.

> The management of the Central Park, directly and through discussions growing out of it, must largely influence customs, fashions, manners, opinions and tastes throughout the country. The differences of opinion which now appear upon the subject are so radical, they touch the value of property of such enormous value, and they are sustained with so much assurance as to leave open to question among all to whom the subject has not been one of special study, whether there are any fixed principles applicable to the treatment of pleasure-grounds public and private. . . . Doubt in the subject is doubt of the value of all study that has been given to the art of landscape gardening by a large number of eminently wise and worthy men and of the utility of the profession of landscape gardening.

Before the work of Mr. Vaux and Mr. Olmsted for the Central Park, there could scarcely be said to have been a *profession* of landscape gardening in America. The condition of the landscape art

[1] See p. 145, *ante.*

in 1857 has been set forth at some length in Volume One.[1] The untimely death of Downing had deprived the country of its literary medium. Downing's young English architect-partner Calvert Vaux of New York, H. W. S. Cleveland and his partner Copeland of Boston, and Adolph Strauch of Cincinnati, were among the very few practitioners with any claim beyond that of gardener or nursery-man. It was the firm of Olmsted & Vaux—later the two men independently and their subsequent partners—which gave the name and the official status to a field which the construction of Central Park proved to be neither architecture nor engineering nor gardening.

The style of landscape design, with its permeating artistic unity, exemplified in the broad meadows and picturesque natural-istic passages of Central Park,—and again in the Prospect Park of Brooklyn, and in the successive rural parks of many other cities,—tracing its lineage to the best existing park-like scenery in America and Europe, became a distinct esthetic conception, an American "landscape school," the principles of which are still valid and accepted in the sense for which Mr. Olmsted appealed in the circular letter quoted earlier in this chapter.

The Inception of the American Park Movement in Central Park.

In their farewell report of 1870 the Commissioners of the Central Park summed up the achievement of the Park which they had guided through its formative years:

> But the rapid advance of property in its immediate vicinity is but a small element of the value of the Park to the City. In its influence as an educator, as a place of agreeable resort, as a source of scientific interest, and in its effect upon the health, happiness, and comfort of our people may be found its chief value. Few cities of considerable population on this continent are now without schemes more or less advanced for the establishment of extensive parks for the pleasure of their people, and it is perhaps not too much to say that these enterprises of our sister cities are owing, in a large degree, to the success that has attended the example of the Central Park.

Two years previously the Commissioners had commented on the spread of parks throughout the country:

[1] See concluding chapter: "American Landscape Gardening in 1857."

There is scarcely a city of magnitude in this country that has not provided, or taken measures to provide, a Park for the pleasure of its citizens. Brooklyn, our neighbor, has one, that differing in its characteristics from our own, yet promises to be of great attractiveness.

Baltimore has laid out and improved its Park under the enlightened action of its Commissioners. Philadelphia has already secured grounds of great extent; enlightened citizens throughout the country already perceive the desirability of procuring conveniently situated pleasure grounds that will accommodate present and future generations, while the necessary space can be acquired within the limits at a reasonable cost; and the subject is under discussion in Providence, Albany, Troy, Cincinnati, Pittsburgh, Chicago, St. Louis and Louisville.

Mr. Olmsted himself, speaking in 1880 before the American Social Science Association,[1] said:

Twenty-five years ago we had no parks, park-like or otherwise, which might not better have been called something else. Since then a class of works so called has been undertaken which, to begin with, are at least spacious, and which hold possibilities of all park-like qualities. Upon twenty of these works in progress there has been thus far expended upwards of forty millions of dollars—well nigh if not fully fifty millions—and this figure does not tell the whole story of cost. . . . Considering that in none of the towns making this outlay the necessity of a park was a little while ago at all felt, a remarkable progress of public demand is thus manifested.

With a large number of parks, undertaken in the twenty-five years of which Mr. Olmsted speaks, he himself had to do, first in collaboration with Mr. Vaux and later independently.[2] Of the immediate successors of Central Park, the present Golden Gate Park of San Francisco is one of the earliest; and for this Mr. Olmsted, while on the Pacific Coast, gave some preliminary advice which he supplemented after his return to partnership with Mr. Vaux. It was, however, in the formation of Prospect Park for Brooklyn that the partners had a real opportunity to utilize the experience gained from Central Park and to produce there what many have felt to be a greater work of the landscape art. There followed in succession a park for Buffalo, the Chicago South Parks,[3] Mount Royal in Montreal, Belle-Isle in Detroit, Franklin Park and other elements of

[1] "Justifying Value of a Public Park."
[2] After 1884, Mr. Olmsted took into partnership his son John Charles Olmsted.
[3] See "The South Side Parks of Chicago: An Appreciation," by W. B. Van Ingen in *Landscape Architecture*, Oct., 1921.

the Boston park system,—for all of these there are published reports and papers, in parts of interest second only to the Central Park and Prospect Park papers,—and parks for Bridgeport, Rochester, Knoxville, and Louisville which carried on the tradition of their well-known predecessors.

The influence of these great urban parks designed as works of the landscape art extended beyond those with which the designers were directly concerned, although the same dangers and difficulties of politics and public misunderstanding of park purposes which beset the development of Central Park often overwhelmed its successors in various parts of the country. In cautioning those responsible for the development of Franklin Park in Boston in 1886, Mr. Olmsted said:[1]

> A study [of park enterprises] will result in a conviction that [the danger] consists mainly in the prevalence, during the earlier years of such undertakings, of vague, immature, conflicting, and muddled ideas of their purpose, and a consequent *tendency to fritter away the advantages of the ground* upon results that pass for collateral, but are really, for the most part, counteractive of their main design. These ideas lead to expectations, disappointments, customs, demands, that become important factors in determining the character of the park. If a notable number of the people, though a minority of all, come to suppose that it is not being prepared to meet expectations they may have happened, even though inconsiderately, to have formed, it is quite possible that their influence will compel the work to proceed upon a fluctuating plan to a degree that would be generally recognized to be scandalously wasteful in any other important class of public works.

A study of American parks would be of great value which should classify them according as they were designed as a whole, left alone, or frittered away. It can fairly be said that while Central Park in some cases influenced cities merely to acquire land *somewhere* for a park, it was the direct means of influencing a considerable number of cities to develop parks according to a unified design, so that they have in their possession today not only breathing spaces but works of the landscape art.

THE INFLUENCE OF PARKS ON OTHER PUBLIC IMPROVEMENTS; CITY PLANNING.

In addressing themselves to the Buffalo park commissioners, Olmsted & Vaux said:

[1] From "Notes on the Plan of Franklin Park."

We think it necessary, first of all, to urge that your scheme should be comprehensively conceived, and especially that features, the desirableness of which are most apparent, should not at the outset be made so important as to cause others, the possible value of which may seem more distant, to be neglected.

For this purpose it should be well thought of that a park exercises a very different and much greater influence upon the progress of a city in its general structure than any other public work. . . .

An immediate effect of the Central Park in increasing the desirability of surrounding land was to create a demand for improved communication between these newer sections and the lower part of the city, in addition to the demand for transportation to the Park itself. The stimulus to the opening and grading of streets in the vicinity of the Park, mapped in the Plan of 1811 but still undeveloped, was constant. And the roads in the new Park set a standard superior to anything yet known in the City.

The significance of Central Park in the cultural life of New York and of the whole country and its stimulation of museums, and other instruments of public education, were commented upon by Mr. Olmsted in the proposed Circular to Experts already referred to.[1]

The Central Park is a work of more than local and immediate importance. The direct outlay of public money already made upon it amounts to upwards of $15,000,000, important parts of it being yet unimproved, encumbered and unused. The expense in which it must indirectly involve the city will be much larger than that of this direct outlay. Great public treasures in addition to those classed with the park are accumulating within and adjoining it. Not only will these circumstances give it extraordinary celebrity but from its situation in the heart of the principal city of the continent it will be brought more under general observation than any other work of its class.

In regard to the growth of public desire for improvements, Mr. Olmsted wrote in 1870[2]:

A few facts will show you what the change in public opinion has been. When the Commissioners began their work, six hundred acres of ground was thought by many of the friends of the enterprise to be too much, by none too little for all park purposes. Since the Park has come into use, the amount of land laid out and reserved for parks in the two principal cities on the Bay of New York has been increased to more than three times that amount, the total reserve for parks alone now being about two thousand acres, and the public demand is now for more not less. Twelve years ago there was almost no pleasure-driving in New York. There are now, at least, ten thousand horses kept for pleasure-driving. Twelve years ago there were no roadways adapted to light carriages. There are now fourteen miles of rural drive within the parks complete and in use, and often crowded, and ground has been reserved in the two cities and their suburbs for fifty miles of parkways, averaging, with their planted borders and inter-spaces, at least one hundred and fifty feet wide.[1]

The land-owners had been trying for years to agree upon a new plan of roads for the upper part of Manhattan Island. A special commission of their own number had been appointed at their solicitation, but had utterly failed to harmonize conflicting interests. A year or two after the Park was opened, they went again to the Legislature and asked that the work might be put upon the Park Commissioners, which was done, giving them absolute control of the matter, and under them it has been arranged in a manner which appears to be generally satisfactory, and has caused an enormous advance of the property of all those interested.[2]

At the petition of the people of the adjoining counties, the field of the Commissioners' operations has been extended over their territory, and their scheme of trunk-ways for pleasure-driving, riding, and walking has thus already been carried far out into what are still perfectly rural districts.

On the west side of the harbor there are other commissioners forming plans for extending a similar system thirty or forty miles back into the country, and the Legislature of New Jersey has a bill before it for laying out another park of seven hundred acres.[3]

[1] Mr. Olmsted made this footnote comment:
"The completion of a few miles of these will much relieve the drives of the park, which, on many accounts, should never be wider than ordinary public requirements imperatively demand."

[2] The reports of the Commissioners of the Central Park and later of the Department of Public Parks dealing with the development of Upper Manhattan are city planning documents of the greatest interest. A list of the earlier of these may be found in "Statistical Report of the Landscape Architect," appended to 3rd Annual Report, D. P. P., for 1873. In this same report appeared the preliminary plan for "Riverside park and avenue." In 1876 Mr. Olmsted as Landscape Architect and Mr. Croes as Civil and Topographical Engineer submitted their joint preliminary report upon the laying out of the 23rd and 24th Wards. All the reports of this series of studies were later printed, including one on local steam transit routes, 1877.

[3] In 1867 a commission was appointed to recommend a site for a park in Newark. The report recommended a park of about 700 acres, including the present Branch Brook Park. The cost of the land and improvements, estimated at a million dollars, was considered too high and the Legislature dropped the matter. The Essex County Park Commission did not come into existence until 1895.—*Information from* Regional Plan of New York.

An early reference to the importance of city planning occurs in the Annual Report of the Central Park Commissioners for 1868:

> Municipalities of various extent have also been stimulated to the discussion of the subject of spacious and convenient thoroughfares, and to their ornamentation, and also to the consideration of the importance of providing for the growth of cities and systematic prearranged plans capable of execution as future years may seem to require.

To the student of the history of city planning in America the consciously studied plans of New York and Brooklyn in the sixties and seventies are of the deepest interest. They show how much earlier than the esthetic impetus to planning from the World's Fair of 1893 lie the beginnings of the present modern movement, and how keenly the planners realized that the design of public parks and of related park systems could vitally affect the structure of those cities in which foresighted citizens dared to follow the adventures of New York.

Some of the passages in the report of Olmsted & Vaux to the Brooklyn Park Commissioners of 1868 are of such enduring interest that they are quoted here, not only as showing the influence of the ramifications of the Central Park experience of its designers only a decade after the original adoption of their plan, but also as foreshadowing various present-day principles of the planning of urban growth.

> In immediate connection with the subject of approaches to the park, arises the question of laying out streets and avenues over that extensive tract of land which lies southerly from and beyond the limits of the park, and which must, at no distant day, become the abode of a vast multitude of people. The importance of attending to this matter at this time is the more obvious from the fact that this tract will soon form a portion of our city, and hence the necessity of projecting its streets and avenues in such a manner as to connect them with our own, consistently with public convenience, and with due regard to the promotion of the public health.
>
> It is of no less importance to our neighbors, that the mistakes and confusion should be avoided which are necessarily incident to the laying out of the suburbs of a large town by individuals, who do not usually act in concert, or with any comprehensive consideration of their common interest. When a plan shall have been prepared, with the advantages of a thorough study of all the topographical conditions of the district, and of its general relations to the city, on the one side, and to the adjoining country

on the other, and with a due consideration of the various requirements which may be expected to arise, as its population increases,
and such plan shall have [been] made a public record, owners of
property will of course conform their transfers of land, and the
erection of houses, to the line of streets and avenues there laid
down, while the corporate authorities will be thereby guided
in the opening, working, and grading of streets and avenues, and
the introduction of water and sewerage thereon. The Commissioners cannot, therefore, withhold the expression of their
unqualified approval of the project of a law which they are
informed will engage the attention of the Legislature at its
coming session, to provide for the laying out of streets, avenues
and public places throughout the county of Kings, outside of the
city of Brooklyn.[1]

In our preliminary report accompanying the first study of the
plan of the park, without making any definite recommendations,
we suggested the leading features of a general scheme of routes of
approach to and extension from the park, through the suburbs, in
which the sanitary, recreative, and domestic requirements of
that portion of the people of the city living at the greatest distance from the park should be especially provided for. In our
annual report of last year portions of this project were somewhat
more distinctly outlined, and the economical advantages were
pointed out, of preparing and adopting plans for the purpose well
in advance of the public demand, which it was intended to antici-
pate, and while land properly situated might yet be selected in
the suburbs of such moderate value that no private interests of
much importance would be found to stand in antagonism in this
respect to those of the public.

Relations of the Park to the Street Arrangements of the City.

Your Board having brought these suggestions before the public,
they have during the last year attracted considerable attention.
One of the minor recommendations has been already taken up by
a body of citizens, and an organized effort to carry it out is understood to be in progress. Under your instructions a topographical
survey has also been made of a section of the ground to which the
larger scheme applies, being that lying immediately east of the
park, and extending from it to the City Line; and a study has been
prepared, also under your instructions, and which is herewith
presented, for a revision of a part of the present city map of this
ground, with a view to the introduction of the suggested
improvement.[2]

The period seems to have arrived, therefore, for a full and

---

[1] This selection is taken from the report of the Commissioners of Prospect
Park, dated Jan. 14, 1868, which precedes the Landscape Architects' report.
The remainder of the selections are from the Olmsted & Vaux report itself.

[2] Eastern Parkway.

comprehensive inquiry as to the manner in which the scheme would, if carried out, affect the substantial and permanent interest of the citizens of Brooklyn, and of the metropolis at large. The project in its full conception is a large one, and it is at once conceded that it does not follow, but anticipates, the demand of the public; that it assumes an extension of the city of Brooklyn, and a degree of wealth, taste, and refinement to be likely to exist among its citizens which has not hitherto been definitely had in view; and that it is even based upon the presumption that the present street system, not only of Brooklyn, but of other large towns, has serious defects, for which, sooner or later, if these towns should continue to advance in wealth, remedies must be devised, the cost of which will be extravagantly increased by a long delay in the determination of their outlines.

.   .   .   .

Inadequate Domestic Access to Suburbs and Parks.

The parks are no more accessible than the suburbs, however, from those quarters of the town occupied domestically, except by means of streets formed in precisely the same manner as those which pass through the quarters devoted to the heaviest commercial traffic. During the periods of transit, therefore, from house to house, and between the houses and the park, there is little pleasure to be had in driving. Riding also, through the ordinary streets, is often not only far from pleasant, but, unless it is very slowly and carefully done, is hazardous to life and limb. Consequently much less enjoyment of the park is possible to those who live at a distance than to those who live near it, and its value to the population at large is correspondingly restricted. The difficulties of reaching the park on foot, for those who might enjoy and be benefited by the walk, are, at the season of the year when it would otherwise be most attractive, even greater, for they must follow the heated flags, and bear the reflected as well as the direct rays of the sun.

But we cannot expect, even if this objection were overcome, that all the inhabitants of a large town would go so far as the park every day, or so often as it is desirable that they should take an agreeable stroll in the fresh air. On the other hand, we cannot say that the transportation of merchandise should be altogether interdicted in the domestic quarters of a town, as it is in a park, and as it now is through certain streets of London and Paris during most hours of the day. On the contrary, it is evidently desirable that every dwelling house should be accessible by means of suitable paved streets to heavy-wheeled vehicles.

New Arrangements Demanded by Existing Requirements.

It will be observed that each of the changes which we have examined points clearly towards the conclusion that the present street arrangements of every large town will, at no very distant day, require, not to be set aside, but to be supplemented, by a series of ways designed with express reference to the pleasure with which they may be used for walking, riding, and the driving of carriages; for rest, recreation, refreshment, and social intercourse, and that these ways must be so arranged that they will be conveniently accessible from every dwelling house, and allow its occupants to pass from it to distant parts of the town, as, for instance, when they want to go to a park, without the necessity of traveling for any considerable distance through streets no more convenient for the purpose than our streets of the better class now are.

We may refuse to make timely provisions for such purposes in our suburbs, and we may by our refusal add prodigiously to the difficulty and the cost of their final introduction; but it is no more probable, if great towns continue to grow greater, that such requirements as we have pointed out will not eventually be provided than it was two hundred years ago that the obvious defects of the then existing street arrangements would continue to be permanently endured rather that property should be destroyed which existed in the buildings by their sides.

.   .   .   .

Influence of the Park on the Value of Property.

The effect of what has already been done, under the direction of your Commission, has been to more than quadruple the value of a certain portion of this land, and we have thus an expression of the most simple character, in regard to the commercial estimate which, at this period in the history of towns, is placed upon the circumstance of convenient access from a residence to a public pleasure-ground, and upon the sanitary and social advantages of a habitation thus situated. The advance in value, in this case, is quite marked at a distance of a mile, and this local advantage has certainly not been attended by any falling back in the value of other land in Brooklyn.[1]

If we analyze the conditions of this change in value, we shall find that it is not altogether, or even in any large degree, dependent upon mere vicinity to the sylvan and rural attractions

---

[1] In connection with the conservation of surrounding land values for the benefit of the City, the Olmsted & Vaux scheme, sponsored by the Prospect Park Commissioners, for a villa neighborhood on land not needed for the Park (doubtless following English precedent) came to naught. This is an early example of the miscarriage of an American excess-condemnation city-planning scheme. Although the designers had legal advice at the time, the Courts ruled that nine-tenths of the land had a bad title because the City could not sell land acquired for a park. The land lay idle over forty years until about 1910 a New York guarantee Company arranged to guarantee the titles.—*Information from* E. M. Bassett, Esq.

An interesting discussion as to the title of the land, and the legal difference between a park and a street will be found in the 10th Annual Report of the Commissioners of Prospect Park, Jan., 1870, pp. 351 f.

of the park, but in very large part, in the first place, upon the degree in which these attractions can be approached with security from the common annoyances of the streets, and with pleasure in the approach itself. If, for instance, the greater part of the park were long and narrow in form, other things being equal, the demand for building sites, fronting on this portion of it, would not, probably, be appreciably less than for those fronting on the broader part. Secondly, the advance in value will be found to be largely dependent on the advantages of having near a residence, a place where, without reference to the sylvan attractions found in a large park, driving, riding, and walking can be conveniently pursued in association with pleasant people, and without the liability of encountering the unpleasant sights and sounds which must generally accompany those who seek rest, recreation or pleasure in the common streets.

There are other things to be valued in a park besides these, but these are the main positive advantages which would make the value of a residence, if upon the park, much greater than if at a distance from it.

How the Advantages of Vicinity to a Park may be Extended.

So far, then, as it is practicable, without an enlargement of the park in its full breadth and compass, to extend its attractions in these especial respects, so far is it also practicable to enlarge the district within which land will have a correspondingly increased attraction for domestic residences. The further the process can be carried the more will Brooklyn, as a whole, become desirable as a place of residence, the higher will be the valuation of land, on an average, within the city, and the lighter will be the financial burden of the Corporation. [Then follows a discussion of the Parkway, so termed, as the solution.]

CHAPTER XIII

THE PARK IN RELATION TO THE CITY PLAN

A GOOD standpoint for a general review of the past and future of Central Park is that of its functions in relation to the ever-changing structure of the city plan. From that general standpoint it will here be discussed in the following five aspects: the designers' conception of its functions as a part of the city plan; success in realizing that conception; failures in the realization of that conception; the test of time applied to the soundness of that conception; and the future of the Park.

THE DESIGNERS' CONCEPTION OF THE FUNCTIONS OF CENTRAL PARK AS A PART OF THE CITY PLAN.

Although they recognized many valuable secondary and incidental functions which the Park might be made to perform, and certain limitations imposed on the performance of its main function by conditions beyond their control,—physical conditions of the site, fiscal and political conditions, and the more or less competing requirements of other necessary elements of the city plan,—the designers of Central Park had from the very outset a clear and self-consistent conception of its main or dominant function, or of its essential "justifying value" as they sometimes called it.

So far as that conception was sound and wise, so far as the objective was attainable without unjustifiable sacrifice of other values, they were absolutely right in their insistence on the principle that the attainment of this dominant objective in the highest practicable degree of perfection should never be sacrificed to secondary considerations however worthy in themselves; just as in the development of a water-supply system no secondary consideration should be permitted to impair its effectiveness for the prime purpose of supplying water of adequate quality and quantity.

Clear and self-consistent as was their conception of the dominant function of Central Park, a full grasp of it is hardly to be obtained without patiently following their exposition of it in the succeeding documents of this volume. But at the risk of some misconception it may be briefly stated thus:

The dominant and justifying purpose of Central Park was conceived to be that of permanently affording, in the densely populated central portion of an immense metropolis,[1] *a means to certain kinds of* REFRESHMENT OF THE MIND AND NERVES *which most city dwellers greatly need and which they are known to derive in large measure from the enjoyment of suitable scenery.*

What qualities of scenery were conceived to be effective for the purpose above stated and to be practically attainable, and what to be ineffective or undesirable for that purpose, and how these conceptions stand the test of time and critical examination will appear below.

Even those who have advocated courses of procedure in respect to Central Park most actively opposed by its designers have no tenable grounds of difference with them on the underlying principle of adherence to some one dominating purpose. They have differed in some instances as to the qualities of scenery which are most expedient under the circumstances for attaining the dominant purpose of refreshment through the enjoyment of scenery. They have differed in other instances in believing that some wholly distinct and different purposes—such as provision for horse-racing, or for athletic sports, or for the erection of armories, museums, hospitals, or other useful buildings on the land acquired for the Park, or for facilitating the general circulation of passengers and goods in the island of Manhattan—are so important, and so difficult of attainment by other means, as to justify the subordination to them of the dominant purpose of the Park as originally conceived. Mostly they have differed in their failure to understand the necessary effect of their proposals on the value of the Park for its dominant purpose, and in their inability to face the facts of conflict and to balance public advantages and disadvantages with patience and broad vision.

Reserving until later a discussion of the special kinds of scenic quality conceived by the designers to be most suitable for serving the dominant purpose of the Park as they saw it, it is worth while to examine their conception of its relation to other important elements of the developing city plan.

[1] As to their conception of the size of that metropolis, see p. 45.

RELATION TO GROWTH OF CITY AND TO OTHER PARK FACILITIES.

It is a common fashion to refer patronizingly and excusingly to the supposed fact that even the more far-seeing men of the nineteenth century had no conception of the scale of growth in store for New York and of the scale of planning appropriate to that growth. On that point, and to indicate that the designers of Central Park looked forward quite definitely to a vast and comprehensive system of recreation facilities for the metropolis, in which system Central Park would be but a single unit properly specialized in function because of the supplementary functions of the rest of the system,[1] the following quotation is significant: " . . . we regard Brooklyn as an integral part of what to-day is the metropolis of the nation, and in the future will be the centre of exchanges for the world, and the park in Brooklyn as part of a system of grounds, of which the Central Park [also] is [merely] a single feature, designed for the recreation of the whole people of the metropolis and their customers and guests from all parts of the world for centuries to come."[2]

This clearly anticipates a scale of urban growth outrunning that of Metropolitan London, then the indubitable "centre of exchanges for the world," with which Mr. Olmsted was closely familiar and which even then had a population of over three million, doubling in forty years. Many references in the Brooklyn and New York reports of the sixties clearly outline in principle a mutually supplementary series of parks and subordinate recreation grounds widely dispersed throughout the metropolitan area and linked together by a system of connecting parkways (including one across the East River by high bridges at Blackwell's Island) of a width, capacity, and scenic quality of which there were then no examples in this country, the whole constituting a recreation service deliberately and comprehensively planned to meet in a well-balanced manner the fairly predictable needs of the entire metropolitan population,—a service such as had not previously been envisaged anywhere.[3] Unfortunately the idea of systematically proceeding in accordance with such a comprehensive park system plan in advance of the extension of streets and buildings, was never fully "sold" to the public authorities, although several sporadic parts of it came into existence.

[1] Cf. the section in the preceding chapter beginning on p. 179.
[2] Report of the Commissioners of Prospect Park, Brooklyn, 1866, p. 94.
[3] Cf. p. 182.

RELATION TO GENERAL STREET TRAFFIC.

The designers of Central Park clearly foresaw a serious conflict between what would be desirable for securing the maximum recreation values from the Park and what would be desirable for convenient circulation of the immense general street traffic that might be expected in central Manhattan within a few decades. Even though they could not foresee the effect of the automobile and of elevator-buildings in stimulating the expansion of street traffic to the limit of street capacity, they were already familiar with full-capacity street traffic in the central parts of great cities, they looked forward to the complete surrounding of Central Park by intensive urban growth with a corresponding intensity of street traffic, and they definitely anticipated a tension of demand for ordinary street traffic movement across and within Central Park that would bear some roughly proportionate relation to the limiting capacity of the surrounding street system, then already fixed in plan.

Mr. Olmsted's thought was sharply focused on this conflict of park desiderata and street-traffic desiderata by the galloping of a fire engine across the Park lands at the very moment when he was studying how to manipulate its landscape so as to produce on visitors an impression of quiet restfulness emphatically contrasting with the turmoil of city streets. Facing the problem squarely, the designers realized on the one hand that it would be incompatible with the economic welfare and convenience of the city to exclude wholly from a central rectangle of the size of Central Park all ordinary street traffic not concerned with the enjoyment of the Park as such, and on the other hand that it would enormously depreciate the value of the Park for its dominant purpose to permit such traffic to mingle indiscriminately with visitors to the Park for its own sake. Apart from the *kinds* of general street traffic seriously disturbing to enjoyment of the Park—such as dangerously speedy and noisy fire-engines and ambulances or lumbering busses, street cars, and commercial trucks—the mere *volume* of additional vehicles thus thrown into the Park might become a serious interference with its value for park purposes.

The solution proposed was twofold: first, to provide reasonably adequate separate facilities for general street traffic by creating a number of sunken transverse roads across the Park[1], not only avoiding all grade crossings with the drives and foot paths of the Park but avoiding intrusion of general street traffic into the park

[1] Cf. pp. 47 and 560.

scenery, and by enlarging the capacity of the streets bordering the Park and improving the paving and other conditions attractive for traffic on those and other possible relief streets;[1] and second, by police regulations and by the arrangement of the Park drives not only to exclude definitely from the Park all classes of general street traffic except so-called "pleasure vehicles" but also to make the Park roads uninviting even for the latter to use merely as rapid thoroughfares, so far as this could be done without a net impairment of the pleasure derived by users of the Park for its proper purposes. This double solution, ingeniously worked out in detail so far as concerns the Park and its bordering streets, was eminently successful for many years. In principle it remains the only solution compatible with adherence to the original dominant purpose of the Park.

Reference has already been made to the largely abortive efforts to correlate with Central Park a metropolitan system of wide parkways having both a recreational function and a specialized highway function. During the sixties and early seventies, however, as we have seen in the preceding chapter, under a stimulus derived from the Central Park work and in part under the direction of the Central Park Commissioners, a number of broad thoroughfares related to the Park were created in the upper part of Manhattan; and in the Bronx there was planned but never executed a fairly complete system of main and secondary thoroughfares and of rapid transit lines on private rights of way, closely adjusted to the topography.[2]

RELATION TO ZONING.

Zoning as we now know it was not thought of in the early days of Central Park. But it is interesting to note in a report of Olmsted and Vaux of 1869[3] a recognition of the importance and value of restrictive covenants "when applied to sufficiently large areas," especially in combination with street planning directed toward the same ends, and especially in the vicinity of parks. This is accompanied by the statement, "It is too late to do anything of this kind in connection with the Central Park."

In view of this alertness of the designers of Central Park in the decade of the sixties to the problem of a planned control of developments on private property in relation to park planning and street planning, it is interesting to speculate on how much more they

[1] Cf. Annual Report, C. P. C., for 1861, p. 6, and for 1868, p. 19.
[2] See report of Olmsted and Croes, mentioned in footnote on p. 181.
[3] See Brooklyn Park Report, Jan., 1870.

might have accomplished in the advancement of American City Planning if they had happened to come in touch with the existing seeds of police power zoning in Europe, which during the next decade Adickes and other German city planners cultivated until at last they flowered into the full Zoning Laws of Germany, reaching America in a highly developed form only after the long slow process of German evolution. The soil was ready in New York for an earlier and perhaps much quicker development of the zoning principle; but the seeds lay buried in French and other statutes unknown to Olmsted and Vaux and their collaborators.

THE KINDS OF SCENIC QUALITIES HELD IMPORTANT FOR THE DOMINANT FUNCTION OF THE PARK.

Returning to the specific dominant function of Central Park, as an instrument for producing certain beneficially refreshing effects on the minds and nerves of city dwellers, what were the qualities believed to be requisite in such an instrument?

It was assumed, in a common-sense, empirical way, that they were to be sought among the qualities of those places to which city dwellers in Europe and America actually resorted with most satisfaction for refreshment from urban strain and weariness. The qualities of such places were subjected to constant penetrating analysis, the results of which are in part set forth among the writings of the designers which follow, and are more definitely embodied in the work of art which they created to accomplish the end in view.

For since that end was to produce an effect primarily psychological,—to give a refreshing enjoyment,—the means to that end was conceived as primarily an esthetic means, as a work of scenic art before all else.

There is an infinite variety in the types of scenery from which city dwellers in fact derive beneficial refreshment of varying degree and kind. They range from the smallest of enclosed gardens to stretches of landscape as vast as the eye can see; they include compositions wholly or mainly architectural, from those most severely rigid in their classic formality to the most romantically picturesque, and likewise compositions without an architectural element in them; they embrace landscapes meticulously designed throughout, from the grandly formal compositions of Le Nôtre to the sedulously informal or naturalistic compositions of the "Landscape Gardening" school which arose as a reaction therefrom in eighteenth century England; and equally they embrace landscapes not consciously designed as such at all but none the less widely appreciated as beautiful and refreshing, whether found in the untouched wilderness or in lands long subdued to human use.

Effectively refreshing scenery—and also dreary unrefreshing scenery—is to be found in all of these and other sorts; but certain rather subtle qualities distinguish scenery of any sort which is generally and effectively refreshing. These qualities cannot be reduced to formulae permitting their mechanical reproduction but they *can* be "sensed," and by real artists reproduced. Some of them can be suggested by words, as was often attempted by Olmsted and Vaux, in the papers which follow, in their effort to guide others toward a consistent pursuit of the one dominant artistic objective which could justify holding such a large unbroken block of land as Central Park out of other urban uses.

Some of these qualities, which they held to be especially important for the end in view, may here be briefly summarized. An appearance of expansive spaciousness was one, valuable inherently and also for its contrast with the prevailingly hemmed-in aspect of most urban scenes. Closely akin to this was a quality in the forms and arrangements of the enclosing masses of such spacious landscapes that is mysteriously suggestive of "more of the same kind beyond," that invites to exploration. Closely allied to this again was a similar quality of mystery and indefiniteness in the enclosure of landscapes not in themselves spacious, but suggestive of continuation into different though harmonious kinds of landscapes. Another of these qualities was a kind of quietness depending on the general absence of details sufficiently exciting and arresting in themselves to make strong individual impressions—even pleasant ones—at the expense of weakening the impression of the whole scene in which they occur. Finally there was one simply physical quality that was held of great importance, directly soothing and refreshing to the nerves for reasons we do not understand, and at the same time refreshing because of its marked contrast with ordinary urban conditions and because of its pleasant associations. This quality was *verdurousness*—the mere fresh green of vigorous turf and profuse umbrageous foliage—something no more beautiful or desirable in the abstract than the beauty of desert sand-dunes or of an exquisite pavement or of athletes on a bare arena, but far more useful for the specific purpose of refreshing ordinary city dwellers by sight of it.

All these qualities may be found in scenery of any of the sorts above cited, formal or informal; but the designers believed that the kind of refreshment in view was obtainable with peculiar effectiveness from certain types of "naturalistic" scenery akin to those which often result spontaneously under pastoral conditions in regions favorable both to trees and to grass,—types characterized chiefly by meadows and glades of turf irregularly intermingled with spreading trees and masses of woodland. Accidently beautiful landscapes of such types have been common, and have been greatly enjoyed, in many parts of the world and in many ages. They were sung by Latin Poets under the designation *nemus*. They are especially familiar in northwestern Europe and the northeastern United States, and their occurrence in the deer parks and pastured forests of England formed a main stimulus to that deliberate manipulation of naturalistic landscapes as things of beauty which in the eighteenth century gave rise to the term "landscape gardening."

The belief of Olmsted and Vaux in the special value of these and kindred types of "informal" landscape compositions for performing the function which they conceived to be the dominant function of Central Park was in part, doubtless, a reflection of the prevailing taste of the times,—characterized by a swing of the pendulum to the Romantic in most of the arts,—but with them it was much more than that. Mr. Olmsted was an unusually independent thinker and a penetrating thinker, and his writings show a keen personal appreciation of the beauty of "formal" landscape compositions, especially of straight and well-proportioned tree-framed vistas, and of self-contained gardens frankly formal in plan. Yet he held strongly to the belief above cited. It was a reasoned belief based on years of critical observation, unbiased at least by any previous personal practice in design that might have wedded him to one particular style.

It was a belief that turned on three other opinions. The first was that the general qualities which appeared mainly effective in making scenery refreshing for city dwellers, as briefly indicated above, although often found singly or in combination in other types of landscape both formal and informal, were apt to be found most effectively combined in landscapes of the pastoral types above described. The second was that these qualities could be artificially secured with more certainty of perfection in such pastoral types of landscape than otherwise. The third was that the obviously rural associations of such naturalistic landscapes, when sufficiently spacious and self-contained, tended greatly to enhance their refreshing value for townsfolk as compared with the urban associations of frankly formal landscape compositions however excellent.

SECONDARY RECREATIONAL FUNCTIONS OF THE PARK RECOGNIZED BY THE DESIGNERS.

The secondary recreational possibilities of the Park which the designers believed to be attainable in considerable measure, under suitable limitations, without impairment of its dominant function of scenic refreshment,—and those which they believed incompatible with that function,—cannot here be fully enumerated; but some of them are worth discussing.

Opportunity for and stimulus to active physical exercise in the open air, under conditions favorable to mental and moral vigor, were prominent in their minds. Walking amidst pleasant surroundings played a very large part in such a program, perhaps a larger part than appeals to the habits of the present generation. It is, however, as obvious now as it was then that, in a given space of land, far more people can get healthful exercise amid pleasant and refreshing surroundings by walking, on paths constructed to withstand constant wear and tear, through unworn and beautifully verdurous surroundings, than can be provided for by any other means whatever.

Horseback riding was largely stressed and was provided for with remarkable ingenuity in the avoidance of conflict between the needs of equestrians and those of other users of the Park, as by the minimimizing of grade crossings. Boating and skating were largely stressed so far as they could be provided for on water otherwise desirable in the landscape of the Park.

Amusements and active play adapted for children were a constant concern. They were sought mainly through means directly contributing to the pleasant qualities of the landscape for others, or at worst neutral in their effect on the landscape,—means which would introduce pleasant kinds of animation without seriously impairing verdurousness or other desired landscape qualities. Subject only to such limitations as might prove necessary from time to time in various places for the general maintenance of verdurousness, the use of the lawns by children and especially by the smaller children whose wear and tear on good turf is much less than that of older children and adults, was to be encouraged and promoted both for spontaneous unorganized play and for organized plays and pageantry. Numerous special devices, some long since fallen into disuse, were contrived for the special benefit of children, the buildings or other special equipment they involved being either woven harmoniously into the general fabric of the scenery or hidden away. Such were the "Dairy" unit, the great arbor, the carousel, the goat wagons, the saddle-donkeys, the toy-boat pool, and the removable equipment for May-Day and other children's festivals.

Subject to somewhat closer limitations as to intensity and continuity of use, in order to avoid serious destruction of the verdurousness of the greater park landscapes, a considerable amount of baseball and other active games by older boys and youths was one of the by-products definitely expected to result from the large open meadows designed primarily for scenic enjoyment and obtainable on the difficult rocky terrain of Central Park only at great expense,—a by-product desirable not only for the youths engaging in it but for the larger public enjoying the animated but verdurous and refreshing scene.

It was quite deliberately concluded that with a population as large as would become tributary to Central Park it was wholly impossible to make provision in it for the entire youthful part of that population to enjoy continuously as much as they might like of baseball playing or other active sports involving hard wear and tear on the ground surface, or to make provision for a large amount of space per capita, without radically subordinating to those ends the dominant scenic purpose of the Park. It was thought inevitable in some cases and expedient in others to provide within the Park boundaries for some other objectives, involving conditions equally incompatible with the scenic qualities proper to the Park, by the process of excision; by deliberately withdrawing certain areas from the landscape of the Park, and using them for these other objectives. In this class were the transverse roads, the widenings of boundary streets, the reservoirs, some service buildings, the carousel, and the site of the Metropolitan Museum of Art. Large areas of bare ground or shabbily worn-out turf, inevitable where active athletic games are constantly played, differ from all of the above except the reservoirs in their extent, and differ from all except the Museum in the absence of any strong logical reason for their location within the boundaries of Central Park. If it had been considered a legitimate charge upon the funds of the Central Park Commission to provide such un-parklike fields for intensive play, the million dollars spent for extending the original area of the Park northward to 110th Street would logically have been spent in acquiring several separate play fields in adjacent parts of Manhattan, where each would have been closely surrounded by the population it was to serve and would have caused less interruption of the street system.

Two other secondary aspects of the Park's functions which the designers stressed were those of affording what they called family pleasures and gregarious pleasures. Except for a few conveniences, in part long since abandoned, that were especially adapted for the convenience of family picnic parties, and the deliberately close association of facilities for little children's amusement with places pleasant for their parents, the former was not specifically expressed in the physical plan of the Park but rather in plans for its administration and for the education of the public in its most effective use. Regard for gregarious pleasures was constantly present in considering all users of the Park as forming the animated part of its scenery, in the manipulation of walks and roads and bridle paths so as to afford to a high degree in certain places the pleasure of seeing throngs of others in holiday mood, while in other places securing a sense of retirement from crowds. In the Mall and Terrace the most specific attempt was made to provide for concentrated gregarious enjoyment, enlivened by music, and in a frankly formal landscape setting considered peculiarly appropriate to that gregarious mood.

Such, briefly, were the objectives which the designers appear to have had in view.

Success in Realizing the Designers' Conception.

In its topography and soil the site of the Park was distinctly adverse to the working out of the designers' main objectives. It was an intricate glaciated confusion of rocky knolls and ridges, small valleys and little fields, and numerous swamps. The soil was generally shallow and none of the best. There were few trees of any important landscape value. Its landscape was deficient in the very qualities of quiet spaciousness and breadth that were felt to be most peculiarly desirable for its purpose. It wholly lacked any outlook on the broad waters surrounding Manhattan, such as added so much spaciousness to the East River park site originally proposed.[1]

But in the course of a single generation, by great practical and

[1] Cf. Part I, Chapter II, p. 28.

artistic ingenuity of design, and by large expenditures[1] for blasting, grading, drainage, soil improvement, planting, and other improvements, and in spite of repeated interference with the work both by political spoilsmen and by high-minded men who did not clearly grasp the underlying artistic intent of the design, these adverse physical conditions were so far overcome as to permit the realization, with a high degree of success, of the conception at which the designers aimed.

Appreciative but discriminating criticism of that success when the park was at its best is contained in the quotations which follow, one from a landscape architect and one from a landscape painter.

Mr. Harold A. Caparn has written[2]:

. . . Everywhere is displayed the utmost resource of the artist and variety of treatment, as consistently as though the true solution of the problem of each part had been found without effort. When conditions are at their best, after rainy weather or in the early morning or evening, there is a wonderful air of calm beauty pervading it all, so that one marvels more and more that such a thing with such a sentiment should exist in New York City. Now, if you travel in any rural district, you will find in all directions the raw material or the motives from which Central Park is made. . . . But, though there is much pictorial beauty, it will be seldom that you find a scene, small or large, that composes well. By composing well I mean not only showing orderly arrangement, just proportion, good lines, and so on, but conveying the impression of a complete picture, "carrying through" as it is called. . . . This is what is done in Central Park; each successive part into which the uneven surface naturally resolves itself is treated according to its own suggestion, with thoroughness and reserve. Buildings and other subordinate objects are carefully set where they will do least harm to the general composition. The ragged countryside planting is arranged in groups or masses or borders with due regard to the habit of the trees, texture, and color of foliage, sky-line and so on. For the rough or divided surface of land is substituted the smooth and continuous lawn, displaying the best contours of the ground, and preserving them unbroken to their logical end.

The following appreciation was written by Mr. W. B. Van Ingen, long a champion and defender of Central Park:

A distinguished New Yorker once said to me (we were in Central Park) that though he had travelled extensively, he had never seen a park where nature had done so much and man so little.

[1] See footnote on p. 95.
[2] "Central Park, a Work of Art," in *Landscape Architecture*, July, 1912.

Yet we know that if the soil and building material placed and replaced in making the park were placed in dump carts and these in single file, the procession would be thirty thousand miles long. Could man well have done more? Yet Mr. Olmsted has been referred to by high authority as the man who preeminently taught us the beauty of natural landscape, and Central Park is, I believe, his greatest triumph. So perfectly is all artifice concealed that the impression of the distinguished New Yorker was justified: it is difficult even in the face of facts, to realize that man had anything to do with the beauty that Nature there displays so profusely.

Fortunately the secret of this seeming paradox is told in two paragraphs, one written by Mr. Olmsted himself, several years before the design of Central Park was thought of, the other by Mr. Vaux, years after it was planned. "What artist," wrote Mr. Olmsted,[1] "so noble as he, who, with far-reaching conception of beauty and designing power, sketches the outlines, writes the colors, and directs the shadows, of a picture so great that Nature shall be employed upon it for generations, before the work he has arranged for her shall realize his intentions." And it was Mr. Vaux who wrote, "In every difficult work, the key-note of success lies, of course, in the idea of thorough subordination but it must be intelligent penetrative subordination, an industrious, ardently artistic, and sleeplessly active ministry that is constantly seeking for an opportunity to do some little thing to help forward the great result on which Nature is lavishing its powers of creation."

Having now the key that unlocks the mind of the men who made the park, we are justified in asking the park to speak for itself. . . . It has always seemed to me that the scene from the terrace out over the lake was planned by the great English artist Turner, that master of the imagination. . . .

. . . And how was it possible men could have reasoned out beforehand that if pin oaks were planted in the woodlands of the Ramble, our memories of their long upright shafts would still be in our minds as we saw the sprawling paulonia trees disporting themselves like arboreal elephants on Peacock Lawn? Contrast, we of course know, is the power plant of the artist, but it's too much to ask us to believe that the two men to whom we attribute the design of the park, could have used memory to emphasize sight. Nature must surely have here conferred an unasked for favor.

I'm thinking now of a French artist, if I mistake not his name was Girard, who used to delight me years ago, with his paintings of flower gardens. Do you know, I really believe he crossed the seas in spirit, and planned that little pool in the Ramble, I saw one Spring, reflecting the beauties of the azaleas and rhododendrons. . . .

. . . I've proved to myself over and over again that Salvatore

[1] Mr. Olmsted often quoted this himself. See p. 50.

Rosa found inspiration for the backgrounds of his pictures, in that almost hidden by-way at the extreme north of the park, where the path leads by rocks purposely placed to conceal robbers. While as for that group of sycamores, south of the Ninety-Seventh Street transverse road, I passed them years and years ago as I trudged to school 'way back in the country.

Was it really Frederick Law Olmsted and Calvert Vaux who made Central Park, or was it Nature herself? I am sure Mr. Olmsted was "the artist so noble" and Mr. Vaux the sleeplessly artistic minister. And how often these faithful workmen argued between themselves how best they could aid Nature. Though I've travelled far and wide, in body and in spirit, through the landscapes created by the world's great master painters, I've taken standards of keenest delight to weigh my impressions of Central Park, only to be convinced that it is one of the great achievements of mankind.

FAILURES IN THE REALIZATION OF THE DESIGNERS' CONCEPTION.

Certain failures of the Park to accomplish successfully what the designers had in mind have been increasingly apparent in recent years. Three groups of these deserve special mention here, reserving to the next section a discussion of their bearing on the suitability of the original conception.

Lofty buildings, looming up jaggedly around the Park, now obtrude themselves into the background of many of its landscapes in a manner wholly unforeseen when it was designed. This tends unquestionably to shrink the scale of the landscapes, to reduce the impression of spaciousness so laboriously sought in the Park, and to weaken the impression of aloofness from ordinary city surroundings,—qualities on which the designers laid much stress.

The volume and at times the speed of automobile traffic on the Park drives, largely of vehicles using the Park as a mere incident in moving to objectives beyond the Park, now seriously impairs the pleasure and safety of visitors to the Park for its own sake, whether on foot or in vehicles. At the same time, as the volume of general street traffic approaches the limiting capacity of neighboring avenues and streets, including those interrupted by the Park, there is in some quarters increasing impatience with such obstruction as the park causes to the free and rapid flow of through traffic. Successive widenings of the Park drives and the introduction of new vehicular entrances from abutting streets not provided in the original plan have tended to increase the first difficulty without appreciably relieving the second.

There has been going on for many years a serious physical

Central Park To-day

Compare the view in 1863 given opposite page 76

deterioration in the Park,[1] especially in its vegetation. The destructive and deteriorating effect of wear and tear under the use, abuse, and misuse of the Park by the public, and of other adverse environmental conditions, has progressively out-matched the opposite effect of favorable conditions and specifically of the administrative efforts which have been made to forestall such damage, to repair it when done, and to secure positive increases in the qualities appropriate to the Park.

The most conspicuous esthetic loss has been the general quality of fresh verdurousness, because of the death, damage, and impoverishment of trees and shrubs and turf, although there have been coincident impairments of many other and less obvious qualities of the landscape compositions.

Associated with the decrease of verdurousness is a pervasive increase of a positively objectionable quality. It is both a result and a true expression of a slatternly and lawless public disregard for, and destructiveness of, fine qualities beneficial to the users of the Park as members of society. It is both a result and an expression of an ever present anti-social or anti-civilized element in human nature. In so far as this quality is noticeably present in one's surroundings, it not only produces a generally depressing psychological effect quite opposite to the refreshing function adopted for Central Park, but by suggestion actually stimulates people to yield to any destructive inner impulses that may arise from this anti-civilized element of their human nature. Every such yielding to destructive impulse tends, by the physical damage it causes, to make the objectionable quality more pronounced except as offset by constructive action, and at the same time reenforces the anti-social elements of the individual who so yields. Whether in a park, in a household, in a whole neighborhood, or anywhere, if the socially constructive forces which act on the physical environment by way of maintenance, repair, restoration, and increase of its finer qualities, and which act upon the people by education and restraint, cannot prevent the increase of these slatternly qualities at the expense of their opposites, the environment is bound to become in so far uncivilizing and injurious instead of beneficially civilizing in its influence.

As an instrument for serving its prime social purpose Central Park has in this way notably declined in its total effectiveness during the last generation, and has certainly fallen far short of

[1] Cf. Chapter XI, *ante*, especially the first and last sections.

exerting the civilizing influence which its designers conceived and hoped for.

The Test of Time Applied to the Soundness of the Designers' Conception.

The question is whether any substantially different conception of the physical means for accomplishing the prime objective of the park would have succeeded better, and how well the degree of success attained or attainable justifies the undertaking of that objective.

The chief shortcoming of the Park to-day as compared with the designers' conception, as just explained, is due to a preponderance of destructive influences over constructive and restorative influences during the latter half of its history, and especially in recent years. After making all due allowance for other factors, such as the inherently somewhat unfavorable soil and atmospheric conditions of the locality, the controlling adverse factor has been the manner and intensity of use, misuse, and abuse of the Park by the public, chiefly the trampling and wearing of the soil and smashing of plants, in ignorance, in self-indulgence, and in wantonness.

The human nature of the people of Manhattan has not greatly altered since the Park was begun. The tendency, under given conditions, to slatternly or wanton destructiveness, to lawless selfishness, is always present, and was recognized at the beginning of the Park as one of the great problems in its design and administration. The same human qualities tended to make slums fifty or sixty years ago as now, regardless of racial and other differences, and tended, then as now, if unrestrained, to make the Park slummy and shabby and to alter its influence from a refreshing and civilizing one to an uncivilizing one. The designers of the Park constantly hammered on the necessity of meeting this ever-present adverse human factor in three ways, none of which could be effective without the others. One was to adapt the physical design and construction of the Park as well as possible to its use by great numbers of people in a manner calculated to give the maximum of refreshing enjoyment without involving excessive wear and tear of a sort destructive to the scenic basis of that enjoyment. The second was to train the public constantly, by instruction and example and by firm disciplinary restraint, to use the Park in that effective manner rather than in a destructive and anti-social manner. The third was constantly to offset such destructive effects as proved unavoidable by diligent maintenance, renewal, and constructive improvement.

The outstanding defect of the Park as an instrument for its purpose is due primarily to gross neglect of the second and third requirements. The economic extravagance of this neglect is suggested by the fact that during the time the Park has been deteriorating in public value for lack of the second and third essentials, the sums annually provided for its maintenance and protection were penuriously limited to an order of magnitude only about a hundredth part of the interest charges on the investment locked up in the Park.

No instrument for serving the purposes of the Park could be highly successful under indefinitely continuing neglect of these two essentials,—proper physical maintenance, and proper control and management of the users. It is true that some kinds of park scenery, as for example the pleasant, gravel-surfaced, formal groves of the Luxembourg Gardens, can withstand unregulated wear and tear with less obviously rapid depreciation than some others; but the difference is marginal. The exquisite orderliness of the Luxembourg groves would rapidly turn to squalor and destruction if *amply adequate* effort were not continually made to restrain the destructive impulses of its less civilized visitors and to make good the unavoidable deterioration. Indeed the part played by perfection of maintenance and of policing in the fine orderliness of the urban pleasure grounds of Paris at their best used to be expressed in the saying that "the guards arrested falling leaves before they could reach the ground."

There is not, nor has there been, any technical or any economic reason, or any reason dependent on the character of its users, why Central Park could not have embodied continuously with a high degree of perfection the physical conditions aimed at by its designers. It may be said that the political and administrative shortcomings which have in fact prevented that result are a definite part of the conditions, and that the designers' conception of the Park is open to the criticism that it was one which could not be realized with adequate success in face of that political fact. Perhaps. But any other means of serving the same general end would have suffered substantially as much from the same political handicap. And it is generally conceded that in spite of any shortcomings the Park has accomplished its purpose effectively enough to have been worth far more than its cost.

The only serious adverse criticisms of the designers' conception are those based, first, on a belief that the aim of providing for a high degree of popular enjoyment of refreshing scenery in the heart of Manhattan is not sufficiently important to justify the necessary price of subordinating other objectives within the Park area (such as the rapid flow of street traffic, or ample provision for athletic activities destructive to verdure); or, second, on the belief that other kinds of scenery would be more appropriate and desirable than those selected, a belief most often accompanied by a plea for a highly formalized or "architectural" type of design.

The first belief appears to be founded mainly on an utter failure to realize how greatly the refreshing function of the Park would be sacrificed by subordination to these other objectives, and on an impatient unwillingness to seek those objectives by means which would not subordinate the esthetic function of the Park.

The traffic problem, for example, clearly can be met by intelligent re-application of the principle adopted by the designers: amplification of the capacity of the bordering streets, and if necessary of the hidden transverse traffic roads, accompanied by such close control of vehicular movements on the Park drives as will discourage its use merely for rapid through travel at the expense of the safety and pleasure of those who resort to it for its proper purposes.

The problem of intensive athletic activities proportionate to the demand, and of other activities incompatible with the effective maintenance of the refreshing quality of the Park scenery, is not so easily met. A wise solution depends on a frank recognition of the real incompatibility of these opposing objectives as dominant purposes within a scenic park, upon measuring the price of providing for these opposing objectives in varying degrees by other means, and on deliberately concluding whether they are worth that price, or if not whether they are at all worth the sacrifice of the dominant objectives which have controlled and alone have justified the enormous present investment in the Park.

The second belief, so far as it is held, appears to be based primarily on the strong personal predilections of certain people for radically different types of landscape design, specifically certain admirable types of formal or architectural landscape, and a certain narrowness of artistic appreciation which prevents them from recognizing any serious artistic merit in compositions of the "naturalistic" type deliberately adapted for Central Park. Their arguments based on special conditions which now affect the Park are therefore somewhat disingenuous and *ex parte*, but they deserve serious consideration on their own merits.

One of these arguments is that, with the development of high buildings in the rectangle which surrounds the Park, its visible frame has become hopelessly un-rural and insistently architectural; that the suggestion of rural aloofness from the city for which the original designers strove is gone beyond recall; and that the artistic discord between these inevitable surroundings and the quasi-rural scenes within the Park demands a *volte-face* involving the more or less complete redesign of the Park in a spirit of frankly urban and architectural magnificence.

It is true that the tall buildings around the Park intrude on its quasi-rural landscapes, dwarf their scale, and seriously impair their former esthetic value. But careful analysis will convince any acute observer that the most distressing feature about the intrusion of these buildings on the park landscapes is not their visible reminder that he is yet in the heart of the city, or even their disharmony in scale: it is the crude and ugly restlessness of the ill-composed skylines which at most points they now present. And it is impossible to conceive of any magnificently dignified formal pleasure ground, perfect in its ordered regularity, around which such a restless disorderly jumble of dominating building masses would not be, as a matter of pure composition, even more distressing and inharmonious than it is in the background of the picturesquely irregular landscape compositions of the Park to-day.

Apart from those who are professionally or otherwise prejudiced to the point of an irrational antipathy against considering any dominantly informal or naturalistic landscape composition as a work of art, it is as true to-day as ever it was that for most city people one of the most refreshing qualities obtainable in a park (if it be sufficiently large to give it in any high degree) is that combination of a sense of spaciousness with a sense of mysterious intricacy, among objects and scenes associated with and suggestive of the distant open country-side, which it was the controlling purpose of Central Park to provide. It still affords a quality so pleasantly in contrast with the normal urban conditions, even where there can be no possibility of the most momentary illusion of being in the unlimited open country, that it is very precious. The most beautiful of frankly urban gardens and architectural parks, delightful as they may be and desirable though they are, do not offer a substitute for it, but an additional and different kind of thing. They can be provided in perfection on areas far less in size than Central Park. And if there be any adequate justification for holding for park uses near the heart of a city anything like so great an area of land in a single block, it is solely in order to provide that one kind of desirable enjoyment which cannot otherwise be had in the city at all.

But even if it were highly debatable, in the abstract on academic grounds, whether a park of the size and situation of Central Park should be dominantly architectural in treatment, that has little bearing on the practical case.

Here is a great and beautiful and useful park of its own kind, a great work of art born of a period otherwise peculiarly unfruitful in great works of art. As such it is a heritage to be sedulously preserved, quite regardless of whether or not it is the particular kind of artistic endeavor to which any given succeeding generation would turn on its own initiative. One does not destroy a Titian or a Rembrandt because one feels more fully in sympathy with the work of John Sargent or of Cazin.

The Future of Central Park.

How far Central Park is to bring an adequate return to the people in the future for all that it has cost, is costing, and will cost, turns mainly on the extent to which the City of New York can overcome the besetting weakness of American democracy,—ineffectiveness of political administration.

It will turn mainly, as it has in the past, upon the extent to which successive administrations realize the importance, and apply themselves effectively to the use, of the second and third of the absolute essentials to the attainment of the end for which Central Park was created. Those two essentials may be restated as: on the one hand, the persistent and adequate management, control, education, and discipline of the people using the complex and delicate instrument which the Park is, so as to make that use socially beneficial as well as individually pleasant, and so as to minimize the physically destructive and socially degrading incidents of that use; and, on the other hand, the persistent, unremitting, and adequate maintenance and renewal of the vulnerable physical elements of the Park and of the accompanying artistic qualities, so as to keep it at a pitch approximating that which would give the maximum returns in public value in proportion to its total annual cost, including the tens of millions of dollars of fixed charges on the investment.

The history of political effectiveness in pursuit of social benefits has been very checkered in New York as in other American cities. In connection with Central Park it has reached, for limited periods, remarkably high levels of foresight and wisdom and tolerably good standards of efficiency, and at other times has fallen very low. It can hardly be said that it shows any decided trend, unless it is away from a more striking alternation of good and bad toward a more nearly continuous and rather inferior mediocrity. At present there seems to be an upward trend and there is now reasonable prospect of much-needed physical rehabilitation in the Park, especially of its long-suffering vegetation.

If only the continuing maintenance of the Park and the management and control of its use by the public can again be put on a reasonably adequate fiscal and administrative basis, it may be predicted with some confidence that the Park can and will be restored to a condition effectively serving essentially the same purposes as those for which it was created, and by essentially the same means as its designers conceived to be most effective for those purposes.

PART II. SELECTED PAPERS OF
FREDERICK LAW OLMSTED AND CALVERT VAUX
RELATING TO CENTRAL PARK

CHAPTER I

THE GENERAL DESIGN

We fortunately have from the designers not only their original explanatory report which accompanied the winning plan, reprinted ten years later with their notes as to progress and changes, but also their review of the design in 1872, after an attempt had been made by the Tweed administration to alter many details essential to the integrity of the Park. This document of 1872 is more illuminating regarding the designers' conception of the Park Plan than any other single paper. It contains the answer as to WHY NUMEROUS SPECIAL FEATURES PROPOSED TO BE INTRODUCED INTO THE PARK *in its seventy years of existence* ARE ENCROACHMENTS, *alien to the spirit of the Park as a unified work of art and destructive to the purposes for which it was formed.*

In attempting to understand what lay back of the designers' conception of a park for the City of New York, it is particularly interesting to include here an early definition of the word park *which occurs in the Olmsted & Vaux report to the Commissioners of Prospect Park (1866):*

"The word park has different significations, but that in which we are now interested has grown out of its application centuries ago, simply to hunting grounds; the choicest lands for hunting grounds being those in which the beasts of the chase were most happy, and consequently most abundant, sites were chosen for them, in which it was easy for animals to turn from rich herbage to clear water, from warm sunlight to cool shade; that is to say, by preference, ranges of well-watered dale-land, broken by open groves and dotted with spreading trees, undulating in surface, but not rugged. Gay parties of pleasure occasionally met in these parks, and when these meetings occurred the enjoyment otherwise obtained in them was found to be increased. Hence, instead of mere hunting lodges and hovels for game-keepers, extensive buildings and other accommodations, having frequently a festive character, were after a time provided within their enclosures. Then it was found that people took pleasure in them without regard to the attractions of the chase, or of conversation and this pleasure was

perceived to be, in some degree, related to their scenery, and in some degree to the peculiar manner of association which occurred in them; and this was also found to be independent of intellectual gifts, tranquilizing and restorative to the powers most tasked in ordinary social duties, and stimulating only in a healthy and recreative way to the imagination. Hence, after a time, parks began to be regarded and to be maintained with reference, more than any thing else, to the convenient accommodation of numbers of people, desirous of moving for recreation among scenes that should be gratifying to their taste or imagination.

"In the present century, not only have the old parks been thus maintained, but many new parks have been formed with these purposes exclusively in view, especially within and adjoining considerable towns and it is upon our knowledge of these latter that our simplest conception of a town park is founded. It is from experience in these that all our ideas of parks must spring."

In 1893, writing to Mrs. Rensselaer, Mr. Olmsted said: "I have had some professional responsibility for close upon a hundred public grounds, but I am not accustomed to class more than twenty of these as 'parks,' reserving that term for places distinguished not for trees or for groups and masses of trees, or for flowers or statues, or roads or bridges, or for collections of these and other fine things, nor for landscapes as painters use the term, nor for anything related to what the word garden formerly meant, and in common popular use means now. I reserve the [word park for places with breadth and space enough, and with all other needed qualities to justify the application to what you find in them of the word scenery, or of the word landscape in its older and more radical sense, which is much the same as that of scenery." [1]

[1] ED. NOTE: Mr. Olmsted then adds a comment of special interest to landscape architects: "(By the way, do you know that Sir Walter Scott protested against the introduction of the word landscape-gardening as likely to confuse two distinct arts: that is to say, the art of gardening and the art of landscape or scenery–making? And, by the way again, did not Milton use the word architecture for the working out of the divine design for the heavens? Architecture is not rightly to be limited to works of buildings. Gardening is rightly to be limited to garden work, which work does not conveniently include that, for instance, of exposing great ledges, damming streams, making lakes, tunnels, bridges, terraces and canals.)" Cf. p. 74, *ante*.

THE PAPERS INCLUDED IN THIS CHAPTER ARE:

Description of a Plan for the Improvement of Central Park (by) *"Greensward" (F. L. Olmsted and Calvert Vaux). New York, 1858. Reprinted with notes as to progress, 1868.—The Particulars of Construction (and planting) which originally accompanied this report may be found in Chapters II and IV.*

Report of Special Committee on Plan, Board of Commissioners of Central Park. May 10, 1858. (Doc. No. 2).—A review of the "Greensward" Plan.

Report as to certain Proposed Modifications in the Plan. To Board from Olmsted and Vaux. May 31, 1858. (Doc. No. 5).—A defense of the "Greensward" Plan against subversive amendments.

A Review of Recent Changes, by the Landscape Architects, 1872. Appendix B, 2nd Annual Report, D. P. P.

‡ *Two letters to the President of the Department of Public Parks from F. L. O., 1886.—A later review of the design.*

In addition to the papers given in this chapter, on questions of the general design, see also Part I, Chapter IV, for passages selected as especially explanatory of the designers' ideals; and Part II, Chapters IV, VII, and XII, for general considerations brought forward in connection with specific improvements proposed or destructive changes averted.

‡ Previously unpublished.

DESCRIPTION OF A PLAN FOR THE IMPROVEMENT OF THE CENTRAL PARK, "GREENSWARD," 1858

(As reprinted, 1868)

Topographical suggestions

A general survey of the ground allotted to the park, taken with a view to arrive at the leading characteristics which present themselves as all-important to be considered in adapting the actual situation to its purpose, shows us, in the first place, that it is very distinctly divided into two tolerably equal portions, which, for convenience sake, may be called the upper and lower parks.

The upper park

The horizon lines of the upper park are bold and sweeping and the slopes have great breadth in almost every aspect in which they may be contemplated. As this character is the highest ideal that can be aimed at for a park under any circumstances, and as it is in most decided contrast to the confined and formal lines of the city it is desirable to interfere with it, by cross-roads and other constructions, as little as possible. Formal planting and architectural effects, unless on a very grand scale, must be avoided; and as nearly all the ground between the Reservoir and 106th Street (west of the Boston road) is seen in connection, from any point within itself, a unity of character should be studiously preserved in all the gardening details.

The lower park

The lower park is far more heterogeneous in its character[1] and

[1] ED. NOTE: The following selection from the Annual Report of the Commissioners of Central Park for 1858, "Topography of the Site—The Lower Park," will give the reader some idea of the condition of the Park lands in 1856 and 1857 prior to the adoption of the "Greensward" plan.—

"When purchased by the city, the southern portion of the site was already a part of its straggling suburbs, and a suburb more filthy, squalid and disgusting can hardly be imagined. A considerable number of its inhabitants were engaged in occupations which are nuisances in the eye of the law, and forbidden to be carried on so near the city. They were accordingly followed at night in wretched hovels, half hidden among the rocks, where, also, heaps of cinders, brick-bats, potsherds, and other rubbish, were deposited by those who had occasion to remove them from the city. During the autumn of 1857, three hundred dwellings were removed or demolished, by the Commissioners of the Central Park, together with several factories, and numerous 'swill-milk' and hog-feeding establishments. Large tracts partially covered with stagnant water were superficially drained, and 10,000

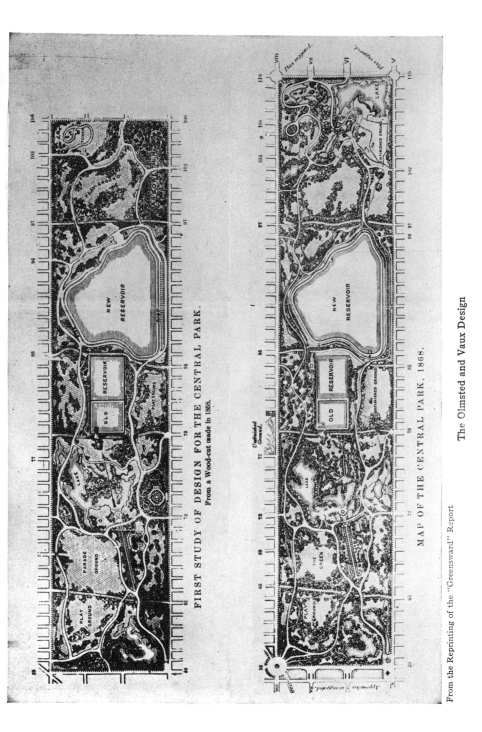

FIRST STUDY OF DESIGN FOR THE CENTRAL PARK.

From a Wood-cut made in 1858.

MAP OF THE CENTRAL PARK, 1868.

From the Reprinting of the "Greensward" Report

The Olmsted and Vaux Design

will require a much more varied treatment. The most important feature in its landscape is the long rocky and wooded hill-side lying immediately south of the Reservoir. Inasmuch as beyond this point there do not appear to be any leading natural characteristics of similar consequence in the scenery, it will be important to draw as much attention as possible to this hill-side, to afford facilities for rest and leisurely contemplation upon the rising ground opposite, and to render the lateral boundaries of the park in its vicinity as inconspicuous as possible. The central and western portion of the lower park is an irregular table-land; the eastern is composed of a series of graceful undulations, suggesting lawn or gardenesque treatment. In the extreme south we find some flat alluvial meadow; but the general character of the ground is rugged and there are several bold, rocky bluffs, that help to give individuality to this part of the composition.

Such being the general suggestions that our survey has afforded, it becomes necessary to consider how the requirements of the Commissioners, as given in their instructions, may be met with the least sacrifice of the characteristic excellencies of the ground.

Preliminary considerations

Up to this time, in planning public works for the city of New York, in no instance has adequate allowance been made for its increasing population and business; not even in the case of the Croton Aqueduct, otherwise so well considered. The City-Hall,

---

cart loads of loose stone taken from the surface and conveyed to the borders of the Park, furnishing materials for the construction, during the winter, of the present enclosing wall. . . .

"Even after the removal of the buildings of all kinds, and the drainage of the pools, the lower park still presented a most confused and unsightly appearance. Before it had been taken for the Park, the grading of streets through and across it had been commenced, and the rude embankments and ragged rock-excavations thus created, added much to the natural irregularities of its surface. A swampy valley . . . extended from the corner of Sixty-fourth street and Eighth avenue to the corner of Fifty-ninth street and Fifth avenue. A similar valley . . . extended from the junction of Seventy-seventh street and Eighth avenue to that of Seventy-fourth street and Fifth avenue. Between Sixty-seventh and Seventy-second streets, and adjoining Fifth avenue, was a tract . . . of ten acres, moderately smooth, and used as a pasture and market garden. A similar tract . . . of nearly equal dimensions, lay midway between the last mentioned one and the west side of the Park. Both tracts were rocky, and a portion of the smaller was a bog.

"The remainder of the lower park was made up of low hills and hillocks, the rock of which they were chiefly composed everywhere cropping out, sometimes boldly, more generally barely breaking through the soil, not unfrequently with a considerable surface, nearly flat, in the depressions of which a few meagre shrubs and grasses struggled for existence. With the exception of portions of the two swampy valleys and the two ten-acre tracts above mentioned, and about three acres on Sixty-sixth street near Sixth avenue, there was not an acre in which the great underlying ledge of gneiss rock did not, in some form, thrust itself above the surface."

the best architectural work in the State, and built to last for centuries, does not at this time afford facilities for one-third the business for which it was intended. The present Post-Office, expensively fitted up some ten years ago, no longer answers its purpose, and a new one of twice its capacity is imperatively demanded. The Custom-House, expressly designed for permanence and constructed to that end at enormous expense less than twenty years ago, is not half large enough to accommodate the present commerce of the city.

The explanation of this apparently bad calculation is mainly given with the fact that, at every census since that of 1800[1] the city's rate of increase has been found to be overrunning the rate previously established.

A wise forecast of the future gave the proposed park the name of Central. Our present chief magistrate, who can himself remember market-gardens below Canal street, and a post-and-rail fence on the north side of City-Hall park, warned his coadjutors, in his inaugural message, to expect a great and rapid movement of population toward the parts of the island adjoining the Central Park. A year hence five city railroads will bring passengers as far up as the park, if not beyond it. Recent movements to transfer the steamboat landings and railroad stations, although as yet unsuccessful, indicate changes we are soon to expect.

The 17,000 lots withdrawn from use for building purposes in the park itself, will greatly accelerate the occupation of the adjoining land. Only twenty years ago Union Square was "out of town"; twenty years hence, the town will have enclosed the Central Park. Let us consider, therefore, what will at that time be satisfactory, for it is then that the design will have to be really judged.

No longer an open suburb, our ground will have around it a continuous high wall of brick, stone, and marble.[2] The adjoining shores will be lined with commercial docks and warehouses; steamboat and ferry landings, railroad stations, hotels, theatres, factories, will be on all sides of it and above it; all which our park must be made to fit.

The demolition of Columbia College, and the removal of the cloistral elms which so long enshadowed it; the pertinacious demand for a division of Trinity churchyard; the numerous instances in which our old graveyards have actually been broken up; the indirect concession of the most important space in the City-Hall park for the purposes of a thoroughfare and the further contraction it is now likely to suffer; together with the constant enormous expenditure of the city and sacrifices of the citizens, in the straightening and widening of streets, are all familiar facts, that teach us a lesson of the most pressing importance in our present duty. To its application we give the first place in our planning.

[1] ED. NOTE: Misprinted *1860* in the text of 1868.

[2] ED. NOTE: The first report on the Central Park, 1856, mentions the "superb views" from high places in the Park.

The transverse roads

Our instructions call for four transverse roads.   Each of these will be the sole line of communication between one side of the town and the other, for a distance equal to that between Chambers street and Canal street.   If we suppose but one crossing of Broadway to be possible in this interval, we shall realize what these transverse roads are destined to become.   Inevitably they will be crowded thoroughfares, having nothing in common with the park proper, but every thing at variance with those agreeable sentiments which we should wish the park to inspire.   It will not be possible to enforce the ordinary police regulations of public parks upon them. They must be constantly open to all the legitimate traffic of the city, to coal carts and butchers' carts, dust carts and dung carts; engine companies will use them, those on one side the park rushing their machines across it with frantic zeal at every alarm from the other; ladies and invalids will need special police escort for crossing them, as they do in lower Broadway: eight times in a single circuit of the park will they oblige a pleasure drive or stroll to encounter a turbid stream of coarse traffic, constantly moving at right angles to the line of the park movement.

The transverse roads will also have to be kept open, while the park proper will be useless for any good purpose, after dusk, for experience has shown that even in London, with its admirable police arrangements, the public cannot be secured safe transit through large open spaces of ground after nightfall.

Foreign examples

These public thoroughfares will then require to be well lighted at the sides, and, to restrain marauders pursued by the police from escaping into the obscurity of the park, strong fences or walls, six or eight feet high, will be necessary.   A public road thus guarded passes through the Regent's Park of London, at the Zoological Gardens.   It has the objection that the fence, with its necessary gates at every crossing of the park drives, roads or paths, is not only a great inconvenience but a disagreeable object in the landscape.

To avoid a similar disfigurement an important passage across the garden of the Tuileries is closed by gates at night, forcing all who would otherwise use it to go a long distance to the right or left.

The form and position of the Central Park are peculiar in respect to this difficulty, and such that precedent in dealing with it is rather to be sought in the long and narrow Boulevards of some of the old Continental cities of Europe, than in the broad parks with which, from its area in acres, we are most naturally led to compare it.   The Boulevards referred to are, however, generally used only as walks, not as drives or places of ceremony.   In frequent instances, in order not to interrupt their alleys, the streets crossing them are made in the form of causeways and carried over on high arches. This, of course, destroys all landscape effect, since it puts an abrupt limit to the view. Some expedient is needed for the Central Park by which the convenience of the arrangement may be retained, while the objection is as far as possible avoided.

The present design

In the plan herewith offered to the Commission, each of the transverse roads is intended to be sunk so far below the general surface that the park drives may, at every necessary point of intersection, be carried entirely over it, without any obvious elevation or divergence from their most attractive routes. The banks on each side will be walled up to the height of about seven feet, thus forming the protective barrier required by police considerations, and a little judicious planting on the tops or slopes of the banks above these walls will, in most cases, entirely conceal both the roads and the vehicles moving in them, from the view of those walking or driving in the park.[1]

If the position which has just been taken with regard to the necessity for permanently open transverse thoroughfares is found to be correct, it follows necessarily that the 700 acres allowed to the new park must, in the first instance, be subdivided definitely, although it is to be hoped to some extent invisibly, into five separate and distinct sections, only connected here and there by roads crossing them; and if the plan of making these thoroughfares by sunken roads is approved, they will, as it appears to us, from the nature of the ground, have to be laid down somewhat on the lines indicated on the plan. If so, the problem to be solved is narrowed in its dimensions, and the efforts of the designer can be no longer directed to an arrangement that shall agreeably use up the space of 700 acres allotted, but to making some plan that shall have unity of effect as a whole, and yet avoid collision in its detailed features with the interesecting lines thus suggested. It is on this basis that the present plan has, in the first instance, been founded. If the sunken transverse roads were omitted, the design would not be less complete in character; but it is, on the other hand, so laid out that the transverse thoroughfares do not interfere materially with its general or detailed effect.

Surface transverse roads

After having planned the park drives agreeably to these views, we observed that three additional moderately direct, transverse roads had occurred. These will afford facilities for crossing the park to all vehicles of classes which it will be proper to admit upon them, such as hackney coaches, and all private carriages; and thus seven transverse roads will be really provided to be used during daylight. Four roads will probably be amply adequate for the

[1] NOTE, 1868.—In execution, the four traffic roads have been carried through the Park in the manner suggested.

night traffic needing to cross the park; but it might be questioned if this number would be sufficient during the day.

The exterior

As it is not proposed that the park proper shall be lighted at night, it is well worth while to consider if the advantages which it offers as an interesting promenade may not yet in some way be obtained at night.

Fifth Avenue

The ordinance that regulates the width of Fifth avenue, provides for an open space of fifteen feet on each side, exclusive of that required for the sidewalks and the roadway; consequently, a space of thirty feet in width is already prepared for on this side of the park for its whole length.

Eighth Avenue Railroad

On the Eighth avenue a similar arrangement may probably be effected, and as there would be no occasion to back up carts against the park side of the avenue, it is feasible to carry the railway tracks close to the edge of the walk, thus leaving a clear space for carriages on the opposite or building side and making the access to the park side more clean and convenient.[1]

Fifty-Ninth and One Hundred and Sixth streets

On the southern boundary it is not desirable to reduce the already moderate width of the carriage way. It is, on the other hand, a question whether, as the streets and the park both, in reality, are the property of one owner—the City—this street should not be ·treated in a similar manner. It will, from its position, be in time rather crowded with traffic, and will, therefore, have some claim to be widened on this ground alone. As a question of beauty of arrangement for the park itself, however, it is conceived that if by this management a more stately character than could otherwise be obtained would be secured to the outer boundaries of the park, it would be cheaply purchased at the sacrifice of a few feet at the south end, off its present length of two and a half miles. In riding along any of the avenues, the eye cannot fail to be struck with the great difference in dignity of effect, between such streets as Fourteenth and Twenty-Third, and those intermediate, and it would be a matter of regret that a source of effect so easily obtained, should be lost in connection with the grand approaches to the park, because it does not happen that its boundaries at present coincide with the wide streets laid out on the working plan upon which the city is being constructed. If, moreover, the advantage of the evening promenade is allowed to be of importance, we

---

[1] NOTE, 1868.—The sidewalks have been treated in execution as proposed, but the suggestion in regard to the railroad has not yet been carried out. In the Brooklyn Park however the intended arrangement has been fully realized.

should be sorry to dispense with this section of it, which would be the only portion having a direct communication from the Sixth and Seventh avenues.

Treatment of boundary lines

For the purpose of concealing the houses on the opposite side of the street, from the park, and to insure an umbrageous horizon line, it is proposed, as will be seen in the plan, to plant a line of trees all around the outer edge of the park, between the sidewalk and the roadway.[1] On approaching the Fifth and Eighth avenue entrances, this line of trees along Fifty-Ninth street will come prominently into view, and have a handsome effect, if the street is widened; but if Fifty-Ninth street is allowed to remain as a narrow street, it is feared that it will be difficult to prevent this boundary line of the park from having a contracted and somewhat mean appearance. Hence, we have thought it proper in our plan to assume the advantage and practicability of this arrangement to be conceded; but, if this should not be the case, it will be readily perceived that it forms no essential part of our design.[2]

On the space originally provided for a sidewalk on the park side of the streets and avenues, there will, in any case, be room for such a line of trees as we have proposed. The continuous exterior mall should by no means be given up, even though it cannot be made in all parts as wide as we have proposed. At many points, and frequently for quite long distances, it will form an elevated terrace, commanding extensive views over the park, of the most interesting character, and a mere parapet-wall three or four feet high, will, in such cases, be all-sufficient for the safety of promenaders and the protection of the park from interlopers.

Fifth Avenue entrance

The finest approach from the city is certain to be along the Fifth avenue, and it has been thought necessary to view with special care the angle of the park first reached from this direction, because it will be generally felt that immediate entrance should be had at this point.[3]

The grade of the avenue has been established so high that considerable filling-in would be required to avoid a rapid descent, but directly this single difficulty is overcome, the ground beyond has great advantages for the purpose of a dignified entrance to the park. A massive rock (*see No. 1 on Folded Map*) that will be found

---

[1] NOTE, 1868.—This feature of the design has been partially carried into execution and is in progress from year to year, as the street and avenue grades become settled.

[2] NOTE, 1868.—In execution, 59th street has been treated as here recommended.

[3] NOTE, 1868.—We submitted a plan for a much needed amplification in this approach during the earlier stages of the work, but the suggestion has not yet been acted on. (ED. NOTE: see Part II, Chapter VI, p. 392.)

in connection with this requisite made-ground, offers a sufficiently large natural object to occupy the attention, and will at once reduce the artificial feature to a position of minor importance.   If, next, we stand upon that portion of the rock which (a little north of the large cherry-tree) is at grade-height, we find that there is another rocky hillock (*see No. 2 on Folded Map*) within a short distance, in the direction a visitor to the park would most naturally pursue—that is to say, towards the centre of the park.   This can be easily reached by slightly raising the intermediate ground; by then sweeping to the right, the natural conformation of the surface offers an easy ascent (by the existing cart-way over Sixty-Third street) to a plateau (two rods west of the powder-house), directly connected with the extensive table-land which occupies the centre of the lower half of the park.

From this plateau (now occupied mainly by the nursery) a view is had of nearly all the park up to the Reservoir, in a northerly direction; and on looking to the south and west, we perceive that there are natural approaches from these directions, which suggest that we have arrived at a suitable point of concentration for all approaches which may be made from the lower part of the city to the interior of the park.

The Avenue

Vista Rock (*see No. 3 on Folded Map*), the most prominent point in the landscape of the lower park, here first comes distinctly into view, and fortunately in a direction diagonal to the boundary lines, from which it is desirable to withdraw attention in every possible way.   We therefore accept this line of view as affording an all-sufficient motive to our further procedure.   Although averse on general principles to a symmetrical arrangement of trees,[1] we consider it an essential feature of a metropolitan park that it should contain a grand promenade, level, spacious, and thoroughly shaded. This result can in no other way be so completely arrived at as by an avenue, which in itself even, exclusive of its adaptability for this purpose, contains so many elements of grandeur and magnificence, that it should be recognized as an essential feature in the arrange-

[1] Ed. Note: From what is said a few lines below about the inherent grandeur and magnificence of an avenue, and from the frequent deliberate use of symmetrically planted trees in later work both by Mr. Olmsted and by Mr. Vaux, it does not appear that they were, precisely speaking, "averse on *general principles* to a symmetrical arrangement of trees."   It probably would be more exact to say, first, that they were averse on general principles to the introduction of symmetrical (or other conspicuously formal) arrangements of trees among the elements of naturalistic scenery, unless done with great discrimination and restraint, with a clear appreciation of the contrast in esthetic character involved, and in pursuit of some well conceived higher unity of design; and, second, that they had a prevailing personal tendency (in harmony with the wide-spread fashion established by the English school of landscape gardening, in the previous century) to prefer the beauty of natural and naturalistic scenery, while clearly and ardently appreciating the greater fitness and appropriate beauty of formal arrangements under special conditions.—F. L. O., Jr.

ment of any large park. The objection to which it is liable is that it divides the landscape into two parts, and it is therefore desirable to decide at what point this necessity can be submitted to with the least sacrifice to the general effect. The whole topographical character of the park is so varied, so suggestive of natural treatment, so picturesque, so individual in its characteristics, that it would be contrary to common sense to make the avenue its leading feature, or to occupy any great extent of ground for this special purpose. It must be subservient to the general design, if that general design is to be in accordance with the present configuration of the ground, and we have therefore thought that it should, so far as possible, be complete in itself, and not become a portion of any of the leading drives. There is no dignity of effect to be produced by driving through an avenue a quarter of a mile long, unless it leads to, and becomes an accessory of, some grand architectural structure, which itself, and not the avenue is the ultimatum of interest. An avenue for driving in should be two or three miles long, or it will be petite and disappointing. We have therefore thought it most desirable to identify the idea of the avenue with the promenade, for which purpose a quarter of a mile is not insufficient, and we can find no better place for such a grand mall, or open air hall of reception, as we desire to have, than the ground before us.[1]

The Promenade

In giving it this prominent position, we look at it in the light of an artificial structure on a scale of magnitude commensurate with the size of the park, and intend in our design that it should occupy the same position of relative importance in the general arrangement of the plan that a mansion should occupy in a park prepared for private occupation. The importance that is justly connected with the idea of the residence of the owner in even the most extensive private grounds, finds no parallel in a public park, however small, and we feel that the interest of the visitor, who, in the best sense is the true owner in the latter case, should concentrate on features of natural, in preference to artificial, beauty. Many elegant buildings may be appropriately erected for desirable purposes in a public park, but we conceive that all such architectural structures should be confessedly subservient to the main idea, and that nothing artificial should be obtruded on the view as an ultimatum of interest. The idea of the park itself should always be uppermost in the mind of the beholder. Holding this general principle to be of considerable importance, we have preferred to place the avenue where it can be terminated appropriately at one end with a landscape attraction of considerable extent, and to relieve the south entrance with only so much architectural treatment as may give the idea that due regard has been paid to the adornment of this principal promenade, without interfering with its real character.

[1] NOTE, 1868.—In execution, this avenue has been planted with elms, as suggested later in the report, and is now called "The Mall."

This avenue may be considered the central feature in our plan for laying out the lower park, and the other details of arrangement are more or less designed in connection with it.

Parade ground

To the west is the parade ground, containing about 25 acres, that may, at a moderate expense, be levelled and made suitable for its purpose;[1] and also some eight or ten acres of broken ground, that will be more or less available for military exercises. Such a broad open plane of well-kept grass would be a refreshing and agreeable feature in the general design, and would bear to be of much greater extent than is here shown, if the lot were of a different shape; but under the circumstances, 25 acres seems as much as can well be spared for the purpose. A military entrance from Eighth avenue is proposed to be made at Sixty-Ninth street, which has been already, at considerable expense, cut through the rock at this point, and offers a suggestion for a picturesque approach, with a portcullis gate, and with the main park drive carried over it at a higher level.

Playground

The natural southern boundary of the table-land occupied by the parade ground is a rapid slope that occurs about in the line of Sixty-Sixth street; in this slope it is proposed to sink one of the transverse roads; and on a level plane below it, stretching to the south, a playground about ten acres in extent is located, as indicated on the plan. We have thought it very desirable to have a cricket ground of this size near the southern boundary of the park, and not far from the Sixth and Eighth avenue railroads, which offer the most rapid means of access from the lower part of the city.[2] In this playground sites are suggested for two buildings of moderate dimensions: one for visitors to view the games, which would be appropriately located on a large rock (*see No. 4 on Folded Map*) that overlooks the ground; and the other (*see No. 5 on Folded Map*) for the players, at the entrance from the transverse road, by which an exit could be obtained from the playground after the other gates were closed.[3] Only one mass of rock of any considerable magnitude would require to be blasted out for the purpose of adapting this ground to its intended purpose; its position is indicated on the plan by a red cross, and the object of its removal will be seen on examination. This part of the design is illustrated in study No. 2. The ground at the southwest corner of the park it is pro-

[1] NOTE, 1868.—A Parade ground was demanded by the schedule of instructions furnished to competitors. In execution this open space under the name of "The Green" has been retained as prominent feature of the design, but has not been and is not intended to be used for military exercises.

[2] [NOTE, 1868].—The playground has been arranged as here recommended.

[3] NOTE, 1868.—The foundation for this building was laid during the last season.

posed to fill in sufficiently to make, on the plan indicated, an agreeable Eighth avenue entrance.

The lower lake

To the south-east of the promenade, and between the Fifth and Sixth avenue entrances, it is proposed to form a lake of irregular shape, and with an area of 8 or 9 acres. This arrangement has been suggested by the present nature of the ground, which is low and somewhat swampy. It is conceived that, by introducing such an ornamental sheet of water into the composition at this point, the picturesque effect of the bold bluffs that will run down to its edge and overhang it, must be much increased;[1] and that by means of such a natural boundary, this rocky section of the park will be rendered more retired and attractive as a pleasant walk or lounge. The proposed effect of this part of the design, as it will appear from the Fifth avenue entrance, is indicated on study No. 1.[2]

The Arsenal

To the south-east of the promenade will be found that portion of the park in which the present Arsenal (*see No. 6 on Folded Map*) is situated. This ground is undulating and agreeable in its character, and will offer pleasant opportunities for shady walks. The Arsenal itself, although at present a very unattractive structure, and only tolerably built, contains a great deal of room in a form that adapts it very well to the purposes of a museum. It is proposed, therefore, to improve its external appearance so far as may be necessary, without changing its shape or usefulness, or going to any great expense; and as it occurs rather near the Fifth avenue entrance, and is, therefore, likely to occupy too considerable a share of attention if left exposed to view from the south, it is intended, as early as possible, to plant in its vicinity forest-trees, calculated to become handsome specimens of large size, and that will, after a few years, prevent the museum from attracting an undue share of attention in the general landscape.

Music-Hall

To the east of the promenade, there will be a half-mile stretch of lawn and trees extending from the vicinity of Fifty-Ninth street to Seventy-Second street, and this will be the dress ground of the park; and in a prominent position on this ground, and immediately

---

[1] NOTE, 1868.—An improvement of the soil and of the skylines of this rocky section, contemplated at the time the plan was made, was last year carried into execution, by means of earth filling on the more prominent summit levels.

[2] NOTE, 1868.—The original requirements of the Commission in regard to boundary and expense necessitated, in the first study, a cramped and unsatisfactory arrangement of the entrances on Fifty-ninth street. We have since made studies for the amplification of each of the principal approaches, and the necessary legislation in regard to the entrance at 8th Avenue and 59th street having been obtained at the instance of the property owners in the neighborhood, this improvement is shown on the map of the Park, dated 1868.

"GREENSWARD" SKETCH NO. 1

(Map showed this view was taken from "Point A," near Fifth Avenue and 59th Street)

"PRESENT OUTLINES"

From photostat of sketch   Retouched by W. B. Van Ingen

"EFFECT PROPOSED"

The Lake in the Lower Park

connected with the grand mall, the site for a music-hall (*see No. 7 on Folded Map*), called for in our instructions, has been set apart; and we have suggested that a palm-house and large conservatory should be added to this music-hall whenever it is built.[1]

This site is recommended because it is conspicuous without being obtrusive, and is easy of access from the promenade and from one of the leading avenue entrances; while, to the north, it commands from its terraces and verandas the finest views that are to be obtained in the lower part of the park. It also overlooks the site which we have selected as most appropriate for the flower-garden (*see No. 8 on Folded Map*) called for in our instructions; and this we consider a decided advantage, as the most attractive view of a flower-garden is from some point above it, that will enable the visitor to take in at a glance a general idea of the effect aimed at.

The Flower Garden

The garden is located in low ground to the northeast of the promenade, and close upon the line of Fifth avenue, the grade of which opposite the centre of the garden is about twenty feet above the present level of the ground; this, for the reasons above stated, we consider a desideratum, and have suggested that over the arcade or veranda that we propose should be built against the east wall of the park in connection with the garden, a structure (*see No. 9 on Folded Map*) should be erected, with an entrance on a level with the avenue, so as to give an opportunity for a view of the garden, both from this level and from another story above it. This idea is not, of course, necessary to the design, and the sketch submitted is merely a suggestion to show what may be done at some future time.[2]

The plan of the flower-garden itself is geometrical; and it is surrounded by an irregular and less formal plantation of shrubs, that will serve to connect it with the park proper. In the centre it is proposed to construct a large basin (*see No. 10 on Folded Map*) for a fountain, with a high jet; other smaller jets are prepared for, as indicated; and, in connection with the north wall, which will be somewhat below the surface of the ground beyond, it is proposed to arrange some such wall fountain as the celebrated one of Trevi. The water for this fountain will, in the present case, be supplied from the skating pond and also from the Reservoir, and will fall into a semi-circular marble basin, with a paved floor. Such a fountain is out of place unless it can be furnished with an ample supply of

[1] NOTE, 1868.—This site is now occupied by a building which we designed for a Ladies' Restaraunt, sites on a somewhat larger scale being reserved for a music-hall and conservatory, which yet remain to be erected.

[2] NOTE, 1868.—While the construction of the park was in progress Messrs. Parsons & Co., who held a contract granted by the Commissioners, employed us to develop this general idea in the form of a two-story glass building, of which the upper section is the conservatory proper and the lower portion is proposed to be used for the exhibition and sale of flowers, but the design has not yet been executed.

water; but, in the position assigned to it on our plan, there will be no difficulty in procuring all the water that can be required for the purpose: and it seems desirable, therefore, to take advantage of the opportunity offered, for the effect of a sculptured fountain of this sort is quite distinct from that produced by a jet d'eau.

A colored plan of this part of the design is illustrated to an enlarged scale on study No. 11.

To the north-west of the promenade is a slope, offering an appropriate site for a summer-house (*see No. 11 on Folded Map*), that in such a situation should have some architectural pretension; and further to the west, near Eighth avenue, is a stretch of tableland, terminated by an abrupt rocky descent, that suggests itself as well suited for a Casino or refreshment house.[1]

From the upper end of the promenade the rocky hill-side to the north, surmounted by Vista Rock at its highest point, comes in full view; and on this rock it will be generally conceded a tower (*see No. 12 on Folded Map*) should be erected—but by no means a large one, or the whole scale of the view will be destroyed.[2] To the north and north-west of the promenade, a tract of low ground is proposed to be converted into the skating pond called for in our instructions; and the picturesque scenery between Vista Rock and the promenade will thus be heightened in effect, when seen from the south side of this lake, of about 14 acres. A terrace approach (*see No. 13 on Folded Map*), as shown on the plan, and on study No. 3, is proposed, from the avenue to the water.[3] This feature, although by no means absolutely necessary, would add much to the general effect, and could be introduced at any future time, if it is preferred at present to treat the ground occupied by it in a less artificial style.

Immediately in the vicinity of Vista Rock is the south wall of the present reservoir. This wall occupies the whole of the middle of the park, and is a blank, uninteresting object, that can in no way be made particularly attractive. We have therefore, thought it necessary to bear this in mind in arranging the general plan, and have given a direction to the lines of drive leading this way from the

---

[1] NOTE, 1868. This ground still remains unimproved, it being the intention to develop the idea referred to in the report, although the plans for the structure are not yet finally decided on.

[2] NOTE, 1868.—The foundations for this work were commenced last season on a rocky promontory which formed a part of the Croton reservoir inclosure when it was expected to be bounded by street lines, but which has lately been added to the park territory, in accordance with our suggestion.

[3] NOTE, 1868.—The architectural treatment of the terrace approach has been developed in detail during the progress of the work, but much of the intended effect still remains to be realized. (ED. NOTE: Mr. J. Wrey Mould was largely responsible for the details of the terrace, while Mr. Vaux was the architect of the general terrace design. Mr. Mould served in a subordinate capacity in the architectural work of the Park for nearly ten years; and after his promotion (about 1869) remained for five years longer. He was removed in May, 1874, but later returned as Architect of the N. Y. D. P. P. Mr. Vaux said of him that his "contributions to the success of the work . . . have been continuous, original and invaluable.")

lower part of the park, that will enable them to avoid the wall of the reservoir altogether.[1] The necessity for doing this has induced us to commence diverting the lines of drive at the south end of the grand promenade, which seems to offer a sufficient reason for so doing, and to lead them afterwards on their northerly course in such a way that they may pass naturally to the east and west of the reservoir. If any drive proceeded in the direction of the line of avenue, and at once crossed the ground proposed to be occupied by the lake, the reservoir would inevitably become the terminal feature of the lower part of the park, and this would be disagreeable. The skating pond will offer a sufficiently natural barrier to this direct mode of proceeding, and will furnish a reason for locating the promenade in its proposed position, and also for terminating it where suggested; and by carrying a road along the edge of the water, an opportunity will be given to lengthen out the drive commanding the principal views in this vicinity; the lake will also help to give a retired and agreeable character to the hill-side beyond, which is well adapted for picnic parties and pleasant strolls. Even if the reservoir did not occur in its present position, the conformation of the ground is such that the roads would naturally take, to a considerable extent, the direction indicated, leaving the centre of the park undivided by a drive.

The management of the ground between the skating pond and Vista Rock[2] appears to be indicated by its form and the character of its present growth. It is well sheltered, and large masses of rock occur at intervals. The soil is moist, and altogether remarkably well adapted to what is called in Europe an American garden, that is, a ground for the special cultivation of hardy plants of the natural order Ericacæi, consisting of rhododendrons, andromedas, azaleas, kalmias, rhodoras, &c.[3] The present growth, consisting of sweet-gum, spice-bush, tulip-tree, sassafras, red-maple, black-oak, azalea, andromeda, &c., is exceedingly intricate and interesting. The ground is at present too much encumbered with stone, and with various indifferent plants.[4] By clearing these away, and carefully leaving what is valuable; by making suitable paths, planting abundantly, as above suggested, and introducing fastigiate shrubs, and evergreens occasionally, to prevent a monotony of bushes, the place may be made very charming. Where the hill-side approaches the lake, sufficient openings are proposed to be left for occasional glimpses, or more open views, of the water; and glades of fine turf are intended to occur at favorable intervals, so as to offer pleasant spots for rest and recreation.

[1] NOTE, 1868.—In execution, the lines have been carried out as here indicated, and as the trees grow up the old square reservoir is less and less thought of as an obstruction in the composition.

[2] NOTE, 1868.—The ground here referred to is now called "The Ramble."

[3] NOTE, 1868.—This suggestion has been partially realized but yet remains to be fully developed.

[4] NOTE, 1868.—Many of these which we have marked for removal, have hitherto, for various reasons, been allowed to remain.

Playground

To the east and south-east of the present reservoir, the general conformation of the surface continues to be of the same easy, undulating character as that to the east of the promenade, and can be treated in a similar manner. The whole space is intended to be occupied with stretches of well-kept turf, with fine groups and single trees, so planted that they may appear to advantage, and not crowd each other. That portion which is immediately east of the reservoir is set apart for one of the playgrounds (*see No. 14 on Folded Map*);[1] and in the strip of land between the main drive and the reservoir wall, a reserved garden (*see No. 15 on Folded Map*) is provided for, with gardener's house attached; this will be needed in connection with the flower-garden already described. On the west side of the reservoir the ground is of an irregular character, which continues past the old and new reservoirs to the upper end of the site. The spaces remaining for park use will, however, be so much contracted by the reservoir walls and embankments, that extended landscape effects are out of the question.

Winter drive

It is intended, therefore, as the soil and situation are adapted to the purpose, to arrange in this locality, a winter drive about a mile and a half in length, and to plant somewhat thickly with evergreens, introducing deciduous trees and shrubs occasionally, to relieve the monotony of effect that otherwise might occur. Large open glades of grass are introduced among these plantations of evergreens, as the effect aimed at is not so much that of a drive through a thick forest, crowded with tall spindling trees, as through a richly wooded country, in which the single trees and copses have had plenty of space for developing their distinctive characteristics to advantage.[2]

Berceau walks

Immediately south and west of the present reservoir, terraces have been already formed, and these can readily be converted into continuous arbors, or berceau walks (*see No. 16 on Folded Map*). Access will thus be provided to all the gates of the reservoir, and the wall will itself be planted out. The effect of these closely shaded walks will also, it is conceived, offer an agreeable contrast to the views obtainable from Vista Rock, in the immediate vicinity.[3]

---

[1] NOTE, 1868.—This tract of ground is now recommended as the site for the formal flower garden in connection with a group of architectural structures that will include music-hall, art galleries, horticultural and other museums, and refreshment rooms on a liberal scale; the intention of allowing military exercises on the park having been abandoned, and the Green serving the purpose of the playground above proposed.

[2] NOTE, 1868.—These plantations have been made as designed.

[3] NOTE, 1868.—The idea of the berceau walk has been carried out in execution on the south side of the reservoir. (ED. NOTE: The berceau walk of trained and clipped Hornbeam, on the model of many such walks in France and England was

Police Station

In the northern section of this locality, and in connection with one of the transverse roads, will be found the house of the Superintendent, the office of the Commission, the police station (*see No. 17 on Folded Map*), and other necessary buildings, such as stables, &c. The site is not far from the one at present occupied by the police, and is thought to be well suited for its purpose. By making a private entrance along the wall of the reservoir, the whole establishment can be immediately connected, by means of the transverse road, with the city streets, and at the same time be central and elevated without being unpleasantly prominent. It is proposed, as will be seen on the plan, to make short connections (*see No. 18 on Folded Map*) from the park roads to the transverse thoroughfare north of the present reservoir, so as to admit of visitors shortening the drive in this way if preferred.

Reservoir ride

The new reservoir, with its high banks, will take up a great deal of room in the park, and although it will offer a large sheet of water to the view, it will be at too high a level to become a landscape attraction from the ordinary drives and walks. It is suggested, therefore, that all round it a ride shall be constructed, and carefully prepared for this purpose only; and although this feature may be somewhat costly in the first instance, it is conceived that the result would be worth the outlay, for the sake of its advantages as a ride over a mile and a half in length, commanding the view of the reservoir, and uninterfered with by the regular drives, although in connection with them at different points.[1]

On the east of the new reservoir, the park is diminished to a mere passageway for connection, and it will be difficult to obtain an agreeable effect in this part of the design, unless some architectural character is given to it. It is not recommended, however, to attempt any such effect immediately, or out of the funds of the Commission, but to accept the high bank of the reservoir as a barrier to the west, for a few years; because it is thought that as soon as this part of the city is built up to any considerable extent, it will not be difficult to obtain an enriched architectural effect, appropriate to the purpose, without expense to the Commission. An arcade, 100 feet deep, could be substantially built, and the drive could be carried above this arcade on a level with the reservoir, and overlooking Fifth avenue, the remainder of the ground being filled in; and it is thought that as this arcade may be lighted from

---

suggested by Mr. Olmsted. At one time it attained a considerable degree of perfection, but its later condition is indicative of the great difficulty of successfully maintaining in American public parks any such effects as this, or pleached alleys, or trained espalier trees, which depend upon *unremitting* skilled manipulation of plants, at the proper season, for an indefinite period of years.—F. L. O., Jr.)

[1] NOTE, 1868.—In execution the design of this separate bridle road has been much amplified.

the rear, and will face a fashionable thoroughfare it will offer, at
no distant period, very valuable lots for stores, or other purposes;
and as it is a third of a mile in extent, it may be a source of revenue,
in rent, to the park fund, instead of a burden on it.[1]

Tower on Bogardus Hill

The north-westerly portion of the park, above the new reservoir, is planned very simply, in accordance with what we conceive
to be the suggestion of the ground.   The evergreen drive is continued nearly to the foot of Bogardus Hill, and then somewhat
changing its character, turns to the east.   At this point (*see No. 19
on Folded Map*) a branch road crosses a brook, that is made to ex-
pand into a pool a little below the bridge; and this road then winds
gradually to the top of the hill, which offers an available site for
some monument of public importance, that may also be used as an
observatory tower (*see No. 20 on Folded Map*).   If as is not improbable, the transatlantic telegraph is brought to a favorable issue,
while the park is in an early stage of construction, many reasons
could, we think, be urged for commemorating the event by some such
monument as the one suggested on the plan, and in study No. 9.
The picturesque effect of a spring of clear water, that already exists
in this vicinity, may be heightened, as suggested in study No. 10.
The central portion of the upper section of the park is left as
open as possible, and can be levelled so far as may be required for
the purposes of the playgrounds indicated on the plan, and on
study No. 7.   At present, it is hardly thought that it would be necessary to make the Sixth avenue entrance to the north; but its position is indicated.[2]

The Arboretum

The north-east section of the upper park is shown as an arboretum of American trees, so that every one who wishes to do so may
become acquainted with the trees and shrubs that will flourish in
the open air in the northern and middle sections of our country.
This arboretum is not intended to be formally arranged, but to
be so planned that it may present all the most beautiful features of
lawn and wood-land landscape, and at the same time preserve the
natural order of families, so far as may be practicable.   The botanical student will thus be able to find any tree or shrub without difficulty.   We have selected this tract of about 40 acres, in the upper

[1] NOTE, 1868.—In execution the simpler plan above suggested was adopted,
and the arrangement will probably remain intact for a number of years.
[2] NOTE, 1868.—The postponement of operations in this quarter was recommended because we found that the 106th street boundary of the park required a
revision, which could not, with propriety, be urged when the competition plan
was made.   The northern limit of the park was, subsequently to the date of this
report, extended from 106th to 110th streets, and so much of the original plan
as applied to the ground to the northward of that here described, was afterwards
modified in order to connect satisfactorily with our design for laying out the
additional territory which was approved by the commission in April [sic], 1863.

angle of the site, so as to interfere with the more special requirements of the park as little as possible. The spot chosen is in some measure separated from the rest of the grounds, by a ridge of land between Fifth and Sixth avenues, and includes the buildings on Mount St. Vincent. The wooden structures would be removed, and the brick chapel converted into a museum and library of botany, similar to that at Kew, but with more specific regard to landscape and decorative gardening. In the park itself there will be numerous specimens of all the trees, native or foreign, that are likely to thrive; but it is proposed to limit this particular collection to American trees, because the space necessary for a complete arboretum would occupy several hundred acres, and also because it will afford an opportunity to show the great advantage that America possesses in this respect. No other extra-tropical country could furnish one-quarter the material for such a collection. In the whole of Great Britain, for example, there are less than twenty trees, native to the island, that grow to be over 30 feet in height; while in America we have from five to six times that number. There are, indeed, already over forty species of the largest native trees standing in the park, which is nearly equivalent to the number to be found in all Europe.

It is proposed to plant from one to three examples of each species of tree on open lawn, and with sufficient space about each to allow it to attain its fullest size with unrestricted expanse of branches; the effect of each tree is also to be exhibited in masses, so as to illustrate its qualities for grouping. Space is provided to admit of at least three specimens of every native which is known to flourish in the United States north of North Carolina; also for several specimens of every shrub; these latter, however, except in particular instances, are not expected to be planted singly, but in thickets, and as underwood to the coppice masses, as may best accord with their natural habits, and be most agreeable to the eye. Further details of this part of the design will be found in the explanatory guide to the arboretum, submitted with the plan, in which the proposed arrangement of all the trees is set forth in order.[1]

The leading features of the plan have now, it is thought, been referred to. It has not been considered necessary to especially particularize the different trees proposed to be used in the various parts of the park. For the purposes of the avenue, the American elm naturally suggests itself at once as the tree to be used; and it is to be hoped that the fine effect this produces, when planted in regular lines, may in a few years be realized in the Central Park.

There is no other part of the plan in which the planting calls for particular mention, except to the south of the skating pond; an opportunity is there offered for an exhibition of semi-tropical trees, and it is intended to treat that portion of the park in the manner

[1] See pp. 335 ff., *post*.

suggested in the study. A list of the trees to be used is appended to the explanation of the arboretum.

The plan does not show any brooks, except a small one in connection with the pool at the foot of Bogardus Hill, which can always be kept full by the waste of water from the New Reservoir. Mere rivulets are uninteresting, and we have preferred to collect the ornamental water in large sheets, and to carry off through underground drains the water that at present runs through the park in shallow brooks.

As a general rule, we propose to run footpaths close to the carriage roads, which are intended to be 60 feet wide, allowing a space of four feet of turf as a barrier between the drive and the path. Other more private footpaths are introduced, but it is hardly thought that any plan would be popular in New York, that did not allow of a continuous promenade along the line of the drives, so that pedestrians may have ample opportunity to look at the equipages and their inmates.

It will be perceived that no long straight drive has been provided on the plan; this feature has been studiously avoided, because it would offer opportunities for trotting matches. The popular idea of the park is a beautiful open space, in which quiet drives, rides, and strolls may be had. This cannot be preserved if a race-course, or a road that can readily be used as a race-course, is made one of its leading attractions.

DESCRIPTIVE LIST OF SKETCHES, ETC., IN PORTFOLIO SUBMITTED
BY OLMSTED AND VAUX WITH PLAN NO. 33 ("GREEN-
SWARD") IN CENTRAL PARK COMPETITION, 1858.

1. View at the Fifth Avenue entrance. (View of Lake from Fifth Avenue and 59th Street—pencil sketches of present and proposed views.) *Reproduced opp. page 224.*

2. Lower playground. (Ball ground looking south. Sketches, present and proposed.)

3. Elm Avenue and Terrace from Vista Rock. (Looking south from Ramble towards terrace—roughly sketched, present and proposed.)

4. Across the Lake towards Vista Rock. (Northeast view from west drive opposite 74th Street towards Vista Rock—large photograph as then and small oil sketch as proposed.)

5. Across the Lake from Vista Rock. (View from Vista Rock southwest across the Lake, opposite view of No. 4—large photograph as then, small oil sketch as proposed.) *Reproduced opp. page 44.*

6. Across the Lake from below Vista Rock. (Nearer view of somewhat the same scene as above—pencil sketches, present and proposed.)

7. Looking south from Bogardus Hill. (Across meadow from high ground opposite 104th Street near Eighth Avenue—pencil sketches, present and proposed.) *Reproduced opposite.*

8. Looking east from Bogardus Hill. (View from same point east—pencil sketches, present and proposed.)

9. Bogardus Hill and Monumental Tower. (View from East Drive opposite 103rd Street looking west—pencil sketch, present, and oil, proposed.)

"GREENSWARD" SKETCH NO. 7

(Map showed this view was taken from "Point G," near Eighth Avenue and 103rd Street)

" PRESENT OUTLINES "

From photostat of sketch   Retouched by W. B. Van Ingen

" EFFECT PROPOSED "

Meadow in Upper Park

10. Winter Drive and Spring on Bogardus Hill. (Picture of spring on Bogardus Hill in pencil. Other sketch, of Winter Drive, missing.)

11. Flower garden. (2 colored views, garden arcade elevation, and plan of flower garden.)

12. Monumental Tower. (The twelfth term in the portfolio is now an oil sketch marked "View from terrace side looking towards Vista Rock showing proposed site for Ornamental water." This is probably the same as No. 12 in the printed list called "Monumental Tower" as there is no reference to any thirteenth item submitted.)

This portfolio of Sketches is now in the possession of the Park Department of the City of New York.

REPORT OF SPECIAL COMMITTEE ON PLAN[1]

(A REVIEW OF THE "GREENSWARD" PLAN, NUMBERED "33" IN THE COMPETITION)

That they have confined their attention to the important structural features of the Park, upon which an immediate determination is necessary to be had if the work is not to be altogether interrupted.

That, as respects the features of the promenade avenue, the exterior wall and the general distribution of lawn, woodland and water, the first premium plan seems to be satisfactory.

That the principal drives, so far as your Committee have had an opportunity of examining the subject, are judiciously laid down.

Two variations from them only have been proposed that would not interfere materially with the general conception of the plan.

As there is no railroad on the Seventh avenue and as it affords the most direct and convenient approach to the Park for carriages coming up Broadway, west of Fifth avenue, it is suggested that a fine carriage entrance should be provided on Fifty-ninth street, opposite Seventh avenue.[2] If this is approved, there should, for the sake of symmetry, be a similar entrance-gate opposite the Sixth avenue. But as the ground at that point does not admit of the entrance of a carriage-road, unless at a great expense, and the loss of some striking natural features, it is proposed that at present a foot-way only should be provided for, leaving it practicable to construct a carriage-road whenever in the future it shall be demanded and be so decided on, by the Commission. The corner of Fifty-ninth street and Eighth avenue is not well adapted to a carriage entrance, the turn from Broadway being an awkward one, the angles very unsymmetrical, and the ground within the Park low. At about Sixty-third street, where the ground is more elevated and an easy and direct connection can be had with the main drive, appears to be a favorable point for the main carriage entrance of the Eighth avenue; and the Committee would suggest, in case an entrance from Seventh avenue is approved, that the entrance at Sixtieth street, on plan 33 be removed to Sixty-third street.

[1] Doc. No. 2, May 10, 1858.
[2] ED. NOTE: Cf. Part II, Chap. VI.

Between Sixty-fifth and Seventy-first streets, the drive on plan 33 approaches closely to Eighth avenue. The drive would be more agreeable if between these two points it were carried with a single sweep (*see No. 21 on Folded Map*) through the interior of the Park; this would contract the parade ground, and carry the drive east of the ravine of Sixty-ninth street. Although the portcullis gate for a military entrance, through this ravine, is a striking and desirable feature, the Committee are not disposed to advise the sacrifice of what they deem to be more essential characteristics of a park, for the sake of advantages for large military displays within it; they would therefore recommend such an alternation in the course of the drive between Sixty-fifth street and Seventy-first street as is indicated in the accompanying diagram.

The Committee consider that the width of the drives, as proposed in plan 33, is greater than is necessary. They are of the opinion that the carriage-way of Fifth avenue is wide enough for a park drive, and that a single foot-path, fifteen feet wide, will be sufficient to be carried side by side with the principal drive. They are also of the opinion that a single bridle-path may, with advantage, be carried side by side with the drive for a considerable distance. As the method of constructing the carriage-road proposed in the description of plan No. 33, adapts it for riding upon at moderate speed, and as an equestrian course, forty-five feet wide, around the new Reservoir, especially prepared for fast riding, upon which no vehicles can intrude, is a part of this plan, the Committee do not deem it necessary that the bridle-road should run continuously through all parts of the Park with the drive, or that it should be wider than is necessary to accommodate four horsemen riding abreast, they recommend that the plan be made to include at least three miles of bridle-road, twenty feet in width, running generally close adjoining the principal drive, but with occasional variations as the surface may best indicate. . . .

Anticipating that considerations of public convenience and of taste will require an extension of the area of the Park to One Hundred and Tenth street, the Committee think it necessary, that before any drives are laid out in the north part of the Park, that it should be known that they are well adapted to such extension.

They recommend, therefore, that the Superintendent be requested to prepare the sketch of a plan for an extension of the Park to One Hundred and Tenth street, connecting such plan with that already presented to the Commission. The preliminary work upon the Park, so far as it can be carried on independently of a plan for laying out the ground, is believed to be completed, and it is questionable if any work is now being done which had not better be left undone.

Before any work upon the plan to be adopted by the Commission can be engaged in, some additional special surveys and working plans will need to be made; before the general drainage of the ground can be undertaken, the necessary grading and the lines of the roads and ponds must be fixed, and the tile will have to be manufactured and brought to the ground; hence it is important, as soon as possible, to definitely fix upon some part of the plan.

The Committee, therefore, recommend that plan 33 be taken as a basis of improvement, and that the Superintendent be instructed to immediately proceed in the construction of the Park, upon the supposition that its main features, with such modifications as the Committee have suggested, are to be carried out, leaving for further consideration whatever it is not necessary to an economical method of construction should be immediately determined on.

In accordance with these views, the Committee offer the following resolutions:

1. Resolved, That the Superintendent be requested to proceed forthwith to form working plans for the construction of the Park, and to stake out the principal features upon the ground.

2. Resolved, That the Superintendent be authorized to call in the service of his associate, (in design No. 33), and such other assistants, not exceeding six in number, as may be necessary to expedite the purpose of the first resolution.

3. Resolved, That the Superintendent be authorized to order tools necessary for drainage, to be made (in value not to exceed $500), and to proceed immediately with the further necessary preliminary surveys for the drainage of the Park, and that at the present time he employ the force now at his disposal in any work which may with advantage be undertaken preliminary to commencing the work of drainage.

4. Resolved, That the Executive Committee be requested to consult with the Superintendent, and to advertise as soon as possible for proposals for furnishing and laying tile necessary for drainage of the Park.

All of which is respectfully submitted.

CHARLES H. RUSSELL } *Special Committee*
ANDREW H. GREEN } *on the Plan.*

DESIGNERS' REPORT AS TO PROPOSED MODIFICATIONS IN THE PLAN[1]

ARCHITECT IN CHIEF'S OFFICE,
CENTRAL PARK, 31st May, 1858.

To the Board of Commissioners
of The Central Park:

Gentlemen:—The amendments[2] which have been referred to the Architect embrace two propositions: one to modify plan 33, and one to supersede that plan by another of an opposite character in its general conception and detailed effect.

[1] Doc. No. 5.
[2] ED. NOTE: Offered by Mr. Dillon. See Minutes, May 24, 1858, for full text.

It seems desirable to separate these two suggestions and to speak of them as distinct from each other, although it will prevent the exact order of the amendments as printed from being followed in this report.

[*Minor Modifications of the Olmsted and Vaux Plan*]

The proposed modifications to plan 33 appear to be, in the first place, No. 3 and 4, 11, 12 and 17. "Strike out the sidewalks for pedestrians on either side the Drive," "all paths for pedestrians," "the ride around the reservoir," "the flower garden," "the music hall, arcade and casino." To these propositions there is no objection, as they are omissions that will not interfere with the general construction of the Park, and may, perhaps, when the work is farther advanced, be considered and determined on to better advantage by the Commissioners.

"5. Truncate the angle formed by Fifty-ninth street with Fifth and Eighth avenues."

The reasons for avoiding in plan 33 the truncated angles in these positions were: first, that it is difficult, if not impossible, to make a dignified architectural entrance on a short truncated angle. In planning a suburban country place of limited extent, occupying an angle of two cross-roads, the idea has been developed by the writer on a small scale with a good result; but it is not recommended as a desirable arrangement for the principal entrance to a large park, because it is thought that these gateways should be designed with reference to the general architectural lines of the other buildings on the streets in which they occur. In the case of the Fifth avenue entrance, the ground suggests the course of drive proposed in plan 33, and the entrance is arranged accordingly, and is also so planned as to leave an ante-park or square outside the boundary in which carriages for hire may wait without obstruction to the thoroughfare. It is thought that many persons who do not keep carriages will be glad of an opportunity to drive in the Park at a moderate expense, and for this reason it has been proposed to introduce the vestibule or ante-Park shown on the plan. A liberally arranged Fifth avenue entrance at Fifty-ninth street on the line proposed by amendment 5, would involve the necessity of a rapid descent into the low ground shown as a lake on plan 33, or this low ground would have to be filled up for a considerable distance at very great expense, and with disadvantage to the general lines of the scenery in this part of the Park.

On the corner of Eighth avenue, the intersection of Broadway, as shown on the city map, cuts up the streets and avenues, into so many irregular three-cornered odds and ends that it was thought advisable in plan 33 to avoid the angle altogether, and to enter the Park opposite Sixtieth street. In point of economical construction, it would be nearly as feasible to make the truncated angular Eighth avenue entrance as any other short of the entrance near

Sixty-third street, proposed to the Special Committee and recommended in their report.

"6. Strike out the cross-drive running north to the commencement of the promenade." This would prevent a circuit drive through the Park, an advantage which it seems desirable to retain.

"14. Strike out the sunken transverse roads." Experience on the Park is already constantly showing the necessity for some contrivance by which direct transit may be secured across the Park for the inhabitants of the adjoining parts of the island, and much dissatisfaction is expressed with the present arrangements, the nature of which the Architect can better explain verbally.

With regard to the necessity for cross-roads that shall not interfere with the Park drives at the point of intersection, and that shall be always open, lighted at night and under the control of the city, all that can be said is included in the report on plan 33, and the designers of that plan are aware of no argument for disregarding the necessities of the case as there presented, or they would endeavor to reply to it. With regard to the detail of construction of those roads, whether they shall at all points where it is practicable be carried somewhat below the surface, or whether they shall, except at the intersections, be made surface roads as far as possible, being separated from the Park only by iron railings, is a question to be decided by a specific examination of the various circumstances of each situation. A further survey, made since the recent action of the Commission adopting plan 33, shows the feasibility and, perhaps, desirability of carrying a considerable proportion of the cross-road above the Arsenal on a level with the general surface by a slight deviation from the course represented on the map.

It is difficult to understand what advantages are proposed to be gained by amendment 14, which proposes that "passage across the Park may be made, but not with such facility of grade and level as to invite passage for purposes of trade or traffic," because such a crossroad is only called for by the necessities of trade or traffic, there being no possible objection to the introduction of pedestrians or private vehicles into any part of the Park.

With regard to the elevated wall proposed, it does not seem to offer any advantages over the plan of more easily concealed walls pertaining to the roads, indicated on plan 33.

Amendment number 16 proposes to strike out the designation for places for parade ground and play grounds. There are obvious advantages to be secured by the adoption of the proposition with regard to the parade ground. It is questionable, however, if the point of concentration for play, suggested in the lower part of the Park, should not be reserved and put in order as soon as possible; all the other situations for play grounds may conveniently be left open for further consideration.

[*Radically New Plan*]

It is difficult to form a judgment on a design for laying out a large park without any illustrative plan and a careful examination of the site with special reference to the leading features supposed to be introduced. The new design roughly indicated in the amendments Nos. 1, 2, 7, 8, 9, 13, 15, necessarily assumes, so far as the portion of the Park above the new Reservoir is concerned, an extension of the boundaries to One Hundred and Tenth street, and as this has not yet been surveyed or mapped, it is impossible to say what would be the best plan for its improvement. The addition of the extra length would lead to some alteration in any plan restricted to the present boundary lines. It is not necessary, however, to consider specifically the upper part of the Park, as proposed to be amended, as it seems to be a repetition, as far as practicable, of the conception [proposed in these amendments] for the lower Park. The leading idea of the plan [thus proposed] for the lower part of the Park is a straight promenade avenue from near Fifty-ninth street to the Reservoir, with entrances at Sixth and Seventh avenues. Two rows of trees of this length would unquestionably be a beautiful feature in itself, and the reasons why the avenue on plan 33 is commenced and terminated at the points indicated, is because, in that situation and with the limitations there assigned to it, it will interfere but little with the present lines of the landscape; while, if extended in either direction, it will destroy scenery, at great cost, which a few months' labor may render far more refreshing and agreeable than the constructed avenue would be after a growth of fifty years. The introduction of the suspension-bridge at the point indicated, merely for the sake of getting across the comparatively slight depression occupied by the lake, would, it is considered, have a forcibly artificial look, that would be out of harmony with the present character of the scenery, which would consequently have to be demolished and made artificial so as to correspond with the new leading feature that is proposed by the fresh plan to bisect it. The wire bridge, with its towers, although doubtless intended to be of elegant design, would destroy the appearance of expanse and the breadth of effect which at present makes this part of the Park so agreeable. If a more rapid and direct communication with Vista Rock is desired than is shown on plan 33, a light bridge can be at any time thrown across at as low a level as possible, between two points a little west of the line indicated by the amendment, but it was designedly omitted on the plan so that the hill to the south of the reservoir might always remain more retired and rural than the ornamental and highly-dressed grounds on the other portions of the site. A simple and unartificial treatment with variety and some degree of intricacy, seems to be preferable in a City-Park to straight lines of trees or stately architecture. These belong not to parks for the people, but to palatial gardens. A tolerably direct continuous walk from the lower end of the Park around the two reservoirs to the upper part of Bogardus Hill, if thought necessary to be introduced, can be at any time arranged without a sacrifice of the present scenery of the Park, or a division of the landscape into two parts by a prominent architectural structure crossing the ravine at Seventy-third street. This could be done in such a way as to avoid bringing the pedestrian in contact with the drives or rides. The walk around the reservoirs is unobjectionable, but it seems undesirable to accept them as important objects for the walk, because they must always be disappointing. They are tanks or cisterns, on a large scale it is true, but perfectly comprehensible and uninteresting after one or two visits of examination. It is considered that they are unfortunately situated, because it is one great purpose of the Park to supply to the hundreds of thousands of tired workers, who have no opportunity to spend their summers in the country, a specimen of God's handiwork that shall be to them, inexpensively, what a month or two in the White Mountains or the Adirondacks is, at great cost, to those in easier circumstances. The time will come when New York will be built up, when all the grading and filling will be done, and when the picturesquely-varied, rocky formations of the Island will have been converted into foundations for rows of monotonous straight streets, and piles of erect, angular buildings. There will be no suggestion left of its present varied surface, with the single exception of the few acres contained in the Park. Then the priceless value of the present picturesque outlines of the ground will be more distinctly perceived, and its adaptability for its purpose more fully recognized. It therefore seems desirable to interfere with its easy, undulating outlines, and picturesque, rocky scenery as little as possible, and, on the other hand, to endeavor rapidly, and by every legitimate means, to increase and judiciously develope these particularly individual and characteristic sources of landscape effects.[1]

Respectfully,

FRED. LAW OLMSTED,
Architect-in-Chief.

[1] ED. NOTE: The following statement by Olmsted and Vaux of the importance of enhancing the effect of broad meadows in the general design is taken from the Brooklyn Park Report for 1865 (dealing with the new Prospect Park).—

"We shall be pardoned for referring to a portion of the Central Park, New York, where somewhat similar conditions [to Brooklyn] formerly existed, and where our views have been adopted and realized. Entering by the turn to the right, at the Merchant's Gate, in a few moments the visitor's eye falls upon the open space called the Cricket Ground, where originally was a small swamp, enlarged at great expense in the construction of the park, . . . by the removal of several large ledges of rock, and now occupied by an unbroken meadow, which extends before the observer to a distance of nearly a thousand feet. Here is a suggestion of freedom and repose which must in itself be refreshing and tranquilizing to the visitor coming from the confinement and bustle of crowded streets. But this is not all. The observer, resting for a moment to enjoy the scene, which he is induced to do by the arrangement of the planting, cannot but hope for still greater space than is obvious before him, and this hope is encouraged, first, by the fact that, though bodies of rock and foliage to the right and left obstruct his direct vision, no limit is seen to the extension of the meadow in a lateral direction; while beyond the low shrubs, which form an undefined border to it in front,

A REVIEW OF RECENT CHANGES, AND CHANGES WHICH HAVE BEEN PROJECTED, IN THE PLANS OF THE CENTRAL PARK:[1]

BY THE LANDSCAPE ARCHITECTS, 1872

LETTER I

A CONSIDERATION OF MOTIVES, REQUIREMENTS AND RESTRICTIONS APPLICABLE TO THE GENERAL SCHEME OF THE PARK.

TO THE HONORABLE H. G. STEBBINS,
   President of the Department of Public Parks:

Sir:—In 1870, the preparation of the Central Park had been fourteen years in progress under the Commission of which you were then President.

A few objects had been accepted as practicable to be associated with the main scheme, suitable provisions for which remained to be established, but the primary construction of the Park in its essential elements, except at the outskirts where joint action with other departments of the city had been required, was complete, and the public enjoyed such use of it as can be had of any park the plantations of which are but just planted, their finer details incomplete, and all parts yet raw and blotchy.

Nearly six million dollars had been expended to bring the undertaking to this point, when the Commission was superseded by the Department under the charter of 1870.

Eighteen months later, another change having occurred restoring you to the head of the administration, it is found that while, in the meantime, little or nothing has been done on the unimproved outskirt ground, numerous alleged defects have been discerned in the plans formerly pursued, remedies for these devised, and to

---

there are no trees or other impediments to vision for a distance of half a mile or more, and the only distinct object is the wooded knoll of Vista Rock (*see No. 3 on Folded Map*), nearly a mile away, upon the summit of which it is an important point in the design, not yet realized, to erect a slight artificial structure, for the purpose of catching the eye, and the better holding it in this direction. The imagination of the visitor is thus led instinctively to form the idea that a broad expanse is opening before him, and the more surely to accomplish this, a glimpse of a slope of turf beyond the border of shrub in the middle distance has been secured. As the visitor proceeds, this idea is strengthened, and the hope which springs from it in a considerable degree satisfied, if not actually realized, first by a view of those parts of the Cricket Ground which lie to the right and left of his previous field of vision, afterwards by the broad expanse of turf on either side and before him, which comes into view as he emerges from the plantations at or near the marble archway (*see No. 22 on Folded Map*).

"The carrying out of this most important purpose in the scenery of the Central Park, owing to the rocky and heterogeneous character of the original surface, involved much more labor, and a larger expenditure, than any other landscape feature of that undertaking."

[1] Appendix B, 2nd Annual Report, D. P. P.

some slight extent carried out, and that the Park stands charged with an additional expenditure of two and a quarter millions of dollars.

At the time the old plans were reviewed and their revision resolved upon, we retained the position which we had held from the beginning of the work, as the professional advisers of the Board in respect to matters of design.

Referring to these facts, you have been kind enough to suggest that an explanation is due from us of the changes which have been thought necessary, more especially as the Annual Report of the Department, while presenting sub-reports from eight junior officers, contains nothing, as you observe, from us and refers in no way to our service.

Thanking you for the opportunity, we shall, as briefly as possible, relieve ourselves from responsibility in respect to the change of plans, and afterwards discuss the occasion and character of this change.

Soon after our re-appointment, in May, 1870, we made a concise written report on the purposes and design of the various structures in progress on the Park, and took several occasions to show our wish to explain these more fully to the new Commissioners.[1] When subsequently we were casually informed of newly conceived projects, we sought opportunity to point out the relations which they would have, and which were liable to be overlooked, to parts of the design already executed, but no reply was made to our requests for appointments for this purpose. As late as November we had not been officially advised of any dissatisfaction with the plans, nor had we been asked to explain those elements of our design which appear from the Report to have been regarded as inscrutable.

On the 25th of November, having then learned, though not officially, that radical changes had been determined on, we addressed a letter to the President of the Department, of which a copy is appended.

The receipt of this was formally acknowledged, but no action taken on the request conveyed, and on the 1st of December, the Department having openly disregarded the terms of its engagement with us, our duties to it were concluded.

The Annual Report of the Department (of the sub-reports attached to which we had no knowledge until you recently placed the printed copy in our hands) embodies a studied inculpation of previous administrations of the Park, the more emphatic charge being that of gross inconsiderateness of the reasonable requirements of the public in the designs of different parts of the work; the specifications of this charge being incorporated in the explanation of various local changes undertaken by the late administration.

The imputations thus made upon the plan of the Park are of a

[1] Ed. Note.—Cf. Docs. No. 10 and 13 of 1870.

class with criticisms which have been constant since the inception of the work; criticisms heretofore more commonly expressed, however, in the form of suggestions and inquiries, and thus with an acknowledgment of incomplete study. As the ground, officially stated, of changes by which not only much previous work is sentenced to be undone, but in which a further expenditure of some millions of dollars is involved, they now demand examination.

By a similar method of criticism, changes equally costly may be demanded and apologized for under every successive administration of the Park.

Its characteristic defect being that it takes no account of the larger number of motives which have influenced the design of the features assumed to be under review, a reply in detail, in which all such overlooked considerations should be set forth, would require a volume much larger than the Report itself. Before attempting a comprehensive reduction of this duty by the development of a general theory of design applicable to the Park, it may be desired, however, that we should fully exhibit this alleged defect.

An example, which will enable us to do so within moderate limits, is offered in a small group of associated objects, in which the motives of design, requiring consideration, are unusually local and limited. First presenting these, we shall then quote the criticism of the Report, and lastly refer to the changes, in this case slight, which have been made with a view of improvement.

Children will come to the Park in large numbers while yet too young to have the tastes and habits with regard to which its arrangements are generally designed, and localities in which they can be more particularly cared for are thus desirable. Ball-grounds have been prepared, in and about which boys have special privileges and special guardianship. Girls and boys, too small to use these, like to flock together also, and it is both better for them and more convenient for their elders that they should be encouraged and facilitated in doing so.

This was one of the considerations to which we have referred; another was suggested by the frightful increase of mortality among very young children which annually occurs in this city about midsummer; the number of deaths of infants, notwithstanding so many are taken out of town, often being double as many in a day about the middle of July as in any day of several previous months. The causes act in part directly upon the children, but largely, also indirectly, by inducing nervous irritation with nursing mothers.

A visit to the country offers the surest means of escaping the danger, and, in incipient stages, the best means of cure of the special disorders in which the danger lies. To most mothers, however, this is impracticable, and the best that can be done is to spend an occasional day or part of a day on the Park. It has been for some years a growing practice with physicians to advise this course.

The whole Park is, of course, open as much to mothers with

children as to any other class; but on a hot day a mother carrying a sick child, and perhaps leading other children, if she follows the throng, is liable to become more heated and feverish through fatigue, anxiety and various slight embarrassments, than if she remained quietly within a close, dark chamber. If she comes with a party of friends, she will be glad to find some quiet nook in which, while others wander, she can be left with her baby. The class of considerations thus suggested had influenced the treatment of several localities, but had been controlling in a larger way than elsewhere at the point in question.

There were here two masses of rock around both of which the main drive passed as a loop. On the borders and in the clefts of these rocks, the ground being impracticable for cultivation, loose thickets of sassafras, dogwoods, sumachs, bitter-sweet, and their common rock-edge associates, had sprung up, so that just here, in the midst of the general bleakness, barrenness and filth of this quarter of the Park site, there was a pretty bit of natural scenery, having a somewhat wild and secluded character. It was designed to follow up the natural suggestions of this class, and by thickening and extending the original sylvan defences, secure a more decided effect of rural retirement.

The advantage for this purpose supplied one ground for the selection of the spot,[1] the proximity of the play-grounds for larger children, another; and that of one of the sunken roads of the Park another; but the main reason for it was the fact that *it was the precise point in the Park which could be reached with the fewest steps* on an average, by visitors coming from the denser parts of the city by seven different lines of railway, and after the Park should be entered, wholly along walks by which the crossing of any carriage road would be avoided. From the Eighth Avenue and the "Belt" lines, access to it could be had by the Park carriages in five minutes; it was ten minutes' walk from the Sixth and Seventh Avenue and Broadway lines, and was approached by six walks, each fourteen feet wide, laid out from as many entrances, to the Park, with no more indirectness than was necessary to avoid with easy curves considerable rocky elevations.

The most noticeable feature of the special local arrangements consisted of a series of seats and tables shaded by trellised vines, so placed as to cover with verdure the larger part of a broad, flat, uninteresting mass of rock, which otherwise would have been a bleak and sterile blot in the view at a point almost of introduction to the more luxuriant landscape in the design of the lower park. A few arrangements for amusing and taking care of children were placed within easy reach, and also a building which had been designated the Dairy (*see No. 24 on Folded Map*), because it was intended to make sure that with a few other simple refreshments for children, perfectly fresh pure milk should be sold in it at a moderate charge. Its

[1] ED. NOTE: This is the "Kinderberg" area for the play of little children (*see vicinity of No. 23 on Folded Map*).

lower story, containing a store-room, ice-room and other offices, not interesting to the public, and accordingly completely concealed from its view, opened upon the sunken road by which its supplies could be received and its waste removed in carts without annoyance to visitors. The upper part, consisting of a sales-room, with a counter for refreshments and the loan or sale of playthings, and a broad gallery, was constructed for coolness and was open to the South breeze which it was found, even when calm elsewhere, would be drawn towards it from the South Pond. A bay of this water, with a bold dark shore opposite, rising to an eminence crowned with firs, was looked down upon, over a narrow glade of turf which, between the rocks and coppices, formed the foreground of a little local landscape promising some day to be quite interesting. Upon the bit of green-sward in front, it had been intended that a cow or two, a ewe with lambs, and a few broods of chickens, should be kept for the amusement of children, and a small stable had been built for them hard by, which also served to mask a dressing-room and water-closet.

It was considered that the same conditions which promised advantages for mothers, especially at midsummer, would be also grateful to convalescents, invalids, and aged persons who should desire to be as much as possible with comfort out of doors, especially in the early spring and late autumn; the Dairy being sheltered on the north, northwest and northeast, by elevations planted with evergreens, and giving upon a warm, dry southern slope, and a walk connecting with it, a quarter of a mile in length, having similar advantages of shelter and geniality.

Although more particularly designed for the benefit of the classes indicated, no attempt to exclude other visitors would have been practicable, nor was any intended. It was simply not desired, by making any of the group of structures unnecessarily prominent, to seem to recommend passers by, who would be likely to enjoy other points of the Park more, to turn off their course and tarry here. A special invitation for people to leave their carriages to obtain meals at the Dairy, was, perhaps, more especially designed *to be avoided*, as the parts of the roadway nearest it were among the most unsuitable on the Park for the stoppage and collection of carriages; and two minutes' drive beyond, a place had been specially prepared where a number might stand together without interrupting the regular movement upon the drive, and visitors in them could be served, if they chose, without alighting. It was thought, however, that people coming to the Park in carriages would frequently find it convenient to leave nurses and children for a short time, as they passed near the Dairy, and there were three convenient routes of access to it from the drive—the distance by the most direct, being less than a hundred paces, by none a hundred and twenty. It had been intended that all the local arrangements should be ready for use before midsummer, and when the new administration took charge in May, the Dairy was well advanced.

Although no inquiry was made of us in regard to this structure, and we did not suspect that any other view of it was taken than that which has been above explained, we twice referred, in written communications to the Department, to the fact that it had been designed as an attachment to the "Children's District," (the various other constructed features of which were once fully enumerated and their relations to it indicated), at the same time urging its immediate completion. The result is shown in the following paragraph of the Annual Report, no other reference to any of the whole group of arrangements being found in the volume:

"The remaining structure in progress was the Dairy House adjacent to the transverse road at Sixty-fifth street, in a very inappropriate location. It is hidden from direct view; *is difficult of access;* and no direct path leads to it from the main drive; so that the criticism is often popularly made that a Dairy building intended for general use of persons frequenting the Park, has been placed, as much as possible, out of sight and reach. Of course, it was necessary to complete it according to the original plans, because it had progressed too far for alteration. It has been finished in accordance with the plans of those who conceived it. It may not, however, be uninteresting to know that this inconsiderable building has cost about fifty thousand dollars—nearly all of it expended before this department took office."

In accordance with the theory of design thus indicated, the Dairy has been used as a common eating-house, no stipulations having been made with the tenant other than apply to the general restaurant at Mount St. Vincent; the stable has been turned into a paint-shop; the coppices thinned and trimmed up, and, with the rocks, put partially out of sight, and wholly out of countenance by rows of prim garden-shrubs. By making gaps in the established plantations, straightening two slight curves of the walks, and planting a granite stepping-stone, twenty feet long on the edge of the drive, it has been opened to view, and the distance to it therefrom shortened six paces.

These changes, as we have said, are comparatively slight. Looking at the building as the authors of the Report had chosen to do, simply as a roadside inn, standing detached from the road, but in their eyes more detached from all else on the Park, if changes were to be made, it is only to be wished that they could have been more efficacious. But slight, or rather feeble, as they are, interpreted by the significant brevity of their explanation, if the building had been leveled, and all the ground around had been plowed and salted, a willing ignorance of the real elements of value in all the work of the neighborhood, and a blind disdain of the study which had been given to the harmonious and equitable adjustment of its several motives could not have been more distinctly manifested.

It will appear probable that those who had taken the responsibility of administering the public trust of this property regarded the building as an item by itself; that they neither knew nor cared for its relations with any other elements of the Park; that they chose, however feebly, to force it into a relation with the drive, for which, by their own declaration, it was not adapted; that the tendency of their policy was to lessen, if not wholly cancel, its value with reference to its characteristic original purposes; and that, when their Report was prepared, they saw no reason to suppose that the public did not, with one voice, consent to and applaud such a method of dealing with their trust.

The construction of the Park has been watched by a large number of intelligent citizens, and more closely than any other public work of the city; it has unquestionably excited more general interest, and been more popular, than any other, and yet it is true that but little weight is commonly given to many important motives of its designs, either in commendations which are heard of it, or in propositions for its amendment.

It is not difficult to partly see how, with the necessarily superficial consideration given to it by most intelligent observers, this happens.

The various works which, since 1857, have been in progress on the site of the Park, may be considered under two classes: one comprehending changes in the surface of the ground and the production of landscape effects, the other limited to the formation of various structures in stone, brick, concrete and metal. Value receivable for the first will only be due in important amount after years of careful culture, and, for the present, few city-bred men can be expected to fully understand wherein the value is to consist. Structures in masonry, on the other hand, often reveal their full design the moment the builders' scaffolds are removed, and the quality of those on the Park has been at all times directly comparable with that of much other work with which the citizens of New York are familiar. The roads on the Park, as fast as opened section after section, were found to be superior to any other roads generally known, and being the only public pleasure roads of the city, they have been greatly frequented and obtained much favorable consideration. It has thus been brought about that encomium and criticism of the Park has alike been mainly directed to works of the second class, and most commonly from points of view in which each of them has been seen in a detached form.

The brick, stone, and iron parts of the Park have thus assumed an importance in comparison with its landscape elements somewhat analogous to that of the solid walls of a public building in comparison with its plaster, paint, frescoes, hangings, and furniture. To most persons they yet, including roads and walks, appear the essential elements of the Park. Take them out, and the Park would seem to be without plan. But leaving them in, from the practice of considering the several structures each by itself, the analogy of a public building would commonly be felt to be defective chiefly in that the plan of the Park is presumed to be much less coherent than that of any building.

It thus occurs that propositions respecting the Park have been constantly made, the like of which are never heard in regard to any public building.

The new Court House has been a great deal discussed during the last few years, but, in all that has been written, a demand has probably not been made that certain of its rooms should be fitted up with billiard tables or suitably for religious services or public demonstrations in anatomy; the lack of a convenient carriage way to the roof or to the lunch-counter has not been complained of, nor has it been proposed to remedy the present cramped, inconvenient and unattractive arrangements for refreshments by devoting the more spacious of the court rooms to this purpose.

The fact that such changes of the plan would in some limited view, be improvements, does not hide the larger fact that the acceptance of but a few propositions of the same character would soon completely ruin the building for the purposes which it has been built expressly to serve, and in reference to which, whatever value it may have is presumed to lie.

But propositions quite as fantastic are not unfrequently made with earnestness in regard to the Park. It has, for example, been seriously proposed that it should be used as a place of burial for the more distinguished dead of the city; that all religious sects should be invited to build places of worship upon it, and often that some central feature should be introduced corresponding in obvious importance to the dwelling in private grounds; that this should be a grand people's cathedral in which all sects might unite in a common litany; that it should be an exhibition and advertisement of the goods for sale in the city; that it should be many other things as diverse in character as the worship of God and of Mammon.

It has been urged that the plan of the Park should be so contrived that an illustration would be presented on a large though miniature scale of the geography of the continent; an illustration of the geological structure of the earth; a living cabinet of botany; a living museum of zoology.

Provided the principal constructions in roads, bridges, arches and buildings are not required to be destroyed, no structure which in itself promises to be in any way valuable to the public, would seem to be thought, by many intelligent citizens, out of place any where on the site of the Park. Thus the location of great buildings in positions where they would utterly destroy the scale of the growing landscape, where they would, indeed, obliterate the most important park features, is frequently urged.

The right has been often claimed to use any part of the Park for any purpose which is lawful to be pursued in the streets of the city; to go any where upon it, either on foot or in any vehicle.

A street railway through the midst of the Park has been called for; steamboats, and even a full rigged ship have been proposed to be placed in its waters.

New roads have been called for, crossing and practically destroying, for their original purpose, the most important features of the design. It has been proposed to widen every principal walk not laid directly along side of a drive, and throw it open to carriages.

A demand has more than once been made for a change in important features of the plan, for no other reason than that particular business speculations would be thereby rendered more promising.

The use of various parts of the ground, assumed to be at present unoccupied, has been asked for horse-races, for steeple-chases, for experiments with sundry new machines, for various kinds of advertising, for the sale of various wares, for popular meetings, for itinerant preaching, for distributing controversial tracts.

Room on which to erect tents, and make enclosures within the Park for circuses, concerts, trials of strength and skill, and all manner of popular exhibitions, has been frequently applied for with confidence.

As the city grows larger, projects for the public benefit multiply, land becomes more valuable, and the Park more and more really central, applications for the use of ground upon it for various more or less plausible purposes, are likely to become increasingly frequent and increasingly urgent, and there will thus be a strong tendency to its conversion into a great, perpetual metropolitan Fair Ground, in the plan and administration of which no general purpose need be recognized, other than to offer, for the recreation of those who may visit it, a desultory collocation of miscellaneous entertainments, tangled together by a series of crooked roads and walks, and richly decorated with flowers and trees, fountains and statuary.

THE ONLY SOLID GROUND OF RESISTANCE TO DANGERS OF THIS CLASS WILL BE FOUND TO REST IN THE CONVICTION THAT THE PARK THROUGHOUT IS A SINGLE WORK OF ART, AND AS SUCH, SUBJECT TO THE PRIMARY LAW OF EVERY WORK OF ART, NAMELY, THAT IT SHALL BE FRAMED UPON A SINGLE, NOBLE MOTIVE, TO WHICH THE DESIGN OF ALL ITS PARTS, IN SOME MORE OR LESS SUBTLE WAY, SHALL BE CONFLUENT AND HELPFUL.

To find such a general motive of design for the Central Park it will be necessary to go back to the beginning and ask, for what worthy purpose could the city be required to take out and keep excluded from the field of ordinary urban improvements, a body of land in what was looked forward to as its very centre, so large as that assigned for the Park? For what such object of great prospective importance would a smaller body of land not have been adequate?

To these questions a sufficient answer can, we believe, be found in the expectation that the whole of the island of New York, would, but for such a reservation, before many years be occupied by buildings and paved streets; that millions upon millions of men were to live their lives upon this island, millions more to go out from it, or its immediate densely populated suburbs, only occasionally and at long intervals, and that all its inhabitants would assuredly suffer, in greater or less degree, according to their occupations and the degree of their confinement to it, from influences engendered by these conditions.

The narrow reservations previously made offered no relief from them, because they would soon be dominated by surrounding buildings, and because the noise, bustle, confinement and noxious qualities of the air of the streets would extend over them without important mitigation.

Provisions for the improvement of the ground, however, pointed to something more than mere exemption from urban conditions, namely, to the formation of an opposite class of conditions; conditions remedial of the influences of urban conditions.

Two classes of improvements were to be planned for this purpose: one directed to secure pure and wholesome air, to act through the lungs; the other to secure an antithesis of objects of vision to those of the streets and houses which should act remedially, by impressions on the mind and suggestions to the imagination.

The latter only require our present attention, and the first question with reference to them is: What class of objects are best adapted to the purpose?

Experience would lead most men to answer that they are chiefly such as give the characteristic charm to gardens, pleasure grounds, and rural landscapes. But some consideration may be required to determine by what mode of selection from among these, and by what general principle of arrangement, the highest practicable degree of the desired effect is to be attained.

It sometimes occurs that certain species of trees grow naturally, under conditions favoring such a result, in forms of extraordinary symmetry, their heads each having the outline of a haycock set upon a straight, perpendicular post. Occasionally several such trees may be found in nature growing together. Any number of objects of that character would have but limited value, if any, for the purpose of the Park, because it is a character more nearly compatible in a tree than any other with the convenience of men when living compactly in streets and houses. Trees of that form might be, and, in fact, sometimes are, grown along the streets of the city between rows of houses.

A series of rose bushes, grown in pots, trained to single stems, sustained by stakes, would have even less value. Trim beds of flowers, such as might be set on a drawing-room table, or in the fore-court of a city dwelling, still less.

A cluster of hornbeams and hemlocks, the trunks of some twisting over a crannied rock, the face of the rock brightened by lichens, and half veiled by tresses of vines growing over it from the rear, and its base lost in a tangle of ground pine, mosses and ferns, would be of considerable value, partly because of the greater difficulty of reconciling the presence of such an assemblage of natural objects with the requirements of convenience in the streets, but mainly because the intricate disposition of lights and shadows seen in the back parts of it would create a degree of obscurity not absolutely impenetrable, but sufficient to affect the imagination with a sense of mystery.

A broad stretch of slightly undulating meadow without defined edge, its turf lost in a haze of the shadows of scattered trees under the branches of which the eye would range, would be of even higher value, and if beyond this meadow occurred a depression of the surface, and the heads of other trees were seen again at an uncertain distance, the conditions would be most of all valuable for the purpose in view, first, because there would be positive assurance of a certain considerable extent of space free of all ordinary urban conditions, and, in the soft, smooth, tranquil surface of turf, of immunity from the bustling, violent and wearing influences which act upon the surface of the streets, and secondly, because the imagination, looking into the soft commingling lights and shadows and fading tints of color of the back ground would have encouragement to extend these purely rural conditions indefinitely.

Considering that large classes of rural objects and many types of natural scenery are not practicable to be introduced on the site of the Park—mountain, ocean, desert and prairie scenery for example—it will be found that the most valuable form that could have been prescribed is that which we have last indicated, and which may be distinguished from all others as pastoral. But the site of the Park having had a very heterogeneous surface, which was largely formed of solid rock, it was not desirable that the attempt should be made to reduce it all to the simplicity of pastoral scenery. What would the central motive of design require of the rest? Clearly that it should be given such a character as, while affording contrast and variety of scene, would, as much as possible, be confluent to the same end, namely, the constant suggestion to the imagination of an unlimited range of rural conditions.

The pleasing uncertainty and delicate, mysterious tone which *chiaro-oscuro* lends to the distance of an open pastoral landscape certainly cannot be paralleled in rugged ground, where the scope of vision is limited; but a similar influence on the mind, less only in degree, is experienced as we pass near the edge of a long stretch of natural woods, the outer trees disposed in irregular clusters, the lower branches sweeping the turf or bending over rocks, and underwood mingling at intervals with their foliage. Under such circumstances, although the eye nowhere penetrates far, an agreeable suggestion is conveyed to the imagination of freedom, and of interest beyond the objects which at any moment meet the eye. While, therefore, elements of scenery of this class (which may, for the present purpose, be distinguished as picturesque sylvan scenery) would both acquire and impart value from their contrast with the simpler elements of open pastoral landscapes, their effect, by tending to withdraw the mind to an indefinite distance from all objects associated with the streets and walls of the city, would be of the same character.

The question of localizing or adjusting these two classes of landscape elements to the various elements of the natural topography of the Park next occurs, the study of which must begin with the consideration that the Park is to be surrounded by an artificial wall, twice as high as the Great Wall of China, composed of urban buildings. Wherever this should appear across a meadow-view, the imagination would be checked abruptly at short range. Natural objects were thus required to be interposed, which, while excluding the buildings as much as possible from view, would leave an uncertainty as to the occupation of the space beyond, and establish a horizon line, composed, as much as possible, of verdure.

No one, looking into a closely-grown wood, can be certain that at a short distance back there are not glades or streams, or that a more open disposition of trees does not prevail.

A range of high woods, then, or of trees so disposed as to produce an effect, when seen from a short distance looking outwardly from the central parts of the Park, of a natural wood-side, must be regarded as more nearly indispensable to the purpose in view—that of relieving the visitor from the city—than any other available feature.

The site of the Park being naturally very broken and largely composed of masses of rock, the extent to which the meadow-like surfaces of pastoral scenery could be introduced in the plan was limited.

It was, then, first of all, required that such parts of the site as were available and necessary to the purpose should be assigned to the occupation of elements which would compose a wood-side, screening incongruous objects without the Park as much as possible from the view of observers within it.

Secondly, of the remaining ground, it was required to assign as much as was available to the occupation of elements which would compose tranquil, open, pastoral scenes.

Thirdly, it was required to assign all of the yet remaining ground to elements which would tend to form passages of scenery contrasting in depth of obscurity and picturesque character of detail with the softness and simplicity of the open landscapes.

There are other elements yet to be considered; but those thus classified and assigned to various quarters of the site alone contribute directly to the general characteristic purpose of the Park, and are, therefore, to be distinguished as its essential elements.

This should be clearly recognized. As neither glass, nor china, nor knives and forks, nor even table and chairs are the essential elements of a dinner, so neither bridges, towers, shelters, seats, refectories, statues, cages for birds and animals, nor even drives and walks are the essential elements of the Park. But as what is well designed to nourish the body and enliven the spirits through the stomach makes a dinner a dinner, so what is well designed to re-create the mind from urban oppressions through the eye, makes the Park the Park. All other elements of it are simply accessories of these essentials.

Accessory elements, by which walking, driving, riding, resting, eating and drinking are facilitated, were also to be required in the design of the Park, in so far as they would be instruments necessary to be used to obtain the benefit of its essential elements.

But if people were to be allowed to straggle at will anywhere upon the ground, and if provision were to be made for their doing so comfortably and with cleanliness, all the ground would need to be specially prepared for the purpose; there would be no turf and no trees upon it, and it would afford no relief from the city. It will thus be seen that these accessory elements of the Park are admissible only where and so far as the advantages they offer in making its essential elements available compensate for any curtailment their introduction may involve in these essential elements. They are desirable to be seen, so far as they aid the essential elements in inviting the observer to rest or move forward in one way or another, as shall most conduce to his recreation. They are undesirable to be seen, so far as they tend to weaken, divide, blot or make patch-work of the essential or natural landscape elements.

The first consideration, then, in a truly critical study of the size, form, and place in the Park of any required construction for the accommodation of visitors was, originally, and always should be, that the degree of display which may be allowed in it should correspond, as nearly as other considerations will permit, with the importance of the need it is designed to meet; this being measured, not only by its average value to each user, but with regard also to the number of those who will have occasion to use it.

The second consideration is, that whatever serves to display an artificial construction required for the convenience of visitors is *undesirable:*

1st.   In the degree in which the border-screen is required to be broken.

2d.   In the degree in which the scope of meadow-surface is required to be broken.

3d.   In the degree in which picturesque passages are required to be disconcerted.

And the location of such constructions as are necessary to convenience should, as far as possible, be regulated by this scale.

But a class of possible accessories requires consideration which are not strictly necessary to make the essential elements of the Park available, yet which may be adapted to indirectly increase the public value of those elements. For example, a great space of ground is not necessary to the performance or the enjoyment of music, but the effect of good music on the Park is to aid the mind in freeing itself from the irritating effect of urban conditions, and by increasing the pleasure of a visit to the Park, it will tend to enlarge the number of visitors to it, and prolong the average period in which the special means of recreation afforded by its essential elements are active. The simple question, then, in regard to the admissibility of musical entertainments on the Park is: will the necessary means of providing such entertainments, as the fixed orchestra, the seats or standing places of the audience, lessen the value of the essential elements of the Park?

Similar considerations will apply to various entertainments which are partially scientific and educational and partially amusing —a cage of monkeys or parrots, for example. But it being understood that to accommodate adequately the numbers of visitors to be expected on the Park, the necessary accessory elements alone must occupy the eye more than is desirable, it may appear that no considerable structures for such purposes can be justifiable.

There are, however, certain localities which may be regarded as exceptional in this respect. They occur from the fact that the Legislature found it convenient to define the legal bounds of this body of the city property by the pre-existing street lines, which do not precisely coincide with the desirable limits of the Park as a work of art, which must nevertheless be all included within them; there are, therefore, along the boundary, several small spaces of ground, buildings within which, if properly designed, will not affect the park landscapes, and which, regarding the Park as a work of art, and with reference to the purpose of affording recreation by scenery from urban conditions, may be considered as extraneous. Questions of height, size and style of building being involved, these exceptional outer districts cannot be here more accurately defined. The extent of such debatable ground is, however, quite limited, and the question of the legitimate occupation and disposition of all parts of the Park site proper need not be complicated in the present discussion by the slight opening thus admitted for exceptions.

We submit that such requirements and restrictions as have been thus developed, commend themselves to common sense as well adapted to secure the desired end of the undertaking of the Central Park.

That the original plans were formed in accordance with them, and that they were respected by the original Commission, has been, as we know, sincerely and intelligently doubted.

We propose, in another letter, to consider the more common grounds of such intelligent doubt before examining the course of alleged improvement which has been more recently adopted.

We are, Mr. President,
Very respectfully yours,
OLMSTED & VAUX,
Landscape Architects.

NEW YORK, January, 1872.

LETTER II

EXAMINATION OF THE DESIGN OF THE PARK AND OF RECENT CHANGES THEREIN

To the Honorable H. G. Stebbins,
President of the Department of Public Parks:

Sir: In the present letter we shall hope to establish the conviction that the restrictions and requirements set forth in our last had been faithfully regarded in all classes of work under the original Commission, and shall afterwards indicate the course with respect to them which has since been taken.

A complete review of all the work being neither practicable nor necessary, we shall address ourselves to points in regard to which intelligent doubt has appeared, and, with reference to the recent works, to such as are most significant of the spirit and intention of alleged improvements.

The preliminary study of the original plan, it will be remembered, was first presented in competition with thirty-three others.[1] One of its distinctions was, that it presented larger unbroken surfaces of turf and of water than any other; it was designated the "Greensward" plan. In actual construction the extent of open pastoral surface had been made even larger than was suggested in the preliminary study. It will not be denied that, wherever it had been practicable to complete the work up to the boundary before the Commission was superseded, the required screening woods had been planted, while one of the criticisms upon the Park has been that, in much of the remaining ground, a wild negligence and seclusion has been suffered to prevail which was not in good taste.

Assuming, then, that with more or less skill the prescribed requirements had been regarded in the design, as far at least as the primary blocking out of natural features is concerned, the question remains, and is one upon which a substantial difference of judgment undoubtedly exists, as to how far, in the subsequent introduction of accessories, or convenient furniture for use, the advantages so gained have been unnecessarily sacrificed?

The architectural features of the Park are numerous and costly, more numerous and costly, it is sometimes said, than those of any other modern pleasure-ground. From this fact, with the influences, explained in our first letter, fixing public attention very strongly upon the architectural works during the period of construction, it has happened that an impression has been very generally adopted, even with qualified judges, that the interest of the Park has been designed to be found largely, if not chiefly, in this class of its works.

The existence of such an impression is placed in very strong

[1] ED. NOTE: See p. 44, *ante.*

light by a not uncommon criticism that these works are so situated as nowhere to be seen to advantage; that they are not individually imposing structures, and that they are never so associated as to produce grand combined effects, such as might have been obtained had a series of boldly projected and well-designed objects of no greater costliness been arranged symmetrically in one noble composition, supported by corresponding plantations, as in the works of the old architectural school of gardening.

Perhaps the existence of the same impression is shown, however, even more strongly, when the Park is spoken of in terms of approval, which could not be applied to natural scenery, as "a magnificent garden," for instance. It has naturally followed, also, from the same impression, and as a retort to misapplied compliments, that regret has been often expressed that the Commissioners had not had the good taste to prefer a plan purely in the natural style.

To persons who have not given special study to this subject, the frequent reference thus made to schools is liable to withdraw attention from the only point of any real importance that these comments prove to be in question, by making it appear necessary to understand the whole art of gardening before it can be intelligently answered. That this is not the case, we shall attempt to make clear by considering upon what purity of style, in a work of the class in question, depends. This may be seen by examining the conditions, and consequent human wants, in which each of the two schools referred to originated.

The architectural style of gardening was in vogue long before the period of Christian civilization; its finest examples probably had been formed in regions of grand landscape features, but of arid climate and with a general aspect of stern, wild and savage nature. The primary motive of design under this school, is, accordingly, to produce a splendid urbanity.

The natural school originated in the last century, and was based on the experience that in northern countries of perennial turf and of gentle topography, modern civilized men, however they may admire the magnificence of the ancient pleasure-grounds, find more refreshment and more lasting pleasure in certain not at all extraordinary types of natural landscape. An extreme statement of such experience is found by Mr. Robinson, in an account by Sidney Smith of a visit to "a very grand place," with which at first he had been enchanted. He says:—"It seemed something so much better than nature that I really began to wish the earth had been laid out according to the latest principles of improvement. . . . In three days' time I was tired to death; a thistle, a nettle, a heap of dead bushes—anything that wore the appearance of accident and want of intention—was quite a relief. I used to escape from the made grounds, and walk upon an adjacent goose-common, where the cart-ruts, gravel-pits, bumps, irregularities, coarse, ungentlemanlike grass, and all the varieties produced by neglect, were a thousand times more gratifying than the monotony of beauties the result of design, and crowded into narrow confines."

The landscape or natural school proceeds upon an analysis of such experiences to design the means of a similar gratification, as far as may be practicable in any given situation, artificially, and to reconcile the means of doing so with the cleanliness, convenience and comfort of those for whom the ground is prepared.

The two schools do not stand in opposition to each other, any more than the shoe-maker and the hatter. The question, if there must be a question of schools, is not, which do you like best? which is most to your taste? or which is the latest fashion? but which, in this or that particular case, promises to provide most toward the fullness of life? and this is wholly a question of special circumstances and conditions.

But as there is no doubt that an attempt to combine motives of such opposite character is sure to produce a feeble result, it is a perfectly reasonable demand that, in a work like that of the Central Park, it shall not be uncertain which has been adopted. Whether the number of architectural and avowedly artificial constructions on the Central Park establishes such an uncertainty, depends on the special motive of each of these constructions, as will be evident from the following considerations:

In all much frequented pleasure-grounds, constructions of various kinds are necessary to the convenience and comfort of those to be benefited; their number and extent being proportioned to the manner in which they are to be used, and to the number of expected users. If well adapted to their purpose, strongly and truly built, the artificial character of many of these must be more or less displayed. It is not, then, by the absence nor by the concealment of construction that the natural school is tested.

On the other hand, the principal elements of scenery in architectural gardens, even of such extreme types as that of Versailles, is found in verdure. It is not, then, by the absence nor the concealment of productions of nature that the architectural school is known. What remains as the essential distinction between the two would seem to be, simply, that in architectural gardening, natural features are employed adjunctively to designs, the essential pleasure-giving elements of which are artificial, while in natural gardening artificial elements are employed adjunctively to designs, the essential pleasure-giving character of which is natural.

It being admitted that the main purpose of the Central Park, as defined in our previous letter, exacts the predominance of natural elements; if this simple requirement in respect to its necessary artificial constructions is kept in view, no further consideration of what, under other circumstances, has been the practice of one school or the other, need enter into a critical review of its design. Neither need the special science of the gardener be brought in question. As Mr. Palgrave, in the preface to his *Essays on Art*, says of judgment upon what are more commonly and conventionally spoken of as works of art: it "is a matter which simply resembles other branches of human knowledge: a certain natural faculty or bias must always be presupposed; with this, as in case of mathematics or of language, taste is obtained by study and observation; and, as in those sciences, leads to a practical power of decision. Some few strictly technical qualities remain, on which the artist alone is a judge. But this exception does not invalidate the criticism of spectators, . . . the technical qualities are only means to a public end, and the question which remains always is, how far do they tend to the object of all the fine arts—high and enduring pleasure."

To a fair understanding of the architectural elements of the design of the Central Park, it is first of all necessary that some effort should be made to realize what extent of accommodation will be required in this particular ground when it shall be in the centre of a city of perhaps two millions of people, surrounded by water and by densely populated suburbs for some distance beyond the water.

Obviously, not only in extent, but in solidity of construction, the means of accommodation which must at times be actually occupied in various ways by visitors will need to be somewhat different from those commonly associated with natural rural scenery. Somewhat different, also, from those required in most foreign public pleasure-grounds—the people of London, Paris, Vienna and Berlin, for example, having each nearly as many thousands of acres to scatter over in pursuit of their recreation as those of New York have hundreds.

By far the most extensive and important of the constructed accommodations of the Central Park are those for convenience of locomotion. How to obtain simply the required amount of room for this purpose, without making this class of its constructions everywhere disagreeably conspicuous, harshly disruptive of all relations of composition between natural landscape elements on their opposite borders, and without the absolute destruction of many valuable topographical features, was the most difficult problem of the design. If any one has doubts of this, it will only be necessary to drive through the Park, pausing at frequent intervals to consider what would be the difference of effect were the groups of foliage, even in their present partial development, thrown back twenty feet on each side, and were the rocks blasted out or the slopes of the surface broken, which will be seen within that distance.

In dealing with this problem, the following considerations had weight. In any roadway much frequented by pleasure-vehicles, and little used otherwise, half a dozen heavily laden carts often cause more divergence from direct movement, and thus more impede such use of it as is chiefly desired, than as many hundred carriages driven at nearly equal moderate speed. A woman attempting to lead a child across the road when it is all crowded with rapidly moving vehicles, will often cause three or four horses to be pulled up to avoid her, and this will oblige others in the rear of them to be turned out of their course; or, if they are near the curb, also to be pulled up to avoid a collision. Consequently, under these conditions, the distance between the curbs will be frequently found, no matter how great it is, inconveniently narrow for those who wish to drive at a steady trot, and a given number of pleasure-carriages will move with greater regularity and be better accommodated in a wheel-way forty feet wide, from which ordinary slow traffic and people on foot are excluded, than in one eighty feet wide to which these sources of obstruction and disturbance are admitted. Again, in crowded thoroughfares, continuous straight-forward movements on the walks is chiefly impeded by people—especially women, children and infirm—who stand fearful and hesitating at the crossings, and whom, under these circumstances, others sometimes find it difficult not to press upon.

These and other observations of similar import, both in our own streets and in European parks, led to the planning of a system of independent ways: 1st, for carriages: 2d, for horsemen wishing to gallop; 3d, for footmen; and 4th, for common street traffic requiring to cross the Park. By this means it was made possible, even for the most timid and nervous, to go on foot to any district of the Park designed to be visited, without crossing a line of wheels on the same level, and consequently, without occasion for anxiety or hesitation.

Incidentally, the system provided, in its arched ways, substantial shelters scattered through the Park, which would be rarely seen above the general plane of the landscape, and which would be made as inconspicuous as possible, but to be readily found when required in sudden showers.

Without taking the present occasion to argue the point, we may simply refer to another incidental advantage of the system which, so far as we have observed, has not been publicly recognized, but which, we are confident, may be justly claimed to exist, in the fact that to the visitor, carried by occasional defiles from one field of landscape to another, in which a wholly different series of details is presented, the extent of the Park is practically much greater than it would otherwise be.

The system was elaborated with great care in detail to accomplish the necessary introduction of its numerous arches and variations of surface, in such a manner as that the ravines and bridges should not appear to have been constructed to order; natural depressions of surface were generally made available for approaches to the subways, but sometimes the construction of picturesque defiles through rock, and even tunneling was resorted to in order to avoid disturbance of important landscape features. In most cases rocky banks were worked up boldly against the masonry of the arches, so that as little as possible of it should be exposed; these banks were planted in such a manner as to obscure it still more. The arches were often so made that a thicket of bushes could be substituted for an obviously artificial parapet. The necessary railing of others was used as a trellis, so that it disappeared under a drapery of twining foliage.

In the majority of cases where, two years ago, the design had not yet been at all realized, we believe that visitors, in passing over the arches, often did so without being aware of it, and in passing under them did so with an experience of gratification. In the single instance where a choice is offered between crossing the drive by the same number of steps upon the surface, or by an arched way, the latter is generally chosen by habitués of the Park.

More than nine-tenths of the so-called architectural objects of the Park have been built as necessary elements of this special system, which had been designed to supply the maximum of accommodation with the minimum of disturbance of its natural scenery, and especially of the more important features of its natural scenery. (In looking across the two principal meadows, in no direction is an archway to be seen. There is one on the edge of a third and smaller meadow, but it is so retired and shaded as in summer to be undiscernible.)

It may here be mentioned that there had been, under the old Commission, but two permanent buildings erected upon or in the edge of the open grounds, and both of these were flanked by groves of trees; one, was a cottage (*see No. 25 on Folded Map*) containing dressing-rooms for ball-players; the other, a small, tent-like structure, the mineral spring pavilion (*see No. 26 on Folded Map*). As yet, the appearance of even such small structures, seen often against the sky and in sunlight, is glaring compared with what it will be when the planted trees shall curtain round and overhang them.

Taking all the architectural features of the Park together, we believe that when the natural elements of the design have been fairly developed, those which had been established under the original Commission will be found to very moderately affect its landscape character, and that rarely will more than one of them be distinguishable from any particular point of view.

It is not to be assumed that in such cases it will always be seen undesirably. It is, to say the least, doubtful if the most effective anti-climax to the lofty buildings and paved levels of the city is to be found in a scene absolutely devoid of evident human handiwork. No authority on landscape design has contended for this. Mr. Ruskin has shown the value of a bridge or a chálet introduced in a representation of even the grandest scenes of nature. Uvedale Price, who, in his zeal for the picturesque, argues that even rudeness resulting from storms, decay and the depredations of beasts should be reproduced by the gardener, cuts trees away to bring a mill, a village spire, or a cottage into his park compositions. Shenstone says, "a rural scene is never complete without the addition of some kind of building."

To determine whether any structure on the Park is undesirable, it should be considered, first, what part of the necessary accommodation of the public on the Park is met by it, how this much of accommodation could be otherwise or elsewhere provided, and in what degree and whence the structure will be conspicuous after it shall have been toned by weather, and the plantations about and beyond it shall have taken a mature character.

Under the peculiar plan adopted in laying out the roads and walks of the Central Park, no one, we believe, who will candidly study it, can doubt that there is a much smaller parting and displacement of the essential natural elements of the Park and a much smaller display of artificial elements than there would needs be, had it been undertaken to provide an equal amount of public accommodation without the architectural constructions of the archways.

Even, however, if a doubt can be maintained on this point, it can be no more than a doubt. Fifteen years ago, the grounds of doubt were very clearly before the administration of the Park, and they were cautiously and deliberately weighed; every argument against the expedient which has since been raised being fully presented and considered before it was adopted. Having been adopted, there is no part of the drive, no part of the ride, and but little of the walk system which is not studiously adjusted to the arches, and planned, in respect to course, breadth, curves and grades, with a constant purpose to avoid leading people on foot to wish to occupy ground on which others have a right to drive horses. That a certain advantage was promised by the arrangement, there has never been a doubt; that a certain advantage is experienced from it, there can be no present doubt. To justify setting aside this advantage, be it considered large or small, after all that has been expended to secure it, there should be clear evidence that some greater advantage is to be gained which cannot be secured without its sacrifice.

The serious and intelligent questionings of the plan of the Park to which we have thus replied, are nowhere recognized in the Annual Report of the Department, but in its undertakings of improvement a disposition to give up the advantages of the archway system has, as we shall show, been quite unnecessarily manifested, while the appliances originally used to avoid undue prominence in its necessary architectural elements have been neglected and in some cases dismantled. In the structures originating with the late administration, indeed, the reverse purpose is evinced; each, no matter how humble its purpose, being made as conspicuous, both by location and design of elevation, as its purpose will allow, and no consideration being paid to the manner in which the natural features will be affected by it, either in scale, color or composition.

The Annual Report, however, contains a series of strictures upon some points of the Commission's policy, of minor consequence, but for a fair understanding of which some explanation seems desirable. It should be remembered that a good deal of forecast had been necessary in regard to the housekeeping work of a place in which the wants of some hundred thousand people would require purveyance, often for several days in succession, and, in which, especially the wear, tear, and litter of that number of visitors would need to be cared for by means and methods which would not be unseemly, would not obstruct their movements and would not interfere with their pleasure. To this end a considerable amount of handy fixtures of the class of dust-bins, tool, store, and other closet-rooms would need to be provided. As an illustration, turf must be kept close or it will run out; the cheapest and best way of keeping it close on the pastoral surface of the Park is to graze it with sheep, and for the sheep thus required, shelter is sometimes necessary. Until the Commission was superseded, old buildings, temporarily left upon the Park for the purpose, and slight temporary structures had been used for these offices. One of permanent character only had been begun, the general barn and stable (*see No. 27 on Folded Map*) which had been so designed and placed that, although its roof, as now completed, is much larger than any other built upon the Park, not one visitor of a thousand has probably ever seen it. It is, at the same time, centrally located, and has direct communication with the streets, clear of the Park drives and walks. The same will be true of the range of workshops which has been begun under the late administration, in a situation and upon a plan previously prepared. Other buildings of this class had been designed to be similarly dealt with. We shall show later that a different policy has been initiated since, in respect to them.

In the original design of the Park, there had been no provision for zoological buildings or yards. Gifts of living animals having been afterwards made to the city, temporary quarters were provided for them in one of the old buildings, formerly occupied as a State Arsenal, and which was used likewise for various administrative purposes. Temporary enclosures were also made for pasturage in two places on the borders of the Park. As the collection gradually increased, mainly from gifts to the city, it became evident that better provision for it would be necessary.

By taking advantage of the circumstances referred to at the close of the preceding letter, and carefully adjusting the required buildings, yards, paddocks, roads and walks to the plan of the Park, a considerable collection of the hardier birds, beasts and reptiles might be provided for without serious encroachment upon its important features; but if a general exposition of the zoology of the world were to be undertaken, including moderately liberal provision for giraffes, elephants, camels and other large tropical graminiverous animals, which, besides airy shelters and strongly enclosed open grounds for a satisfactory exhibition of their characteristic movements and habits in summer, with ample approaches and accommodations for crowds of lookers-on, need also roomy and artificially warmed winter apartments, it was seen that, with all possible skill in the arrangement of these appliances, the Park must be grievously injured with respect to its essential purposes. It was also seen that it would be a measure of economy to bring all required buildings for tropical animals near together for convenience of heating.

The suggestion was, therefore, made and adopted that a piece of unimproved land belonging to the city, lying near the Park, should be placed in the hands of the Commission—such parts of it as were needed, to be occupied by the tropical section of a popular zoological exhibition.

The impression is very emphatically conveyed in the Annual Report, that the ground given to the Commission in accordance with this suggestion, is wet, cold, and impossible to be drained, and that this consideration, which makes it utterly unsuitable for the purpose, had wholly escaped our attention. As the late administration itself proposed to erect buildings for men and women upon the same site, it is hardly necessary to refer to this argument further than to state that surveys had been made and two distinct plans of drainage, with estimates, prepared, either of which was perfectly feasible. There was no formidable difficulty in making it dryer, more sheltered and warmer than any ground upon the Park.

Besides living animals, the Park had been made a receptacle for a variety of gifts to the city: some of them illustrations of art, others of history, others of science.

The policy of your Commission had been to cautiously foster the formation of collections mainly by the voluntary associated action of citizens, in which, through its negotiations, the public should be secured certain rights, rather than establish museums to be solely managed by the civic authorities.

A question had arisen as to whether any suitable buildings or building sites could be offered for this purpose; and this leading to the inquiry where on the Park *a large range of buildings could be placed at the least disadvantage to its essential elements*, a plat of ground east of the old reservoir had been indicated. The reason for this selection was that a large range of buildings at this point would be seen from no other point of the Park, the locality being bounded on two sides by the reservoir walls, on a third by a rocky ridge, and on the fourth by exterior buildings, while the whole of the territory thus enclosed was too small for the formation of spacious pastoral grounds, and was less well adapted and less required than any other equal space for contrasting picturesque effects.

Public interest had been rapidly increasing, and public agitations rapidly growing and tending to comprehensive and liberal combination in respect to these associated and incidental purposes of the Commission's work; and although the time was not thought to have arrived for a definite and final study of plans, it was seen that some extensive public or semi-public buildings, in connection with the Park and on city property, would soon be called for, in the basements and courts of which it was not unlikely that some of the necessary accessories of the Park would be incidentally provided. Under these circumstances, the policy of the Commission being a waiting one, temporary accommodations continued to be patched up and used for many purposes, more and longer than was consistent with its own convenience or perfect efficiency of management for the time being.

The old arsenal (*see No. 6 on Folded Map*), for example, was found a useful make-shift during the period of construction, but was regarded as a conspicuously ugly and ill-placed building. A part of the permanent buildings to which its contents would be transferred, had already been begun; projects for others were forming. Pending the question of its evacuation and demolition, expense had been as much as possible avoided in fitting it for its temporary duties, and, so far as its exterior was concerned, outlay had been chiefly directed to subduing its color, making it less conspicuous by reducing its height, and training over it the vines which the late administration has torn down and uprooted. The same temporizing policy led to the maintenance of various humble arrangements which are dealt with in the Annual Report, as if they were permanent, prominent and characteristic elements of the Park.

Most of the structures really permanent in character, which were built by your Commission are unquestionably well built, and, like all firm and well-built permanent works, they were honestly costly. A doubt is admitted whether, in respect to arrangements of temporary convenience, a somewhat more liberal policy would not have been more economical. On the other hand, while there can be no question of the great improvements made in this respect under the late administration, there may be a question whether their costliness is fully justified. But this is a matter of minor consequence, and we now turn to the main question of the alleged improvements of the permanent elements of the Park.

During fourteen years the whole work of the Central Park centered, as has been shown, upon three branches of a single purpose: first, the putting out of view of exterior buildings by a suitable disposition of tall growing trees; second, the formation of a series of broad, simple meadow surfaces, with, when practicable, such a disposition of umbrageous trees, without underwood, as would render their limits undefined; third, the development of a series of landscape passages *strongly contrasting* with those of the pastoral and high wood districts in complexity of grouping, and the frequent density, obscurity, and wild intricacy of low growing foliage, especially on broken and rock-strewn surfaces. The permanent accessory elements of roads, walks, arches, and other structures had been located and designed in strict sequence and subordination to these purposes; as little as possible to conflict with them, as much as possible to support them.

The question now before us is, how have these purposes been served during the last year and a half; how far has the value which had been gained previously been increased, and in what degree, with reference to these purposes, has the design of the Park been improved by the changes made?

First: as to the screening woods?

The Department has done nothing to advance, and but little practically to thwart this branch of the design, but it has published the declaration (page 20 of the Annual Report) that it is an illegal undertaking; that an unobstructed view across the Park from any house that may be built around it is one of the rights of the owners of the adjoining land that cannot be interfered with for the public benefit. In that case, unquestionably, much of the work which has been done upon the Park, under the late administration itself, as well as previously, had been worse than wasted, for much earth and rock has been heaped up, as well as trees planted, which must have this illegal effect, and it would seem to be necessary for compliance with the requirement, to reduce its surface everywhere to the level of the adjoining street.

Second: as to open landscapes?

The Department has begun the erection of a large series of buildings, which is intended to be followed by the construction of a series of small yards, of walks between them, and of lines of trees following these walks, upon the largest meadow of the Park. The first of the houses may be seen, exteriorly nearly complete, about 400 yards south of Mount St. Vincent. The meadow is intended to entirely disappear, and in defending its course (pages 23 and 280, Annual Report) the late administration has not considered the landscape value of this opening worth mentioning. The argument of the defence is based, as we have shown, upon a fallacy.

In the site of the lower Park there were originally two spaces besides those excavated for water, where, by the reduction and covering with soil of a few comparatively small ledges of rock, it was possible to obtain some expanse of landscape. One was at a lower elevation than the other, and they were separated by a rocky ridge and rapid slope. Along this slope it was thought necessary, for reasons of exterior convenience, that one of the roads for common business purposes crossing the park should be carried. This was graded eight feet below the natural surface, and a ledge to the north of it having been blasted out for the purpose, an opening about 200 feet in width was thus secured, by which the range of the eye from both sides was greatly extended, looking from the south, considerably more than half a mile. Walks leading from the main walks were laid out near the edge of the sunken road, from which however the masonry of its walls was concealed. A row of English elms "breaking joints," with a row of silver maples, pruned as street trees, to long naked trunks, has been planted by the late administration, following the lines of these walks. The effect, if they should be allowed to grow as intended, will be to completely close this opening, previously secured at so much expense.

Third: as to the more picturesque elements?

It must be admitted that the plantations of the Park, and particularly the more picturesque plantations, at the period of the change of administration, did stand, as claimed in the Annual Report, in need of extensive revision. The construction of the Park had proceeded by districts, one after another being taken up in succession. From the time in which drainage and grading work began, until the roads and walks of any district were finished, was generally a period of from two to three years. It was necessary to finish roads and walks before the ground adjoining them could be surfaced and planted. As soon, however, as roads and walks were finished, the public eagerly thronged upon them. The desire was strong with the Commission that when this occurred the impression produced by the appearance of the adjoining ground should not be so disagreeable as it was likely to be if left in the extremely rough and cumbered condition which the border of a road under construction must have. It often happened that the first opportunity of clearing them occurred very late in the planting season; in the spring, so late that only coniferous trees could be planted safely.

The Commission had declined to adopt the policy urged upon it at an early day to establish a large and varied nursery of its own. It began with the trial of some not very successful experiments to obtain its trees, like brick, stone and cement, by contracts to the lowest bidder. It had been found impossible, through ordinary channels to obtain many desired trees and plants, and especially to obtain anything like the number of many that was required. Of some that were then costly, there was a certain doubt, since wholly removed, that they would endure the climate of the Park, at least until its surface should become less bleak.

These and many other considerations (some of which are indicated in the printed document of the Commission, No. 4, of 1859, pages 5 and 6),[1] led to a habit of occasionally giving a temporary finish to the ground, and often to the planting of unsuitable trees, especially strong conifers, which would serve to give it a fresh, green appearance, and at once cover its nakedness, with the intention of subsequently removing them to the outer parts of the Park.

Owing to successive changes of policy of other departments of the city, the finishing of the outer parts of the Park was delayed, and for this and other reasons the necessary measures for securing an adequate supply of many desired plants had not yet been taken when the Commission was removed. It sometimes happened, therefore, that only the central or interior members of the principal masses and groups of planting had yet been planted, while cheap lots of the commonest nursery stock had been dropped in along the borders of the drives and walks in front of them.

With similar motives, indigenous trees and shrubs had been suffered to remain untouched in some localities, where, when full

---

[1] Ed. Note: Given in our Part II, Chapter III, pp. 307 f.

grown, they would destroy important landscape compositions, and these had already partly overgrown and obscured some points of interest.

The intended revision, by the removal of temporary material and the introduction of finer detail, the cutting away of low growth in some cases, the establishment of low growth in others, had, it cannot be denied, been in many parts postponed longer than was desirable.

A vigorous remedy for this neglect has, during the last year been in progress.[1] The result is frequently, that in parts of the Park in which intricacy of low growth and picturesque obscurity had been required by the design, the natural underwood has been grubbed up, the original admirably rugged surface made as smooth and meadow-like as ledge-rock would allow, and the trees, to a height of from ten to fifteen feet, trimmed to bare poles.

The object of these operations is stated in the Annual Report to have been that of securing "a circulation of air," "opening beautiful views of lawn and scenery," and clearing the Park of "cat-briars and tangled weeds." The undergrowth removed was, in fact, largely of indigenous azaleas, clethra, cephalanthus, and the commonly associated interesting wood shrubs, with plenty of asters, gentians, golden rod and the like. No shrubbery or low growth seems to have been valued unless it could be seen within a clean-edged dug border.

The extent to which this kind of improvement has been carried, is partly indicated by the fact that the quail, both Eastern and California, with which the Park was well stocked, and which were breeding in it freely before the destruction of the covers, have now almost wholly disappeared.

The bolder rocky parts of the Park had been in some cases, especially in the more recent work, left with a smooth surface of turf or of clean, bare ground between and about the base of the rocks, and with smooth, turf-covered flanking slopes, conditions scarcely ever seen in nature, incongruous and uninteresting. The intention had been to give a temporary finish to these parts that would save a destructive wash of the surface; and afterwards, at a convenient time, to add peat and wood earth, and bring to them a large number of low plants from the mountains, ferns, mosses and creepers. Nothing like this has been done, but the late administration has, in some of these cases, undertaken an improvement

---

[1] ED. NOTE: Cf. the resolution (Minutes, D. P. P.) presented by Commissioner Dillon and finally passed on Dec. 20, 1870 (Pres. Sweeny and Comrs. Hilton, Field, and Dillon all voting for it):

"That the Landscape Gardener be requested to reform the present planting of the Park upon the principle that distance, expanse, and extent of vision should be constantly aimed at; that in all cases where the soil will permit an undergrowth of grass the trees should be thinned out for their better development; and that shrubbery which obstructs the view and impedes the circulation of the air, and is not necessary to conceal imperfections, should be especially avoided."

by the introduction of a variety of beds in arabesque patterns, planted with flower-garden annuals.

On the borders of the open ground, where the indigenous trees required thinning, an additional number have in some cases been planted, and in others an improvement has been attempted by lopping off lower limbs in the manner before described, so as to lessen their umbrageousness and produce the character of street trees.

A large number of structures have been projected, some planned, and the plans of others, half built, recast, but to show how little respect has been paid to the requirements originally recognized in this class of the accessories of the Park, it will be sufficient to refer to two buildings for the humblest purposes, which have been projected, planned and completely constructed since the removal of the original Commission.

No one can visit the Park without having his attention called to a structure (*see No. 28 on Folded Map*) placed on a slight elevation, where, in the original design, the principal meadow view from the north part of the Mall was designed to become dim under large trees, which were also to hide the buildings on the Eighth avenue, which lies sixty paces beyond. It consists of a central building, two stories in height, with low wings, extending diagonally on each side toward the Green, and terminating in two handsome pavilions of greater elevation. It has throughout a high pitched, slate roof, decorated with turrets and gilded iron work; the walls are of pressed brick, with trimmings of cut blue stone and polished granite, and its general aspect suggests a large English parochial school. Its cost has been $70,000. It is officially designated a "sheepfold," and its ostensible purpose is to provide a shelter, *at night* and in severe winter weather for the sheep used to keep down the grass on the adjoining Green. The pavilions at its ends, however, are designed for the use of visitors, and it has been intended that portraits of sheep and specimens of wool should be hung upon their walls. It is expected, as stated in the Annual Report, to be "a great attraction to all classes." It can, nevertheless, only be reached by footmen, after crossing the Bridle Road *on the surface* at a point where, owing to its grades and curves, a rider would not see persons crossing before him until too close upon them to pull up a galloping horse. So little was this objection to the site and arrangement valued, that when the attention of the Department was called to it officially, it obtained no attention. A flower-garden was designed to be formed in front of the sheep-shed, between which and the door to its public rooms the Bridle Road passed.

A "cottage" may be seen a little to the north of this edifice. It is situated between two branches of the Bridle Road, which must be crossed on the surface by every one visiting it.

Situations for both these buildings, free from this objection, in which they would have been more convenient for their purposes, and much less obtrusive, might have been found within a stone's throw of their present positions.

On the drive east of the old reservoir, one of the archways of the walk system has been lengthened: in rebuilding its end, the original arrangement, by which a screen of shrubbery was carried across the arch, entirely concealing the artificial work, has been changed, a broad platform of blue stone, with a substantial iron railing, substituted and the face of cut stone work over the arch has been doubled in depth.

The Central Park, on account of the narrowness of its site and the way in which it is broken by the reservoirs and numerous rocky ledges, and because of the constructions indispensable to the convenient and harmonious use of it, in divers methods and under various circumstances, of the vast body of people of all classes, which will need to be accommodated when the centre of population, now four miles away, shall be in the midst of it, could not be given a landscape character of as much simplicity, tranquillity and unsophisticated naturalness as, for its primary purpose, was desirable. If the work done upon it during the first fourteen years was designed, without undignified tricks of disguise, or mere affectations of rusticity, to get as far as practicable the better of these difficulties, and secure as much as possible of this desirable character as we have given reasons for claiming, all that has been done and projected since has been directed by the reverse motive and necessarily to the waste of what had before been gained.

In judging what should now be done with the Park, there are a variety of minor considerations which seem to require more attention than, in public discussions, they always receive.

The Central Park is not by any means to be the only place of resort in the city for pleasure-driving and walking. To say nothing of the smaller grounds now in use, at least twenty miles of shaded "boulevards" are already laid out upon the island, besides four notable pleasure grounds, which remain to be prepared. From two of these grounds, and from a number of points in the boulevard system, views much more grand than any on the Central Park will be permanently commanded, and each of the pleasure grounds will be likely in some respects to excell the Central Park in beauty.

The boulevards, five miles of one of which, 150 feet wide, is nearly complete in its constructive features, will offer much better opportunities for a display of equipage and for general public promenade than can be presented in the Central Park.

No part of any of the lands now owned by the city on the island is suitable to be formed into a parade ground, which the present Governor has declared to be a necessity of the city, the demand and agitation for which has already been heated and is sure to occur again and with increasing force.

Four broad avenues of communication running parallel with the principal drives of the Park, are now under construction, and will in a few years be open to public use. These will withdraw an important element of the travel that now passes through the Park.

As population increases and lodges nearer the Park, those who will resort to it for a short stroll on foot or for lounging and resting—who will require walks, seats and shelter—will increase in number much more rapidly than those who come to it in carriages and on horseback. It may in time even be superseded as the fashionable promenade, but, unless greatly mutilated and mismanaged, in no other grounds can there be offered any comparable degree of simple rural effects or of advantages, in that respect, of relief from the city. This special quality of value, then, in the Central Park, should be carefully guarded against a disposition to extend the wheel-ways, or crowd the limited open spaces with artificial objects of interest which would soon have greater value elsewhere.

The value of the Park to the city will be greatly affected by the degree in which good nature and a liking for good order and decorum prevail among those who resort to it. Nothing is so unfavorable to an increase of its value in this respect as temporary, make-shift, incomplete or imperfectly finished arrangements by which the convenience and comfort of visitors is affected and their esthetic impressions are confused. The best means of education in good order is good order.

The walks, especially the concrete walks and gutters, borders of the walks, wooden foot bridges and wood work generally, are now in bad order, and partly from neglect of timely repair, much of their original material will require to be replaced. The present condition of the various works of all classes, executed from eight to fifteen years ago, demonstrates the superior economy of the more substantial and, in the first cost, more expensive structures, and also of a judiciously liberal policy in maintenance.

The existing arrangements for supplying refreshments in the Park are temporary and incomplete: the buildings in which they are served are none of them adapted to be used precisely as they are at present.

The Central Park was designed in all its parts to be closed at night-fall, and to be environed by a walk thirty feet wide and six miles long, to be brilliantly lighted for a night promenade. The time must soon come when if the Park proper is left open at night, it will be impossible by any practicable force of police to prevent the occurrence of frequent crimes and gross outrages upon it. The advantages for clandestine purposes offered in its numerous coverts of rock and foliage, will tend not only to bring the Park itself into disrepute, but to form a bad neighborhood about it. The attempt, recently projected, to light it with gas, while the cost in original outlay and continuous expense would be very great, could not possibly make it a safe or decent place of resort at night. The difficulty of closing and clearing it will increase the longer it is left open after dark. It can hardly be closed, however, at least to carriages, until the adjoining avenues are made ready for use.

The due return for what has already been expended in the Park undertaking, remains not only in abeyance, but, as recent experience has shown, in special peril, so long as the completion of its deferred works is delayed.

Of these there are three classes: First, those dependent on works outside the Park proper. Until, for example, the grading of Eighth avenue is complete, a body of trees within the Park, of the first importance in its landscape design, must remain unplanted, although they will need thirty years' growth to fully realize their purpose, and the trees with which they are to combine, and with which great inequality is undesirable, have already been planted ten years.

Second, those which are yet but vaguely projected, and the location and extent of which, so far as they are to come on the Park at all, is undetermined, as the proposed museums of science, of art, and of living animals.

Third, the refinement and filling out with delicate detail of the present but roughly sketched-in landscape design, especially by suitable horticultural treatment. This, which would not be very costly work, may and should be at once diligently prosecuted.

The increased value of life in this city which has been thought to be promised in the Park, and the expectations of trade, population and wealth to be held and attracted to it, returns more to the city treasury, through its effect on the value of real estate, than the cost of acquiring the Park, as it now stands, has taken from it.

It is quite possible that a large additional outlay may be made on the Park with the eventual result of abating and disappointing the expectations which have been formed of it.

On the other hand, not only may the highest estimates hitherto entertained of its value be realized, but by well directed outlay, they may, profitably, be very much enlarged.

We are, Mr. President,

Very respectfully yours,

OLMSTED & VAUX,

Landscape Architects.

NEW YORK, February, 1872.

TWO LETTERS, 1886

LENOX, MASS., 20th May, 1886.

THE HONORABLE HENRY K. BEEKMAN,
President of the Department of Public Parks, New York.

Dear Sir:

You have asked me to state on what terms your Board could arrange to take counsel with me on several matters. With regard to this request I beg to offer the following observations:

1. The general design of the Central Park was determined twenty-nine years ago. It was controlled in important particulars by conditions that have since disappeared, by legal enactments since abrogated and by instructions from a Board of Commissioners just organized and new to their duties. Limitations and requirements were thus imposed on the designers some of which the Commissioners soon recognized to have been unfortunate. A number of the purposes required to be provided for have since been abandoned and provisions have been introduced in the Park for purposes not then entertained. The surroundings of the Park have greatly changed. The character of the city and the manners and customs of its people have greatly changed. The mere ground space of the Park has become of immense value and is looked upon greedily from many points of view and with reference to a great variety of tastes that might be gratified and interests public and private that might be served upon it. Not a hundredth part of the accommodations for which demands may thus be made could be provided for without destroying the value of the Park for the purposes to which it was originally adapted and wasting the results of the outlay that has been made for them. For some additional purposes, however, provisions may probably be wisely introduced; and provisions for some of the original purposes may be wisely enlarged, but the adjustments of the original design needed for these ends can be made judiciously only with much caution and close study.

2. Fourteen years ago, the preliminary outlines of a plan for a promenade and a Park, were suggested to your predecessors, in general, but imperfect, adaptation to which a large outlay has been made upon the Riverside property of the city, not at all under the superintendence of the designer. In most important particulars the design has been mangled. It is yet but half carried out. Annexations have been made to the property and a reconsideration, revision, enlargement and development of the design for treating it is greatly needed. What is thus required cannot be well provided in a piecemeal way. It must have comprehensive study.

3. The history and present condition of the Morningside property of the city are much the same with those of the Riverside, except that less work has been done upon it.

4. Several times during the last eight years I have been asked

by different Park Commissioners if I would accept a commission to prepare plans for detached portions of each of these parks, and have stated my unwillingness to do so for the reason that it would imply a degree of assent to a method of managing them of an essentially temporizing and time-serving character, inadequate and sure to have wasteful and disastrous results.

5. In view of the circumstances and considerations that have thus been sufficiently set forth it would seem to me best that an engagement should if practicable be made with the original designers of the three parks, under which engagement a general review and report would be prepared upon their present conditions and the improvements and additions desirable to be undertaken in them. With this in view, I respectfully suggest that it should be proposed to Mr. Vaux, who is equally responsible with me for the original design of the Central Park, to resume with me the position and duties that we formerly held for a series of years under your predecessors to their satisfaction and with results generally satisfactory to the public. This was a consulting position, the title of it being that of Landscape Architects Advisory. I have since held and am now holding a similar relation to other important public works.

6. It would, during the following year, be our duty, under such an arrangement, to make the review of the parks and the report upon them that I have suggested to be desirable and this would include duties to be rendered one after another, in the form of provisional or preliminary reports, as soon as should be found practicable, as follows:

(a) A preliminary plan with respect to the proposed entrance at the northwest corner of the Central Park.

(b) Enlarged and improved provisions for riding in the Central Park.

(c) Methods for the radical improvement of the plantations of the Central Park and their constant better management.

(d) A study of the present condition of the park lakes and other waters with advice as to their improvement.

(e) A consideration of the demand for the enlargement of the drives of the Central Park.

(f) A consideration of the demand for additional walks in the Central Park.

(g) A consideration of the Menagerie question.

(h) A consideration of the alleged malarial conditions of the park and their remedy.

(i) A consideration of the present practicability of certain improvements of the Central Park formerly had in view but postponed because of difficulties believed since in a great measure to have disappeared.

(j) Preliminary plans for Riverside Park.

(k) Preliminary plans for Morningside Park.

(*l*) A study of improved connections between the Central, Riverside and Morningside Parks.

(*m*) A consideration of public properties lying exterior to the parks.

(*n*) Such additional matters especially in respect to conditions necessary to the proper realization of adopted designs, as may be found desirable to be reported upon.

7. All other engagements that I have made of the character above contemplated have provided for a term of service of three years and I think it highly desirable in the interest of the parks that that which may be made with you should be.

The duty of the first year, involving as it would unusual professional responsibility in advice as to the recasting in many important particulars of designs for very costly works, already in considerable part worked out, would be extraordinary, but with Mr. Vaux's assent, I should be willing to make an engagement for three years at the same rate of compensation per annum that we formerly received, namely, $5000, and on the same terms in all essential respects.

It is to be presumed that we should be allowed needed assistance of the Superintendent, the Surveyors and other employees of the Department in obtaining the data necessary to the preparation of our plans and report, necessary travelling expenses and expenses for draughting, and that the printing of our report with necessary maps would be done under our direction at the cost of the Department.

As I was advised that the Commissioners wished to obtain an understanding of my views independently of Mr. Vaux I have not, before writing this communication, consulted with him. I have at no time since I left the service of the Department nine years ago conferred with him on the subject. If advised that such an arrangement as I have suggested would be acceptable to your Board, I will ask his assent to it and be prepared to close an engagement and enter upon its duties, as speedily as possible.

(F. L. O.)

10th June, 1886.

THE HONORABLE HENRY K. BEEKMAN,
President, etc.

Dear Sir:

We have the honor to reply to your letter of 4th instant.

1. Parts of each of three costly properties of the city, the Central, Riverside and Morningside parks are within six hundred yards of a common centre. If the three had been brought together

the value of the combined property would be considerably greater than that of the three separately. This consideration not having been regarded in determining their boundaries, the next best thing to do would appear to be that which your Board has in view, the adaptation of certain existing streets to the purpose of connecting pleasure roads and walks, bringing the three properties into one circuit.

2. With regard to the proposition to enter at an early day upon the work necessary to make the Riverside and Morningside park properties available for use, it is to be considered that the city can have no profit from these properties until operations are carried out that have not yet been begun; that their value will depend almost entirely in trees to be grown upon them that cannot be planted until these operations are ended, and that after they have been planted the profit of the entire property in each case will be increasing at a constantly advancing rate of increase. Unquestionably a general plan for their improvement should be settled upon as soon as this can be done with due forethought and deliberation, for the situation in each case presents difficulties to be overcome with economy only by ingenious expedients yet to be devised.

3. As to the Central Park the need for a comprehensive review of its plan and of various projects of alleged improvement to be made in it has for some time been obvious. The original plan has not yet been fully carried out. Features have been introduced in a manner making it impossible that it should ever be carried out in all respects. Important elements of the plan have been so marred in execution as not to serve the purpose originally had in view, and the public respect for the design and confidence in the pursuit of it has in various ways been much impaired.

But the reason commonly given for urging a revision of the plan is based mainly, in our judgment, on mistaken premises, and as reference is made to it in your letter, much as we should like the opportunity of making such a review as you suggest, we should be sorry to have you engage us for the purpose without a clear understanding of the point of view from which we should proceed.

The reason in question may be stated in this form:

Since the Central Park was planned the city has gained greatly in population and wealth and the character, tastes and modes of life of its people have greatly changed. What was adequate for their wants at that time cannot be supposed to be so now. Therefore it is but reasonable to assume that a sweeping revision of the plan is now needed.

This reasoning would give occasion not only for upsetting such results as have been gradually gained at great cost during the last thirty years on this park but for radically revising the plan of all parks of growing cities at certain intervals.

That the facts of the case may be realized it is first to be considered that under the name of parks undertakings may be set about for innumerable purposes. Those to be provided for in one park may differ as widely from those of another as the purposes to be served in building a hotel from those to be served in building a church. Whether and in what way the plan of a park needs revision, therefore, is wholly a question of the particular purposes assigned to be met by that particular park. A park planned with reference to one set of purposes will be as bad as it possibly can be with reference to another.

Hence in planning a park to be found on any given body of land, the first thing to be done is to limit and fix the purposes to be had in view.

The purposes that were determined to be had in view in planning the Central Park were not to be fully well served until in various parts of the site (then mainly a body of rock without trees and without soil in which to grow trees) there should be great numbers of trees with a spread of branches and standing in relations one to another that could not be expected to be attained in less time than forty years, nor, except through processes to be patiently and steadily pursued during that time for the purpose. Accordingly the plan in all its parts was devised with reference not in the least to what the city then was or to the manifest wants of the day but to what the city might be expected to be and its probable wants after a period of forty years. As the degree of the forecast thus used is now rarely realized by those who discuss questions of revision we will recall a few illustrations of it.

One is to be found in the four streets carried through the park by subways as a means of avoiding the disturbance and vexation that would otherwise be caused in time by currents of all sorts of street travel crossing the lines of pleasure travel. This element of the plan imposed cruel restrictions with respect to provisions for its main purposes and made the work of designing these in a satisfactory manner greatly more difficult. The sunken roads were very costly. They delayed the opening of the park to use and were a ground of antagonism to the plan with all who were indisposed to carefully consider what their value would be after many years. There was not the least immediate need for them. Even now not a tenth part of the advantages to be eventually expected from them is realized and yet it is plain that if they had not been provided and the plan of the park proper had not been accommodated to them the most important measure for the improvement of the property at this time would be one for their introduction, even though it involved a revision of the plan of the park of a much more radical, destructive and costly character than anyone thinks of proposing.

Another illustration of the fact is to be found in the numerous archways by which the greater number of visitors moving through the park on foot are led to avoid crossing or following the driveway and riding ways. Were it not for the precautions taken in this respect at a time when the number of private pleasure carriages and riding horses used in the city was not a hundredth part as great as at present, the pleasure roads of the Park might have been double the width they are without accommodating the use now made of them nearly as well as they do.

One other fact of similar significance may be stated. Some of those who regard riding as a matter of supreme importance are disposed to think that the provisions they find in the park for the purpose were devised with reference to the demand of the period when the plan was made. The fact is that at that time not half a dozen citizens of New York kept riding horses and among the innumerable suggestions offered as to what should be provided for in the park there was not one from any quarter for a bridle road. Yet the space then proposed by the designers to be given to bridle roads was larger than that of all the bridle roads of all the parks of London and in three years after the plan had been settled upon, more had been done at the Central Park for the encouragement of pleasure riding than had been done in ten times as many years in all the other cities of the world. Even with all that has since been done elsewhere for the purpose, there is not yet another city that has made as complete, as varied, as costly, or, all things considered, as good provisions for pleasure riding as had long ago been planned by us to be offered to the citizens of New York. And it must be remembered that New York is now acquiring lands in which it is to be presumed that much larger and more perfect provision will be made for this form of recreation in which the interest of the great body of its taxpayers and voters is very slight indeed.

It is perfectly true that there are defects in the existing provisions. It is not true that they are defects of ignorance of what is desirable or of neglect of careful study to secure the best that it has been wise to aim at under all the circumstances. The bridle road is unfortunately winding. It is to be regretted that the course before a rider is as much concealed as it often is but there is not a curve in the road that was not compelled by overruling considerations of the safety of riders and the pleasure and convenience of the public generally in the park. It has always been recognized to be most desirable to have a Rotten Row and a grand promenade in the Park. But conditions of topography and the requirements of general convenience have interposed obstacles that in the opinion of successive Park Commissioners could not be overcome except at a cost not to be justified. We should be glad to find your Board able to take a different view.

With the caution thus offered against mistaken assumptions we shall proceed to consider how it well may happen that a careful revision of the plan of the Central Park as it exists today may be pressingly desirable.

The profit of nearly all classes of public as well as of private works is dependent largely upon the degree in which deferred ends are kept continuously in view. If before a certain point has been reached a work has been carried on with a view to the requirements of a church and later to those of a hotel, the result will be a structure built at excessive cost, to be kept at excessive cost, and not nearly as well adapted to any desirable purpose as it might have been.

The cost of forming the Central Park has been much more than it would have been, the maintenance of it excessively expensive, and in no particular do the citizens of New York obtain nearly the value from their outlay upon it that would otherwise have been due them, because of the pressure constantly brought to bear upon their agents to disregard the principle thus illustrated. The particulars in which the plan is lost sight of or deliberately put aside are seldom particulars of striking importance. There has perhaps been but one instance in which any considerable overruling of the plan has been plainly seen to be impending that public opinion has not been so strongly expressed against it as to force the purpose to be abandoned, but one little thing after another has been done, and a general spirit nursed, tending by the multiplication of departures in detail from the lines necessary to be followed in order that the ruling purposes of the plan may not fail to be realized, of which the outcome is in many respects disastrous to the original ends of the work.

To show how this comes about more than might be supposed, it may be observed that from the beginning there have been annual changes in the composition of the Park Commission. Of the thirty Commissioners who have come suddenly from pursuits in no way preparing them to deal with technical questions of park management to take active part in the management of the park, no two have entered upon their duties with the same ideas of the purposes to be served by it, and no one has retired from these duties after a few years' experience without very different ideas of what purposes it is desirable and practicable to attempt to serve from those he originally had. The greater number of Commissioners have at first considered that the most important part of their duty was to make the park more agreeable not by providing for its uninterrupted growth and development upon plans already formed but by the addition of new features of special and immediate interest to some particular division of the public: the riders, the drivers, the walkers, the skaters, the curlers, those who are fond of croquet, or archery or lawn tennis, or cricket or baseball; those who have a special interest in exotic plants, in flowers, in perennials, in specimen trees; those who think the park is too shady, those who think it is too sunny and so on. With every change in the composition of the Commission there has been more or less bending of the ruling purpose of the Department in respect to such features, and it has happened repeatedly that a considerable amount of work has been done with a view to a particular result and before this result was reached regard for it has so changed that the plan for attaining it has been abandoned. In this manner hundreds of thousands of dollars have been thrown away. And this is not the worst of it.

As a general rule every new undertaking of the class indicated has given a certain degree of satisfaction to a small portion of the public but at a loss to the great body not generally recognized at the time. Because of the large aggregate outlay into which the city has been led for the accomplishment of results of this character to be quickly realized and applauded by those particularly interested in them and because of the attention diverted to these results, undertakings of which the results were to be more slowly realized, and which it was therefore desirable should be prosecuted as rapidly as possible—undertakings of far more general and lasting importance—have been neglected, delayed, advanced listlessly and intermittently, and conditions have been allowed to be established making it finally impossible to carry out the original plan with respect to them.

It is now, therefore, an exceedingly complicated and difficult question in what degree it is judicious to attempt to return to the original design, in what respects to abandon it, in what respects to add to it and in what respects to accept and make the best of the revisions that have, without comprehensive purpose or regard for the future interests of the city, been drifted into.

As to the scope of the revision desirable, this is to be said: In the further management of the Central Park one of three courses must be pursued.

First, it may be managed with little continuous regard to any general design but in a time-serving, desultory, piecemeal way, largely by compromises between differing views of what at any time shall be thought desirable to be rapidly accomplished.

Second, it may be managed with a steady purpose to pursue the ends originally selected to be had in view and with reference to what the larger part of the outlay upon it has been expended, so far as the opportunity for doing so with economy has not been destroyed.

It is with a view to this course if any that we should expect to be of service to you.

But, thirdly, as the population and wealth of the city are multiplied and the park becomes less a central than a "down-town" park, it may be questioned whether the difficulty of maintaining it suitably to the ends had in view in the original plan will not so increase as to render that purpose impracticable.

In view of the constantly recurring demands that provision shall be made for the better accommodation of visitors in certain particulars, not a tenth of which can be made within the area of this park without destroying its value for its original purposes, the question thus presented should have the gravest consideration.

The prime object of the park as originally had in view was to provide for the mass of the population unable to go as much out of town as would be desirable, a retreat as completely rural in character as the circumstances would admit. The proportion of those who use the park in carriages relatively to those who use it on foot will be constantly lessening in the future, yet the number of carriage visitors will be constantly increasing. It may yet come to

Photograph by Edward Heim

Winter Scene, from West Side of the Lake

Looking just north of the Bow Bridge

1924

be double or quadruple the present number. What will happen then? Even today complaint is made that the drives are not wide enough and we understand that the Department is constantly pressed to enlarge them. Once already it has yielded to such pressure and widened a considerable stretch of road, destroying many of the finest trees on the ground in order to do so, and readjusting walks and other features to the injury of the rural character of the ground.

Suppose, then, another enlargement of the drives having been made, the carriage-using part of the public shall have continued to increase and to live near the park so as to use it more freely proportionately to its numbers and that demands again came for yet another enlargement, and so again and again, what is the final result to be? Plainly it is only a question of time when the park will no longer have any value as a rural retreat. Nay, it is but a question how far the process shall be carried to make that which will take the place of the Central Park, a series of broad, hot, glaring desert driving places, with strips of grass and trees between them as unrural as a conservatory or a flower garden.

We have wished simply to suggest toward what ends a large class of the demands tend that are addressed to your Department, for the most part privately, by persons who, having no public responsibility in the premises, naturally take narrow and short-sighted views of the duty of the Commissioners.

Before dropping the subject, we will refer to the fact that while London has been growing densely all about Hyde Park and Kensington Garden, while it has been doubling in population and while fashion has been crowding all about these grounds and the throng of carriages entering them has enormously increased, no material enlargement has been made of the park drives. They are yet generally narrower than those of the Central Park and if filled with carriages would altogether contain not half as many as the Central Park drives as originally laid out would accommodate. The drives, rides and walks of the system of parks which you have in contemplation to form by connecting Riverside and Morningside with Central Park and which can be made ready for public use in two or three years, will not only comfortably accommodate several times as many people in carriages but several times as many in the saddle and several times as many on foot as the corresponding ways of Kensington Garden, Hyde, Green and St. James' Parks and there is no probability that there will ever be a quarter as many people living within three miles of this group of the pleasure grounds of New York as within the same distance of those named of London.

The fact is that the enjoyment of rural scenery, or of any approach to rural quiet and tranquillity, cannot well be provided for in the midst of a city by arrangements that will also provide in a perfectly satisfactory way for the pleasure that people take in great throngs, in making displays of fine dresses, equipages, horses and horsemanship, and in watching such displays. Nor is the enjoyment of rural scenery as a counteractive to the irritating effect of confinement over-long to urban scenery to be satisfactorily associated with such gorgeous floral displays as many urge that the Commissioners may with advantage make on the park, especially on a park formed in accommodation to such a rugged, wild and intractable topography as the Central Park has been. We cannot have our cake and eat it. Hitherto, the park has offered little of rural charm but now, three-fourths of the forty years upon which the designers reckoned for the development of its foliage having been passed, it will be found that the artificial features, so generally supposed, with the greatest possible misconception of their purpose, to have been introduced as objects of decoration, are, except in two or three special cases, scarcely noticeable, not at all intrusive and wholly subordinate in interest to the broader rural elements of the work.

If the city is to throw away the advantage that has thus been gained,—if a different sort of park, adapted to serve a widely different leading purpose from that had in view in the original laying out of the drives, rides and walks, the planting on their borders, the grading and outlining of the lawns and the massing of the woods,— it will be far better that the work of providing it should be taken up deliberately, plans for it devised comprehensively and with a fair counting of the cost, than that it should proceed in the scattering, unpremeditated, stealthy way thus far pursued.

Having thus explained our view of the situation, if your Board should still desire to engage our services as proposed in your letter, we suggest that the best arrangement for the purpose would be one similar to that twice before made with us since we relinquished our first position of general superintendence of the Central Park and which the records will show to have worked satisfactorily to those making it and to the public.

Under such an arrangement our duty would be to give the Department our best judgment on problems of general design of the Central, Morningside and Riverside Parks and the proposed connections between them and to such extent as we should think to be desirable upon methods necessary to the prosecution of the work consistently with the designs. [*Terms stated as in letter of May 20 above.*]

The Department to take no action modifying the intended effect of works that have been advanced upon our designs until after opportunity has been given us to report upon propositions for such action.

If these terms should be satisfactory to your Board, we have only further to request that methods may be adopted for carrying out the arrangement in as prompt, simple and direct a manner as the laws permit.

[Written by F. L. O. evidently to be signed also by C. V.]

CHAPTER II

CONSIDERATIONS OF CONSTRUCTION AND COST

The experience of Mr. Olmsted as Superintendent of the Central Park prior to his submission with Mr. Vaux of the "Greensward" plan undoubtedly caused him to realize more than any of the other competitors the importance of the construction estimate for so large and complicated a piece of work. The report, "Particulars of Construction and Estimate," which accompanied the plan by Olmsted and Vaux, has therefore an historical importance which justifies its reprinting here.[1] The paper of 1859 on the increased cost entailed by changes in the original plan and by opening the park to the public during construction is also of great interest. But the essential difficulty of accurate estimate, and the political impediments to the realization of the park in accordance with any estimates made, are revealed in the letter of 1861 to the Board, regarding the costliness of politics in the park's construction, although this letter merely sketches the difficulties, which are more fully revealed to the reader in the famous document Spoils of the Park *(see Part I, page* 117). *Politics again can be held responsible in 1875 for the niggardly course against which Mr. Olmsted argues in his letter of October, following the action of the Board of Estimate in cutting almost in half the appropriations required for the Parks. This letter can well be quoted today in the campaign to end the "penny-wise pound-foolish" policy which has reduced Central Park to its present unhappy condition.*

THE PAPERS INCLUDED IN THIS CHAPTER ARE:

Particulars of Construction and Estimate for a Plan of the Central Park. 1858.—To accompany "Greensward" Plan. (See ante.)

Report on Construction of certain parts of the work on the Park by contract, by the Superintendent (F. L. O.) May 14, 1858. (Doc. No. 7.)—Recommending work to be done by days' work, and material procured by contract.

[1] This report seems not to be generally known. It was discovered bound in with the reports on competition plans in a pamplet volume in the New York Public Library. See footnote, p. 44, *ante.*

281

Report upon the Changes made in the original plan and their cost by Architect-in-Chief (F. L. O.). July 7, 1859. (Doc. No. 1.)

‡ *Letter regarding classification of work for estimate, to Supt. Eng. Grant from F. L. O. January 20, 1861.*

‡ *Letter regarding costliness of political interference in the construction of the Park, to Board from F. L. O. March 28, 1861.*

‡ *Letter regarding results of undue reduction of appropriations for Park maintenance, to President of Department (Mr. Stebbins) from F. L. O. October 30, 1875.*

‡ Previously unpublished.

PARTICULARS OF CONSTRUCTION AND ESTIMATE, 1858[1]

Order of Construction.

Drainage should be at once commenced, and ought to be completed as soon as possible, because the wetness of the ground which the drainage is to remedy, and the trenches that will necessarily be open during the construction of the drains, will hinder other operations.

The excavations for ponds and all the heavier grading, should be done at the same time with the draining.

The excavation for the drives and walks should also be carried on at the same time; not their complete construction; because the stone which will be brought to the surface in grading, draining and trenching, will need to be selected, to furnish, in part, the material for their construction.

The process of deepening and enriching the soil should follow close upon the drainage; because the narrow trenches formed in draining give facilities for the general trenching of the ground, and the last action in the drainage work can be made the first of the trenching work.

After the present season, tree-planting may be prosecuted at some portions of the park at any time when the season will permit.

Drainage.

Thorough drainage often costs twice as much as it should do, from an inconsiderate arrangement of drains, and the use of improper tools, and unnecessarily expensive materials. It is a scientific operation, and can only be properly carried on after a special study of the ground has been made for the purpose. As no experimental drainage survey has yet been made, it would be premature to offer a detailed plan for this part of the work, but it is recommended that tubular tile should be used, with collars for the most part, and that these should be placed not less than three feet below the surface, and rarely more than four. The direction of the drainage lines should be, as far as practicable, at right angles to the bases of the slopes. The first series of drains will not require pipes of larger calibre than $1\frac{1}{4}$ inches, and the trenches necessary for pipes of this size being narrower than for the 2 inch pipes ordinarily

---

[1] ED. NOTE: Accompanying the "Greensward" plan, No. 33. See Part II, Chapter I, "Description of a Plan, etc.," p. 214.

used, a saving in this particular, as well as in first cost will be effected. The soil in all parts of the park not reserved for ponds, and not furnished with natural drainage, as for instance, by subjacent sloping rocks, should be underlaid with these pipes, not more than forty feet apart; omitting such rocky ground as will not require to be drained by small pipes, there will be little less than 500 acres through which the parallels should be extended.

The annexed estimate of the cost of drainage has been made, after comparing the character of the park land with other sites of which we have had experience, and allows a fair margin for the uncertainty of the subterranean conditions.

Draining 500 acres at $60 per acre - - $30,000.

Improvement of the Soil.

Much of the land in the lower part of the park has been occupied by market gardeners and dealers in offal, and has in consequence been already enriched to some extent. In many places the surface is even now covered with a rich deposit of organic matter, as yet but partially incorporated with the soil. Such is the case on a portion of the slope south of the Reservoir, at the head of which, apparently some large establishment has been in operation, from which streams of fertilizing matter have escaped. The same is the case on some parts of the slopes between Sixth and Seventh avenues in the extreme south of the park.

The adjoining low grounds which we have proposed to excavate for ponds, contain rich soil, and this, when drawn out, and properly distributed where most needed on the slopes referred to, will sufficiently enrich them. Fifty acres may probably be thus provided for. The rest of the ground in the lower park is, on the whole, not in especially bad condition, but most of the soil on the upper park is quite poor. The deepening of the soil in all parts of the park is highly necessary, and the sub-soil must be loosened and fertilizing materials mingled with it.

An experience in bringing land of a similar character to that of the park, to a condition in which trees and shrubs are found to develop rapidly and thrive perfectly, leads to the opinion that an outlay of $150 per acre may possibly be required, exclusive of the cost of drainage, to make such a garden soil upon the park as would be desirable.

If we assume 50 acres to be already provided for, as above mentioned, 100 acres for roads, ponds, building sites, &c., 50 acres of rock, and 150 acres for the reservoirs, we have 400 acres left to be improved, and this at $150 per acre amounts to $60,000.

Trees and Shrubs.

It will be observed that our plan makes at once available the greater part of the trees and shrubs at present growing on the park site. In the upper park this is no inconsiderable advantage, for these trees, although valueless for transplanting, being, for the most part, grown from old stools, are, nevertheless, calculated to be healthy, and in every way satisfactory, if allowed to continue in connection with their parent roots until they have attained full size.

The avenues of the promenade, as already stated, are proposed to be formed of the American Elm, a tree of distinct character, remarkably well adapted for the purpose, and peculiar to this part of the world. It has the vigor and vitality of a young tree until it has grown to be of large size, and will, therefore, bear to be successfully transplanted for immediate effect.

An avenue of considerable dignity may thus be formed with the American elm, sooner, we believe, than with any other tree.

The trees on the map are shown, for the sake of distinctness and accuracy, merely in *plan*, and may thus, in some instances, appear to stand openly and scattered. They would, however, in any natural horizontal view, compose in masses more or less dense.

The planting generally is designed to give from the greatest number of points of view, within the park, the broadest effects of light and shade which can be obtained upon the ground, and to produce the impression of great space and freedom, while at the same time the visitor may keep in dense shade if he prefer it. We have thought it necessary to pay particular attention to this point, having observed, that townspeople appear to find, in broad spaces of green sward, over which they are allowed unrestricted movement, the most exhilarating contrast to the walled-in floors or pavements to which they are ordinarily confined by their business.

Planting.

In any calculation for expenditure in planting, it will evidently be necessary to include a far greater number of trees than will ultimately remain in the park, or than ought to be shown on any plan made to illustrate a completed result. We allow:—

150,000 trees, at an average price of 33⅓ cents,...............	$50,000
And for 150,000 shrubs, average price of 16 cents,.............	24,000
For extra sized trees, to be planted for immediate effect,........	25,000
And for the planting and cultivation of trees,.................	120,000
	219,000

Drives and Walks.

It is proposed that the principal driveways shall be sixty feet in width. This is the width of the grand drive in the Prater of Vienna, and of the most frequented drives of the Bois de Boulogne. It admits of six lines of carriages being driven at moderate speed, side by side. Much wider roads, however fine in themselves, are incompatible with a rural character of landscape.

After a long continuance of rainy weather, the best road is found to be one composed of small broken stone, packed firmly as a rock, and the deeper the better.　Such a road is, however, far less agreeable under all ordinary circumstances, than even a common earth road, if the latter is kept tolerably smooth, on account of the jar and noise which the solidity of the stone occasions.　This will be appreciated by any one who is in the habit of driving out upon our macadamized avenues, and from them into the country roads. It is invariably the case where a portion of a broad earth road is macadamized, that the earth track, except after bad weather, is much more driven upon than the stone.　Such it will be remembered was the case with the old Third avenue road.

It would be undesirable to entirely forego this advantage of earth roads in park drives, which are chiefly used in fine weather, even if stone roads were the only ones which could be depended upon to be tolerably good after heavy rains.

This, however, is by no means the case.　After rain, clay roads, it is true, must be slimy, and even on the best gravel roads the traction will be slightly increased; but this is, really, no objection to gravel roads for pleasure carriages, to which the additional resistance would be inappreciable.　Roads of binding gravel are always excellent—better for pleasure-driving than any other—so long as their foundation is firm and unyielding.　Ordinarily, however, the earth below works up every Spring, and the whole road becomes soft and rutty.　It is very commonly attempted on private grounds to provide against this by laying a stratum of stone under the gravel, which, if the road is much used, serves only to increase the evil, for the gravel stone sinking through the clay more readily than the larger stone, the latter, in obedience to a well-known law, work to the surface.　There is one method of using large stones, however, which was first practised by Telford on the Holyhead road, and which supplies a perfectly unyielding road foundation.　The stone should be from 8 to 12 inches in length, and from 6 to 8 in breadth; irregularly rhomboidal in form, and moderately soft, are better than extremely hard stone for the purpose.　Stones of this description are found in great quantities upon the park.　Several stacks of them gathered from the trenched ground of the middle nursery, are now, or lately were standing below Seventy-First street, midway between the Fifth and Sixth avenues.　We observe them also on the recently trenched ground in the north part of the park.　A quantity large enough to make all the roads of the park, and useless for any other purpose, will evidently be brought to the surface whenever the ground shall be ditched or trenched.

The proper method of employing these stones, having first prepared a suitable road bed, is to set them by hand on their broadest ends, closely, side by side; then tó crowd or ram other smaller stone in the large interstices, which will be left.　This process being carried on over the whole roadbed, a rude pavement is formed, the stones of which being wedged in their places, cannot work up, as stones laid flatwise, constantly will, under the pressure of wheels.

Believing that a road, of binding gravel, laid upon a foundation of this kind, well drained, will be much more satisfactory for pleasure drives than any other, we have endeavored to ascertain whether a gravel of the right description can be procured for the present purpose, at a moderate cost. Large portions of the park are underlaid by a compact gravelly sub-soil, and there are within it some beds of tolerable gravel. One of these beds will, probably, be encountered by the lower transverse road, and may possibly furnish a considerable quantity of fair quality. None, however, seems to be found in the park, or in the vicinity of New York city as good as it is desirable to obtain. An excellent gravel, which was used in the construction of St. John's Square, is brought from Philadelphia. The cost of this, however, puts it out of the question for our purpose. The slate-gravel of the palisades will not endure the action of wheels. We have, as yet, found none that would answer nearer than Kingston Creek, on the Hudson. This gravel, (a specimen of which, taken at random from the bed, and not screened, is herewith submitted,) is of good color, very even, and we have ascertained that it packs remarkably well. It can be loaded into sloops from the creek banks, and delivered on the North River wharves, at one dollar a cubic yard. It can thence be transported to any part of the park, by two-horse wagons, at 50 cents a yard. The surface of the drive is proposed to be made of this material, and to give it more complete solidity, a central portion is intended to be formed of road metal, six inches deep, for a width of twenty-four feet. The whole to rest on the foundation described, which is to be covered at the sides four inches deep, with such gravelly material as may be obtained in grading for the road-bed.

(The superintendent of the Harlem Railroad has proposed to supply any amount of good clean gravel, that may be needed for the park, at a considerably less rate than is allowed in this estimate, but has failed to furnish a specimen in time to be submitted with the plan).

The necessary embankments for the drives will be furnished by the excavations, without additional cost, except in certain instances, where they may also be provided, without cost, from the adjoining transverse road excavations.

For the grading and construction of road-bed, an average expenditure is allowed, per mile, of....................	$3,840 00
Foundation to be laid by hand as described, including arrangements for the removal of surface water, per mile........	7,000 00
(Where rock bottom is found, the artificial road foundation will be omitted; but as the cost of drainage, &c., may, in these cases, be greater than usual, no deduction from the estimate for the foundation is made on this account.)	
Centre, twenty-four feet of road metal, two inches size, six inches thick, per mile...............................	6,101 33
Carried forward.............	$16,941 33

Brought forward............. $16,941 33

The hardest stone which can be readily procured should be taken for this purpose; but there does not appear to be a large quantity of the Diorite, which is at present being broken on the park, remaining in its vicinity; and it is probable that resort will need to be had to some other rock, to furnish even the limited quantity of metal required by this plan. If, on trenching the ground, an unexpected amount of Diorite boulders should be exposed, this stone may be used exclusively for the purpose; but it must be broken more cheaply than by the present method. Consultation with a mining engineer, shows us that a stamping-mill, such as is used in the gold-fields of North Carolina, (and which, with a five-horse power steam-engine, would cost less than $1,000.) would break Diorite (first suitably sledged) to the requisite size, at a cost not probably exceeding one half the price of the work now done in stone breaking for the commission.

Probably, however, there will be no occasion to resort to this process, and either the gneiss rock broken on the park, or the debris of quarries will be obtained at an equal reduction on the present cost of the Diorite metal.

We have, therefore, estimated the road metal, spread and rolled, at the rate of $2 60 per cubic yard.

Layer of the local gravel, or of gravelly sub-soil, four inches deep on the foundation, each side of the road metal, eighteen feet wide, per mile..............................   355 28

(i.e. 2,368½ cubic yards, at 15 cents per yard).

Layer of good Kingston gravel, two inches over the road metal, four inches on the wings, per mile....................   4,725 75

(i.e. 3,150½ cubic yards, at $1 50 per yard).

Rolling and keeping in order for say three years, per mile....   500 00

Making a total per mile, sixty feet wide, of................. $22,522 36

On the plan, there are seven and a half miles of this width, which, at this price, will cost........................ $168,917 70

And 4,000 feet of roads, forty feet wide, at $15,015 per mile...   11,386 65

Walks and footpaths are calculated at an average width of twelve feet.

Grading and draining, per mile.................... $1,600
Bedding with unbroken stone, per mile...........   960
Covering with gravel, per mile...................   1,700
Rolling and keeping, three years per mile..........   150

Total cost per mile.............................$4,410 00

Fifteen miles of walk at $4,410 .... $66,150 00

Making a total for roads and walks, of.................... $246,454 35

Transverse Roads.

Nothing in the act defining the trust of the Board of Commissioners of the Central Park, can be construed as requiring it to provide any public roads across the park. If they are furnished, it will be purely as a matter of convenience to the business of the city, and they should therefore be considered under an entirely different head from that of its parks or places of recreation. They will in no way subserve, but, on the contrary, rather interfere with the purposes of the fund, which the commission is exclusively charged to expend. Although, therefore, from a proper foresight in regard to public convenience, competitors have been required by the commission to make provision for this contingency, and it will doubtless be willing to cede such portions of the park land as may be necessary, it can hardly be supposed that it will consent to withdraw from its fund the sum necessary to be expended in their actual construction. The three lower roads should, however, for evident reasons of economy and convenience, be made at the same time with the park. The transverse road at Ninety-Seventh street may possibly be unneeded for many years, and only requires at present to be recognized in the general scheme of planting.

The cost of the transverse roads has been calculated as follows:

Excavation, Tunnelling, and Mason work.

First (65th to 66th st.),	$27,025
Second (79th to 79th st.),	43,200
Third (86th to 86th st.),	16,000
Fourth (97th to 97th st.),	12,350
Walling sides (additional to above),	26,000
Sewering, Lighting, and Paving,	80,000
Total,	$204,575

The embankments which have been unnecessarily made upon the park, for the extension of Seventh avenue and of Sixty-Third street, are intended to furnish most of the material for the needed elevation near the entrances at Fifty-Ninth street and Fifth avenue and at Sixtieth street and Eighth avenue. The soil and earth necessary at these points, however, is supposed in our estimates to be obtained from without the park, at a price of 25 cents a yard. At this price it may be carted from beyond Hamilton Square, near which there is much private land which must be removed to a depth of 15 feet before it can be built upon.

The earth required for the elevated ride around the new Reservoir, is supposed to be brought from between Avenue C and Second Avenue, south of Eighty-Sixth street, at which locality it has been ascertained that the requisite quantity can be had for the moving of it. The cost of this is calculated at 25 cents a yard. Tan bark for the Reservoir ride is supposed to be brought from the neighborhood of the Catskill Mountains at a cost of $7,600. It can, perhaps, be procured nearer and cheaper.

Some portion of the low ground, west of the new Reservoir, is intended to be raised. This is necessary in order to secure drainage, which must lead westwardly through an existing culvert under the aqueduct, the floor of which is above the present surface of the ground referred to. This will require about 16,667 cubic yards of filling, at 25 cents, $4,166 75.

In widening Fifty-Ninth street, near Fifth avenue, stone is supposed to be dumped in such a manner as to form a slope from 30° to 60°, and the same plan is to be followed wherever the established grade of the street is four or more feet above the natural surface of the land within the park. Earth is to be dumped together with the stone, and a sufficient quantity must be secured on the surface to permit a growth of small trees and shrubs. The expense of a regular retaining wall will thus be saved, and the effect, in connection with the trees upon the exterior wall, will be to add much to the apparent extent of the park.

Exterior Wall.

In these cases it is to be expected that, eventually, a parapet wall, of somewhat enriched character, will be made upon the edge of the mall, as suggested when treating especially of that portion of the plan. For years to come however, a wall, somewhat like the one which has already been built around the park, but less massive, and furnished with a coping of quarried stone, will be entirely appropriate and sufficient. The body of such a wall would be formed from a selection of the materials of the present one, which will require to be demolished, whenever the grading of the streets and avenues is perfected.

We should propose to build the wall seven feet high, wherever the surface of the park is more than that height above grade. The bank immediately within the wall to be sloped from the base of the wall on the inside, at an angle varying according to its material, from 20° to 50°, so as to prevent danger of land slides, and to admit of the growth of shrubs or creepers on the slope. Soil to be deposited within the angle of the slope and the wall, in which, as in a pot, or elevated border, choice shrubs should be planted.

It is supposed that the rock and earth which would be obtained in forming the slopes just described, together with the stone not otherwise appropriated, which will be brought to the surface in draining and trenching, and in excavating and tunnelling for the drives, walks, and transverse roads, would be sufficient to form the slopes which we have previously proposed to take the place of retaining walls.

We reckon this quantity to be 125,000 loads, which will cost about
7 cents a load, or...................................... $8,750
For rebuilding and improvement of wall in the manner proposed
(average $2 per yard)................................. 21,180

For slopes and walls $29,930

Bridges.

Two large bridges have been provided for in the estimates for transverse roads (one being the rock over a tunnel, the other of mason work in connection with a tunnel). Seven other bridges are required, which it is proposed to build of timber. These should be as inconspicuous as possible and it is designed that they should be plain truss bridges, supported in the centre. At a cost of $4,000 each, they will be perfectly substantial and enduring. A small, but handsome stone arch, to cost say $500, will be wanted in McGowan's pass, and two foot bridges, at $250 each,

For bridges, total..................................... $29,000

The excavations for ponds will amount to about 100,000 yards,
entirely of earth and loose stone, which, at 16 cents a yard,
is... $16,000

As the sub soil of the sites is a stiff clay, little expense for puddling is
apprehended, and the sub soil and loose stone removed in
excavation, will furnish material for the "heads"; but to allow
for unexpected difficulties, these items are placed at......... $5,000

For ponds, total..................................... $21,000

Buildings.

Buildings are scarcely a necessary part of a park; neither are flower-gardens, architectural terraces or fountains. They should, therefore, be constructed after dry walks and drives, greensward and shade, with other essentials have been secured, and the expenditure for them should be made with entire reference to the surplus funds at the disposal of the commission after the park is constructed. If it were necessary to regard these features as of paramount importance, they might readily absorb two-thirds of the whole fund at the disposal of the commission: we consider them, however, as entirely subordinate to the main idea, and in our plan the music hall, Italian terrace, conservatory, flower garden and fountains, are but accessories of a composition in which the triple promenade avenue is the central and only important point. We merely indicate appropriate sites for these minor features, and suggest the style in which they may, when required, be constructed.

Similar remarks apply to fences and gates, lodges, dressing and refreshment houses, &c. The expenditure absolutely necessary for all this class of constructions need not exceed $50,000

Estimate [Summary]

Draining..	$ 30,000
Formation of ponds.............................	21,000
Water conveyance...............................	20,000
Improvement of soil............................	60,000
Trees and planting..............................	219,000
Carried forward..........	$350,000

Brought forward..........	$350,000
Roads and walks..	246,454
Widening 59th Street..................................	10,000
Grading at entrances..................................	20,000
Levelling and forming parade ground.....................	12,000
Levelling and forming play grounds.......................	5,000
Levelling and forming promenade and hall site..............	5,000
Formation of ride about New Reservoir....................	71,368
Filling west of New Reservoir...........................	4,166
Exterior walls and slopes...............................	29,930
Formation of turf......................................	20,000
Bridges...	29,000
Lodges and gates......................................	50,000
Alteration of Arsenal and Fifth Avenue entrance to same......	8,000
Alteration of Chapel and preparing Museum................	5,000
Music platforms, arbors, and seats........................	5,000
Casino..	6,000
Military entrance......................................	3,000
Martello tower on Vista rock............................	1,500
Present expenditures...................................	140,000
Salaries and running expenses...........................	100,000
Total estimate for construction of Park................	$1,121,418
Garden and fountains...................................	20,000
Terrace and fountains..................................	20,000
Superintendent's house and offices........................	12,000
Fifth Avenue entrance lodge and gate (additional)............	10,000
Gardener's house, green house, and reserve garden...........	5,000
	$1,188,418
Surplus for extra buildings and contingencies (including transverse roads $204,575),................................	311,582
Total amount....................................	$1,500,000

(Following the estimate, a second part of this Particulars of Construction was devoted to a "Descriptive Guide to the Arboretum." See Part II, Chapter IV, page 335.)

REPORT ON CONSTRUCTION BY CONTRACT.[1]

May 14, 1858.

It is obvious that there is much to be done on the Park, which it would be impracticable to have properly executed under contract; tree planting, for instance. The objections which will at once be

[1] From Superintendent, F. L. O. Ordered to be printed July 15, 1858, as Doc. No. 7.

perceived to having trees planted by contract, apply, in a greater or less degree to nearly all the work to be done on the Park; very little work is to be done, that is to say, in which the constant exercise of taste and judgment as well as of skill and industry will not be required; and this taste and judgment can not well be contracted for.

It is considered desirable, even with regard to the construction of the roads, that the designer should be left free to improve the plan as the work progresses, from suggestions afforded by the partial construction of the roads; such suggestions are so likely to occur, that it is the custom of many landscape gardeners to make no special preliminary surveys, but having determined the general direction of a pleasure drive, to fix its curves and grades definitely only from day to day, as point after point is reached. It was in this way that the drives at Greenwood were laid out, and although a moderately exact preconception of the final result should be formed before commencing the work, it is undesirable to undertake to fix the lines, curves, grades, or even the method of construction with that degree of precision which would be necessary before contracts for the roads could be made.

It is apparent, also, that if made in connection with other parts of the work to be done, the roads can be constructed with less labor than if undertaken as a distinct enterprise. Thus the trenching of the ground is expected to supply material for the roads; the number of men and carts which will be required to remove this material within a limited time, will be much greater for one acre than for another, because one acre will supply double as much as another.

It will therefore be desirable that the power should be had to draft men and teams from one branch of the work to another, as from day to day may be found best. Changes of weather will produce similar necessities. Sixty carts are now engaged for work on the Park. It has not been practicable to work any of them this week, the ground being too wet to admit of their carrying full loads on the low ground, where they would otherwise have been engaged. If roads had been under construction there would have been, yesterday, nothing to prevent the whole number working upon them, the high ground being firm and the earth to be shovelled from the roadbed being in a condition to work more cheaply than usual.

If the same interest governs the progress of road construction and all other work to be done, it will be usual to carry on grading for all other purposes as closely as possible to the work of construction upon the roads in order that an interchange of material may be cheaply made. But no agreement in terms could be made for such a purpose, and no contractor could be forced to accommodate his progress to the progress of the Park towards completion, in other respects than the subject of his contract.

In order to secure the performance of contract work in a satisfactory manner, the expense of superintendence would need to be about as great if the work should be done by day's labor.

Another objection occurs to contracts generally, from the introduction which they would effect, of bodies of laborers, under a different government, with different wages, hours of work, privileges, requirements and customs from those which will belong to the regularly hired laborers of the Commission. It is supposed to be for a reason of this character that walls have been built to separate the work upon the new Reservoir from that upon the Park.

On these grounds it is not advised that any considerable division of the work to be done on the Park should be accomplished by contract.[1] It will, however, probably be best to obtain most of the materials to be procured for use upon the Park by contract, as also for the work of masons and other mechanics.

REPORT ON CHANGES FROM ORIGINAL PLAN AND THEIR COST.[2]

*To the Board of Commissioners
of the Central Park:*

Gentlemen:—

A resolution of the Board, of the 16th of June, requests the Architect-in-Chief to report whether any, and if so, what changes have been made in the original plan, and what has been the increased cost occasioned by such changes.[3]

It is proper to say, that the plan, as originally presented to the Commission, did not assume to be a working or exact plan, but simply a study or sketch for a plan, as was the case with each of the previous plans, and with all but one, it is believed, of the others before the Commission. A plan adapted to be followed exactly would have required an elaborate survey, such as it would have been impossible, save by employing several engineers, to have

---

[1] ED. NOTE: The contract question was thoroughly canvassed in the Board. While a minority report favored the contract system, a majority, including the President, were satisfied with Mr. Olmsted's reasons against contract construction and with the progress of work under his superintendence. The President concluded:
"The results at which the undersigned has arrived are, in brief, that it is not expedient to disarrange or suspend the work as at present organized for a period of time necessary to perfect the specifications and preliminary examinations that must precede and accompany a system of contracts. . . .
"The construction of the Park proper is the first object of this Board, and from this duty it should not be diverted by visions of costly fountains or marble structures. A constant and careful watchfulness over its expenditures will enable the Board to secure its primary object—a Park with walks, rides and drives without violation of law, and with the approbation of those who are to enjoy its annually augmenting attractions." (Doc. No. 10).
[2] Doc. No. 1 of July 7, 1859.
[3] ED. NOTE: It shoud be noted that by Act of Legislature, April 2, 1859, the upper part of the Park was extended from 106th St. to 110th St., in accordance with recommendations of the designers.

obtained within the period given to competitors for forming the plans.

The principal changes of the plan consist, as shown on the accompanying maps, of the introduction of the Bridle-road, a considerable increase in the length, and a change in the courses of the walks, and an entire change in the position of the Drive east and south of the Play-ground, and along the west side of the Park, as far north as Seventy-second street. With the exception of the changes recently ordered by the Board near Fifty-ninth street, between Sixth and Eighth avenues, the above specified alterations of the plan were laid out under instructions of the Board, of May 18th, 1858, reported September 9th, 1858, endorsed by the Executive Committee, and assented to by the Board, September 16th, 1858. They have involved considerable changes of the surface, and of the treatment of ground, from that had in view in the original study. . . . They have also led to the introduction of bridges for carrying the Bridle-path and the walks clear of the Drive. The region of the Ramble has been much more thoroughly improved, and a more extensive system of walks made through it, than was originally contemplated; the capacities of the ground not having been entirely obvious until test-pits and experimental cuttings had been formed, and the ground somewhat cleared of worthless matters. . . . The Central Pond has been considerably enlarged, and its outline changed, as in the process of excavation the rocks were found to give invitation. Knowing nothing of the subterranean rock forms, it was, of course, impossible to establish the best outlines, and it was not practicable to obtain such knowledge until after the adoption of a general intention of work. Changes will also have been made in the outline of the lower Pond, the final survey for which cannot even yet be completed. The attention of the Executive Committee was called to each of the above operations in their early stages, and they were approved by that Committee in September last.

It is not now possible to form an estimate, which would have any practical value, of the difference of cost which these changes have occasioned. It has before, on more than one occasion, been reported to the Board, that without able assistants employed expressly for the purpose, it had been and would be impossible to state with an approximation to certain accuracy, the cost of any particular portion or portions of the work. The Board has seen fit to require or provide means for this service only in regard to the Transverse Roads—a very careful separation of all expenditure properly chargeable to which, from all other work with which they connect, is now made every day, an Assistant General Foreman being employed exclusively and constantly in the duty of obtaining the data for this account.

Each of the improvements upon the original plan involves a larger expenditure than was contemplated in that plan, and it was for that reason, and that reason alone (as was explained to the Committee of the Board under the advice of which the Board has acted in adopting them), that most of them were not included in the original plan. The change of the line of Drive on the west side is an exception, but the lines of the original plan were required by the specifications of the Board demanding a parade-ground of a certain fixed area. This also was explained to the Board at the time the change was ordered.

For the same reason that it was not possible to make working plans it was still less practicable to prepare, previous to the competition of designers, anything like accurate estimates. The Commission required an expression of opinion from each designer that it was possible to execute all the different parts of his or her plan in such a manner that the whole would not cost above an allotted sum. From the peculiar nature of the work, this involved, for almost any plan, simply a question, throughout, of the quality of workmanship to be assumed. . . .

The Board has not, at any time since the work upon the ground according to the plan commenced, evinced in its instructions to the Architect-in-Chief any expectation of fully completing the Park in all its parts and details together, within a definite period of time, or a fixed amount of expenditure. It is not, and has never been, possible to undertake to do this with confidence, not because the materials and labor necessary to make a park must, under all circumstances, have cost more than that sum, nor because the time would have been insufficient, if the field of operations were clear, but because there were obstacles while the construction of the New Reservoir was to be in progress, and the adjacent streets and avenues remained ungraded or in the process of grading, in the non-existence of proper outlets for water, and the incomplete system of sewerage of the adjoining part of the island, and in various other circumstances, which could not be immediately overcome, except at great and otherwise unnecessary cost. On the supposition that all work intended to be done in the neighborhood of the Park, and within its limits, was to have been pushed forward with the same energy which all desire to have employed on the Park itself, the Park might possibly be completed in every particular directly contemplated in the plan, within the time allotted to this Commission, and within the sum allowed for its expenditure.

The work, however, cannot be expected to be completed, as things are, in all parts and all details, under the present law, and it has been necessary to determine how the most complete park possible to be obtained with the fund at the disposal of the Commission, and within the time allotted for its duties, can be best secured. The Architect-in-Chief entertains the opinion that it is best to finish such portions as are most needed, and which will together make the most complete park, in a manner which shall give the most lasting satisfaction, and involve the least practicable future expenditure for alterations and repairs. Such a policy the Architect-in-Chief considers to have governed all work on the Park hitherto. It would have been easy to have greatly reduced the expenditure, or, rather, to have made more immediate show of a tolerable finish, by carrying the drives at various points with heavier grades, and less agreeable curves, by leaving large flat masses of rock from a few inches to a foot below the surface of the lawns, the bad consequences of which would be but occasionally apparent, by making the foundation of the walks less substantial, and their under-drainage less perfect; by neglecting to excavate about rocks having picturesque features hidden under a worthless deposit, etc. The course pursued has been directed, however, as is believed, by a judicious economy, looking to the future. The Park will not only at once be much more satisfactory and valuable to the city, but its improvement in such particulars as have been enumerated, and in many others, which would unquestionably have been demanded in the future if now neglected, will have been made at a moiety of the cost which would be necessary to accomplish them when once the lawns have been formed, the trees established, and the public admitted, while the specific features of detail that will have to be for a time omitted (such as the flower-garden) are not absolutely necessary requirements in a park, and can be constructed at any time, at as reasonable cost as now.

There always has been, and there now is, a considerable cost incurred, which would otherwise be unnecessary, in forcing to rapid, and, at the same time, substantial completion, certain parts of the Park, in obedience to the well-understood wish of the Board and of the public that as soon as possible it might be made of some direct value to the public.[1] The principal work upon more than three-

---

[1] ED. NOTE: This policy was in agreement with that expressed by the Board in the following statement:

" It also seemed to the Board clear, that the construction of the Park would be much more economically and much more speedily accomplished by carrying on all classes of structure at the same time, and that it was the duty of the Board to construct the work placed in its charge in such a manner as to combine beauty of design, with solidity and permanency of structure.

" In furtherance of these views, and, as it is believed, in obedience to the dictates of a sound economy, a request was made of your Honorable Body for its sanction of an application to the Legislature, for further provision of means to complete the Park. This request was met on the part of both Boards of the Common Council with an unanimity of approval that was peculiarly grateful to those charged with the labor and responsibility of the conduct of the Park; and the Board take pleasure in acknowledging the cordial co-operation and encouragement it has received in the carrying on its work at the hands of your Honorable Body, from the commencement of the work to this time.

" The policy of opening for public use portions of the Park as they are completed, has thrown upon the Board the necessity of providing out of the moneys placed at its disposal, the means of maintaining and keeping in order these completed portions.

" The current expenses of maintaining and keeping the Park in order, should be provided from a fund other than that provided for construction.

" The Board has had under consideration the subject of the expense of maintaining the Park, and will endeavor to establish a system of licenses for franchises and privileges, that will yield a revenue to the Park without in any respect obstructing or taxing its free enjoyment in all departments. Licenses for refreshment rooms, for perambulators, or Bath-chairs for invalids, to be allowed on the

quarters of the whole area of the Park may be expected to be completed, and the public, in some measure, given the enjoyment of it, in fifteen months from the beginning of work, instead of four years, as contemplated in the estimates of the designers. The additional cost is not occasioned by the employment of an unwieldy mass of laborers, the Architect-in-Chief believing that, as at present organized, no saving could be made by reducing the force, except in the convenience of obtaining and turning to the best account materials obtained in excavation, in keeping open and unincumbered the most direct routes of transit for materials, in using machinery of construction a second time instead of duplicating it, and in the more careful distribution and preparation of different qualities of materials, especially of soils and manures, the poor supply of which obliges a constant resort to costly expedients.

Central Park, July 5th, 1859.

Respectfully,

FRED. LAW OLMSTED,
Archt.-in-Chief and Supt.

CLASSIFICATION OF WORK FOR ESTIMATES.

January 20th, 1861.

To W. W. GRANT, ESQ.,
    Supt. Eng.

A scheme of work to be done on the park between Feb. 1st and Dec. 1st, 1862, with estimate is to be prepared as soon as practicable. The work is to be classified[1] under heads of excavation, filling, road

---

walks, and for boats on the lake, may all be made to yield a revenue, and relieve the city of a part of the annual cost of maintaining the Park."—From 3rd Annual Report, C. P. C., 1859. (A typical list of receipts from concessions and sale of products of the Park may be found in the 12th Annual Report, C. P. C., 1868, p. 16.)

    [1] ED. NOTE: The classification of maintenance expenses is also of interest, as given in the 9th Annual Report, C. P. C., 1865, page 16:—

" The accounts of the expenses of the maintenance of the Park were several years since classified for the purpose of convenience, and to secure and preserve their correct record in detail.

" This classification comprehends the following heads:

1. Roads.	9. Thorough Drainage
2. Walks.	10. Traffic Roads.
3. Plantations.	11. Masonry.
4. Turf.	12. Tools.
5. Water.	13. Buildings.
6. Ice.	14. Miscellaneous.
7. Surface Drainage.	15. Gate-keepers.
8. Irrigation.	16. Park-keepers."

In the 5th Annual Report, 1861, there is an early discussion of classes of maintenance expenses, following the statement that by Act of March 19, 1860, an estimate for maintenance and government of the Park was authorized to be made. See p. 39 of this report for analysis of maintenance expenses, 1861.

bottoming, superstructure, drainage, trenching, surface grading, etc., etc., and each head into local sections, and each local section into progress sections. The local sections should be so limited in size (except as in the case of bridges when it would be impracticable) that the total estimate on each section should not exceed $4000, and the progress sections should each constitute an estimate of the rate of progress of the expenditure to be made on each section by quarters of expenditure, showing to what point each sum of one-quarter of the whole sum estimated to be expended will carry the work. The whole to be arranged with reference to a system of accounts by which the work can be checked and if necessary its plan modified, if it is found to be exceeding the estimates.

[F. L. O.]

COSTLINESS OF POLITICAL INTERFERENCE IN THE CONSTRUCTION OF THE PARK.

NEW YORK, March 28, 1861.

*To the Board of Commissioners
of the Central Park.*

Gentlemen:

Much less was accomplished on the park last year than you had intended and the cost of what was accomplished was much in excess of your estimates.

The park as hitherto designed cannot be completed, at the rate of the cost of what was done last year, within the amount to which the expenditure of your Board has been limited.

After being convinced of what I have now announced to you, in January last, I presented my resignation of the office of Superintendent. The President and a majority of the Board and of the Executive Committee having been informed of the circumstances which led me to do so, at the request of the President and a majority of the Executive I subsequently withdrew my resignation. I state this here that it may be seen why I have not sooner brought a matter of so much gravity before the Board. The only accounts in detail which could be had as a basis for calculating were so meagre and untrustworthy that a clear and definite exhibition of the state of the work, and of the specific items in which the estimates had been exceeded, could not be given. Until a more thorough analysis could be made, it was not thought best to occupy the Board with matters the discussion of which there appeared no reason to believe would serve any good purpose.

After much labor I find it still quite impracticable to prepare a statement in detail of the cost of the work of last year. The reason is simply that no specific account of the expenditure of labor upon different parts of the work has been kept except upon the transverse roads, beyond the rough record which almost from the beginning of the work I have required each foreman to give me in the form of a daily report. Many of the foremen are ignorant; some of the best can barely write and are quite unable to make any but the simplest entries. These reports therefore are too indefinite and untrustworthy to furnish a proper basis for accurate calculations. Owing to the want of all other provision for a record of cost, and to the insufficient means of superintendence in general, it is not now practicable to draw up an accurate statement of account between the different parts of the work. Nor can the general conclusions of two months study of such data as exist be presented in a useful form to the Board, except as they bear upon a few broad questions of policy.

A few such conclusions I shall now offer:

To complete the park in all respects as has hitherto been intended, with as good workmanship as has hitherto been secured, at the rates of cost of last year, and with a safely liberal estimate on work and materials of kinds not hitherto largely used, would cost more than the sum which the Commission is pledged not to exceed by 32 per cent.

It is practicable to vary the plan as it has formed itself in the minds of the designers, in particulars to which the Commission has not yet given definite attention, in such a way that without mutilating it or essentially changing it the estimate of cost may be reduced from what it should be for the design and as hitherto entertained and estimated upon. It is also practicable to adopt in the upper park a ruder workmanship and cheaper method of construction in some particulars.

At the beginning of operations on the park I expressed the opinion that the required work could be done cheaper by the direct employment of the workmen under the superintendent than by the contract system. Influenced in some measure by my judgment, as the given records show, the Board directed me to employ the necessary force directly and has hitherto resorted to the contract system only as an exception. I think it due to myself to now say that I do not consider that a fair trial of the system of labor which I had intended to approve as the alternative of the contract system has ever been had on the park, and I protest against being held as approving and recommending it. If the Board holds me to have been responsible for the economy of the work of the park, and is justified in doing so, then I have been culpably neglectful of my duty in that I have allowed myself to be constrained to constantly employ incompetent and inefficient men. Not grossly and totally incompetent and inefficient men, but men whom I should not have employed if I had been required to employ only the most competent and efficient men whom I could procure. Not one man in ten of all employed on the work has in my opinion obtained employment there because he was competent and efficient and for no other reason. The Commission has the credit of conducting its work free from the vice of politics. The park is not made to administer to the strength of any political party, but men and officers are and have been from the beginning employed on the park from considerations not of economy and efficiency but of policy, just as truly as in the Custom House or the City Hall, and the park has never been free, but has been constantly cursed and disgraced with the vice of politics. It is so now and it will probably continue to be. I have no reason to think that there is one member of the Board who does not believe this to be necessary; no member of the Board has evinced a desire that it should be otherwise.

For myself, after a close observation during four years of the working of this political system I am satisfied that, looked upon merely as a policy, it is a bad policy, the purposes intended to be accomplished by it being on an average as much set back as advanced by every appointment that is made. What is a favor to one man brings about a cause of offence by preventing the appointment desired by another; a bad man is appointed as a favor, and his subsequent necessary discharge, his malice and false reports, do more harm than his appointment did good, simply with reference to the friendship of those intended to be conciliated. I am speaking now of the matter without any regard to economy, but simply to policy as ordinarily considered in the advice I receive as to the employment of officers and men. I repeat that I believe that no purpose of the Commission is served by it in the average of all cases. I may not be competent to properly judge of the matter, and I do not ask that my opinion should outweigh that of any Commissioner, but I think it proper in discussing the general policy of the Board to distinctly express it. It has not been formed carelessly, or without a certain amount of familiarity with all the circumstances of the case.

As to the additional cost of the work caused in this way it is difficult to form anything like an exact estimate. It is not by any means limited to the difference in the direct value of the men employed and of those who might be employed at the same wages; it is the indirect influence of the system which costs the most, the discouragement of personal exertion, the demoralization which comes from it, and which unconsciously affects every man on the work from myself to the water-boys. I acknowledge myself affected by it, and I do not believe there is an officer on the park who would answer upon his honor that he had not at times reserved the expenditure of his best powers for the park from the reflection that appointments, promotions and discharges were made from other considerations than they are upon works conducted purely upon commercial principles. If this is the case with the superior officers it is ten-fold more so with the foremen, policemen and working men. It is the opinion of those whose long experience on other works as well as our own gives reason for respecting their judgment that the vice of politics in the form in which it exists on the park costs the public $200,000 of every million expended. I have no reason to believe, and I do not believe, that this is an exaggerated estimate. If the Commission could unanimously determine and persist in the determination that the work should be conducted absolutely upon the principles which would govern an honest and humane contractor in the management of a similar work, it is my deliberate conviction, after much reflection, that this amount would be saved, that in the end trouble and annoyance would be saved, and that any purpose of the commission would be better accomplished than by any other course.

I should like to have the work fairly placed in my hands, with the same liberty to secure efficiency in its management which is possessed by those who directly manage the greater part of this city's expenditure for work. I believe that it is possible to secure as cheap work for the Commission as these contractors secure for themselves and to save their profits. I should like to fairly try this, but I have been too often told that I did not understand or did not adequately appreciate the necessities of the Commission to expect this, and I do not ask it. I do ask however that this question and the questions which should follow it may be once more thoroughly considered by the Board, and if it is thought impracticable to secure a very decided change in the direction that I have indicated, that I may be definitely relieved of the responsibility of the superintendence of the work of construction. What I have now said I have said to no member of the Board before, nor have I advised with any Commissioner before presenting it to the Board. It is no more than I believe to have been required of me by my duty as the servant of the whole Board and of that which the Board represents.

This matter is one which interests my personal feelings, and I have desired to urge my request in a more definite form, but I would not venture to do so without acquitting myself of the responsibility of overstepping the proper limits of my duty. For this reason I advised with the President, as he yesterday stated, and it is with his approval that I ask the Board to appoint a special Committee with instructions to report at a future meeting, to be called for the purpose of considering their report on the general feasibility of the plan of operations now had in view by the superintendent and especially upon the following points:

1st. Whether any and if any, what modifications or additions to the plan, or omissions from it, are at this time desirable to be made by the Commission.

2nd. Whether the alterations in the method of construction referred to in the report of the Superintendent should be forbidden.

3rd. Whether it is practicable to conduct the work hereafter, especially with respect to the employment of officers, foremen and men, with simple and direct regard to its economy and with no more consideration for the wishes of those not employed on it than is usually to be expected of an honest and humane contractor under a commercial operation.

4th. Whether it is best to give and secure to the Superintendent the authority and means to so conduct the work.

5th. What measures can be taken for this purpose which while giving him freedom to act efficiently and according to his own necessities without waste of time in matters of form, will also secure a proper account of expenditure, and enable the Comptroller to exercise authority whenever there shall be due occasion to arrest unauthorized or excessive rates of expenditure.

Respectfully,

[F. L. O.]

RESULTS OF UNDUE REDUCTION OF APPROPRIATIONS FOR PARK MAINTENANCE.

Hon. H. G. S.[1]   30 October, 1875
   President, etc.,

Sir:

I have the honor to reply to your communication of this date, in which reference to the action of the Board of Apportionment proposing to allow the sum of $375,000. for the maintenance expenses of the parks and places of the city instead of $647,760. the sum applied for and certified by the Department, to be necessary for this purpose. You ask me to state what would be the result of the adoption of this proposition. Disregarding the value of the land, the property of the city in parks and places, were it all run to waste would cost to replace from fifteen to twenty millions of dollars. This property has been mainly acquired at the expense of a debt. There is no justice in throwing this debt on the future tax-payers of the city, except the property of the city in Parks and places above the value of the land. The justification of this debt lies in the intention of the city to hold the property for the benefit of the future population. To maintain its value a certain amount of watchfulness against damage and of labor in timely repair is constantly necessary.

The maintenance fund of the Department is designed to provide for this as well as for keeping the grounds in condition for the use and benefit of its present citizens.

If processes of damage are quickly recognized and the means of arresting them promptly used, the expenditure for the purpose may be kept within moderate limits. If they are overlooked and neglected the elements of deterioration rapidly increase in power, which deterioration will have to be made good, and the damage to

[1] Ed. Note: Mr. Stebbins, from a pencil draft kept by Mr. Olmsted.

the value of the property in time becomes such that it can only be made good by costly reconstructions.

The force hitherto employed has as a rule been little more than sufficient to perform the duties necessary to keep the parks in fair condition for immediate use, and the repair of damages and arrest of damaging processes have been neglected.

The wastefulness of the policy which permits this is illustrated in the almost complete crowding out of the fine perennial grasses, of which the turf of the Central Park was once composed, by coarse, poor, lustreless annual grasses and weeds; in the death of thousands of perennial plants, the cultivation and watering of which has been necessarily suspended for want of force in the dry season; in the necessity of applying to the legislature for a special fund to make good the losses resulting from the inability of the Department to make timely repairs upon architectural structures, and in the considerable destruction or pilfering of the city property which has occurred in the parks, which losses the Department has been able only in part to replace.

In these and nearly all other particulars except those of the roads and walks, the park has been in the condition of a farm "running down." As a general rule the "running down" process has begun where the work paid for by borrowed money—i.e., the proceeds of construction bonds—has ended.

The lack of sufficient means for the prompt arrest of sources of injury to various architectural structures when they were first discernible, and the immediate repair of damages while they were yet inconsiderable, has demonstrably added a much larger amount to the city's debt than has been saved to current taxation.

If the present rate of wages continues, the force to be employed next year, under the proposition of the Board of Apportionment will be much less relatively to the area to be maintained than ever before.

It will result that the Department will be compelled either to discontinue some of the customary expenditure for the immediate gratification of the public, as for example, for the maintenance of the museums, the menagerie, the skating pond, the Central Park roads and walks during the winter and to close some of the smaller parks, as Mount Morris, Reservoir and Stuyvesant, or to carry still further the wasteful process of neglecting repairs where the results will not be immediately felt by the public.

Respectfully,

[F. L. O.]

CHAPTER III

PROFESSIONAL DUTIES OF DESIGN AND SUPERINTENDENCE

In this chapter we have a document, hitherto unpublished, which at once throws light on the professional practice of landscape architecture in Europe about 1860 and reveals Mr. Olmsted's own clear understanding of the practical difficulties encountered in undertaking such professional work on an unaccustomed scale in this country. This letter offering his resignation in 1861 also contains a vivid statement of his conception of design,—*of the part which "creative fancy" must play in the work of the landscape architect.*

In the second letter of resignation, in 1873, following the Park Department's reorganization, the position of the professional adviser seemed to Mr. Olmsted about to become untenable; and he therefore quite frankly reviews the difficulties and analyzes the effect on park construction and maintenance which the divorce of "design" from superintendence has produced. This tentative resignation, being laid on the table by the Board and not producing any improvement in the situation, Mr. Olmsted two months later re-submitted his resignation, but enclosed a By-Law under which he would be willing to undertake certain further duties of design for new work on the City's parks, without his being involved in matters of management.[1] The resignation was again laid on the table, and subsequently Mr. Olmsted consented (as he said in Spoils of the Park) *"to resume service under the Commission upon a modified arrangement, vindicating my professional standing and securing me against another similar experience."[2]*

---

[1] Minutes, D. P. P., September 17, 1873. The enclosed suggested By-Law was as follows: "The duty of Landscape Architect shall be to prepare designs for all new work on parks and places and submit the same to the Board for approval; the Chief Engineer, Architect and Landscape Gardener shall be under his orders so far as required for this purpose and no changes of plan shall be made or construction undertaken until the Landscape Architect shall have reported thereon."

[2] Cf. Part I, Chapter X, p. 132. In the Revised By-Laws of 1873–74 the Landscape Architect is made head of the Office of Design and Superintendence, and the Landscape Gardener is to act under his direction as regards the "ornamentation and embellishment" of parks and places.

These letters and Spoils of the Park *tell the story of Mr.* Olmsted's *harassing struggle for twenty years to secure such a form of superintendence for the Park that the design might be steadily and sympathetically brought to realization.*

THE PAPERS INCLUDED IN THIS CHAPTER ARE:

Duties of a Chief-Executive of a great Park. Selection from Report on European Visit, by F. L. O. 1859. (Doc. No. 4.)—Suggests desirability of having duties homogeneous, and executive unencumbered by political pressure.

‡ *Letter offering F. L. O.'s resignation as Architect-in-Chief and Superintendent of the Central Park, because of ambiguous duties. January 22, 1861.—Discusses lack of trained technical staff working under the chief professional adviser.—Resignation later withdrawn and expunged from official records.*

‡ *Letter analyzing difficulties in current executive system with reference to construction and maintenance, to one of the Park Commissioners from F. L. O. May 25, 1872.—Points out lack of coördination between duties of superintendence and those of design.*

‡ *Letter offering F. L. O.'s resignation on ground of his untenable position as executive officer, under proposed reorganization, to President of Department (Mr. Stebbins). July 3, 1873.—Draft marked in F. L. O.'s hand: "Reasons for declining in advance an ambiguous position."—Resignation laid on table.*

‡ *"An explanation of the main divisions of responsibility under the late executive organization," memorandum by F. L. O. Spring, 1874. —Marked in his own hand: "Theory of Organization." Prepared in connection with request for full account of works in progress under cognizance of the Office of Design and Superintendence.*

‡ Previously unpublished.

SELECTION FROM REPORT ON EUROPEAN VISIT[1]

Grateful to the Commission for its past confidence, and willing to give my best endeavor to the execution of any duty which it may require of me, I think it proper at this time to express the conviction, that the Park would be much benefited if the duties which the chief executive officer of the Board has hitherto been forced to personally undertake, were of a more homogeneous character. The Board, it is true, has not prescribed duties for the Architect-in-Chief and Superintendent, except in special cases, but for that reason, every duty for which the Board has not appointed some other officer is understood, by all who are not employed in the Park, to devolve upon him. Every citizen, therefore, who wishes to have dealings with, or employment upon, or information about the Central Park, applies personally to the Architect-in-Chief and Superintendent. . .

The consequence has been, that the Architect-in-Chief has had no hour in which he could be secure from the harassment of discussion, conversation, or correspondence, upon topics utterly at variance with his most important duty, the execution of which involves a calm exercise of the imagination, and a just consideration of beauty and a large economy. It is impossible, without effort too great to be long sustained, to do justice to the opportunities offered by nature in designing the work, and to properly oversee and direct its progress, when at any moment it may be necessary to listen to a story of the calamities which have forced an individual to apply for employment, or to read the letters which have been procured by such an one from any charitable person able to write, whom he may have been able to persuade to assist him, or, what is worse, to recollect, at any time afterwards, the exact grounds on which an application has been rejected, or to recall the evidence and debate with an indignant friend the propriety of the discharge of a poor man who has been deemed insufficient in the duty which has been assigned him. I think I do not underrate the importance of duties of this kind. On their proper performance the popularity of the Park is greatly dependent. But their performance is hardly compatible with the proper performance of the other and even more important duties of the Architect-in-Chief, who should be at liberty to spend a large part of his time upon the ground and in the offices of the work, watching, and personally directing the work, especially as it approaches the form in which it is to be left.

[1] 1859, Doc. No. 4.

These more important duties, by the pressure of the other class of duties, chiefly connected with details of management, have therefore been necessarily performed almost by stealth, never, except as storms or holidays gave rare opportunity, with any possibility of the deliberation and absorption of mind to which they were entitled. The less important class of duties have, consequently, of necessity been attended to with some impatience, and with even less of the deliberation to which they were entitled.

The great kindness and readiness to give time and labor to furnish the information which I have desired, at every office in Europe, at which I have called, has made me more conscious of what I deem a defect in the organization of the service of the Commission.

The new duties devolving upon the Superintendent, as portions of the Park come into their final public use, will hereafter make it still more difficult for him to give his personal attention to details connected with the mere supply of labor of the rudimentary construction. It is certainly desirable that he should control individuals, directly or indirectly, so far as is necessary to make sure that the ideas of the design can be executed by those employed, and to prevent waste through the continued employment of incompetent persons. I submit to the generosity of the Board, also, that he should be allowed perfect freedom in selecting those who are to be his personal aids or whose work must be personally superintended by him, and on whose capability and efficiency he is entirely dependent in his endeavor to accomplish the primary purposes of the Board. . . .

I take this opportunity, then, before resuming the duties with regard to appointments, from which I have been, by the favor of the Board, temporarily relieved, in my personal capacity, to request, and, as my professional duty, to recommend, that the office of the Architect-in-Chief and Superintendent may have attached to it the unqualified power of selecting the individuals who must be immediately responsible to it, or with whom, in the nature of the case, the person holding it, however they are appointed, must deal directly, and that it may be relieved from the necessity of its occupant's personally superintending and answering for the details of the employment of all other persons in the service of the Board. [1]

In cases authorized by the Executive Committee, I have this week given permission to persons to sell refreshments [2] and hire skates upon the pond. I have delayed furnishing them with formal licenses from an opinion that such licenses should be made a source

---

[1] To prevent misapprehension, I desire to say more explicitly, that the responsibility *to the Board*, of employing an effective and economical working force, is not what is found incompatible with proper attention to other duties, but the incessant demands upon the Architect-in-Chief and Superintendent, to answer personally to individuals, for all the details of the duties growing out of the responsibility of recruiting and disciplining the working force of the Board.

[2] ED. NOTE: Doc. No. 6 of 1860 (not here reprinted) refers to the matter of Refreshments in the Park.

of revenue, and doubting if I should be justified in inserting a provision for that purpose, without express permission from the Board.

The offices at Seventy-ninth street are now extremely inconvenient, and will soon be scarcely tenable. I request permission to make the necessary arrangements for their removal to the building at Mount St. Vincent.

LETTER OFFERING MR. OLMSTED'S RESIGNATION, 1861.

CENTRAL PARK, January 22nd, 1861.

To the Board of Commissioners
of the Central Park.

Gentlemen:

I cannot without a sacrifice of self respect any longer allow myself to be held responsible for the duties implied by the designation, Architect-in-chief and Superintendent of the Central Park.

I must apologize for the tardiness of this acknowledgment. It has been owing to the reluctance with which under any circumstances I should leave the Central Park.

If I could be charged with any specific duties of design or of superintendence, or of both, being responsible directly to you and having sole control, the necessary means for a true and honorable performance of those duties, I could nowhere in the world put to better use such talent as I possess or live with more satisfaction to my tastes and inclinations than on the Central Park.

I have no right to claim nor would it become [me] to request from you a position more agreeable to myself than that which by your kindness and your perhaps too favorable judgment of my abilities I now occupy.

I am prepared, therefore, to withdraw entirely from your service, and shall do so, whenever it may be convenient for you to permit me, with sentiments of gratitude to each of you personally for which I have never more felt the occasion than at the moment of this writing.

I present my resignation of the office of Architect-in-Chief and Superintendent, to take effect from the date of your next regular meeting, holding myself at your service, however, until further orders, for such of the duties of my present office as I am able to execute satisfactorily to myself.

At the bottom of the most important function of my office, Mr. President, there must be something which you cannot buy in any market, of good quality, merely for money. It is a natural, spontaneous, individual action of imagination—of *creative fancy*. I mean that the best conceptions of scenery, the best plans, details of plans—intentions—the best, are not contrived by effort, but are spontaneous and instinctive and no man would be worthy of my office, who did not know that he must depend for his best success less upon any strong effort, than upon a good instinct. There are circumstances favorable to the action of this good instinct, and there are circumstances unfavorable to it. There are circumstances under which no amount of good intention and hard labor will produce good design. What would you think of a landscape painter who staid in town all summer, ever so industriously dabbing at his canvas? But what is most necessary to really good design is a satisfaction in the work for itself and not merely in what it may buy or purchase. I say then I cannot do my duty as it ought to be done, without having some enjoyment in it, and it's wrong for me to pretend to be doing it when I am conscious that my ability to do it well is in any considerable degree impaired. The work of design necessarily supposes a gallery of mental pictures, and in all parts of the park I constantly have before me, more or less distinctly, more or less vaguely, a picture, which as Superintendent I am constantly laboring to realize. Necessarily the crude maps which are laid before you are but the merest hints of the more rigid outlines of these pictures, of these plans.

I shall venture to assume to myself the title of artist and to add that no sculptor, painter or architect can have anything like the difficulty in sketching and conveying a knowledge of his design to those who employ him which must attend upon an artist employed for such a kind of designing as is required of me. The design must be almost exclusively in my imagination. No one but myself can feel, and without feeling no one can understand *at the present time* the true value or purport of much that is done in the park, of much that needs to be done. Consequently except under my guidance these pictures can never be perfectly realized, and if I am interrupted and another hand takes up the tools, the interior purpose which has actuated me will be very liable to be thwarted, and confusion and a vague discord result. Does the work which has thus far been done accomplish my design? No more than stretching the canvas and chalking a few outlines, realizes the painter's. Why, the work has been thus far wholly and entirely with dead, inert materials: my picture is all alive—its very essence is life, human and vegetable. The work which has been done has had no interest to me except as a basis, as a canvas, as a block.

   ·   ·   ·   ·   ·   ·

Now, Gentlemen, with regard to the staff of Superintendence. As I have said, I never have indicated what *I* felt to be necessary in this respect that I have not seen that you thought me extravagant. I do not believe, Sir, that since my appointment a month has passed that I have not been told that it appeared as if I had too large a number of engineers and clerks and so on, and that I had better get rid of some of them.

Photograph by Edward Heim

1925

The Gorge at the Pool

Now, Gentlemen, who is the proper judge of what I need in this way? You or I? If you hold me responsible for errors of estimate, for excess of expenditure, I am and *no one else;* and if you constrain me in this respect, you relieve me of that responsibility. I am no longer Architect, no longer Superintendent. You have taken the duties which those titles imply away from me. You have assumed them.

Your Board had it once under consideration to employ Mr. Alphand, or Mr. Kemp, or Sir Joseph Paxton for the duties which subsequently devolved on me. If either one of those gentlemen had undertaken the laying out and general supervision of the park he would undoubtedly have brought some portion of his professional staff with him—because such assistants as those gentlemen are accustomed to employ are not to be *had* here.

I have been in their offices and I *know* what sort of assistance they have—but you have the evidence in your own hands—look at the paper sent you by Mr. Alphand, or that from Mr. Austin of London. I saw the man who drew up the latter in London and obtained much information from him direct. He occupies a very subordinate position in Mr. Austin's office, but you have but one man in your employment, but one man who is able to prepare for you such a paper as that, and that man is myself. There is not another man in the park to whom I could hand over such a duty, except —— there is not another man in the park who has the necessary education and training for it. Why, so far as I know, I have had but two men at any time who had ever been on work like ours before, of my office assistants there is not one who had ever seen a park. I say, Gentlemen, that if you had employed Alphand or Kemp or Paxton, or Sir William Hooker, or any of the men to whom such a work as this would have been assigned in Europe, any man of established reputation for such work, here, if there had been any, they would have had their own staff of practiced professional assistants, would have undertaken the whole business of Superintendence in their own way, with their own men, and then in the usual course of such a business, they would after a time have brought in their bill for Superintendence and traveling and incidental expenses—the Superintendence being a certain fair percentage on the outlay for which they *had been responsible.* That is the usual way. I won't say that it is the only way in which men of established reputation would have served you, but it is the usual proper and many times the best way, very likely the cheapest way, for good work. Well, Gentlemen, if such a bill were presented to you at this time and footed up to say $100,000 would you refuse to pay it, as an exorbitant charge? Indeed you would not, Gentlemen, for a little investigation would satisfy you that it was a very moderate professional charge. . . . But what does your own architect superintendence—*purely architect* superintendence cost? . . . It has not cost you 2%. I don't believe it has cost you 1%. Is there any good reason why you should pay less than private individuals? You have better work, more substantial, better considered. I happen to know what Mr. Vaux's professional earnings were last year. He was paid over $10,000—entirely for plans and superintendence of buildings and grounds. Of this you paid him a quarter. Do you think you only took from a quarter of his expenditure of time, thought, study, anxiety? I know that you took a good deal more than *half*, and yet I have had more than one intimation that Mr. Vaux should give more time to the park. . . .

It was a different thing, when we commenced. That is true, I had no professional reputation, no professional standing, except what you had given—or rather, given me the means of gaining myself. It was natural—perhaps wise—to distrust my judgment, to distrust my talent—to distrust somewhat even my honesty perhaps.

You could not even then, Sir, doubt my ability to organize and control, efficiently and economically contról your work for I had, Sir, then already brought out of a mob of lazy, reckless, turbulent and violent loafers a well organized, punctual, sober, industrious and disciplined body of 1000 men. . . .

And now, I say, after three years trial of me I feel that if you are now unwilling to trust my judgment, to trust confidently and implicitly to my judgment, in such matters as I have referred to, it is time you were rid of me altogether. I feel this, Sir, I feel it, and I have felt it and spite of my sincere respect for you, spite of my real love for the park, and in spite of my personal habit of discipline and loyalty, which is a very strong and inherent element of my character, feeling this as I have done it has been impossible for me to give you the true and good service which my conscience demands that I should do if I continue to receive your pay[1] and to wear the title of Architect-in-Chief, Superintendent, or anything like it.

Let me ask then, if you will not think it improper for me to take up an old question of your own, let me ask, what is the proper business of your commission? I mean, what business with advantage, economically, efficiently, can your Commission undertake to perform directly? In 1858, Mr. Dillon, Mr. Belmont and Mr. Fields took the ground that the Commission *having adopted* the plan, appointed their Executive Officer and assumed to give him powers necessary to carry out the plan, had no longer any functions to perform with reference to the park, but those of cashiers and accountants. Those were the words of Mr. Dillon's report, "cashiers and accountants." Manifestly the fact was overlooked that the Commission was a legislative body; the mistake was also made, (and the same error has since occasionally led to some confusion of words

---

[1] ED. NOTE: Mr. Olmsted's pay at this time was $4000 per annum.

in the debates of your Board) of considering that the plan of the park was at that time complete, speaking technically. The Commission had seen nothing and acted on nothing but a study, had adopted nothing but the outline of a plan. I know, that some of the competitors pretended to finish a working plan for the park, but that was an absurdity. Working plans for the park could not have been formed, fully and usefully in a year's hard labor of a dozen engineers. Although the Commission had in common parlance adopted a plan, there was much yet remaining to be determined about the plan, much which it was not right to leave wholly to the judgment of their Architect and Superintendent, and there were considerations of general policy. Sir, on account of the relations of the Commission with the Common Council and the State Legislature and on other grounds, which rendered it inexpedient for the Commission to hand over to its Superintendent that entire general control in all respects which a commercial body, an independent and self-sustaining corporation, having the same purposes in view, would have done. . . . for the sake of economy, efficiency and success. But theoretically Mr. Dillon and his associates were right. And still right, practically right, if his proposition is limited by a reservation of the exercise of functions from the Executive such—not as ordinary prudence requires, for ordinary prudence requires none—but such as the special and unusual relations of your body required that it should sometimes exercise itself and directly. I say that ordinary prudence, ordinary commercial prudence required the reservation of no functions from your chief executive except those of cashiers and accountants—only so far as I have made exception—because, Sir, when ordinary prudence requires a corporation to interpose and interfere with its executive, in a work of this character, then ordinary prudence goes further; it requires that they should supercede him altogether. He is the round man in the square hole, and they made a mistake when they got him to lay out, plan, and carry on the work of this character. *Why*, a work of this character? Because, Sir, this work is eminently one of design and Congress might as well engage a clever draftsman like Mr. Ehninger or Mr. Darley to sketch a historical cartoon for a panel of the rotunda of the Capitol, and then get a good colorist like Mr. Ginoux or Mr. Page to paint it. Mr. Ginoux or Mr. Page wouldn't do it. Why some Western Committee once actually proposed something of that kind to Mr. Page, as I recollect he told me when I was in Rome, but he laughed at them and declined to serve them, as any man fit for your work would refuse to serve you on such terms.

All comparisons are imperfect, and involve some error on close scrutiny. I don't say that this does not, or that the inference is to be perfect and unqualified. . . . But the general conclusion from the practice of other bodies having similar duties, and from your own experience seems to me to confirm and establish the theoretical proposition that—*having fixed upon certain prudential limits and holding your designer most rigidly to account within those limits,* you should trust as largely as is by any means compatible with your duty as cashiers and accountants, to *his* prudence, to *his* judgment and not to your own, or to that of any committee, or any man of you—but to his judgment and his prudence, *as to details.* So long as you employ him at all, it is absolutely necessary to your success that—fixing for your own safety's sake certain general limits—in details of his duty you should deal with him confidently —generously—even generously—even, over-looking unless very distinctly offensive to you or largely wasteful, overlooking what may appear to you in such details errors of judgment or taste, whims, fancies, which you can only regard as personal idiosyncracies because in all works of art, in a crude and incomplete state there appear always unaccountable touches, which when finished, completed and brought into a good light, are suddenly recognized as strokes of genius. If your designer has any genius in him, Sir, it will show itself in that way, in little details where he acts as it were instinctively, where at all events, he could no more explain and demonstrate beforehand, the absolute necessity of the expenditure of the last sixpence that does the business, than a graceful woman could give an anatomical demonstration and explanation of her every graceful movement.

The President required of me perfect frankness tonight. If I am too frank, he is responsible for it. I promised that I would be frank with you. You very well know that up to this moment I have *not* been *entirely* frank with you, and if I said nothing more you would not believe that I had been perfectly honest.

[F. L. O.]

DIFFICULTIES IN CURRENT EXECUTIVE SYSTEM

NEW YORK, May 25th, 1872.

My Dear Sir:

As you seemed surprised at my expressions of despondency in regard to Central Park, in our conversation with Mr. Green, after the last meeting of the Board, I wish to make the following explanation. There will be nothing in what I shall write that I have not often said to you in effect before, but if I have failed to do so with sufficient distinctness and emphasis, which I think hardly possible, it is because the present organization and methods of business of the Department were designed as you have often said for an *ad interim* purpose—to bridge over the gap between the withdrawal of Mr. Sweeny and Mr. Hilton from the Board and the reorganization of the city government expected to be made by last winter's legislature, by the readiest and simplest means possible.

When you asked me in November last if there could be any

doubt that it would be best to abolish the system of "bureaus" under which the work of the Department had been organized, I replied that a considerable change in that respect was probably desirable but that I would far prefer such a system to that which had preceded it, under which the efficient management of so complicated a series of works as the Department had in hand was in my judgment quite impossible. That system was abolished and the arrangement of the executive service with reference to construction and maintenance is now, broadly considered, as follows:

The authorization of, or orders fof, all work proceed from the President through a Staff composed of, 1st, an Engineer whose executive duties are confined to the boulevards and streets; 2nd, an officer styled Superintendent of Parks, who has exclusive control of all the working force and equipment, except so much as is under the Engineer.

The orders and permits of the President are in part given in the form of endorsements upon drawings, specifications and requisitions prepared by the Landscape Architects. Much the larger part of the force engaged on the Central Park, however, is employed on work which does not proceed on drawings or written specifications. For example, the shaping of the surface of banks and the finishing surface of nearly all earth work and the disposition of rocks upon it with reference to landscape effect; the application of manures and the seeding, mowing, rolling and weeding of turf; the spading, forking, raking, etc., of dug borders and the disposition of herbaceous plants upon them, the constant repairs, ordinary and extraordinary, and the watering and cleaning of roads, walks and gutters; the thinning and pruning of trees and shrubs; the replacing or reinforcement of decaying wood work; the painting of iron work, etc.

The character of the park, its beauty and fitness for the purpose it has been designed to serve; in one word its value to the public, is to be far more affected by the work of this class to be done upon it than by all that is to be done upon accurate drawings and specifications.

Whether such work is well or ill done, whether the ideal in view in the direction of it is or is not that which has been had in view in the structural work which has preceded it, whether it is directed to the development in every part of the park of special local qualities of landscape or the rubbing down of the whole to a common insipidity of tolerable neatness, depends theoretically upon the President. But commonly the sole act of the President with reference to all this class of work is his endorsement of requisitions prepared by the Superintendent and the enlistment of the force placed at the discretion (in this respect) of the Superintendent. The judgment of the President is no more exercised with regard to the greater part of the work than is that of the President of the United States in regard to the medical treatment of sick seamen in the East India Squadron.

The Superintendent is required to consult no one and practically has no superior in respect to all this most important class of work, any more than has the surgeon of a frigate when afloat in regard to the dispensing of medicines. The Landscape Architects are allowed to attempt his instruction if they choose but it is entirely optional with him whether he shall be in any respect guided by their instructions.

With regard to the greater part of this class of work however the Superintendent himself exercises no judgment, it being necessarily left to subordinates—chiefly four deputies styled foremen, each of whom is responsible under the Superintendent for what is done on a certain territorial divison and who has a certain force of men, horses, implements and supplies placed at his discretion for the purpose. The Landscape Architects may attempt the instruction of these deputies but it is optional with them and with the Superintendent whether they shall be in any degree influenced by such instruction.

But this is not all; the present Superintendent and his deputies were each selected by the present Landscape Architects for very different duties, and the nature of the duties which they offered to undertake and for which they were, each when of middle age, selected, indicates for what duties they are qualified. The Superintendent recommended himself simply for the duties of a "walking boss," and his deputies as foremen, for the rudest labor of the preliminary grading and blocking out of the design of the park. They were excellent men for the class of duties required of them in those capacities.

There has been but one motive in placing all the work of the park under them, it is simply to guard against the waste of labor. They know this; great care has been used to impress them with the conviction that they owe everything to their ability simply in this respect. They are trained and habituated to regard this, the prevention of indolence and of what in their judgment would be a misdirection of labor, as the chief end of their offices. Accordingly what they are most on the watch against, what most excites their indignation and impatience is what they call "pottering," that is to say work in which there is no evident, constant exertion of the muscles and the results of which are not at once palpably evident and measurable. It is true that since they came upon the park they have been educated to regard certain results of work as valuable and in skill to direct labor to those results, but what they have gained in this respect by no means fits them for producing such results as are needed in the park.

There is a large amount of work, the lack of which detracts vastly—I mean literally millions of dollars—from the value the park has been designed and partly prepared to have, with regard to which these men are not, never have been, and never can be competent to receive instructions; and with all respect, you will allow me to say that the Board is no more justified in asking its Landscape Architects to finish a park by instructions given to such assistants than the owners of a ship to ask her captain to sail her with mates who had never been on blue water.

It is true that there are two men on the park of special standing, and of whose qualifications as landscape gardeners, judging wholly by their own representations I have spoken with satisfaction. It is true that in the force under the deputy superintendents there is a certain number of working gardeners and that the deputy superintendents have been instructed by the Superintendent to let these men perform certain operations under the instructions of the head gardeners, while the head gardeners again are allowed to receive instructions from the Landscape Architects. The Superintendent professes that it passes his comprehension why this does not supply all that the Landscape Architects want. But is it reasonable for the Board to require that the Landscape Architects should make the requirements of the most subtle and ineffable part of a very original and elaborate work of art comprehensible to a man who is wholly unprepared by education, training, habits and tastes to the study of means for such a purpose. That is the ground, as I understand it upon which you have placed yourself. For example in February last I submitted to you a schedule of work which I stated was more important to be taken up early in the spring and to be carried steadily through than any other that could be undertaken and that it would require a special force with a special organization. You told me afterwards that you had consulted the Superintendent and that he estimated that the work would require a thousand men. I answered that I would be content to undertake it with a special force under such superintendence and subdivision of duty as I should arrange, of three hundred. You said that if that would be sufficient, I could have them. Afterwards, however, you told me that the Superintendent was very unwilling to have such a special force organized and thought that if a sufficient number of men of the regular force were placed from day to day under the orders of the head gardeners it would be sufficient. I assured you that it would not and finding in March that the *ad interim* arrangement was likely to last through the planting season at least, and recognizing your aversion to any considerable change in the actual method of Superintendence for the time being, I submitted a scheme for a method of organizing a much smaller force of gardeners with the least possible change from the existing arrangements which would admit of the slightest hope of success. You approved of this scheme; it was briefly presented to the Board and assented to by the Board. The Superintendent was advised of your will that a constant force of twenty men, and a force of one hundred to be detailed daily when wanted from the force in command of the deputy Superintendents (foremen), should be placed under my orders. At the end of the month, the most essential element of the scheme not having been carried into effect, he was asked for an explanation, when he simply and squarely refused to carry it out, saying it was his business why. Being subsequently asked in your presence for an explanation, he said that so much of the scheme as had not been carried out was, in his judgment, unnecessary.

And with no other explanation, than that the Superintendent was unable to understand what desirable objects were to be accomplished by any essential change in the arrangements to which he had been accustomed, the organization remains a model of efficiency, perhaps, with reference to such results as the mind of the Superintendent has conceived to be desirable, but which the Landscape Architects assure you does not contain the skeleton of such an organization as it is absolutely essential (to a due finish of the work) should be prepared, picked over and revised, instructed and disciplined for the purpose.

The *ad interim* Board has become permanent, and the prospects of an organized staff of officers, each member sufficiently qualified and respectable to be treated with confidence in the matters of his own special study and responsibility (without which it is simply impossible for such large and varied duties as are placed in your Department to be satisfactorily met) are far from brightening.

[F. L. O.]

ANOTHER LETTER OF RESIGNATION, 1873

NEW YORK, July 30th, 1873.

TO THE HON. H. G. STEBBINS,
President, Department of Public Parks.

Dear Sir:

On leaving town last week you handed me a copy of a draught of proposed Byelaws for the Department of Parks, lately adopted in Committee of the Whole, under which the office of Design and Superintendence, of which I have been the head, is done away with and independent offices constituted respectively of Landscape Architecture, Landscape Gardening and Police. You called my attention to these provisions and stated that it was the intention that I should be retained with the title of Landscape Architect in a position of General Superintendence of the works of the Department. You observed also that Commissioners were disposed to respect my judgment and wishes and that a principal advantage of the proposed changes was supposed to be that, under them, I should be relieved from onerous non-professional cares and allowed to give my attention more completely and effectively to higher and more congenial duties. You thought that if the changes proposed would be unwelcome to me, a full statement of my views would undoubtedly induce some modifications of them.

Knowing my views as well as they do, that the Commissioners should, with their friendly feelings toward me, have thought such changes desirable in the Byelaws of the Department leads me unavoidably to the conclusion that their mature judgment will not accept the conditions on which alone I am willing to hold any such general responsibility under them as is proposed.

In complying with your request, therefore, I shall do so not with the motive which you suggest but rather that I may make this fact as evident to them as it is to me, and that further waste of time in the consideration of impracticable measures may be avoided.

In my recent engagement with the Department I had, as you know, one purpose constantly before me, in view of which alone I had been induced to give up my private business. I had reason to suppose that this purpose was to be adopted by the Commissioners but for various reasons, never wholly satisfactory to me, I have from time to time been asked to forego its pursuit. I have never for a moment entertained the idea of doing so after the permanent reorganization of the Department had been accomplished.

The purpose to which I refer grows out of the fact that in my judgment the Central Park fails to give the public anything like the value which should be realized from the work done upon it, and equally fails to justly represent the design for the merits and the faults of which Mr. Vaux and I are held accountable.

To understand why it thus fails, the manner in which the design has been developed from the first pen and ink study adopted by the Park Commission in 1858 and the manner in which the designers have superintended its execution must be considered.

Immediately after the adoption of the study "as a basis of a plan," an office was constituted which I was invited to accept, as representative of the designers, and which was defined by a unanimous vote of the Board, as follows: "He shall be the Chief Executive officer by or through whom all work on the Park shall be executed and shall have the government and supervision of all employees at the Park." I was then authorized to call on my partner Mr. Vaux for assistance; to employ a staff of engineers and architects of my own selection and such force of artisans and laborers as could be engaged advantageously. It was also made my duty to enlist, instruct and superintend such force of Keepers as I thought necessary to the requirements of the enterprise. I was then directed to proceed with the construction of the Park "on the basis of the adopted plan, subject to such modifications as might be suggested from time to time by the Board." (*Vide* Minutes, 1858–9, page 37).

I objected to the title given my office which was that of "Architect-in-Chief of the Central Park" because I was not an architect; I was answered that the term implied better than any other the kind of responsibility which the Board meant to put upon me, namely a *professional* responsibility for the result that would be realized from the work which I was to organize and superintend.[1]

[1] ED. NOTE: In a letter to Mr. Vaux from California, 1863, Mr. Olmsted wrote: "I had a will—an ambition, or plan of life, in connection with the park, by which my conduct had been greatly moved before I knew you. Under its influence I had obtained the position of Superintendent of the Park—this before I

The analogy of my duties with those of an architect of any great undertaking, such as a public building of cost corresponding to that of the Park, was very incomplete, chiefly for this reason; there are great numbers of men specially educated as architects, and an architect about to undertake the detailed planning and Superintendence of a building, no matter how extensive, can almost instantly organize a staff of experienced men who with very little instruction from him shall be fully prepared to give him effective assistance both in preparing working plans and in inspecting and directing the work of carrying them out. Then, in the actual operations, he has also no difficulty in finding men who are not only fitted by much experience to understand his plans and specifications but who are all ready with suitable classified bodies of workmen to carry them out, each taking a different part; such for example are master stone-cutters, masons, bricklayers, carpenters, plumbers, and painters. It is rare that there is any thing in the design that cannot be clearly put into the minds of this class of assistants, though in the finishing details, in delicate sculptured decoration of an original and novel motive for instance, there may be some difficulty and the architect may need to look beyond the common organizations of contractors to be satisfactorily served, and then in a measure to educate the workmen in his own feeling.

Now, there were really no men in New York who had had experience in the preparation of detailed plans of such a work as the Central Park was designed to be, and there were no suitable trade arrangements for it. It must be considered also that an artist dealing with trees and plants has to adapt his work to the vicissitudes of seasons and other transient conditions of growth and that his processes are necessarily longer processes than those of an architect,

---

knew you, before I entertained the idea of having anything to do with the design or with you. When I took the office I supposed Viele to be the designer, the designer to be the Engineer in Chief. By the order constituting my office I was made in certain respects independent of the Engineer and by presumption of the designer. My office extended in its term beyond that of the execution of the design. By express terms I was made responsible for the use to be made of the completed park—independent of the designer. . . .

"But you know that the advantages offered in the office of the Superintendent for spending a good deal of my life in the park, being with the people in it, watching over it and cherishing it in every way—living in it and being a part of it (whatever else there was) were valued by me at a valuation which you thought nonsensical, childish and unworthy of me—but it was my valuation of them and not yours which was concerned—and that this was something deeper than a whim you know, for you know that it existed essentially years before it attached itself to the Central Park as was shown by the fact that while others gravitated to pictures, architecture, Alps, libraries, high life and low life when traveling I had gravitated to parks—spent all my spare time in them, when living in London for instance, and this with no purpose whatever except a gratification which came from sources which the Superintendence of the Park would have made easy and cheap to me, to say the least, every day of my life. What I wanted in London and in Paris and in Brussels and everywhere I went in Europe—what I wanted in New York in 1857, I want now *and this from no regard for Art or fame or money.*"

dealing in such materials as brick and stone. For all these reasons the necessary personal labor of the head of such a work as the transformation of the site of the Central Park into such a pleasure ground (perhaps the most elaborately studied public ground in the world) was of a much more varied and burdensome character than that of the Architect of any building, no matter how large and complex its design. It was thought necessary also for political reasons that the work should for some time be driven as hard as possible, until at least the main features of the plan should be finally stamped on the ground. During the first three years working-plans and instructions were provided and a sufficient supervisory force trained, for the employment, during most of the time, of from two to nearly four thousand workmen. Under this pressure, of course, nothing was done that could be postponed without hazard of immediate unpopularity, which would be hazard of failure and of transfer to unfriendly and destructive hands, such as finally took possession of the work in 1871.[1]

---

[1] ED. NOTE: In retrospect Mr. Olmsted took a more cheerful view of the results of his management of the construction of Central Park. The following extract is from a letter written in 1890:

"Thirty-three years ago, I had an order to take general charge of the improvement of a piece of real estate that had cost five million dollars. The order provided that nothing should be done upon the work, except under my instructions; that no man should be employed or retained in employment, except by me; no payment made except on my certificate; no reports from the work received that I did not sign or countersign. The work was to be driven with all practicable speed. When it was well under way, I had nearly four thousand men employed. It was to be an intimate combination of such work as is commonly directed apart, respectively, by engineers, architects and horticulturists. Thus, there was to be grading, quarrying, dam-building, sewering; there were to be many costly bridges on all sorts of foundations; there were to be numerous small buildings; there were to be many miles of heavy retaining walls, many miles of roads. Three hundred thousand trees were to be planted on ground, the greater part of which was a bare ledge of granite and another considerable part a swamp.

"The organization and discipline of such a complex work was one of unusual difficulty. I had to deal with strikes and riots at the outset, and continuously with all manner of efforts by unscrupulous men to destroy discipline and to harass, browbeat and influence me to aid political and personal projects. There was no end of plots and intrigues for this purpose, and several times I was placed by misrepresentations under the harrow of legislative investigating committees. The last of these started with a hostile purpose, employed experts to make searching examinations of the work in every aspect; its plans, construction, management and accounts. The experts swore that the work was the best of its kind in every respect of which they had any knowledge and that the reports upon which the investigation had been ordered were wrong in every particular, and the committee at length reported that the force was well directed and under rarely good discipline.

"But as to my success, perhaps the simplest evidence may appear in the fact that, while I never directly or indirectly suggested that my pay should be increased, my salary was from time to time advanced until it came to be more than six times as much as it was at the start.

"Probably the reason of this advance lay largely in the means I used to guard against fraud and inefficient service and the success of them; to illustrate which I may mention that I invented and carried into practice a system of time-keeping and accounts which operated so well that it was afterwards adopted and is yet in use by the United States Government."

With these conditions by the spring of 1861 the work had, in nearly all parts of the ground, been brought to a certain stage of progress. The ruder and solider constructions were mostly completed, the trees designed to form the principal masses of foliage had been set out; the first planted trees and shrubs were beginning, through their rapid growth, to take character in masses. Visitors on foot began to find shade and seclusion and to foretaste the recreation which the place was designed to provide; the number of visitors was becoming rapidly larger and the difficulties of keeping were increasing. It was time to make a general advance to a second stage; to bring up lagging elements of a character not to be presented in a black and white plan but on which the merit of the design and the value of much of the heavier work was even more dependent than on those elements which had already gained a settled popular favor for the enterprise. To proceed with these, the designers' instructions to the overseers and workmen needed to be more elaborate and direct; a process of education rather than of instruction was in fact required. This made modifications of the original organization desirable and made it necessary that the general superintendent should disengage himself from certain affairs in order to give more personal attention and exercise more efficient control of others.

But just here so many difficulties occurred, difficulties represented to be largely political, that the designers found themselves no longer allowed the means for meeting what they deemed to be their professional responsibilities and, the war coming on, I withdrew from the Park to other duties and Mr. Vaux soon followed me.

On the breakdown of what is known as the "Ring" government in 1872, we were invited to resume the position of Landscape Architects to the Department having in charge the Central Park pending the reorganization of the City government under a new charter from the legislature. The expectations that this would be soon accomplished failed. On the adjournment of the legislature, a change in the administration of the Department became necessary; it was thought desirable that I should temporarily assume the duties of President and Treasurer as well as of General Superintendent. I did so reluctantly and held them until the autumn when the organization was again changed and I took the office which I have held since but, all the time, as I have before said, under conditions baffling to my purpose.

Since a comparatively early stage in the formation of the Park, therefore, it has had no efficient professional superintendence, and for want of it has been growing up in many respects unfortunately. For this reason and because of the peculiar character of its design, the kind of superintendence which it now requires is not professional superintendence at arms' length merely or by means of drawings and specifications but a direct, controlling, educational superintendence, similar to, though on a much smaller scale, than that which I originally exercised. Such, at least, is my sincere conviction and I will stand in no position before the public, in which I may seem to acquiesce in an arrangement which directly overrules my conviction and squarely sets aside my most earnest professional advice in this respect.

The effect of the proposed byelaws will be to "relieve" me, by the abolition of my present office, from the imperfect control I have hitherto had over the work upon the plantations of the Central Park, and to form an office of landscape gardening under which a force of gardeners is to be organized by another man, not to be of my selection and not to be responsible to me but to be selected by my non-professional superiors; to receive his instructions directly from them and report directly to them. Why it is preferred that orders and reports should pass over my head in respect to this division of the Department's business and that they should not do so in respect to such matters as the setting of foundations on quicksands, the choice of tiles for a house flooring or the management of bears and wolves, I do not know. While, therefore, I should not have been wholly taken aback by a proposal for an office, independent of my superintendence, of engineering or of architecture or of zoology, and while I should not have objected to an independent office of nursery and exotic gardening, which would establish a desirable special responsibility and facilitate accuracy in accounts, I can find in this proposition of an independent organization of landscape gardening only a very striking evidence of a radical difference of judgment between myself and the Commissioners in respect to the present requirements of the Park. There could have been but one proposition in the present state of affairs which would have made this more evident and that would be a proposition for such changes as are intended to be made in respect to the service of attendance on visitors in the Park.

I say "in the present situation of affairs," and I must show what this is. After the gardeners, of all the divisions of your service the only one which, nominally under my instructions, I have reported to be utterly inadequate for the duties which, in the design of the Park, were assigned to it, has been that of the Keepers' force. Among its defects the following were notable:—1st, a want of comprehension on the part of the officers of what it should accomplish and their consequent inability as well as indisposition to rightly instruct the men; 2nd, their want of confidence and skill in discipline; 3rd, the insufficiency in numbers of the force; 4th, a habit throughout the force of looking to the influence of irresponsible persons, and to furtive and surreptitious means for maintaining or bettering their position. It became my duty under orders of the Board to undertake a reform of this force, *one month before the new charter went into effect*, and under what otherwise would have been a hopeless load of difficulties. I was completely dependent on the Captain, and the Captain had reason to believe that if he continued to hold his place it would be for other reasons than my opinion of his fitness and efficiency in it. I had been required to select and take the responsibility of the discharge of a large number of men, nearly all of whom pressed applications on the Department for a restoration backed by influential politicians, newspaper men and other friends, and all of whom were answered that the matter was in my hands. The means taken for reforming some of the bad habits of the force required increased exertions of all the men and officers. Their selfishness was accordingly enlisted against them and a class of means was at once employed to prevent their success such as is commonly used to accomplish personal purposes with political bodies in this city. False reports were propagated by anonymous letters and otherwise and an impression was industriously sought to be established that in consequence of the new arrangements of the Park had become a wholly unsafe and improper place of resort for decent people. At length a collection of such reports studiously and shrewdly prepared and likely if at all credited, to do much harm in various ways, was given to the public in an influential journal.

This was done at a moment when the Board which had ordered the changes was broken up and another about to be formed with a majority of new Commissioners. On the strength of the statements made, public indignation was attempted to be excited by an inflammatory harangue against the old Board and certain advice proffered to the new Board.

At the suggestion of the two Commissioners who were at the moment my only official superiors in the Department, I then for the first time came directly before the public as the responsible supervisor of the business in question and pledged my personal character that the statements made were false and the expressions of opinion unworthy of respect.

The advice given was more especially this: that a Committee of the Board should consult the Superintendent of Labor on the Park, that it should consult the Captain of the force; that it should consult the men, that it should not consult the lieutenant for the reason that he did not make common cause with the men; that the Captain should receive his orders only from the Board, that the men should constantly carry clubs, that the round system should be abolished and the theorist who led to its adoption be made to attend to his proper business.

Since then a Committee of the Board *has* consulted the Superintendent of labor, *has* consulted the Captain of the force, *has not* consulted the lieutenant, *has* received communications directly from the men, of the contents of which I have not been informed, *has* recommended that the office of lieutenant be done away with, that the Captain receive his orders only from the Board, that the men constantly carry clubs, that the round system be abolished, and that I be given more leisure for what are deemed my strictly professional duties.

I of course adopt your view of the motive of these propositions, but the motive makes little difference as to the significance which under the circumstances they must have. I do not mean their significance with the public, for this I conceive concerns the honor of the Commissioners more than mine, but their practical significance with reference to the business of the Department.

As a responsible executive officer with large experience, in divers undertakings, of the difficulties of carrying out important general orders through influence on the wills of thousands of subordinate agents of every degree of intelligence and moral strength, I naturally estimate the importance of their significance at a somewhat higher rate than the Commissioners may have done. And yet, I think the Commissioners could hardly have been unconscious that no officer whom they might hereafter employ would ever again as willingly as before, undertake duties that would necessarily be disagreeable to and unpopular with his subordinates, or that there would be no corrupt or weak man in their employment in whom they would not seem to strengthen a too prevalent impression that eye-service, chicanery and the cultivation of influence with politicians and the press will pay much better than strict attention to and faithful and intelligent performance of the duties assigned to him by any agent standing between him and the Board. I believe that considerations of this class are of much consequence in the management of public business, that economy is more dependent on them than on many others that get more public attention. But these observations apply chiefly to the question of the timeliness of the action of the Committee, beyond which lies one perhaps of greater importance.

Under the Ring government, what I had with the approval of the Park Commissioners originally organized and trained as a body of "Park Keepers," with great care to establish the understanding that their principal duty was to aid, instruct and restrain honest but often inconsiderate visitors in their use of the Park—that of arresting criminals being *incidental to this*—was definitely transformed into a "Police" and assimilated as closely as possible in all respects to the ordinary street police of the city. The effect in any judgment was extremely bad on the men and far from conducive in any way to the public interests. Criminals were no better guarded against than before while honest people fared worse. With the approval of the last Board I have accordingly made some efforts to bring the force back to its original idea. The action of the Committee in restoring the title of *police* to it and at the same time withdrawing it from my influence looks I presume to an abandonment of this purpose—probably on the ground which has lately been publicly urged that it is an impracticable theory. I will only remark that if it is so, I can see no justification for the present *imperium in imperio* which exists on the park in respect to the matter of police. There would be obvious advantages in the Department's abandoning the maintenance of any distinctive force and allowing the Police Commission to take its appropriate responsibility in this respect in regard to the parks as well as other portions of the city. The convenience of rapidly enlarging the number of policemen on the park upon occasions when it is much thronged, by details from adjoining precincts would be one of no little value, and a continuous service through the park of the horse-patrol, now separated by it into two divisions, would also have clear advantages. But from the first, the design of the Park has assumed a very different class of attendance on visitors from that of ordinary policemen, and my professional judgment has been often expressed to the Board that there is nothing so important for the justification of the design as a Keeper's force under such management as was originally intended. The Committee has probably considered that a superintendence of the police arrangements of the Park was no part of my professional superintendence. I have not found that absolute independence can well be established between professional and unprofessional superintendence in any incomplete work of the peculiar character of the Central Park. One must be subordinate to the other, else conflicts of authority will occur and neither can then be efficient. A general oversight of the public use of the Park is certainly no more unprofessional to me than half the business which I have been asked to do by the present Board, and the Keepers are so many aids of this duty.

It is to be considered also that the business of organizing and training park keepers was mine before the plan of the Parks was adopted and before I became its architect; such efficiency for its distinctive duties as the force has ever had has been due to the training which I secured to it. I have never heretofore been asked to assume any responsibilities of Superintendence that the Keepers were not placed under my orders. You say, and I have been assured by the other Commissioners, that the principal object of the proposed changes is to relieve me from unprofessional cares; a significance seems however to be attached to this word more narrow than I am willing to accept. A profession according to the dictionary is the business a man professes to understand. The business which I profess to understand and for which I have offered the city of New York my services is that of providing means for safe and convenient recreation with a view to a gain in health of great numbers of people on grounds called Parks. It is not a business the science of which many men have comprehensively studied. There are hundreds at your service who have studied practical engineering and architecture and gardening as separate businesses and with reference to other objects, much more than I, but I know of no man living who has given more study to this business of forming public parks or who has had a longer and more varied experience in the practice of it than I.

Let it not be said that on this ground I seek to usurp the functions of the Commissioners themselves. The question is not *what* they shall trust, but *whom;* not, on what points shall they be advised by a subordinate but by what class of subordinates shall they be advised. . . .

On this, I have simply said that there are no points on which the

Central Park comes so far short of what was originally intended as in these two, of the Superintendence of the plantations and the Superintendence of its public use; there are none, therefore, which I have so much felt the need of personally superintending. I have always testified to the satisfactory superintendence of the roads and of all the ordinary work of the mechanics and laborers. I have never sought to resume my former direct superintendence of these parts of your business. I have been glad to be relieved of them; there are other parts of your business of which I should be willing to be relieved. But in respect to the superintendence of the plantations and the keeping of the park, in the sixteen years since I was first made its Superintendent I have never asked relief.

Shall I add that in that time, I have never asked for any other office than that of Superintendent of the Central Park; never have asked for promotion, for an increase of salary; that I have asked for no patronage, contracts or perquisites. I have asked personal advancement or personal favor never in any way except as it was to be found in an improved management of the Park *in these two particulars.* I have offered within two years to take an office in which I should be allowed proper advantages for this purpose at less than half the rate of pay which has since been given me, without my solicitation, for undertaking duties in which it was necessary I should forego this purpose. I have been willing, as your Committee on ByeLaws was informed before its action, to lay aside all other duties and take these alone. I have been willing as they also were informed to assume the responsibility for all other duties of design and superintendence in addition to these that might be desired provided only I should not be made dependent on men as my immediate assistants in whose competency and good will to second me I could have no sufficient confidence.

That the Commissioners should then, so quickly and confidently, as the first step in the organization of the Department make up their minds to withdraw just these two elements of their business and no other from my superintendence makes it plain that they must have different aims in the general management of the Park from those which I recognize to be desirable.

Under these circumstances I cannot believe that they would be long satisfied to retain me in the position of general professional responsibility with respect to the Park which they at present have in view, and I think that upon reflection this will even now be as evident to the Board as it is to me.

Respectfully yours,

FRED. LAW OLMSTED.

MAIN DIVISIONS OF RESPONSIBILITY IN THE PARK ORGANIZATION

It has been the business of the Office of Design and Superintendence to develop the plans of improvement adopted by the Board by advancing new details from time to time as the work progressed; by digesting working plans and specifications or instructions of various forms; by setting out the work and by superintending its progress. It has been the intention of the Board that it should so far control and direct all work as to be responsible for the character of the result and especially that details should be fitting and harmonious with the ruling motives of the general design to which they are subordinate.

The Treasurer has been responsible for the economy of purchases, and of contracts for work.

It has been the intention of the Board that the Office of Design and Superintendence should have a qualified accountability for the character of the result of all work done on parks and places and for the sufficiency of the public accommodations in them in all respects including their keeping. The qualifications of this responsibility are such as have been fixed by special instructions of the Board to the L. A. and by the action or failure of action called for by the L. A. of the Treasurer and Superintendent of Parks.

The Treasurer is responsible for the supply of tools and materials required for the prosecution of the work; the Superintendent of Parks is responsible for the economy of the workmen directly employed by the Department. The Office of D. and S. has therefore no control over the rate of progress of any undertaking and is responsible with respect to its progress only so far as the Treasurer, the Superintendent of Parks and the contractors for work or supplies depend on it for plans, requisitions and instructions.

The Superintendent of Parks has had control of the working force of the Department and been responsible for the economy of labor employed in carrying out the orders given him.

To put any project or plan in the way of realization, according to the character of what is needed to advance it, either orders have been given to the Superintendent of Parks to employ the park force to that end or the Treasurer has been called upon by requisition to make contracts or purchases. With the issuance of such order or the rendering of such requisition, the function of the Office for the time being terminated. When informed however that a contract had been made, it became its duty to inspect and superintend the manner of its execution, no payments being made on contracts without evidence satisfactory to the head of the Office that the terms of the contract had been fulfilled and the consideration of the required payments received and a certificate to this effect being made on each bill by an expert whose competency was attested by the head of the Office.

Where improvements were to be made by the park force, it has been the duty of the Superintendent of Parks to make requisition for the necessary tools and materials for carrying out his order the responsibility for providing them resting with the Treasurer and the responsibility of the Park Superintendent for progress being suspended for the time being.

[1874]   [F. L. O.]

CHAPTER IV

THE CHOICE AND CARE OF PLANTATIONS

The reports and papers on the Central Park plantations fall into two groups: those dealing with the early selection and arrangement of plants to be used, and those suggesting the ideals to be sought in developing the plantations and the methods of administration for securing the care necessary to realize these ideals in the Park. The earlier group, including also passages from more general papers setting forth the design of the Park (see Part II, Chapter I) and especially Mr. Olmsted's last survey of the Central Park planting with Mr. Harrison in 1889, are somewhat known already; but none of the group on "gardener organization" were published. These represent the long struggle in which Mr. Olmsted engaged to secure a specially-trained force devoted to the maintenance of plantations (as distinct from roads, buildings, turf, etc.), and in which he was successful for only a brief period, followed by gradual deterioration of the finer passages of park planting. These papers, therefore, have great importance in view of the present-day need for a thorough-going horticultural rehabilitation of the Park.

THE PAPERS INCLUDED IN THIS CHAPTER ARE:

Report from Superintendent (F. L. O.) relative to Trees. October 20, 1857. (Doc. No. 11.)—Selections from.

Descriptive Guide to the Arboretum, accompanying "Greensward" Plan. 1858.

Letter regarding the inspiration from tropical scenery for park planting, to Mr. Pilat from F. L. O. in the tropics. September 26, 1863.[1]—Discusses the possibilities for securing tropical effects in the Central Park plantations.

‡ Letter regarding improvement of planting details, to President of Park Department (Mr. Sweeny) from O. V. & Co. November 12,

[1] Printed in *Landscape Architecture*, Apr., 1915.
‡ Previously unpublished.

1870.—Suggesting replacement of temporary planting with finer material contemplated by the design.

‡ *Letter regarding progress work, to Mr. Ryan, Superintendent of the Park, from F. L. O., enclosing memorandum of planting instructions to Mr. Demcker. February 27, 1872.—Explaining skill necessary to carry out designers' conception of Central Park planting.*

‡ *"Superintendent of Central Park to Gardeners." Draft of Circular by F. L. O. Undated, but about 1873.—On the true purpose of the work of the gardening staff.*

‡ *Two letters on "Gardener Organization" to President of Park Department from F. L. O. June 5, 1875, and July 8, 1875.*

‡ *Letter regarding false economy in maintenance of plantations, to Commissioners from F. L. O. September 18, 1877.*

Observations on the Treatment of Public Plantations, more especially relating to the use of the axe, by F. L. O. and J. B. Harrison. 1889.

In addition to the papers given in this chapter, for a consideration of planting in relation to the general design see also Part II, Chapter I, especially pages 230 ff. and 265 f.; and for a discussion of shade in the Park, see Part II, Chapter V, Doc. No. 36, page 379.

It may also be of interest to note in connection with this chapter Mr. Olmsted's recollections of the earliest plantings on the Park: "I have a note that the first tree was planted on the Mall . . . October 17, 1858 [1] *. . . In 1859, 1,700 trees and shrubs were planted out; in 1860, 34,000; in 1861, 52,000. If I recollect rightly, in 1859 the trees east of the playground and green, those about the Mall and east of it, and on both sides the 72d Street entrance road were planted; also many of those in the upper part of the Ramble. The following spring the shrubs in the Ramble and the evergreens in the southwest part of the park. In the fall most of the remaining deciduous trees in the lower park. In 1861 the evergreens of the winter drive (West drive from 79th Street to 102d) and most of the shrubs on the lower park."*

The Annual Report of the Central Park Commissioners for 1863 paints the following picture: "The earlier planting has already become dense and vigorous. Its varied foliage, beautiful at all times, affords seclusion and shade grateful in the warmer months; in the spray of its branches numerous native birds find home and refuge."

---

[1] Cf. Annual Report, D. P. P., 1873, p. 311.
‡ Previously unpublished.

REPORT RELATIVE TO TREES [1]

It is impossible to form an estimate which will have any value, of the numbers of the different sorts of trees which will be wanted for the Park, until the plan is finally determined on. But it may be supposed that in the greater part of the Park the natural characteristics of the ground will be accepted and turned to account; and an opinion may be expressed as to the style of planting which would best comport with these characteristics, and of the sorts of trees which this style will require. It will probably best meet the purpose had in view by the board in calling upon me for a report on the subject, if I state the conclusions to which I should myself thus arrive, and indicate the number of the different sorts of trees which would seem to me to be indispensable, at the very outset of the planting.

In the rugged portion, comprising nearly three-fourths of the surface of the first section, the stiffer forms of evergreen trees will best accord with, and set off, the picturesque rocks which are the marked feature of the landscape. The Hemlock and Black Spruce will probably be preferred as the predominating trees, wherever it is practicable to supply and retain the deep, loose, rich, black soil which they require; and on the steeper slopes and higher ground the Norway Spruce. On portions of thin soil, over, and in the clefts of, masses of rock, the European Larch, Scotch Fir and American Arbor-vitæ, and in the more sheltered low-ground, especially if a portion of this is occupied by a pond, as proposed by the chief-engineer, the Deciduous Cypress, the White Cedar or swamp Arbor-vitæ and the Red and Black American Larch or Hackmatack would both harmonize with the scenery and be most sure to flourish. Most of these trees will be wanted in large quantity elsewhere in the Park, but here they are likely to be employed as the groundwork of the planting, various other trees being used, each in smaller numbers, to heighten local effects.

[1] ED. NOTE: Made at the request of the Board by Mr. Olmsted soon after his appointment, and printed as Doc. No. 11, 1857. In addition to these selections dealing with trees more particularly as elements in the design of the Park, and with the securing of suitable trees in quantity in the United States and from abroad, this document contains an interesting "Schedule of Catalogue Prices for certain Trees at the Principal Nurseries in the United States, France, England and Scotland," covering the trees recommended for purchase. It is of interest to compare with these lists of plants available for order, the *Catalogue of Plants Gathered in August and September, 1857, in the ground of the Central Park.* By Charles Rawolle & Ig. A. Pilat. (Published as booklet in 1857). Cf. p. 77.

On many accounts it will be found best to plant this part of the Park earliest; and as it will be an advantage to have had the trees in a nursery near at hand, for at least a year before setting them in the position they are intended to occupy permanently, I think it would be safe to obtain for the purpose, as soon as may be found convenient, at least 3,000 Norway Spruce, 3,000 Hemlock, 500 Black Spruce, 500 Larch, 500 Arbor-vitæ and 150 of each of the others I have mentioned.

In the transition from this rugged ground to the table-land of the second section, the softer evergreens will be appropriately used and 300 of the White Pine and 150 each of the Scotch, Corsican, Pinaster and Cembra Pines may be safely purchased at once.

Nearly a third of the second and third sections is now occupied by a young grove of Deciduous trees, and no large number of any particular sort will be needed to be introduced among these. The artificial style will probably be adopted, or at least approached, as indicated on the plan of the Chief Engineer, in the eastern parts of these sections, for which choice lawn and avenue trees will be wanted, and in the western part, evergreens of the sorts suggested for the first section will be most appropriate. European Larch, Arbor-vitæs of different varieties, the Silver Fir and others of the smaller Firs, will best grow on the rocky terrace west of the reservoir. The park soil seems particularly obnoxious to the Balsam Fir, not one of twenty specimens growing upon it being in sound condition.

In the fourth section there is again much fine young wood of the native deciduous species admirably grouped by nature. The largest and finest trees of our climate can, however, be employed here in great numbers—Hickories, Oaks, Elms, Beeches, Chestnuts, Ashes and Maples especially. The same trees will be wanted also for groups and detached planting on the lawn-like ground which will probably be made on the gentle slopes and level portions of the second and third sections. Those varieties of these species, therefore, which are most uniformly healthy, simple in outline, and dense and retentive of foliage, may be safely obtained in large quantities. I should think that at least 1,000 of each would be needed next autumn.

At the first planting season after any portion of the drives or footpaths are laid out, such shrubs as the following (the Superintendent of Planting would doubtless add largely to the list) will be wanted in large quantity. Several thousand of each may be procured at once with unquestionable advantage: Honeysuckle, Kalmia Latifolia (the Laurel of New England), Dogwood, Privet, Hawthorn, Buckthorn, Osage Orange, Magnolia Glauca, Obovata, Conspicua, and all the varieties which are certainly hardy and healthy in the climate; Lilacs, Dwarf Horse-chestnut, Missouri Currant, Virginia Fringe, Spirea, Syringa, Hydrangea quercifolia,

Viburnum, Althea, Acacias, Indigo-bush, Deutzia Scabra, Weigela Rosea, Japan Quince, Daphne Mezerium, Burning-bush, Laburnum, and every smooth-leaved evergreen that will surely endure the climate.

I have confined myself to an enumeration of trees, which, in my judgment, will be indispensable to at least the numbers given, merely as a basis of the landscape planting; which will, therefore, be the first required for use, and which it will be an important advantage to the landscape-gardener to have growing in a nursery on the park. If there is yet time for the preparation of the ground, and for proper painstaking in their selection, I should strongly recommend them to be procured this season, and at all events I should advise that ground be drained, fertilized and trenched, in order to receive them early in the spring. Besides getting those I have mentioned, it would be well to select immediately the finest trees which can be found, at a moderate price, in any nurseries which can conveniently be visited for the purpose, to the number of at least 1,000 Mountain Ash; 1,000 Dogwood; 1,000 Sweet Gum; 1,000 Horse-chestnut; 500 Linden; 200 Silver Poplar; 200 Weeping Willow; 200 Button-Wood; 100 Lombardy poplar.

. . . .

It will probably be found that the trees which are ordinarily used in the United States as shade and road trees, and which consequently are imported, or propagated, extensively by our nurserymen, can be obtained from the American nurseries better than from the foreign. These are the trees which will be wanted in largest quantity, and which it will be most important to get of size, well nourished, and in healthy, thrifty condition.

. . . .

A considerable importation of evergreens will probably be found unavoidable. Our nurseries have extremely small stocks of a very great variety of evergreens, which some of the European nurseries keep on hand in much larger quantity, because they are required on precisely such occasions as this, in the planting of a park or garden of the first class, an undertaking much more common there than here, as well as by a class of wealthy amateurs, not yet found in the United States, who form collections of evergreens, or winter-gardens in their private grounds. The greatest number of varieties of evergreen trees and shrubs to be found in the catalogue of any nurseryman in the United States does not, I believe, exceed eighty—some of the foreign nurseries have eight hundred.

For similar reasons, European nurserymen propagate a better assortment of varieties of deciduous trees than ours.

. . . .

It may be true that many of the varieties named in the European catalogues have no especially valuable qualities and that many of them are unsuited to our climate (though in most cases, this remains to be tested), but it is also true that with the addition of those which cannot be got here, the gardening artist has it in his power to produce landscape effects with a degree of precision and delicacy which without them it would be hopeless for him to attempt.

* * * * * * *

DESCRIPTIVE GUIDE TO THE ARBORETUM [1]

As Proposed in "Greensward" Plan

The general arrangement of the arboretum is exhibited on the plan. The principal walk is intended to be so laid out, that while the trees and shrubs bordering it succeed one another in the natural order of families, each will be brought, as far as possible, into a position corresponding to its natural habits, and in which its distinguishing characteristics will be favorably exhibited. At the entrance, marked "W" on the plan, we place the Magnoliaceæ, associating with them the shrubs belonging to the orders Ranunculaceæ, Anonoceæ, Berberidaceæ, and Cistaceæ. The great beauty of these families entitles them, if no other reasons prevailed, to a very prominent place on our grounds. In pursuing the path which enters here, we find on our right hand the order Tiliaceæ, with the shrubs belonging to the orders Rutaceæ, Anacardiaceæ, and Rhamnaceæ. On each side of the walk groups succeed, composed wholly of the order Sapindaceæ. Next to the right, planted on high ground, among large rocks, we come to the natural order, Leguminosæ, distinguished for the beauty of its forms and the lightness of its foliage, and not less in some species for the exquisite fragrance and delicacy of its blossoms.

At the next turn of the path, we come upon the Rosaceæ. The shrubs of this order being very beautiful, we have placed many of them singly, as well as in thickets between, and over, the large masses of rock, which here occur on both sides.

Next, we reach the order Hamamelaceæ, represented by the only tree of the order, Liquid Amber Styraciflua, with shrubbery consisting of Calycanthaceæ, Grossulaceæ, Saxafragaceæ, Hamamelaceæ, and Araliaceæ.

On the right of the path and nearly in front of the chapel, comes the family Cornaceæ, which contains but two large trees, Nyssa Multiflora, and Nyssa Uniflora. But to compensate for its meagerness in this respect, this and the following orders, Capri-

---

[1] Ed. Note: This guide formed the second part of the document accompanying the "Greensward" Plan, by Olmsted and Vaux, entitled: Particulars of Construction and Estimate for a Plan of the Central Park. For the first part, see p. 283, *ante*.

foliaceæ and Rubiaceæ, contain some of our finest shrubs, which are well placed upon smooth slopes.

Next in order and occupying a large space upon the dark, fertile soil of the Harlem flats, which here extend into the park, we find the natural family, Ericaceæ, possessing but one large tree, Oxydendrum Arboreum. This order is remarkable for the beauty of its shrubs, which are so peculiar to this country, that, when planted by themselves abroad, they form what is called an American garden, one of the choicest ornaments of the higher class of English country-seats.

At the next turn are arranged three natural orders, represented by one tree each: Aquifoliaceæ by Ilex Opaca, Styraceæ by Halesia Tetraptera, and Ebenaceæ by Diospyros Virginiana. With these are the shrubs of Styraceæ, Sapotaceæ and Verbenaceæ. At the left hand of the walk, stand singly two specimens of our finest flowering tree, the Catalpa Bignoniodes (Bignoniaceæ), which has no shrubs immediately associated with it. Next, the Oleaceæ, with shrubs belonging to Thymeleceæ; some of them scattered on a large open lawn, and some gathered in copses upon a rocky hill side. On another part of the same ledge will be seen the only species of the Laurel tribe which belong to our climate—the Sassafras officinalis, and Benzoin odoriferum (Lauraceæ). The specimens will be numerous, standing both singly and in clusters.

The arboretum walk here approaches and soon crosses the One hundred and Second street entrance to the park, which will thus in the regular sequence of the natural orders be furnished with a canopy of the American elm, bordered by the other fine trees of the order, and shrubs of Elægnaceæ, Santaraceæ, and Empetraceæ.

South of the entrance road stands singly and in an isolated group, the Platanus occidentalis (Platanaceæ). Scattered on a grassy declivity, follow the Juglandaceæ. Growing as they grow in our pastures, no tree is more beautiful in groups or singly than the hickory, and shrubbery of any kind among them would be out of place.

The oak may be almost called an American tree, as in no other country are the species half so numerous. On this account, as well as for their great beauty, it has been thought proper to give them much open space. A few shrubs of Cupuliferæ and Myricaceæ form the underwood of the mass which will shut out the view towards Fifth avenue, which here passes at an elevated grade.

To these succeed the order Betulaceæ, the graceful birches, and Salicaceæ, which includes the poplars. Finally, are brought in our various American Coniferæ. Only single trees are provided for in this section, as masses of each are elsewhere arranged in the park.

INDEX TO ARBORETUM

∗ The large capitals correspond with letters on the map.

TREES

A. Magnoliaceæ.

1.	Magnolia glauca.
2.	" macrophylla.
3.	" acuminata.
4.	" Frazeri.
5.	" umbrella.
6.	Liriodendron tulipifera.

B. Tiliaceæ.

7.	Tilia Americana.
8.	" heterophylla.

Camelliaceæ.

9.	Stuartia Virginica.
10.	" pentigyna.
11.	Gordonia larianthus.

C. Sapindaceæ.

12.	Æsculus glabra.
13.	" flava.
14.	" Pavia.
15.	Acer saccharinum.
16.	" Pennsylvanicum.
17.	" dasycarpum.
18.	" rubrum.
19.	Negundo aceroides.

D. Leguminosæ.

20.	Robinia pseudocacia.
21.	" viscosa.
22.	Cladrastus tinctoria.
23.	Gymnocladus Canadensis.
24.	Gleditschia triacanthos.

E. Rosaceæ.

25.	Prunus scrotina.
26.	" Pennsylvanica.
27.	" Virginiana.
28.	Pyrus coronaria.
29.	" angustifolia.

F. Hamamelaceæ.

G. Cornaceæ.

30.	Liquidambar styraciflua.
31.	Nyssa multiflora.
32.	" uniflora.

H. Ericaceæ.

33.	Oxydendrum arboreum.

I. Aquifoliaceæ.

34.	Ilex opaca.

Styraceæ.
Ebenaceæ.

35.	Halesia tetraptera.
36.	Diospyros Virginiana.
37.	Catalpa Bignonioides.

K. Oleaceæ.

38.	Chionanthus virginica.
39.	Fraxinus Americana.
40.	" pubescens.
41.	" viridis.
42.	" sambucifolia.
43.	" angulata.

L. Lauraceæ.

M. Urticaceæ.

N. Platanaceæ.

O. Juglandaceæ.

P. Cupuliferæ.

Q. Betulaceæ.

R. Salicaceæ.

S. Coniferæ.

44. Sassafras officinale.
45. Benzoin odoriferum.
46. Morus rubra.
47. Maclura aurantiaca.
48. Ulmus fulva.
49. " racemosa.
50. " Americana.
51. " alata.
52. Celtis occidentalis.
53. Platanus occidentalis.
54. Juglans cinerea.
55. " nigra.
56. Carya olivæformis.
57. " alba.
58. " sulcata.
59. " tormentosa.
60. " microcarpa.
61. " glabra.
62. " amara.
63. Quercus prinoides.
64. " illicifolia.
65. " nigra.
66. " palustris.
67. " rubra.
68. " coccinea.
69. " tinctoria.
70. " falcata.
71. " castanea.
72. " alba.
73. " obtusiloba.
74. " macrocarpa.
75. " Phellos.
76. " imbricaria.
77. " aquatica.
78. " bicolor.
79. " Prinus.
80. Castanea viva.
81. " pumila.
82. Fagus ferruginea.
83. Ostrya virginica.
84. Betula lenta.
85. " nigra.
86. " excelsa.
87. " papyracea.
88. " alba.
89. Populus grandidenta.
90. " heterophylla.
91. " monilifera.
92. " angulata.
93. " balsamifera.
94. " tremuloides.
95. Larix Americana.
96. Thuja occidentalis.

S. Coniferæ.

97. Cupressus thyoides.
98. Abies Canadensis.
99. " alba.
100. " nigra.
101. " balsamea.
102. " Fraseri.
103. Pinus inops.
104. " Tæda.
105. " strobus.
106. " rigida.
107. " mitis.
108. " pungens.
109. " resinosa.
110. Taxodium distichum.
111. Juniperus communis.
112. " Virginiana.

SHRUBS

A. Ranunculaceæ.

Atragene Americana.
Zanthorhiza apiifolia.

Annonaceæ.

Asimina triloba.
" apiifolia.

Berberidaceæ.

Berberis vulgaris.
" Canadensis.
Mahonia aquifolium.

Cistaceæ.

Helianthemum Canadensis.
" corymborum.
Hudsonia ericoides.
" tomentosa.

B. Rutaceæ.

Zanthoxylum Americanum.
" Carolinianum.
Pelia trifoliata.

Anacardiaceæ.

Rhus typhina.
" glabra.
" copallina.
" aromatica.

Rhamnaceæ.

Rhamnus lanceolatus.
" alnifolius.

C. Sapindaceæ.

Staphylia trifolia.
Æsculus macrostachya.
Acer spicatum.

D. Leguminosæ.

Amorpha fruticosa.
" canescens.
Robinia hispida.
Cercis Canadensis.

E. Rosaceæ.

Prunus Americana.
" Maritima.
" Chicasa.
" pumila.

E. Rosaceæ.

Spiraea opulifolia.
" salicifolia.
" corymbora.
Rubus odoratus.
Rosa setigera.
" Carolina.
" lucida.
" blanda.
Cratægus spathulata.
" cordata.
" apiifolia.
" coccinea.
" tormentosa.
" crus-galli.
" flava.
" paroiflora.
Pyrus arbutifolia.
" Americana.
Amelanchier Canadensis.

F. Calycanthaceæ.

Calycanthus floridus.
" lævigatus.
" glaucus.

Grossulaceæ.

Ribes Cynosbati.
" hirtellum.
" rotundifolium.
" lacustre.
" prostratum.
" floridum.
" rubrum.
" aureum.

Saxafragaceæ.

Hydrangea arborescens.
" quercifolia.
" nivea.
Philadelphus inodorus.

Hamamelaceæ.

Hamamelis Virginica.
Fothergilla alnifolia.

Araliaceæ.

Aralia spinosa.

G. Cornaceæ.

Cornus florida.
" circinnata.
" sericea.
" stolonifera.
" asperifolia.
" stricta.
" paniculata.
" alternifolia.

Caprifoliaceæ.

Symphoricarpus occidentalis.
" racemosa.
" vulgaris.
Caprifolium sempervirens.
Lonicera ciliata.
" cærulea.
" oblongifolia.
Diervilla trifida.
" sessiliflora.
Sambucus Canadensis.
" pubens.

G. Cornaceæ.
Caprifoliaceæ.

H. Ericaceæ.

Rubiaceæ.

Viburnum nudum.
" prunifolium.
" Lentago.
" obovatum.
" dentatum.
" pubescens.
" acerifolium.
" panciflorum.
" opulus.
" lantanoides.
Cephalanthus occidentalis.

Gaylussacia brachycera.
" dumosa.
" frondosa.
" resinosa.
Vaccinium Oxycoccus.
" macrocarpon.
" stamineum.
" cæspitosum.
" uliginosum.
" erythrocarpon.
" Vitis-Idaea.
" Pennsylvanicum.
" Canadense.
Vaccinium vaccillans.
" corymborum.
Chiogenes hispidula.
Arclostaphylos Uva-ursi.
" alpina.
Epiygæa repens.
Gaultheria repens.
" shallon.
Leucothœ axillaris.
" Catisbei.
" recurva.
" racemosa.
Cassandra calyculata.
Andromeda polifolia.
" floribunda.
" Mariana.
" ligustrina.
Clethra alnifolia.
" acuminata.
Kalmia latifolia.
" angustifolia.
" glauca.
" hirsuta.
Menzieria ferruginea.
Azalea arborescens.
" viscosa.
" nudiflora.
" calendulacea.
Rhododendron maximum.
" punctatum.
" Catawbiense.
" Lapponicum.
Rhodora Canadensis.
Ledum buxifolium.

I. Aquifoliaceæ.

Ilex decidua.
"   monticola.
"   verticillata.
"   lævigata.
"   glabra.
Nepomanthes Canadensis.

Styraceæ.

Styrax grandifolia.
"   pulverulentula
"   Americana.
Symplocos tinctoria.

Sapotaceæ.

Bumelia lycioides.
"   lanuiginosa.

Verbenaceæ.

Callicarpa Americana.

K. Oleaceæ.

Forestina ligustrina.
Tetranthera geniculata.

Thymelaceæ.

Dirca palustris.

M. Eleagnaceæ.

Shepherdia Canadensis
"   argentea.
Eleagnus argentea.

Santalaceæ.

Pyrularia oleifera.

Empetraceæ.

Empetrum nigrum.
Corema Conradii.

P. Cupuliferæ.

Corylus Americana.
"   rostrata.
Carpinus Americana.
Myrica gale.
"   cerifera.
Comptonia asplenifolia

S. Coniferæ.

Taxus Canadensis.

MEMORANDUM FOR PSEUDO TROPICAL PLANTING

Sassafras officinale; magnolia purpurea, glauca, auriculata, &c.; andromeda arborea; catalpa; ailanthus; paulonia; morus rubra, alba; liquid amber; papaw; persimmon; dorca palustris; together with a variety of broad leaved plants for the water's edge; such as simptocarpus fœtidus, veratrum viride, orentium aquaticum, and saracenia purpurea.

INSPIRATION FROM TROPICAL SCENERY FOR PARK PLANTING

LETTER FROM MR. OLMSTED TO MR. IGNAZ A. PILAT. CHIEF
LANDSCAPE GARDENER OF CENTRAL PARK.

PANAMA, September 26, 1863.

My dear Mr. Pilat: I have never had a more complete satisfaction and delight of my love of nature than I had yesterday in crossing the isthmus. You will remember that I always had a reaching out for tropical effect,[1] but I found the reality far beyond my imagination, resting as it did upon very inadequate specimens, hastily and imperfectly observed. I constantly wished that you and Mr. Fisher[2] were with me, and much more I wished that we could have seen five years ago what I saw yesterday, and received then the same distinct lesson which I did yesterday, and of which I certainly had some sort of prophetic feeling, and desire to avail myself in some of our study of the park planting. The groundwork was not extraordinary to us, the topographical characteristics not differing essentially from those of the park; yet the scenery excited a wholly different emotion from that produced by any of our temperate-zone scenery, or rather it excited an emotion of a kind which our scenery sometimes produces as a quiet suggestion to reflection, excited it instantly, instinctively and directly. If my retrospective analysis of this emotion is correct, it rests upon a sense of the superabundant creative power, infinite resource, and liberality of Nature—the childish playfulness and profuse careless utterance of Nature.

This is what I felt most strongly, and, after my excitement was somewhat tempered, I naturally fell to questioning how it was produced, and whether, with materials that we can command in the temperate regions, we could to any marked degree reproduce it. I think that I was rather blindly and instinctively feeling for it, in my desire to give "tropical character" to the planting of the island, and luxuriant jungled variety and density and intricate abundance to the planting generally of the lake border and the Ramble and the River Road. Of course, it is the very reverse of the emotion sought to be produced in the Mall and playgrounds region —rest, tranquillity, deliberation and maturity. As to how it is caused —I mean how the intensity of it which I yesterday experienced is occasioned by any details which I can select in tropical scenery—it is unnecessary to ask, if we can assume that these details do naturally contribute to it. Taking it for granted that they do, what is there here that we have not something similar to, or that by management we can bring something that we have to resemble?

[1] ED. NOTE: Cf. memorandum for pseudo-tropical planting, accompanying "Greensward" Plan, 1858, *opposite.*

[2] ED. NOTE: It has not been possible to ascertain whether or not this is a misspelling for Mr. Fischer mentioned in footnote on p. 353.

First, we have nothing that will resemble cocoanut or date palms (none of our established materials) or bamboo. These are the most striking things we see. But does this esthetic effect of the tropical scenery depend greatly upon them? In the center of the isthmus we passed considerable intervals where palms were absent from the foreground. The tropical picture was much less complete as merely a picture of the tropics, but the sense of the luxuriance of nature produced was not less complete. Indeed, I think the association of the palm with the open, flat monotonous desert, and with many scenes of barrenness, as on the rocky, parched and sterile coast of Cuba, makes it not absolutely essential, but only favourable to this impression. The banana or plantain is a great help and is of the greatest possible value, but it appears only occasionally, and is also not indispensable though more desirable than any other of the family. On the high grounds, especially, there was often nothing of which we have not a typical representative in our scenery; the great difference being that we have no scenery in which there are not qualities which are altogether absent here, and we have no scenery in which those qualities which are common to both are seen in anything like the same profusion and combination. I frequently thought, looking at any ten or twenty square feet of which I saw before me, and omitting the palms, it would only be necessary to assemble various bits of scenes to have a complete scene resembling and producing in considerable degree the moral effect of a scene before me. Palms or palm-like trees were never out of sight, though sometimes, as I said, absent from the foreground. Well, it was then a great satisfaction to find that the trees most markedly different from our common temperate-zone trees, at a little distance, could not be distinguished from what we were trying to get and what we know it to be possible to get on the island. It is true, nature uncontrolled, except by a most rare accident possibly, never quite gives us the palm, or palm-like tree in our distances,—but she sometimes comes near it. By selection and special treatment, we can then produce trees, which, seen at a distance of a couple of hundred feet, shall lead a man to say, "I have seen such trees before only in the tropics."

This is what we are aiming for on the island. Wherein are we wrong? As far as the palm-like effect is concerned, only in not pushing our plan far enough. The length of stem and smallness of head is more than I had supposed, often more marked than I had supposed, I mean at a distance, the trunk frequently is imperceptible, and you see the head apparently floating unsupported. The trees growing in this way are not palms or not all palms, but in their foliage so nearly like the Ailanthus that at no great distance (as a landscape painter would depict them) you would not know them apart, at least an average observer would not. Another of our prominent trees on the island, the Aralia, is, if I mistake not, itself in several varieties, actually present and frequent and not unimportant in the minor scenery of the isthmus. I saw these two trees (something resembling the Ailanthus and the Aralia) on the shore of lagoons and rivers and on islands in these, not a few hundred yards away, not differing at all from those on our island, except as they stretched themselves higher toward heaven and had smaller bunches of plumes at the top. I saw also great lengths of shore, where the immediate border of the water consisted wholly of shrubs and grass or herbage, which would in the middle distance of a picture be perfectly represented by a copy of a bank, very densely grown (horizontally over the water) of our Holly-leaved Barberry and beds of Sweet Flag and Tiger Lily with vines running through and over them. These vines are thinly leaved with leaves like Kalmia, but longer, and a blossom like a white Convolvulus. The only noticeably frequent blossom or flower at all conspicuous was not to be distinguished a few rods off from the Convolvulus, sometimes white and sometimes purple. A speck of scarlet was sometimes seen in the herbage, but I could not catch the form. There were also great broad leaves of the color of the Skunk Cabbage and others which I could not distinguish from the Paulownia. A small tree was sometimes seen also having exactly the effect of the Paulownia four to five years old in rich soil. These then are all details which (seen across water) we can very well produce.

Other plants, of the general density, form, size and best color of the Berberis aquifolia, including some of broader leaf and greater pliancy, are mixed with that. The Forsythia and the Oriental Magnolias represent closely other shrubs which I saw distinctly by the roadside. I saw also, as it seemed to me, our Wild Raspberry, the fragrant variety, one purple dark leaf of the same form (a single shrub of Purple Barberry would meet the effect in a bank). I saw also our common rushes and the Cat-tail Flag, but without seed-stems. Of many scenes, there was no other marked detail. Of trees which I could distinguish in the general body of foliage, there were besides those spoken of, what I suppose to be Tamarinds, not essentially differing in landscape effect from our Honey-locust, and one resembling in its structure our Sycamore, with a thinly scattered foliage of leaves like the Magnolia grandiflora; I almost think it is that, grown very large and straggling under tropical heat. There were glaucous-leaved small trees which the Magnolia glauca would tolerably replace and all the varieties of Magnolia, generally growing in clusters and not large, much the most marked of these not differing from our great-leaved Magnolia when young and in rich soil. Young shoots of this growing as it would if from a stool with the different stems cut down one or two every year, and none growing over five years, would give what was of most value of the great-leafed trees not palms and not of the Paulownia character. I saw no great-leafed trees more than twenty feet high, always excepting palms. As a general rule, in the landscape, these and whatever trees there were, were lost completely (as individuals) in the intricacy of whatever went to make up the mass of luxuriance, but especially under the all-clothing garment of vines and creepers.

You know how we see a single tree—most frequently a Juniperus Virginiana—lost completely under the Cat-briar. Frequently—generally—the whole forest is lost in the same way here. You often see nothing but the foliage of the vines, and this is generally so small and delicate in detail that you distinguish nothing individual except in the immediate foreground. Palms and everything are lost under it. As far as I could make out, the largest and highest trees were completely covered with a most delicate vine with a close narrow long leaf, gray-green in color, or more likely with a small white or gray blossom, which gave that effect. When growing over shrubs or small trees, a hundred feet distant, it was not essentially different in landscape effect from the Clematis as we often see it showered over a Sumach.

If you could have large spreading trees like the Chestnut or Sycamore growing on a steep hillside, and completely cover them with Clematis as the Sumach is covered, only here and there little branches and twigs of the other trees I have mentioned pushing up through, you would have the effect of the tropical forest much as I saw it yesterday across the Chagres River. There are all sorts of other vines. I saw, as I suppose, the yellow jessamine (of Georgia) and the Trumpet Creeper, but the Virginia Creeper would at a little distance answer better the purpose of what was more common. But also there were many more delicate in structure and smaller leaf, but larger and more cord-like in trunk. Very often it seemed as if hundreds of cords (½ inch) were stretched from every part of the great spreading tops of trees, fifty to a hundred feet to the ground. All large trees seem to have strained themselves to the utmost to get their foliage away from the smothering density of the ground-growth, the smaller trees and shrubs, but not to have been able to get away from the vines and creepers. Thus there is often, as it were, an upper and a lower growth, of which the Cocoanut Palm growing out of a jungle, but itself overgrown by the creepers, is the extreme type. There are parts of the Ramble where you will have this result in a considerable degree after a few years, the lower stratum being a few shrubs that will endure the shade and the upper low-spreading topped, artificially dwarfed trees assisted by vines. I don't doubt that in the interior of these forests you would find spots where the ground-growth was killed by density of shade and the trunks only supported a canopy or extended parasol, rendered complete and impervious by the vines and by the absence of shade above. The theory of adaptation of varieties thus accounts for the palm-like growth of so many tropical trees and shrubs or sub-trees. Our Sassafras as it grows in the Sassafras grove in the Ramble, is a perfectly tropical tree in character. But for the tropical or tropic-like scenery, you must get the utmost possible intricacy and variety and can have no breadth or mass of color or simple continuity of outline.

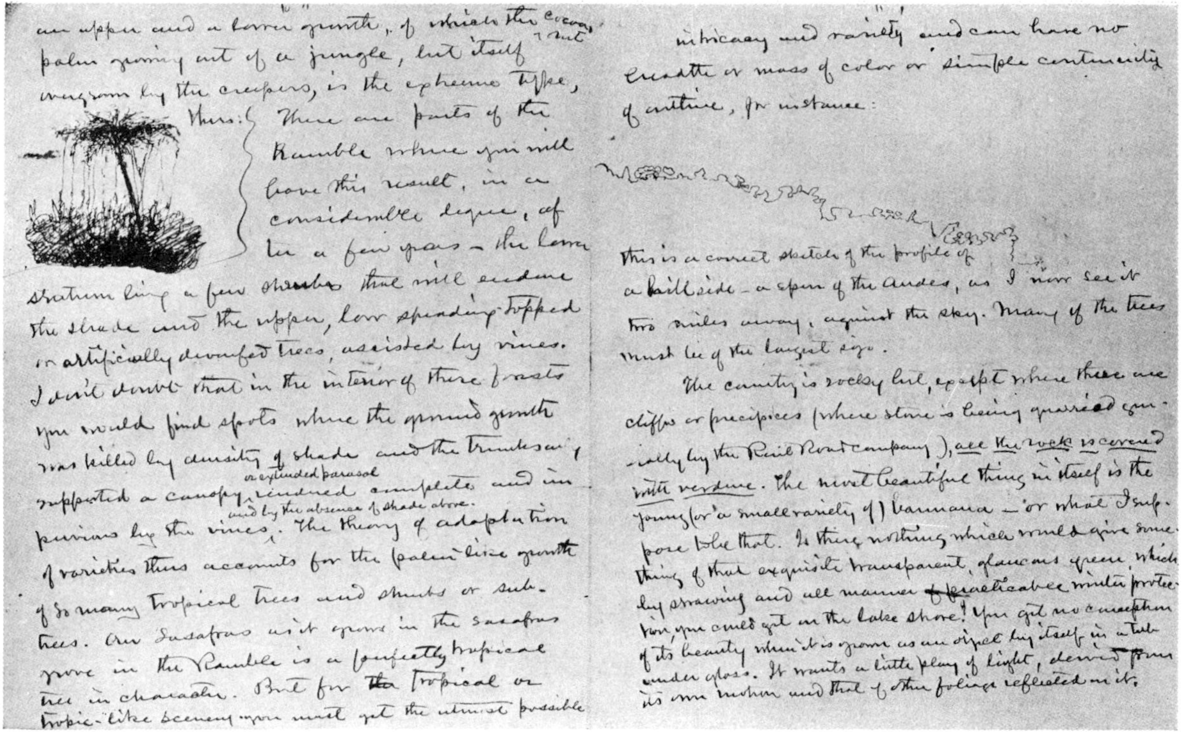

"an upper and a lower growth," of which the cocoa-nut palm growing out of a jungle, but itself overgrown by the creepers, is the extreme type, thus: There are parts of the Ramble where you will have this result, in a considerable degree, of [illegible] in a few years — the lower stratum being a few shrubs that will endure the shade and the upper, low spreading-topped or artificially dwarfed trees, assisted by vines. I don't doubt that in the interior of those forests you would find spots where the ground growth was killed by density of shade and the trunks sw[illegible] supported a canopy, or extended parasol, rendered complete and impervious by the vines, and by the absence of shade above. The theory of adaptation of varieties thus accounts for the palm-like growth of so many tropical trees and shrubs or sub-trees. Our Sassafras as it grows in the sassafras grove in the Ramble is a perfectly tropical tree in character. But for tropical or tropic-like scenery you must get the utmost possible

"intricacy and variety" and can have no breadth or mass of color or simple continuity of outline, for instance:

This is a correct sketch of the profile of a hillside — a spur of the Andes, as I now see it two miles away, against the sky. Many of the trees must be of the largest size.

The country is rocky but, except where there are cliffs or precipices (where stone is being quarried generally by the Rail Road company), all the rock is covered with verdure. The most beautiful thing in itself is the young (or a small variety of) banana — or what I suppose to be that. Is there nothing which would give something of that exquisite transparent, glaucous green, which by drawing and all manner of practicable winter protection, you could get on the lake shore? You get no conception of its beauty when it is grown as an object by itself in a tub under glass. It wants a little play of light, derived from its own motion and that of other foliage reflected on it.

Courtesy of *Landscape Architecture*

From Mr. Olmsted's Letter to Mr. Pilat, 1863

The country is very rocky but except where there are cliffs or precipices (where stone is being quarried, generally by the railroad company) all the rock is covered with verdure. The most beautiful thing in itself is the young (or small variety) Banana, or what I suppose to be that. Is there nothing which would give something of that exquisite transparent glaucous-green which by strawing and all manner of practical winter protection, you could get on the lake-shore? You get no conception of its beauty when it is grown as an object by itself in a tub under glass. It wants a little play of light, derived from its own motion and that of other foliage reflected on it. I assume, as I said at starting, that as a general rule, these things which I have mentioned as the most obvious parts (except those clearly out of our power to produce) which combine to constitute tropical scenery all help to that emotion, the root of which seems to be a profound sense of the Creator's bountifulness. I don't know how, without considering the probable reason (in the tropics) for this upper growth of certain and many trees, we can be led to this emotion by witnessing it, but I am inclined to think that it plays its part without this reflection being induced, as well as everything else. Therefore, in trying to make the best of our materials to the same purpose, I should not neglect to use it—to train up by continual selection of a leader and pruning off anything below its junction with the trunk, until a very unusual height was attained and so on by knife and training and manure. I think we could get objects to represent all the prominent details. Then general richness of soil and the removal or covering up and making intricate with vines and creepers of everything else, would under favorable natural circumstances, I believe, produce an effect having at least an interesting association with or, so to speak, flavor of tropical scenery and I should hope some little feeling of the emotion it is fitted to produce. For this purpose, however, we must make much of trees of the smallest size and large shrubs, and consequently must subject all large trees to peculiar treatment, so as not to destroy the minor scale of the landscape, and also not to crowd out and destroy the important small trees by shade.

If I were, after this experience, in your place on the park, I should aim to have something of this character all around the lake, but especially on the east shore of the main lake. We always, or at least originally, intended to get water-plants in there. The mass of foliage on the shore opposite and to the north of the island is, I think, more monotonous than was originally intended—very much. Is it too late to break into it and reducing the surface in some places to the water-level, get flags and coarse water-grasses and lilies, etc., to grow? On the island, I would cut away all the deciduous growth which inclines to run more than four feet high, except the Aralias and Ailanthus and push these as high as possible (except also the vines, of course). I question whether I would keep the cedars, but if I did, I would confine them in a network of vines to the narrowest limits consistent with the life of the lower foliage. I would remove from the island the Deciduous Cypresses. The adjoining bank I would, if it were possible, treat in the same way for a short distance, and then make sure of great intricacy above and a water edge (where Flags would not grow) of over-hanging glossy (with spots of glaucous) foliage. I would have every rock (and evergreen) in this immediate vicinity shrouded under Cat-briar or Clematis, completely so. Of course I would get in the Indian Corn here and there if I could. I think the Sorghum would have a canelike effect, would it not? And of course I would have some show of the Ailanthus and the cut-down Pau-lownia along the edges, as well as Callas, etc. By callas I mean plants having the general appearance of callas. I was delighted the last time I was in the park, with the appearance of the Cy-presses on the west shore and thought I would be glad to have the masses of them enlarged. Would it not be well to move those on the island for that purpose? I did not like the Weeping Willow at the bridge, but don't mind their being tried. Cut them away when you feel like it. I would have the Catalpa and the Paper Mulberry once or twice more repeated along the lake-shore. I thought the knife was badly wanted to bring out the dark on the point opposite the terrace and at a few other points. I meant to have said all this to you and more, but had no time.

I hope you will continue to pay particular attention to the en-richment of the soil on the intermediate border of the lake, especi-ally where the rocky parts are. Up to this time there has been no part of the work which has disappointed me more than these rocky and stony parts of the lake-shore, particularly the bay opposite the terrace and the east side of the point, the north bay and the west side of the passage to the crypt, where the blasting drill-hole is still seen and where the richest luxuriance of foliage was wanted, there is rawness, bareness, and sharpness of form, and poverty. Couldn't you have some large pocket-holes blasted or quarried near the water's edge in those rocks in the north bay, the crypt-cove and the terrace bay and fill them with rich soil so as to get vines growing over them from beneath? By some means or other the bareness of those rocks should be overcome whatever its cost, for it detracts greatly from the value of all that has been done about them.

Off Cape Corrientes, October 6th.

Since the above writing, we have landed at Acapulco and Man-sanillo bay in Mexico, and I have strolled a little among the trees. I find the true palms seldom except in groves and clusters by them-selves, generally in low alluvial ground, and what I have said above is confirmed, except as the distinctive character of tropical foliage is less on the Mexican coast than at the isthmus. We have coasted for days within short distance of the shore. What I chiefly feel that I have above disregarded or neglected to refer to, is the peculiar beauty in tropical landscape which is due to the frequent cavernous depths of shade, to the constant recurrence of these on the forest slopes. You can easily see how these result from the circumstances I have mentioned; the umbrella-like trees, over-hanging dense undergrowth and the vines making a drapery, all natural ravines and cliffs of rock and caverns of rock, which form the characteristic topography of this coast as of parts of the Italian and English coasts, being thus clothed with foliage. The play of light and shade even at noonday is most refreshing. One can often hardly believe that the forms of foliage are not artificial, so like are they when seen at a distance in effect of light and shade to the old clipped arbors and boweries and hedge figures. You have all this in some degree about the crypt and the rustic arch and with care to push the vines and coax the branches over, so as to get, not merely caverns and depths of shade, but caverns of foliage, dark and yet reflecting light at every leaf-point, and depths of shade in green, such as elsewhere in our climate we see only in gray and brown, you will get it perfectly. When you do, to the utmost extent that is possible with the materials which the climate allows you to use in those situations, I believe it will be a revelation of beauty to the people, and even to gardeners and artists, for although in some, indeed in many particulars, they have the advantage of us in England, in their materials, especially dark and glossy foliage, they can not approach us in materials for canopy and drapery effects of foliage, and there are few situations where soil, exposure and rocky skeletons can be so happily com-bined for the production of this class of effects as in the Ramble and along the lake-border. I have seen my ideal of the treatment of several points, done by the unaided hand of Nature (with the tropical sun) a number of times this morning and as I never saw before.

Please tell Mr. Green that I fully intended to have spent a day with him on the park before I left, and regret that I was so pressed as to be unable to.

With regards to Mr. Fisher and Mr. Rolland,

Very truly yours,

FRED. LAW OLMSTED.

IMPROVEMENT OF PLANTING DETAILS

Nov. 12th, 1870.

THE HON. PETER B. SWEENY: [1]

Pres. Dept. Public Parks:

Sir:

A good deal of work was done some years since in the dis-position of earth and rocks upon the Central Park with the in-tention of producing results which have so far been allowed to

[1] ED. NOTE: The draft of this letter is marked on the back in Mr. Olmsted's writing: "Not acknowledged or noticed."

remain incompletely provided for. To carry out the original intention plants are in some cases required, the practicability of getting and establishing which under the conditions fixed was thought at the time to be open to some question. As also they could not be purchased at the nurseries it was deemed best not to make the special arrangements which would be necessary for procuring them until a later period when all of the ground designed to be planted with them should be prepared. This, however, now having been done and as now also we are able to answer positively from the results of trials elsewhere, for the entire feasibility of the original intention, we should be glad if you would instruct the proper executive officer of the Park to discuss with us suitable measures for carrying it out during the coming year. The sites to be planted are at present either bare or occupied by a few coarse indigenous plants which have fully served their temporary purpose and are now inappropriate to their situations; and we are confident that the changes which we should recommend while they would not be very great or expensive would add much to the public satisfaction in the Park.

Your obedient servants,
OLMSTED, VAUX & CO.

PROGRESS WORK AND PLANTING INSTRUCTIONS

Feb. 27th, 1872.

MR. C. RYAN,
Superintendent's Office,
Central Park.

Dear Sir:

Several thousand trees and a large quantity of small plants, seeds, etc., are expected to arrive from Europe in the course of a month, which Mr. Demcker should be prepared in every respect to dispose of promptly and with all possible care. Please see that he lacks no reasonable advantage for this purpose.

I enclose a memorandum intended to give Mr. Demcker an outline of the work of an unusual character, besides the above, which is expected to be done under his direction during the coming season and largely during the next two months. I am very sorry indeed that it has not been practicable to have more of it done during the winter.

The Park has suffered great injury, which it is even now impossible wholly to retrieve, through the neglect of timely thinning of the plantations and the maltreatment of the last year and a half. If a very energetic and skilful course of improvement is not pursued this year, the difficulty of recovering the lost ground will be greatly increased.

If you read the memorandum, you will see that a year's growth in the standing plants to be affected in one way or another by the operations would add much to the cost of what is intended and that, provided the force employed is directed with reasonable efficiency and with due skill and judgment, the sooner the work is done the less it will cost.

You will also see that nearly all this work must be laid out and superintended with a high degree of purely technical knowledge and expert judgment and skill. No one man could meet the requirements of superintendence unless he had trustworthy, intelligent and expert assistants, as the force employed must be considerable and adjustments requiring taste and delicacy as well as mere gardening skill and industry will be required in operations in widely separated parts of the Park simultaneously.

So far as my judgment or wishes are entitled to any respect in the management of the Central Park this will be regarded as the most critical and important work remaining to be done in the Park. Were it necessary to spend a million dollars to secure the highest practicable degree of skill and efficiency in its management I know of no other way in which it will ever be as important that it should be used. The value receivable for all that has hitherto been expended depends upon the skill with which it is done. A few hundred or a few thousand dollars is of small consequence if the result ultimately obtained is to be materially better.

These being my views I want you to aid me with your best judgment as to the course to be pursued to secure the requisite degree of skill. From the beginning of the work we have never had anything like a suitable organization for it. Because we had not, the original planting work was never properly done.

I have not made up my mind what would be best, but it seems to me necessary that a man of thorough technical training and large experience and observation of plants should be in control of the work and should by every means be made to feel that *if he is not the master of the business it is his own fault.* It is not sufficient that others should think he is, but that he should fully realize it himself.

I suppose that Mr. Demcker must be our man, if for no other reason, because it is now too late to take the risk of any unknown man. As far as mere technical *knowledge* is concerned I have no doubt of his being efficient. We must take all necessary risk of his understanding what is wanted in detail and being able to make his assistants understand it and to keep them to it.

The main thing at the outset is that he should see what he has undertaken, appreciate the full weight of the trust to be put in him and be fully prepared to meet it.

I have already partly taken his views of the assistance he will require but I do not upon reflection think that they were well considered or that he fully saw what was to be undertaken. I have therefore written out this resumé of the verbal instructions previously given him in order to put the business all at once fully before him. After he has had time to think it over, I want with you to question him and finally discuss the best arrangements. Please hand the memorandum to him.

Yours truly,

FRED. LAW OLMSTED.

MEMORANDUM RELATING TO CERTAIN WORK TO BE DONE, AS SOON AS POSSIBLE, UNDER GENERAL DIRECTION OF MR. DEMCKER.[1]

1. The North Meadows, the green and the Play ground, except where large rocks prevent, are to be bordered by scattered trees, singly and in small clusters or loose groups, all of kinds which will grow large and spread widely; that is to say with characteristic park trees. They are to be formed with low heads but not so low that sheep cannot graze under them. Oaks and such as have horizontal limbs should be trimmed with a trunk clean to height of about seven feet. Those which, like the American elm, branch more obtusely upward, may be allowed to branch lower. Trees on these grounds which have been trimmed to long naked trunks are to be shortened in to force new lower branching. Groves of trees on the border of the meadows (as those near the Mineral Spring Pavilion—*see No. 26 on Folded Map*), where either branches or roots are generally interlocking or likely soon to do so, are to be thinned to groups, clusters and single trees, with sufficient intervals to favor the desired general open park effect. In thinning those are to be spared when practicable which are likely to have long-lived, low branches; others, such as black oak and sassafras to be generally cut out. Where shrubs have been set in the borders of these open grounds, unless to screen out some inharmonious object (as a barren rocky knoll) they are to be removed.

2. The above instructions in regard to trimming do not apply to trees intended for the shade of the walks and drive, the branches of which must be kept sufficiently high not to interfere with the passage required by the public on these ways, but trees trimmed unnecessarily and excessively high are to be headed in to force new branching.

3. Where trees have been planted at a regular distance from the edge of a drive or walk and at regular intervals, as in ordinary road-side planting, this character is to be changed, either by mak-

---

[1] ED. NOTE: The copy of this memorandum given to Mr. Demcker bears his notes as to the progress of the work, as follows: "(1) Partly done except topping the trees; shrubs not planted this spring.—(2) done according to this information.—(3) done so far as possible for this spring.—(5) only the trimming of spruces and some planting done.—(6) many of such trees are taken away.—(7) 6 arches have been planted according to instruction.—(9) is done according to instruction.—(10) this work is done as far as the material is found.—(12) we have not on hand such plants at present." There is also a separate record in Mr. Demcker's hand of "Proposed plantings for the Arches over Transverse Roads," evidently prepared in pursuance of section 7.

ing some slight shift of position, or the entire removal of the majority. Those allowed to remain will generally require heading in to force lower growth.

4. The last paragraph does not apply to trees on the outer walls, the trunks of which have been trimmed too high but the improvement of which may be postponed.

5. Hedge plants (spruces) on the transverse roads which are overgrown are to be reduced and trimmed with reference to a flat face flush with the retaining wall below them. Gaps are to be filled as far as possible by thinnings from existing plantations, trees with one side well filled to the bottom being preferred. These hedges are to be backed with a thicket chiefly of conifers and low thorny shrubs, the conifers will be mostly supplied by thinning. The transverse roads not hitherto planted are to be treated in the same way.

6. Spruces, Thuyas and fastigiate conifers standing so near walks and drives that they will interfere with passage unless the lower branches are cut off, or so shortened in as to give them an ugly distorted character, are to be removed. Smaller conifers, as yews and retinosporas may sometimes be substituted for them; more frequently, especially on the winter drive, thickets of bayberry, winterberry, inkberry, hollies, kalmias, andromedas, mahonias, tree box, fiery thorn, etc.

7. The last class of plants (but only such as are thoroughly hardy) is especially to be set on all the arches of the transverse roads, in loose hedges to form permanent screens thick from the ground. This is a matter of imperative importance this season. The part of the screen which will be visible from the park is to be irregular and natural in character.

8. Clusters and groups of coniferous trees throughout the Park generally require numbers to be removed to secure the health and good development of the lower branches of those which will remain.

9. The middle parts of the Ramble in a line from the Terrace to Vista Rock are to be cleared of trees. The rocks in the upper part of the Ramble are to be made permanently visible from the terrace. Tall trees are to be retained and encouraged in the outer parts; dark evergreens on the nearer parts of the ridges, right and left, with a general gradation of light foliage upon and near Vista Rock. The recently made moss gardens are to be revised and the ground rendered natural by the removal of some of the boulders, making larger, plainer surfaces, and by the introduction of more varied and common materials. Evergreen shrubs, ferns, moss, ivy, periwinkle, rock plants and common bulbs (snowdrop, dog tooth violet, crocuses, etc.), are to be largely planted in the Ramble, and while carefully keeping to the landscape character required in the general view from the Terrace, and aiming at a much more natural wild character [1] in the interior views than at

[1] ED. NOTE: Cf. a letter from Mr. Olmsted to Mr. Fischer, superintending gardener, March 14, 1875:—

present, much greater variety and more interest of detail is to be introduced.

10. Rock edges and clefts at various points, particularly the following, viz: in the Ramble; on both sides of the drive near the Sixth Avenue entrance; South of the Playground between the Dairy and South pond; North of the green; East of the Mall; between the Arsenal and the Mall; along the watercourse of the upper park, the bridges and lakes; and on the drive north of Observatory Hill, are to be dressed with peat and wood earth and planted with ferns, mosses and Alpine plants.

11. Of the trees now standing in groves, except on the border of the larger turf surfaces, the poorer class need to be taken out, the others often to be headed down to remedy the effects of the mistaken trimming of the last two years, and generally these plantations should be given a naturally dense or obscure bottom character, by encouraging low growth and planting in underwood irregularly.

12. Wherever, in the parts of the Park which have been planted, owing either to density of shade or the presence of rock and general roughness of surface, fine close turf will either be out of character, liable to die out from drought or very difficult to mow, thickets of low mountain shrubs, broom, furze, heaths or mats of vines or herbacious plants, such as asters, gentians, lobelia, hepatica, southern-wood, camomile, tansy, vervain, wild arum, wake-robin, epigea, Solomon's-seal, golden rod, lysimachia, lycopodium, convolvulus, vinca, are to be diligently introduced in patches and encouraged to completely cover the surface.

13. The patches of shrubs are now generally much too garden-like. They are to be made more natural and picturesque, especially those on hillsides and broken ground by taking out some of the plants when there are many together of one kind, and introducing others; more upright growing of fastigiate species in some parts and many more low and spreading species (such as Forsythia suspensa, Rubus odorata and brambles) in others. Shrubs growing together must be made to blend more both by the means above suggested and by special pruning for the purpose, also by introducing clematis, lycium, wistaria, honeysuckles and for immediate effect convolvulus, vetches, etc.

14. Norway spruce and other spirey-topped trees are soon likely to be too conspicuous, prominent and controlling on much of the winter drive. In thinning these plantations, pines should

---

"I send you Robinson's *Wild Garden*, as I promised. I have marked various passages in the first 40 pages, which be so good as to observe attentively. Robinson expressed the views I have always had for the Ramble, the winter drive district and the more rocky and broken parts of the park. There can be no better place than the Ramble for the perfect realization of the wild garden and I want to stock it in that way as fully and as rapidly as is possible."

A good description of the wild planting of the Ramble as it appeared a few years earlier may be found in *A Description of the New York Central Park*, 1869, pages 107 and 131.

be more generally given the front place, and, in the place of some of the spruces, yews, mountain pines, Cembran pine, glaucous and weeping red cedar, retinosporas, cryptomeria, etc., are to be introduced. The West drive north of 79th Street is to be made more cheerful by the introduction of a much larger number of such deciduous trees as by the character of the spray, color of bark or their berries will be interesting in the winter and will also associate well with the conifers; as birches, mountain ash and red-twigged dogwood. Evergreen and other shrubs as mentioned in paragraphs 6 and 12 are also to be largely introduced in this district.

Where the tops of ridges have been planted with spirey topped conifers, as that west of the South pond, a portion of them are to be removed and pines substituted so as to establish a more quiet and flowing sky line.

"SUPERINTENDENT OF CENTRAL PARK TO GARDENERS"[1]

The work which has been done in getting ready that part of the park which is now out of sight, underneath the turf, trees and bushes, gravel and water (including the purchased material such as the drain and water pipes), is equivalent to the labor of 1,000 men during a period of sixteen years. The sole use of all this work is that of a foundation for something to be formed upon it and much the most important part of this something is to be produced by work to be hereafter done by and under the direction of the district gardeners. Upon the intelligence and efficiency of the district gardeners therefore, the value of the immense preparatory work which has been already done is dependent. So far as they work with different general motives or to obtain a different class of results from those for which the preparatory work was designed, that work will have been wasted. Even, therefore, when it would be possible to aim at something better than was originally intended, it will be the part of an honest man to pursue that intention and make the best of it. Different and better purposes of gardening should be reserved to be worked out on ground where so much has not already been done for the purposes which have been in view in the Central Park.

It is, therefore, desired that the district gardeners should understand and intelligently adopt these original purposes and exert all their ability in a sincere endeavor to carry them out.

The object of this paper is to present a few leading points of these purposes with cautions against certain wrong views which many gardeners will be likely to hold.

The land and the construction of the park has not only cost the people of the city a great deal and its keeping up is not only to cost

[1] ED. NOTE: Prepared by Mr. Olmsted about 1873. Cf. references in Minutes, D. P. P., 1873–74, pages 618 and 629.

a great deal, but the taking of so many building sites and the stopping of so many avenues and streets, and causing people to go so much further around in their business than they would have otherwise needed to, is a serious inconvenience. Every gardener should understand and bear in mind what all this outlay and inconvenience is for. It is not simply to give the people of the city an opportunity for getting fresh air and exercise; if it were it could have been obtained by other means than those to be provided on the park at much less cost. It is not simply to make a place of amusement or for the gratification of curiosity or for gaining knowledge. The main object and justification is simply to produce a certain influence in the minds of people and through this to make life in the city healthier and happier. The character of this influence is a poetic one and it is to be produced by means of scenes, through observation of which the mind may be more or less lifted out of moods and habits into which it is, under the ordinary conditions of life in the city, likely to fall.

As a general rule the more there is that is natural and simple, and the less there is that is apparently artificial or suggestive of the work of men, the better the scenery would be adapted to this purpose. For this reason, if there were but a few persons to be benefitted, it would be better that there were no roads or bridges or buildings; but the object being to offer the benefits of the park to a great many thousand people, of all classes and conditions, it is necessary to make extensive provision for their accommodation and to occupy a good deal of the ground with appliances for this purpose. So far as this consideration does not apply therefore, it may be said that the object of all the work that has been done on the park is to induce the formation, chiefly by the growth of trees and plants, of a considerable variety of natural landscape scenery, —the rocks and water help to the same end, and the roads, walks, seats and other prominent structures are meant to be only such as will help the people the better to enjoy it.[1]

It is desirable that all who are allowed to use discretion in making or directing work in, on, or among trees, plants and turf in the Central Park, in order that they may proceed safely and intelligently without requiring constant instruction as to details of their duty, should understand what is the use of the Park and in just what way everything with which they will have to do will best help to make the Park better for that use.

To foremen, gardeners and others who may have discretionary duties in the Central Park:

There are certain general considerations which every man who is given any discretion in taking care of the Park should all the time bear in mind.

1st—The people who are to visit the Park this year or next are but a small fraction of those who must be expected to visit it

---

[1] ED. NOTE: Cf. Part II, Chapter IX, p. 472.

hereafter. If the Park had to be laid out, and especially if it had
to be planted with reference only to the use of the next few years,
a very different general plan, a very different way of planting and
a very different way of managing the trees, would be proper from
that which is required. No man is to use the discretion given him
to secure pretty temporary effects at the expense of advantages
for the future.

2nd—The special value of the Central Park to the city of New
York will lie, and even now lies, in its comparative largeness.
There are certain kinds of beauty possible to be had in it which
it is not possible for the city to have anywhere else, because on no
other ground of the city is there scope and breadth enough for them.
Such beauty as there is in a flower bed, such beauty as there is
in a fir tree or a cluster of fir trees, can be enjoyed on any piece
of flat ground of a quarter of an acre, can be had even in the back
yard of a city house. The seven hundred acres of the Central
Park can be better used. That which is expected to be especially
valuable on the Central Park is the beauty of broad landscape
scenes and of combinations of trees with trees and with rocks and
turf and water.

No man is to use the discretion given him to secure pretty
little local effects, at the expense of general effects and especially
of broad landscape effects.

3rd—It must be remembered that what is good and beautiful
in one place may be far from good and beautiful in another.

A great number of visitors have to be provided for in the Park,
for this reason the ground has to be cut up with roads and walks
and encumbered with frequent buildings and other structures and
appliances. Rocks have to be placed and trees and shrubs planted
in some degree so as to fit these artificial features and with a view
to convenience and economy in maintaining order. But, except
for this reason, every bit of work done on the Park should be done
for the single purpose of making the visitor feel as if he had got
far away from the town. Except in these things which are designed for the comfortable accommodation of visitors, the less
anything that is seen appears to have been dressed up by human
hands, the better.

To secure interest, it is necessary that some parts of the Park
should strongly contrast with others. As far as space will allow,
therefore, smooth, simple, clean surfaces of turf on which the
light falls early and the shadows are broad and trees which have
grown freely with plenty of room to stretch out their limbs are
intended to be brought in contrast with surfaces which are much
broken and on which there is a great profusion of lines and colors
and lights and shades, and with trees and bushes and plants which
have grown in a somewhat crowded way, bent and mingled together
as they generally are where native plants thrive on rough ground,
especially if the soil is rich and neither over dry nor over wet.

The perfection of such meadow and glade surfaces is found in nature only in the spring, when the turf is still short and growing evenly, but by shaving the grass closely at frequent intervals, this perfection can be nearly maintained through the summer. Consequently in preparing those parts of the ground where this effect is wanted, the surface without being so flat as to be evidently artificial, can hardly be made too fine or too smooth and even nor can the turf afterwards be kept too free of any plant except the grasses, nor the grass be kept too short, or be too smoothly rolled. But with the same general object in view precisely the opposite sort of treatment is required in other places. In these the surface should be more or less rough and rude, the trees and shrubs should grow more or less in bunches, there should be a great variety of character in them, some standing up and some struggling along the ground; instead of a smooth turf surface of clean short grass there should be varied sorts of herbage one crowding over another and all running together without any order, or there should be vines and creepers and mosses and ferns. There will be places where these two kinds of ground should play into one another and the surface and the plantations be of an intermediate character.

Gardeners and others are apt to think that work which would be regarded as excellent in a pleasure ground connected with a private house, or in a fine flower garden, must also be excellent anywhere in the Central Park. This is a great mistake.

For example, it is intended in the mall to give accommodations for a large number of visitors walking together and to let them have as open a prospect as is possible under the circumstances. To make this purpose obvious and to carry it out completely, the ground immediately adjoining the broad walk cannot be too evenly or flatly graded, the turf too fine or closely kept, nor the trees too carefully arranged to afford the largest degree of shade with the least degree of obstruction to the view. But a similar treatment of the ground and a similar disposition of trees is desirable nowhere else in the park.

. . . .

The main features [of the Park are] already outlined. What remains is to cure some defects, foster the right growth of what is art, and add beauty and interest of detail.

"GARDENER ORGANIZATION" [1]

5th June, 1875.

To the President:

Supposing that the proposed reduction of wages for the working force shall be carried out I wish to offer certain observations relative to the organization of the force for gardening on the parks.

All the work of the parks may be divided under three classes.

[1] ED. NOTE: From rough drafts so marked in Mr. Olmsted's hand. Cf. Minutes, 1875–76, page 138.

Plantations

1st.—Work similar to that ordinarily ordered by engineers and executed by common laborers under the immediate direction of foremen who have been trained to their business in a similar class of works, as on railroads and canals.

2d.—Artisan's work executed mainly by mechanics organized in squads or gangs according to their trade, each trade working under the immediate direction of a man more highly educated and skilled in that trade than his subordinates.

3d.—The horticultural work of the Park including such earth work as directly affects the development of the horticultural elements of the Park. For the proper performance of this a much larger range of knowledge and more cultivated skill is required than for that of ordinary mechanics, but for certain reasons of convenience of management this department of the park work upon which the value of all the rest depends, has not been organized as that of other craftsmen has been, but has been principally done by men enrolled with the common laborers and under the direction of the common foremen uneducated in and indifferent to the craft of the gardener.[1] There has always been an officer nominally filling the function of a head gardener and a foreman of gardening under him, but he has had no force exclusively under his command adequate for a tenth part of the amount of work of this class actually done; he has not known from one day to another what work it would be in his power to have done in the next; and much work has been done both by gardeners and laborers under the direct order of the foreman by ordinary laborers with or without the knowledge, consent or approval of the head gardener by which the horticultural character of the park has been radically affected. That it has been a mistaken policy to allow this and that its apparent economy has been deceptive can be demonstrated on the ground, and I can not think it necessary to argue the proposition that all garden work if it is not to be done by gardeners should at least be directed and supervised by gardeners.

To make it possible to fix the responsibility for all garden work definitely upon some individual gardener and that each such responsible gardener should be properly instructed and held to account by the superintending gardener, it is essential in my judgment that there should be territorial divisions for the ordinary care of each of which a gardener should be assigned, under whom all other necessary labor for ordinary maintenance garden work should be done.

This was the theory under which the present rank of division gardeners was formed, but of the theoretic divisions there is nothing left but the name nor have the so-called division gardeners any fixed duties distinct from the gardeners not so distinguished.

There were last summer 8 division gardeners receiving $3 a day, but in the winter three of them were reduced to the rank of gardeners at $2.50 a day.

With a view to an organization adapted to the ordinary constant requirements of the parks and at the same time to a reduction of the rate of wages in this department of the work corresponding to that in other departments, I recommend that the Board authorize the employment of 8 Division gardeners at 30 cts. an hour (the present rate being 37½ cts.), and of 9 gardeners at 25 cts., the present rate being 31¼ cts.—[F.L.O.].

———————

8th July, 1875.

To the President:
Sir:

In continuance of the matter of my report of June—which now lies on the table—I recommend a reorganization of the gardening force of the department as follows:

1st. That for gardening maintenance purposes 8 districts be formed; 6 to be in the Central Park, the small parks to form one, and the nursery and hot houses, one (but Morris Park to remain as at present).

2nd. For each gardening district a division gardener to be in immediate charge of all gardening work on his division and responsible for the care of its trees, shrubs and plants, turf excepted. His time to be taken and reported as the time of Division Gardeners is at present by the maintenance foreman of the ground in which his division is included.

3rd. Two gardeners and two garden laborers to be enrolled with each division gardener and to be at his orders whenever he shall require their service; at other times to be at the orders of the foreman, by whom their time shall be returned as heretofore.

4th. The above gardening force to be under the exclusive orders of the superintending gardener, and nothing to be done on ground occupied by trees, shrubs or plants except under his orders or with his approval.

5th. Additional laboring force, carts and other means, when certified by the superintending gardener to be necessary for his work, to be provided as may be directed by the Superintendent of Parks.

6th. The wages of division gardeners to be 40%, and of gardeners 15%, greater than that of ordinary laborers.

These arrangements are approved by the superintending gardener and the Superintendent of Parks.

Respectfully,

F. L. O.
Landscape Architect.

FALSE ECONOMY IN MAINTENANCE OF PLANTATIONS

*To the Board of Commissioners
of the Department of Parks:*

Gentlemen:

Apprehending that a further reduction of the park force may be necessary before winter, I beg to make the following statement.

Last year, contrary to what I had understood to be a fixed policy of the Department, the larger part of what is called the Gardening force was suddenly removed,[1] leaving several districts of the Central Park without a single man upon them who had ever had instruction, training or experience or the slightest ground of pretence of competence in respect to the most important duties to be performed in them.

I suppose myself to be employed by the Department mainly with respect to those duties and to be its professional adviser upon them, but the removals were made without my knowledge and neither I nor the Superintending Gardener had a suspicion that a reduction of this part of the force was contemplated nor had any preparation been made for it. The removals were made without knowledge as to the relative value of the men thrown out or those retained.

The course thus taken was adopted, I do not doubt, suddenly, in an emergency, in some degree inadvertently and without forecast of the consequences. But in view of it, I think it my duty to say in advance of any possible similar emergency the coming season, that it is essential to the economical management of the plantations that there should be a *constant* force of honest, competent men, each familiar with his own ground and carrying on continuous processes upon it. The loss of a man of this class cannot be repaired by a new one in two years' time, as well as that of a foreman, a policeman or a clerk in any position can in two months'.

The work done by and through the diminutive force of gardeners is the only work which distinguishes the business of the Department of Parks from that of other Departments of the City Government, and for this business the oldest and best foremen that are now or ever have been in the park are as ignorant and helpless as the commonest laborer.

The usual and necessary late autumn, winter and spring work upon the plantations having been last year omitted, there is now nothing to be done in the park so imperative as the work which can be done only by the gardeners, and there is no work to be done by any other men that cannot more wisely and prudently be neglected.

[1] ED. NOTE: It was not until September, 1875, that Mr. Olmsted secured from the Board authority to organize even a meager special force for the care and development of plantations on the Park. (Cf. Minutes, D. P. P., 1875–76, page 261.) This force was allowed to operate scarcely a year.

A complete suspension of work on all the roads, walks, buildings and turf for a year or two, however wasteful and calamitous it might be, would leave no injury that could not by large special expenditure be repaired in a single year. The continuous neglect of the plantations would cause injuries which no expenditure could ever make good.

Respectfully,

FRED. LAW OLMSTED.

Landscape Architect.

New York, 18th Sept., 1877., (Cf. Minutes D.P.P., 1877–78, page 311).

OBSERVATIONS ON THE TREATMENT OF PUBLIC PLANTATIONS, MORE ESPECIALLY RELATING TO THE USE OF THE AXE.[1]

BY F. L. OLMSTED, *Landscape Architect,* and
J. B. HARRISON, *Corresponding Secretary American Forestry Congress*

It has been said of our old frontier settlers that they seemed to bear a grudge against trees, and to be engaged in a constant indiscriminate warfare with them. If this were so a strong reaction has since set in, of which a notable manifestation appears in the fact that with regard to no other matter pertaining to the public grounds of our cities has public interest taken as earnest, strenuous and effective a form as in respect to the protection of their plantations against the axe.

It has occurred repeatedly of late years that ladies and gentlemen, seeking their pleasure during the winter in public parks, have chanced to see men felling trees, and have been moved by the sight to take duties upon themselves that nothing else short of a startling public outrage would have led them to assume. Sometimes they have hastened to stand before a partly felled tree and have attempted to wrest the axe from the hand of the woodsman. Oftener they have resorted to the press and other means of rousing public feeling, and not unfrequently a considerable popular excitement has resulted. At the time of such excitements a strong tendency has appeared in many minds to assume that the act of tree-cutting marks those who are responsible for it as unsusceptible to the charm of sylvan scenery, and to class them with the old indiscriminately devastating pioneers.

We say that such manifestations of public spirit in respect to the protection of plantations have been frequent. They have occurred, for example, within a few years in Brooklyn, Boston, Washington and San Francisco. They have in some cases affected

---

[1] ED. NOTE: Boston: T. R. Marvin & Son, Printers, 1889. For the circumstances giving rise to the preparation of this report, see p. 164, *ante.*

legislation. They have appeared in the halls of Congress, and statesmen have had part in them. Since the planting of Central Park there have been several in New York. The leaders in them have often been citizens deservedly high in public esteem, more than commonly well equipped with general information, liberally educated, of good social standing and wide influence.

Naturally an effect of such manifestations of public sentiment has been to make those in direct superintendence of public plantations, and the governing boards supervising them, extremely reluctant to use the axe. In some cases, for years not a tree has been cut down; in others only decaying trees which were prominent eye-sores or dangerous to passersby, and even when these were to be dealt with the work has been done in stormy weather, when it was little likely to be observed by visitors, and care has been taken to put the fallen wood out of sight as soon as possible. To guard against the provocation of public feeling even in such extreme cases, a standing order has been made by one Park Commission that not a tree should be cut in its plantations till leave had been granted for it by a majority vote of its Board. One of the best trained and most successful tree growers in the country having been dropped from the service of this Board, a member of it gave as the reason for his dismissal that he had been too anxious to obtain leave to cut out trees. In another case the effect of the agitation was such that a laborer refused to fell a tree when ordered, fearing that he would be punished for it as for a crime.

Early this Spring there was a movement in New York partaking of the character of those which had gone before. In the opinion of some having part in it, trees had been felled in Central Park to an extent, and with a degree of unfeeling indiscrimation and disregard of the landscape effects with a view to which they had been planted and grown, that called for the severest condemnation.

Some difference of opinion having been developed in the course of the proceedings to which this movement gave rise, it was thought desirable that an opinion should be obtained from experts other than those to whose judgment the Commissioners had been leaving the matter. To this end the undersigned were selected,—one the Secretary of the American Forestry Congress, the other one of the designers of the Park, and for forty years a tree grower. The request to them was made in behalf of the West End Improvement Association, the Torrey Botanical Club and the Park Commissioners. The duty which they assumed was to review the plantations of the Park, and report how far the tree-cutting upon them had been in accordance with the requirements of the park design and with approved professional practice.

While no sensible man will deliberately maintain that a tree can never be wisely removed from a public plantation, it will be seen from what has been said, that a public sentiment is liable to be cultivated, the effect of which, in numerous instances, may be to keep trees standing for years that might more wisely be cut, and in a general way to *prevent the free exercise of any specially competent judgment upon the question.*

Hence, instead of simply reporting our own view of the particular case that we have been asked to consider, we have thought it better that we should set forth by quotations what may be regarded as the Common Law view of the duty, in respect to the cutting of trees, of a professional public servant to whom has been given the direction of plantations. We venture to say that no man, however well informed he may be in other respects, can have a respectable understanding of this duty to whom such precepts as are about to be cited are not familiar. It is greatly to be desired that knowledge of them and faith in them should be more generally diffused than it is at present among leaders of public opinion in all our cities. In view of the circumstance that New York has a large scheme of new parks and park improvements before it, a publication of them may be hoped to be useful.[1]

1. It is in the act of removing trees and thinning woods that the landscape gardener must show his intimate knowledge of pleasing combinations, his genius for painting, and his acute perceptions of the principles of an art which transfers the imitative, though permanent beauties of a picture, to the purposes of elegant and comfortable habitation, the ever-varying effects of light and shade and the inimitable circumstances of a natural landscape.—*Repton.*

2. The old adage, "PLANT THICK AND THIN QUICK," holds as good now as centuries ago.—*Douglas.*

3. Fully half the number of plants inserted per acre should be removed by the time that the most valuable are twenty-five feet high.—*Grigor.*

[1] Among those to be quoted are the following: *Loudon,* J. C., author of Arboretum Britannicum, the Cyclopedia of Gardening, and many other standard technical works; *De Candolle,* Augustin, an eminent botanist, friend and co-worker with Cuvier and Humboldt; *Lauder,* Sir Thomas Dick, editor and commentator upon the works of Price and Gilpin; *Whately,* Thomas, a member of the British Parliament, and author of the first standard work on Modern Gardening; *Cobbet,* William, author of "Woodlands" and various famous works on Rural Economy; *Repton,* Humphrey, author of several works on Landscape Gardening and the most distinguished English landscape designer of the present century; *Smith,* C. H. J., author of a treatise on Parks and Pleasure Grounds; *Speechly, Grigor, Main* and *Brown,* authors of well-known treatises on Plantations; *Emerson,* G. B., author of a treatise on Trees, prepared at the request of the Legislature of Massachusetts; *Brisbane,* Gen. J. L., U. S. A.; *Hough, Scott* and *Bryant,* authors of works on Tree Planting and Landscape Gardening, published in the United States; *Fernow,* Editor of U. S. Government Reports of Forestry; *Sargent,* C. S., Professor of Forestry in Harvard University and Superintendent of the Forestry Division of the United States Census, 1880; *Hall,* J. H., State Engineer of California; *McLaren,* John, Superintendent of Golden Gate Park, San Francisco; *Beal,* Wm. J., Professor of Horticulture, Agricultural College of Michigan; *Fay,* J. S. and *Forbes,* J. M., notable citizens of Eastern Massachusetts who have been in direction of plantations, one above thirty, the other fifty, years; *Douglas,* Robert, the oldest and most successful large planter in North America, his plantings in the arid regions of the far West alone amounting to over three million trees.

4. For the best results, we must plant thickly, keep removing, some here some there, perhaps adding others.—*Beal.*

5. Thinning is one of the most indispensable operations.—*Brown.*

6. Of the implements required to produce a fine tree the axe is certainly the first and most important.—*Sargent.*

7. We now come to the most important consideration connected with forestral questions, that of thinning the trees.—*Hobbs.* (Report to American Forestry Congress, 1886.)

8. They go on vegetating but hardly growing. The remedy is obvious. *Every year* they need to be thinned.—*Emerson.*

9. Though they are still far short of their growth, they are [from neglect of thinning] run up into poles, and the groves are already past their prime. —*Whately.* (Criticism on Cleremont Park.)

10. A natural growth of pine which was thinned when six years old showed an increased rate of accretion three times as great as that of the part not thinned, which was also deficient in height growth.—*Fernow.*

11. Wherever systematic thinning has been applied the crops are of nearly double the value at a given age. We divide the several plantations into three portions, and thin one portion regularly and systematically each year successively.—*Brown.*

12. It is an undeniable fact that the weakly, unprofitable, and therefore unsatisfactory state of a large extent of plantations is to be attributed to the neglect of systematic thinning. We frequently see woods growing upon the best land, matured when only some sixty years old: This arises from neglect of systematic thinning.—*Brown.*

13. At all stages of a plantation, spaces should be gradually allowed, according to the growth of the trees, which, with some sorts, in favorable situations, extends till the plantation is eighty years of age.—*Grigor.*

14. The thinning may be continued gradually as the trees grow larger. —*Bryant.*

15. *Hough* gives a table showing the number of trees held, as the result of long experiments, by the German Government Department of Forestry, as desirable to be left in thrifty plantations after a growth of from thirty to one hundred years. The number to remain at fifty years is less than half that at thirty, at one hundred years less than half that at fifty.

16. To form fine ornamental groves or most valuable woods, the trees should be planted thickly, and when they have attained a sufficient length of bole, thinned gradually till each individual tree enjoys a sufficient share of light and air to bring it to its utmost magnitude and perfection.—*Main.*

17. *Loudon*, in Arboretum Britannicum, concludes from an examination of the cultivated larch plantations of the Duke of Athol, that in the most successful practice seven trees out of eight will have to be thinned out in the first twenty years, and quotes *De Candolle* as having reached a similar conclusion from observations in France.

18. *Lauder*, (in a note upon Gilpin's Forest Scenery), says that to make an artificial plantation which shall ultimately resemble a natural plantation, "the best way" is to so manage as that "by a frequent and judicious use of the axe, the best individuals, and those most calculated to associate and harmonize together, are left in permanent possession of the ground." "This

mode, be it understood," he adds, "requires constant attention—an attention unremitting from the earliest years of the plantation, till nothing remains but the permanent trees; otherwise, from too long confinement or other causes, stiff and unnatural forms may be produced."

19. Nurses are surplus trees or shrubs introduced into the plantation for a temporary purpose, for the occupancy of the ground to shelter and protect the permanent plants and to aid in forming them into well shaped trees. Unless care be taken to subordinate these nurses they will be likely to overwhelm the more valuable plants.—*Brisbane.*

20. Experience shows us that the oak would make but a slow progress for a number of years were it not for some kind nurses; the birch seems to answer that purpose the best. After the birches are cut down there is nothing more to be done but thinning the oaks, from time to time, as may be required.—*Speechly.*

21. *Cobbett* records in "Rural Rides" that he saw at New Park two plantations of oaks, one twelve years old, grown with nurses, the other adjoining, on land thought to be better, twenty years old without nurses. The second "was not nearly so good as the first."

22. White pine cannot endure our prairie winds if standing exposed, and the same holds good on our Eastern Coast; but intermixed with Scotch pine they have succeeded admirably; the Scotch pine making the most rapid growth during the first five years were overtopped in less than two years [afterwards] and cut out, leaving the White pines to occupy the ground. —*Douglas.*

23. When the nurses consist of inferior kinds, they should generally be all removed by the time that the plantation arrives at the height of fifteen or twenty feet.—*Loudon.*

24. From the time that all the nurses are removed, in each of the subsequent thinnings, those trees should first be cut down which appear to press on their stronger and more healthy neighbors, and to deprive them of the room and nourishment needful to their increasing growth.—*Smith.*

25. Addressing the Southampton Chamber of Commerce, Mr. *T. W. Shore*, urging the importance of a School of Forestry, observed that the management of the New Forest was "a national disgrace." "Look," he said, "at the many thousands of young trees choked by their nursing pines." "So many young trees killed before they are grown, and see the pines growing so large and thick as to be at the present time actually killing each other."

26. Consistently with this, Mr. *Gladstone*, speaking on the same topic in the House of Commons, referred to a popular "superstition," which caused the thinning of plantations to be too much neglected, as the most serious difficulty to be overcome in an improvement of British tree-growing.

27. Now we have trees whose natural habits would produce heads of foliage twenty-five to thirty feet across, at ten to fourteen years of age (and which were planted four to eight feet apart, with the view of gradually cutting out full two-thirds of the number within the years down to this time), still standing in the groups as planted—spindling, bare-stalked saplings within the groups and one-sided shams around the margin thereof; in many cases not a single well-developed specimen in the whole group. In this respect the main large clumps of the older trees are rotten shams, which in

a few years, because the individual trees are spindling, weak and light-rooted, and with foliage and branches high up the trunk only, will commence to blow down wholesale. These trees were never intended to stand permanently in such places. There are thousands which are serving no other purpose than to ruin others.—*Hall.*

28. I have charge of several hundred acres in forest and ornamental tree growths. My practice has been to plant thick, and thin as soon as the trees showed the slightest indication of interfering with one another. The result has been most satisfactory. Where this work [of thinning] has been neglected, the result has been disastrous.—*McLaren.*

29. I find the older plantations in very bad condition, which is the result of the neglect of thinning. They are planted thick for various reasons, but have been allowed to stand as planted until the lower branches have died off, and the trees spindled up to their stems. I have seen whole acres of conifers die off in a single year from these causes [neglect of thinning].—*McLaren.*

30. Mr. *Forbes* planted extensively fifty years ago, and, on account of the extreme bleakness of the site, under the advice of Mr. Downing, as he writes, "*very thickly;*" but he adds "the axe has been used vigorously *every year*, and a look at the plantations at this time will convince everybody that this was absolutely essential." Of certain other plantations he says: "They were nearly ruined for the want of courage with the axe." "The trees are fast becoming broomsticks with branches on top."

Most trees are gregarious in extreme youth, from habit transmitted through many generations; they love company, and only thrive really when closely surrounded. Close planting is essential, therefore, to insure the best results. As the trees grow, the weaker are pushed aside, and finally destroyed by the more vigorous, and the plantation is gradually thinned. This is the operation which is always going on in the forest when man does not intervene. It is a slow and expensive operation, however, and the result is attained by a vast expenditure of energy and of good material. The strongest trees come out victorious in the end, but they will bear the scars of the contest through life. The long, bare trunk, with a small and misshapen head—the only form of a mature tree found in the virgin forest—tells of years or of centuries of struggle, in which hundreds of weaker individuals may have perished, that one giant might survive. But man can intervene, and by judicious and systematic thinning help the strong to destroy the weak more quickly, and with a less expenditure of vital force. Thick planting is but following the rule of nature, and thinning is only helping nature do what she does herself too slowly, and therefore too expensively. This is why trees in a plantation intended for ornament, like those in a park or pleasure-ground, should be planted thickly at first, and why they should then be systematically thinned from time to time; and it is because this systematic thinning is altogether neglected, or put off until the trees are ruined for any purpose of ornament, that it is so rare to find a really fine tree in any public place or private grounds.—*Sargent.*

It will be observed that all agree that in good practice trees are planted originally much closer than it is desirable that they should be allowed to grow permanently, and that, from every well-planted large body of trees, some are removed every year [or at most every few years] up to at least eighty years. This for centuries has been the established custom in Great Britain and on the continent of Europe, and it is approved by every American to whom the subject has been one of anything like professional study, whether with reference to the object of sylvan charm of scenery or simply that of growing the largest amount of wood in the shortest time.

Upon this point, we have not, with considerable search, found one man with any claim to be regarded as an authority, differing from those we have quoted. Many writers on Landscape Gardening say nothing about it; but this evidently because they assume that their readers will be of a class not needing to be advised of a principle so well established.

Undoubtedly authorities differ a little in their views as to the extent to which, in the management of plantations for landscape-effect, the thinning process should be pursued. But such differences mainly represent varying degrees of susceptibility to the charm of one or another variety of sylvan scenery, and a consequent disposition to give more prominence in writing to one or another. We may observe that if there can be considered to be two schools in this respect, we should ourselves be classed with that which favors the less uniform use of the axe, and which believes in sometimes sacrificing more of the chances for long and perfect development of trees to the result of a more playful disposition and greater variation of companionship of them. We should, more than some, guard in thinning against making any tree individually conspicuous. We would not have the least confusion between the purpose of a Park and the purpose of an Arboretum.

But no difference in this respect among those who have carefully studied the results of varying practice during many years, subtracts, in the slightest degree, from the unanimity with which they condemn all such management of plantations as it is the tendency of public sentiment to compel public servants to adopt. Instead of saying that if men are seen to be cutting trees out of a plantation there is a presumption of ignorant or unfeeling management, which, practically, is the prevailing disposition with those expressing the most affectionate interest in our parks, they are agreed in teaching that whenever a year passes in which trees are not cut out of any extensive plantation, there is ground for presumption—a very strong presumption—that the management is ignorant or neglectful of its most important duty.

The fact is, nevertheless, that until men, whether non-professional commissioners of public plantations or non-professional planters on their own private account, have learned better by costly lessons of personal experience, they are generally much indisposed to plant as thickly as is necessary, and still more indisposed to allow plantations to be thinned as is desirable. Often, therefore, plantations become and remain crowded to a degree which brings many of their trees to death, or to a decrepit and slowly dying condition, and which draws all others into such forms that, even if by a late use of the axe they are at last given ample branch and root room, they are precluded from taking advantage of it. They come to be of senile habit, and it is no longer possible for them to contribute to broad, rich and harmonious compositions of foliage.

The question then will often arise:—What can best be done in places where trees have been more or less seriously injured by crowding;—in what degree is their restoration to be wisely aimed at;—to what extent will it be more judicious to clear the ground and replant? A landscape architect who has had probably as large a private practice as any other in the country, says that no other question oftener comes to him, and no other is a greater tax upon his professional resources. It is easy in any given case, for a shallow, conceited quack to settle it flippantly; it is easy to settle it indolently; it requires experience, close study and sagacious foresight to determine the best practicable settlement of it. Upon this point we present a few additional quotations:—

1. Speaking of a case where due, gradual thinning had been neglected, *Grigor*, in his Treatise on Forestry (Edinburg, 1868), says: "Although a thinning is now going on, it is doubtful if the trees left will make much more progress." "The only question is whether it would not be better to clear the trees off at once by rooting them out. Had the ground been in a conspicuous position I should have had no hesitation in recommending that course, for, however common, few scenes more unsightly are to be met with than the display of unshapely trees struggling for existence, and diseased through mismanagement."

2. *Loudon* quotes a passage from *Lang*, urging the importance of timely thinning, observing that if neglected "*the plantation will inevitably be ruined.*"

3. If thinning is delayed too long, the stems will be slender and feeble. Dead and dying trees should be taken out whenever found.—*Hough*.

4. Considerable loss is frequently sustained by producing through long confinement tall trunks without a proportionate diameter; and unless the soil is very congenial and the trees of great vigor, they are often slow to become stout or shapely when ample space has at last been afforded to them. —*Grigor*.

5. The first thing to be decided is the amount of *clean cutting* to be done,—what had better be entirely removed in order that something better may be developed.—*Scott; Advice as to the Renovation of Old Places.*

6. It is very difficult to determine how to treat plantations that have been neglected in thinning. It is a bad job, and you can only hope to prevent further ruin, but not to entirely remedy that which is now so painfully apparent to anyone who knows about trees and their cultivation. *The trees in some parts are so far gone that they cannot be saved to good purpose. Better cut out spaces* within such groups and around the margins, fertilize the

soil, trench it over, plant new trees, and as they grow *cut away the balance of the old ones.—McLaren.*

7. If I were again to set out young trees among the old woods, *I should cut the latter all down clean.—J. S. Fay.* (Experiments in Tree Planting, U. S. Forestry Report, 1877.)

8. When any plantation has stood long without being thinned, particularly such as are composed of coniferous trees, it is, we may say, impossible to recover it.—*Brown's Forester.*

9. This plantation in place of being thinned gradually . . . had been subjected to a severe thinning all at once. When a pine plantation has been mismanaged in this way, the proprietor should never hesitate but have it cut down at once and the ground replanted.—*J. B. Webster,* in London Garden, April 13, 1889.

We are now prepared to take up the case of the last winter's management of Central Park. What the designers of this Park had in view as to the treatment of its plantations may be inferred from the following passage in a report of theirs. Writing in advance of certain advised plantations, they said:—

They are to be thinned out gradually as they come to interlock, until, at length, not more than one-third of the original number will remain; and these, because the less promising will have constantly been selected for removal with little regard to evenness of spacing, will be those of the most vigorous constitution, those with the greatest capabilities of growth, and those with the greatest power of resistance to attacks of storms, ice, disease and vermin. Individual tree beauty is to be but little regarded, but all consideration to be given to beauty and effectiveness of groups, passages, and masses of foliage. The native underwood is to be planted in thickets and allowed to grow in natural forms, enough of it being introduced to prevent (in connection with the grouping of trees and interspaces of groups, to be formed by the process of thinning the tree plantations), a grove or orchard-like monotony of trunks. [1]

But in much of the planting of the Park not only were several trees planted of each kind designed to remain permanently, with the object first, of protection, second, of selecting that to remain which should prove most promising of long life and vigor under the circumstances, but nurses were also planted among them. At the time of the earlier planting, the commercial nurseries of the country were overstocked with imported Norway Spruce, and plants of it could be bought by the thousand, of unusual size, at low rates. They were therefore much used as nurses, especially in the bleaker parts on the west side and where the planting was designed to be largely of white pines and hemlocks, which when young grow very slowly and often die if not well nursed.

When the time came for gradually removing these nurses and

[1] General plan for the improvement of the Niagara Reservation, by Frederick Law Olmsted and Calvert Vaux.

thinning out the less promising of other trees, the necessary work was restricted within exceedingly inadequate limits, and, as has been stated, at times, was for years wholly suspended. Consequently but a small part of the thinning needed was ever done. Numbers of the spruces intended to serve only as nurses from three to six years, remained on the ground after twenty years; some remain yet, after thirty years, and the pines and hemlocks that they were designed to foster have long since disappeared;—either smothered to death or cut out because dwarfed, sickened and mutilated by the oppression of the spruces.

Of the spruces thus brought into undesigned prominence, the late Governor Horatio Seymour stated, from experience on his own farm at Utica:—

They grow rapidly when young, but become ragged and thin when they have got to be of any size. Their effect in groups is bad, as their sharp, tapering tops give them a weak, ineffective aspect.

Probably there are localities in which this condemnation would be found too sweeping, but the Central Park is not one of them. Whenever a Norway spruce has proved worthy to remain, it would appear to be because of an exceptional vigor of constitution, and individual adaptation to the local circumstances. A large majority of all planted in the Park fell into a dwindling condition before they had come to be twenty years old. Four years ago it was observed that much the larger part of those originally planted had disappeared, but many quite dead ones remained; many more were barely alive, and these were disagreeable objects, disgraceful in themselves to the management, but much more disgraceful in the ruin they had made of what would otherwise have been beautiful plantations, contributive to charming passages of sylvan scenery. Fourteen years ago the professional adviser of the Park Department at the time made a report to the Commissioners, going over much of the ground of the present paper, including in part the citations from eminent tree-growers that have been given above, in support of his statements. He pointed out [1] that the neglect of thinning had already gone far to destroy some of the most important plantations, and that if it continued it was but a question of time when the best thing that could be done, would be to clear considerable areas of ground and replant them.

This report was not published, but as a result of it a special force for thinning was allowed to be employed, and during an inclement season, when few visitors passed through the Park, within less than a month's time, more trees were felled than there had been altogether, probably, in ten years before. The advantage gained where the thinning was most resolute is now conspicuous.

[1] ED. NOTE: Cf. Minutes, D. P. P., 1874-75, page 549, recommending Messrs. Fischer and Bullard for thinning plantations on the Park.

It may be seen, for example, on the rising ground, between the two lobes of the North Meadow, the most park-like part of the Park; again on the north side of the eastern half of the road crossing the Park at Mount St. Vincent; on the borders of the drive mounting Bogardus Hill from the south; near the drive opposite Summit Rock; on Cherry Hill and at a few other points. A few complete clearances and replantings were made at this time. A group of hemlocks northwest of the Great Reservoir, for example, occupies ground in which a previous plantation had been ruined by the overgrowth of Norway spruce, the latter having been also ruined a little later, by their crowding of one another. It can be seen that these hemlocks have not been growing thriftily. This is because, in dread of a repetition of the first experience, they were planted too openly.

Within a month the public indignation was excited and the Commissioners ordered the work to be stopped.[1]

Not one man with the slightest pretentions to be regarded as an expert in Sylviculture has ever been employed in the service of the Park Department, without making efforts to obtain leave to thin the plantations, or without giving warning that a time was approaching when, if more thorough thinning than the Commissioners were willing to allow, should not soon be made, some of the most important bodies of trees would be ruined, and nothing would remain but to exterminate them and replant the ground.

When we were last passing through the Park before our recent visit, we had observed numbers of dead trees; larger numbers in a dying, and whole groups in a feeble, gaunt and dwindling condition, due to neglect of thinning. It had seemed to us probable that the time was passed when any process of thinning could be successfully used with them. Reading the reports sent this spring, with the request that we would review the plantations, we had been led to suppose that extensive clearings had accordingly been made, and that the principal question that we should have to consider would be whether such clearings had been carried too far, and had been of the insensate character alleged.

On the 20th of March we made an examination of the plantations of the Park, passing nearly from end to end of it four times, walking through all the localities to which our attention had been particularly invited, and bringing under close review all parts of the Ramble and other interior and secluded districts.

It was nowhere apparent to us that trees had been lately removed inconsiderately or without regard for the motives of the original plan. At a number of points what might be regarded as

---

[1] There is probably no direct connection between the circumstances, but it is worthy of note that immediately following the public protest against the thinning of the Park plantations, of last winter, a bill is introduced to legislate the Commissioners responsible for it out of office. There may be no direct connection, but if public sentiment had been alive to the real character of that work, would those who instigate legislation have been as ready for the move?

small clearings were found. We saw no reason for doubting that the trees removed in these cases had been ruined for the purpose that had been had in view in the planting of them, by neglect of thinning, and that it had been intended to replant the ground; and at one point we actually found men, so early in the season, beginning the work of replanting.

We saw not a few trees, which in our judgment must die before many years, standing in positions where, if allowed to remain, they will greatly retard the growth of others which if uncrowded would yet become long-lived and umbrageous. It is fair to assume that not a few failing trees thus doing mischief show an incomplete work of improvement.

It was estimated in a report sent us that the quantity of wood cut on the park during the last winter would measure little short of 250 cords. The plantations of the Park are mainly in the form of narrow belts and groups of irregular outline, alternating with spaces of rock, turf, water and roadways; these vacancies being larger on the whole than the planted spaces, so that a large proportion of the trees are open on two sides to light and air. The planted ground was well-drained; the soil taken from the uncovered rocks and the road and water spaces was added to its original soil; many parts had been occupied two years before the planting by small market gardens; the whole was liberally treated with a compost of dung and limed peat, and with phosphates, and finely tilled to a depth of twenty inches. It has since been frequently top-dressed. The trees have been generally growing with extraordinary rapidity. The extent of the planted ground is estimated at 400 acres. The principal tree-planting of the Park was made in 1858, '59 and '60. Having been before thinned much too scantily, would it be thought, by experienced tree-growers, that the taking out of two or three hundred cords of wood from such plantations, at the end of thirty years, was, as has been supposed, an excessive amount?
We cannot think that it would.
Considering how large a proportion of all the felled trees were probably of dead, dying or greatly enfeebled condition, we doubt if they would have borne this year two per cent. of the entire leafage of the Park. We are of the opinion that before midsummer the expanse of leafage that will be gained by new growth will be more than equivalent to all that has been cut off in the winter's thinning. (Let anyone passing through the Park six weeks hence ask if the foliage seems less in amount than it did at the same period last year.)
It is, however, more important to consider the lasting effect. As to this we do not think that a man can be found, of extended experience in plantations of a character corresponding with those of the Park, who, knowing the facts we have recounted, will have

the least doubt that the body of foliage on the Park must within two years be considerably larger than it would have been, had the two or three hundred cords of trunks and limbs taken out last winter been left standing.

We have taken for granted that it has been intended to replant various small areas which, because of the destruction by crowding of the originally designed low foliage, were at the time of our visit of dreary aspect. It hardly lies within the duty assigned us, but we may be permitted to add that there are many parts of the Park where ground not now shaded by trees might much more suitably be occupied otherwise than it is. About a hundred paces east of the Springbanks Arch (*see No. 29 on Folded Map*), on the south side of the road, there is a piece of ground of thin soil partly broken by rock, which is charmingly overgrown with low bushes and creepers. It has had much of its present pleasing character for at least twenty-five years, and in that time the annual cost of keeping it has not probably been a fiftieth part as much as the average annual cost of keeping an equal area of the open turf and high shrubbery-studded spaces of the Park. In our judgment a somewhat similar covering would be desirably substituted for turf in many of its smaller openings, which it is never well should be crossed by visitors; in nearly all those, for example, of the Winter Drive and the hill north of it, which are now at large expense kept by lawn-mower and hand-rake, smooth, smug and tame, incongruously with the general character of the designed local scenery. Some slight indications of a desire for improvement in this direction were apparent to us. Should they be liberally followed up, the result, in connection with that of a more courageous management of the old plantations, would, at comparatively small expense, accomplish more for the beautifying of the Park than all that has been done for the purpose in many years. It may be well to say at this point that we have had no recent communication with anyone in the service of the Park, and none for years on the subject of this report. In speaking of the intentions of the management we mean only what is naturally to be surmised in that respect.

At first view it will seem remarkable that complaints so specific and so sweeping as those we have considered should be made by persons of a high degree of general intelligence without any support in the actual facts of the case. It will perhaps be thought hardly credible that the common impression and sentiment of the great body of good citizens as to what is desirable in the management of plantations should be in such direct conflict with what we have shown to be the general conviction of all lovers of natural scenery to whom the question has been one of professional study.

The explanation of the mystery is to be found, we suppose, in the fact that the management of a large park is an art the principles and methods of which are much further from being generally comprehended, even by cultivated men, than is commonly supposed. On this point we offer one more quotation bearing directly upon the particular point of management as to which expert opinion has been asked:

> To give such general rules for thinning as might be understood by those who never attentively and scientifically considered the subject would be like attempting to direct a man who had never used a pencil to imitate the groups of a Claude or a Poussin.—*Repton.*

And yet it is most undesirable that public-spirited citizens should be led to relinquish any degree of interest that they may now feel in the management of the public grounds of our cities. It is most desirable that they should manifest still greater and more searching interest; that they should influence the management more directly, constantly and effectively. But to do so wisely will require a seriousness of thought upon the subject such as it yet seldom obtains. It will also require a degree of respect for the technical responsibility involved that few have yet begun to realize to be its due.

CHAPTER V

ROADS, WALKS, AND RIDES

In the original "Greensward" report[1] submitted with the winning plan, the designers made clear the distinction between the system of ways intended to lead the visitor pleasantly around the Park for the enjoyment of its beauties, and the "Transverse Roads" intended to carry business traffic directly and inconspicuously from one side of the Park to the other. The conception of the transverse roads is not set forth in any separate document, but is best explained in the original report and in the passages quoted in our Appendix relating to the Viele Case (see page 560). Of the documents given here, the first is of special interest as emphasizing the importance of grade separations between the park ways used for different purposes,—which is, indeed, a logical extension of the principle involved in the transverse roads,—the non-interruption of all kinds of pleasure traffic, as well as the non-interruption of landscape effect.[2]

The document of April, 1872 is important in connection with various proposals more recent than those occasioning the report, in that it analyzes the demand for a broad direct trunk-line walk from south to north, through the Park, and shows the kind of landscape value sought for by the designers in the adopted devious system. The last document, somewhat complementary to the one just mentioned, contains passages again defending the Park scenery from a long straight slash. At the same time, this report sets forth the essential requirements for a formal promenade in a park,—which may often be more readily met along its borders, as Mr. Olmsted here proposes.

Another question which frequently arose and which became acute in the eighties was the widening of the Park drives, adequate in 1863

---

[1] See Part II, Chapter I, pp. 218 and 258.
[2] "The sunken roads in the Central Park, . . . were laid out with the utmost care to avoid any perceptible break of the surface of the ground where it would be visible to visitors. Where they cross a line of view, it is usually at a distance of more than a quarter of a mile from the observer."—Brooklyn Park Report, 9th, for 1868.

but in 1883 characterized as "demonstrably unable to accommodate visitors." Mr. Olmsted's last official word on this subject was given in March, 1890, at a meeting of the Board, where he reported verbally "in relation to the proposed widening of the Central Park drives, . . . that in his opinion such widenings would not result in such improvement as would warrant the expenditure, which would necessarily be a large one, and that it could not be done without sacrificing certain topographical features of the park."

In visiting Central Park with a view to comprehending the designers' ideals, the reader may be helped by Mr. Olmsted's answer to an inquiry as to driving routes for seeing the park to best advantage: "The Central Park was laid out with a view to giving the greatest satisfaction when seen in driving northward on the west side, southward on the east side. In driving to the north on the east side, south of Mt. St. Vincent, few of the better landscape features are to be seen at all and the best scenery only by glimpses over the left shoulder. "The drive along the west side is apart from this consideration much the more interesting. After the leaves begin to fall, its advantage is conspicuous."

THE PAPERS INCLUDED IN THIS CHAPTER ARE:

Letter regarding the System of Walks and Rides to be laid out in the Park, from F. L. O. September 9, 1858. (Doc. No. 11).—Selections describing plan to encompass grade separations between walks, rides, and drives.

Report on Communication between the Terrace and the Reservoirs, and on the deficiency of shade on the drives and walks of the Central Park, by F. L. O. April 16, 1872. (Doc. No. 36.)

Report on the Proposed New System of Walks in the South-East Quarter of the Central Park, by F. L. O. December 11, 1872. 3d Annual Report, D. P. P. Appendix J.

Report on the subject of a Promenade, consisting of a drive, ride, and walks, arranged side by side, in the Central Park, by F. L. O. December 3, 1875. (Doc. No. 67.)

THE SYSTEM OF WALKS AND RIDES[1]

GRADE SEPARATIONS

SEPTEMBER 9, 1858.

To the Board of Commissioners
of the Central Park:

Gentlemen,—To obtain walks which shall be for long distances exclusively and uninterruptedly devoted to pedestrians, and a ride preserved in a similar manner for equestrians, (except around the Reservoir,) it must be necessary to lay out all the principal drives, rides and walks of the Park in lines having a continuous northerly and southerly course, nearly parallel with each other and with the avenues of the city, or, these different lines of passage must at certain points of intersection more or less frequent, cross over or under one another by means of bridges. I have already been obliged to express my opinion to the Board, that the former method could not be reconciled with the structural principles of the plan first adopted as a basis of operations, and that it is as desirable that all the lines of travel for one purpose should be occasionally connected so as to form circuits and trans-communications within the Park, as that each should be uninterfered with by any lines appropriated to a different purpose. In preparing the details of the plan, therefore, the latter plan has been pursued.

. . . Over four miles of moderately level walk, exclusive of that upon the Reservoir wall, may . . . be formed in the lower park alone, in which the walker can have no apprehension of being met or crossed by a vehicle or horseman.

. . . The length of the ride . . . proposed in the Lower Park, would be nearly two miles, and the rider, though passing at intervals near to and concurrently with portions of the drive, as desired by the Board, will find his way nowhere crossed by any road or walk. The arched passages proposed for both the walks and ride will be at an average distance of about three-quarters of a mile apart, and in every case but two, they occupy positions in which artificial embankments with culverts beneath them will be otherwise required, so that the expense of constructing them will be chiefly that of the mason-work.

Respectfully,
FRED. LAW OLMSTED.

[1] Selections from Doc. No. 11.

378

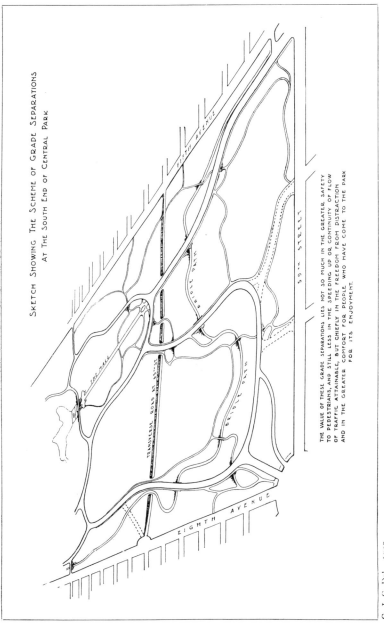

SKETCH SHOWING THE SCHEME OF GRADE SEPARATIONS
AT THE SOUTH END OF CENTRAL PARK

THE VALUE OF THESE GRADE SEPARATIONS LIES NOT SO MUCH IN THE GREATER SAFETY
TO PEDESTRIANS, AND STILL LESS IN THE SPEEDING UP OR CONTINUITY OF FLOW
OF TRAFFIC ATTAINABLE, BUT CHIEFLY IN THE FREEDOM FROM DISTRACTION
AND IN THE GREATER COMFORT FOR PEOPLE WHO HAVE COME TO THE PARK
FOR ITS ENJOYMENT.

G. J. C. Del. 1927

COMMUNICATION BETWEEN THE TERRACE AND THE RESERVOIRS[1]

THE DEFICIENCY OF SHADE ON THE DRIVES AND WALKS OF THE CENTRAL PARK

To the Hon. H. G. Stebbins,
President of the Department of Public Parks.

Sir:—Two resolutions of inquiry have been addressed to us from the Department: one in respect to the feasibility of more direct and ample means of communication between the Terrace (*see No. 13 on Folded Map*) and the Belvedere (*see No. 12 on Folded Map*) of the Central Park; the other in respect to the general deficiency of shade in the Park and the means of its improvement in that regard.

We present a skeleton map showing two courses of walk, one or the other of which would probably be followed by anyone anxious to get to the Belvedere as soon as possible after leaving the Terrace.

The grade of the walk which leads eastwardly from the Esplanade below the Terrace, after passing the foot of the Lake, although it is carried in a winding course up the hill, is perhaps inconveniently steep. It has been badly washed at this point, and having, in some changes made since its original construction, been laid with a high crown and the concrete at its sides having given way, its designed width is now practically much contracted. It needs to be completely relaid with a better concrete.

When its reconstruction is undertaken, we would suggest the introduction of steps, and recommend the adoption of a nearly flat cross-section, with improvements of the side drainage. By these means, without changing its course or making it any more obtrusive or subversive of the natural features, or breaking in upon the general walk-system of the Ramble, a considerably larger number of people could pass over this walk in a given time with ease and convenience, than at present.

We can recommend no other alteration in the plan of either of these routes of walks, by which the purpose in view would be served.

Various propositions have at different times been urged, manifesting convictions which may be presumed to be less fully represented by the resolution, with the direct requirement of which we have thus complied. Holding these convictions in sincere respect, we shall take the present occasion to briefly indicate the relation in which the propositions in question appear to us to stand to the design already in great part carried out.

It is urged that a broad, direct walk, forming in effect a trunk line, through the midst of the Park, from south to north, is a public

[1] Doc. No. 36, 1872.

requirement of paramount importance. It is also claimed that the Reservoirs, being geographically central, and the grandest objects in the Park, the walk or walks leading to and from them should be distinguished by unusual breadth, directness of course, and otherwise.

As the required south and north central walk would lead directly to the Reservoirs and then necessarily divide, passing around them on their walls, the two propositions may be considered as essentially one.

That feature of the Park, as it exists, which is known as the Mall, is considered a satisfactory provision, as far as it goes, for the required central trunk line of walk, while the Belvedere is regarded as emphasizing the entrance from the south upon the Reservoirs by an architectural porch, which, if somewhat awkwardly designed for this purpose, is a distinct recognition of the eminent importance of the position to which attention is thus enforced. But between the Belvedere and the Mall, and between the Mall and the south end of the Park, the existing arrangements are found very imperfect, and it is urged that these defective links in the plan should be improved by measures adapted to establish, as far as possible, a plain and straightforward thoroughfare in place of, or in addition to, the present devious and divided walks.

There is room, undoubtedly, for an intelligent difference of judgment upon the question whether the advantages which might have been secured by accepting the Reservoirs as features of great value in the design of the Park, and by establishing a grand avenue from north to south, through the midst of the Park, were such as to outweigh the disadvantages which would have been thereby entailed. We do not propose to argue this question, but shall consider it our present duty simply to aid the Board in judging how far there is a reasonable probability that the advantages which may originally have been promised by such an arrangement, can now be obtained in any valuable degree, without an unjustifiable sacrifice of other classes of advantages which, wisely or unwisely, have thus far been preferably had in view, and the nature of which we shall, for this purpose, hope to sufficiently indicate.

The territory appropriated to the Park was a parallelogram two miles and half in length, and but half a mile in width. The Reservoirs stood in the midst of it, extending, at their broadest point, nine-tenths of the distance across it, with walls so high, that the two parts of the Park thus essentially separated were necessarily to be considered as wholly distinct fields of landscape. Although works of much interest, the grounds upon which the interest of the Reservoirs was to depend were essentially different from those upon which the interest of the Park was expected to chiefly lie. If, therefore, in passing through the Park, especially on foot, and slowly, the visitor was to be led along the walls of the Reservoirs, he would have three distinctly separated experiences:—

First, the lower rural experience; then the unrural, but very striking experience of the passage of the Reservoirs; then a second rural experience in the upper Park.

The prospective value of the Park, as a distinct property of the city, was assumed to lie chiefly in the extent of continuous rural experience which it would be possible to obtain in it. Consequently, this division of the site by the Reservoirs was not considered a fortunate circumstance. It would have been better, in the judgment of the designers, if the Reservoirs had been situated *on one side* of the Park, rather than in such a way as to so nearly divide it.

But the Park territory really encloses the Reservoirs; and although the strips of ground to the east and west of them are very narrow, it was thought not to be out of the question, on the west at least, to form such a passage between the north and south rural divisions that, seen in succession, they would produce the impression rather of a single work in two parts than of two separate undertakings. It was thought to be possible, that is to say, that in the mental experience of a visitor passing from the south to the north park, the Reservoirs might be practically *put on one side*, and the design of the Park is intended to make the most of this possibility.

It was anticipated, however, that the majority of foot visitors coming to the Park from a distance, would not be inclined or able, after reaching it, to walk more than three or four miles through it in any single visit. A walk by the most direct course that could be established from the south end of the Park to the middle of the north division, returning upon the same track, would be over five miles in length. Consequently, it was to be anticipated that, to most visitors, an experience of the Park on any one occasion would be limited by the Reservoirs.

The special recreation of a park (in distinction from a mere garden, avenue or promenade), being mainly obtained through an exercise of the mind following upon suggestions presented through the eye, it was deemed desirable that every advantage should be taken of the natural features of the lower Park to establish spacious landscape effects, and also to lay out walks which, within a limited compass, would present a strongly contrasting series of rural experiences.

The ground south of the Reservoirs is thus designed with a two-fold purpose:—First, as a part of a large park of which the other part is to be found, not by pushing from the locality of the Terrace directly across the water, up the opposite hill and along the high walls of the Reservoir which crowns it, but by a devious rural route; and second, as a Park complete and offering varied and extended, but harmoniously related rural experiences within itself.

The form, size and position of the Belvedere and the Terrace, the treatment of the Esplanade below the Terrace, and of the Ramble and all the ground below the Belvedere, the outline of the Lake and the position of the Bow-bridge (*see No. 30 on Folded Map*), all are designed mainly to serve the latter purpose by making the most of the distance and by emphasizing and aggrandizing the natural difference of landscape character between the locality of the level central district and the northern hilly, rocky and picturesque district of the lower Park.

The Mall was described in the report accompanying the plan when it was first presented to the Commission as being a feature of the proposed park corresponding in special distinction to the mansion in private grounds. That is to say, instead of being introduced as a channel or stage in a channel, to something beyond, it was designed to be a central feature, complete in itself, and to which, as to a dwelling or abiding place, the general walk system of the Park should be tributary. Of course, technically speaking, it had no objective points; and while walks were made to diverge from it in various other directions, rectangularly and diagonally to its axis, none were formed directly outward from its ends. On the contrary, the theory of proceeding through it, and right on from it toward the Belvedere was distinctly precluded by ending it on a body of water, and extending a bay of this water as far as possible in the direction of the Belvedere.

In elaborating the preliminary study, this general conception of the relation of the Mall to the walk system of the Park as a whole, so far from being abandoned, has, with the approval of the Board, been even more decidedly emphasized.

Again; the Belvedere is not the special objective point of the walks leading out right and left from the esplanade of the Terrace; on the contrary, it is designed that the visitor, in pursuing these, shall be made equally welcome, whether he shall be disposed, first to go to the upper Park, keeping away from the Ramble; second, to saunter through the Ramble; or third, to make a circuit of the Ramble, so as to return by a different route from that which he followed in coming up. In the latter case only is the Belvedere designed to be brought invitingly before him.

It will thus be seen that every practical expedient in architecture and in gardening has been used to effect a series of purposes which are really antithetical to that which we assume to have been had in view in the resolution of your Board.

––––––––––

With regard to the deficiency of shade on the Park, it is to be observed that in laying out a park, the question of the most desirable disposition of the trees is one which precedes rather than follows that of the arrangement of the communications, and that the communications should be accommodated to the plantations quite as much as the reverse.

It should also be considered that the site of the Park was at the outset almost completely destitute of shade, and was a piece of ground in which the difficulties of establishing shade with trees were unusual. The parts of the Park immediately adjoining the boundaries, the space east of the old Reservoir, and some stretches of the borders of the Bridle Road have not yet been fully planted. Elsewhere through the Park the trees now seen have been growing in their present positions, on an average, but ten years; they were, when set, generally young nursery stock, transplanted from a distance to a soil largely made by mixing crude materials for the purpose upon a foundation of rock. Under these circumstances it was to be expected, and was expected; that they would for a few years grow but slowly. They are now generally in thrifty condition, and, except where timely thinning has been neglected and an upright habit encouraged, their lateral branches are ready to push rapidly. Their growth in the first five years did not add as much shade to the Park as it will now probably in one, nor would an additional planting of a thousand saplings give as much more shade as the Park will gain through the growth of those already planted, in a single month, if the season should be favorable, this summer.

We cannot regard it as desirable that there should be continuous shade upon all the roads and walks, or believe that to obtain shade at every point, the scenery of the Park may with advantage be divided, as it would have been had the plans of the late administration been carried out, into a series of contracted apartments. Assuming that passages of sunlight are admissible, the question is whether, under the present design, they will be too frequent or too broad. By the time the trees now planted and designed to stand shall have reached a fair middle-age development, a man in going all through the Park will have to pass a hundred yards on completely unshaded walks, scarcely more than once in any mile, not as often as three times in two miles. More than nine-tenths of the whole length of the Drive, Bridle Road and Walks will be overhung in whole or in part, before many years, by the foliage of the trees now planted.

We do not think that more trees should be planted for the sake of immediate shade, but that if more means of shade are temporarily required, they should be supplied by vines on trellises, or by awnings.

Respectfully,

OLMSTED & VAUX.

New York, April 16th, 1872.

PROPOSED NEW SYSTEM OF WALKS IN THE SOUTH-
EAST QUARTER[1]

DEPARTMENT OF PUBLIC PARKS,
OFFICE OF DESIGN AND SUPERINTENDENCE,

NEW YORK, 11th December, 1872.

TO THE HON. HENRY G. STEBBINS,
President of the Board.

Sir: On June 19th, the undersigned was requested to report
as to the obliteration of a walk leading from the Drive to the
Museum,[2] and to suggest a plan in relation to approaches to the
Museum from the main Drive.

A great number of visitors entering the Park on Fifty-ninth
street, from the Sixth, Seventh and Eighth avenues and, on the
west side of the Drive, from Fifth avenue wish to visit the Museum
and Menagerie, and a majority of all who do so, both in going
and returning, strive to make their way across the Drive at some
point between the Scholar's Gate and the Mall. The Drive is here
more thronged, horses are more difficult to control, and it is more
annoying to drivers to be compelled to pull up to avoid footmen
than anywhere else on the Park. Most of these visitors also
attempt to cross the Bridle Road, and not a few to follow the Bridle
Road, using it as a walk, between the Ball Ground and the Museum,
putting themselves in danger and greatly annoying riders. Visitors
to the Croquet Grounds and swings on the east side often take the
same courses. The opening of the Lennox Library, the Conservatory and the Art Museum will add to the number; and the need,
recognized in the resolution, for some better means of communication from east to west, through the district in question, will not
cease with the removal of the Museum and Menagerie.

With the present arrangements, not only is the crossing of the
Drive and Ride on the line of walk which it is proposed to obliterate,
highly objectionable, but the attempts to cross at other and forbidden points are so frequent, that if half the keepers at any time
on the Park were employed to prevent it they could not be entirely
successful. As things are, visitors may be seen on any fine day constantly disregarding the rules in this respect, which, both in the
minds of visitors and of the officers and keepers of the Park, are
thus brought into contempt. The disorder and injury which directly and indirectly results is much to be regretted, and the question
of a remedy has had prolonged attention.

[1] From 3rd Annual Report, D. P. P., 1873, Appendix J.
[2] ED. NOTE: This was the old Arsenal, then used as a Museum (*see No. 6 on
Folded Map*).

The only way in which the present difficulties of communication in this quarter can be adequately overcome is by the introduction of another arched passage across the Drive and Ride. In fact, by no other plan can any essential improvement be secured upon the present objectionable arrangements, until, at least, the Menagerie and Museum shall have been removed.

The line of the present walk leading across the Ride from the Museum offers favorable conditions for an archway, as the required excavation would be wholly in an embankment of earth formed above the natural surface, and the material to be removed would all be needed close at hand in preparing the ascent needed to the arch over the Bridle Road. The map hereto appended, marked A, shows the position of the arches as thus suggested, and also the new lines of walk which it would be practicable to form in connection with them. Three different routes are suggested for reaching the proposed arch (*see No. 31 on Folded Map*) from the entrance walk from the Scholar's Gate; the walk leading from the Sixth avenue entrance along the shore of the pond is extended to the arch and beyond it, so as to give an improved approach to the Mall as well as to the Museum and Menagerie.

By a small foot-bridge (*see No. 32 on Folded Map*) at the narrows of the pond, a much more direct line of communication is opened between the Museum and all the southeast parts of the Park and the south entrances on Sixth, Seventh and Eighth avenues. The walks proposed to be formed for this purpose lead across the peninsula and open an interesting district from which the public has hitherto been excluded.

Another sketch (B) shows how the ground now occupied by the Museum and Menagerie Buildings would probably be laid out after their removal, and it will be evident from it that the works now proposed, though especially desirable while those buildings remain, would be a great permanent convenience.

It is proposed to build the arch under the Drive of rough stone. Its estimated cost is $50,000. It is proposed to cross the Bridle Road with a light span of iron, similar in character to those which have been made over it at other points, and the cost of which has been five to seven thousand dollars. At present rates it is estimated that this work would cost $10,000.

Respectfully,

FRED. LAW OLMSTED,

Landscape Architect.

REPORT ON A PROMENADE

DEPARTMENT OF PUBLIC PARKS,
OFFICE OF DESIGN AND SUPERINTENDENCE.

NEW YORK, 3d December, 1875.[1]

TO THE HON. HENRY G. STEBBINS,
President of the Board:

Sir,—The want has long been recognized of a place in the Central Park arranged suitably for a promenade, side by side, of drivers, riders and walkers under conditions favorable to a certain degree of social enjoyment. It has also been recognized that it would be a grave error to provide an arrangement for this purpose, which, while likely to establish a custom and stimulate an irresistible public demand, should fall far short of satisfying it. It has been considered especially that any considerable sacrifice of the results of the expenditure already made on the park in order to gain such an imperfect arrangement, would be unpardonable. Whether any of the existing constructions of the park can be so far improved and supplemented as to supply what is needed, and, if not, how much it would be necessary to sacrifice in order to introduce entirely new constructions for the purpose, was therefore to be determined upon a careful forecast of the detail of conditions which would be favorable or otherwise to the enjoyment of those engaging in the promenade. There are three constant elements of such enjoyment to be considered, one being that of the spectacle; the second, that arising from recognition of friends and observation of special objects, as faces, dresses, horses and equipages; and the third, that of such personal conversation as is possible for those moving side by side in a crowd.

Every person present becomes a part of the spectacle, and may contribute to each of the other two elements. The position and movements of each person is consequently a matter of interest to every other present. It is desirable, therefore, that during the hours of the promenade, the ground used for the purpose should be well filled. It is desirable that there should be a continuous movement of all engaged, and that the attention of none should be unnecessarily held to other matters in such a way as to interfere with the enjoyments which are special to the promenade. The more the movement of each person is regulated with reference to the enjoyment of all by fixed conditions, and the less by the constant effort of his individual judgment; the more the vision of each over the promenade before him is unobstructed, and the more complete and extended his command of the spectacle, the greater will be the enjoyment of all.

Whenever obstructions, however slight, occur, tending to

[1] Doc. No. 67.

suddenly arrest movement at particular points, or to hinder or to make unnecessarily indirect the movements of individuals, and especially of carriages and riding horses, the consequence will be at one place crowding, apprehension of collisions, and more or less demand on the attention of each person near by to the circumstance, and at another breaks and gaps in the spectacle and the irregularities of movement to which these would invite. The turning of carriages on the promenade, their entrance upon it, and their withdrawal, create more or less unavoidable disturbance; therefore, there should be no frequent opportunity or temptation for these movements; at the same time the space prepared for the promenade should not be so long that its necessarily restrained movement would become very tedious before those entering upon it could, if they desired, escape, and move more at will.

The following specifications of requirement are readily deducible from the above considerations:

1. A devious course is to be avoided; the more nearly straight the promenade the better.

2. A steeper grade than one in forty and much variation of grade is to be avoided. A "hogsback" is particularly objectionable. The more nearly level the promenade the better.

3. No other thoroughfares should cross or intersect the line of the promenade.

4. There should be no necessity for driving freighting vehicles over it late in the day.

5. Its direction should not be such as would bring the sun in the eyes of those resorting to it late in the day.

6. All parts of it should be as much as possible shaded late in the day.

7. At each end it should be practicable for visitors to do either of three things with the least possible confusion and disturbance, and with reasonable ease and convenience, viz.: To turn around and continue on the promenade; to make an excursion in the park beyond the promenade and out of its crowd; or, lastly, to quickly leave the park on the shortest course home.

8. The promenade should be fully half a mile in length and will desirably be somewhat longer.

9. The total space to be occupied by the drive, ride and walks cannot well be less than 150 feet in breadth.[1]

According to the degree in which these desiderata can all be combined in any arrangement it will be likely to prove permanently satisfactory, while in so far as one or more of them shall be secured at the sacrifice of others the public demand designed to be met will be greatly increased but not adequately fulfilled.

In 1872, after the return of the present President of the Department from Europe, the subject was, at his request, more

---

[1] This allows 60 feet for the driving-way, 40 feet for the riding-way, 40 feet for two walks and 10 feet for two rows of shade trees.

thoroughly canvassed than ever before. After demonstrating objections to two suggested plans, which were recognized to be conclusive against them, I was then asked to select the least objectionable route to be found in the South Park and prepare a definite plan for laying it out. In doing so I was assisted by Mr. Vaux, and the plan which resulted has been seen by all the Commissioners of the Department. It has never been formally presented to the Board, however, because of its acknowledged numerous defects and the injury, which would unquestionably result from undertaking to carry it out, to the park as it now stands.

The conclusion of the study then given the subject may, therefore, be stated as follows:

That no plan at all adequate to the requirements of the city in a promenade can be carried out on the South Park, except at a cost in direct outlay and in the waste of results of outlay already made, for which its value would be no sufficient compensation.

Bearing in mind and giving but their just weight to each of the desiderata that have been enumerated, and considering a few broad general facts of the topography of the park, the conditions which enforce this conclusion are easily recognized.

The South Park is one mile in length from north to south and half a mile in width, and is divisible topographically into three tolerably distinct elevated ranges and two intermediate valleys, all trending across the line of the greater distance. Each range of high ground is a continuous ledge of rock, with a coating of earth, for the most part artificially laid on, not exceeding two feet in average depth.

The difference of elevation between these ranges and the valleys which divide them is from thirty to ninety feet. It is only by circuitous courses or by heavy rock cuttings and embankments that roads of tolerable grade can be carried from north to south, and only by crossing these existing roads and numerous walks, lawns and plantations, that a moderately direct road of even a third of a mile in length could be made from east to west. In either case the reduction of a space of ground 150 feet in width and the necessary length, so nearly to a plane surface as would be necessary to the purpose, could only be accomplished by the destruction of the most valuable landscape features of the ground.

Difficulties similar in character to those which have been indicated are found in all of the North as well as the South Park, and also in the strip of ground through which the communication with it from between the two is carried on the west. The only space where they do not obtain in the property under the control of the Department is that of the straight, narrow belt of land on the east side of the great reservoir. The drive which passes along this belt has already been selected by the public as more nearly than any other meeting the requirement of the promenade, and this in spite of the fact that there is neither a walk nor a bridle road alongside of it.

It is not only more traveled by carriages than any other on the park, but late in the day they are often driven back and forth upon it as on a proper promenade. The reasons for its use in this manner are: 1st, that it is straight; 2d, that it is level; 3d, that late in the day it is shaded; 4th, that it does not look toward the setting sun.

Observing that speed of movement was more checked by the conflux of carriages here than elsewhere in the park, the Commissioners of 1871 thought to make an improvement simply by widening the wheelway, giving no consideration to any other public requirement of the locality, and accomplishing the little that was attempted with such narrow study of the circumstances that the relation of the widened drive to adjoining objects was left incomplete, unsymmetrical and offensive to the eye. To adapt the arrangement to the purpose for which the public is obviously inclined to use the locality, the straight reach of drive needs to be still further widened and, if possible, lengthened, and a broad walk and riding-way to be formed adjoining it. To gain the necessary space for this purpose without encroaching on the reservoir it would be necessary to appropriate a part of the sidewalk on the west side of Fifth Avenue, to remove and reconstruct the present retaining wall, and to give increased height as well as breadth to the embankment on which the drive is now carried. I present a preliminary study of a plan in which these, with several minor improvements, are proposed. If this plan were carried out every one of the desiderata of a promenade would be realized in full degree almost precisely as they have been stated.

Certain objections to the proposition are obvious: First, that of its cost; second, that of the distance of the locality from the present centre of residence of the city; third, that the length of the promenade (being barely half a mile) is rather less than is desirable. The fact that it is now more resorted to for carriage exercise than any other part of the park, shows that the second objection already has no very important weight; with the advance northward of population it will annually have less. The fact, again, that whenever the improvement of Riverside Avenue is made; the city will be possessed of another promenade nearly a mile in length, and better in all important respects than any other in the world, lessens considerably the weight of the third objection.

That the promenade would adjoin Fifth Avenue may be considered an advantage, as an alternate route is thus provided for those who may wish to pass rapidly north from the South Park when the promenade is crowded and the less occasion is left for the intrusion upon it of an undesirable class of vehicles. The entrance at the south end from the avenue would meet a local demand which has been the subject of repeated memorials to the Department.

I submit this study to the consideration of the Board as indicating the least objectionable way of providing for a public demand which is likely to increase, and any less complete arrangement for meeting which would probably prove temporary, and therefore more costly, and in all respects objectionable.

The work could now be all put under contract at $250,000.

Respectfully,

FRED. LAW OLMSTED,
Landscape Architect.

CHAPTER VI

BOUNDARIES AND ENTRANCES

Since much of the area secured for the Central Park necessarily had to remain in an unfinished state for some years,—not strongly differentiated from surrounding vacant land and little protected from the incursions of neighboring goats,[1]—the Central Park Commissioners found the establishment of a substantial boundary highly important. As to the character of the boundary treatment, there was room for debate, especially in the anticipated problems of park administration. In Mr. Olmsted's letter of 1860 to the Board, he discusses this enclosure in relation to the use of the Park by the public, particularly the prevention of entering or leaving the Park at improper places and in the hours after nightfall when the Park was unlighted. A wall in some form finally appeared to be the most economical and practical boundary. The early low wall hurried together by the end of 1859 was therefore gradually superseded in sections by a permanent wall, adapted to the elevations of the Park boundaries and designed with reference to appearances from the surrounding promenade. The ungraded condition of the streets bounding all but the southern part of the Park prevented permanent construction on stretches of wall and on certain gates for many years. Even in 1886 this enclosing wall seems not to have been wholly built, judging from urgent references in the park records to pieces yet to be finished.

The original "Greensward" plan indicated the number of entrance gates as twenty. It was early deemed appropriate that these entrances should be named in some way more appealing to popular imagination than a numerical designation taken from the neighboring streets. An abridgment of the Committee Report on Nomenclature is here printed. It is interesting to note that the names chosen appear on a Park map for the first time in the Board's report for 1865. A few of these names have been changed, but the scheme survived and has recently been

[1] Cf. Part I, p. 33.

brought to public attention by the Central Park Association[1] *in its campaign for the restoration of the Park.*

The Nomenclature report of 1862 hinted that suitable architectural and sculptural treatment of the entrance gates was to be expected in the course of years, by public-spirited gifts as well as from the Park funds. Almost immediately, however, it was felt that the entrances to the Park on 59th Street should be given the dignity their importance and greater use demanded. In 1863 plans secured by competition for the four entrances at Fifth, Sixth, Seventh, and Eighth avenues were referred to the Board's Committee on Statuary, Fountains and Architectural Structures. Of these the drawings by Richard M. Hunt were rather hastily selected and approved, but nothing was done to carry out his very elaborate projects.

After the close of the Civil War, in 1866, Mr. Hunt published a book[2] *containing illustrations of his designs and a protest addressed to the Commissioners of the Park against their failure to undertake construction of the gates as approved in 1863. At that time and in the intervening period, there had been considerable public controversy about the designs, particularly on the ground that they were entirely incongruous with the Landscape Architects' design of the adjacent park areas. It should be said that Messrs. Olmsted and Vaux,*[3] *who had recently re-entered the service of the Park, were strongly against Mr. Hunt's designs, and, at the request of the Commissioners, subsequently submitted drawings themselves. These, in turn, although less grandiose, met with delay and inaction on the part of the Commissioners.*

The taking of more land for adequate approaches at the southerly Fifth and Eighth avenue corners of the Park was more or less bound up with the question of gates. Before 1870 the Circle at Eighth Avenue had been authorized; and although the taking of the entire block from 58th to 59th Street at Fifth Avenue was voted down, a considerable amount of land for a plaza had been secured.

A history of the ultimate elaboration of the Central Park entrances would be too full of detail and debate for this present work. Increased and changed use of the Park has forced a form in many cases different from that shown on the original plan of the Park, although the preservation of the road system has kept the essential scheme of gates the same.

---

[1] See *The Central Park*, 1926, p. 87 ff. The Committees of the Association are designated by the gate names.

[2] *Designs for the Gateways of the Southern Entrances to the Central Park,* by Richard M. Hunt, Member of the American Institute of Architects. New York, D. Van Nostrand, 1866.

[3] See Mr. Vaux's letter to the *Evening Post,* May, 1865, referred to on p. 75.

Whether the Park as an esthetic whole has gained or lost by the postponed architectural treatment of its boundaries and entrances is perhaps a question.

THE PAPERS INCLUDED IN THIS CHAPTER ARE:

‡ *Letter regarding boundary treatment of the Park, to Board from F. L. O. April, 1860.—Discusses kind of barrier desirable between main park and outer promenade.*

Report on Nomenclature of the Gates of the Park. By Standing Committee on Statuary, Fountains, and Architectural Structures, of the Board. April 10, 1862. Doc. No. 2—By Messrs. Stebbins, Russell, and Green. (Abridgement).

Letter submitting Study for Sixth and Seventh Avenue Entrances at Fifty-ninth Street, to Board from O. V. & Co. March 29, 1869. Appendix H, 13th Annual Report, C. P. C.

‡ Previously unpublished.

BOUNDARY TREATMENT OF THE PARK

OFFICE OF ARCHITECT-IN-CHIEF & SUPT.,
CENTRAL PARK, April, 1860

To the Board of Commissioners of the Central Park.

Gentlemen:

The city has imposed upon your Board in addition to the duties originally assigned to it by the Legislature, with regard to the Central Park, the duty of also laying out and forming an outer park of no inconsiderable size. Including the portions which you have determined to unite with it from the park proper, this outer park will contain an area as large as the Battery, Bowling Green, the City Hall Park, and Hudson Square united.

It is not desirable that this outer park should be separated by any barrier more than a common stone curb from the adjoining roadways. It is still more undesirable in the interest of those who are to use it that it should be separated more than is necessary from the interior park. It will offer to these a broad shaded promenade more than twice as long as from the Battery to Union Square, in immediate proximity to and associated in design with the scenery of the main park. The trees which grow upon it are used in the design as a part of the scenery of the main park, adding to its beauty, attractiveness and value. The scenery of the main park should much more be made to add to the beauty, attractiveness and value of the outer park. As far as it is practicable the two should be incorporated as one whole, each being part of the other. The value of this outer park cannot be estimated at less than $3,000,000. Whatever separates it from the interior park detracts from its value and equally detracts from the value of the park itself. If a close fence six feet high intervened between the park and the outer park, it would by and by be felt to be cheaply purchased for the sake of removal, at the price of $5,000,000. Assuming that a barrier is necessary for police purposes on this line, the more it fills the eye, the more it crosses the landscape, the more it is seen either from one side or the other, the more it is a nuisance, the more it detracts from the value of everything else you do, the less valuable becomes the park. The more modest, unobtrusive, insignificant it is, the less will it interfere with your general purpose, the less will it injure your design, the more will be its value, and the greater the value of both the park and the outer park.

The object of the barrier is to prevent people from entering and leaving the park at improper times [and places]. It can have no other good object. If the present arrangement of allowing the public to use the park till eleven o'clock at night is to be continued, there is not the slightest use in any barrier at all. It will be not only an entirely useless expense to establish it, but an expense the only result of which will be an injury to the park. It will constitute an eyesore and an inconvenience and has nothing whatever to recommend it. Experience, however, must soon lead to such a modification of the present ordinance that while carriages may be permitted to pass through the park, after dusk only the outer park will be open at night to use for sauntering, resting and walking. Experience has shown everywhere in Europe that public grounds must be closed at nightfall, unless they can be very well lighted and policed; otherwise rapes, robberies and murders are frequent. A similar experience here even with our small and open and well lighted public places, has led to the closing of Union Square at night and to quadrupling the usual police force on the area of the City Hall Park. The mere current expenses of a prudent lighting of the park with gas lights will not be less than $1,000,000 per annum, or five times as much as is at present expected to be expended for its maintenance in all other respects. There are the gravest objections, however to the introduction of gas pipes through the park, aside from the enormous cost of laying them. Trees for instance seldom flourish and generally die young in the vicinity of gas pipes. The additional cost of adequately lighting of the outer park need not exceed $5,000 per annum and with a suitable barrier the police expenses of the park will be 75 per cent. less than would be necessary even if the park were well lighted, if the present arrangement should be continued.

On these grounds I assume that a barrier will be necessary,[1] and for the reasons I have given previously, I further take it for granted that the Board will wish this barrier to be of the slightest and most inconspicuous character that can be made to answer the purpose.

An insurmountable barrier is not practicable to be had. Even the fence of the garden of the Tuileries, which is the most formidable one that I have seen, would not detain a man of ordinary strength and skill, who had a strong determination to surmount it, two minutes, and the effort would be neither fatiguing nor painful. Such a fence around the Central Park would cost more than the whole sum at the disposition of the Commission. I say, therefore, that a fence which would be really a formidable obstacle to a determined man is not to be aimed at. All that is required is a

---

[1] Ed. Note: Cf. discussion of exterior wall, in *Particulars of Construction and Estimate*, 1858, Part II, Chapter II, p. 290.

perfectly distinct demarcation between the main and the outer park, which cannot be crossed accidentally, or without sense of effort and inconvenience, or without a deliberate intention of breaking the law.[1]

The style and appearance of the barrier so far as it must be seen, should have some relation to whatever else is seen in connection with it.   It should therefore change in character correspondingly with each very striking change in the character of the scene of which it will form a component part.   There is not the slightest occasion for uniformity in the fence because unlike many other situations, as the Tuileries garden for instance, or any of our City Squares and Parks, the position of the fence of the Park will be such that nowhere can it be seen except a little at a time.

Of all sorts of barriers which could be used by far the worst, artistically, is the ordinary spiked iron fence.   In expression and in association, it is in the most distinct contradiction and discord with all the sentiment of a park.   It belongs to a jail or to the residence of a despot who dreads assassination.   Mr. Ruskin in a recent work asks what it means and answers: "Your iron railing always means thieves outside or Bedlam inside.   It *can* mean nothing else than that.   If the people outside were good for anything, a hint in the way of fence would be enough for them; but because they are violent and at enmity with you, you are forced to put the close bars and the spikes at top."

I consider the iron fence to be unquestionably the ugliest that can be used.   If on the score of utility, it must be used then the less the better, and certainly where used, it should not be elaborated and set up on high, and made large and striking as if it were something admirable in itself, and had better claims to be noticed than the scenery which it crosses and obscures.   Where used, the less it obtrudes itself the better.   It should be no larger in any way than is necessary and should appear nothing more than is necessary to guard people from going where they should not go.   Unfortunately an iron fence is the cheapest upright fence of a substantial and permanent character which can be used, and where it will not bar the promenader on the outer park from any beautiful prospect over the main park or cause him to look at it like a confined madman through a grated window, it will probably be thought best to use it. Wherever practicable I should flank it on the park side with a hedge. The most elegant form of iron fence, if my reasoning and feeling is right about it, would be a simple series of $\frac{3}{4}$ inch iron bars six feet high, six inches apart, firmly attached at each end to rails and posts of the same character.   This would be as little offensive as an iron fence of the requisite strength could be, and with the hedge would

---

[1] Ed. Note: In Doc. No. 2 of 1862-3, the Commissioners do not favor a fence, but recommend a wall of Dorchester stone, with gateways of the same, the walls below grade being of native stone.   In a memorandum of the 70's Mr. Olmsted refers to "five miles of a beautiful enclosing wall of stone," the cost included in that of the Park.

accomplish every desirable purpose required as well as the fence of the Tuileries and at one-tenth the cost. It may be questioned if a strong wooden paling of a rustic character would not be better than either. . . .

Where the outer park is graded at a higher elevation than the adjoining ground of the main park and commands a view over it, a high fence of any kind would be as much out of place as a grating over a beautiful picture or before a drawing-room window. If the outer park were formed on a causeway-wall above the park at a height of eight feet or more, no other barrier against ingress or egress would be needed, as no one would ordinarily leap a distance of eight feet perpendicularly without an object, and it is more difficult to climb an eight-foot wall than to surmount an ordinary iron fence of twice that height. A guard in the form of a balustrade or banister would be needed to prevent accidental falls and this would add to the depth to be leaped by one attempting to enter over it. If eight feet is enough to deter a man from carelessly undertaking this, and an iron banister be set $3\frac{1}{2}$ feet high, $4\frac{1}{2}$ feet of wall would then be sufficient. It would perhaps be too easy to attempt to get out of the park by grasping the banisters and pulling up by them. This would be obviated by a hedge planted at the foot of the wall. Such a method of separating the interior and exterior portions of the park is much better than any other which has been suggested and should be adopted wherever practicable. In some situations, a balustrade with a cut stone coping and base course might be substituted for the iron banister with great advantage. With a dead-wall of brick, masked by a hedge, this would not be too expensive. I have not been able to obtain any satisfactory plan of substantial fence in which the use of both iron and brick could be dispensed with which would not cost more than it is prudent to appropriate for this purpose.

Where cliffs, or vertical walls of rock more than eight feet high, bound the outer park toward the park proper, no other barrier is required. I propose only to excavate niches at intervals of about ten feet, and to guard these with iron railing, within which ivy can be planted, and at a proper height trained over the face of rock. This will be the most beautiful as well as the most economical barrier of the park. Unfortunately it is practicable but for a short distance.

NOMENCLATURE OF THE PARK GATES[1]

*To the Board of Commissioners
of the Central Park:*

The Standing Committee on Statuary, Fountains, and Architectural Structures, to whom was referred the subject of the nomenclature of the Park, respectfully report:

. . . .

That the Park is to be enclosed, seems to have been assumed in the action of the Board, although the intention is not yet expressly declared.

There are examples of Parks, in populous cities, without enclosures; but the necessity for a permanent enclosure to the Central Park, for the preservation of order and the protection of property, can hardly be questioned.

The character of this enclosure, as yet undetermined, will necessarily be decided by the extent of means at the disposal of the Board; but whatever style or material may be adopted, it is evident that entrance ways will be required at proper intervals, and preparation has accordingly been made for them in the general arrangement of the design.

These entrances are twenty in number, some of more immediate importance, and others destined always to be in a measure subordinate, because of the lesser currents of ingress and egress that they are designed to accommodate, but all requiring to be arranged with primary respect to the public convenience, and with a certain degree of architectural fitness.

Immemorial custom has sanctioned the practice of giving names of dignity to the gates or entrance-ways of cities, which, in ancient, as in more modern times, were walled.

. . . .

The same considerations that give names as convenient designations of locality to the gates of cities, obtain in a great place of public resort like the Park, and the popular convenience will manage somehow to affix local names that cannot readily be effaced, unless appropriate ones are suggested, and supplied in season by the proper authorities.

. . . .

While this question of nomenclature requires careful adjustment in connection with every part of the Park, its importance is more particularly evident in the case of the entrance gateways, as they will naturally attract a large share of public attention, and be constantly spoken of by name, on account of the conspicuous purposes they serve, and the prominent position they occupy; it is

[1] Doc. No. 2, 1862.

therefore desirable, not only that they should be made as agreeable as possible in design, but that they should be named in accordance with some simple but comprehensive plan that will fully meet the every-day wants of the public, and at the same time be unobjectionable in other important respects.

The monotonous numerical system used to distinguish the thoroughfares of New York is at once felt to be unsuitable for Park use, and but few suggestions of much greater value appear to be offered by other metropolitan cities.

.   .   .   .

It will, moreover, in all probability, be thought desirable that the Park itself should, in some way, indicate the special nomenclature to be used; it may, therefore, be worth while to consider whether it offers any leading ideas of sufficient scope and general interest to deserve expression in the names of the different entrances, and of a character that will readily admit of varied artistic treatment in the gateways themselves.

Although, as already stated, there are twenty entrances to the Park, special interest attaches to the four gateways on Fifty-ninth street, because they directly face the large portion of the city already built up, and are always likely to be the most thronged.

Their position thus seems to require that the names by which they are to be known, should collectively express a single idea that will admit of further development in detail in the other less prominent gateways.

The construction of the Park has been easily achieved, because the industrious population of New York has been wise enough to require it, and rich enough to pay for it: to New Yorkers it belongs wholly, and these four principal gateways may, perhaps, be allowed to recognize this proprietary right, and to extend to each citizen a respectful welcome.

.   .   .   .

If an attempt is made to analyze the various industrial pursuits of a large city like New York, it will be found that they may be easily grouped under a few leading heads.

We have, first, that portion of the population whose sphere of usefulness is manual labor. This large and important class contributes to the prosperity of the community all the hard, positive, tangible work that is done, and it deserves, on entering the Park, a hearty and respectful recognition. . . . The word "Artizan," . . . seems to present the whole idea in its more comprehensive and desirable aspect, and is, perhaps, the most characteristic title that can be used.

In close connection with the industrial idea suggested by the term "Artizan," will be found another which may be readily conveyed by the word "Artist." . . . In this class will naturally be included all whose pursuits are directly connected with the idea of "Design," either in the leading arts of music, painting, architecture, and sculpture, or in the numberless supplementary arts. . .

The next important generalization that suggests itself, is that expressed by the word "Merchant.". . .[to cover] many different names, such as "Banker," "Broker," "Importer," "Trader," "Agent,"· "Director," "Store Keeper." The prosperity of every community must necessarily depend to a great extent on the successful development of the general idea that is embodied in these various terms, and as the city of New York is the commercial centre of the whole country, it is especially desirable that it should find an adequate recognition in connection with the Park.

There seems to be yet one other class of laborers who cannot be correctly distinguished, either by the term "Artizan," "Artist," or "Merchant," and this is the class that includes the Poet, the Divine, the Statesman, the Lawyer, the Author, the Editor, the Teacher, the Physician, the man of Science, and all in fact, whose contributions to the welfare of the community, are of a specially intellectual character.

The word "Scholar," perhaps expresses the generic idea with sufficient completeness, and if we add this term to the three already mentioned, we have a group of four names bearing a mutual relation one to the other, and embodying in a general way, and on an equal footing, so far as the Park is concerned, all the industrial ideas that are entertained in a civilized community.

In the remaining gates, the dependence of the city on the whole country may be recognized, and its connection with other cities and other countries acknowledged; the importance of the domestic relations may be dwelt on, and the idea may be set forth that for the sake of peace, we must yet be prepared for war.

The first industrial idea outside of the city that seems to demand our attentive consideration, is that connected with the cultivation of the soil, for the sustenance of the metropolis is entirely dependent on agricultural labor, . . . through the patient care and prudent foresight of the tiller of the soil, and if it is desired to lay particular stress on this characteristic idea of providence and forethought, it seems to be more simply and completely conveyed by the familiar word "Husbandman," than by any other term. If, however, it is preferable to express only the general idea of cultivation, this entrance may take the name of the "Cultivator's" gate, or the "Agriculturist's" gate. In the event of the plan being carried out which was suggested some time since for widening to one hundred and fifty feet the Seventh Avenue, north of One hundred and tenth street, and planting it with several rows of trees; the point at which this shaded country-like road will meet the Park, seems to be the most appropriate for the gate intended to be illustrative of country life.

  .   .   .   .

It is evident . . . that every well organized community must contain within itself the elements of an army prepared, whenever the necessity arises, to strike boldly in defence of its just rights, and without doubt the claim of the "Warrior" to the grateful recognition of the city of New York will be at once allowed.

The "Warrior's" gate may, with propriety, be situated on the north side of the Park, facing Washington Heights, and in the immediate neighborhood of the old fortifications, that will continue to be preserved within the boundaries of the people's pleasure-ground.

The vocations which are followed by men who find in untamed and uncultivated nature a suitable field of action, are so various, that they require to be grouped under several distinct heads.

Thus we have the "Hunter" and the "Fisherman," both individual pursuits that contribute largely to the wants of the community.

The term "Woodman" may represent all the labor that is devoted to procuring such important staples as lumber, bark, charcoal, pitch, tar, rosin, and turpentine; and the term "Miner" seems to include the workers in coal, and the different ores, and also the quarrymen or miners of stone.

The prosperity of every metropolis depends to an important extent on the channels open to it for ready communication with the rest of the business world. In a city with such an immense shipping interest as New York, one branch of this idea will be typified by the "Mariner," who is forever carving out a new public highway over the ocean, the river, or the lake, and the other equally important branch will be represented by the "Engineer," who provides the community with all the facilities it possesses for overland transportation, and also contributes to its welfare in many other ways. The highroad, the plankroad, the railroad, the canal, the breakwater, the dock, the tunnel, the viaduct, the aqueduct, and the reservoir are all called into existence by his skill and indomitable perseverence, and there can be no question but that general ideas conveyed by the terms "Mariner" and "Engineer," deserve a ready appreciation in connection with such a public work as the Park.

The Mariner's gate should perhaps be situated in the immediate vicinity of the highest ground contained within the Park limits, so that on entering or leaving it a suggestive view may be offered of the hills beyond the harbor in the distance, and of the two busy rivers that float by the city.

The Engineer's gate may with some propriety be placed on the east side of the new reservoir, where . . . the good cause of temperance and cleanliness requires that the plan of the people's pleasure-ground shall conform closely to the lines of an equally popular, but more strictly useful, engineering work.

Having thus generalized all the preeminently practical pursuits of life, . . . it is fitting that a welcome should be extended to the men who devote their energies to having new discoveries that enlarge the field of human action and add to the value of civilized life. The labors of such men as Columbus and Hendrick Hudson can never be forgotten. . . .

The example set by them has, however, been so diligently followed, that a glance at the numerous expeditions that have been undertaken by Americans within the experience of the present generation, is sufficient to establish the claim of the "Explorer" to a cordial recognition.

Akin to this idea, and yet widely differing from it, is that of the "Inventor," whose labors are devoted to the study of natural laws, and to a searching analysis of the various mechanical possibilities that are within the scope of human effort. . . .

The various industrial ideas that are constantly working to the advantage of a metropolis, having been thus typified, it seems desirable in a public work like the Central Park, to give attentive consideration to two ideas of a somewhat different character, before proceeding to the embodiment of the domestic relations.

The one is, that the city, although metropolitan by position, is cosmopolitan in its associations and sympathies, and is ever ready to extend a courteous welcome to all peaceably disposed "Strangers," or "Foreigners"; . . . this welcome being offered, however, not merely as a matter of courtesy, but as a recognition of the fact, that it is highly important, both to the general and the particular interests of the whole nation, that its cities should be visited, and its institutions studied and comprehended by intelligent and industrious travellers from other countries. . . . The Foreigners' gate may also, in its sculptural decoration, directly acknowledge the obligation that the owners of the Park are under to liberal and disinterested men of other nations, like Lafayette, for instance. . . .

It seems desirable . . . to have one gate to the Park, that, under the name of "All Saints," will respectfully acknowledge the importance of the influence that is exercised, to a greater or less degree, over the whole community by the pure and holy men of all ages. . . .

Although the Park is intended to afford ample opportunity for personal relaxation and repose to all the hard-working and energetic representatives of manly labor, it has another class of individuals to provide for. . . .

It aims to provide within the city limits an extensive rural play-ground, and a country experience generally, for the whole domestic circle, so that, in future, "The Boys," "The Girls," "The Women," and "The Children" may all have an opportunity to escape at intervals, from the close confinement of the city streets, and to spend pure and happy hours in direct communication with the beauties of nature.

The Park is already used freely, and enjoyed heartily by troops of young children, and the Children's gate will help to keep in mind, the fact, that, in the course of the next twenty years, the whole army of industrious workers, who are now vigorously laboring for the general welfare, must have received large reinforcements from the band of little ones. . . .

The Boys' gate and the Girls' gate will convey the idea that ample opportunity for physical development is considered a necessary part of the free educational system of the city, and will recognize the fact that it is not thought sufficient for the young students of either sex to be liberally provided with schools, school-teachers, and school-books, but that they must also be induced to study freely the works of nature. . . .

.   .   .   .

In the Women's gate, it is not intended to convey the idea that the various industrial pursuits recognized at the other entrances to the Park, are followed by one sex only, . . . but it is desired to express in an especial manner, a sense of the all-important services that are rendered by women in their domestic capacity alone. . . .

A list of twenty names is thus obtained that seems to be somewhat appropriate for the object in view. We have the Artizan, the Artist, the Merchant, the Scholar, the Cultivator, the Warrior, the Mariner, the Engineer, the Hunter, the Fisherman, the Woodman, the Miner, the Explorer, the Inventor, the Foreigner, the Boys, the Girls, the Women, the Children, and All Saints. . . .[1]

The artistic adaptability of the general system of nomenclature above suggested, has already been proved, and worthy types of the Miner, the Trapper, and the Sailor, are now in existence, that have been conceived by American artists.

At present, it would only be desirable to arrange the gateways with a view to possible elaboration hereafter, for although it can scarcely be considered within the proper scope of the Commissioners to provide out of the Park funds, artistic decoration of a really high character, at all the various entrances, an outlet may readily be left open for future effort in this direction by private subscription, and if such an opportunity is offered in connection with a popular system of nomenclature, it will probably, in course of time, be accepted and improved, for each separate gateway will have a special claim to the affectionate consideration of some particular portion of the community.

.   .   .   .

Dated New York, April 10th, 1862.

H. G. STEBBINS,⎫
C. H. RUSSELL, ⎬ *Committee.*
AND. H. GREEN,⎭

[1] ED. NOTE: The following present gates represent changes from the original names proposed: Farmer, instead of Cultivator; Army and Navy, instead of Warrior; Pioneer, instead of Explorer; Stranger, instead of Foreigner; Prophets, instead of All Saints. The Fisherman and Inventor are omitted.

STUDY FOR SIXTH AND SEVENTH AVENUE ENTRANCES[1]

NEW YORK, March 29, 1869.

To the President of the Board of
Commissioners of the Central Park:

Sir,—We send herewith a study that is intended to serve as a further illustration of our plan for the re-arrangement of the Sixth and Seventh avenue approaches to the Park at Fifty-ninth Street.

Since this plan was laid before you, in 1866, extensions of territory on a liberal scale have been secured, in accordance with our recommendation, on the city side of the Fifth and Eighth avenue gateways, and the question of a corresponding enlargement at the two intermediate points will doubtless, therefore, at some time engage the attention of your Commission.

The relative positions of the Sixth and Seventh avenue entrances coincide with each other so precisely that the accompanying study is applicable to both localities. The design for the building, however, and even the details of the plan may be somewhat varied, without interfering with the general idea.

The main fact we have to deal with is a gateway situated at the point where a broad city avenue is abruptly terminated by the wall of a great park, evidently a salient conjunction of circumstances, and a conspicuous architectural opportunity.

It is to be borne in mind in this connection, that a shaded walk forty feet in width, adjoins the Central Park wall along the line of Fifty-ninth street, and that the entrance under consideration is for visitors on foot only; also, that a horse railroad is laid down in the centre of the avenue, which is a main artery for metropolitan travel, and that the cars now stop short of the Park, on the down town side of Fifty-ninth street, while a belt railroad of secondary importance occupies the whole line of curb in front of the broad walk, and hinders visitors arriving in carriages from being set down comfortably at the Park gate.

Fifty-ninth street must, in time, become a crowded thoroughfare, because it will have to accommodate half the cross town travel which will be stopped by the Park between the south line and the traffic road at Sixty-fifth street. Consequently the point will be a critical one where the railroad avenue meets this busy street, and ample provision should be made for an accumulation of vehicles in the immediate vicinity of the Park entrance.

Architecturally considered, the position is one that seems to warrant almost any degree of liberality in its conception, for a time must come when the whole neighborhood will be filled up with handsome houses, and it will be easy then to raise funds for large structures of this specific character.

[1] 13th Annual Report, C. P. C., 1869, Appendix H.

Under these circumstances our suggestion is that the avenue between Fifty-eighth and Fifty-ninth streets be sufficiently widened to form a public place of liberal dimensions, that the railroad be re-arranged as shown on the plan, and that the gateway be designed in the form of an arcade or shelter erected for the convenience of the public, over the wide sidewalk, in front of the Park entrance.

Hoping that the general idea thus embodied may meet with a favorable consideration,

We remain, sir,

Yours respectfully,

OLMSTED, VAUX & CO.
Landscape Architects.

CHAPTER VII

THE USE AND ABUSE OF THE PARK BY THE PUBLIC

From the first the Commissioners of the Central Park intended to make of it a thoroughly democratic institution. In their final report of 1870—when the old Commission was about to be ousted under the new "Ring" charter—we find these words:

"The gratification, within justifiable limits, of the people has been the end sought to be obtained . . . It offers wide opportunities and abundant facilities for exercise, for rest, for rural suggestion, and for perceptive education.

"The amusements are so classified that all ages and tastes may be gratified. No exclusiveness obtains. Freedom of access to all parts of the Park, under the necessary restrictions, has been the policy in its management." [1]

But the use of a public park—like Liberty itself—can be made equitable only by a fair apportionment of the amount of freedom to be permitted to each class of visitors. The Commissioners were quick to see and explain that complete freedom of use for any one class meant the destruction of other reasonable possibilities for use. As early as 1859, in their third report the Commissioners thus expressed the motive of the Central Park Plan.

"The primary purpose of the Park is to provide the best practicable means of healthful recreation, for the inhabitants of the city, of all classes. It should have an aspect of spaciousness and tranquillity, with variety and intricacy of arrangement, thereby affording the most agreeable contrast to the confinement, bustle, and monotonous street-division of the city. It should, that is to say, as far as practicable, present to the eye a charming rural landscape, such as, unless produced by art, is never found within the limits of a large town; always remembering, however, that facilities and inducements for recreation [2] *and exercise are to be provided for a concourse of*

[1] Cf. the letter to Wm. Robinson, 1872, Part I, p. 96 f.
[2] The word *recreation* is used here, not in its present-day restricted connotation implying active sports, but in its original sense. Here recreation is *contrasted* with exercise.

406

people, and that the object of the scenery to be created is only to further the attainment of this end in the most complete and satisfactory manner. No kind of sport can be permitted which would be inconsistent with the general method of amusement, and no species of exercise which must be enjoyed only by a single class in the community to the diminution of the enjoyment of others."

In a later report (1863) the Commissioners recognize the variety of tastes to be satisfied:

"The Park is an enclosed ground devoted to such popular amusements as can, with proper regard to the convenience and pleasure of the general public, be enjoyed in the open air.

"This area is situated in the centre of the city, having a population not altogether homogeneous, reared in different climes, and bringing to the society of the metropolis views of labor and ideas of social enjoyment differing as widely as the temperature of the various countries of their origin. A day's work in the large cities of Europe, and a day's work in New York, are not the same; the amusements and routine of the daily life of the Sicilian and Scotchman are dissimilar. Each brings with him the traditions and the habits of his own country. The work of fusing the people of differing nationalities into a homogeneous body can be accomplished only during the life of two or three generations, and it would be difficult to prescribe rules that would satisfy these dissimilar tastes and habits.

"The most that can be attained at the Park, is to afford an opportunity for those recreations or entertainments that are generally acceptable, and to exclude such as will, though perhaps acceptable to a considerable number, in practice impair the attractions of a common place of recreation to much larger numbers.

"It is daily observation, that individuals, even of the same nationality, reared in the same city, have, by reasons of difference in education or from other circumstances, acquired habits so diverse as to render the entertainments that afford gratification to one unsuitable to another.

*"*THERE IS, HOWEVER, A UNIVERSALITY IN NATURE, THAT AFFORDS A FIELD OF ENJOYMENT TO ALL OBSERVERS OF HER WORKS.*"*

To enjoy Nature in the Park the series of naturalistic pictures must remain unspoiled. When ball clubs petitioned to usurp the broad green meadows, the Commissioners replied:

"It is obviously impossible that the ordinary play of these clubs should be allowed on the Park; the space is not sufficient. The Park

has attractions to those that visit it, merely as a picture; people walk, and drive, and ride there, not only because the walks, and ride, and drive are superior, but because the eye is gratified at the picture that constantly changes with the movement of the observer. Whatever defaces or injures this picture makes it less attractive to the great mass of visitors, and should, for the general good, be excluded.

"The lawn, the flowers, the trees, the water, all combine to form this picture, and each adds to its attractiveness.

"If the trees are cut and broken, if the waters are stagnant, if the flowers are trampled, or if the grass is beaten down and tracked, the picture is in so much rendered unattractive, and the enjoyment of the great mass is thereby diminished." (1861).

"It seems difficult for them to realize that the large open surface of turf that, to the cultivated taste is among the most attractive features of the Park, can have any other use than that of a playground.

"Nothing is more certain than that the beauty of these lawns would soon be lost, and that they would be rendered disagreeable objects, if these games were to be constantly played upon them.

"If the play of one club is allowed, others will demand the same privilege; and these clubs are so numerous, that if space were provided for the ordinary practice of their games, it would tend to depreciate the attractions of the Park to the far greater number who visit it for the refined pleasures that its landscape affords to those who are sensitive to natural beauties.

"These spacious open glades will, with the growth of each successive year, present a more marked and grateful contrast with the planted parts of the grounds.

"It is not to be inferred that they are wastes without use because they are not walked upon; both the plantations and the wide sweep of the lawn are essential to the completeness and the variety of the scene; their largest use is in the gratification they afford to those fitted for enjoyment of this nature; and this use is not to be diminished to accommodate sports, of themselves innocent and worthy of encouragement, but participated in by comparatively few persons." (1865.)

To further the enjoyment of the Park as a picture, as a place for rambling and picnicking and boating in summer and for skating in winter, as a concert ground, as a place of promenade in carriages and on foot, as a pleasant and safe riding ground, as a rural resort for young children, and, with limitations, as a playground for boys and girls, the Commissioners did all in their power. Guidebooks were encouraged to be sold in the Park as early as 1860 to unfold its various attractions; carefully selected concessions, such as refreshment stands, the boat service, the donkey rides, and the carriage service [1] *were calculated to meet popular demand without undue disturbance of landscape charms. The concerts begun by private funds in 1859 drew thousands, and became (1863) a publicly-financed feature quite consonant with the Commissioners' ideals.* [2]

Nevertheless the increasing use of the Park was not accompanied by an increasing popular care in preserving the qualities which made it precious. In this chapter we find the papers addressed by Mr. Olmsted to the Commissioners—whose ideals he had been largely instrumental in developing—showing the steps which the governing authorities of the Park must take to secure their investment from continuing depreciation. It is significant that all of the documents regarding destruction of turf were called forth after abuses had been engendered during the demoralizing period of "Ring" rule.

As a preliminary to these papers it is illuminating to read the early regulations or "ordinances" of the Park, published in 1859.

"Be it ordained, by the Commissioners of the Central Park:

"All persons are forbidden—

"To enter or leave the Park, except by the gate-ways;

"To climb, or walk upon the wall;

"To turn cattle, horses, goats, or swine, into the Park;

"To carry fire-arms, or to throw stones or other missiles within it;

"To cut, break, or in any way injure or deface the trees, shrubs, plants, turf, or any of the buildings, fences, bridges, or other constructions upon the Park, or to converse with, or in any way hinder, those engaged in its construction;

"No animal shall travel on any part of the Central Park, except upon the 'ride' or 'equestrian road,' at a rate exceeding seven miles an hour. Persons on horse-back shall not travel on the 'ride' or 'equestrian road,' at a rate exceeding ten miles per hour.

"No vehicle shall be permitted on the 'ride' or 'equestrian road,' the same being devoted exclusively to equestrians; nor shall any vehicle, horse, or animal of burden, go upon any part of the Central Park, except upon the 'drive,' and other carriage and transverse roads, and upon such places as are appropriated for carriages at rest.

"No animal or vehicle shall be permitted to stand upon the 'drive,'

---

[1] A park-controlled carriage service had to be installed in 1868 to obviate the annoyances from hiring ordinary carriages outside the Park.

[2] Cf. Part I, Chapter V, p. 66 f.

or carriage-roads of the Central Park, or any part thereof, to the ob-struction of the way, or to the inconvenience of travel, nor shall any person upon the Central Park solicit or invite passengers.

"No hackney coach, carriage, or other vehicle for hire, shall stand upon any part of the Central Park for the purpose of taking in any other passengers or persons than those carried to the Park by said coach, carriage, or vehicle.

"No person shall expose any article or thing for sale upon the Central Park, except previously licensed by the Board of Commis-sioners of the Central Park; nor shall any hawking or peddling be allowed on the Central Park.

"No omnibus, or express wagon, with or without passengers; nor any cart, dray, wagon, truck, or other vehicle carrying goods, mer-chandise, manure, soil, or other article, shall be allowed to enter any part of the Central Park, except upon the transverse roads.

"No threatening, abusive, insulting, or indecent language, shall be allowed on the Central Park, whereby a breach of the peace may be occasioned.

"No person shall be allowed to tell fortunes, or play at any game of chance, at or with any table or instrument of gaming, nor to do any obscene or indecent act whatever on the Central Park.

"In case of emergency, where life or property is endangered, all persons, if required so to do by the Superintendent, or any of his assistants, shall remove from the portion of the Central Park specified by the Superintendent or his assistants, and remain off the same till permission is given to return."

THE PAPERS INCLUDED IN THIS CHAPTER ARE:

‡ *Letter regarding the posting of Park rules, to A. H. Green from F. L. O. November 3, 1860.*

‡ *Letter suggesting music from the water, to A. H. Green from F. L. O. August 26, 1861.—The band to be placed on a float.*

‡ *Regulations of the boat service of the Central Park. April, 1861.—Draft in F. L. O.'s hand.*

Circular of inquiry regarding Park Lighting. July 15, 1872, signed by F. L. O., Pres. D. P. P.

A Handbill addressed: To Those having the care of Young Chil-dren (1872), signed by F. L. O., Pres. D. P. P.

‡ *Communication on concessions in the Park, to President of the Board from F. L. O. October 6, 1875.*

Use and Abuse of Park

Report on Applications for Appropriations of Ground in the Central Park for special purposes, by F. L. O., Landscape Architect. May 14, 1874 (Doc. No. 58).—Recommending the adoption of certain resolutions by the Board.

‡ *Papers regarding the difficulties of preserving green turf, to President of the Board from F. L. O. I. May 15, 1874. II. May 18, 1875.—With suggested restrictions in use.*

Report on Damage to Park by Crowds at unveiling of Halleck Statue, to President of Board from F. L. O. May 16, 1877.—Discusses unsuitability of rural parks for military functions.

‡ Previously unpublished.

POSTING OF PARK RULES

November 3rd, 1860.

Dear Sir:

In compliance with a request of your note of 30th ultimo, I send you an enclosed copy for two posters. These contain all which I deem necessary to be posted at frequent points within the park, and I have thought it best the cautions for the drivers and riders should be separated from those required by strollers upon the grounds, as it will allow smaller posters to be used and there is little fear that the drivers will offend while driving except in the matter of speed. If they leave their carriages they will meet the other poster and that it may not be passed unnoticed, it should be on paper of another color. The instructions as to stopping and waiting carriages without being imperative will favor a good custom and prevent unnecessary crowding of the roads. I think the road poster had better be printed on a white sheet about 12 x 18. This will allow rather more distinctness than is in the present bill (the large green one) which is successful I think in that respect.

I advise that these posters be set in a glazed frame, the border being a plain flat cleat which will be screwed on to hold the glass. The commonest window glass will answer. If merely pasted or glued to a board the posters are either washed off, or become dirty and more or less illegible at the first rain.

I propose that each gate keeper and park keeper be supplied and required to carry a copy of the complete ordinances. The gate keepers will prevent persons entering with loose dogs, with firearms, flowers, led horses, etc., and if required will show the ordinance. A poster on these points is unnecessary unless at the gates.

The offences of telling fortunes [and] gambling are so unfrequent (no arrests for these having yet been made) that unless persisted in after being noticed by a keeper it is unnecessary to prosecute for them. A verbal warning or exhibition of the ordinance in the keeper's pocket copy is all that is necessary. I omit these therefore from the general poster for the walks and grounds for the sake of conciseness.

To make this poster answer for all of next summer, I should add the words (I have in pencil) "except of the Commons," to the caution to keep off the grass, then, by calling all turf ground which is not to be reserved by the generic name of "Common," and setting a sign with the word only, whenever the walks lead on to such ground the duty and privileges of visitors in respect of grass will be sufficiently defined. Local names could still be attached to the open turf, as "the cricket common," etc.

After much study of the concourse difficulty, I have concluded that it cannot be entirely remedied except by a complicated and expensive arrangement, and that this would destroy the attractiveness of the place. The approved plan should be adhered to, and a sign to the following effect be exhibited at the entrance on Concert afternoons (next year).

"Carriages will not be allowed to stand in such a manner as to prevent others from passing them, except while the band is playing. To prevent collisions and disturbance all carriages are required to rest while the band is playing."

By instructing the keepers to rank the carriages of those who wish to rest, in such a manner that there will always be a lane for moving carriages, between the ranks of the standing ones, which is easily done, and then when the band begins to play closing a gate at the entrance, or in any other way stopping ingress and egress, the place will contain as many carriages as is practicable to accommodate by any other means. It simply requires some skill on the part of the keeper. I propose, while I continue to be necessarily so much confined as I now am, to give each of the keepers some instructions personally with regard to the management and control of carriages, horsemen and women in this and in other circumstances where there is likely to be crowding and confusion.

The name "Concourse" had better be given up, since it appears to be a misnomer and is likely to lead to an impression which is not favorable to order and will be disappointing. The locality, I would call "The upper terrace," and class the carriage part of it, with other similar spaces, "carriage rests" or "resting places" as I have termed them in the poster, "waiting grounds" if you prefer, or "waits" or "restings,"[1] designating each also specifically as "the upper terrace rest," "the circle rest." The word step (carriage step) applies to the step proper and not to the space and as carriage steps merely will be found at various other places, this term applied to spaces would lead to confusion. On the other hand we would have carriages directed to wait or rest, only at these spaces, so that a proper direction to them would never fail.

FRED. LAW OLMSTED,
Architect-in-Chief & Superintendent.

A. H. GREEN, Esq.

---

[1] ED. NOTE: Mr. Olmsted could not foresee that the terms which he meticulously seeks for "carriage rest" would in these present days of automobiles be lost in the "parking space" of our looser phraseology.

MUSIC FROM THE WATER

CENTRAL PARK, August 26, 1861.

Dear Sir:

I tried in vain both last Saturday and Saturday before to find a position where I could hear the music. The crowd was larger last Saturday than ever before and so dense that it was impossible for me to penetrate it. It was not at all practicable to enforce the ordinances, and groups of people too large to disperse could not be prevented from forming on the grass. On the hillside west of the Terrace, I think they did no harm and it would be well now to put the sign of "Common" there and on the "Green." After the concert I made a trial of music from the water. The band was placed in a boat successively at the points A, B, C & D.[1] Standing at the landing and at the foot of the staircase of the Terrace, it was found that the music was heard best and most distinctly when the band was at the greatest distance, or nearest the base of the rocky amphitheatre opposite, viz, at the point A. It was heard more distinctly at A than at B and probably at every point within the sweep of the hills rising from the water opposite the point A, than at any point, when on the Mall. Mr. Dodsworth[2] and others who were present were of the opinion that this would be the case with regard to every point indicated by the mark X on the map. As large an audience could be accommodated, scattered at these points, as on the Mall, and as promenading would be practicable, there would not need to be a crowd at any one point. Would it not be well to place the band at these points for the next concert? The same platform at present used placed on some casks could be used. It should be anchored, and if the wind is high, brought near the south shore. If a crowd should be apprehended on the north shore the nearest walks could be shut off. The music would be heard well within the arcade [of the Terrace], where seats might be placed. The whole Ramble is now pretty well shaded before 5 o'clock; so that with this accommodation, I doubt if the awnings would be needed. If they were, and are in their present position too far off, they could be accommodated on both sides the fountain place.

Yours respectfully,

FRED. LAW OLMSTED,
Supt.

A. H. GREEN, Esq.,
Treas. & Comptroller.

[1] ED. NOTE: No copy of the accompanying map was found.
[2] ED. NOTE: Director of the Band. There is an interesting piece of music composed by him entitled "The Central Park March," 1865. The cover of this bears several vignettes of Park views, in colors.

REGULATIONS OF THE BOAT SERVICE[1]

There will be two classes of boats designated respectively, according as they are to be used, passage boats and Call boats. From the first day of May to the first day of November every day when the weather is not stormy, a passage boat will leave the Terrace at 10 o'clock, make a complete circuit of the lake and call (if required) at each landing, returning to the Terrace within 45 minutes from the time of leaving. Another passage boat will follow in at the most half an hour; thereafter one will leave the Terrace at least once every half hour and make the circuit of the lake in like manner until within half an hour of the closing of the Park. Whenever any boat on leaving the Terrace has taken 12 passengers or whenever it shall be necessary for the proper accommodation of the public, a boat will follow in 15 minutes.

At each regular landing a flag staff 18 feet in height is to be placed . . .

. . . At each landing there will be an inscription painted thus: "Boats call at this landing for passengers once in 15 minutes when the red flag is hoisted on this staff, and once in 30 minutes when the blue flag is hoisted. Fare for any distance not exceeding one complete circuit of the lake (a mile and a half)—Ten cents."

. . . .

Passage boats shall not carry more than 12 adult passengers at once or more than 2,000 lbs. weight. Whenever any one of the passenger boats is carrying 12 passengers and no one else shall wish to leave it at any of the landings, that landing having been approached within 20 feet may be passed without a stop and whenever no one within the boat wishes to leave at a landing which has been approached within 20 feet and no one at the landing wishes to enter the boat, the landing may be passed without stopping.

The call boats are to be upon the waters of the Park whenever it is open to the public between the 1st of April and the 15th of November, and are to be held at the service of all persons calling for them; the first person calling to be first served; a boatman always going with the boat. These boats are not to carry more than 6 passengers each.

. . . .

The officers and keepers of the Park are to be conveyed in both classes of boats, whenever they require this assistance in the performance of their duties, free of charge.

Neither class of boats is to approach within ten feet of the shore except at the regular landings.

[1] Draft of April, 1861. Regular boat service on the lake began June 24, 1861, operated by Mr. Dick. See Part I, p. 66.

Nothing is to be thrown in the water from the boats and whatever is thrown in by passengers inadvertently or wantonly must be taken out if practicable by their boatmen.

The boats and their furniture must be kept clean and in good order and overhauled and painted whenever and in such colors as shall be required by the Superintendent. . . .

Each boat is to have an appropriate name approved by the Superintendent properly inscribed upon her.

There must be in attendance during the hours in which the park is open to the public in the boating season a sufficient number of boatmen to accommodate persons applying for the use of boats.

The boatmen are required to be in all respects capable and experienced in their duty, good swimmers, of sober habits and be respectful and obliging in their deportment, they are not to use tobacco in any form. Whenever on duty they will wear a suitable uniform which is to be provided by the Superintendent.

Boatmen and all persons employed regularly in the boat service of the park are deemed to be engaged in the service of the Com'rs of the Central Park and are to be governed when on the park by the same rules of order and discipline as far as applicable to them as the police force of the park. They will be under the orders of the Superintendent or parkkeepers when required.

FRED. LAW OLMSTED,
Architect-in-Chief & Supt.

INQUIRY REGARDING PARK LIGHTING

DEPARTMENT OF PUBLIC PARKS,
NEW YORK, July 15th, 1872.

There being a desire that the Central Park in this City should be lighted with gas and thrown open to public use at night, information is sought bearing upon the question of the expediency of the proposition. The park in question is a piece of ground two and a half miles long by half a mile wide, and will be entirely surrounded by the City. Its topography being highly varied and in parts wildly rugged, it includes sharp rocky ridges and ravines, precipitous ledges, and passages of cavernous obscurity. Over fifty miles of winding roads and foot-ways have been formed in it. It has been planted generally in a picturesque manner, and contains the most varied collection of trees and shrubs on the continent, many of them being exotic. The plantations are now generally from ten to fifteen years old.

The designers of the Park assumed that more would be lost than gained by keeping such a ground open at night, and believed that the attempt to so light it with gas as to make it safe and decent for public use would be destructive of its trees. They therefore

Photograph by Edward Heim

1926

Rowing on the Lake

Looking from the Point toward the Boathouse

arranged outside its walls a walk thirty feet in width, with a carriage way forty feet in width, both to be well lighted with gas, and forming a public promenade for night use seven miles in length, looking at frequent intervals into the Park over a low parapet.

The inconvenience of going around the Park, when closed at night, was obviated by the construction of four sunken roads through it (so walled and arched over that the Park could not be entered from them) which are lighted with gas.

There are in the City numerous other public grounds openly planted and designed to be lighted for night use, and ten miles of "Boulevards," 150 feet in width, and now under construction.

There are two points upon which advice is sought.

1st.—Whether experience indicates that a ground of the extent and character thus described, in the central part of a city of a million of people will be found, when gas-lighted, to be a desirable place of popular resort at night, or whether the occurrence of accidents and offences against morality and decency is likely to be seriously larger within it than in the streets and other public places free from coverts of rock and low foliage?

2nd.—Whether experience indicates that the number of gas-lights which would be necessary to secure a satisfactory degree of convenience and safety in the public use at night of such a ground would be seriously harmful to its trees?

Any information on these points will be thankfully received.[1]

FRED. LAW OLMSTED,
*President of the Department of Public Parks
of the City of New York.*

"TO THOSE HAVING THE CARE OF YOUNG CHILDREN"

(A HANDBILL OF 1872—AN EARLY EXAMPLE OF PARK PUBLICITY)

Young children, when confined to the city during the summer, generally suffer in health, and are specially liable to fall into dangerous disorders of the bowels. When it is impracticable to make a visit of some length to the country with them, great advantage will be gained by spending the greater part of a day occasionally in the open air, and under conditions otherwise favorable to health. Arrangements have been made by which this can be done easily and cheaply by great numbers on the Central Park.

The attention of those interested is particularly invited to four points: The Dairy, the Ramble, the Great Hill, and Mt. St. Vin-

---

[1] ED. NOTE: A considerable number of replies, mainly from Germany, were received, giving various opinions. Central Park was allowed to be open at night in 1873 until nine o'clock in winter (except during the skating season when the time was extended to midnight) and eleven o'clock in summer. Cf. ordinances given p. 464, *post.*

cent, at each of which there are private accommodations for women and children (with the attendance of a woman), which may be used without charge. At the Dairy and the Great Hill there is turf on which young children are allowed to play, and shaded seats; fresh, pure and wholesome milk is furnished at 5 cts. a glass, and bowls of bread and milk for children at 10 cts.

A drive of five miles may be taken through the Park in one of the Park Carriages, which are to be found at the south entrances on Fifth Avenue and Eighth Avenue, for 25 cts. a seat; no charge for children in arms.

A sail of nearly a mile in length may be taken around the Lake for ten cents.

The Dairy is ten minutes' walk from the Sixth and Seventh Avenue entrances on the south. The Sixth and Seventh Avenue, the Broadway and the Belt lines of horse-cars take passengers from the lower part of the city directly to these entrances for five cents. Children not living near either of these lines may be taken to the Park by the Second, Third, Madison, Eighth or Ninth Avenue lines, changing to the Belt line at 59th Street. They will thus reach the Sixth Avenue entrance, which is nearest the Dairy, at the cost of ten cents.

The Eighth Avenue line takes passengers within five minutes walk of the house on the Great Hill, near which there are advantages for family pic-nics, for eight cents.

The Eighth Avenue may be reached from the eastern part of the city by the "Belt Line," the "Green Line." running through Fourteenth Street, and the Grand Street line.

It is advised that children should not remain in the Park after sunset.

Fred. Law Olmsted, <i>President,</i>
Department of Public Parks.

CONCESSIONS IN THE PARK

New York, 6th Oct., 1875.

To President:
  Dear Sir:

The Board having referred to me the communications of ——— Snow and ——— Lucas on the subjects respectively of pony and donkey service on the Central Park, proposing enlargements of the same and an addition of pony carriages and sleighs, I beg to report that it is unquestionable that both donkeys and ponies have afforded amusement and recreation to numbers of children and satisfaction to their parents.

There are, however, objections to all business of this class of which the more important may be classed as follows:

1st.—That they tend to create demands which it is impossible to meet without obstructing and interfering with other interests with reference to which the park has been more particularly designed, and proper accommodation for which on the park is an established right of the public.

For instance, the Mall is an appurtenance of the park expressly made to be used as a shaded promenade by visitors on foot. It is sometimes insufficient for the convenient accommodation of the numbers who enter it for this purpose. In consequence of its crowded condition at such times the police of the park represent that it is often impossible to enforce the ordinances of the Department, and the attempt to restrain visitors from striking off upon the turf is abandoned; the turf is ruined and the value of the Mall for its purpose and the beauty and usefulness of the park are thus greatly and permanently injured. The Department has licensed a man to run goat carriages on the Mall. At the periods when there is the largest demand for its use for its primary purpose, and it is found insufficiently large for this purpose, there is also the greatest demand for the use of the carriages. It may be assumed that each carriage with its driver in passing through a crowd puts out of the way directly and by the disturbance it creates twelve persons walking. This with the droppings of the goats, the groups of children with their parents and nurses and interested spectators standing at the two ends of the route, would, if the number of carriages was to be made equal to the demand for carriages at all times, most seriously diminish the value of the Mall as a promenade and tend to promote disorder and greatly injure the park.

The number of the carriages being limited as it is, it sometimes happens that children are kept waiting their turn for a ride for some time and in such cases their parents complain that the management is bad. Fortunately the management of the business is at this time exceptionally good, the licensee is not disposed to make more of it than is consistent with other uses of the park and takes every proper means to pacify instead of to stimulate and urge demands on the Commissioners for an increase of privileges.

The history of the Schultz and Warker contract for supplying mineral waters in the park is an illustration of what may occur where a licensee is otherwise disposed, numerous petitions, memorials and remonstrances having been at various times addressed to the Department urging that additional privileges tending to the enlargement and greater profit of this business should be granted and its refusal to meet these special demands having been made the occasion of unfair and unjust newspaper criticism.

I believe that there has never been a case in which a license has been held for a year that the holder of it has not solicited, and few cases if any where he has not obtained, privileges, concessions and advantages not at first asked for or designed to be given him.

Another objection to the introduction of such business in the park is that, as a matter of practice and experience, it is obviously very difficult to have it regulated and managed in a manner favorable to the interests of the public except so far as those interests consist precisely with the immediate direct and temporary private and personal pecuniary interests of each particular licensee.

The ordinary influence of competition to provoke and secure ingenuity, enterprise, taste, skill and energy in overcoming difficulties in the management of a business is lacking in all cases where a monopoly is by license of the Commission granted to any man for supplying a public requirement in the park and the only provision for counterpoising this disadvantage which the Commission possesses is that of the vigilance, activity, and determination of its officers and its own sustained resolution in enforcing to the last possible limit in spirit and letter the provisions of its contracts.

It is a matter of fact that the Commission has never been able to make its officers feel a responsibility of the slightest value in this respect. Even the formal conditions on which licenses are granted are seldom attempted to be enforced, when the contractor finds any unexpected difficulty in carrying them out.

Mr. Dick has had a license for exclusively providing boats for use on the lake for the last 16 years. On condition of enjoying a monopoly of the business he originally undertook as the result of a long debate, to meet a variety of distinct stipulations, designed for the better enjoyment of the park by the public, not only by those paying him a fee and using the boats, but for all those on shore as well as those afloat. On one ground or another the enforcement of the large part of these stipulations has been from year to year postponed and unenforced. And yet Mr. Dick is in personal character, in close attention to this business, in disposition, and ability to meet the obvious demands of the public in his special business, all that could be desired, and the most satisfactory man with whom the Commission has ever dealt.

The carriage business affords another illustration of the same tendency to let a man as soon as he has obtained a business foothold in the park, manage his business with reference to its special and immediate requirements and not with reference to the general and sustained interests of the public in the park as a whole.

There are stipulations in the contract with Clapp & Platt, which was entered into by them after a long consideration of these stipulations, as the most important and essential conditions of their treaty with the Department that they have never made the first motion toward carrying it into practice. If they had complied with them, one of the petitions now before the Board would never have been presented.

In smaller kinds of business like that of the ponies and donkeys and baby carriages and the Camera Obscura the difficulty of securing a constant close efficient and exacting superintendence of details on the part of officers of the Board, has been much greater than in such as make more display and get more public attention.

(A detailed consideration of specific cases followed. The letter is signed FRED. LAW OLMSTED.)

APPLICATIONS FOR APPROPRIATION OF PARK GROUND[1]

CITY OF NEW YORK,
DEPARTMENT OF PUBLIC PARKS,
OFFICE OF DESIGN AND SUPERINTENDENCE.

14th May, 1874.

TO THE HON. HENRY G. STEBBINS,
    President of the Board:

Sir:

The last two applications made to the Board, and referred to me to report upon, for the use of ground on the Central Park, are as follows: One for the practice of archery by a club of young ladies; another for instruction in natural science by telescopes and microscopes. A third has since been received, and is yet not acted upon, for use of ground for quoiting.

Each of these propositions is in effect a repetition of many which have preceded it in past years, and is in contravention of the established policy of the city in respect to the Park, which should be in no degree departed from without mature consideration, and the adoption of general rules applicable to all similar propositions. There have been three instances in which this policy appears to have been overruled, viz., in the photographic booth of Mr. Rockwood, in the camera obscura of Mr. Raphael, and in the custom of adults playing croquet on the East Green. Each of these inconsistencies is, in my judgment, unfortunate, yielding little advantage to the general public, adding to the difficulties of maintenance, and presenting a standing suggestion for innumerable encroachments on the Park. If every exhibition which had "a tendency to reveal the truths of natural science," and every form of recreation which had a "healthful and graceful character" were to be admitted on the Park, it is certain that in a few years but little would be left of the Park proper. The perplexity in which the Board is now placed in dealing with the question of the Zoological collection, is an illustration of the danger of a lax management in this respect.

The question of rules expedient to be adopted in regard to the use of the Central Park for plays and games was much considered for a period of nine years before the established policy was fixed, nor was it finally settled upon until after several of the Park Com-

[1] Doc. No. 58.

missioners had had an opportunity of observing the working of customs prevailing on several parks in Europe and some experience had been obtained at home. The first public declaration of the conclusions finally reached was made in the Tenth Annual Report, from which an extract is appended below.

It was decided that the city should undertake to provide ground, as far as practicable, for the playing of the school children of the city on the Central Park, and for school children only, and this conclusion has since been maintained.[1]

Out of the 860 acres included in the bounds of the Park, not more than sixty acres, or less than a fourteenth of all, consists of turf spaces of more than one acre in extent clear of rocks and trees. It is certain that these will soon be insufficient for the number of school children who will ask for play-room upon them, and indeed the spaces allotted to the boys in the south park are already found inadequate.

That the spaces of turf are not larger is no fault of the Commissioners responsible for the plan of the Park, as may be inferred

---

[1] Circular to Principals of Schools from OFFICE OF THE BOARD OF COMMISSIONERS OF THE CENTRAL PARK, 31 Nassau Street, New York, October 20, 1867.

The Commissioners of the Central Park, carrying out their intention with respect to out of door exercises on the Play Grounds of the Park, as heretofore communicated to the Board of Education, have, during the past three years, endeavored, by observation, to determine to what extent these exercises can be allowed without injury to the lawns, and without impairing their attractiveness in the landscape.

It is intended to confine the privilege of playing upon the grounds of the Park to children attending the Schools of the City; and it is the desire of the Commissioners of the Park to make this privilege, as far as is practicable, dependent upon regular attendance and good standing of the pupil in the School. To this end, the co-operation of School Officers and Teachers is desired, in order that the advantages of these arrangements may be extended to those only who will use it properly, and that the influence of the teacher may be made available to secure the proper behavior of their pupils while at the Park.

It will be readily seen that the large numbers that will desire the use of the grounds will render it essential for the preservation of order that the Regulations of the Park be strictly observed. These Regulations are simple, and intended to secure the convenience and gratification of all . . .

Applications for permission should be signed by those desiring to play, addressed to the Commissioners of the Central Park . . . accompanied by a certificate . . . signed by the Principal of the School at which they attend. . . . .

While these arrangements are specially designed for pupils of the Public Schools, those of private schools making similar applications and bringing a similar certificate from their principals, will be afforded equal advantages on the grounds.

The Commissioners of the Park desire that it be expressly understood that these arrangements are still experimental, and that they will be modified or suspended from time to time, or altogether discontinued, as experience may prove necessary for the proper appearance of the Park, or if they are found to conflict with its convenient enjoyment by the general public. ANDREW H. GREEN, *Comptroller of the Parks.* (Mr. Green was particularly interested in co-operation with the Schools, since he was President of the Board of Education when appointed a Commissioner of the Central Park. The plan of allowing school children to play on the Park was reported very successful in 1868, some twenty thousand children having enjoyed the privilege that year.)

from the fact that in the adopted design they were proposed to be much larger than in any one other of the thirty-two offered in competition with it, and that in actual construction, by generous expenditure for the purpose, more turf has been gained than was originally proposed.

As applications of the same class as those now under consideration are of increasing frequency, I respectfully suggest that the Board consider whether it may not be best to refuse permission for a continuance of the photographic establishment, the camera obscura and of croquet playing for adults, and the adoption of resolutions of the following character:

Resolved, That the Department will not give, set apart or rent any ground in the Central Park to be used by adults for any games or plays, and that children to whom permits are issued shall be allowed to use the grounds set apart for them only when this may be done, in the judgment of the Superintendent, without injury to the turf, and under suitable restrictions and police control.

Resolved, That the Board will not give permission for any exhibition, show or entertainment on the Central Park for the admission to which a fee, charge or gratuity of money is to be collected.

Resolved, That the President is requested to inform all applicants who may desire an appropriation of the ground in the Central Park for games for adults, or for exhibitions, of the rules adopted in the passage of the above resolutions.[1]

With respect to the application for the provision of ground for the exhibition of a telescope and microscopes on the small parks, the same objections do not apply as to that for the use of ground in the Central Park; but it is obvious that no such exhibition can be had on the walks of any of the small parks without causing an obstruction to passage, and if it is considered desirable that entertainments by which money is to be made should be had upon them, it would seem to be better that ground should be prepared expressly for the purpose, clear of all lines of thoroughfare, and that a rent, however trifling, should, in each case, be exacted for its use; otherwise the demands upon the Board for similar privileges will be unlimited in number, and the refusal of any will be regarded as an evidence of unjust favoritism toward those preferred.

Respectfully,

FRED. LAW OLMSTED,
Landscape Architect.

[Extract appended from the 10th Annual Report, pp. 34 to 40, 1886.]

On the whole, it may be said that up to this time the influence of the Park on the amusement of skating has been beneficial, for it has directly encouraged habits of active winter exercise in both

---

[1] ED. NOTE: The Board passed the resolutions, May 20, 1874.

old and young, and, indirectly, has stimulated invention and assisted in the development of a new branch of home manufacture. It has, moreover, by degrees, taught many of its former visitors to be almost entirely independent of it, and has induced them to undertake and carry to a successful issue, by private subscription, schemes that would otherwise never have been thought of as possible or desirable.

It is not to be inferred from the great success that has attended the skating-ponds, that similar general use of the playgrounds of the Park would be equally advantageous. It may seem but a very simple matter to throw open the grounds for use; but it is to be remembered that while ice is a substance which, when worn and cut out by the skaters, renews itself, and its surface can be refitted for use by inexpensive machinery, the tender verdure that constitutes the turf, when worn, is not readily restored to a condition that renders its appearance agreeable. Further than this, all the spaces of the Park that are available for playgrounds are limited in extent, and any use of them as playgrounds should be subordinate to the principal idea of the design, which is to provide an agreeable recreating ground for the whole community.

If a considerable number of people of the city were impressed with the importance of out-of-door exercise for themselves and their children to a degree that would lead them to provide the opportunities for it at their own cost and charges, the necessity for the park playgrounds would be largely diminished; but the taste for these out-of-door sports is but very limited, and it has been deemed proper so to regulate the use of this portion of the park as to stimulate and develop a taste for them.

With this object in view, opportunities for the use of the playgrounds have been extended to the school-boys of the city, who will be likely in after-life to keep up the habits they have formed at the Park, and become members of organizations whose accommodations are provided from their own means.

The use of playgrounds of the Park for exercise and the extent to which the lawns will admit of that use, has been the subject of further observations and attention.

In a communication heretofore made to the Board of Education of the city, suggestions were submitted by the Commissioners of the Park looking to such an extent of the use of the lawns as was admissible by the children of the public schools.

It was deemed impracticable to satisfy the requirements of the numerous cricket, ball, and other adult clubs within the area of the Park, and at the same time preserve in the grounds an appearance that would be satisfactory to the much more numerous class that frequent the Park for the enjoyment of the refined and attractive features of its natural beauties. While it is obvious that the practice of these clubs cannot be allowed in the Park without destroying some of its chief attractions, yet there is undoubtedly a degree to which play can be admitted.

The problem is to ascertain this limit and to establish such regulations as will control it.

It was thought that, by extending the privilege to boys attending the public schools, the Park might be well made a valuable ancillary to the educational system of the city. The number of children would be sufficient to occupy the grounds to the fullest extent practicable. No unfriendly allegation of favoritism to one class or another would have any foothold for mischief. The children that attend the schools are the children of the people; with the assistance of their teachers, the privilege of the Park play could readily be made an inducement to regular attendance at school and to diligence in study.

Giving effect experimentally to these views during the past season, facilities for play have been extended to considerable numbers of the boys of the schools. At a late period in the season a circular was addressed to the principals of the schools, stating the arrangements of the Commissioners of the Park in this regard.

At one part of the season, play was allowed on the playgrounds for two days in each week; at a later period, on three days in each week; and the increase of applications for play was such as to require the space known as the "green" for the same purpose. 7,520 lads have played on the grounds, and there is every reason to believe that all the facilities that can be extended at the Park for this class of exercise, will be required and fully used by the youth of the city.

The development of this idea will not be limited to boys. It is intended next season to set apart one or more grounds where the girls of the schools can play at croquet and other games under regulations adapted to their amusement and protection.

The Commissioners of the Park do not know of any instance of a satisfactory appearance being maintained in a public park where the play of games is generally allowed on the grass.

Unsatisfactory results are certain to follow such play on the Central Park; and in the effort to pursue a medium course where so many interests are concerned, they will be careful to provide and maintain such thorough regulations as shall ensure that the enjoyments in which the public now participate shall not be diminished.

Convenient arrangements specially adapted to the amusement of a still younger class of children . . . who are not yet quite equal to the sturdy conflicts of the active games that interest the older boys have appeared to be desirable.

With the view of satisfying this apparent need, the Commissioners have made on the lower Park somewhat extensive arrangement for their accommodation, and designed to afford them opportunities for amusements suited to their age. A structure (*see No. 23 on Folded Map*), of adequate dimensions of a rustic character, is in process of erection at an accessible point. It will be partially closely roofed as a protection from sun and rain, and partially of an open framework to be covered with foliage. A smooth floor of 110 feet in diameter is contemplated, with benches, blocks, and other small facilities for children's amusement.

This arbor-like structure is subdivided into compartments and corridors of divers shapes and dimensions by wide rustic seats or lounges, introduced between the uprights, in each of which tables are placed for the use of the children; the general aim being to provide for a number of groups, each of which can have the advantage of the accommodation without interference with the other.

Around the outside of the structure is an open verandah, unoccupied by seats or tables, affording a running stretch of several hundred feet. In the immediate vicinity is the dairy, from which will be dispensed milk and other light and simple refreshments. A small, secluded green sward is provided, upon which children can tumble about when sunshine favors.

This feature, which has been for some time in contemplation, is now being carried out on a tract of ground east of the playground, and south of the Mall. The situation has been chosen, after careful deliberation, because it is comparatively isolated, and interferes with no other part of the design; it is not remote from the southerly boundary of the Park, and is easily approached by the protected system of footwalks from the Fifth, Sixth, Seventh and Eighth avenue entrances at Fifty-ninth street.

No difficulty or danger will attend the passing to and from of the children and their attendants, even when the Park roads are crowded with vehicles.

The Park, as a whole, is undoubtedly expected to afford to the citizens of the metropolis, day after day, and year after year, a succession of views of rural character so real and genuine as to convey very positive ideas in regard to natural scenery, even to a person who might never see anything more country-like than will ultimately be contained within its limits; and this, in connection with the opportunity it offers for a social enjoyment of fresh air and exercise, is perhaps the most important service that it is calculated to perform in a direct way. Hill and dale, wood and water, grass and green leaves, are the natural food and refreshment of the human eye—an organ of sense so delicately adjusted as to require something more than dull colors and uninteresting forms, and is but little ministered to, in a pleasant way, in the portion of the city devoted to plain, straightforward business, or even domestic routine.

Indirectly, however, the influence of the Central Park as an educator of the popular taste, in regard to natural scenes, works in the same way as it has been shown to do in reference to the more easily defined amusement of skating, and as it may doubtless be made to do in other matters, such as music, playgrounds, zoological gardens, museums, &c.

DIFFICULTIES OF PRESERVING GREEN TURF

15th May, 1874.

HON. H. G. STEBBINS,
President, Dept. of Public Parks,

Sir:

Experience shows that if the present customs are maintained with the increased number of visitors using the Central Park, it will soon be impossible to keep the turf in tolerable condition, and as the beauty of the Park depends more upon success in this respect than any other [1] and the difficulty of changing customs increases the longer they are perpetuated and the larger the number of people to whom they are familiar, it is respectfully suggested that additional restrictions on the use of the turf should now be ordered.

With a view to a practical consideration of the question the following propositions are respectfully submitted, in the hope that they may be referred to a committee and that the superintendent may be consulted in regard to them.

First that the East Green should no longer be used as a croquet ground but that croquet playing should be allowed on the Ball Ground at places where the turf is not worn, to be alloted to parties for the day, by the superintendent, or the man in charge of the ground under him, on days when the ground is not to be used by the school boys.

Second, that the only grounds hereafter to be used as "Common" in the lower park, shall be the Ball Ground and the Green; the turf on the middle ground and the East Green being reserved. If this is deemed too great a restriction for the present, I strongly

---

[1] ED. NOTE: In the 7th Report of the Central Park Commissioners for 1863, we read:

"The landscape is arranged to please the eye; it presents a picture more exquisitely pleasing to the mind through the sense of vision, than the most distinguished work of any master. Is the lawn the less beautiful because it cannot, without destruction, be made a footpath, a drill-ground, or a place for ball play?

"A much larger number of persons derive gratification from the appearance of the lawn well preserved, than could be by the practice of any special amusement that would destroy it. Who would think of condemning a bed of violets with its pervading fragrance, because he cannot walk upon it? The blades of grass that united, make up the lawn, can be enjoyed without pressing them under foot.

"It is not to be denied that there is a pleasure found in walking on a lawn; the change from the rigid pavement to the slightly yielding turf is agreeable, especially to residents of a city it is a sensation not often attainable sometimes prohibited, and therefore more sought for and desired.

"In the wide reaches of grass in the country, where but few people are assembled, this pleasure may be indulged, but it is one of many gratifications that can only be most widely enjoyed in rural neighborhoods; its practice by multitudes in cities within limited spaces, will soon destroy the lawn, and ruin its otherwise perennial power to gratify the sight." Cf. the notice to the public of Liverpool given in footnote on p. 6, *ante.*

recommend that the middle ground or turf of the Mall be not made Common on concert days, but only on Sundays, as more than 25,000 persons now walk from end to end of the Mall at least twice on every afternoon of a well attended concert, and the turf has to sustain the mar of at least 30,000 pairs of feet. It is impossible that it should be kept in good order, even at much greater expense than is now put upon it, while subject to such usage, and yet there is no place in the park where the maintenance of perfect neatness is as important as it is on the Mall. The much enlarged gravelled space about the music pavilion and the new fixed seats, which will be first open to use this summer, offer a better opportunity than is likely to occur again for accomplishing this necessary change.

If it is to be done, much care should at first be taken to secure to visitors a knowledge of the new rule, and to aid the police in enforcing it, by sign boards and special temporary barricades.

I also recommend a reissue of the hand bill [1] used some years ago for the instruction of the public in regard to the privilege of using the turf with, if the above suggestions are adopted, such modifications as may now be desirable.

REPORT ON TURF

18th May, 1875.

Hon. H. G. S.,
   President,

Dear Sir:

The attention of the Board has frequently been called to the manner in which the turf of the Central Park is abused and to the need of more effective measures for preserving it, especially to the necessity of employing a large number of men with the duty of cautioning visitors against breaking the rules for its proper keeping. Two years ago the Board adopted a plan under which a great improvement was gained but from a necessity of reducing expenditure for maintenance, it was soon discontinued, and during last summer the misuse of the turf continued and was, as I reported in September, greater than ever before. It followed that during the dry weather fully a quarter of all the turf of the larger open spaces of the South Park was trodden out and eradicated; the soil having no protection was pulverized by those walking on it and blew away in dust. I earnestly beg that the Commissioners will now personally examine these grounds and observe the result. [2] The surface is very uneven owing to the depressions formed as above described and what should be and once was a smooth even fabric of fine close

---

[1] ED. NOTE: A copy of this has not been found.   [2] Cf. p. 432, also p. 105.

turf is a patch work consisting of three parts of poor and tufty grass with one of brown bare earth. The bare parts will probably now soon green over with weeds and annual grasses, which will alternately wither and brown and spring up and become temporarily verdant according as the weather shall be hot and dry or cool and moist. These annuals having feebler roots and being in all respects less tough and fibrous than the proper turf grasses will wear out under foot more rapidly and the process above described will, if it is allowed to continue during the present summer, extend further. The result will be that although in the early summer the park will still appear green and promising, at that period when it is most resorted to by the mass of the people of the city and it is most important that its appearance should be cheerful and refreshing, it will lack the element most essential to its beauty and without which it can have but little rural charm. To repair this loss in the most direct, rapid and effective way, the ground should be broken up, finely tilled and re-seeded. A fine fresh turf might thus be had next year, but the small fund at the command of the department must for the present prevent any such thorough operation; the next best thing is to level up the worst depressions by the addition of fine soil, and to rake in the seed of good perennial grasses on all the bare and thinner parts.

It would be of no avail to do this if the ordinary use of the turf shall be allowed this year as the tender young grass would be at once trodden to death.

If such use is discontinued,—if the public can be kept off and the turf be allowed a few months respite from wear,—it may recover a tolerable condition. If such use cannot be discontinued it is certain to present a dreary and stultifying appearance, and to bring dis-credit to the government of the city by mid-summer of the centennial year.[1]

That the difficulty may be better understood, I will repeat and state more fully in what way the turf is abused. First, however, it may be necessary to observe that the greater heat and drought of this climate is most unfavorable to the maintenance of good turf as compared with that of Great Britain, and the north of Europe, during a certain period, usually in August. The grasses here lose their ordinary elasticity both in blade and root, their vitality is low and under pressure and friction may be completely exhausted. The dryness of the soil at this period is in the Central

---

[1] ED. NOTE: In May, 1876, the question of the use of turf being acute, Mr. Olmsted wrote to the President of the Board:

"Sir, There has been much difference of opinion as to the proper use and management of the turf of the public parks and that of the Central Park particularly is now in such condition that a review of the subject would be opportune. I submit the suggestion to your consideration whether it would not be advisable to seek counsel upon it from some persons who have not been in the employment of the Department and who have a standing with the community as authorities on the botanical and horticultural questions involved?"

Park greater than elsewhere because of the fact that it has nearly everywhere a shallow made soil laid upon a solid flooring of rock. Almost anywhere for example on the green and between the elm trees of the mall, when the ground is saturated with moisture a walking stick may be thrust down to the rock. When these grounds were prepared it was intended to provide a system of watering by the method in use in the Bois de Boulogne, but the plan which I laid before the Board for this purpose was rejected, partly to avoid the expense of the piping and partly because it was thought that at the season when alone it would be necessary the city could not spare the water for the purpose. Even with watering, however, no such use as the public has here demanded and the Department allowed is made of the turf in the Bois de Boulogne.

The misuse of the turf which has resulted in its present condition as above described has been of three kinds: first, in the days when the public school boys are allowed to play on the ball-ground and the green, hundreds of others, many of them beyond the school age have mingled with them. Norman Manning says there often are as many as 50 and sometimes as many as 200 full grown men who have been on the green at once, most of them rude fellows, who by main force take possession of considerable parts of it, practically excluding the boys and depriving them of their legal rights. On any fair day the number of men and boys has commonly been much larger than should have been allowed.

2nd.—On days when it has not been legally permissible to walk on the turf it has been much trespassed upon. It is so now. While examining the turf of the ballground this morning—there being but few visitors yet in the park—I saw in ten minutes 15 persons crossing parts of it illegally, without caution, protest or reprimand. Two of them were lying down in a conspicuous position during all of the time. I am informed that last Saturday a party of boys were for some time playing ball there and I myself checked a party going on with bats, evidently with the intention of playing.

3rd.—Many walk across the turf, especially near the edges of the walks without reflection that they are doing it an injury or transgressing any rule. This chiefly occurs when the walks are crowded and knots and clusters of people stand so as to force others wishing to move rapidly to step off.

As soon as the turf is thus trodden smooth at any point, especially if a distinct foot path is formed, every visitor seeing it reasonably assumes that when so many have been allowed to go before him he is free to follow. In a hot day especially, the turf, or the bare ground where the turf has been, is more agreeable than any prepared walk can be, consequently once partially formed the wear upon these foot ways is very rapid.

Experience shows that greater standing, sitting and passing room is required at some points and I should recommend measures for this purpose, if I did not know that the department was so stinted in its means that it would be useless. But such measures would help but little.

There are two ways in which the abuses which have been described may be guarded against. First, by fencing in the walks of the parks. To a certain extent this is done already and the foremen responsible for the condition of the turf, shrubs and plants, knowing that it is the only effective means which they are at liberty to use are inclined to resort to it much more. It is a means which destroys the charm of the park as the pleasure ground of the people and which proclaims that it is impossible to secure a proper regard for regulations absolutely essential to its preservation except by physical force,—a proposition which the earlier experience of the park demonstrated, in my judgment, to be fallacious and unjust.

The other means of guarding against these abuses is that of properly distributing a sufficient number of men, who, incidentally to other occupations, shall have the duty of cautioning visitors against disobeying the laws, of interrupting and remonstrating with those engaged in doing so, and in case of need of causing their arrest.

It is utterly futile to expect the park police as at present organized to accomplish the purpose. The Board has sought in vain to obtain means for enlarging its number and has been compelled on the contrary to reduce it. It is insufficient for the proper regulation of the use of the roads alone.

Runaways and collisions owing chiefly to disregard of the rules are of almost daily occurrence, and by each one of them the lives of innocent and orderly visitors are put in peril. Five persons were thrown out or knocked down last week, and one lady dangerously injured. A runaway horse has been able to pass at full speed for a distance of more than two miles through the park and out of one of its most frequented gates without arrest. As for the interior walks I have frequently been for hours upon them without seeing a single man having a sign of authority to caution or warn visitors or to help them on their proper ways. It is so evidently absurd to interfere with a single visitor in doing what hundreds of others may be doing, that the regulations for preserving the turf and tender plants are practically regarded by the keepers themselves as a dead letter.

I will add that it is also practically impossible for the foremen to repair damages as fast as they occur and to keep the park in as good order as has been usual, with the present force employed. Notwithstanding an unusual degree of activity and industry, there is not a single class of all the work of the department that is not now behind hand, or a single division of the park that is adequately manned. The roads are not sufficiently watered and their more rapid wear in consequence will cost more than the wages of the additional force required for watering them.

There is but one working gardener rated and paid as such for

each 100 acres of the park, and for the care on an average of more
than 50,000 trees and shrubs, to say nothing of the herbaceous
plants.   The gardeners report from every division of the park the
stealing of plants; the withdrawal of the gate keepers from two
gates as a measure of necessary reduction of force is at once followed
by an invasion of goats, some of them driven in by their owners
to browse on the shrubs and girdle the young trees.   They may
easily damage the park in a single hour to an amount ten times
their value to their owners, and much more than the wages of the
watchmen who would be required to guard against them.

I mention these facts that the Commissioners may be the better
prepared for the inevitable consequences of the present policy of
the city in reference to the park.   It is absolutely necessary that
the force should be still further reduced in order to keep the expenses of the department within the limit fixed by the Board of
Apportionment, or that this limit should be practically unchanged
by a reduction of wages.

With respect to the turf, I must advise the Board that the ball-
ground and the mall cannot be put in a condition to be used this
summer as heretofore, without causing such injury to them as will
destroy their value [1] and as cannot be properly repaired except by
breaking up and reforming them another year.

I believe that it would cause the least privation to the public
and the least dissatisfaction to suspend ball playing and croquet
playing and the usual Saturday and Sunday free range over all the
turf of the South Park during the present year.   The North
Meadows might be prepared for the use of the school boys while
the ballground is recruiting.

Respectfully,

[F. L. O.]

[1] ED. NOTE: We find in a Memorandum as to Observation of the Turf by
Commissioners, May, 1875:
The President reported that since the last meeting a majority of the Commissioners had visited the Central Park and examined the condition of the turf
as then requested by the Landscape Architect, and proposed that the following
statement of their observations be entered on the minutes:
"It is found that on a large part of the ball ground, the East Green where it
has been used as a croquet ground, the ground adjoining the Mall where walking
has been allowed on Saturdays and Sundays, and on all other grounds subject
to foot wear, the turf of the park is now in large parts dead while in other parts
the fine and suitable grasses have been superseded by undesirable annuals and
coarse grasses; that in other places, where the turf has been protected from foot
wear, it is still in fair condition.   That these and other circumstances demonstrate that the use of the turf hitherto permitted has been excessive and that
greater restrictions need to be placed upon it than have hitherto been thought
necessary."

DAMAGE TO PARK BY CROWDS[1]

NEW YORK, 16th May, 1877.

THE HON. WILLIAM R. MARTIN,[1]
President of the Department of Public Parks,

Sir:

On the 9th inst. the Board was informed that the statue of Halleck (*see No. 33 on Folded Map*) was intended to be unveiled on the 15th, and that plans had been formed for the occasion for the carrying out of which its sanction and aid were needed.

It was ascertained that the committee having the matter in charge had already made an engagement with the President of the United States, and numerous distinguished persons, to take part in the proceedings, and also to associate with them a military display under the form of an act of courtesy to the President. A thousand invitations had been printed and mainly sent out, each promising a secured seat for two persons; sixty special guests of the committee were also to be provided for upon the platform or in reserved seats adjoining it.

These arrangements had been so far advanced that, on the whole, it seemed best to take the risks of carrying them through than to attempt to have them changed. [A detailed account of arrangements for handling the crowd and of the way things worked on this particular occasion follows, from which only a few excerpts are here given.]

. . . The force available for preserving order consisted of a captain and fifty men of the 7th Regiment, and the lieutenant of the park keepers, three sergeants and sixty-nine uniformed privates.

. . . From the enclosure of the seats near the platform southward to the end of the Mall there was a mass so dense that one of the park keepers who undertook to carry a prisoner through it, states that for a distance of fully 250 feet no one could move in it except by pressing others back. Many women begged to be assisted in getting out. A great many people, mostly women and children, when they came near enough to see the standing crowd, turned aside or back and made their way through the vines, shrubs and evergreens, seeking either a place where they could sit in the shade or where the passing crowd could be overlooked. . . . Boys climbed into the trees, and girls, to pass away the time, made garlands of flowers and leaves, which they picked as if in the wild woods.

. . . The gate keepers report that at times the people came in like a mob, in such numbers that the attempt to count or estimate them was abandoned. The general report is that never before

[1] Minutes, D. P. P., May 16, 1877.

had half so many been seen passing in. The influx continued till the end of the ceremonies, when the current was suddenly reversed.

.   .   .   .

As the President appeared on the platform there was a general movement toward it, with loud and continuous cheering and clamor, in the midst of which several of the iron frames of the settees gave way, and a number of persons leapt or were pitched into the but half-filled enclosure. The reserved seats were instantly occupied, and there was for a few moments considerable crowding and confusion within the enclosure, but no violent rush, and fortunately not the least panic. The band played the opening piece of music, the assembly became quiet, and the exercises went on in regular order.

At their close the President and his party returned without difficulty to their carriages, and the military column formed and moved out of the park, followed closely by the greater part of those present.

To these minutes we shall add some general observations.

The day was fair, the temperature warm for the season, but not oppressive, and the park in the richest possible condition of foliage and bloom. The so-called "Carnival" procession in the forenoon had been extensively advertised, and had brought in a great many people from the country who had made it a part of the plan of their holiday to visit the park. A considerable proportion of the men present had their wives and children with them, and throughout all of the crowd there were many women. The proportion of decided roughs was nowhere large, and that of quiet, civil and well-disposed people nowhere small. The spirit of the crowd as a body was patient, good-natured and accommodating. With a very few individual exceptions, there was not only a willingness but an evident goodwill and effort to meet the requirements of the authorities, and to maintain such a degree of order and decorum as was appropriate under the circumstances. We did not hear a harsh word, nor witness any violence. We did not see a drunken man, and not a personal injury to any one has been reported.

In view of all these facts it is gravely significant, and we trust that the lesson will not be overlooked, that as with respect to all the special regulations which are necessary for the development of the park as a place of rural recreation, *the crowd was essentially a mob, lawless and uncontrollable.* Had the whole police force of the city been on the ground, it could have done little toward protecting the property which it is the essence of the department's special trust to preserve. Judging from all experience, it would have made no attempt to do so. The keepers of the park, who are supposed to be trained especially for this duty, looked upon the most flagrant offences against the ordinances of the department in thousands of instances under an impression apparently that they were for the time being suspended.

An hour after the military had left the ground we saw keepers repeatedly pass by a group, mainly of children, who in their play were trampling upon and about a piece of rockwork, the crevices of which were filled with delicate plants in bloom and the edges fringed with ferns and mosses. The life of these was stamped out, and in places the ground was left beaten hard, and without a tinge of green remaining.

We saw women and girls breaking off branches of lilacs loaded with bloom, and others carrying aloft bundles of similar branches, passing out of the park by way of the police station, perfectly oblivious of the fact that it subjected them to arrest and punishment. We asked two men openly breaking the law, if they knew that they were doing so; both answered smilingly that the law just then was not of much account.

Long after the President and the military had disappeared, people, especially children, continued to rove off the walks, quietly breaking down and trampling over shrubs and vines, and seemed surprised when remonstrated with.

The turf in the park was in the best condition for hard wear, growing rapidly, and the ground neither moist nor dry. The trees and shrubs were also sappy and pliant, and bent to force as they would not at any other season. The crowd centered at the point where it could least do harm, the surface of the ground being level, covered for a large space with turf and gravel, and bearing no shrubs or low branched trees.

For all these reasons the damage done was comparatively slight, and every pains being taken to repair it as rapidly as possible, under favorable conditions of weather, it is now hardly to be noticed. The turf was soaked with water, and except where the crowd was densest, warm moist weather following, will generally recover. There are hundreds of spots from one to two, or three, feet across, however, where it has been tramped out completely, and the soil ground to dust. These will not, probably, again green over this year unless it be with coarse annual grasses and weeds.

Forty of the settees were smashed, the iron frames of six being broken. The statues between that of Halleck and the south end of the Mall were loaded with men and boys when the President passed, but suffered no harm. Had there been any delicately cut stone work in the vicinity like that at the Terrace it would have been ruined. No limbs, but hundreds of small branchlets, were broken from the trees.

The city has expended, within the area of the park, nearly ten millions of dollars, and, if it is closely considered for what purpose, in the last analysis it will be found to be to produce certain influences on the imagination of those who visit it, influences which are received and which act, for the most part, unconsciously to those who benefit by them. These influences come exclusively from the natural objects of the park as they fall in passing them into relations and sequences adapted to the end in view. The value of the park is greater or less according to the success with which arrangements for this purpose have been made. If the value of the natural elements is lessened, the value of the artificial, as the roads, bridges and arches, lessens correspondingly. With the increase in beauty and influence on the imagination of the one increases the value of the city's property—the amount of the city's income—in the other. A much higher degree of beauty and poetic influence would be possible but for the necessity of taking so much space for that which in itself is not only prosaic but often dreary and incongruous, that is to say the necessary standing and moving room for the visitors.

The area thus appropriated in the park is considerably more than a hundred acres, and much study has been given to the object of distributing it in fair proportion to the requirements of the public in different parts, and of keeping it as inconspicuous as practicable. Its extent can nowhere be enlarged, nor can the public be allowed to occupy unprepared ground without destruction and waste of what has been laid out for the main object in the natural elements.

Whenever, therefore, the park is used for any other than its primary purpose, and especially for spectacles entirely foreign to it, like that of a military display, which tend to concentrate visitors, the regulations designed with reference to that purpose are necessarily, in a greater or less degree, out of place, and are overruled; its custodians, as well as its visitors, become accustomed to regard them without respect, customs suitable to paved streets or commons override them, and the result, directly and indirectly, is incalculably wasteful of the public property.

Respectfully,

FREDERICK LAW OLMSTED,
Landscape Architect.

JULIUS MUNCKWITZ,
Superintendent D. P. P.

CHAPTER VIII

THE PARK KEEPERS' FORCE: MANAGING THE PUBLIC

The general conception held by Mr. Olmsted of the close relation between park management and park design (as set forth in Part I, Chapters VI and VIII, see pages 78 and 99) was based not only on his experiments in the Central Park but also on his early study of police systems in Europe. The same principles which we find elaborated in his Instructions to Keepers, 1873, appeared in the poster of March 12, 1859, entitled: Rules and Conditions of Service of the Central Park Keepers. Mr. Olmsted considered that the management of the keepers' service at that period (1859) was reasonably successful. In 1872, after the upheaval caused by the Tweed Ring, Mr. Olmsted reported that the unsatisfactory conditions were largely due to politics, and the reorganization which he proposed was in reality only a readjustment of his original scheme to the growth of park attendance, with more energetic measures to ensure the vigilance of the keepers' force. The misuse of the park in the seventies which these documents decry foreshadows the deplorable conditions of today. If those responsible for park administration can fully enter into the reasons underlying the requirements for a keepers' service, as Mr. Olmsted sets these forth, they will possess the key to the most effective utilization of parks as instruments of human service.

THE PAPERS INCLUDED IN THIS CHAPTER[1] ARE:

‡ *Letter as to policing of Park, to Board from F. L. O.   1860. Requesting increase of number of keepers.*

Report relative to the Police Force of the Department, by F. L. O. October 24, 1872.   (Doc. No. 41.)—Suggestions for improving policing.

Instructions to the Keepers of the Central Park.   1873.   (Prepared by F. L. O.)

Report on the Changes recently made in the Management of the Keepers' Force, by F. L. O.   July 17, 1873.   (Doc. No. 47.)

---

[1] See also F. L. O. letter to Mr. Stebbins, July 30, 1873, given in Part II, Chapter III, p. 318.
‡ Previously unpublished.

POLICING OF THE PARK

To the Board of Commissioners of the Central Park.

Gentlemen:

The robbery of a child upon the park has been reported and complaint is made of the inadequacy of the police force. Names and obscene words are frequently found of late cut or marked on the structures of the park and the offenders are seldom detected. At the same time the keepers consider themselves overtasked and there is no doubt that the service required of them is more fatiguing than that of the Metropolitan police force whose pay is considerably greater than theirs. There is no ground of complaint, however, against the keepers individually; as a rule they perform their duty zealously. The system of inspection is such that habitual carelessness, neglect or inactivity cannot occur without detection and consequent dismissal. I think this is now well understood in the force.

It remains for the Board to judge whether the force is directed advantageously or whether it is inadequate in number for its purpose.

The number of persons visiting the park is many times greater in the afternoon and especially in the latter part of the afternoon than in the morning: many times greater on Saturday than on other working days, and double on Sunday what it is on Saturday. The proportion of careless and evil disposed persons is greater when a larger number of persons are on the park than when the visitors are few. For this reason the number of keepers kept on active duty in the morning is very small in order that the largest possible force may be thrown out in the afternoon and evening. During six hours in the forenoon two men patrol the lower park; during six hours in the afternoon twenty-two. A reserve for special duty of those not on patrol is constantly at the station house. The remaining ten men of the force are on the park during twelve hours of the night, the whole being in active duty most of the time, but each man getting from two to four hours rest between 12 and 4 o'clock. On rainy days the period of out-of-door duty of those coming on duty in the afternoon is lessened. During the skating season the whole system is necessarily changed. When the ice was most frequented, a large proportion of the men were last year required to be on their feet from twelve to eighteen hours a day.

On Sunday men selected from the foremen of the working force are employed as a reinforcement of the regular police.

Some deductions from the force above indicated always occur on account of absences. Leave of absence with pay is never given; leave of absence without pay seldom except on account of illness or death in the family of the applicant. Absence without leave is a matter of discipline. Absence on account of illness, or injury even when the injury has been incurred on duty involves loss of pay. Nevertheless from two to seven men daily fail to appear at roll-call. In fine summer weather the average number absent is two; in the autumn, five; in winter somewhat more. The usual causes of absence are foot soreness and intermittent fever. The real force employed is thus more than seven per cent. below that authorized by the board and this appears by the pay rolls.

In the morning, there is but one patrolman for fifty acres of the lower park or one to a mile and a half of the completed walks and drives. During the afternoon, one to 30 acres of the completed ground, exclusive of the Ramble; one to 8 acres in the Ramble, or one to each three-fourths of a mile of the drives and walks in use. The upper part of the park is not patrolled, but is incidentally inspected at frequent intervals by keepers and especially by the officers when returning from duty below, or by special details drawn from the reserve at the station when the active duty is not severe. The disproportionate force distributed during certain hours of the afternoon is required by the distraction and interruption to systematic watchfulness of each patrolman, occasioned by the constant enquiries made and the cautions and directions needed by those who visit the park at that time. It would be very unfortunate if the great body of visitors should notice the rarity with which the guardians of order, decency and personal safety were seen and the impression should thus be gained that a very inadequate police was maintained on the park. It is my constant endeavor by all means in my power to secure a contrary reputation for the park.

The wanton defacement of the various structures to which I have referred occurs chiefly I believe on Sundays and holidays and can only be prevented by the almost constant attendance of a man at each point on those days. Owing to the leaning and handling of dirty and sweaty persons, tobacco-spitting, the deposit of broken fruit and waste of all sorts of eatables, and other filthy practices voluntary or otherwise, the summer houses, seats, balustrades, balconies of the bridges are frequently forbidding to cleanly persons, who are thus deprived of what they deem their rights upon the park. These structures should be cleaned thoroughly every morning, and should be visited for the same purpose once or twice during the day. Water closets and urinals and the walks leading to them, of which there will soon be several established in the park, will especially need a service which could not be altogether well performed by the regular keepers consistently with their other duty. Nor can this class of duties be well and consistently attended to by the officers of the working force. They are properly included in the public duties of the park.

Besides the park keepers, there are at present 12 gate keepers. A petition of the gate keepers recently handed me accompanies this communication. It was composed by one of their number, and the simple statement of facts which it presents is worthy of the attention of the Board. The duties of the gate keepers at first very easy are not important and demand, especially at certain gates, but little less exercise of good judgment than those of the park keepers. The gate keepers are at present required to be at their posts from 11 to 12 hours together every day, including Sundays. This is more than it is right under ordinary circumstances to demand of any man. The entrances to the park should however be watched during all the time the public are allowed or expected to visit it, which according to a vote of the Commission will hereafter be from 15 to 18 hours a day. The ordinances of the Commission cannot be enforced unless the gates are attended by two sets of men, one relieving the other. That men at all fit for the duty required of the gate keepers can be hired at 90 cents a day can only be accounted for on the ground that in this city there are always those so driven by extremity of destitution, that after long experience of disappointment they are willing to undertake any duty offered them at any rate of compensation. I feel obliged at present to make the demand upon the gate keepers as light as the necessities of the park will admit of. It would obviously be better if the duty of the gate keepers could be performed by the regular park keepers. I am unwilling however to ask from the Commission so large an increase of the police expenditure as this would require. But the gate keepers should at least be brought under stricter discipline, their standard of deportment and manners advanced, they should be uniformed and their pay should be enough to enable them to live, if not comfortably at least as well as common laborers.

I suggest that the Board authorize the number of gate keepers to be increased to double the number of gates needed for the convenience of the public, their pay to be at the rate of 15 cents an hour, or $1.50 per day of ten hours, out of which one dollar a week may be withheld for the necessary expenses of uniforming them. If then, the ordinary period of duty should be ten hours a day, and the gates should require attendance fifteen hours a day, there would be a squad of twelve men, who could be daily employed for five hours in cleaning and caring for the various structures, seats and other movables of the park, cleaning the shores of the pond from drifting dirt, the care of the fowls and the removal of rubbish dropped by visitors. There are daily other duties for which such a squad is needed, which cannot be enumerated, but which arise from various accidents and which would come more properly and economically under the police management of the park, than of the superintendence of the regular work of construction or repair. The temporary guardianship of the summer houses, bridges, etc., required on Sundays and other special occasions would also be provided for by this organization.

In December last, during my absence in Europe, and without suggestion from me, the Committee on Salaries and Offices recommended that the number of park keepers should be increased to fifty; the recommendation was not at that time acted upon by the Board. As a second pond will need to be guarded during the skating season of the coming winter, in view of the excessively severe duty demanded of the keepers last winter, I am constrained with much reluctance to increase the expenditure of this department, [and] recall the attention of the Board to that recommendation.

I am of opinion that the use of two horses would add much to the efficiency of the police, if used for patrol duty on the drives during promenade hours. It is impossible for footmen to overtake horses driven fast or running away, and it is often impossible to stop them if seen from before, when a horseman riding the same way, can with a certain hold put himself alongside them and catch their bridle. Many fast drivers escape the keepers at present, greatly to their mortification, and the injury of their prestige. But if the Board are unwilling to put these views on trial I earnestly recommend that one horse and equipments be placed at my disposal for police use. The field inspection of the police, if made three times in the twenty-four hours as I think it should by the Inspector, involves a walk of at least eighteen miles. This cannot be accomplished thoroughly, with regularity in all matters, and it frequently happens that the captain from footsoreness is rendered quite unfit for his duty and is not able to make a single round in the day unless he can obtain the use of a horse. The duty of the sergeants is often equally severe. An inspection on horseback, from the greater distance at which the keepers may be seen and the rapidity with which they may be approached, is much more effective than a foot inspection. If two horses are supplied for the force, I should employ one of them for a night and one for a forenoon inspection, and both for patrol duty in the afternoon.

I have the honor to report to the Board that I am mainly recovered from the illness resulting from a fractured thigh and that I have this week had the pleasure of personally inspecting nearly all the work going on upon the park. The important work of the season, the deciduous planting, I shall be able, I trust, to personally superintend, the maps and plans therefor as far as yet complete having been prepared or revised by me during my confinement.

Respectfully,

FRED. LAW OLMSTED.

[1860]

REPORT ON POLICE FORCE[1]

The Central Park is planned upon a motive which, in the very freedom it offers the visitor, assumes the exercise on his part of a degree of circumspection and restraint to avoid the abuse of its advantages, such as would have been unnecessary had they been more commonplace.

The difficulty of adequately instructing and reminding the visitor of its exactions in this respect was, from the outset of the work, known to be the most vulnerable point in the undertaking. The means adopted for the purpose were, however, for a series of years, so far effective as to give increasing assurance of the practicability of success, the only apparent danger ahead being that, through political corruption, unskillful administration or improvident parsimony, the force of park-keepers should become insufficient for its required duty, either in numbers or in training and discipline.

The public seemed not only to submit to the enforcement of the necessary regulations, but to welcome the means used for that purpose, and pride was taken in the belief that the park was to present an exceptionally creditable exhibition of orderliness and decorum, as well as of finish and good keeping.

A lawless habit was rare among visitors, and it was apparent that even men of reckless disposition and unaccustomed to polite restraints upon selfishness were under influences when in the park which dissuaded them from a misuse of its privileges.

The admonitions of the keepers were generally received in good spirit and willingly heeded, and when this was not the case by-standers were often prompt to reprove the offender and applaud the representative of the law.

It was to be expected, as the city should in effect be brought nearer, year by year, to the park, and it thus came to be more easily, familiarly and numerously visited, that the means used for instructing and reminding visitors of their duty would be found less effective, and would require enlargement, if not modification of character.

The average attendance at the park having already reached thirty thousand a day, and apparently increasing at a more rapid rate than ever before, it is wise, at this time, to inquire how far the requirements of the plan as to the conduct of the public in its use, continue to be met.

After careful study of the matter during the last year, it is found that a change has occurred greatly for the worse.

The park is much misused, and this not merely by men of lawless ways, but even more by people whose appearance indicates orderly habits and a disposition to regard the common interests of the community.

Regulations which for the general convenience are most nec-

[1] Selections from Doc. No. 41, Oct. 24, 1872.

essary to be observed, are often obeyed in a way which conveys a protest and reproof to the policemen enforcing them; more often, openly disregarded.

Even the children playing on the skating-pond and ball-ground are latterly manifestly much more rude in their ways than they were a few years ago—more ready to violence, and more apt to commit wanton injury upon the objects provided for their accommodation and gratification.

If what has been lost in this respect shall not be speedily recovered and a reverse tendency established, the distinguishing elements of advantage which this park has been supposed to possess over others will, with the rapidly-increasing numbers of visitors, become elements of disadvantage; the money which has been and is now being spent in their development will have been wasted, and sooner or later a new park will have to be made upon the ruins of that hitherto designed, adapted to recreation of a less refined character, and in which there shall be little to lose through mere carelessness and rudeness.

To get the better of this danger is the most important duty before the department, for the reason that there can be no waste of the city's wealth controllable by the board equal to that which will result from the use of inadequate means for the purpose.

Many reasons for the change in the habits and disposition with which the park is used might be indicated, none of them involving the supposition that a change has occurred in the character of the people rendering them less amenable to reasonable requirements, and most of them referrable to the fact that the park was for two years under a government indifferent to the danger and strongly disposed to vary from the methods of its previous management in every way practicable.

The principal cause, however, must be believed to be that, notwithstanding the fact that the total sum of wages paid for police service was, during the period just referred to, increased in larger proportion than the increase which had occurred in the number of visitors, the means of instructing and reminding visitors in an effective way, of what, for their own satisfaction as a whole, would be desirable in their methods of using the park, have not been enlarged correspondingly.

More particularly the growth of an indisposition to yield gracefully to reasonable requirements may be accounted for on the supposition that, in the scarcity and lack of vigilance of keepers, disregard of some of the park ordinances passes so frequently unnoticed, that when, by chance, an attempt to enforce them is experienced, it seems a capricious exercise of authority.

.   .   .   .

For reasons, which it is hoped have thus been sufficiently stated, a reform of the police arrangements of the Central Park is advised, of which the following would be leading features.

1st. The reduction in numbers of the present regular force, chiefly through the enforcement of a higher standard of duty and the dismissal of men convicted of offences indicating unfitness of constitution and habits for the service needed; perhaps, also, by the dismissal of all men who have not shown positive evidence of special fitness for the service. This to form the only constant force for police duty and to serve as a central and superior body in a larger organization.

2d. The organization of a body of men to work constantly through the day, in taking care of walks, seats and houses throughout the park, who shall be uniformed and systematically instructed to guide, inform and caution visitors, as occasion offers, incidentally to their work. This element would be employed on police service only in fair weather, expenditure for that purpose, so far as it was concerned, ceasing with storms, and being at all times relative in amount in some degree to the number of visitors.

3d. The organization of a larger body of men selected from the gardeners and laborers of the park and their training in the same duties, so that when the park is more than usually thronged, all or any desirable part of them can be quickly drawn from work, uniformed by a light overall suit, and distributed as circumstances may require.

. . . .

Respectfully,

FRED. LAW OLMSTED,
Treasurer.

October 23d, 1872.

INSTRUCTIONS TO THE KEEPERS OF THE CENTRAL PARK[1]

The following

GENERAL ORDER FOR ORGANIZATION,
RULES OF CONDUCT,
CONDITIONS OF HOLDING APPOINTMENTS, AND
GENERAL OBSERVATIONS,

have been approved by the Commissioners, and ordered printed for the instruction of the Keepers of the Central Park, who will be required to be familiar with their contents. Each copy issued to the force is the property of the Department of Public Parks, must be held solely for his own use by

[1] Printed by order of the Commissioners of the Department of Public Parks, 1873.

the Keeper receiving it, must be preserved in good order, and returned when called for.

Fred. Law Olmsted, L. A.,
General Superintendent.

Office of Design and Superintendence,
February 20th, 1873

DEPARTMENT OF PUBLIC PARKS

General Order for the Organization and Routine of Duty of the Keepers' Service of the Central Park.

Branches of the Service

The organization for attendance on visitors in the Central Park will consist of three branches, with the superintending officers.

First.—*Patrol-keepers*, whose duties will require much activity of movement, and who, besides attending directly on visitors, will act as sub-officers for the other two branches of the service.

Second.—*Post-keepers*, who will be chiefly stationed at gates and other posts.

Third.—*Extra-keepers*, who will be uniformed workingmen, for the most part charged with keeping in order each a certain division of the walks with the connected structures, and who will incidentally to this duty assist in preventing the misuse of the Park under their view. The number of extra keepers to be placed on duty will vary according to circumstances.

There will be a special body of watchmen for the care of the Park after visitors leave at night.

Patrol-Keepers

Organization of Patrol-keepers.—The Patrol-keepers will be organized in three sections; one for morning duty, which will take the care of the Park from the night watchmen; one for evening duty, which will take the care of the Park from the morning section, and one for reserve duty, which will ordinarily be used to strengthen the evening section.

Each man will be specially assigned for each period of duty, some to a designated beat ("beat duty"); others to a designated route ("round duty").

Beat Duty

"*All-Day Beats.*"—There will be four regular all-day beats, as follows:

First.—The Harlem beat will be the drive from the Farmer's Gate to Mt. St. Vincent, with all the ground to the eastward and so much to the westward as is under observation from the drive.

Second.—The Hill beat will be the drive from the Warrior's Gate to the Glen Span, with all of the ground on both sides of it west of the Harlem beat.

Third.—The Ramble beat will be the whole of the Ramble.

Fourth.—the Terrace beat will be all of the ground from the East to the West Drive, between the Lake, on the north, and the walks north of the Green, and south of the Music-stand, on the south.

Keepers assigned to the Harlem and Hill beats will make a close inspection of the gates upon them once every hour.

Other beats and posts of duty will be established at the discretion of the commanding officers.

Evening Beats.—There will be a series of beats to be covered (by the reserve section) after 7 P.M., which will be designated on a map.

ROUND DUTY

Routes.—Routes for round duty will be respectively designated the West and East routes according as the keeper is required to pass northwards on the east or west side of the Park. Each will be more particularly defined hereafter. In each, the circuit drive is to be followed, with certain regular diversions (directed below) and such others, as it may appear to the keeper will enable him better to accomplish the purposes in view. Each route may be easily passed in two hours and a half, but not less than two hours and forty minutes is to be used. If regular time is made, ten minutes can ordinarily be occupied in rest at the stations. Between the beginning of one round and the beginning of the next there will thus be a period of two hours and fifty minutes.

Routine Inspections.—In the course of each round inspections will be made of two classes: close and passing inspections.

Each patrol-keeper on round duty will make a close inspection of one-half of the gates he passes, and a passing inspection of the other half. In the close inspection he will observe, in approaching the gate, if the post-keeper is attentive to his duties; he will see that the walk and border is clean within fifty feet of the gate each way, and, if not, direct it to be made so. He will see that the post-keeper is tidy in his appearance and wears his uniform properly, and require the correction of any faults. He will examine the post-keeper's book and judge if he has been keeping correct accounts. He will write his number and the time of his inspection in the book. In the passing inspection the patrol-keeper will come near enough to distinctly see the post-keeper. If he appears to require no instruction or assistance, the patrol-keeper may then pass on without approaching nearer.

Passing inspections will be made of all post and extra keepers on or near the route, as will be more particularly directed later.

.   .   .   .

ASSIGNMENTS FOR ROUND DUTY

There will be six regular series of rounds for the patrol keepers, the first series beginning at 5:30 A.M., the last series at 7:40 P.M.

The morning section will supply keepers for three series of rounds, the first beginning at 5:30 A.M. The evening section will supply keepers for the three series of rounds beginning at 2 P.M. The reserve section will be used to increase the number of keepers on round duty from 2 P.M. to 7 P.M., or for other duty, as occasion may require.

The keepers assigned to round duty will proceed in succession, one following another at an interval, the length of which will vary with the number of men available for duty, an adjustment for this purpose being made by the station sergeant as the different squads report for duty, according to the number of men reporting, as will be hereafter directed.

DAILY ROUTINE OF MOVEMENTS

Morning: All-day beats.—Four keepers are to be sent from the station at 5.30 A.M. to occupy the all-day beats. In going north they are to proceed by different routes; one by the West Drive and one by the East to Mt. St. Vincent; one by the Dene Walk and the Mall to the Terrace beat, and the fourth by the Dairy, the Middle Drive, the Lake Concourse and Bow Bridge to the Ramble beat. Those assigned to the upper beats will report to the sergeant at the sub-station before going on them. (At 1.55 P.M. eight keepers are to report for duty at the station, and to be sent out to relieve the first on the all-day beats. These will hold them until the hour for closing the park.)

Morning: Round duty.—At 5.25 A.M. one-half the keepers assigned to morning round duty are to report at the station. At 5.30 A.M. one is to be sent out, the rest following in a regular sequence, alternately on the east and west routes. The length of the intervals will depend on the number of keepers ready for duty, as many intervals of equal length being made between 5.30 A.M. and 6.55 A.M. (85 minutes) as there are keepers—thus, if there are five keepers, the intervals will be seventeen minutes; if four keepers, twenty-one minutes; if three keepers, twenty-eight minutes.

At 6.50 A.M. the second half of the keepers of the morning section are to report for duty at the station; at 6.55 the first is to be sent out, and the others in succession at regular intervals, dividing the time till 8.20 A.M. (85 minutes) by the number of keepers ready for duty.

At 8.10 A.M. the first keeper sent out will be due on his return; at 8.20 he is to be sent out on his second round; the time from 8.20 to 11.10 A.M. (170 minutes) is to be divided by the full number of keepers on round duty, and those returning from the first round are to be sent out on the second as nearly as practicable at the successive intervals thus indicated. The first round of the second series is to be completed at 11 A.M., and the third to begin at 11.10.

If, on account of making an arrest, or other necessity, any keeper on round duty is prevented from keeping his place in the sequence, his place is to be taken with as little delay as practicable by the next following.

In all cases of disarrangement of the sequence, the officer in charge of the station will shorten rests and hasten movements, so as to secure the nearest approach to the regular order in the disposition of the whole body of keepers, on round duty as is practicable.

The keeper making the first round will, in regular order, complete his third round at 1.50 P.M., and unless there is an extraordinary necessity for further service, will then be dismissed for the day; others of the section on morning duty will be dismissed as they return, in regular succession.

Evening: All-day Beats.—Three men will be taken from the evening section and three from the reserve section for the all-day beats, the Ramble and Terrace beats, each being divided for evening duty into two. These will report for duty at 1.55 P.M., and between 2 and 2.05 P.M., will be sent out; care being taken that no two proceed in company after leaving the station.

Evening: Round duty.—At 1.55 P.M., one-half the remainder of the evening and reserve sections will report for duty. The keepers for round duty of the evening section will be sent out at intervals determined by the same method as before directed to be used for the morning section, the first at 2 P.M., the west and east routes being taken alternately, as before. If the reserve section is not required for special duty (as will be the case on concert days, etc.), it will be sent out in the same way on round duty—a keeper of the reserve section leaving the station one minute after each keeper of the evening section, but taking the east route when the keeper of the evening section takes the west, and *vice versa*. Thus, one-half the keepers of each section will be sent on each route.

At 3.20 P.M. the remainder of the evening and (ordinarily) of the reserve sections will report for duty, and the process will continue as above, the first keeper for round duty of the evening section going out at 3.25 P.M. The second series of evening rounds will begin at 4.50; the third (for the evening section only) at 7.40 P.M.; the keeper assigned to the first evening round will end his last round at 10.20 P.M., and be dismissed, and the others as they come in, in regular succession.

ASSIGNMENTS FOR EVENING BEATS

At 7 P.M. the keepers of the reserve section on round duty, wherever they may be, will discontinue that duty and proceed each man to the evening beat previously assigned him, where, until the hour for closing the Park, he will patrol the walks, from which, at 7 P.M., the extra keepers are to be withdrawn.

GENERAL SUPERVISORY DUTIES

Extra keepers, not in charge of houses, will each have a district of walks to cover. Outside the all-day beats, some part of each extra keeper's district, and generally the larger part, will be open to view from the route of the patrol-keepers on round duty, and it will be the duty of the patrol-keepers, whether on round or beat duty, to watch for occasions to instruct or assist each extra and post-keeper whom he passes. The patrol keeper on round-duty, will try to make a passing inspection on every round of each extra keeper on the Park who is not within the all-day beats; but is not required to accomplish this purpose when it will involve a break of sequence. Short diversions from the drive, at the discretion of the patrol-keeper, for better observation of the walks, the meadows and the water, are allowed and desirable. Shelters and urinals on the beats are to be inspected by the beat-keepers every half-hour, and each of those within fifty paces of the routes is to be inspected by each patrol-keeper on round-duty at least as often as every second time he passes it.

Patrol-keepers are directed, for the most part, to follow the drive, because by doing so, and judiciously crossing from side to side, according to circumstances, they may observe, and may bring themselves to the notice of, a larger number of walking visitors than in any other way, as well as because they will thus best superintend the post and extra keepers. Care must be taken not to let attention be drawn too much from their more important duties in these respects by the carriages on the drive. All necessary directions and cautions to drivers may, generally, be given by gestures and without stopping. So long as visitors are in carriages they are little liable to misuse the Park to its serious injury. They are, therefore, of secondary interest in park-keeping.

SHIFTING SECTIONS

A shift of sections will be made monthly, the morning section becoming the evening section, the evening section the reserve, and so on.

SHORTENING FIELD FORCE

In stormy or extremely inclement weather, when there are no visitors for recreation on the Park, the Captain, and, in his absence, the Lieutenant, may put two beats in one, divide periods of beat duty, and lengthen the intervals of sequence in round duty at his discretion; all held at the station may then be placed under drill or instruction, and the usual time of dismissal for the day anticipated.

LEAVE OF ABSENCE

Leave of absence, except for less time than one period of duty, is to be granted only to keepers on the reserve section, but exchanges may be made between keepers of the morning and evening sections and the reserve, as a preliminary to leave of absence.

TEMPORARY VACANCIES

When absences occur in the morning and evening sections without leave, as may happen from illness, the vacancies will be made good as soon as practicable by transfers from the reserve.

Vacancies occurring in the evening section will in all cases be immediately filled. Vacancies in the morning section may be temporarily made good by transfers from the post-keepers; vacancies in the post-keepers being filled by draft on the extra keepers.

POST KEEPERS

The post-keepers will be organized in three sections; one to cover the gates during the first half of the day; another to cover the gates during the second half of the day, and the third to cover such other posts, at and during such periods of time as may be designated from day to day by the officer in command, it being intended that the keepers composing it shall be generally posted during the afternoon at points within the Park where visitors are most apt to crowd, and to need assistance, advice and caution.

REVISED AND ADDITIONAL RULES FOR THE CONDUCT OF PATROL AND POST KEEPERS

The rules and customs of the keepers' force heretofore established, not inconsistent with the present orders, will continue to apply to patrol and post keepers. The following are in part old rules, which have fallen to some extent into neglect, or which are now given a more defined form than they have hitherto had. They are hereafter to be exactly followed and rigidly enforced.

Note.—Keepers in uniform, waiting orders at the stations and elsewhere, and not called for, will be on "waiting duty." After being dispatched from the stations, whether in proceeding to posts, on posts, on beats, on rounds, or carrying orders or messages, they will be on "active duty."

I.—Wearing the uniform will signify that a keeper is on duty, and subject to the rules and discipline of duty in all respects.

II.—No outer clothing is to be worn on duty except the prescribed uniform.

III.—No part of the uniform is to be worn out of the stations without all parts.

IV.—No keeper is to wear the uniform or any part of it out of the stations, unless he is prepared in all respects for active duty.

V.—No keeper is to wear any other clothing which is likely to be mistaken for a part of the uniform, even though his own property, and when off duty.

VI.—Post keepers, on whose posts watch-boxes are placed, may enter the boxes and remain standing in them, in a position suitable for observation, in stormy or very inclement weather, when few visitors are passing. They may shift and deposit over-clothing in the watch-boxes, as required by changes of weather. They may also enter and stand in them for a space of not more than ten minutes, while eating a lunch, once during each period of duty. They are forbidden to enter the watch-boxes for rest or shelter except as above authorized. They are forbidden when in the watch-boxes to sit or lounge. Patrol keepers, on route duty, will carry no food with them from the station, will receive none, and will eat none. Patrol-keepers while on beat duty will receive no food, and if they find it necessary to take sustenance will temporarily exchange duties with post keepers on gate duty, and follow the rule applicable to that duty.

VII.—From the time that a keeper comes on active duty, until he reports and is dismissed, or returned by his officer to waiting duty, including all of the time in which he shall be in uniform, out of a station or office of the Department, he is to carry and deport himself in a vigilant, decorous and soldier-like way. When proceeding to a post or beat, or when on route duty, he is to move at a quick march, or if there is special need to move slowly for observation, he is to carefully avoid any appearance of sauntering or listlessness. He is to seek no shelter, and to occupy no position or locality unfavorable to his duty of preventing the misuse of the Park, and aiding and giving confidence to visitors in its proper use. Nor is he, without special necessity, to enter any building or take any position or action in which he may appear to others to be seeking his own ease or comfort, or disengagement from activity and vigilance.

When illness, a call of nature, or any irresistible necessity would otherwise prevent a compliance with these requirements, he is to call on and temporarily resign his duty to some other member of the force; to an extra keeper if no other is available. This is to be done formally, and with a statement of the reason; he is at the same time to remove his shield and put it out of sight. He may afterwards return, if able, replace his shield, and resume his duty. The time of the resignation and resumption of duty is to be noted and reported, with other particulars, by both keepers.

VIII.—He is not to try to surprise visitors; is not to play the detective; is not to move furtively or use slyness, in any way, for any purpose.

IX.—He is not to suffer himself to be drawn into private conversation.

X.—He is not to engage in disputes or discussions on questions of his duty or that of visitors, or other matters.

XI.—To lessen the liability of falling into conversation, not required by his duty, and of an appearance of neglect of duty, he will, while in necessary communication with others, stand in the position of "attention," or if in movement, will take special care to maintain a brisk and vigilant carriage.

XII.—He is not to address visitors in a loud voice, when occasion for doing so can be avoided by his own activity.

XIII.—He is not to exhibit ill-temper, vexation, impatience or vindictiveness in manner, tone of voice, words or acts.

XIV.—The authority to make arrests is to be used with extreme caution; only when to refrain from using it will bring the law, as represented by the keeper, into disrespect, or be followed by other results harmful to general public interests.

XV.—Persons to be arrested, and while under arrest, must be saved from all unnecessary indignity.

XVI.—When the keeper is obliged, for the vindication of the law, to use force, he must be cautious to avoid unnecessary violence or harshness.

XVII.—The worst criminal having a right to a hearing by a magistrate before condemnation to punishment, the punishment of offenders can be no business of the keeper. No conduct or language toward a visitor, which conveys *an intention of punishment*, is therefore, under any circumstances, to be justified.

XVIII.—The Captain or Lieutenant will, as soon as practicable after every arrest, inquire into the cause and motive of it, the manner in which it was made, the language used, and the treatment of the prisoner from first to last.

XIX.—Keepers are not to carry clubs, unless by special order, and are not, under any circumstances to carry pistols, or other weapons, concealed or exposed.

XX.—Two members of the force will never move side by side in company, unless under orders of an officer, or to meet a special necessity. If, by chance, two come side by side, both proceeding the same way, the one who has the highest number on his shield will quicken, and the other moderate speed, until there is a space of at least one hundred paces between them.

XXI.—Patrol keepers meeting on the drive, and having no occasion of duty for verbal communication, will pass on opposite sides, each taking the left (because by so doing, each will face the nearest approaching carriages).

XXII.—When a section or squad is to move in a body, and no officer with it, the keeper having the lowest number on his shield will be in command, military order will be preserved, and no talking allowed.

XXIII.—A keeper finding visitors sick, swooning, sun-stricken, deranged, paralyzed, in stupor, or apparently drugged or intoxicated, may suspend all other duty in order to help them either to find relief or to leave the Park. If they can in any way be disposed of with more kindness to themselves and less annoyance to others or injury to the Park without bringing them to the station, that way is to be preferred. In urgent cases they may be taken to the nearest cottage, or other suitable shaded or sheltered place, and an extra keeper or other trusty messenger sent for a surgeon or to obtain a conveyance.

XXIV.—When persons are found not in their sober senses and inclined to disorder or violence, keepers are not to consider whether they came so by intemperance or otherwise, but to regard their condition as an infirmity, the evils of which it is their duty for the time being to skilfully restrict as far as they can.

XXV.—The action of the Commissioners in establishing different grades of responsibility and authority in the keepers' force must be rigidly respected by all its members. That habits of subordination and respect may be cultivated and guarded, a proper reserve and formality of manner must be preserved in the intercourse between those of different ranks.

XXVI.—Conduct, language and manners tending unnecessarily to provoke or foster jealousies, prejudices or ill-will between different members of the force, whether of the same or of different ranks, by which a spirit of mutual support and co-operation would be discouraged, are to be studiously avoided. The intrusion of personal interests, and especially of personal differences between keepers into proceedings of official duty is strongly reprobated.

XXVII.—Officers and keepers of each rank may suspend those of a lower rank, and may discontinue suspensions made by those of a lower rank, in every case reporting their action as soon as practicable to their own superiors. A keeper suspended while on active duty will remove his shield, and report at the station as soon as practicable thereafter. Suspensions are to be made only where there is an appearance of grave fault or incompetency for duty, and those making them are to be held to strict account for the grounds of their action.

XXVIII.—It is the duty of officers to watch for, consider and report errors or neglect of duty in the conduct of their subordinates. It is not the duty of keepers to watch for faults in their officers or in one another, and it is inconsistent with their duty to countenance useless grumbling, or idle reports, gossip or scandal tending to insubordination or the injury of their officers or comrades.

XXIX.—When a keeper, against whom no charges are pending, has knowledge of grave misconduct on the part of an officer, or reasonable grounds of complaint against an officer, it will be proper for him to make the same known to that officer's superior without unnecessary delay. But after charges have been made against any keeper, and while they are pending, it will not be proper for him to bring accusations against those making them or the witnesses to be examined, unless this is necessary to his own vindication, in which case the accusations must be made in writing, formally and specifically, so that due notice may be given those accused.

XXX.—The resignation of no member of the force will be accepted while a charge is pending against him.

CONDITIONS OF HOLDING APPOINTMENTS

By resolution of the Commissioners of the Department of Public Parks the following are established as conditions of holding an appointment as patrol or park keeper. Any keeper failing to comply with them will forfeit his position:

I.—A keeper shall be engaged in no other business, trade or calling, but shall hold himself ready for keeper's duty, when required by his officers, at all times.

II.—Each keeper shall carry out all lawful instructions from persons placed in authority over him, in good faith, according to their true intent and meaning to the best of his understanding and ability.

III.—He shall not, upon any occasion, or for any reason, take money or any gratuity from any person without the express permission of the Commissioners.

IV.—He shall not seek to obtain promotion or favor from his officers or the Commissioners by the aid or interposition of others, or on other grounds than that of his just credit for intelligent and faithful service.

V.—He shall enter into no agreement, intrigue or understanding with others to bring about the discredit or the advance of any member of the force.

VI.—He shall not seek to evade or prevent a fair trial of himself or other keepers when charged with delinquencies.

GENERAL OBSERVATIONS OF THE CONDUCT REQUIRED OF THE KEEPERS OF THE CENTRAL PARK

Among the circumstances which have obliged considerable changes to be ordered in the regulations for the keeping of the Park, are the following:

After the dismissal of more than a third of the force, represented by its officers to be its least promising members, and after much effort to secure improvement under existing rules, a satisfactory appearance of vigilance, discipline and activity in a keeper on duty has remained exceptional.

Moreover, although a keeper, while on his beat or post, rarely comes under the observation of an officer unexpectedly to himself, instances have continued to be disgracefully common of keepers seen by their officers under conditions raising a strong presumption of intentional neglect of duty.

It has been but too evident, from these and other circumstances, that a habit of disregarding the just claims upon them of the Commissioners and of the public, had been strongly established with many members of the force, and, that under existing arrangements, the Commissioners have been unable to enforce a faithful compliance with the contract which is, in effect, made between themselves and each keeper at his appointment, and which is renewed and ratified whenever the keeper puts on his uniform.

This being a duty resting on the Commissioners second in importance to no other, as will be later shown, the subject has, for sometime, been one of constant and close study, with a view to new arrangements on a sounder basis.

Most of the cases of apparent neglect of duty reported, have been found, after investigation, to divide more or less distinctly, into three classes:

First.—Those in which the keeper has frankly confirmed the statement of the officer, acknowledged himself at fault, and in which it has been probable that the error was a casual one, quite out of his usual habits.

Second.—Those in which the statement of the officer has been essentially confirmed by the keeper, and some reason given for the apparent neglect, which has been assumed by the keeper to be a justification of it.

Third.—Those in which the keeper has either admitted the facts, as represented by the officer, or has denied only some quite unimportant particulars of them, but has seemingly not recognized that they established any neglect of duty.

There has really been but a single instance of the first class; that of one of the oldest of the keepers, whose character has always been, and is, of the highest. Of the second class of cases there have been many. The following are examples of the grounds on which justification for an admitted relaxation from, or temporary putting aside of, duty, has been commonly claimed:

1st.—Compulsion of heat, cold, or storm; sickness, fatigue, or exhaustion from exposure or excessive tours of duty.

2d.—Calls of nature.

3d.—Hiding from visitors while eating, or when making some change or adjustment of clothing.

4th.—Receiving necessary food from home, and standing apart to converse with the person bringing it.

5th.—Communication with other keepers.

6th.—Civilities to a friend.

7th.—Trying to detect a visitor in wrong-doing.

It has been evident that if, in the comparatively few cases of neglect of duty which would come under official notice, it should continue the case that the keepers, called to account, had only need to assert that they were acting under some one of these classes of alleged necessities in order to clear themselves, men wholly unfit for the business, with no pride in it, and no sense of honor in relation to it, might remain in the force for years, and the requirements upon them be easier than they would be upon the true men.

One object of the changes now to be made is to debar such excuses for neglect of duty.

It will be readily seen that most of them are precluded under the new rules, and that they are so in a manner which involves no excessive requirement of self-control or endurance. The keeper who offers them, hereafter, will show either that he does not know his business or that he is incompetent for it.

As for the first, it is intended that every man appointed or retained as a keeper, shall have such strength of constitution, vigor, stamina and muscles, as he must have to bear his share in meeting all the obvious requirements upon the force as a whole, without excessive strain or discomfort.

The surgeon certifies that all who have been retained on the force are so at this time.

This being the case, in determining what the Commissioners may reasonably require of each man, it is to be remembered that they provide him with outer clothing more or less fitting to the season but that he supplies his own under-clothing, and can wear thick or thin; single, double or triple layers as in his judgment may most conduce to his comfort. No man is required to report for duty when he is unwell. Consequently, when a man reports for duty, he is supposed to be clothed as nearly as possible suitably for his period of duty, and to be in sufficiently vigorous condition to bear any exposure or discomfort to which a change of weather occurring within it would subject him. If, then, he is found to be inactive; to be taking rest or shelter; to be throwing off or adding to his dress, except as regularly provided for, he makes one of two things evident; either that he is physically disqualified for his duty, or that he prefers to disobey orders rather than endure the measure of fatigue and discomfort which is involved in the obligations he has assumed with his uniform.

In either case he shows that he cannot rightly be retained in the employment of the Commissioners as a keeper.

Under the new arrangements, most of the patrol keepers will regularly call at a station, where, when necessity exists, they can be excused from duty by an officer, as often as once in every hour and a half. Special provisions are made in the rules for those who will not do so. Post keepers will be in communication with patrol keepers at least every half-hour, and will be constantly within signalling distance of an extra keeper. In case of real necessity, therefore, any member of the force can soon get another to take his place under the rules.

Failing to do so, suspension, abandonment or neglect of duty cannot be attributed to illness, unless it shall be of so sudden and prostrating a character as to require the immediate aid of physician. Of this, the only evidence which can be considered conclusive will be that of the surgeon.

In the third class of cases it has been evident that, if the keeper's statements were sincere, it had been possible for men to hold appointments for some time in the force with scarcely the least idea for what purposes it is maintained by the Commissioners, and whose conduct had, on the whole, probably tended to promote that which they had been paid for aiding to prevent.

Hereafter no man will be retained on the force who cannot be made to realize that it is the smallest part of his duty to avoid being absent from his place, and while in it to perform those few acts, for which he may find occasion as a common officer of the law. No man can be retained who fails to understand the special purposes of the system of park keeping, or how he may steadily contribute to those purposes without a moment's intermission during all of such time as he is on active duty.

That there may be the less excuse for failure, the purposes of the system and the method by which they are chiefly to be promoted will here be explained in the most elemental way, at the same time the error of certain habits into which there has been much tendency to fall will be exposed.

The Park Commissioners are trustees and managers for the whole body of owners of a large amount of public property. Their business with it is of two kinds, first, that of forming parks; second, that of keeping them.

The first of these duties employs many the more men, costs much the more money, and makes greatly the larger show to the eye, but the second is the graver responsibility, and the Commissioners are to be holden to a stricter account if the arrangements they make for it are ill-judged, or if they delegate it to faithless or inefficient agents.

What is here meant by the keeping of the Parks in distinction from the forming of them, and why it has so much more importance than the comparative extent of business would indicate may be suggested by an illustration:

A man may buy and fit up a costly house, but if, after he has done so, he finds coal and ashes scattered over his carpets, if decorated ceilings are stained and marred, if pictures are defaced, if books and dishes are piled on his chairs, windows and doors kept open during storms, beds used as tables and tables as beds, and so on, all that he has obtained for his expenditure will be of little value to him for the time being, and the possibility of its ever again being made of much value will lessen with every day that such misuse is suffered, through *inefficiency of housekeeping*, to prevail.

In the same way a park, as in the case of the Central Park, having been formed and furnished with a great variety of appliances, each, like chairs, and tables, and beds, and dishes, and carpets, and pictures in a house, designed to be used in a different way and for different ends, though all for the one general end of the comfort of the occupants, whatever value the owners are to enjoy for the twelve million dollars or more they have laid out upon the park will depend on the prevention of misuse, which again is a question of the efficiency of the park-keeping.

For example, rock has been removed, drains laid, deep soil formed and fine, short greensward gradually established upon the soil in certain places in order to secure that particular form of gratification which may be produced by a rich color and texture of turf, and by the contrast of this color and texture with that of other associated objects. To a limited extent and under certain conditions, the turf may be trodden upon without injury, but if walking upon it were generally allowed, the particular object for which much labor during many years has been thus expended would be wholly lost. Hence it is an imperative part of the business of the Commissioners to prevent this misuse of it.

Again, the Park is furnished with a bridle-road, the object being to have a place where horses can be ridden with a free hand and at a rapid rate of speed. This is forbidden by law any where else in the city, because nowhere else have arrangements been made by which it could be done with safety. In the Park they have been, at great cost. This bridle-road might be used by people in carriages or on foot, but it is not necessary to the comfort of any one that it should be, as there are on the Park above nine miles of road much better adapted to driving, and nearly thirty miles better adapted to walking; and, as to drive or walk upon it would greatly injure its value for its special purposes, it is the business of the Commissioners to prevent such misuse of it.

Similar illustrations might be multiplied by the hundred, and keepers must realize that every foot of the Park's surface, every tree and bush, as well as every arch, roadway and walk has been fixed where it is *with a purpose*, and upon its being so used that it may continue to serve that purpose to the best advantage, and upon its *not being otherwise used*, depends its value.

There are ways, however, in which the Park may be misused, not so distinctly definable as those above illustrated, the general nature of which may be indicated as follows:

The Park is not simply a pleasure-ground, that is, a ground to which people may resort to obtain some sort of recreation, but a ground to which people may resort for recreation in certain ways and under certain circumstances *which will be conducive to their better health.*

Physicians order certain classes of their patients to visit the Park instead of prescribing medicine for them, because, they need first of all the tranquilizing influence upon the nerves which they may find in it, and the insensible advantage which is gained in this way by thousands who visit it without this purpose definitely in view, but whose strength and powers of usefulness are thus increased, and whose lives thus prolonged, constitutes its chief value.

Any conduct which tends on the whole to restrict this value is a misuse of the Park, and in considering what conduct would have this effect it must be remembered that a large majority of all the inhabitants of the city are women and children, sickly and aged or weakly, nervous and delicate persons, and that the Park is adapted to benefit none so much as those who have barely the courage, strength and nerve required for a visit to it.

Incidentally to the prevention of misuse in the two forms which have been indicated, it is required in the keeping of the Park, that such assistance should be given to visitors as is necessary to their profitable use of it.

Those most needing assistance (in the way chiefly of directions, information and advice) will be people of home-keeping habits, retiring disposition, helpless, sensitive, modest. The difficulty here is not in supplying all necessary advice that shall be asked, but *in giving those most needing to obtain advice the confidence to ask and accept what they need.*

From all that has been said it will be seen that the administration of this most important part of the Department's business does not turn simply upon the question, by what means can the misuse of the park be prevented? but that it must also be considered how the agencies employed for this purpose may best aid the proper use of the park, and especially how trustfulness in the means of prevention and confidence in the use of the aid to be provided may best be inspired.

There are apt to be certain preconceived ideas in the minds of those who have not studied the subject which stand in the way of sound convictions as to the methods by which the park can best be kept and, that they may be removed, it is desirable that the following considerations should be well weighed.

There are frequent occasions when the number of visitors on the Park is many times larger than is usual. The walks and seats being then crowded the temptation to each visitor to pursue his pleasure out of the beaten tracks, and so to misuse the Park in various ways, is correspondingly greater than usual. To employ a sufficient number of keepers on such occasions to guard every point where these temptations will occur, and to give a caution or check directly and personally to every one who might need it, would be wholly impracticable.

But even if it were practicable, it will be evident that the pleasure and value of a ramble in the Park would be destroyed, and, instead of a tranquilizing, an irritating effect would be produced if at every turn a visitor were to be made to feel himself superintended in all his conduct like a lunatic by his keeper, or a child by its nurse.

It is not, then, by the frequent overhauling of visitors that the park is to be successfully kept.

There have been many occasions when each keeper employed within the gates of the Park has had to cover a space on an average of fifty acres, most of these spaces abounding with bushes, hollows and rocks favorable to those wishing to escape notice while misusing it, and when there will have been on each such space three or four thousand visitors. If it could be supposed that any considerable part of these visitors were influenced by positive hostility to the purposes of the keeper, it will be apparent that the evidences of misuse which they would leave behind them would be much greater than they ever have been. To see this more clearly, however, let a common example of misuse be studied.

Certain spots have been prepared in a peculiar manner, with a view to secure a luxuriant growth of ferns and wild flowers in association with rocks and other adjoining objects. There are some of the owners of the Park to whom the intended effect would give great delight, aiding them to forget their troubles, momentarily at least, and producing something of the good result which a visit to the mountains brings to a fagged-out man or a jaded woman. The places have been carefully selected and prepared so that it need be little, if any, inconvenience for visitors to avoid walking on them, and so that the plants, once well established, will in a great degree take care of themselves. The danger in this case that the intended result will not be attained, is chiefly this, that a few persons, perhaps one in ten thousand of all who pass near any such place, will tramp across it, and in so doing, stamp out the life of the plants, or will, one by one, pick and misappropriate the flowers to private use. They have no more right to do either than to pick their neighbor's pockets, throw stones at his windows or vitriol at his coat. Yet, of the comparatively small number of visitors who will crush out the life of the ferns, or steal the flowers, it will certainly be a still very much smaller number who are capable of being led intentionally to do any such wrong to their neighbor.

The truth is, then, that even of the comparatively small number of those who would make such a misuse of the Park, much the larger part are capable of being tempted to it only because having had no occasion, under ordinary circumstances, in walking along the streets, or when in the country, through the woods and fields, to consider the rights of others in the way that is necessary in the Park, it fails to be clear to their minds that they will be wronging others when they feel the impulse to such misconduct.

There is the same explanation often to be made even for people who carry themselves rudely in the Park, disputing loudly with one another, using threatening, profane or obscene language, crowding others off the walks, excluding others unnecessarily from seats, and so on. It is not with intention of troubling others that they do these things, but in most cases from sheer unmindfulness that others are being unpleasantly affected by them.

But a little further thought will satisfy the keeper that not only is it to be fairly presumed that visitors, as a rule, are indisposed to misuse the Park, but that they have an active desire and intention to avoid its misuse. Consider, for example, how much pleasanter it is in a hot summer's day to step on turf than on gravel or concrete walks, yet how few, comparatively, make a practice of stepping off the walks upon the turf whenever they have reason to think they might do so without danger of reproof from a keeper.

Even of the more lawless class a larger number commonly keep within the bounds of decent use of the Park than, when it is an easy matter to keep out of the sight of a keeper for hours together, can be accounted for by the mere danger of reproof or arrest. In what other way can it be explained that bad men, abandoned women and mischievous boys make no more misuse of the Park than they do?

Let the keeper who is at all doubtful of the answer ask himself, if he were going with a friend to a theatre, or a church or a funeral and while walking the streets should be smoking or engaged in a warm debate and talking loudly with his friend, whether he would be at all likely to continue smoking or talking aloud after entering the house? or, supposing that by any mischance he did so for a moment, whether he would continue long to do so? If not, let him ask himself again, why he would not wait until admonished or threatened with arrest by an officer of the law?

Reflection will satisfy him that he would be led by the silent and unconscious influence of others present to regard the custom and proprieties of the occasion and the place. A little more reflection will further satisfy him that no man however hardened, no woman however brazened, is wholly proof against such an influence. Remembering then, that, on the other hand, this class has not often much to gain by any marked defiance of custom or propriety in the Park, it will be seen that its protection rests almost wholly on the loyal disposition of the great body of visitors to side with the keepers in discountenancing its misuse.

Keeping this last consideration in mind, let the keeper imagine a man entering the Park, fully aware that he does so as one of its rightful owners, under obligations to no one; that, presently, through heedlessness or ignorance, he disobeys some rule for its proper use; that immediately a man whose livery shows that he is one of his servants, employed for his pleasure and paid with his money, accosts him, not, as it appears, with a purpose to respectfully aid him toward a better understanding of what is due to others, as one gentleman might manage to aid another who was a stranger to him, but as a watch-dog might accost a sneak-thief growling, and with a look of seizing hold of him. Suppose that the visitor has not only been so treated himself, but has observed similar conduct on the part of other keepers toward other visitors, and that both experiences have been often repeated. Let the keeper consider whether a desire will not grow with this visitor to take care of himself when he is in his Park, and no thanks to anybody; whether a disposition to try conclusions with the whole force of keepers, to see whether they shall prevent him from going where he likes and behaving as he pleases, will not be established in his mind?

To fully realize the danger of thus enlisting the self-respect of visitors against the purposes of the force, it must be remembered that there are many Jacks-in-office who, commanding but little of the respect of others in their own proper persons, enjoy to presume on the respect of others for any slight authority of law with which they may be briefly clothed, and that, consequently, there has grown up a common and not unreasonable predisposition in the public mind to find all public servants, more or less officious and meddlesome.

Now, if the keeper sees that it is not by activity in reproof of misuse, or by exciting fear of his authority to arrest, that he is chiefly to contribute to the efficiency of the force for its purposes, it must also be plain to him, without argument, that the occasional sight of a man who is simply distinguished from men in general by a badge and some peculiarities of clothing, is going to check misuse of the park very little. It will also be plain to him that a visitor, knowing that men so distinguished are the only representatives of those who are charged with the duty of keeping the park, and who sees one of them lounging listlessly, talking with friends, making himself comfortable, and who reflects that he is maintained in this way of living at public expense, is likely to have his respect for the ordinances established by the Commissioners to prevent the misuse of the park is no way increased.

But, now, let the keeper who cannot see what way is left to him for contributing to the object of the force, suppose that a visitor has, through some previous observation, come to be aware that there is an organized system for aiding visitors to avoid its misuse and for giving them all needed directions for its use; that in whatever part of the park he has been he has, at intervals, found agents of this system, and has observed a striking uniformity not only in their attire but in their carriage and manner, making it evident they were acting under common authority, common instructions, and with a common responsibility strictly enforced.

Suppose that they had invariably appeared to him watchful, vigilant, active and with their minds so fully occupied with their business of keeping the Park that they could think of nothing else. That whenever any one of them had been seen addressing a visitor, it had been obviously because it was his duty to do so, and that whomsoever he found occasion to address, a swaggering, impudent man, or a poor shrinking girl, and for whatever purpose, to check a misuse of the Park or to show the way to a seat, it had been with a manner of studied official respect.

Suppose that having himself had need occasionally for some information or advice, and having applied to keepers for it, it had been given with no more words than necessary, but with all desirable fullness, accuracy and clearness, and with perfect courtesy: not with an air as if it were a matter of grace with the keeper, nor with a hurried, irritated manner, as if he were impatient of it, but simply as if it were a constant duty for which he had carefully prepared himself, and in which he had no right to do otherwise than as well as possible.

It will be readily seen that one result of such an experience would be that, to this visitor, every Park-keeper would distinctly represent the general, permanent and legal interests which he possessed, in common with all other citizens, in the Park, in distinction from the momentary, selfish, illegal, individual interests which alone can be served through its misuse.

If then, at any time, such a visitor were carelessly misusing the Park, the mere sight of a keeper would be sufficient to recall those larger, deeper, nobler interests to his mind, and self-respect, instead of prompting him to persist in a spirit of defiance, would lead him to cease from the misuse, and to proceed in the proper use and enjoyment of the Park with more consideration.

If, on the other hand, he were misusing the Park through ignorance, and the keeper should ask him to desist, the request, so far from being felt as a personal affront, would be received with all respect and cheerfully complied with.

But if this would be the result of such an experience of keepers with one man, it would equally be the result with thousands—with the great body of fairly well disposed visitors—and thus the force of custom would act, out of the keeper's sight, in resistance to the misuse of the Park, with a strong, constant pressure, upon even the more recklessly selfish class.

It can not, then, be too strongly borne in mind, that any conduct which tends to wound the self-respect of visitors tends also to promote a disposition to misuse the Park, and that, in so far as there is anything in the appearance of a keeper at any moment while he is on active duty, which seconds those general influences of the Park, by which the self-respect or civic pride of the citizen is gratified, he will at that moment be actively contributing to the general purpose of the organization.

Moreover, it may be fairly estimated that however slight such influence may be at any particular moment, on any particular visitor, the sum of all the influence which each keeper may so exert will be a larger contribution to the general end which he has undertaken, as the business of his life, to serve, than he will be able to make in all other ways.

It is very desirable that the officers of the force, especially, should realize that the great difficulty with which they have to contend is just here, in the proneness, that is to say, of keepers, in common with mankind in general, to have too little respect for or faith in influences which operate quietly and graciously, and to magnify the importance of acts of which the results are direct and obvious; in the proneness, also, of keepers to imagine that their usefulness lies in what each man accomplishes from day to day, by himself, rather than in the ultimate results of a system to which any contributions that any one of them can make will be chiefly valuable in proportion as he sustains a general influence proceeding from all with whom he is placed in co-operation.

The points more important to be fixed in the keeper's mind of what has been said may be recapitulated as follows:

First.—The most pressing responsibility upon the Commissioners, with reference to the Central Park, is that of the prevention of its misuse.

Second.—The degree in which the Park will be wilfully and gravely misused corresponds to the degree in which any misuse of it will be given the apparent sanction of custom, through thoughtless and slight misuse of it.

Third.—The keeper can do little towards preventing misuse of the park, by arrests or by threats or admonitions addressed personally to visitors.

Fourth.—What is chiefly to be relied upon for keeping within necessary limits the thoughtless and slight misuse of the park, and through all this misuse, is the impression which may from time to time be produced on the minds of well-intentioned visitors by the mere presence and manner of the Park-keepers.

Fifth.—This impression will be valuable for the purpose in proportion as it is uniform, and as it manifests systematic vigilance, order, discipline, considerateness and courtesy.

Sixth.—The Commissioners cannot afford, in justice to their own responsibility, to retain men in the position of keepers who fail to contribute constantly, when on active duty, to such an impression.

ORDINANCES APPLICABLE TO THE ORDINARY USE OF THE CENTRAL PARK

The Board of Commissioners of the Department of Public Parks, this thirty-first day of March, A.D. 1873, adopt and ordain the following ordinances for the use of the Central Park, to be observed by all persons not in the service of the Department.

I.   No one shall enter or leave the Park except at the established entrance ways, nor shall any one enter or remain in it after eleven o'clock at night, during the six months beginning May first; nor after nine o'clock at night during the six months beginning November first, except as, on special occasions, its general use may be authorized beyond the regular hours.

II.   No one shall climb upon or in any way cut, break, injure or deface any wall, fence, shelter, seat, statue or other erection, nor any turf, tree, shrub, or other plant, nor throw stones or other missiles, nor discharge, fire or carry any firearm, fire-cracker, torpedo or fire-works, nor make a fire, nor play any musical instrument, nor offer or expose things for sale, nor post or display any sign, placard, flag, banner, target, transparency, advertisement or device of business, nor solicit business or fares, nor beg or publicly solicit subscriptions or contributions, nor tell fortunes, nor play games of chance or with any table or instruments of gaming, nor make any oration or harangue, nor utter loud threatening, abusive or indecent language, nor do any indecent or obscene act.

III.   No quadrupeds except those placed in the Park by the Commissioners, and except dogs when controlled by a line of suitable strength not more than six feet in length, and horses and others used for pleasure travel, shall be driven or conducted into the Park or allowed to remain in it.

IV.   The drive shall be used only by persons in pleasure carriages or on horseback; the ride only by persons on horseback; animals to be used on either shall be well broken and constantly held in such control, that they may be easily and quickly turned or stopped; they shall not be allowed to move at a rate of speed which shall be alarming or cause danger, nor under any circumstances at a rate of speed on the drive of more than seven miles, nor on the ride of over twelve miles an hour; and when any park-keeper shall deem it necessary to safety, good order, or the general convenience, that the speed of an animal shall be checked, or that it should be stopped, or its course altered, and shall so direct, by gesture or otherwise, it shall be the duty of the rider or driver of such animal to follow such direction; and no horse or other beast of burden or draft shall be driven or suffered to stand anywhere, except on the drive or ride.

V.   No hackney-coach or other vehicle for hire shall stand within the Park, for the purpose of taking up passengers, other than those whom it has brought in.   No omnibus or express-wagon, and no wagon, cart or other vehicle, carrying, or ordinarily used to carry merchandise, goods, tools or rubbish, and no fire-engine or other apparatus on wheels for extinguishing fires shall enter or be allowed upon any part of the Park.

VI.   No military or target company, and no civic, funeral or other procession, or a detachment of a procession, and no hearse or other vehicle, or persons, carrying the body of a dead person shall enter, or be allowed on any part of the Park.

VII.   No person shall bathe or angle, or take fish, or send or throw or place any animal or thing in or on the waters, or disturb or annoy the birds or animals in the Park.

VIII.   No person shall go on the turf except when and where the word "common" is posted as an indication that at that time and place all persons are allowed to go on it.

IX.   No person shall bring into or carry within the Park any tree, shrub, plant or flower, nor any newly plucked branch or portion thereof.

X.   When necessary to the protection of life or property, the officers and keepers of the Park may require all persons to remove from, and keep off any designated part thereof.

XI.   On the arrest of a person in the Park, he shall be forthwith conducted to one of the keepers' stations, the officer in charge of which shall determine whether he shall thence be conveyed before a magistrate or be discharged.

By order of the Board of Commissioners of the Department of Public Parks.

HENRY G. STEBBINS,
President.

F. W. WHITTEMORE,
Secretary.

REPORT ON RECENT CHANGES IN MANAGEMENT OF
THE KEEPERS' FORCE[1]

.   .   .   .

The designers of the Central Park aimed to provide, or rather
to retain and develop, in it certain elements of interest and attraction which, if they were successful, would be almost peculiar to
itself. They saw, from the beginning, that the danger of failure
lay chiefly in the liability of misunderstanding, misuse and misappropriation of these elements of the design by the public. They
saw also quite as distinctly sixteen years ago as now, that in this
respect the practicability and value of their plan turned upon the
question, whether a keepers' service *adequate to its special requirements* could be maintained upon it. The Commissioners adopting
the plan were distinctly warned of this. I, myself, stated to them,
in full Board, that I should be unwilling to take any responsibility
in respect to the Park unless assured that I would be allowed to
exact a degree of faithfulness, activity and discipline in the keepers'
force that would be extraordinary in any service of the city.

And I now affirm, that every dollar that has been spent this
far on the Park, or that can be spent on it, without changes in
plan, uprooting its very foundations, will have been spent on the
assumption of a much more efficient keepers' service than has ever
yet been had upon it. Otherwise not a line of the Park would
have been laid where it is, not a tree planted where trees now
stand. Otherwise, it has been a mistake from the beginning.

And the deplorableness of this mistake is not to be measured
by the millions of dollars that will have been thrown away upon it,
or the deprivations which will result from it to the people of New
York. This park is, in many respects, an experiment, by the
results of which the welfare of vast numbers of people in other
great cities than New York cannot fail to be affected.

I have indicated the grounds of this claim in a paper read at
the Lowell Institute, in Boston, in 1870, and printed in the *Journal
of Social Science* of that year, and can barely give a clue to it here.

The growth of great cities, which began in Europe with the
rise of trans-oceanic commerce in the sixteenth century, and which
has lately, in all civilized countries, been so greatly stimulated
by the inventions of the steam-engine, the railway, the steamship
and the telegraph, brings with it great evils and dangers.

The old parks of the great cities of Europe have come to be
within them by accident, and their adaptations to popular use
are in every case limited, desultory and ill-combined. Experience shows, nevertheless, that they serve the purpose of mitigat-
ing and limiting the special evils of great cities, in varying but

[1] Doc. No. 47., July 17, 1873.

always notable and important degrees. Setting aside the elements of accessibility, local sanitary conditions and others, there is reason to believe that they are thus valuable in the ratio in which they chance to be so formed as to allow multitudes of people to experience the enjoyment of pastoral and sylvan scenery, and to the degree of that special enjoyment which they are adapted to furnish.

It follows that there is good reason for believing that had a true nature-loving art been applied to this purpose, in the formation of a park from the outset, in the choice and disposition of trees, in the arrangement of roads and walks, and of other structures required for the comfortable accommodation of multitudes of visitors, and had liberal expenditures been directed to this purpose, with as profound study and as much skill as it has been to the supplying great cities with palaces and prisons, fortifications, monuments, museums and statues, the result would have been beneficent beyond computation.

That it is worth while for civilized communities to use their wealth in this way; that humanity and patriotism and religion require that every community which occupies territory in which it is reasonably certain that a great city is to grow, should, if necessary, at some sacrifice of immediate convenience and comfort and prosperity, begin the formation of a park of this comprehensive and artistically complete character, is a conclusion that no intelligent man, who will carefully study the effect on the people of the existing few and almost chance-formed city parks of the world, can resist.

Yet the demonstration of experience is lacking, and if the design of the Central Park is ever realized, will be first found in its realization. If, then, there is ground for the conviction held and stated by the designers, that the practicability and value of their plan is to turn upon the question whether a keeper's service can be maintained upon it adequate to its special requirements, neglect to secure this one condition involves much more than a waste of resources and a calamity to the people of New York. It must necessarily cause discouragement to enterprise in the same direction everywhere, and is a wrong and misfortune to the civilized world.

. . . .

Few persons fully comprehend the purposes of a park, and still fewer, especially of city-bred persons, fully appreciate the conditions upon which the real value of the various elements of a park depend. It requires some little reflection to understand that nearly all that is agreeable and refreshing at present on the Central Park would speedily disappear if practices, harmless elsewhere, were to be continued in it; if the multitude of visitors were to move through it, for example, as freely and inconsiderately as visitors at a watering place are allowed to move through the neighboring woods and fields.

The Central Park is necessarily peculiar in this respect, and must be used with certain special restraints, because of the means employed in it to overcome the naturally harsh and forbidding landscape quality of much of its rocky surface.

It is with reference to the prevention of ignorant and inconsiderate misuse of the park that the keeper's force chiefly needs to be organized, instructed, trained and disciplined. If it is sufficient for the part required of it, in the design of the park, in this respect, it will certainly be sufficient for protection against crime. And if its members are trained or allowed to hold the notion that their chief duty is to bring criminals to punishment, they will never serve the purpose of their organization effectively.

A clear understanding of this principle must lie at the foundation of any wise provisions for the keeping of the park.

Nevertheless, as the danger of the misuse of the park for criminal ends is a much more definite and obvious one, and the necessity of certain conditions, which have not recently existed in the keeper's force, is just as clear with reference to it as to the more important duty, I shall now ask attention especially to this class of dangers inherent in the plan of the park.

They exist more especially in the opportunities which it presents for ready concealment, for slipping quickly out of sight of others, for lying in ambush, for dodging and doubling on a pursuer, and for temporarily putting articles carried by hand out of sight.

To measure the importance of guarding against this class of dangers in the park, let it be considered that the larger part of the advance which has occurred in the value of real estate adjoining the park since its design began to be understood, and which amounts to a sum of $160,000,000, has grown out of a conviction that, for persons of great wealth and of certain social habits, a family residence near the park will be more attractively situated than anywhere else on the continent, while the number of this class is likely constantly to be larger than the number of such sites that will be available to meet the demand.

If the grounds of this conviction are analyzed it will be found that they do not, by any means, lie wholly in the expectation of the outlook toward the park which will be commanded from houses so situated, for the advance in value applies to sites from which no view of the park can be obtained, but that they exist largely in the presumption that it will be safe, healthful and pleasant for women and children to walk from their houses into the park, as they would into their private grounds, when living in a country house. In short, it is assumed that in a residence near the park, there may be combined greater advantages of the city, with less of its disadvantages, especially to women and children, than anywhere else, and in this assumption the actuality of an immense amount of the nominal wealth of many of the capitalists of this city is absolutely dependent.

Suppose, then, that such statements come once to be generally believed, as were lately published in the *Tribune*, as to the danger of robbery, and of insults and outrages to women in the park; as to the frequency of criminal assignations in it, as to the use made of it by great numbers of common prostitutes, as to the prevalence of wantonly mischievous, lawless, reckless and brutal manners among its visitors, and as to the practical immunity from arrest which ruffians of every stamp feel themselves to enjoy in it. Clearly such a state of things, or an evident dangerous liability to such a state of things, would almost certainly lead on to a financial disaster, through which the city would lose much more than all that has been spent on the park.

What, then, are the qualities required in the keepers' force to supply a sufficient insurance against such a liability? I wish to gain and hold the attention of the Commissioners at this time to one only, or rather to one class of qualities.

Places of sylvan seclusion on the park are so numerous, and are so distributed, that anything approaching a constant police surveillance of visitors is out of the question. So far, then, as those who come into the park are to be prevented, either from careless misuse of it, or from indulgence in mischief, vice and crime, by fear of police interference, it will be from the estimate they are led to form of the chances of a keeper's coming, within a given time, in sight of any particular spot from which he was previously at a distance. Their calculation of these chances will start with two factors: first, a certain number of keepers; second, the degree of their activity. If there were thirty times—I mean literally so—as many keepers on duty as there ever yet regularly have been, it would be but one for an acre, and if each of them were to stand as a sentry, or to move at an even slow pace back and forth on a given strip of road or walk, several hundred men might easily be engaged in illegal, licentious and rascally acts on the park, with perfect confidence that they would not be detected.

Thus it will be seen that the value of a keeper depends, first of all, on the impression which he produces on the mind of observers of *activity* in his duty; for upon this impression will be the estimate found of the liability that he or some other keeper will be looking at any particular spot of ground within a given time.

I ask the Commissioners to keep this essential requirement of the keepers' force continuously in mind—this prime necessity of a habit of activity during the whole period of duty.

It will be obvious, without argument, that the necessary number of men for the service will never be secured, who will, from a simple sense for obligation of their wages, and from their own understanding of the necessity, at once fix themselves in such an active habit as is required, and constantly maintain it.

The force, then, needs officers able and disposed to instruct the keepers in this respect, and to enforce their instructions by a sufficient discipline. When it is considered how the keepers are to be scattered; that they are to be for the most part alone, out of view of their officers; that they are liable to fall in with friends; that they have to be out in all weathers; that parts of their beats will be much exposed to the sun, or to wind and rain, others sheltered, it will be seen that the sufficient discipline must be unusually exacting.

Nor is argument necessary to show that the difficulties of establishing and enforcing such a degree of discipline as is required are very great; nevertheless I must ask the Commissioners to reflect for a moment on what, under the circumstances, is the chief difficulty.

The effect of political patronage—of the doctrine "to the victors belong the spoils"—has been to gradually familiarize the public mind with the idea that any public office or employment is a privilege and a favor, and it has been, from the first, difficult to make any man in the employment of the Board believe that he owes his employment to the fact that it is supposed that he will render better service of a certain kind, for a certain price, than any other man who can be obtained; it has been difficult to overcome the notion that the money paid him is only in part the wages of the labor or service he renders and that the remainder is given him to purchase the favor or satisfy the demand of some person, party, club or class, or possibly out of personal regard or charity toward himself or his family.

It was only by great toil, and at some political peril for the whole undertaking, that this difficulty was overcome as it once has been, at least in a great degree, in respect to the keepers' force.

.   .   .   .

If the Board should be disposed to trust me further with it [the executive management of the keepers], there are several improvements which I have many years had in my mind, and for which I should be glad, in due time, to ask its consideration. For the present I should recommend that, as soon as its general policy is firmly settled, the force should be recruited to the full number assumed in the present organization, which would require the promotion of one man from the position of post to that of patrol-keeper, and an addition of twelve post-keepers. I have not heretofore recommended this to be done, because, in the condition of expectancy, and demoralization in which the force more or less has been of late, the education of new men would begin under great disadvantages.

I should advise that a portion of the recruits be obtained by promotion from the extra keepers, if men can be found among them who are able to pass the proper examination. I should also advise that the additional force for the small parks, recommended in a report now lying on the table of the Board, be at once organized under the immediate direction of a discreet officer detailed for that purpose from the Central Park force, and that the place of such officer be supplied, by promotion from the ranks. I should recommend that the subject of a small mounted force have early consideration.

But all these are details of no pressing importance. What is first of all wanted is that every man, and especially every officer, should be made to believe that this new Board cares to know nothing about him except what he is worth in himself for the business of park-keeping; that this new Board will have a strong and sustainedly strong policy with reference to this business, which will be carried out in every detail with a single eye, energetically, resolutely and without fear or favor.

Hitherto, at least for the last two years, every standing order has been regarded as tentative, every act of authority as the manifestation of a purpose of no significance except for the moment. The thoughts of the force, from top to bottom, instead of being upon the means of satisfying the organic requirements of the public interests, have been upon the question, who are to be the next Commissioners and who is to have "influence" with them?

Whatever else is to be done for its improvement, means must be taken for putting it under much more careful education and much more thorough discipline. The manner in which the men shall be disposed, the time and place in which each shall perform his duty, is a matter of wholly secondary consequence to this.

Respectfully,

FRED. LAW OLMSTED,
Landscape Architect and General Superintendent.

CHAPTER IX

BUILDINGS IN THE PARK

Writing in 1895, Mr. Olmsted gave his mature opinion on buildings in landscape parks:

"ARE NOT FINE BUILDINGS, STATUES, MONUMENTS, GREAT ADDITIONS TO A PARK?"

"NAY, THEY ARE DEDUCTIONS FROM IT."

"DO THEY NOT ADD GREATLY TO THE VALUE OF THE CENTRAL PARK?"

"NAY, THEY TAKE MUCH FROM ITS VALUE AS A PARK. THEY WOULD BE WORTH MORE TO THE CITY IF THEY WERE ELSEWHERE."

This conviction represented a considerable change from early opinion on the use of park land.

Almost fifty years before, when Andrew Jackson Downing urged in the Horticulturist *a park for New York, his conception included monumental buildings; and the competition program put forth by the Commissioners of the Central Park called for a site for a future hall for exhibitions, concerts, etc. The impression seems to be current also that an art museum was originally provided for in the Park, although this is not strictly true.*

In the description of the "Greensward" plan by Olmsted and Vaux, the old arsenal building was designated as a museum, and a music hall combined with a conservatory was to be located near Fifth Avenue. The area now occupied by the Metropolitan Museum of Art was designated as a Playground. During the first few years of the Park, there were numerous communications regarding a museum of natural history, a museum for the New York Historical Society, and so on, especially after 1859 when a law had been obtained allowing gifts and bequests for museums, galleries, etc., to be under the jurisdiction of the Central Park Board. It was the feeling of the Commissioners that "institu-

tions of this kind are desirable and would be fitly placed on the park.'' [1]
*It was not until 1868 that a " Museum of Antiquities and Art" was
specifically authorized by an Act of Legislature; and, even after long
negotiations between the New York Historical Society and the Commissioners, the site was not decided on until 1872,—approximately the
site now occupied by the Metropolitan Museum.* [2] *Thus, although the
possibility of a museum was had in mind and its present site was the
result of the development of the uses of the Park over a period of fifteen
years, yet one could hardly say that a site for a Museum of Art was
actually included in the original plan.*

*That the Commissioners presently began to recognize dangers in the
placing of buildings in Central Park is evident from their last annual
report before they were swept out of office by the Tweed Ring:—*

"*The architectural development is thus far mainly of a character
that is required for the immediate comfort and pleasure of the visitor to
the Park itself, and little of it can be styled grand or magnificent, the
aim being to secure, wherever possible, quiet, unobtrusive effects
that will harmonize with the character of the scenery and help the
visitor to free himself from thoughts of business and city activities.*

"*The preliminary questions involved in the establishment of the more
extensive architectural structures necessary for museums of natural history and of art, and for the proper arrangement of zoological gardens,
aquaria, and of astronomical and meteorological observatories, have
been much considered, and, after elaborate study, conclusions have been
reached, based upon the essential conditions of such establishments
under our form of government, and in accordance with the peculiar
organization of American society. The way is thus left comparatively
clear for the successful establishment of this class of institutions, thus
placing the city of New York in proper relation with the great movement of the age in the interest of science and art. The Park is not to
be regarded as so many acres of ground upon which structures can be
indiscriminately placed, but rather as an extensive city domain,
arranged in every part as to its various uses with special reference to the
needs of those who are to occupy it. It is a single establishment supplying a complex need in a great city, and if mistakes or failures are to be
avoided, each department must be located and arranged with strict*

[1] 3rd Annual Report, C. P. C., 1859, pages 11–13.
[2] 2nd Annual Report, D. P. P., 1872, page 4.

regard to the requirements of its own particular necessities, and with due consideration as to its external effect on the whole design." [1]

The Commissioners as early as 1864 had gone on record as to the subordination of buildings to the landscape:

"*So far as is consistent with the convenient use of the grounds, vegetation should hold first place of distinction; it is the work of nature, invulnerable to criticism, accepted by all, as well the cultivated as the ignorant, and affords a limitless field for interesting observation and instruction.*

"*There is not only fitness in this idea, but there is safety. All artwork is the subject of animadversion; much of it sinks beneath observation; it is the fortune of but very little of it to escape wide censure, less of it finds permanent acceptance. Such as finds a place in the Park in answer to the demands of convenience and pleasure should therefore be subordinate to its recognized natural features and in harmony with them, not impertinently thrusting itself into conspicuous notice, but fitly fulfilling the purposes for which it is admitted.*" [2]

The designers of the Central Park in discussing buildings for the new park in Brooklyn (Prospect Park) explained their view in including a museum in their plan.

"*When we were preparing the design of Central Park, we advocated the retention of the building near the Fifth avenue and Fifty-ninth street entrance, formerly used as an arsenal, simply because it would probably, if retained, be found to be of sufficient value to be converted into the nucleus of a museum, and although it was very inconveniently located for any such purpose, taking the proposed landscape effects of the park into consideration we felt that the opportunity was one that ought not to be lost. Our suggestion was adopted by the Commissioners, and the Historical Society has since asked for and obtained possession from them of this site and this building, with the understanding that it is to be improved and converted into a public museum at the expense of the society.*

"*This illustration is presented with no purpose of favoring the introduction of large structures of this character within the limits of a public park, but rather to show that they ought in some way to be provided for in season.*" [3]

[1] 14th Annual Report, C. P. C., 1870, pages 11–12.
[2] 8th Annual Report, C. P. C., page 26.
[3] Brooklyn Park Report, for 1865.

In other words, if the problem of providing adequate sites for such needed public buildings is faced and solved concurrently with the problem of providing landscape parks, the latter will be much less in danger of piecemeal mutilation.

In 1872, when the landscape architects reviewed the changes in their design made by the Tweed Commission,—which had altered certain structures in the heart of the Park, so as to make them assertively prominent,—Olmsted and Vaux had this justification to offer of the sites assigned to the Art Museum and other buildings during the earlier periods of their responsibility.

"There are, however, certain localities which may be regarded as exceptional in this respect. They occur from the fact that the Legislature found it convenient to define the legal bounds of this body of city property by the pre-existing street lines, which do not precisely coincide with the desirable limits of the Park as a work of art, . . . there are, therefore, along the boundary, several small spaces of ground, buildings within which, if properly designed, will not affect the park landscapes, and which, regarding the Park as a work of art, and with reference to the purpose of affording recreation by scenery from urban conditions, may be considered as extraneous. Questions of height, size and style of building being involved, these exceptional outer districts cannot be here more accurately defined. The extent of such debatable ground is, however, quite limited, and the question of the legitimate occupation and disposition of all parts of the Park site proper need not be complicated in the present discussion by the slight opening thus admitted for exceptions."[1]

The criterion for determining whether any building is justified in the Park was also stated in the landscape architects' review of 1872.

"To determine whether any structure on the Park is undesirable, it should be considered, first, what part of the necessary accommodation of the public on the Park is met by it, how this much of accommodation could be otherwise or elsewhere provided, and in what degree and whence the structure will be conspicuous after it shall have been toned by weather, and the plantations about and beyond it shall have taken a mature character."

"This should be clearly recognized. As neither glass, nor china, nor knives and forks, nor even tables and chairs are the essential ele-

[1] Cf. Part II, Chapter I, p. 253. It is interesting to note that both the Metropolitan Museum and the Museum of Natural History were designed by Mr. Vaux, one of the designers of the Park itself.

ments of a dinner, so neither bridges, towers, shelters, seats, refectories, statues, cages for birds and animals, nor even drives and walks are the essential elements of the Park. But as what is well designed to nourish the body and enliven the spirits through the stomach makes a dinner a dinner, so what is well designed to recreate the mind from urban oppressions through the eye, makes the Park the Park. All other elements of it are simply accessories of these essentials."

The full discussion from which the above passages were taken should be read with care, since nowhere else is there a better statement of the true subordination of buildings to the essential elements of a landscape park.[1]

THE PAPERS INCLUDED IN THIS CHAPTER ARE:

Report from Olmsted, Vaux & Co. relative to works in progress on their designs. June 7, 1870. (Doc. No. 13.)—Relates to buildings under way when control of Park was taken over by the Tweed Ring.

Report on Boat and Refreshment Houses on the Lake of the Park, by F. L. O. December 26, 1873. (Doc. No. 55.)—Discusses practical requirements in relation to effect on park scenery.

---

[1] Cf. Introduction to Part II, Chapter XII, pp. 518 ff.

REPORT FROM OLMSTED, VAUX & CO., AS TO WORKS IN PROGRESS, 1870[1]

No. 110 Broadway, June 6, 1870.

Peter B. Sweeny, Esq.,
President, Department of Public Parks:

Sir—

In accordance with instructions embodied in resolution adopted May 31, we have to report that no work "subject to the control of your Board" is now being progressed with under our immediate direction.

In regard to the designs mentioned in our communication to the Executive Committee, we have to report that the building called *The Diary (see No. 24 on Folded Map)* is one of a series planned in connection with the Children's Department *(see vicinity of No. 23 on Folded Map)* in the lower Park. This series consists of the Boys' House *(see No. 25 on Folded Map)*, on the Play-ground, which is completed, with the exception of a platform and some woodwork, forming part of the design, and that can be added at a cost of $525. *The Carousel (see No. 34 on Folded Map)*, a structure prepared for the amusement of children, which has not yet been commenced on the ground, but for which a location has been arranged in reference to an engagement entered into by the former Board for the construction of the building on an approved plan at the cost of a lessee. *The Rustic Shelter (see No. 23 on Folded Map)*, one hundred feet diameter, complete, with the exception of an additional protecting rail, which experience shows should be added to the southern opening. *The Children's Cottage (see No. 35 on Folded Map)*, with cow stable underneath, which has been constructed with washrooms, etc., for both sexes, and an ante-room, arranged for the sale of toys, a feature of the plan that as yet remains unused to the detriment of the general design.

The Dairy completes the series, and is a stone structure, the cellar of which connects directly with one of the traffic roads, it being the intention that the building should receive its main supplies from the exterior of the Park. The Dairy is intended to serve as a refreshment room for adult visitors, and for the furnishing of sup-

[1] Doc. No. 13, D. P. P.

plies to parties of children who will congregate in the rustic shelter and in the play-grounds. The completion of this building, as designed in accordance with an estimate prepared in conjunction with the Architect-in-chief, will cost $3,000.

THE CONSERVATORY TERRACE

Our original design for the Park contemplated an extensive structure (*see No. 9 on Folded Map*) at the point occupied by the foundation work now in progress for the Conservatory Terrace. While the general design of the Park was in progress, an agreement was made by the Board with Messrs. Parsons & Co. to erect at their expense a conservatory combined with a building for the sale of flowers, in accordance with a design prepared by Mr. Vaux for them, as their architect, and approved by the Board. The laying out of the adjoining ground was accordingly adapted to this conspicuous feature of the design, and a sheet of water that might reflect the glass building was introduced, and some other accessories, including a terrace to connect the structure with the water line. Messrs. Parsons & Co. were unable to fulfil their engagement, and the design for the Conservatory remains unexecuted, the plans resting in the hands of the architect. *The Terrace* forms part of the accessory work prepared for execution as a part of the Park design, and its completion, in accordance with an estimate prepared in conjunction with the Architect-in-chief, will cost $22,500.

THE BELVEDERE

In our original design for the Park a towerlike structure (*see No. 12 on Folded Map*) was contemplated at this important point. At that time, however, the rocky promontory within the Reservoir inclosure was excluded from the Park, and the axial line of "The Mall" had to be adapted to the fact that this exclusion might continue.

After a number of years the right to add this promontory to the Park territory was obtained, and it was possible and desirable to place the Tower somewhat farther to the north. It also became evident that every available opportunity should be taken advantage of to give facilities for the gathering and shelter of a number of visitors in an informal picturesque way at this attractive point; the present plan was therefore prepared, adopted, and the foundation work executed. As it would be out of character to prepare for any rich architectural work at this point, which is the antithesis to the *Terrace*, and as it was a site of too great prominence to justify apparent cheapness of design, the work, though rough in actual surface, has been executed with special care and accuracy, so as to attract some attention as a piece of stone-work.

Courtesy of Charles Downing Lay

A Rustic Shelter on a Rocky Ledge

The completion of this building as designed in accordance with an estimate prepared in conjunction with the Architect-in-chief, will cost by the day about $96,000, taking present work as a basis for calculation, but a fair class of work may be contracted for at a proportionately lower estimate.

THE PALÆOZOIC MUSEUM

This building is the first of a series which it is proposed should be introduced with great caution from time to time as needed in connection with the outer boundary plantations of the Park. It is thus intended to utilize the broad shaded avenue promenades at night, as these buildings might be lighted by gas and approached directly from the sidewalk either by day or evening, additional foot entrances being thus furnished, the door-keepers taking the place of gate-keepers. This building is designed to contain a special collection of gigantic forms of rehabilitated animals now being modeled and executed by Professor Hawkins. The building has been sunk ten feet into the ground, so that it may not be a prominent feature in the landscape when seen from the interior of the Park, and the roof is designed for the same reason, with a somewhat flat pitch. The completion of the work, as designed in accordance with an estimate prepared in conjunction with the Architect-in-chief, will cost $270,000.

There is one other design to which we have given study, which was not referred to in our letter to the Executive Committee, as no work has been done on it as yet. We refer to *the Astronomical Observatory*, intended to be built on the high ground at the northern extremity of the Park. The accompanying study has been in process of preparation, in conjunction with Professor Henry Draper. It is entirely immature, and is only allowed to accompany this report for the immediate purpose of aiding us to comply fully with the terms of the resolution of May 31. Study has been given to the question of position and general plan of a large structure to accommodate scientific, historical, and artistic collections on the Park. Also with reference to a refectory on the west side of the lake, the present arrangements for refreshment being not only imperfect, but inconsistent with the requirements of the general design. The study given to these questions is not, however, in a form to be more particularly referred to in this report.

Respectfully,

OLMSTED, VAUX & CO.
Landscape Architects.

BOAT AND REFRESHMENT HOUSES ON THE LAKE[1]

26 Dec. 1873.

To the Hon. S. H. Wales.

I have . . . been instructed to report on the subject of the boat and refreshment houses on the lake of the Park.

The subject is intimately related to several others of prime importance, and I wish to place, as fully as practicable, before the Board the considerations which have led to the existing arrangements, and those which will govern my recommendations.

The project of a boat-house is a recent one, having grown out of complaints and reports of inconvenience to the public, made in 1872 by the contractor for the boat business, which reports were confirmed by the Superintendent and by personal observation.

The subject being under study, suggestions of the contractor and of the Superintendent that other objects should be combined with plans for a boat-house were considered, the site of the present movable skating-house being visited for the purpose by Mr. Vaux and myself in their company. We afterwards invited the Commissioners to inspect the lake with us that they might the better understand the matter, and they did so.

The necessity of removing the principal boat station from the esplanade (*see No. 36 on Folded Map*) being conceded, it was agreed, after examination of the shore, that at no point could provision for the ordinary boat business be made as convenient and as inconspicuous as at the point on the east bay, opposite the Trefoil Arch (*see No. 37 on Folded Map*). This site (*see No. 38 on Folded Map*) was accordingly fixed upon. The principal objection to it was one which applies to every site that could be thought of for the purpose, namely, that any building, no matter how low, set upon it would be interposed between visitors and a view of the lake, and that it would tend to crowd the nearest walk with persons waiting for the boats, and watching their departure and arrival. The plan of the house afterwards approved was designed in adaptation to the site, and, in order to compensate for the interruption of the view from the walk, and better accommodate those who should wish to wait in the vicinity, the roof was made a deck to be covered with awnings and furnished with seats, so that the advantages for looking over the lake, instead of being diminished, should be increased. A project for an additional temporary shelter near this point, for use during the skating season, being before the Commissioners at the time this plan was presented, it was pointed out to them that the proposed boat-house was adapted, incidentally to its main purpose, to very well serve this object. Its construction was then immediately ordered, with a view to use the following winter. . . [An account of

---

[1] Doc. No. 55, dated Jan. 7, 1874.

the delays which prevented work from going forward for nearly a year]. . . The question of site was again reopened, and with the suggestion that an addition should be made to the plan with a view to better accommodations for the public during the skating season, referred to me to report upon. I am informed that the suggestion relates to a proposition formerly urged and decided against, for saving the annual cost of taking down and setting up the present skating-house at the south end of the main lake, by the substitution for it of a permanent structure. This annual cost is estimated to be about $2,000. The building is not yet five years old, and as some improvement has been added to it every year, is probably now nearly, if not quite, as good as new. It was built in adaptation to the site it occupies.

The boat-house will contain a certain amount of enclosed space, and a certain amount of space covered but not enclosed. The skating-house contains a cubic space, entirely enclosed, ten times as great as that of the boat-house, and five times as great as that covered, added to that enclosed by the boat-house. To design accommodations of corresponding capacity to those of the skating-house, as a supplement to those of the boat-house would, of course, be to treat a large affair as secondary to a small one. The boat-house is designed in adaptation to a different site from that of the skating-house, and its construction is now so far advanced that it would now be but little more practicable to make any considerable alteration or addition to its plan if it were standing in its proper place instead of being stored in the shop.

So far as the purposes hitherto had in view in the plan of the boat-house itself are concerned, the facts before recited show that there has been no lack of deliberation in determining its site, or of study in preparing its plan, and that the result of repeated reviews of the question by different minds, has always been the same. I shall assume, therefore, that further discussion of this question is not required, and that the only matter now needing to be debated is whether the Department should undertake the construction of a permanent restaurant building on the shore of the lake, and associate accommodation for the boating business with it.

As a means of improving the boating business and the restaurant business, the plan has everything to recommend it. It by no means follows that the public would thereby be better served. In this case, as always, and with every project of alleged improvement for the Central Park, the Commissioners are bound to bring the matter to the test of this question: *"Will the Park, through the plan proposed, be made more valuable as a substitute to the mass of the people of the city for a visit to the country—as affording the greatest possible healthful change of scene, of air, of mental associations, from those to which they are subject under the ordinary conditions of city life."*

The use of boats must be regarded as that of a convenient and attractive form of carriage by means of which this primary use of the lake, in its effect on the mind of the visitor, is greater than it would otherwise be.

The use of a refreshment house in the summer, if required at all near the lake, must be regarded as that of relieving the visitor, by the satisfaction of his hunger, of what would otherwise detract from his enjoyment of its scenery.

The lake, as an element of scenery, must be considered to be not merely the water of the lake but the margins, by reason of which it is anything else than a reservoir. The use of the lake, as a skating-pond, though not necessarily in the least opposed to its primary use, is diametrically different from it. The ice, in fact, is simply a temporary floor for an amusing and healthful exercise during, on an average, but one-tenth part of the year, when the use of the lake for its primary purpose is almost entirely intermitted. The skating-floor being movable, and this use of the lake being a temporary one, wholly different from the more important and general use for which its margins have been designed, the special and peculiar accommodations which the public require on its margins are also temporary and movable, arriving and departing with the ice.

As to their character, it is to be remembered that a majority of the visitors who are attracted to the shores of the lake during the winter are not skaters, but find their chief amusement in watching the movements of the skaters. For this purpose, elevated positions overlooking the main body of the ice, are desirable. All such positions are very bleak, and visitors standing upon them are liable to be excessively chilled, and, much more than the skaters, need temporary shelter, refreshments and other means of restoring warmth. What is required in a structure in connection with the ice is not, therefore, simply that it may be entered directly from the ice by skaters, but also, and more particularly, that it shall be convenient for the larger spectator class. It is also desirable that a comfortable place of observation overlooking the main field of ice shall be provided for ladies, and that all the accommodations shall be conveniently accessible to persons approaching from carriages or on foot along the higher ground back from the shore.

It was for these reasons that the Commissioners abandoned the original arrangement of a number of small movable houses and tents, scattered at various points on the shore of the lake, each set up, owned and managed by a different person, licensed under suitable regulations for the purpose. This arrangement, faulty in some respects, had the advantages of establishing a healthy competition in the business of supplying refreshments, of dividing the mass of persons to be accommodated, and thus lessening the danger of concentrating a great crowd at one point, of affording a variety of accommodations adapted to persons of different tastes and means, and of much smaller demands on the maintenance fund.

The inconvenience of this system, however; its failure to meet the requirements which have been enumerated, and especially the fact of its forcing the spectator class to come to the level of the ice, were thought to be such serious defects, that in 1867 plans of a single building were ordered to be prepared, with the design of wholly superseding it.

To fully meet the specified requirements, it was necessary that the proposed building should be of two stories, and situated with one front on the water's edge of the main lake. It was also necessary that it should be placed on the south side of the lake, as will be seen in the following reasons: 1st. Because a person facing the sun, as one would do at times anywhere but on the south side, when looking upon the field of ice is blinded by the glare. 2d. Because neither on the north, east or west sides of the lake is there any open space nearly large enough for a building of the required size. 3d. Because only on the south and west sides are there direct foot approaches from the cars, and only on the south side are the walks leading toward the lake ample and direct from the principal entrances. 4th. Because only on the south and west sides could a building be approached by carriages, and only on the south side, without causing serious obstruction to the ordinary use of the main drive. On the south side a large concourse for carriages overlooking the lake was a part of the original design, and had been long in use, summer and winter.

In the preparation of the required building plan, the architects of the Commission considered that the crowd which would concentrate at any single building would on occasions be so large that, to avoid great inconvenience and disorder, all the accommodations must be spacious, and two plans were offered, in succession, each of which was rejected before the reduced plan, on which the present building has been constructed, was submitted. In construction, this plan was further reduced and greatly injured in effect and convenience. Experience shows that the evils of the arrangement are fully as great as the architects imagined that they would be, and no Commissioner who will attempt to enter and pass through the house, obtain refreshments, and make such other use of it as it is designed to serve, on any winter day when the ice is specially attractive, will fail to be disgusted with its inadequacy.

Considering it, then, to be demonstrated that if this concentration of the refreshment and other business of the movable house is necessary, a smaller structure than that at present used for the purpose is out of the question, and that the only satisfactory position for a large house on the lake is at its south end, in connection with the concourse and the main approaches from the east and south entrances, an examination of the ground at any time will further satisfy the Commissioners that nowhere else is there room for it, except in the exact position now occupied.

A little study of the lake from all sides, in summer, could not fail to satisfy them also that any permanent building of the size, or of half the size, of the boat-house, in that situation, to say nothing of such a building as would be required to combine the accommodations of the present movable house with those of the boat-house, would be utterly inconsistent with the primary purpose of the lake as before defined. A glance toward the present building, from the balcony bridge, will even now make this sufficiently manifest, but it should be remembered that the topography of the ground surrounding the lake is such that the space between the lake concourse and the lake shore, now shut out of view by the building, affords the only situation in all the Park where, in summer, the eye falls upon a body of water in association with a quiet slope of green sward. It should be observed that special arrangements for enjoying it from several points of view were included in the design, and have been established at considerable expense, and that the object of thousands of details of the general plan would be subverted by the introduction of such an object at the point in question.

Again, looking from a point south of the skating-house, it will be seen that the only broad, general view of the lake to be had from a carriage would be much encroached upon, and the designed effect entirely ruined by the introduction of such a feature as the boat-house.

I trust that it has thus been made sufficiently evident that the proposition to combine a restaurant with the boat-house, and to make the combination serve the purpose of the present movable skating-house, should not be entertained.

In regard to the permanent arrangements for supplying needed refreshments on the Park, it may be well here to say that the original design of the Park in this respect has been perverted through the use of temporary expedients, familiarity with which gives them the effect of permanence and of bad design. The Casino (*see No. 39 on Folded Map*), east of the Mall, for instance, was not built for a general restaurant; the arcade of the Terrace was not designed to be used as a shop for the sale of ice cream and soda-water. Neither of these structures is adapted to its present uses, and the present use of both interferes with the use for which they were designed.

The present arrangements for provisioning the public on the Park are, in short, inadequate and most unsatisfactory, and the need of improving them has been often urged by your landscape architects as well as by your contractor for providing refreshments.

Spacious refectories will be desirable in connection with the Museum of Natural History and the Museum of Art. Besides these, there are needed smaller houses each containing a counter and a few tables at which ices and simple refreshments, rather than full meals, can be obtained, and from which there will be access to retiring rooms, respectively for women and for men, on the general theory of the plan lately presented the Board for a building in Madison square. Buildings of this class, with low roofs, could be so placed that while one could always be reached by a short walk by visitors needing to make use of it, in whatever part of the Park they might be, they would yet be scarcely seen by those who had no occasion to look for them. Two necessary buildings, each covering a space of 16 x 30 feet, were last year placed in positions where they have since been passed within 100 feet by a large majority of all the visitors to the Park without being seen, and without causing the slightest offense. All necessary refreshment rooms, privies and urinals can be arranged so as to be perfectly convenient without being obtrusive or injuring the rural character of the park.

. . . .

Respectfully,

FRED. LAW OLMSTED,
Landscape Architect.

CHAPTER X

THE PROPER FUNCTION OF STATUARY IN THE PARK

Of the two documents bearing on this subject, the first is of unusual permanent interest because it furnishes a well-considered statement of the criteria by which park boards may determine the appropriateness of monuments and statuary in park designs. The report,—signed by Mr. Church, the artist[1], by Mr. Vaux, and by the President of the Board, and undoubtedly having the collaboration of Mr. Olmsted,— revises and amplifies the former rules which had been in course of formulation since the Committee on Statuary of 1860 began its work. Directly after the Civil War, in the Annual Report of 1867, there is a statement of the Commissioners' opinion as to the inclusion of memorials in the Park which is worth quoting:

"*The Commissioners of the Park have been thus guarded in dealing with this subject (7th Regiment Monument) because they have deemed the Park not an appropriate place for sepulchral memorials; it is for recreation and pleasure; its especial aim and object is, by all justifiable means, to dispel from the mind of the visitor, once within its enclosure, thoughts of business and memories calculated to sadden or oppress. It is a pleasure-ground. The beautiful cemeteries in the vicinity of the city offer abundant opportunity to commemorate, by appropriate memorials, the virtues of those who are passing away from the strifes and distinctions of the cabinet or the field.*

"*It will, on the whole, perhaps, always be wiser to defer the admission of monuments intended to commemorate individuals chiefly characterized by an active participation in any questions upon which the public mind is divided with a greater or less degree of vehemence, until time determines whether they are of those reputations that briefly flame and flicker, or of those whose lives of sacrifice and labor have formed characters that all ages delight to honor.*"

An amusing account of some of the early difficulties which the

[1] See p. 92, *ante.*

Commissioners *encountered in dealing with proferred gifts may be found in the* Description of the New York Central Park, *1869. (See Bibliography)*

THE PAPERS INCLUDED IN THIS CHAPTER ARE:

Report of the Committee (of the Board) on the subject of Statuary on the Central Park. April 25, 1873. Printed as Doc. No. 46, July 17, 1873.—Finally adopted with additions (noted on page 493) at the meeting of the Board on October 18, 1876, and incorporated in the By-Laws as Section 5, Article III.

Communication on a Proposition to place a Colossal Statue at the south end of the Mall in the Central Park, from F. L. O. and C. V. March 4, 1874. (Doc. No. 57.)

REPORT OF COMMITTEE ON STATUES IN THE PARK[1]

DEPARTMENT OF PUBLIC PARKS,
OFFICE OF DESIGN AND SUPERINTENDENCE,
NEW YORK, 25th April, 1873.

To the Board of Commissioners
of the Department of Public Parks:

At the request of the Board, the undersigned have considered the subject of Statues in the Central Park, with a view to the determination of some general rules which shall govern the question of accepting and disposing of them.

During the first half of this century but one statue was placed in the public places of this city, and it may be difficult to believe that the offer of such costly and substantial presents to the public is likely to be at all frequent in the future. A consideration of certain facts will, however, show that the inclination to this form of benefaction has, with the progress of wealth, luxury, and a taste for refined enjoyments, been very rapidly increasing.

It is less than ten years since the Drive was opened through the Park; the improvement of some important sections of the grounds is not even now begun; the larger portion is yet in a sketchy state, and a few residences are but now beginning to be occupied at one end of its border.

Nevertheless, we find that already more than twenty works of sculpture—the majority full length statues in bronze—have been formally offered to the Commissioners, and it is known that the tender of a number of others is likely soon to be made. During the same period three other statues have been paid for by voluntary contributions and set up elsewhere in the city. Another is at this time in the sculptor's hands, and still others are projected.

In nearly every instance, those offering a statue have designated the position in which they would have it stand, and, in the majority of cases, have made the concession of their selected position a condition of the gift. At least two offers have been withdrawn because the Commissioners hesitated to promise what was thus required; one of these coming from a man who proposed to make the statue of a

[1] Doc. No. 46.

relative the central object of the Mall. On two other occasions, the positions fixed by the Commissioners have been refused, with some feeling, by those offering statues, and, in several, the Commissioners have been requested to remove well grown trees in order to give greater prominence to a selected site.

It will thus appear probable, first: that before the design of the park is at all maturely realized, the number of statues for which positions will be sought upon it will be very great; and, second: that if the question of placing them is in each case to be determined without reference to defined and strongly established rules, narrow considerations of temporary expediency will almost necessarily have undue weight, both with respect to the choice of statues for the park, and to the positions which they shall be allowed to occupy. Rules applicable to the question can be established only by a consideration of the major purposes of the park, and of the essential properties by which it serves those purposes. The main popular want to be ministered to in a large park situated like the Central Park, with respect to a great city, is the natural craving of its residents for opportunity to exercise a variety of capacities for enjoyment which must necessarily remain unused, and through disuse tend to feebleness or distortion under the ordinary limitations of a city experience, however rich this may be in other respects. Three things should be supplied in a park not to be had in the city elsewhere: First, air, purified by abundant foliage. Second, means of tranquilizing and invigorating exercise, as in good quiet roads and walks, kept free from the irritating embarrassments of the city streets. Third, extended landscapes, to refresh and delight the eye, and, therefore, as free as possible from the rigidity and confinement of the city and from the incessant emphasis of artificial objects which inevitably belong to its ordinary conditions. The chief difficulty of a park enterprise is to meet the latter requirement as fully as desirable.

In a well drained and cultivated territory extending over several miles, the air naturally remains fresh and pure, and a liberal area of ground planted with shade trees at intervals along properly constructed roads and walks, can hardly fail to offer good facilities for healthful out-door exercise. But the preparation and preservation of the best possible landscape effects will always depend on a series of conditions of a subtle and delicate character, that are much more liable to be interfered with and encroached upon.

If a park, as a whole, is to be considered as a work of art, it is in this direction, then, that it most needs to be carefully protected; for the demands of the special art of which it is an example must always have the first claim to consideration.

The essence of the park, that is to say, must be in its landscapes. If, as years elapse, the pictorial effects prove to be as broad, well-marked and varied as was possible under the circumstances of the site, a corresponding measure of success is assured. If, on the other hand, a general impression is conveyed to the eye of a series of groups with comparatively small features, and crowded with details and accessories, the result will be a failure, however beautiful the details and accessories in themselves may be.

The Central Park labors under marked disadvantages in this respect. Its actual dimensions in acres do not seem small, but the spaces of turf or water that have to be depended on to establish the required impression of indefinite extent and comparatively open landscape, are very contracted.

The first practical deduction to be derived from this review of the facts is, that in the consideration of all propositions for adding to or altering its details and accessories, the due relation and subordination of the various parts to the general design require to be constantly borne in mind, and as this relation can hardly be understood and appreciated without much special study, and is liable not to be at all distinctly recognized by those who may represent a proposed new statue, the duty of the Board is obvious to reserve to itself the question of location for decision after each work has been accepted on behalf of the city. It is equally obvious, that while there must be difficulty in establishing rules which shall neither be too restrictive to be endured nor too lax to be of any practical value, it is certainly dangerous to proceed without reference to fixed standards when dealing with delicate questions of art, by which the character and value of so important a public property as the Central Park is to be permanently affected. It is the duty of your Committee, therefore, to seek to reduce the general views which have thus far been presented, to a form in which they may be definitely applied to particular cases.

Positions are likely to be sought for two classes of statues; First, those designed expressly for a commemorative purpose, as the statues of Shakespeare, Scott, and the allegorical figure Commerce. Second, those designed to present objects of beauty or dramatic interest, as those of the Indian Hunter, the Falconer and the Tigress.

The first, when worthy to be brought upon the Park, are entitled to positions of dignity; and it is desirable, also, that the feelings which they are intended to inspire should be sustained and supported as far as possible by other objects to which they shall stand in some easily recognized relation.

It is with this view, as well as to avoid the intrusion of artificial objects of any class not locally necessary as a matter of public convenience, upon the natural scenery of the Park, that it has hitherto been contemplated that portrait or commemorative statues should be placed either in immediate association with the entrance-ways or in juxta-position with the formal lines and avenues of the Mall.

With regard to the entrance-ways, it is not desirable that the gates should be built until other and substantial improvements have been made in the neighborhood of each. When this period arrives, it is to be assumed that an outlay may be commanded sufficiently liberal to secure structures of a satisfactory architectural character, with unexceptionable positions for noble statues and other works of sculpture illustrating the class of human interests from which the gate in such case takes its name.

When, as in the case of the bust of Humboldt, which has been placed at the Scholars' Gate, or the statue of Commerce, near to the Merchants' Gate, a satisfactory position shall at once be found in connection with the appropriate entrance; a work of sculpture may at the outset be placed in its final position, although the architectural features of the general design of the entrance and the companion figures that are expected to be placed opposite or adjoining it are yet entirely lacking.

When, on the other hand, owing to the little use yet made of the appropriate entrance-way, or the unfinished and unsuitable condition of the ground near it, no satisfactory position is thus immediately found for a statue, it may be placed on the Mall, but with the distinct expectation that it shall be removed when the appropriate gateway shall be built, and a suitable position made for it.

In determining the position of such works of the second or more distinctly idealistic class as shall be worthy of a place at all upon the Park, the point chiefly to be guarded against is, that they shall not dominate the landscape, and thus put those considerations in the subordinate place, which in the main work have throughout been assumed to be primary considerations; that is to say, of sylvan or idyllic interest; antithetic to those in which the mind of man is the larger element, as in architectural and gardening work as well as sculptural. It is probably impracticable to lay down any rule of more definite application in this respect than that no position shall be given to a statue in which it shall be a prominent object from a distance, or in which, when regarded from the front, it will divide or obstruct the view of any of the few expanses of the Park.

There is no class of works of art of which so few are found permanently satisfactory as statues, none which, if awkward, ungraceful or unfitting to the situation in which they are placed, are so obtrusive and unsatisfactory.

Although it may not be denied that works of sculpture, even if inartistically conceived and executed, may be of considerable interest to some persons, from an association of ideas in connection with the subjects represented, or that they may have a strictly archæological claim to attention, if relics of another age; it may yet be laid down as a general rule, so far as the Department of Public Parks is concerned, that no statue can have a just claim to a position in any portion of the public pleasure-grounds of the city unless it is a work that has artistic merit of so marked and individual a character, that its introduction can be completely justified on that ground alone. As it is to be anticipated that the liberality of citizens will hereafter lead to a multiplicity of offers to contribute works of sculpture for erection in the Central and other city parks, and as it may be difficult at times to decide the exact line that ought to be drawn in respect to the art character of the work under consideration, it is suggested, that to make this rule a practical one, it should be determined that when any statue of importance is offered to the Department, the Landscape Architect shall be instructed to confer with the President of the National Academy of Design, the President of the American Museum of Art, and the President of the American Institute of Architects, in regard to its artistic value, and to make a report to the Board on the subject prior to any action being taken.

If it becomes the settled policy of the Department to require that their acceptance of any work of sculpture should be without qualification as to time or place of erection on the park, and if in some such manner as has been indicated the critical value of every important work is determined before the proposition in regard to it is acted on by the Board, there will be no universally valid reason for a refusal to receive statues in honor of living men.

With the view, however, of avoiding, in a simple manner, the difficulties and evils that might otherwise arise, it seems desirable to make it a fixed rule of the Department to postpone any action in regard to the erection of a portrait statue till five years after the death of the individual it is designed to commemorate.

We are convinced that if the suggestions which have thus been made should be adopted as by-laws, so that they could not be hastily put aside, and if the Board were able to answer applicants and enquiries by reference to them, the park would thereby be protected from serious evils, and much agitation, trouble and heart-burning be saved.

The following is a recapitulation of these suggestions in a form for consideration as by-laws or rules, and which are thus recommended for adoption:

First.—Before any engagement is made to place a statue, or allow a statue to be placed, on the Central Park, it shall be seen in a finished condition, or in the form of a finished model, and a judgment as to its merits, as a work of art, shall have been requested of the respective Presidents of the American Academy of Design, the American Museum of Art, and the American Institute of Architects.

Second.—The determination of a site for any statue shall be reserved until after its acceptance.

Photograph by Edward Heim

Bethesda Fountain on the Terrace

Third.—On each side of the main walk of the Mall, on a line with the statue of Scott, now placed, a series of statues may be ranged, commemorative of men or of events of far reaching and permanent interest. At or near each of the gates of the park, portrait or commemorative statues may also be placed, appropriate to the name of the gate. Portrait or memorial statues shall hereafter be placed nowhere else in the Central Park. [1]

Fourth.—Statues or sculptured works designed to represent objects of beauty, or dramatic and poetic interest, may be placed at any points in the park where they shall not dominate a landscape, or, when seen in front, divide the view over an expanse, lawn or glade.

Fifth.—A statue, commemorative of any person, shall not be placed in the Central Park, nor accepted with a condition that it shall be placed in the Central Park, until after a period of at least five years from the death of the person represented. [2]

FREDERIC[K] E. CHURCH.
CALVERT VAUX.

HENRY G. STEBBINS,
Pres. and Ex. Of. of Com.

[1] ED. NOTE: At the end of Third, the rules as adopted in 1876 add: except in close connection with the buildings of the American Museum of Natural History, and of the Metropolitan Museum of Art, and at the request of their respective Boards of Trustees.

[2] ED. NOTE: Two paragraphs were added at the end:

Statues to be placed on the Mall shall be of bronze, and of heroic size. Colossal statues shall not hereafter be placed on the Park.

Plans and elevations for the pedestals of statues to be placed on the Park, shall be submitted to, and approved by, the Department. They shall be of granite, of simple outlines, and free from the elaborate decorations. They shall not exceed in height above the surface of the ground one-half the height of the figure to be placed upon them. They shall have no inscription except one in front designating the subject commemorated and its period, and one in the rear recording the date of the presentation of the statue, and designating in the simplest terms from whom it was received. The letters and figures required to be used in the front shall not exceed 4 inches, and those in the rear 2 inches, in height.

PROPOSITION TO PLACE A COLOSSAL STATUE AT THE SOUTH END OF THE MALL[1]

DEPARTMENT OF PUBLIC PARKS,
OFFICE OF DESIGN AND SUPERINTENDENCE,
New York, March 4, 1874.

To THE
HON. S. H. WALES,
*President of the Board of Commissioners
of the Department of Public Parks:*

SIR:—You ask us to report in answer to the following question:

Is it desirable that a statue, which with its pedestal would be thirty feet in height, should be placed in the centre of the oval plat of turf at the south end of the Mall of the Central Park?

The position, outlines and color of every object in this part of the Park, as in every other, have been studied, first by reference to the main purpose of the Park, and afterwards with reference to special local purposes, consistent with and more or less contributive to that paramount purpose.

It may be assumed that the desirability of the introduction of any additional object at any point can best be determined by a similar process of study.

We shall consider the proposition, therefore, with reference, first, to the general design of the Park, and afterwards to the special design of the Mall, and other local conditions.

In providing for recreation from the effects of constant urban confinement of the people of a great city, it would but for one reason be better to have several comparatively small grounds rather than a single large one. This reason is that a sense of escape from the confinement of buildings and streets is in itself an important element of the desired recreation, and that the degree in which this is produced depends largely on the extent of open country which can be brought into view. The site of the Central Park was unfortunately selected with no regard for this desideratum, and happened to be divided in the middle by the reservoirs and further subdivided by rocky hillocks in such a way that in but few places was there any general rural view more extensive than might be found in a tract of land but one-tenth as large. It has consequently been a primary object in its design to get the better of this most conspicuous defect of the site, and to take the utmost advantage of such opportunities as were offered in the topography to make the visitor feel as if a considerable extent of country were open before him.

Such opportunities were therefore made key-points in the design of the park.

[1] Doc. No. 57.

Of these key-points, the locality in question was considered to be of the first importance, for the following reasons:

The eminence at the southwest corner of the reservoir, called Vista Rock, is the most distant natural object which can be seen from any point in the southern part of the park; and the Drive south of the Mall, is the nearest point to the entrance from Fifth avenue at which it can be brought into view. A little to the right and left of the line of view towards it from this point, large rocky elevations shorten the prospect by more than one-half. Further to the right and left, the prospect opens again much more broadly, but not to so great a distance. The strongest effect of distance can only be had, therefore, for a moment in passing this spot; and it was, in the estimation of the designers, worth so much that, to the enhancement of the possible impression it might make on the visitor, every element of the plan for long distances about it was subordinated. Not only, for instance, were the lines of the Mall, and the choice of trees upon it and its borders, controlled by this motive, but it influenced the courses of all roads and walks south of Seventy-second street; it led to the very costly excavation of large bodies of rock, and determined the selection of trees and color of foliage nearly half a mile away. The towered structure on Vista Rock itself was placed where it is and designed, by its grey colors and the small proportions of its elevated parts, solely to further this purpose.

The middle line of the vista of the Mall is the line on which all these operations centre, and in looking along which everything tends most to favor the desired impression. The space proposed for the base of the statue centres on this line of view, and if occupied as proposed, would interrupt it at a short distance from the most southerly point of observation.

It is obvious, then, that the adoption of the proposition would be a direct repudiation of the primary motive of the general design.

It may be said that the view would still be open on either side. It is true that it would, but aside from the fact of its being divided and narrowed by the introduction of the statue, if an object of the character proposed were so placed in the foreground the intended importance of the distant elements of the scene would certainly be lost.

So far also as the statue would be visible to those passing on the drive, their attention would be drawn by it to a lofty object near at hand and of course withheld from the distant scene below upon which it has heretofore been assumed that every means should be used to concentrate it.

With regard to the special purpose of the Mall, it is the only place in the park where large numbers of people are expected to congregate in summer, the walks elsewhere being designed for continuous motion with seats and spaces of rest for small clusters of persons only.

Walks from all sides lead towards the Mall, the principal approaches being carried by arched passages under the carriage roads: this element of the design of the park, therefore, stands, with reference to all others, as the hall of audience to the various other rooms, corridors and passages of a palace. Although the elms by which it is to be completely arched over and shaded are as yet not nearly half grown and but two of the many objects of art, by which its dignity is expected to be supported and its perspective effect increased, are yet placed along its borders, it even now begins, in popular use, to assume its designed character. On a fine day in summer thousands of people who have been walking rapidly while in the various approaches to it, here move more slowly, often turning and returning, and the seats which are then placed at its side with accommodation for several hundred persons are often fully occupied.

The proposition is to place a colossal statue in the middle of the south end of this grand hall of the park *with its back set square to the people.*

The impropriety of such an arrangement is plain.

But it is also to be remembered that a colossal statue in the proposed position would tend to establish a scale to which no other object in the vicinity has been or can be adapted. Relatively to it the adjoining walks and plats and the spaces between the trees would seem cramped and mean. It would have the effect of dwarfing and, so to speak, of casting in the shade the statue of Shakespeare and all others which are designed to be placed in the vicinity, of which there are four now provided.

With reference to the value of what has already been acquired in the park, it is thus clearly not desirable that the proposition should be entertained.

We shall proceed to consider, whether, setting aside the fact that by far the greater number of visitors to the park would see only the back of the statue, the position proposed for it is one adapted to its favorable and dignified presentation.

On the elliptical plat of turf to be occupied there are four trees, and in the design of the park there are no more important trees upon it. They were the very first, or among the very first, planted on the park, and their trunks have already grown to be over one and a half feet in diameter. In a few years they will be three feet. The entire figure of the statue would be elevated above the point at which the branches spread out from these trunks.

If the base of the pedestal at the ground should be a square of about fifteen feet, as is probable, one of these trees would stand opposite each corner, at a distance from it of fifteen feet, and a quartering view of the statue from any greater distance would therefore be wholly obstructed.

Nearly at the same range, but a little more toward the front, stand two other trees of the same character; still further toward the front two more, all of which, as will be plainly seen by the annexed diagram,[1] would be between the statue and the carriage-way, and

---

[1] Ed. Note: This diagram was not found.

the most distant less than eighty feet from the base, and within equal distance, laterally, there are several others.

These trees have suffered from ice storms while young, and were, unfortunately, trimmed up under Mr. Sweeney's administration; their heads have consequently not yet grown in fair proportion with their bodies, and are not well filled out, but it is only necessary for an observer walking around them to-day to imagine what they will be in June, five years hence, to be convinced that there is no point of view in which, during the summer, the proposed colossal statue would be even visible at the distance, and from the positions in which a colossal statue at the proposed elevation should be seen to the best advantage. If it were to be set up even two years hence, as it has been suggested that it might be, with a view to the centennial anniversary of Independence, and an audience were to gather as large as greeted the unveiling of the Shakespeare statue, not half of those assembled would be able to see the head of the figure.

If such a statue had been expected to stand in the proposed position, and the designers of the park had, at the outset, been instructed to arrange the foot approaches to the Mall, and to set the trees about the position in such a way that only the pedestal would be conspicuous, the result would be very much what it is.

Even were the dozen trees, which have been referred to, away, the position from which the statue would be seen to the best advantage is at the meeting of three carriage ways, and the busiest and most disturbed place in all the park, so much so, that it has long been the custom to station a keeper upon it to prevent people on foot from attempting to cross it, and to guard against collisions. Such a spot is certainly not one to be selected for the worthy contemplation of a great work of art.

The views which have thus been expressed as to the motives which should be controlling in respect to every object introduced at or near the point in question, are those adopted by the Park Commissioners before the first stroke toward the construction of the park was ordered. To show this, we quote from the explanation of the plan published by the Commissioners in 1858:—"From this "plateau a view is had of nearly all of the park up to the Reser- "voir, in a northerly direction, and in looking to the south and "west we perceive that there are natural approaches from these "directions, which suggest that we have arrived at a suitable "point of concentration for all approaches which may be made "from the lower part of the city to the interior of the park. "Vista Rock, the most prominent point in the landscape of the "lower park, here first comes distinctly into view, and, fortunately, "in a direction diagonal to the boundary lines, from which it is de- "sirable to withdraw attention in every possible way. We there- "fore *accept this line of view as affording an all-sufficient motive* "*to our further procedure.* . . .

"The idea of the park itself should always be uppermost in

"the mind of the beholder. Holding this general principle to
"be of considerable importance, we have preferred to place the
"avenue [or Mall] where it can be terminated appropriately at
"one end with a landscape attraction of considerable extent,
"and to *relieve the south entrance with only so much architectural*
"*treatment as may give the idea that due regard has been paid to*
"*the adornment of this principal promenade, without interfering*
"*with its real character.*"

Mention should perhaps be made of the fact that a statue
has once been offered to the Commissioners of the Park, with the
expectation that they would place it on the spot now in question.
The Commissioners declined to do so, and the offer was withdrawn.

Respectfully,

FRED. LAW OLMSTED, ⎫ Designers of the
CALVERT VAUX, ⎭ Central Park.

CHAPTER XI

THE ZOO

The story of the Zoo in Central Park resembles that of the camel which pushed its head under the Arab's tent. Only in the case of the Park, there were always defenders who succeeded in pushing the camel back before it had done irreparable damage. Of all the papers here published, the last, a letter in the form of a catechism, is the most instructive and also the most entertaining. The visual incompatibility of zoological buildings with park scenery designed to produce broad landscape effects, and the difference in their essential purposes, are here summed up; and this letter—equally applicable to-day to other forms of enterprises proposed for the Park—happens to be the last official paper on Central Park which we have from Mr. Olmsted's hand.

THE PAPERS INCLUDED IN THIS CHAPTER ARE:

Report on Provision for Zoological Collections in Manhattan Square, by Olmsted & Vaux. 1866. (Last document in 10th Annual Report, C. P. C.)

Circular letter against location of Zoo in Central Park meadows, signed by F. L. O. and C. V. December 16, 1870.—Reasons why proposal made by Tweed Ring Park Commissioners should not be adopted.

Report on the Disposition of the Zoological Collection of the Department, by F. L. O. (and C. V., consulting). October 11, 1873. (Doc. No. 51.)

Report as to possibility of combined Zoological and Botanical garden in the Park, by F. L. O. January 2, 1878. (From Minutes.)— Discusses the only site not involving undue sacrifice of other park features.

Letter as to purpose and site of Zoo, to President of Park Department (Mr. Hutchins), from F. L. O. March 18, 1890. Printed as Doc. No. 117, March 27, 1890.—In question and answer form.

PROVISION FOR ZOOLOGICAL COLLECTIONS IN MANHATTAN SQUARE[1]

To the President of the Board of Commissioners
of the Central Park:

Sir,—We presented some time since for your consideration, a plan to connect the established system of Park walks with the section of territory under the control of the Commissioners, formerly known as Manhattan square, and we now submit a preliminary study for laying out the additional tract thus proposed to be brought into direct communication with the grounds that have been already improved.

The Archway, designed to provide a passage through the Eighth avenue embankment at the point of junction, is intended to be of such liberal dimensions, that visitors will be enabled to walk to and fro with entire freedom.

The embankment itself is, however, so elevated, that it must always act as a barrier to any general view in connection with the interior of the Park, and the landscape effects of the nineteen acres added on the west side of the avenue will therefore be entirely isolated from those already carried into execution on the east side.

Although this is on some accounts to be regretted, it evidently allows of a more individual treatment of the new territory than would otherwise be advisable, and the study now made is intended to show how this tract of broken, irregular ground can be adapted to the special purposes of a Zoological Garden.

It will scarcely be thought desirable that the Central Park Commissioners should undertake to provide the public with a collection of living specimens which shall be scientifically complete, but, on the other hand, it seems eminently proper that the Park should contain within its limits, a collection representative of the animal kingdom so liberally arranged, that it will afford ample gratification and entertainment to the public generally and at the same time be especially valuable, as an adjunct to the Common School system of education.

The hardy grazing animals are proposed to be kept in various detached paddocks at different points within the original ground of

[1] ED. NOTE: No date is given for this, but it is the last item in the Annual Report, C. P. C., for 1866.

the Park: the district under consideration being reserved for tropical specimens which require special accommodation and treatment.

As the land belongs to the City, and is a portion of the public pleasure ground of New York, the general impression conveyed by its improvement, should undoubtedly be that the whole area, however it may be laid out, is open freely to citizens and strangers without charge; and public walks similar to those in the Park are, with this view, arranged in the present plan to skirt the various paddocks and exercising grounds intended for unacclimated specimens.

As, however, on the other hand, the larger structures required for the accommodation of the collection will contain but a limited amount of standing room for the public, it seems desirable to reduce the temptation to use these buildings as lounges for idlers, and they are therefore so located in our design, that whenever expedient, a charge may be made at the door for admittance, without seriously interfering with the impression of general publicity which should be conveyed by the collection as a whole.

If admittance to all the buildings were made free on Saturdays, and a small fee were collected on other days, the convenience of the public at large would probably be better consulted than if either arrangement were adopted invariably: the main object of the suggested charge for admission not being to provide a fund for the support of the institution, but to prevent the buildings from being habitually occupied by visitors little interested in the collections. The system once established in reference to the large buildings, could, of course, by the issuing of proper tickets, be made to apply day by day to any isolated structures that might be found in practice to be overcrowded when left entirely free to the general public.

In the study submitted, one of the first considerations has been to secure an open landscape effect of sufficient extent to give character to the whole design, and the central stretch of level ground between Eighth and Ninth avenues is therefore unencumbered by any buildings and is laid out with lawn and trees and an ornamental pool of water, which would be available for the uses of aquatic birds and animals.

The largest building, intended specially for the accommodation of carnivorous specimens, is situated near the north boundary of the property, so that it may have a full south frontage and be sheltered from the cold winds by the private residences to be erected on the other side of Eighty-first street, which is proposed to be widened twenty feet. In this situation it would be seen at once as the terminus of the northerly view by all approaching from the interior of the Park, and a somewhat smaller building placed near the Ninth avenue line would furnish a satisfactory boundary to the view in a westerly direction across the central open spaces already referred to. In the prominent positions assigned to them on the edges of the property, these structures would close up the most important landscape outlines suggested by

the present configuration of the ground, and if elegantly designed,
would help to improve the general artistic effect.   It is very desirable, however, that the interior of a zoological garden should not seem
to be crowded with artificial structures, and with the exception of a
museum for stuffed specimens that could be entered from Seventy-
seventh street, all the other necessary accommodations are proposed
to be provided in buildings of a character so unobtrusive that they
would, in connection with the proposed plantations, be comparatively inconspicuous.

The building for carnivorous specimens can be entered either
from the Park or from Eighty-first street, and is proposed to be
arranged as indicated in the annexed diagram,

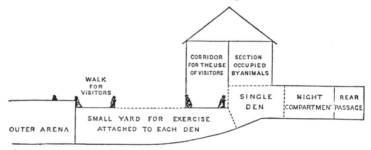

DIAGRAM FOR ZOOLOGICAL BUILDING

so that each den may have its small open yard, which will connect
with an arena of much larger dimensions, intended for occasional
use by the animals, singly or in pairs, during the warm weather. It
is anticipated that a higher standard of health will thus be secured
to the menagerie, and that visitors will derive a great advantage
from seeing in turn the various wild beasts moving about the
large airing courts in a comparatively untrammelled way.   Such
portion of the principal building as is not shown to be connected
with the arenas would be suitable for reptiles.   The Monkey tribe
would probably occupy a part of the building on the westerly
side.   The arrangement proposed for the smaller buildings may
be gathered from the study, which in its present stage of development, is only intended to illustrate the leading ideas that we think
should control the design.   No exact sites are indicated for the
Elephant, the Bears, the Hippopotamus, the Aviaries, &c.   We
desire rather to present for consideration at this time the general
plan of single or double buildings with airing courts attached, and
laid out in irregular plots, of varying size, partially planted.   This
arrangement is adapted to a great variety of specimens, and may be
modified to any extent in detail.

It will thus be seen that the more ferocious animals, and those
requiring at all times an unusual degree of heat, are provided for in
buildings of considerable size, located near the outskirts of the

property, but that the aim has been to make an informal arrangement of the Zoological Garden as a whole, so that the attention of visitors passing through the grounds may be easily concentrated on individual specimens, instead of being distracted as is usually the case, by a great variety of interesting objects seen in close proximity. It will also be observed, that the proposed informal arrangement allows of a far more rural and park-like general effect than would otherwise be practicable.

Respectfully,

OLMSTED & VAUX,
Landscape Architects.[1]

CIRCULAR AGAINST THE ZOO IN CENTRAL PARK MEADOWS

No. 110 BROADWAY,
NEW YORK, December 16th, 1870.

Sir:

The accompanying statement is intended to be sent to the public press, but we trust that you may be sufficiently interested in the facts it recites to excuse our taking this way to invite your special consideration of them.

The proceedings referred to occurred three weeks ago, and we cannot think that their import has been generally comprehended. The feature of the Central Park proposed to be superseded has, we believe, been heretofore universally regarded with favor. By many it has been esteemed the most attractive and promising of future value of any. The purpose which its suppression is intended to

---

[1] ED. NOTE: There is a jotting relating to this report in Mr. Olmsted's hand, dated March 22d, 1867:.

"Mr. Green called at our office and asked detailed advice with reference to operations which he appeared to contemplate undertaking immediately upon the Zoological ground. Mr. Green said that it had not and that he did not propose to lay it before the Board. Mr. Vaux asked if our general plan had been passed by the Board. Mr. Vaux reminded him that it had been addressed to the President, and said that the plan dealt with problems of great difficulty and importance, our solution of which should be well considered and adopted with a clear understanding, or difficulties and misunderstandings in regard to details would inevitably occur in the future. He replied that if he (Green) were willing to take the responsibility in this respect, he saw no reason we should concern ourselves with it. He argued the inexpediency of laying the plan before the Board at considerable length. Finally, Mr. Vaux very emphatically refused to consent that any use should be made of the plan until it had been formally laid before the Board, and said that we would not supply working drawings until the general plan should have been approved by the Board.

"Mr. Green then reopened a discussion of the general plan, in the course of which he hinted at a plan for leasing the ground to some one who should undertake to maintain a zoological collection to which the public should be admitted upon payment of fees."

serve is one which we have no reason to doubt could be equally well met elsewhere. Provision for it was not required by the Commission in the original plan, and the site being none too large for the simple purposes of a park, we did not recommend its introduction. When, however, the frequent gifts of living animals accepted by the Commission made it evident that accommodation for a considerable collection of them would eventually be necessary, we advised that the adjoining property of the city, Manhattan Square, an area of nineteen acres, should be taken for the purpose, the hardier grazing animals only being provided for in such open spaces, exterior to the circuit drive of the Park, as were of minor importance with reference to its primary motive. The suggestion was approved and construction upon it had begun, when the Commission was abolished last spring. Since it was made the City has taken steps to acquire several hundred additional acres of land for public pleasure grounds, the treatment of which, so far as we are informed, has not been determined.

Your obedient servants,

FRED. LAW OLMSTED,
CALVERT VAUX,
Designers of the Central Park.

NO. 110 BROADWAY,
NEW YORK, December 16th, 1870.

At the meeting of the Department of Public Parks, on November 22nd, a change in the plan of the Central Park was agreed upon, for the purpose of introducing accommodations for the Zoological collection of the city upon the ground known as "the Meadows," in the upper Park,[1] and provision was made for the design and execution of the necessary constructions.

We held at that time the office of Chief Landscape Architects Advisory to the Department, under an engagement which was to terminate in a few days by a resolution of the Board, and as we had no official knowledge of the contemplated revision of our design, we addressed a letter to the President.[2]

.   .   .   .

As our engagement terminated at the end of November, and we have received no fresh communication from the Department, two sessions of which have since been reported, we think it right now to call the attention of citizens interested in the subject to the character of the proposed change.

The defect of the Central Park is a lack of breadth and repose.

---

[1] 1st Annual Report, D. P. P., 1871, page 278 ff.
[2] ED. NOTE: See Part I, Chapter VII, p. 89.   The letter was merely acknowledged.

This defect grows out of the natural limitations fixed by the original rocky surface of its site, and from the necessity of providing structurally, for the convenience and safety of great throngs of people in a public pleasure ground that is expected finally to be situated in the heart of a densely populated city.

The impracticability of making, in either section of the Park, open spaces of greensward as large as desirable was recognized from the outset, but as much as possible was done to gain ground in this direction, and the central meadow stretches are the result in the upper Park. They supply two connected spaces, each about a quarter of a mile in extent, partially separated by a mass of rock and almost completely surrounded by a border of indigenous trees which are already beginning to take on umbrageous forms and to cast broad shadows over the now well-established turf. These meadows constitute the only broad space of quiet rural ground on the island which has been left undisturbed by artificial objects, and much labor has been expended to render practicable the preservation of their present general character.

A Zoological Garden must be made up to a considerable extent, if not altogether, of small scattered buildings and small fenced yards, it requires little breadth or unity of surface in its site, and it must be adapted to recreation of a completely diverse character from that which this ground has been prepared to serve. It would therefore, in our judgment, be a fatal mistake to plant a ceaselessly growing institution of this kind even on the borders of the ground in question.

FRED. LAW OLMSTED,
CALVERT VAUX.

DISPOSITION OF THE ZOO[1]

DEPARTMENT OF PUBLIC PARKS,
OFFICE OF DESIGN,
October 11th, 1873.

To THE HON. S. H. WALES,
President of the Board.

Sir:—As the question of a plan for the ultimate disposition of the collection of living animals belonging to the city is complicated with other questions requiring early discussion, at your request the following statements and suggestions are respectfully submitted as a report to the Board.

Under the old Board of Commissioners of the Central Park the chief features of a plan had been adopted, of which an outline

[1] Doc. No. 51.

was published in the Annual Report of 1866, page 42, and in a communication from the Landscape Architects appended to the same document, page 149.[1]

In this plan accommodations were to be furnished for all animals requiring artificial heat during the winter, on Manhattan Square; others were to be provided for in different parts of the Central Park; these two grounds then being all the territory under the control of the Commissioners.

Under the administration of Mr. Sweeney,[2] in 1871, this plan was discarded, and it was determined to form within the Central Park a zoological garden of the general character of those of the principal towns of Europe. Under the second Board of the Department of Public Parks this plan was, in its turn, set aside, for the reason that it involved the complete diversion from its original purpose of the best part of the Central Park. A large building which was nearly completed was ordered to be removed and the ground restored to its former condition. Manhattan Square having, in the meantime, been devoted by law to other purposes, the first plan, in so far as that ground is concerned, cannot be resumed.

There is one consideration by which, with but a single exception, the plans of all the European collections of this class have been affected, which consideration, so far as at present determined, would not apply to that in custody of the Department. They are the property of societies, and though more or less aided by governments, are largely dependent for their means of support on the entrance fees paid by visitors. In the inception of the enterprise the collection has been established on land offered to the society by governments, or obtained on a lease for a long term of years at a low rent. The plans for the disposal of the animals have been accommodated to the conditions of such sites as were thus available. With the subsequent growth of the collection, new buildings generally have been placed wherever space could be conveniently made for them, and not where they were otherwise most desirable. Various features have also been introduced among the accommodations for the animals, having no appropriate association with them, but intended to occupy the ground in the manner best calculated to increase the income of the society.

Setting aside all considerations of this class, which directly and indirectly have influenced the arrangements of the European collections, it is to be observed that the conditions of health and convenience of management and satisfactory exhibition which should be fulfilled in a plan differ with different animals. The feline animals of the tropics, for instance, must be confined in strong cages within a building, the air of which can be artificially heated. The grazing animals of temperate regions should have

---

[1] See p. 500, *ante.*   [2] *Sic.*

shelters essentially similar to those of our ordinary domestic animals, with considerable spaces of open ground in which they can be turned out during the day.   In this view it is clearly better to take detached pieces of ground, each of which shall be well suited to the requirements of some one division of a collection, *rather than place any at disadvantage within one general enclosure.*

With respect to the management of public grounds, within which provision for a collection of animals is required, a division of the collection between several localities offers some decided advantages.

A given length of ordinary park-walk, say 100 yards, will comfortably accommodate 1,000 people moving at different rates of speed and in opposite directions.   If double this number undertake to pass over it at the same time, the difficulties of preserving order and securing a tolerable degree of convenience and comfort will have increased in much greater proportion than the increase in number of the people.   Consequently, the more a given number of objects of interest with[in] a park are separated, and the more the number of visitors seeking them is divided and led to take different routes, the less the difficulties of management, the greater the convenience and comfort of the public.   The less, also, will be the crowd standing at any time before any object of interest and, consequently, the better the opportunities of observation.

In the specifications of the plan for the laying out of the Central Park no provisions were required for the exhibition of animals and, in the present stage of the development of the plan, it would be utterly impossible to find suitable accomodations for all the divisions of a collection as large and varied as any of the more important ones of Europe.   There are however spaces of limited extent, on each of which a certain division might be provided for satisfactorily.

For example, the proposition has already been favorably considered by the Commission to establish suitable sheds on the hillside facing south, between the East Drive and Fifth avenue, near the line of One Hundredth street, for the grazing animals now kept on the ground near Fifth avenue at Eightieth street, lately appropriated to the Art Museum, and to assign the valley to the southward, between the hillside and the fourth transverse road, as the grazing ground for such animals.   The suggestion has also already been made that the meadow between the Reservoir and the fourth transverse road be appropriated to sub-hardy grazing animals, such as the antelope; suitable buildings for their summer and winter accommodation being erected on the north side of it, at which point they would be inconspicuous and obstruct no extended views.

It is now further suggested that another division of the collection might be satisfactorily accommodated on the proposed esplanade of Morningside Park, in a building of the following description:

A conservatory 450 feet long, and, in the main body, 60 feet wide and 30 feet high, consisting of a quadrangular hall with a pavilion at each end. The glass of the roof and sides to be movable, so that in summer the whole or either of the three apartments may be thrown open and the atmosphere within the house, whenever desirable, made the same as that without. The temperature in winter to be heated and regulated as in an ordinary green-house and ventilation to be accomplished by the apparatus now commonly used in large hospitals, to be driven by a steam engine, which would also serve to supply water for fountains and general distribution throughout the building. Exotic plants to be grown from the floor and trained along the rafters as vines in an ordinary grapery; the whole building thus forming a winter garden and sanitarium. The central parts of the two pavilions to be occupied by aviaries; the central parts of the main hall by a series of double cages 24 feet square; these cages to be appropriated to the feline tropical animals. It will be observed that the advantages for securing cleanliness and ventilation for such animals are very great, and that each will be under observation by spectators from three sides at once. Such a structure, so situated, will be out of sight from the nearest private buildings, nor can any tainted air or noise of the animals reach them. The greatest length of the building will be in a line almost exactly north and south, and the sunlight from both sides will fall directly upon the animals. It will offer no obstruction to the view, and, though very low, will have an elegant and brilliant character. It is completely protected on the north and west by high walls of rock.

Respectfully,

Fred. Law Olmsted, L.A.
For himself, and
Calvert Vaux,
Late Consulting L.A.

POSSIBILITY OF COMBINED ZOOLOGICAL AND
BOTANICAL GARDEN[1]

New York, 2d January, 1878.

To the Board of Commissioners
of the Department of Public Parks:

Gentlemen,—The present menagerie (*see No. 40 on Folded Map*) of the Department has become what it is by successive desultory steps taken with no view to permanence or completeness in any

---

[1] Minutes, D. P. P., January 9, 1878.

respect. It is so placed as to be a serious injury to the Central Park; it is ill arranged, ill equipped, not adapted to economical maintenance. Under these circumstances, though closely, prudently and skillfully managed, it adds a weight to the annual appropriations for the Park which tends unjustly to the public discredit of its administration.

The existing objections to it will be more obvious as its slight wooden buildings fall more and more into disrepair. The cracks and openings caused by the shrinkage, decay and warping of timber in them are now so many and so large that after another year, should an extraordinarily severe winter occur, it will be hardly practicable to keep the tropical animals alive, unless considerable and expensive rebuilding is undertaken. The Board can, therefore, not long hold to a waiting policy with respect to it, but will be compelled to adopt some radical measure.

Still more unsuitable and economically indefensible, except as makeshifts, have been all the arrangements hitherto employed by the Department for purposes such as are met by the well-known Floral and Exotic Public Gardens of Europe.

The Park Commissioners of different periods, always expecting that some permanent and well-arranged plan would soon be carried out, have tentatively entertained two radically different classes of projects, one having in view the management of the proposed gardens by the city direct, the other the management of them by an association especially formed for the purpose.

With reference to the first class, four different localities have been successively appropriated, plans adopted suitable to them, and twice operations have been begun in carrying out these plans. Each of these appropriations has at last been reconsidered, and all of the plans abandoned. With reference to the second class, numerous organizations have been undertaken, and two have been so far matured as to obtain special acts of legislation, but no one has been able to secure such concessions, assistance, and privileges as its promoters thought necessary to success, and all are now defunct.

During the last three years I have been asked to report upon five projects, some of one of these classes, some of the other, on neither of which has the Commission as yet taken definite action. As the subject is likely to be further agitated during my intended absence, I propose at this point briefly and without extended argument, to state certain general conclusions which, in my judgment, may be wisely adopted.

1st. New York demands advantages corresponding to those found in the acclimatization, zoological, botanic, and horticultural gardens of other metropolitan cities.

2d. The best way to secure such advantages would be one in general accordance with the policy which has been heretofore adopted and which is already, to a certain extent, in successful operation in the American Museum of Natural History and the Metropolitan Museum of Art.

3d. This policy would lead to a contract between the city and a society, for the purpose, under which the city would give the society the use of land and aid in obtaining buildings and collections, while the society would give the public the use of the same at certain times, gratuitously, and at others in payment of moderate admission fees, and would undertake the current expenses of the enterprise.

4th. Botanic or exotic gardens need to have many of the same plants and the same appliances as zoological gardens. A zoological garden, as generally managed, is, to some extent, a botanic garden, and each of the propositions for a zoological garden, now before the Department contemplates a combination of botanic and zoological interests.

In view of the difficulty which has been experienced in raising the necessary capital to start either a zoological or a botanic garden on an adequate basis, and in view of the objections to inclosing any more of the area of the Central Park than is necessary for the purpose, it is not wise to contemplate, at present, two or more distinct gardens—one for zoology, others for different branches of botany or floriculture—each to be aided by the city.

5th. No garden of the kind proposed could be established on the Central Park without taking away from the public advantages for which a high price has been paid. Nowhere in the middle parts of the park, nor on its southern borders, could such a garden be placed without great waste and disastrous results. Not even on its more northern borders could any body of land be taken for the purpose which would not be found cramped, and, in some respects, inconvenient—requiring large outlays to make it satisfactory.

6th. On the other hand, no garden of the class contemplated would be likely, for a long time to come, to make adequate returns through admission fees, if situated much further north than the Central Park.

7th. Under all these conditions, the Department would be justified in providing, wherever it shall be found practicable by the method proposed, for the more immediately useful, attractive, and popular departments of a combined zoological and botanic garden upon the Central Park, taking land for these purposes in which the buildings could be so arranged as not to break up the broader landscape scenes, and recovering for the Park the land now occupied by the menagerie.

8th. But it is desirable in addition to this, that the Department should designate some considerable tract of suburban land as a public ground to be specially reserved for an arboretum and horticultural garden, and, perhaps, other scientific uses in the future. Suitable land for such a purpose may be found in that portion of the new wards, the plans of which remain to be determined.

9th. Having in view a Zoological and Botanic garden to be situated in the Central Park, which would compare favorably with the best in the world in respect to popular entertainment and instructiveness, though lacking space for scientific completeness, a site should be sought within which a considerable extent of surface would be found with (1) an exposure to the south, (2) protection from northeast, north and northwest winds, (3) perfect drainage, (4) ample flowing water supply, (5) direct association with a considerable pond or broad body of water, which would lie within the same enclosure.

10th. The only ground in other respects available where these advantages are offered in the Central Park lies on the west side of the Park, south of the great hill, from Ninety-sixth to One hundred and fifth Streets. A garden might be found to which this locality would be central, containing from twenty to thirty acres, in which the necessary buildings and fences of a zoological and exotic garden would be inconspicuous, if not wholly invisible, from any part of the park proper. No other equal space of ground upon the park could be taken for the purpose of a zoological and botanic garden with less sacrifice of advantages for the proper general purposes of the park.

In conclusion, I beg to urge that if the Commission is of opinion that it is necessary to appropriate some portion of the Central Park to a zoological garden, and any association can be found, having public interests in view, like the existing organizations managing the Natural History and Art Museum and not looking to pecuniary profits, which is able and disposed to assume due responsibilities in the matter, it is very desirable that negotiations with a view to the lease for the purpose of the ground I have indicated, should be entered upon at an early day.

Respectfully,

FRED. LAW OLMSTED,
Landscape Architect.

THE PURPOSE AND SITE OF THE ZOO—A CATECHISM[1]

BROOKLINE, MASS., 18th March, 1890.

THE HONORABLE WALDO HUTCHINS,
President of the Department of Public Parks
of the City of New York.

Dear Sir:—

At the meeting of your Board on the 12th instant, a few questions were addressed to me to which I could not at once make satisfactory reply. Having since traced upon the ground the plan then before you for a zoological garden in Central Park, and having refreshed my memory on certain points, I beg leave to submit a

[1] ED. NOTE: From draft in Olmsted letter book.   Printed as Doc. No. 117, March 27, 1890.

written report on the subject.   I propose to give it the form of
questions and answers the better to recall the general line of inquiry
pursued at that meeting, but I will first show briefly how I believe
the problem of a zoological garden for the city has taken the form in
which it is now presented.

Originally, the Park Commissioners did not intend that any of
the territory at their disposal should be used for such a purpose.
It was expected that the old Arsenal, with which the land taken for
Central Park was encumbered, would soon make way for the screening plantations required by the design of the Park, as a limit to the
eastward view from the Fifth Avenue entrance-ways.   Pending its
removal, when a few small animals were received, most of them
having been, I think, pets of children who had died, or who were
leaving town, temporary place was provided for them in the Arsenal.
As additional animals were, from time to time, presented, the
Commissioners, never liking to decline gifts to the city, had pens
and sheds prepared for some outside of the Arsenal.   At a later
period, the Director was allowed to make the collection more
interesting by exchanges; and, still later, by purchases; and so, by
successive, unpremeditated steps, the present conditions have been
gradually approached.   Considering how largely the process has
been one of makeshifts and temporizing expedients, that the result
has come to be as valuable as it is, and as little discreditable to the
city, must be attributed to the sincere devotion and rare discretion
of Dr. Conklin, who, from the beginning, has been responsible for
almost everything in the history of this affair that is not to be
regretted.   There have been many projects for placing it on a substantial, permanent footing.   I recall twelve schemes for this
purpose that have had some consideration by the Department.
At least three of these have been successively adopted by the Park
Commissioners and afterward abandoned.   Several thousand
dollars were expended in preliminary work with a view to carrying
out one of them; afterwards, several thousand more in removing the
result and restoring the ground to its previous condition.

As often as the subject comes to be searchingly discussed, it is
recognized that New York is going to be a much larger city than it
is at present; that no institutions to be useful to the mass of its population will be for many years adequate that are not projected on a
larger scale than they need to be in order to meet such wants as have
been established in past experience; and that the progress of zoological enterprise is likely to make such advances in the future that
no accommodations that would be provided for present necessities
can be expected to be long satisfactory, unless so situated that
they can be afterwards considerably enlarged by spreading out and
covering additional ground.

Moreover, it is felt that if a zoological garden is to be established
as a governmental institution, the City ought not to be satisfied
with a place for it that is not more than tolerably adapted to the
purpose.   It is felt that, with respect to the health and comfort of

the animals, at least, a site should be found in which ideal conditions are fairly approached.

The difficulty has always been to find such a place that is not further removed than is desirable from the present centre of population of the City, and which can be used without too large a sacrifice of property valuable for other purposes.

I will proceed to consider the present proposition with reference to this difficulty.

Question: Having particularly in view the health and comfort of the animals, what should be looked for in a site for a zoological garden in the climate of New York? *Answer:* 1st, A good part of its surface will desirably slope to the South, providing a sunny exposure; 2nd, There will be nothing to the immediate southward of it to prevent its being swept by southerly breezes; 3rd, There should be, on the other hand, a protecting rise of ground to the North of it; 4th, It should have a freely permeable soil; 5th, There will desirably be a running stream or a flowing pool of water within it.

Question: Are these desiderata found in the site now in view? *Answer:* Not one of them; 1st, its surface slopes to the northward, which is the worst possible exposure; 2nd, There is a ridge running along its southern boundary which would deflect the summer breezes from its surface; 3rd, There is no elevation shielding it from the northerly winds; 4th, It has a cold, impermeable soil and a hard-pan subsoil; 5th, It has no permanent surface water.

Question: Considered with reference to the health of the animals, is the site now occupied better or worse than that to which it is proposed that they shall be removed? *Answer:* Better, because it has a southern exposure and is protected from northerly winds by adjoining higher ground.

Question: Is there any other objection to this proposed site than those which have been stated? *Answer:* The main objection remains. This is that, in its present condition, that ground serves the leading purpose for which the land of the Park as a whole was bought by the City better than it would if occupied by the proposed garden.

Question: Is there any portion of the Park that is more crowded, or in which the people, and especially the children, find more amusement than in that portion of it occupied by the Zoological Collection? *Answer:* None, yet it is less crowded than a negro minstrel show often is, and is less amusing, especially to the small children, than a Punch and Judy performance would be. Any number of things more amusing, and that would collect larger crowds might be provided for the people by the City at much less cost than the Menagerie.

Question: If the leading purpose of the Park is not the amusement of the people, how can we come at what it is? *Answer:* It is plainly a purpose to further which it has been thought not unreasonable to take more than ten thousand building lots out of the heart of a great commercial town, to close twenty miles of its streets and to expend millions in operations of which the general effect will be the production of woods and meadows.

Question: And what can such a purpose be but a purpose of amusement? *Answer:* If it is to be called amusement, it is plainly not any kind of amusement that could just as well be provided within the space that would suffice for a theatre or for a zoological garden. If the purpose had been to provide for a great number of means of amusement, in that sense of the word, it would have been much less inconvenient and costly to have had sixty places of amusement well distributed, each of the area of two city blocks, with slight local closing of streets, rather than one place sixty times as large, with the closing of fifty streets, all in one quarter of the city and that a central quarter where the interruption of travel would be most inconvenient to all.

Question: With what purpose could such a proceeding have been rationally decided upon? *Answer:* Only with the purpose of providing great numbers of people living in a compactly built town all around such a place, with an opportunity to get quickly out of the scenery of buildings, streets and yards into scenery to be formed with a view to supplying a refreshing contrast with it; a contrast with it to be refreshing more particularly because of its having a more spaciously natural aspect than it would be possible for scenery to have, the scope of which was limited to a less spacious field of operations for the forming of scenery.

Question: Admitting such to be the proper and only justifying purpose of so large a park, could not the essential requirements of a zoological garden be reconciled with that purpose? *Answer:* Possibly.

Question: Does the Garden of the Zoological Society of London interfere with such a purpose in Regent's Park? *Answer:* It does. That Park would much better serve such a purpose if it had as much more interior, open, meadow-like space as is taken up by the Zoological Garden. The scenery of the Bois de Bologne also would be much more refreshing than it is, if, in its interior parts, there were two or three broad, quiet, open glades, with turf spreading out from them under openly disposed, stately, umbrageous trees, the entire space of such open ground being equal to that which has been leased for the Garden of the Acclimatization Society.

Question: How then might the requirements of a zoological collection be provided for in the Park, as you say they might, without seriously interfering with the distinctive purpose of the Park? *Answer:* Suppose a park in the interior of which there are open areas large enough to establish a character of landscape spaciousness and to allow that form of beauty to be enjoyed which can only be had in looking to a distance across broad openings of woodland. In the shadow of the outer wooded parts of such a park, the structures necessary for the zoological collection might be so disposed that they would stand veiled from view across the openings and not be in any way obtrusive upon the natural scenery.

Question: Could the necessary buildings of the Zoological Garden be so placed upon the site now under consideration by the Board without interfering with the object of the Park? *Answer:* They could not. In nearly every acre of Central Park there were originally swells and ridges of rock projecting from the general surface at frequent intervals. Wherever there was a chance to obtain an open space of turf by a moderate amount of blasting out of some of these protuberances, such blasting was done and loam was deposited in place of the rock blown out; and in this way meadow spaces gained. Trees were then planted in the borders of these spaces, in openings of ledges and on their outer edges. As these trees, properly thinned, grow to stateliness, they will form natural landscape compositions with one another, with the ledges and with the flatter turfy spaces, and as such compositions are seen across the openings, they will have a peculiarly refreshing and park-like beauty. But the process that has been described was a terribly costly one. Hence, the removal of the rocky ridges was not carried so far but that the Park is greatly defective in respect to landscape spaciousness and breadth of tranquil surface. Every good opening, therefore, that has been secured by the process described is to be highly valued and scrupulously cherished.

The little meadow north of the Reservoir is one of these open spaces. There are numerous oaks with other trees growing along its rocky borders. They have been little crowded, their branches spread horizontally and they are taking superbly umbrageous forms. They give fair promise to be in time the stateliest trees on the Park.

Question: Could the plan for the Zoological Garden now before the Board be carried out without the destruction of these rocky elevations and of the trees grouped about them? *Answer:* It could not. The main walk of this plan could not be made without blasting out several hundred feet in length of ledges and breaking up a rocky surface twenty or thirty square feet in area; not without destroying numbers of trees that are now growing between and adjoining these ledges. These trees have not suffered from crowding as have most of the trees on the Park, and being fully thirty years old, are already treasures, several being oaks of the first class, of which there are all too few on the Park.

Question: Is, then, the plan now before the Board to be considered a very bad plan? *Answer:* Having regard to the purpose of providing a village of pretty houses adapted to the lodging of animals, on each side of a broad, straight avenue, it is a good plan, entirely creditable to the talented architect who has evidently designed it for that purpose. That which is bad in the matter is simply the necessity of destroying, for such a purpose, so rare an opportunity of securing, in the middle of a great city, a perfect bit of charming, picturesque, pastoral scenery, such as there will surely be at this point in a few years, if nature is allowed to keep on her present course.

Question: Can a less objectionable place be found on the Park for the Zoological Garden? *Answer:* The ground which the City was once advised by the American Natural History Society to appropriate to the purpose is much less objectionable. This ground lies west of the Winter Drive between 98th St. and 104th St.

Question: In what respect is it less objectionable? *Answer:* A part of it, several acres in extent, has a southerly aspect, is open to southerly breezes and is sheltered by much higher ground on the north. It contains a considerable body of water with beautiful rock-bound and tree-shadowed banks. The necessary buildings could be so placed in it as to be comparatively secluded and almost completely shut out of any of the open prospects of the Park by existing well grown trees, mostly low-bottomed coniferous trees.

Question: Are there any situations in the Park that would be more objectionable for the Zoological Garden than that to which the present plan applies? *Answer:* There are as many as five, and two of them have repeatedly been urged as very desirable places for the purpose by citizens of high standing and of large influence, politically and otherwise. So great is the danger that with annually recurring changes of membership in your Board, some one of these will eventually be taken, and the Menagerie be established upon it before public opinion realizes what is to be lost, that it is with reluctance that I advise against this last project, as a means of assurance against one even more objectionable.

May I be allowed to add that I strongly sympathize with the desire that there should be a fine, permanent exhibition of animals near the centre of the City, and regret exceedingly that I cannot think that a more than tolerable place can be made for it in Central Park, except at a sacrifice of that which is even more desirable than such an exhibition would be. Central Park will not much longer be found over-large for the simple purpose for which it was originally designed, and for overcoming the natural obstacles to which the City has made such large outlay. It is only by a strenuously conservative policy that this outlay will not be wasted.

Your obedient servant,

FRED^K. LAW OLMSTED,
*Landscape Architect in
Consultation.*[1]

[1] ED. NOTE: On August 6, 1889, we find that Mr. Olmsted was addressed as Consulting Landscape Architect to the Department of Public Parks (Calvert Vaux being Landscape Architect), and his advice sought on matters in the Central Park. Cf. Part II, Chapter I, pp. 272 ff.

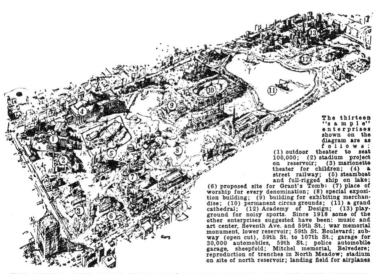

The thirteen "s a m p l e" enterprises shown on the diagram are as f o l l o w s : (1) outdoor theater to seat 100,000; (2) stadium project on reservoir; (3) marionette theater for children; (4) a street railway; (5) steamboat and full-rigged ship on lake; (6) proposed site for Grant's Tomb: (7) place of worship for every denomination; (8) special exposition building; (9) building for exhibiting merchandise; (10) permanent circus grounds; (11) a grand cathedral; (12) Academy of Design; (13) playground for noisy sports. Since 1918 some of the other enterprises suggested have been: music and art center, Seventh Ave. and 59th St.; war memorial monument, lower reservoir; 59th St. Boulevard; subway (open cut), 59th St. to 107th St.; garage for 30,000 automobiles, 59th St.; police automobile garage, sheepfold; Mitchel memorial, Belvedere; reproduction of trenches in North Meadow; stadium on site of north reservoir; landing field for airplanes

HOW CENTRAL PARK MIGHT HAVE LOOKED IF THE INVADERS HAD NOT BEEN DEFEATED
A few of the unsuccessful attempts to divert the park from its primary purpose, as visualized by "The New York Times"

Reproduced from *The American City Magazine*

CHAPTER XII

VARIOUS ENCROACHMENTS PROPOSED AND WARDED OFF

"*The Park is a ground appropriated and arranged for the enjoyment of all the classes that inhabit a great city, and the design has been so to plan and arrange it that the visitor may immediately on entering be led . . . to divest himself of the thoughts and reflections that attend upon city business life, and to give himself up to an hour of undisturbed recreation.*

"*Whatever in such a scheme properly aids in the transition of the mental operations from business to pleasure or recreation is valuable.*

"*The Park is visited by millions—citizens and strangers; the natural beauties of the landscape, of tree, shrub, and flower, of brook, meadow, and beetling cliff, as they appear, changing with the varying seasons, afford more satisfaction to a larger number of people than any other use to which the acres could be devoted; and it is not too much to say that experience has fully shown that ideas of this nature that underlie the whole design have been generally comprehended and accepted. . . .*

"THESE ARE CONSISTENT WITH CERTAIN OTHER USES, BUT NOT WITH ALL OTHER USES, AND NO ONE OUGHT TO DESIRE TO IMPAIR THE ATTRACTIONS OF THE PARK BY INTRODUCING OTHERS THAT ARE INCONSISTENT AND IMPRACTICABLE." [1]

"*In the inception of an entirely novel undertaking, like that of the establishment and management of a great city Park, the Commissioners expect that new questions will continually arise, and that new schemes, having, perhaps, some valuable elements to commend them, will be urged by persons not altogether familiar with the whole plan and object of the Park. It will be the study of the Commissioners to dispose of these questions, so far as they have the power, with sole reference to the general enjoyment, keeping in mind that the chief*

[1] 13th Annual Report, C. P. C., 1869.

object for which the Park was instituted, and with reference to which it has been laid out. . . ." [1]

The history of Central Park is full of attempts to appropriate ground for uses inconsistent with its avowed purpose. In the earlier days of the Park, this original purpose was clearly had in mind by the Commissioners, who themselves constituted a committee of defence. But as the Park came under less wise and thoughtful management, and as land became more precious and the vacant acres of the Park more coveted, the strength of thoroughly aroused citizens' committees, working through the press and the Legislature, has been necessary to defend what is now the only remaining stretch of open landscape on the Island of Manhattan.

The variety of proposals to utilize ground in the Park has been endless. In the five years to 1863, enough applications had been made to the Commissioners to call forth the following comment:

"Having become the resort of large assemblages of people, the Park is considered too advantageous a field for advertising to be neglected by those who would force their wants or wares upon the public attention at every turn. The regulations on this subject have been enforced thoroughly, and these practices are thus far kept in abeyance. If all the applications for the erection and maintenances of towers, houses, drinking fountains, telescopes, mineral water fountains, cottages, Aeolian harps, gymnasiums, observatories, [and] weighing-scales, for the sale of eatables, velocipedes, perambulators, Indian work, tobacco, [and] segars, for the privilege of using steam-engines, snow-shoes, [and] ice-boats, and for the use of the ice for fancy dress carnivals, were granted, they would occupy a large portion of the surface of the Park, establish a very extensive and very various business, and give to it the appearance of the grounds of a country fair, or of a militia training-field. A catalogue of applications to use the lawns, the trees, the roads, the walks, and the waters, for purposes entirely foreign to the objects of the Park, and utterly incompatible with its preservation, would give some idea of the ease with which the Park could be overrun if these applications met with favor." [2]

In 1872 when the Landscape Architects wrote their "Review of Recent Changes," there was an even longer catalogue of attempted invasions. (See pages 247 f., ante.)

In 1886, after various encroachments on the Park had been re-

[1] 7th Annual Report, C. P. C., 1863.
[2] *Ibid.*

sisted[1] *the* NEW YORK TRIBUNE *in a leading article* (*January 10*) *recalls the thousand and one projects urged on the Commissioners.*

"*Persons of quality who delight in steeple-chasing, and those who pursue the fleet anise-seed bag in its lair, have had an eye upon the rolling meadows and dense coppices of the Park as an inviting field for manly sport. Commissioners have been petitioned to throw open the Park as a parade ground for our citizen soldiery, and space has been asked for tents and enclosures for popular exhibitions, circuses, shooting-matches, and trials of strength and skill. Eminent educators have urged that the Park should be planned on the model of a map of our native land, with miniature states, lakes, and rivers, with every physical and geological feature complete, so that the children of the public schools could be turned loose thereon to study geography in its most attractive form. It has been proposed that each religious sect should be invited to build places of worship there; that one section should be set apart for a World's Fair, and another section as a den for wild beasts, and again that a vast building should be erected there as a sample-room and advertisement for all the wares the merchants of the city have to sell; that the lakes should be enlarged so as to float a full-rigged ship where the great maritime city of the continent could train sailors for our merchant marine; that it should be transmuted into a burial-place for the country's distinguished dead, an experimental farm in the interest of scientific agriculture, and a permanent Metropolitan Fair Ground.*

"*Now, if the Park is only a big scope of unimproved ground, it is natural that people of different tastes should desire to pre-empt a quarter section here and there for the particular business or pleasure in which they are chiefly interested. For this reason, the people who drive their own carriages, or are able to hire one occasionally, have clamored for widening the wheelways, to give them ample space to roll around and be seen. Other citizens, in less fortunate circumstances have asked that a street railroad be run up through the centre of the Park, so that they might view it from the economical and democratic horse-car.*"

The placing of Museums in the Park and the extension of the Zoo threatened the park landscape, as we have seen in Chapters IX and XI. Among the other most important attempted encroachments[2]

---

[1] Cf. Part I, Chapter, XI, p. 162.
[2] An interesting article, "The Attacks on Central Park," by Robert Wheelwright, published in *Landscape Architecture*, October, 1910, summarized proposed invasions to that date. See further references given in footnote on p. 164, *ante*.

have been a *military parade ground* (several times), a *huge hotel on Mt. St. Vincent*, a *wide speedway* for trotting horses the length of the west boundary of the Park, a *permanent World's Fair*, building sites for the *National Academy of Design*, an *Exhibition Hall*, a *place of worship* for every denomination, a *grand cathedral*, a *great war memorial*, a *music and art center*, a *stadium*, a *subterranean garage for 30,000 automobiles*, a *landing field for airplanes*, and an *open-cut subway* along the west side.

In 1918 the *New York* Times [1] published an imaginary bird's-eye view of the Park showing how it would look if thirteen of the principal projects had been carried out. The Park was pictured almost completely covered with buildings!

Of all the projects during Mr. Olmsted's lifetime, none seems to have aroused more violent public opposition than the Speedway, which was authorized by the Legislature in 1892. It was an earlier out-cropping of this proposal that called forth Mr. Olmsted's letter to Mr. Dana, of the *New York Sun*, given in this chapter. So great was the storm of protest against the Speedway that just twenty-eight days after its passage the bill was repealed. Present defenders of the Park would find encouragement in reading a booklet entitled "*The Central Park Race Track Law was Repealed by Public Sentiment*" (1892).

The great legal bulwark against further encroachments on the Park is the decision of the Court of Appeals in 1920 against the lease of the Arsenal by the Park Commissioner to the American Institute of Safety as a Safety Museum. The Court held that the "educational" character of the exhibition was not in conformity with "park purposes," which it defined in detail. This decision is quoted in full in Appendix II of this volume.

The present organization guarding the Park's integrity is the Central Park Association, formed in 1926 as an outgrowth of the Parks Conservation Association which had led the fight on behalf of the parks during the Hylan administration. The little book, "*The Central Park*," setting forth the new association's aims and plans, concluded with the following words:

"*If the congestion of 1851 required the erection of Central Park, the greater congestion of 1926 requires its ample restoration and perpetual maintenance and protection.*"

[1] See illustration on p. 517.

THE PAPERS INCLUDED IN THIS CHAPTER ARE:

‡ *Letter regarding real purpose of Park in relation to subversive new projects, to C. V. from F. L. O. November 4, 1883.*

‡ *Letter giving reasons against Speeding Track in Central Park, to Paul Dana from F. L. O. December 22, 1890.*

"*The Justifying Value of a Public Park*": *Selections from paper before American Social Science Association, 1880, by F. L. O.—Giving a criterion for determining appropriate uses.*

‡ Previously unpublished.

REAL PURPOSE OF THE PARK IN RELATION TO SUB-
VERSIVE NEW PROJECTS

BROOKLINE, MASS., 4th Nov., 1883.

My dear Vaux:

I am sorry that I cannot be in New York tomorrow.

The special difficulty of the park in city administration lies in the ordinary unreadiness to regard it otherwise than as a body of land held for a variety of purposes, vague and variable. Because of this misty background every year in its history some project of a ruinous tendency has had the warm support of many good men, the advantages to be gained by it seeming to them for the time to stand out with such perfect clearness that they have seen no room for debate on the question. Yet the fact is that much the larger part of the appropriations made in twenty-six years on account of the park have been asked for ostensibly with reference to one comprehensive purpose—that of providing such small measure as is practicable so near at hand of natural, verdant and sylvan scenery for the refreshment of town-strained men, women and children, especially in those conditions of life that preclude resort to scenery of absolutely unsophisticated nature.

Accepting this as a good purpose and what has been done as not wholly misdirected with reference to it, when a project is urged for the occupation of any part of the park territory for a special purpose, as for military displays, botanical or zoological shows, the promotion of good fellowship on the road, a World's Fair, running horses or what not, two questions are to be asked:

First, taking a fair look ahead, does it now seem that the entire remaining territory held under the name of the park is larger than is desirable to be held exclusively for the central purpose above defined? Second, to the estimated cost of what is proposed, how much should be added to represent what is necessarily to be set aside of expenditure previously made with a view to this central purpose?

As to the latter question it will always appear on due reflection very foolish to assume that where little has been expended little can be wasted It might be said of all that part of a man's overcoat upon which no velvet or buttons, braid or stitching had been expended. The most valuable parts of the park are those which because of their natural fitness for the central purpose have required the least modification of their original condition. In truth, the design of all other parts has been determined with reference to these and to appropriate them to other purposes is to wipe out that upon which the value of everything else depends. No proposition could be more revolutionary, more wasteful, more extravagant.

Experience indicates that it is only necessary to have public attention adequately called to this consideration to compel all such projects to be relinquished.

When my counsel is invited about the Park, I do not like to be altogether silent with regard to a danger more difficult to cope with which lies in the state of mind that confuses a purpose of decorating ground on principles analogous to those of the upholsterer or the milliner's trade with the purpose of gaining the charm of natural scenery. The two purposes have hardly more in common than those of painting and sculpture but are so constantly confounded in public discussions that it would seem that hardly more than a germ of sound public opinion on the subject yet existed. The result is an opening for innumerable follies of detail to go unrebuked.

Yours truly,

[F. L. O.]

REASONS AGAINST SPEEDING TRACK IN CENTRAL PARK

22nd December, 1890.

Dear Mr. Dana:[1]

I have received your note of the 15th instant and am sorry that I could not reply sooner.

I would like to indicate the point of view from which I regard the proposition to sequestrate a part of Central Park for a Speeding Track.

Thirty-five years ago, when I lived several months in London, most of the people could yet, by less than an hour's walk from their homes, get into charming fragments of rural scenery, saunter in lovely lanes, or by old foot-paths through fields, and find many pretty wild flowers. On Sundays, I have met thousands of its people rambling with their children in these places. Last year an English physician visiting us told me that all I had known of this sort had been long since destroyed; that the eating up of rural suburbs went on much faster than the increase of population, and that it was already useless to look for a wild flower within twenty miles of Bow Bells. Henceforth, a large part of the people of London would live and die without ever having seen a suggestion of rural beauty, except such as might be provided in public parks.

[1] Mr. Paul Dana of the *Sun*.

Because of the great space occupied by water, and for other reasons, before New York shall have nearly the present population of London, a much larger territory will have been dis-ruralized.

It is now generally held to be desirable that cities growing to be great should make timely provisions through which their future people shall not be compelled to go out from them to obtain some degree of soothing rural influences.

It is now also held, but as yet less generally perhaps, that such cities should be possessed of open areas to be used for various sports, or manly and blood-stirring recreations.

Provisions suitable for one of these purposes are not to any considerable extent suitable for the other. On the contrary, the preparation of a given piece of land suitable for one of them makes it unsuitable for the other.

It is unfortunate that the word park, without any discriminating prefix, is popularly applied to pieces of ground used for various and incongruous purposes. When a man says: "I am going to the park," he may mean to a baseball park, a deer park, an oyster park, or a park proper, that is to say, a rural park. So if a man chooses to say a park is not complete unless it has provisions for all sorts of sports, he is not to be put down with dictionaries.

An astute, successful and wealthy gentleman said to me a year ago:

"You have provided in the park means of recreation of different kinds for a good part of the population; for those who like to walk; to ride; loiter in slow-going carriages; for those who like boating, skating, curling, tennis, ball-playing, and even for children who like to use merry-go-rounds, scups and goat carriages. Now, I and certain other citizens and tax-payers do not care for any of these. Our form of recreation is the driving of fast horses with light vehicles at a much faster rate of speed than is allowed, or than would be safe on the crooked roads you have made in the park. Why should we be discriminated against? Why have we not as much right to be provided with facilities for the enjoyment of the one form of recreation in which we are interested as those who have taken up tennis, or skating, or cycling, or pedestrianism, or driving slowly, or riding, for their recreations?"

And the view thus indicated is undoubtedly held by many intelligent citizens of New York. But it must have been adopted thoughtlessly. It has no legal foundation. The fact is, although I cannot show you verse and chapter for it, or any clear, legal records, the territory of the park was bought, the plan of the construction of the park devised, and many million dollars spent upon the park, with no purpose of making it a place of general, miscellaneous out-of-door recreation, as thus assumed, but for the purpose of making it *a place of rural recreation*. The roads have been laid out with the object of developing and exhibiting the rural capabilities of the territory to the utmost. Thirty costly archways and bridges have been built exclusively with the same motive;

i.e. to provide for the convenient passage of great bodies of people through it in various directions, without making the lines of passage excessively conspicuous or otherwise smoothing out unnecessarily the natural inequalities. The same is true of the Ride, the walks, the buildings, the boats, as well as the modeling of the ground and the planting. I do not mean to say that there was, at the outset, not the least confusion of mind on the point, much less that there has never been any waste of money in consequence; but I do say that all such cohfusion has, as yet, no general effect except such as would result from occasional diversion of the main current of purpose.

How then is it to be accounted for that provisions should now be found on the park for playing baseball, skating, tennis, for archery, music, the menagerie, and so on?

I answer that it has been thought that, to a certain extent, provision for these sports and these other forms of recreation might be made incidentally, subordinately and harmlessly to the provision made the main ruling purpose of the park. I admit that the question has often been a practical one, to just what extent provision should be made for some of these sports without lessening the value of the park for its controlling purpose, and that, in my judgment, there have been errors in this respect, but, with perhaps one exception, these errors have been errors of judgment, not intentional repudiations of the main principle. They have established no ground for the assumption that the park is not fundamentally an institution for providing, as far as practicable under the circumstances, that enjoyment of rural scenery of which the growth of the city was rapidly depriving its people.

Ground having been taken by the city for this particular purpose, and having been fitted for this purpose, at an outlay of many million dollars, that ground is reasonably to be regarded as an institution established for that purpose. Those given charge of such a property are then Trustees for that purpose. Because a respectable or a powerful body of citizens think that it would be a good thing to break into this property and apply some of it to another purpose, those Trustees have no more right to yield to this view than they have to sell parts of the property and apply the proceeds to any other purpose. To do so is a distinct breach of trust. It is by far the most important duty of the Commissioners serving as Trustees to defend the property against all such movements.

Bodies of officially irresponsible men who have thoughtlessly adopted a different opinion have always been besieging the Park Commissioners to appropriate pieces of the park for all sorts of other purposes, more or less obviously antagonistic to the preservation of its rurality.

In the last thirty years I do not think that there has ever been a period of two years in which there has not been a strong and respectable movement to destroy some part of the park for its original purpose in order to establish provision for some other form of recreation than that for which it was established. At one time it is a Military Parade Ground; then a Zoological Garden; then a Botanical Garden; then a Palm House and Winter Garden; then an Arboretum; then a Sub-tropical Garden; then a Museum of History; then an Exhibition of Fat Cattle; then one of Rhododendrons, and so on.

Many of these schemes, through the influence of specious argument, and because of presumed political necessities, have been very nearly successful. The Commissioners have more than once voted favorably to some of them. But, after due deliberation and consultation, they have all been at length defeated with the single exception that a large piece of ground (not essentially a part of the landscape of the park) was once given up to an Art Museum—an act now generally regretted.

If half of these schemes had been successful, the park would before this have entirely lost its designed rural character. It would have been subdivided into a hundred sections, each appropriated to some special sport or amusement, with only decorative trimmings of foliage and flowers; lacking all unity; lacking every element of breadth, repose and sylvan composition.

A purpose more clearly apart from, and inconsistent with, the original comprehensive purpose of the park could hardly be devised than this of a Speeding Track. A place which would have been less likely to be chosen for such a purpose than that proposed, were land to be bought for it, could hardly have been selected on the island. No one would have thought of it if it had not been for the chance of stealing the necessary land out of the park and so saving the expense of buying a suitable site for it.

The demand for a Speeding Track has not been as long continued, nor nearly as popular and strong as the demand for a Rotten Row, or as that for widening the East Drive with the object of making an ampler place of Parade for carriages. Fair provision for both of these latter projects might be made with much less outlay, and with much less injury to the rurality of the park, than for that of a Speeding Track.

If you yield to the demand for a Speeding Track, you yield the principle, adherence to which has thus far alone prevented the complete ruin of the park for its established purpose. It may be asked: Would not provision within the city for athletic recreations be more valuable than provision for a sauntering place for the enjoyment of rurality of scenery?

I think not; but what if they would? Would any man in his senses have chosen the site of Central Park for them? A site in which there was not an acre of flat ground, or of ground not broken by outcrops of rock? All these sports require places of flat surface and of even a somewhat elastic surface. The places for them must in no case be crossed by people not engaged in the sport. A Speeding Track a mile and a half long (from 71st St. to 101st St.) on the west side of the park, to be adapted to the purposes of a Speeding Track, would not only require the destruction of valuable existing natural scenery and the blasting out of an immense quantity of ledge rock, but also either the closing of eight of the present entrances to the Park, or a great amount of ugly tunnel and bridge building, to carry travel over or under the Speeding Track. After all had been done, it would be a poor Speeding Track and movements would follow in a few years for additions to it and for improvements upon it, involving great further cost and great further injury to the rural character of the Park.

You ask if there is any other locality in which a Speeding Track could be made. I answer, none where the acquisition by the city of the necessary real estate would not involve large expense.

Is it practicable to get the city to stand this expense at this time?

You can judge of this better than I can, but I should say that an attempt to steal a strip of the poor, narrow Central Park site shows that the movers for the Speeding Track have no confidence that it would.

But there is a larger question, and it is easier to get the interest of the public of New York in a large question than in one affecting the interest of any comparatively small class of the population. The larger question is, whether it is expedient or possible to secure for the city, South of the Harlem at 155th St., a place adapted to sports and athletic recreations, including those to which a Speeding Track is necessary, and which would also supply a place for great assemblages and for exhibitions of value to the city, but not desirable to be placed on broken, rural ground?

A few years ago I felt quite sure that it was, and I have often advocated such a project. The land I have had more particularly in view for it was the Harlem Flats north of the Park. But I suppose that the necessary area there has already become of such value that it would be a bold proposition to acquire it.

Is there a suitable site to be had *anywhere* at a cost that would not stagger the city?

I have lost touch with New York now too much to answer that question offhand.

I think that if I were in your shoes, I should be inclined to draw up a paper setting forth the great desirability of at once providing a place for athletic sports and recreations, recognizing that the constantly growing demand for such a place cannot begin to be met in Central Park, except by a repudiation of its present leading purpose and a costly destruction of what has been gained for it, and concluding with a draft of a resolution directing the appointment of a Committee to ascertain where a site for such a ground could be had, south of 155th St., at the least cost, with a plan for the ground adapted to the site and an estimate of the cost of the real estate and of its construction.

Any action less thorough and comprehensive than this will be paltering, shuffling, dilly-dallying and makeshift. It is a thousand times better to deal with the whole problem squarely than to have it coming up piecemeal, as hitherto it has been every year.

Such a Committee should be empowered to employ good real estate experts, a special clerk, et cetera.

Very truly yours,

FRED^K. LAW OLMSTED.

"THE JUSTIFYING VALUE OF A PUBLIC PARK" [1]

(GIVING A CRITERION FOR DETERMINING APPROPRIATE USES)

. . . While the few public properties which had the name of park with us, twenty-five years ago, did not differ from others known as greens, commons, or yards, yet the word had a meaning by no other so well given. Scores of times I have heard plain country people, Northern and Southern, Eastern and Western, describe something they had seen as "park-like," or "pretty as a park," or as "a perfect natural park." It might be Blue Ridge table-lands, oak openings further west, mesquit-grass prairies beyond the Trinity, or passages of the Genessee Flats or Connecticut Bottoms. What did the word mean? Nothing in the least practical. It reported nothing of the soil, of the water-power, of quarries, or quartz lodes. It told of a certain influence of *conditions solely of scenery*—soothing and reposeful influences. If we trace back this use of the word, it will carry us to the immigrations of the early part of the seventeenth century, before the replanting of English parks under the urgings of Evelyn, the Royal Society, and the Admiralty, when there were generally broader spaces of greensward within them, and yet more of spacious seclusion from all without than even at present.

I beg that this significance of the word may be kept in mind a little while.

Twenty-five years ago we had no parks, park-like or otherwise, which might not better have been called something else. Since then a class of works so called has been undertaken which, to begin with, are at least spacious, and which hold possibilities of all park-like qualities.

. . . .

. . . The reflection may be made that a widespread popular movement is not, naturally, all at once perfectly clear-headed, coherent, and perspicuous in its demands. In other words, it is hardly to be supposed that the popular demand represented in parks has yet taken the fully mature, self-conscious form of thor-

[1] Selections from paper before American Social Science Association, 1880.

oughly reasoned purposes and principles, and has insisted on an accurate embodiment of them in the works ordered. It is more reasonable to assume that it has not.

I wish to present this assumption in a practical form. Let me suppose that a man has become possessed, near a town, of adjoining properties comprising one or two farms, with marsh land, wood-land, pastures, mill-pond, quarry and brick-yard. It is crossed by roads, upon which there is some pleasure driving; the pond is used for skating, the hill-sides for coasting, the pastures for kite-flying, base-ball and target-firing; snipe are shot in the marshes, rabbits trapped in the woods. There are neglected private properties so used for recreation by the public near most of our towns. Now, suppose that the man dies, leaving an infant heir; twenty years afterwards the heir dies, and the entire property is to come by will to the town on condition that the town spends half a million dollars to make it a park. Suppose the old roads are improved and furnished with sidewalks and shade trees; the brickyard fitted for a parade ground, the marsh for a rifle range; and that the quarry, with masonry and gates added, becomes a town reservoir. Part of the ground is taken for a cemetery; a statue of the former owner is set on the highest hill; a museum and public library take the place of the homestead; an armory is provided, a hospital, poor-house, high school, conservatory, camera-obscura, prospect tower, botanic and zoological garden, archery, lawn-tennis and croquet-grounds, billiard-house, skating-rink, racket court, ten-pin alley, riding-school, Turkish bath, mineral springs, restaurants, pagodas, pavilions, and a mall, terrace, and concert garden. Suppose that the town has spent its half million, several times over, in these things, and that the courts can have found reason (I know not how) to decide that the condition of the bequest has been complied with. Suppose that a due part of all the town outlay in the premises has been set down in the town books to old accounts, so far as applicable, as to account of waterworks, street improvements, schools, hospitals, and so on; and that, after all, there is found something which must be charged under the new head of "parks."

Now, suppose that a question is raised whether this expenditure has been made in good faith, with reference to the proper objects and distinctive value of a park, and has been judiciously and economically directed, and that a popular judgment (not a technical court judgment) is asked upon the issue, what would be the result? Few men would have a sufficiently clear idea of the objects and the conditions of value of a park to form judgment; those who had would differ widely in their ideas, and most of the more judicial and properly leading minds would hold such ideas as they had with enough of doubt to make them slow either to fully support or decisively condemn those responsible. This, unquestionably, would be the case much more than it would in regard to any other large matter of town expenditure.

· · · · · · · · ·

The simplest statement of purpose that courts would unhesitatingly accept or public opinion stand agreed upon, and, even then, not as a complete statement, but only as true so far as it goes, would be this: "A public park is a ground appropriated to public recreation."

Observe, then, that most of the public properties known as parks contain provisions for other purposes than recreation, and even opposed to recreation. Again, waiving the question how far these are legitimate parts of them, observe that recreation is so broad a term, and means so much more to some than to others, that to devote public funds to recreation is little less than to give a free rein to the personal tastes, whims and speculations of those intrusted with the administration of them.

We must fall back on usage. What, then, does usage prescribe?

In one European public park we find a race-course, with its grand-stand, stables, pool-room, and betting ring; in another, popular diversions of the class which we elsewhere look to Barnum to provide. In one there is a theater with ballet-dancing; in another, soldiers firing field-pieces at a target, with a detail of cavalry to keep the public at a distance.

Attempts to introduce like provisions in several of our American parks have been resisted under the personal conviction that they would tend to subvert their more important purpose. In some of our parks, nevertheless, arrangements have been made for various games; concerts and shows have been admitted; there have been military parades; and it is impossible to find any line of principle between many favored and neglected propositions.

Usage, therefore, in this respect, decides nothing.

Asking what usage prescribes as to the simpler forms of recreation, we shall find that one ground, classed among public parks, consists of dense woods, with a few nearly straight roads through it, while others have open, pastoral landscapes, with circuitous drives, rides, and walks; that the interest of one centers in an extremely artificial display of exotics and bedding plants, while another bids fair to be equally distinguished for its fountains, monuments, statues, and other means of recreation in stone, concrete, and bronze. Yet another is so natural and unsophisticated you can hardly use it in dry weather without choking with dust, or in wet weather without wading in mud.

Again, usage determines nothing.

What this laxity leaves us liable to, and how much may be safely presumed upon the public's confusion of mind, is shown by the fact that in one case, when local opposition was found to be inconveniently strong against the location of a smallpox hospital anywhere else, the difficulty was overcome by placing it in the midst of a park.

.   .   .   .

. . . To all the economical advantages we have gained through modern discoveries and inventions, the great enlargement of the field of commerce, the growth of towns, and the spread of town ways of living, there are some grave drawbacks. We may yet understand them so imperfectly that we but little more than veil our ignorance when we talk of what is lost and suffered under the name of "vital exhaustion" . . . But that there are actual drawbacks, which we thus vaguely indicate, to the prosperity of large towns, and that they deduct much from the wealth-producing and tax-bearing capacity of their people, as well as from the wealth-enjoying capacity, there can be no doubt.

The question remains whether the contemplation of beauty in natural scenery is practically of much value in counteracting and alleviating these evils, and whether it is possible, at reasonable cost, to make such beauty available to the daily use of great numbers of townspeople? I do not propose to argue this question. I submit it . . . as one needing discussion; for if the object of parks is not that thus suggested, I know of none which justifies their cost. On the other hand, if the object of parks is thus indicated, I know of no justification for a great deal that is done with them, and a great deal more that many men are bent on doing. That other objects than the cultivation of beauty of natural scenery may be associated with it economically, in a park, I am not disposed to deny; but that all such other objects should be held strictly subordinate to that, in order to justify the purchase and holding of these large properties . . . cannot be successfully disputed.

I will but add that the problem of a park . . . under the view which I have aimed to suggest . . . is mainly the reconciliation of adequate beauty of nature in scenery with adequate means in artificial constructions [for] protecting the conditions of such beauty, and [for] holding it available to the use, in a convenient and orderly way, of those needing it; and the employment of such means for both purposes as will make the park steadily gainful of that quality of beauty which comes only with age.

APPENDIX I

CHRONOLOGICAL TABLE

Including Important Dates in the History of Central Park[1]

1851 *April.* Mayor Kingsland recommended the Common Council to consider the question of a public park for New York. Committee of Common Council reported favorably and recommended Jones' Wood for the purpose.

July. Act of Legislature (ch. 529), providing for a park at Jones' Wood. (Later repassed and repealed.)

August. Committee of Common Council recommended a change of the site.

1853 *July.* Act of Legislature (ch. 616) passed, taking site of the present Central Park, south of 106th Street.

November. Commissioners of Estimate and Assessment appointed under the Act of July.

1855 *March.* Resolution passed by Common Council favoring a reduction of the area vetoed by Mayor Fernando Wood.

1856 *February.* Report of Commissioners of Estimate and Assessment confirmed, and the title of the City to the site of the Central Park, south of 106th Street, established.

May. Mayor Wood and Street Commissioner Taylor appointed by the Common Council a Commission for the management of the Park; Egbert L. Viele appointed Chief Engineer; Washington Irving, Charles P. Briggs, James Phalen, and Stewart Brown, appointed Advisory Committee. Topographical survey of the ground ordered. Special Police appointed.

1857 *April.* Act of Legislature (ch. 771) passed, establishing the Board of Commissioners of the Central Park. Board organized. J. E. Cooley, President.

June. Andrew H. Green elected Treasurer.

August. Workmen employed to clean the ground of stones and rubbish, and open surface drains; work begun on the 12th.

September. F. L. Olmsted appointed Superintendent. Competitive designs for laying out the Park invited by public advertisement; 500 men at work.

December. 1,120 men at work.

---

[1] As much as possible of this Table has been taken from Mr. Olmsted's own "Chronological Table of the progress of the Park undertakings," published in Statistical Report of the Landscape Architect, 1873. (3rd Annual Report, D. P. P.)

1858 *February.* Special Police disbanded. Appointment of 24 Park-keepers.

March. Ordinances for the government of the Park adopted.

April. Competitive designs received on the 1st; prize awarded to "Greensward" (Olmsted and Vaux).

May. Plans publicly exhibited 30 days. Work ordered under the prize plan. F. L. Olmsted appointed Architect-in-Chief of the Central Park.

August. 2,000 men at work.

October. First tree planted in the Park on the 17th.

November. 2,600 men at work.

December. Water let into the Lake. First skating on the Park.

1858. The planting done this year was chiefly on the Mall and in its neighborhood, the East Green, and the Ramble.

1859 *January.* First curling on the Park.

April. Act of Legislature (ch. 101) passed, providing for the extension of the Park to 110th Street.

May. Old Boston Post Road through the Park closed.

June. The Ramble declared open to public use by advertisement of the Commission; 3,000 men at work.

July. First concert in the Park (by private contribution); first deer presented to the Park; 3,800 men employed.

August. Vista Rock Tunnel cut through, work upon it having been continuous for several months, day and night.

November. 3½ miles of drive declared open to public use; Lake completed; first transverse road open to public use.

December. Construction of the Park south of 79th Street announced by Commissioner to be "complete."

1859. During this year 10 viaduct arches completed; 7 miles of walk constructed; 10 miles of drainage-pipe laid; 17,300 trees and shrubs planted, including most of the deciduous trees south of 79th Street; plan prepared for extension to 110th Street; average force of laborers employed, 2,977.

1860 *May.* Swans presented to the Park by the City of Hamburg.

June. Committee of State Senate investigated the management of the Park.

September. 2,500 men at work.

October. Swans presented from London.

1860. During this year 16,200 trees planted, including most of the deciduous shrubs and evergreen trees south of 79th Street; average force of laborers employed, 1,328.

1861 *January.* Proceedings to acquire title to ground north of 106th Street discontinued.

April. Volunteers quartered in the old arsenal in the Park; regular boat service on the Lake commenced.

June. Proceedings for extension of the Park to 110th Street renewed.

1861. At the end of this year, carriage road in public use 7 miles; total length of drainage-pipe laid in Park, 62 miles; of water-pipe, 13½ miles. During this year the 59th Street Mall (previously formed by widening the street on the Park side 40 feet) was planted; enclosing wall of Park commenced on 59th Street; average force of laborers employed, 650; 52,700 trees and shrubs planted, including winter-drive district and most of the deciduous trees north of 79th Street and south of 110th Street.

1862 During this year average force of laborers employed, 560; trees and shrubs planted, 74,730; Mount St. Vincent used as an Army Hospital; Music Pavilion erected at the Mall.

1863 *April.* Report of Commissioners of Estimate and Assessment in the proceeding to acquire title to land for Central Park north of 106th Street, confirmed.

May. Olmsted and Vaux resigned from connection with Central Park.

September. Deer presented to the Park by the City of Philadelphia.

1863. During this year average force of laborers employed, 492; the expense of the music during the season was paid by the Commission, which heretofore had been defrayed by private contribution; number of visitors to the Park, 4,326,500.

1864 *April.* Two Regiments of the National Guard illegally paraded in the Park; Manhattan Square annexed to Central Park by Act of Legislature. (ch. 319.)

1864. During this year English Sparrows were introduced on the Park (7 pairs); 20,000 trees and shrubs planted; average force of laborers employed, 541; number of visitors to the Park, 6,120,179.

1865 *June.* Statue of Commerce presented.

July. Olmsted and Vaux reappointed.

December. The Loch completed and filled.

1865. During this year average force of laborers employed, 341; the drive and ride were completed; school-boys were allowed to play ball on the Park, and the building of the enclosing wall was continued to a total of 15,544 feet (about 3 miles); number of visitors to the Park, 7,593,139.

1866 *August.* Harlem Meer completed. "Kinderberg," rustic shelter for children, built.

1866. During this year average force of laborers employed, 256; trees and shrubs planted, 17,700; elms planted in Fifth Avenue Mall; number of visitors to the Park, 7,839,373.

1867 *June.* Belvedere commenced.

October. Bronze of the Tigress presented; boys' play-house commenced.

1867. During this year average force of laborers employed, 241; the first hot-house erected on the Park, and the meteorological observatory established; number of visitors to the Park, 7,227,855.

1868 *June.* Palæozoic Museum commenced.

December. Bronze statue of the Indian Hunter, by J. Q. A. Ward, presented.

1868. During this year average force of laborers employed, 396; trees and shrubs planted, 6,800; number of visitors to the Park, 7,089,798.

1869 *February.* Bust of Humboldt presented.

April. Statue of Columbus presented.

September. Dairy commenced. Merchant's gate commenced.

November. Movable skating-house at Lake and curling-house at Conservatory water built.

1869. During this year 12,522 trees and shrubs were planted; the average force of laborers employed was 1,179; a Museum of Natural History was established in the Arsenal; steam rollers were first used on the Park roads; boys' play-house first in use; number of visitors to the Park, 7, 350,957.

1870 *May.* Charter of 1870 (ch. 137) took effect; first meeting of the Board of the Department of Public Parks on the 3rd; Board organized. (Tweed Ring Administration.)

June. Zoological Gardens ordered to be laid out; day's work reduced to 8 hours in conformity with Act of Legislature (ch. 385, 1870). Carrousel ordered.

September. Ground plan of Conservatory approved, and the foundations ordered to be prepared.

October. "Sheepfold" commenced.

November. Olmsted and Vaux resigned.

December. Building of the Palæozoic Museum ordered to be discontinued.

1870. During this year "Dairy" opened to use; average force of laborers employed, 1,587; number of visitors to the Park, 8,628,826.

1871 *April.* Stables and workshops commenced; reorganization of Park-keepers' force.

November. Reorganization of the Board; Olmsted and Vaux reappointed; work discontinued on Zoological Gardens, Deer House, Conservatory, etc.

December. Park-keepers' force reduced by the discharge of 54 keepers.

1871. During this year average force of laborers employed, 2,970; number of visitors to the Park, 10,764,411.

1872 *May.* F. L. Olmsted President of Department of Public Parks (in absence of Commissioner Stebbins, until October); Deer House removed.

October. Carrousel removed to its present location.

November. Park-keepers' force ordered to be reduced and extra keepers to be employed from the laboring force.

1872. During this year number of visitors to the Park, 10,873,839.

1873 *May.* Construction work generally discontinued for lack of funds; Bethesda fountain inaugurated.

June. Reorganization of the Board under the charter of 1873 (ch. 335); construction work resumed.

October. Revised system of rules adopted for the regulation of the force of Park-keepers.

1873. During this year number of visitors to the Park, 10,060,159.

1874 *April.* Number of Park Commissioners reduced to four (ch. 300).

1875 *March.* Construction work temporarily suspended for lack of funds. Maintenance continued.

1876 *November.* Mr. Green, friend and defender of the Park, removed as Comptroller of the City of New York.

1876. "The building of (Central Park), in its principal features was completed." [1]

1877 *May.* Unveiling of Halleck Statue (see *ante*, page 433) and military display causes damage to Park. Commissioners resolve that the regulations prohibiting military parades and unusual crowds be henceforth rigidly adhered to.

---

[1] E. H. Hall in American Scenic and Historic Preservation Society Report, 1911, page 478. He adds, "The park, however, has never really been finished."

1878 *January.* Office of Design and Superintendence abolished. Mr. Olmsted dismissed.

1881 *January.* Park threatened by proposed World's Fair scheme. Act of Legislature made exhibitions in Park illegal (ch. 208).

1882 *February.* Pamphlet "Spoils of the Park," by Mr. Olmsted, published.

1883 *January.* Mr. Vaux resigned as Superintending Architect.

1884 During this year an enlargement of the building for Museum of Art was approved, and a new foot entrance at Eighth Avenue and 92nd Street authorized.

1885 During this year reconstruction of Plaza at Fifth Avenue and 59th Street completed. Samuel Parsons became Superintendent of Parks.

1886 During this year work on the enclosing wall was actively proceeding.

1888 *January.* Mr. Vaux's appointment as Landscape Architect to the Department of Public Parks effective on the 1st.

    1888. During this year plans were prepared for the permanent landscape improvement of the northernmost part of the Park. Also the Park Board held hearing on public speeding drive on west side of Central Park, but denied petition as "subversive of the uses and ends for which the Park was created and is maintained."

1889 *September.* Park Board against reviving proposals for World's Fair in Central Park.

    1889. During this year Mr. Olmsted and Mr. Harrison reported on plantations in the Park and pamphlet "Use of the Axe" published.

1890 During this year there was constant agitation about the location of the Zoo in the Park. Mr. Olmsted consulted about this and also widening of the Park drives, which he advised against.

1892 *March.* Speedway Act passed.
    April. Speedway Act repealed, through pressure of public opinion.

1897 Under Greater New York Consolidation Act, government of Central Park came within province of Park Commissioner for Manhattan and Richmond (see page 538).

1920 Decision of Court of Appeals, by Judge Pound (229 N. Y., 248) forbidding the use of the Arsenal in the Park for a Safety Museum. "Central Park should be kept open as a public park" (see page 551).

1926 *January.* Formation of the Central Park Association.

    March. Report of Fifth Avenue Association to the Board of Estimate and Apportionment setting forth causes of Park's deterioration.

1927 *February.* The sum of $1,000,000 was laid aside by the Board of Estimate and Apportionment for the rehabilitation of the Park.

APPENDIX II

LAWS RELATING TO CENTRAL PARK

1853–1892

The first law authorizing the City of New York to take and lay out "certain lands for a public park" was passed by the Legislature of the State of New York on July 11, 1851, specifying land in the Nineteenth Ward, known as Jones' Wood. This law was repassed in slightly different form on July 21, 1853, but finally repealed on April 11, 1854. Meanwhile the act had been passed (July 21, 1853) declaring land in the central wards of the city "to be a public place." After this act, and prior to the passage by the State Legislature in 1857 of the act creating the Commissioners of the Central Park, the Common Council of the City of New York had, in 1856, passed two ordinances for the Park's financing and temporary government. In order to show the status of the Park during this interim period, these two ordinances will be interpolated in historical sequence in the following digest.

The "Laws respecting the Central Park" may be found compiled, together with the laws relating to other works under the control of the Department of Public Parks, in a pamphlet published by the City in 1870 after the so-called Tweed Charter had gone into effect. An earlier compilation of laws, together with the full report of the State Senate Investigation Committee of 1860, may be found appended to the 4th Annual Report of the Commissioners of the Central Park. In the marginal references of Chap. 410, Laws of 1882, will be found an index to previous legislation, and in the Consolidation Act itself, a summary of the laws then in force.

The date 1892 has been selected to conclude our Appendix of Laws because this was the year of the passage and the repeal of the notorious Speedway Act (see pages 163 and 524, *ante*), after which date we find no laws enacted relating specifically to Central Park within the period covered by this volume.

It is of interest to note that under the Greater New York Consolidation Act of 1897, the Department of Public Parks was completely reorganized on the borough system and that the government of Central Park and other parks on the Island of Manhattan came within the province of the Commissioner for Manhattan and Richmond, the other two Commissioners who composed the Board governing respectively the Borough of The Bronx and the Boroughs of Brooklyn and Queens. The Park Board was required under the Consolidation Act to appoint a landscape architect "whose assent shall be requisite to all plans and works or changes thereof respecting the conformation, development or ornamentation of any of the parks, squares, or public places of the city."

1853, Chapter 616. *An act to alter the map of the city of New-York, by laying out thereon a public place, and to authorize the taking of the same.*
Passed July 21, 1853.

§ 1.   "All that piece or parcel of land situate, lying, and being in the twelfth, nineteenth, and twenty-second wards of the city of New-York, bounded southerly by Fifty-ninth-street, northerly by One Hundred and Sixth-street, easterly by the Fifth-avenue, and westerly by Eighth-avenue, is hereby declared to be a public place, in like manner as if the same had been laid out by the commissioners appointed in and by the act of the Legislature, entitled 'An act relative to improvements touching the laying out of streets and roads in the city of New-York, and for other purposes,' passed April 3, 1807; and the map or plan of said city is hereby altered accordingly."

§ 2.   "The mayor, aldermen, and commonalty of the city of New-York are hereby authorized to take the said piece of land for public use, as and for a public square," pursuant to act of April 9, 1813, and amendments thereto, etc.

§§ 3–4.   Five Commissioners of Estimate and Assessment appointed. Three may act.

§§ 5–6.   Damages may be allowed.   Payment of damages awarded due immediately on confirmation of report of Commissioners.

§ 7.   For payment of damages in excess of sums assessed by Commissioners on parties, etc., deemed benefited by the opening of such public square or place, Mayor, Aldermen, and Commonalty may raise amount by loan "by the creation of a public fund or stock, to be called 'The Central Park Fund,' which shall bear an interest not exceeding five per centum per annum, and shall be redeemable within a period of time not exceeding forty-five years after the passage of this act, and for the payment of which the said piece of land, so as aforesaid to be taken, shall be irrevocably pledged."

§§ 8–10.   Mayor, etc., to determine value and number of shares of stock; sale authorized, etc.   Interest to be paid by taxation.   Provisions of act to regulate finances of City of New York, June 8, 1812, to apply.

1856 (Feb. 29.)   An ordinance[1] to create funds for the payment of the Public Place entitled "The Central Park."

Loan of $2,867,000 at five per cent.

1856 (May 21.)   An ordinance for the regulation and government of the Central Park.

Section 1.   "The Central Park, until further action of the Common Council, or the Legislature, shall be under the control and management of a Board of Commissioners, to consist of the Mayor and the Street Commissioner, who shall be termed the 'Commissioners of the Central Park'."

Sec. 2.   "The said Board shall have full power to govern, manage, and direct the said park; to consult, examine, and determine upon the plan for the improvement thereof; to lay out and regulate the grounds; to pass and make rules for the regulation and government thereof; to appoint such gardeners, engineers, surveyors, clerks and laborers as may be necessary; to prescribe and define their respective duties and the amount of their compensation, to be fixed by the Common Council."

---

[1] Only copy known to be in existence of Proceedings of Board of Aldermen and Board of Councilmen for 1856, containing these ordinances, may be found in the New York Municipal Reference Library.

Sec. 3. "The said Board shall, semi-annually and in the months of January and July, in each year, and at any time when so requested by either Board of the Common Council, make to the Common Council, a full report of their receipts and expenditures on account of said park."

Sec. 4. "It shall be lawful for the Comptroller and the Collector of the City Revenue, by and with the permission of the said Board, to let any buildings, and the grounds attached thereto, now being within said park, until the same shall be required for the laying out and regulation thereof, when the said buildings shall be removed, except such as may be used for the purposes of the park; but the proceeds thereof shall be placed to the credit of the fund at the disposal of the Commissioners, for the improvements therein referred to."

Sec. 5. "It shall be lawful for the said Board of Commissioners, to sell any buildings, improvements, and other materials, now being within said park, which, in their judgment, shall not be required for the purposes of the park, or the public use."

Sec. 6. "The proceeds of buildings, improvements or materials sold, and the rent of buildings and lands let, as hereinbefore authorized, are hereby appropriated for the purposes of this ordinance, to be disbursed by the Comptroller upon requisition of said Commissioners."

1856 (July 18.) An ordinance making an appropriation for the improvement of the Central Park.

$100,000 appropriated.

1857, Chap. 388. *An act authorizing the Mayor, Aldermen and Commonalty of the city of New York to widen Broadway or Bloomingdale road, between Fifty-seventh and fifty-ninth streets* . . . Passed April 13, 1857.[1]

Section 1. Broadway to be widened whenever deemed desirable "to improve the access to Central Park."

1857, Chap. 771. *An act for the regulation and government of the Central Park, in the city of New-York.* Passed April 17, 1857.[2]

Section 1. Land taken for a public place confirmed by order of Supreme Court, February 5, 1856, shall be known as "The Central Park."

§§ 2–3. Park to be under exclusive control and management of a Board of Commissioners, to consist of eleven persons, who shall be styled "The Commissioners of the Central Park." Commissioners named (see page 33, *ante*).

---

[1] Amended by Chap. 757, Laws of 1866.

[2] In Report No. 25 of the competition volume (mentioned on page 44), ascribed to R. Graves formerly of the Central Park, the following interesting bit of unwritten history occurs:

"When the Central Park act of 1857 (under operation of which the park is now governed) passed the Committee of Conference of the Senate and House, and was by them handed to their chairman for its final passage, there was included in the act at the end of section 7, the following clause:

" 'The Commissioners, in conjunction with the Street Department of the city, are hereby authorized *to make and adjust permanent grades*, and determine the permanent width of the avenues and streets, and the sidewalks and roadways thereof, bounding the said park, and adjust the grades of all streets affected thereby. And no house or obstruction shall hereafter be erected beyond the front lines of the avenues and streets thus widened.'

" I took a copy of this clause from the act, then in possession of the Chairman, within five minutes after the Conference Committee adjourned. By some strange conjuration the bill was reported to the Senate *with the clause above quoted stricken out*—passed that body, and also the House before the discovery was made. The Session (next day, I think) adjourned sine die."

§ 4. The Board "shall have the full and exclusive power to govern, manage and direct the said Central Park; to lay out and regulate the same," etc.

§ 5. A misdemeanor for any Commissioner, directly or indirectly, to be interested in any contract, etc., connected with the Park.

§ 6. Full annual report to be made.

§§ 7–8. Leasing of buildings until removal necessary and sale of materials now on Park land to be allowed, and proceeds devoted to improvement of Park.

§ 9. "No plan for the laying out, regulation and government of said Park shall be adopted or undertaken by the commissioners, of which the entire expense, when funded, shall require for the payment of the annual interest thereon a greater sum than one hundred thousand dollars per annum."

§10. "The mayor, aldermen, and commonalty of the city of New-York, shall from time to time create and issue a public fund or stock, to be denominated 'The Central Park Improvement Fund' . . . and the said Park shall be and the same is hereby specifically pledged for the redemption thereof."

§ 11. For payment of interest on stock, money to be raised by taxation.

§ 12. How and where moneys of Commissioners are to be deposited, and interest to be secured for same.

§ 13. Exchange of certain lands with Croton Aqueduct Board authorized.

§§ 14–15. Commissioners to pass ordinances "for regulation, use and government" of Park. Violations of these to be punished.

1859, Chap. 101. *An act to alter the map of the city of New York, by laying out thereon a public place, and to authorize the taking of the same* (extension of Park to 110th Street).   Passed April 2, 1859.

Section 1. Land, 106th Street to 110th Street between Fifth and Eighth avenues, declared a public place.

§§ 2–12. Provisions for Commissioners of Estimate and Assessment, financing by a public stock, "The Central Park Additional Fund" redeemable within forty-five years, interest to be raised by taxation, etc.

§ 13. The said public place with the piece of land mentioned in act passed April 17, 1857, shall form "The Central Park," and shall be subject to all provisions of that act.

1859, Chap. 349. *An act to amend an act . . . passed April 17, 1857, and further to provide for the maintenance and government of said Park.*
                                                Passed April 15, 1859.

Section 1. Of the act of April 17, 1857, section two is amended to read:

§ 2. "The said Park shall be under the exclusive control and management of a board of commissioners to consist of not less than seven, nor more than eleven persons, who shall be named and styled 'The Commissioners of the Central park.' A majority of the said commissioners in office, for the time being, shall constitute a quorum for the transaction of business, and no action of the board shall be final or binding unless it shall have received the approval of a majority of the said board then in office, whose names shall be recorded in its minutes."

Section 2. Section three of said act is amended to read:

§ 3. "The commissioners of the Central park now in office, and such person as shall be appointed to fill the existing vacancy in said board, are hereby continued and constituted the said board of commissioners; they shall hold their office as such commissioners for five years from the passage of the act hereby amended. No member of said board shall receive any compensation for his services except the president or treasurer, but each commissioner shall, nevertheless, be entitled to receive for his personal expenses in visiting and superintending the said park, a sum not exceeding three hundred dollars per annum. In case of a vacancy, the same may be filled by the remaining members of the board for the residue of the term then vacant, and all vacancies occasioned by expirations of terms of office shall be filled by the mayor, by and with the advice and consent of the board of aldermen of the city of New York."

Section 3. Amendment of section five, misdemeanor to be pecuniarily interested in contract. Oath of office to be taken.

Section 4. Section nine is amended to read:

§ 9. "No plan for the laying out, regulation and government of said park shall be adopted or undertaken by the commissioners, of which the entire expense, when funded, shall require for the payment of the annual interest thereon a greater sum than one hundred and twenty-five thousand dollars per annum."

Section 5. Interest on stock.

Section 6. Deposit of moneys.

Section 7. Debt is not to be created by commissioners or employees, except with express authority of board in meeting convened.

Section 8. Repeal of inconsistent provisions.

Section 9. "The office of either of the said commissioners who shall not attend the meetings of the board for three successive months, after having been duly notified of said meetings, without reasons satisfactory to said board, or without leave of absence from said board, may by said board be declared vacant."

Section 10. "Real and personal property may be granted, devised, bequeathed or conveyed to the mayor, aldermen and commonalty of the city of New York, for the purposes of the improvement or ornamentation of the Central park in said city, or for the establishment or maintenance, within the limits of said Central park, of museums, zoological or other gardens, collections of natural history, observatories or works of art, upon such trusts and conditions as may be prescribed by the grantors or donors thereof, and agreed to by the said mayor, aldermen and commonalty; and all property so devised, granted, bequeathed or conveyed, and the rents, issues, profits and income thereof, shall be subject to the exclusive management, direction and control of the said board of commissioners of the Central park."

1859, Chap. 363. *An act to alter the map or plan of the city of New York.*
Passed April 15, 1859.[1]

Section 1. Seventh Avenue between 110th Street and Harlem River to be widened to 150 feet.

§ 2. Said part of Seventh Avenue to be laid out and regulated under the supervision of the Commissioners of the Central Park.

---

[1] Interesting as first of city planning enterprises laid on Central Park Commissioners arising out of their success with undertaking the Park itself. References to laws authorizing subsequent planning enterprises will not be included.

1860, Chap. 85. *An act for the construction, regulation, maintenance and government of the Central park . . . and to provide additional means therefor.* Passed March 19, 1860.

Section 1. Public stock to be created for "The Central Park Improvement Fund," the annual interest of which shall not exceed $150,000, but not more than one-third of stock to be issued in any one year.

§§ 2–3. Interest on stock to be paid from moneys raised by taxation. Moneys to be deposited, interest on these to be allowed, etc.

§ 4. Commissioners shall transmit to Board of Supervisors an estimate of the amount of money required each year (not exceeding $150,000 in any one year) for maintenance and government of the Central Park.

1860, Chap. 256. *An act to incorporate the American Zoological and Botanical Society.* Passed April 10, 1860.

Section 1. Incorporators named (including F. L. Olmsted).

§§ 2–10. Powers, organization, officers, qualifications for membership, etc.

§ 11. "The board of commissioners of the Central park in the city of New York are hereby authorized and empowered to allow the said corporation hereby created, to establish within the said Park, the zoological and botanical garden contemplated by this act; and, to that end, the said board of commissioners may allot, set apart and appropriate suitable and proper grounds within the said park, in the position, and of the dimensions to be determined by the said board of commissioners, not exceeding sixty acres, for the said garden;" corporation to have access to grounds and to use rent free under conditions and terms to be agreed on, etc.

1861, Chap. 88. *An act to amend an act . . . passed April 15, 1859, and further to provide for the construction, maintenance and government of the said park.* Passed March 27, 1861.

Sections 1–2. Commissioners of the Central Park now in office to continue for five years from expiration of present term. They may fill in any vacancy occuring in their number.

§ 3. "The said board is hereby authorized to take and hold any gifts, devises or bequests, that may be made to said board, upon such trusts and conditions, as may be prescribed by the donors or grantors thereof, and agreed to by said board, for the purpose of embellishing or ornamenting said park;" and shall make annual report of gifts, etc.

1862, Chap. 46. *An act to improve the Central Park in the city of New York.* Passed March 25, 1862.

Section 1. "The commissioners of the Central Park in the city of New York are hereby authorized to set apart and appropriate to the New York Historical Society the building within said Park heretofore known as the New York State Arsenal, together with such grounds adjoining the same as the said commissioners may determine to be necessary and proper for the purpose of establishing and maintaining therein by the said Society a museum of antiquities and science and a gallery of art."

§§ 2–5. Power to alter building, gallery to be accessible to the public, buildings to revert to Central Park if museum is discontinued, etc.

1863, from Chap. 227. (City Tax Levy.) Passed April 24, 1863.

§ 4. Authority given to Commissioners of Central Park to obtain money on faith of certain stock. Comptroller of city to issue stock, etc.

1864, Chap. 319. *An act in relation to Manhattan square in the city of New York.* Passed April 23, 1864.

Section 1. Manhattan Square annexed to Central Park under control of Commissioners. Eighth Avenue to be kept open. "Commissioners shall have power to establish and maintain on the said piece of ground, or any other part of the Central park, a Botanical and Zoological garden," etc.

1865, Chap. 26. *An act for the improvement, maintenance, regulation and government of the Central Park . . . and to provide additional means therefor.* Passed February 10, 1865.

Section 1. City of New York to create a public fund to be denominated "The Central Park Improvement Fund," limited to sum of which annual interest not to exceed $100,000.

§§ 2–4. Moneys for interest to be raised by taxation, deposit of moneys, advances in anticipation of issue of stock, etc.

§ 5. Gifts, devises, etc., to zoological or botanical gardens, etc., to be controlled by the commissioners of the Central Park, etc.

§ 6. Board to determine condition of admissions to gardens.

§ 7. No military encampment, parade, drill, review, etc., to be held in the Central Park.

1866, Chap. 757. Act to amend act authorizing "Public place or circle" at Broadway, 59th Street, and Eighth Avenue. (Act of April 13, 1857.) Amendment passed April 21, 1866.

"To improve the access to Central Park."

1867, Chap. 580. Act in regard to grading and widening of Eighth Avenue. Passed April 23, 1867.

Specific directions for grading Eighth Avenue between 59th and 122nd streets given, and also for widening of Eighth Avenue between 103rd and 107th streets; also for building a supporting wall on the easterly side of said avenue and "to slope off or terrace the part of the surface of the Central Park immediately behind the said supporting wall; and to establish an entrance into the Park opposite to the said bridge," etc.

1868, Chap. 478. *An act to authorize the commissioners of the Central Park to set apart a site for a Museum of History, Antiquities, and Art.* Passed April 29, 1868.

Section 1. "The commissioners of the Central Park, in the city of New York, are hereby authorized to set apart and appropriate to the New York Historical Society, upon such conditions as they may deem expedient, such portion of the grounds of the Central Park lying between the Fifth avenue and a line parallel therewith, and not exceeding three hundred feet distant westerly therefrom, and between the northerly line of Eighty-first street and the southerly line of Eighty-fourth street, continued westerly at right angles with said avenue, as the commissioners may determine to be necessary and proper for the purpose of establishing and maintaining therein by the said society a Museum of History, Antiquities, and Art."

§ 2. "The said society may, at its own expense, erect on the said grounds, after the same shall have been set apart and appropriated in accordance with the first section of this act, a building for the accommodation of said museum, the plan and elevation of which shall, before its erection, be submitted to the said commissioners of the Central Park, and no building shall be erected by said society on said ground until the plan and elevations thereof have been approved by the said commissioners of the Central Park; and all rights and privileges that may be granted, set apart, and appropriated by said commissioners of the Central Park to said New York Historical Society, shall become absolutely void and of no effect if said society shall fail to erect and complete said building within the time that may be limited by said board of commissioners of the Central Park for so doing."

§ 3. "The museum contemplated in the first section of this act, when so established, shall be accessible to the public under proper regulations to be adopted by the said society, approved by the said commissioners, and not inconsistent with proper administration and management of the said park."

§ 4. "The evidence of setting apart and appropriation of the said grounds within the said park to the said New York Historical Society, for the purpose aforesaid, shall be a resolution to that effect adopted by the said board of commissioners, duly acknowledged by one or more of the officers of the said board to be designated by the said board for that purpose, and recorded in the office of the register of the city and county of New York."

§ 5. "If the said New York Historical Society shall so establish their said museum of history, antiquities and art, then so long as they shall continue there to maintain the same they shall occupy and enjoy the said building and the grounds so to be set apart and appropriated to them for the purpose aforesaid, free from rent, assessment or charge whatever therefor, and if the said society shall at any time hereafter for any cause discontinue their said museum of history, antiquities and art, in the said building or on the said grounds, then any building whatever, erected under the provisions of this act, and the said grounds before set apart and appropriated, shall revert to the said Central Park for the general purposes thereof; but the said society shall in such case be permitted to remove therefrom the said museum and all its property other than such building."

§ 6. "The act entitled 'An act to improve the Central Park in the city of New York,' passed March twenty-fifth, eighteen hundred and sixty-two, is hereby repealed, and all resolutions and other acts or evidences of appropriation or setting apart any ground within the limits of the Central Park, to the said New York Historical Society, heretofore made by the said commissioners of the Central Park by virtue of said act or otherwise, are hereby declared to be void and of no effect."

1868, from Chap. 853. (City Tax Levy.) Deficiency appropriation for maintenance and government of Central Park.

1869, Chap. 350. *An act to authorize the erection of a Soldiers' and Sailors' Monument in the city of New York. . . .*   Passed April 27, 1869.

On request of the Commissioners of the Central Park, appropriation authorized for Monument, to be located and erected under charge of said Commissioners.

1869, Chap. 595. *An act to authorize the erection and maintenance of an observatory in the city of New York.*   Passed May 5, 1869.

Section 1. "The Board of Commissioners of the Central Park are hereby authorized to erect, establish, conduct and maintain on the Central Park, in said city, a meteorological and astronomical observatory, and a museum of natural history, and a gallery of art, and the buildings therefor, and to provide the necessary instruments, furniture and equipments for the same."

1870, from Chap. 137. (City Charter.) *Act to reorganize the local government of the city of New York.* Passed April 5, 1870.

Article Fourth: *Of the co-ordinate city departments generally.*

§§ 29–30. Heads of departments to be appointed by the Mayor, including Department of Public Parks.

Article Twelfth: *Of the Department of Public Parks.*

§ 94. "The department of public parks shall control and manage all public parks and public places above Canal street, which are of the realty of the city of New York."[1]

§ 95. "This department shall be under the charge of a board, to consist of five members, who shall be appointed by the mayor, and shall respectively hold office for terms of five years."

§ 96. "All provisions of law which provide for the maintenance and government of the Central Park, or grant powers and devolve duties upon, (or award allowance for carriage hire to,—*these words repealed by sec.* 15, *chap.* 383, *laws of* 1870) the commissioners of the Central Park, (or provide salary for the comptroller of said park,—*these words repealed by sec.* 15, *chap.* 383, *laws of* 1870) shall apply to the department of parks hereby established, and to the commissioners and comptroller thereof respectively."

1870, from Chap. 383 (City Tax Levy). *An act to make further provision for the government of the city of New York.* Passed April 26, 1870.

Department of Public Parks

(Extract from Section 1.) Maintenance and government of Central Park, $250,000; for arrears for year 1869, $27,357.08; west line of Central Park, adapting same to line of Eighth avenue, $25,000.

§ 15. "No member of the board of the department of public parks shall receive any salary or other compensation for his services in any capacity connected with said department. The said department of parks is hereby directed to perfect the boulevard on the southerly side of the Central park in Fifty-ninth street, by removing therefrom the railway tracks of the North, East, and Central Park Railroad Company, and permission is hereby given to said company to lay double tracks in lieu of tracks so removed, in Fifty-eighth street, to connect suitably with their other tracks now laid in the Eleventh and First avenues. The road or public drive laid out on the map or plan of the city of New York, by the commissioners of the Central park, pursuant to the provisions of chapter five hundred and sixty-five, laws of eighteen hundred and sixty-five, shall hereafter be known as 'The Boulevard,' and shall be wholly under the care, management, and control of the department of public parks, and as to the use thereof the said department shall have, possess, and enjoy all the powers now or hereafter possessed, enjoyed, or exercised by said commissioners in respect to the Central park in said city."

§ 16. "All parks and public grounds south of Canal street, shall hereafter be under the control and management of the department of public parks, and nothing in any act contained shall be deemed, construed, or taken to abrogate or impair any powers or duties conferred on the said department of public parks, 'by virtue of article twelve of chapter one hundred and thirty-seven, laws of one thousand eight hundred and seventy,' and all acts conferring powers and devolving duties upon the board of commissioners of the Central park are hereby transferred to and conferred upon the said department of public parks, but no action of the board composing said department shall be deemed final or binding unless it shall

---

[1] Amended by § 16, Chap. 383, Laws of 1870, q.v.

have received the approval of a majority of the said board whose names shall be recorded in its minutes. The department of public parks is hereby authorized to include in the estimate, which said department is authorized to make for moneys required for the maintenance and government of the Central park, such further sum as may be annually required for the maintenance, government and improvement of the several parks, roads and avenues under the control of said department."

1871, Chap. 290. *An act in relation to the powers and duties of the board of commissioners of the department of public parks, including provision for the several public parks, squares and places, under the jurisdiction and direction of said department, in the city of New York.* Passed April 5, 1871.

Comptroller to issue stock for improving parks and squares, also for observatory in Central Park. Erection of a building for Museum of Art authorized, also building for Museum of Natural History, both on Manhattan Square or "any other public park, square or place in the city."

1873, Chap. 335. Passed April 30, 1873.

Article XII: *Of the Department of Public Parks.*

§ 83. "The department of public parks shall control and manage all public parks and streets immediately adjoining the same above Fifty-ninth street, ʰand public places, which are the realty of the city of New York, except the buildings in city hall park, and save as herein otherwise provided; and shall have all the powers and duties belonging to the department or commissioners of parks not inconsistent with the provisions of this act, and the laying out and preparing maps and plans *for the construction of* [1] all streets, avenues and drives above Fifty-ninth street."

§ 84. "This department shall be under the charge of a board to consist of five members, who, except those first appointed, shall hold their offices for five years, unless sooner removed as herein provided. The persons first appointed shall be appointed and hold office for one, two, three, *four* and five years respectively, unless sooner removed as herein provided."

NOTE: In § 27, it was provided that city departments should make reports to the mayor once in three months, which reports shall be published in City Record.

1873, Chap. 757. Amending Chap. 335. Passed June 13, 1873.

In § 83, omit words "for the construction."
In § 84, word "four"[2] to be struck out.

1874, Chap. 300. Passed April 30, 1874.

§ 2 amends Chap. 335 of 1873, § 84 to read:
"The department of public parks on and after the first day of May, one thousand eight hundred and seventy-four, shall be under the charge and control of four commissioners," etc.

---

[1] *Phrases in italics* were stricken out by the amendatory Chap. 757.
[2] From § 25 of Chap. 335, it would appear that the President of the Department of Public Parks should hold office for six years, which would call for this amendment to § 84.

1875, Chap. 351. *An act to provide means for the establishment and equipment of the building erected on that portion of Central park formerly known as Manhattan square.* . . . Passed May 15, 1875.

Building for the purposes of a Museum of Natural History.

1875, Chap. 608. *An act to make further provision for the payment of further expenses of the local government of the city of New York.*
Passed June 21, 1875.

Public fund or stock authorized to be known as "City Parks Improvement Fund" up to $575,000 (in addition to other funds) the moneys realized from this to "be applied only to the construction and improvement of said parks, squares and public places, and the completion and repair of architectural structures in the Central park."

1875, Chap. 619. *An act in relation to the powers and duties of the department of public parks of the city of New York.* Passed June 21, 1875.

Commissioners authorized "to set apart as much ground as may be deemed necessary by them, upon that portion of the Central park lying on the easterly side thereof, opposite Fifth avenue from Seventy-ninth street to Eighty-fifth street" for the "American College of Music." [1]

1878, Chap. 385. *An act to provide means for the equipment and furnishing of the building erected on that portion of the Central park, in the city of New York, east of the old receiving reservoir, under the provisions of chapter two hundred and ninety of the laws of one thousand eight hundred and seventy-one for the purposes of a museum and gallery of art, and for the removing thereto and establishing therein the collections of the metropolitan museum of art.* Passed June 3, 1878.

1881, Chap. 208. *An act restricting the right to grant, use or occupy the Central Park, in the city of New York, for the purposes of a public fair or exhibition.*
Passed May 4, 1881. [2]

Section 1. "It shall not be lawful to grant, use or occupy, for the purposes of a public fair or exhibition, any portion of the Central Park in the city of New York."

1882, Chap. 410. *An act to consolidate into one act and to declare the special and local laws affecting public interests in the city of New York.*
Passed July 1, 1882.

Chapter XIII: *Department of Public Parks.* (§§ 668–703.)

§ 680. (1881, Chap. 323, § 1.) "The board of commissioners of the department of public parks is hereby authorized to complete the entrances on the Eighth Avenue at Seventy-seventh and Eighty-first streets to the westerly drive and on the avenue between said streets to the transverse road. The plans for said improvements may be prepared by the trustees of the American Museum of Natural History, without cost to said city, subject to approval of said board of commissioners."

§ 682. (*see* 1862, Chap. 319, § 1.)

§ 690. (1871, Chap. 290, § 6.) "The commissioners of public parks may organize and appoint a force to be known as keepers of the Central park, and the several public parks, squares, and places in the city, to consist of such number of men as the board may, from time to time, deem necessary to preserve order" . . . etc.

---

[1] This project was abandoned and the same ground was later assigned to the Metropolitain Museum of Art.

[2] Not returned by the governor within ten days after it was presented to him, and became a law without his signature, May 4, 1881.

§ 692. (*see* 1865, Chap. 26, § 7.) (1871, Chap. 208.) "It shall not be lawful to grant, use, or occupy for the purposes of a public fair or exhibition any portion of said park."

§ 693. (*see* 1869, Chap. 599, §§ 1–2.)

§ 694. (*see* 1864, Chap. 319, § 1.)

§ 695. (*see* 1865, Chap. 27, § 6.)

§§ 696–697. (1876, Chap. 139, §§ 1–2.) Contracts with American Museum of Natural History and Metropolitan Museum of Art to be continued.

§ 698. (1881, Chap. 375, § 1.) Enlargement of Metropolitan Museum of Art authorized.

§ 700. (*see* 1859, Chap. 349, § 10; 1861, Chap. 88, § 3; 1865, Chap. 26, § 3.)

§ 702. (1873, Chap. 756, § 7.) $30,000 per year, out of park maintenance moneys, allowed for care, etc., of collections referred to in §§ 696 and 697.

1885, Chap. 106. Department of Public Parks may enlarge building plans, etc., for Metropolitan Museum of Art in Central Park.

Passed April 3, 1885.

1886, Chap. 317. *An act extending the jurisdiction of the department of public parks in the city of New York over a portion of Fifth avenue.*

Passed May 11, 1886.

Department of Public Parks to have exclusive control[1] of maintenance of Fifth Avenue from 59th Street to 110th Street, "and the same shall be deemed a portion of Central park."

1886, Chap. 421. *An act authorizing the mayor, aldermen and commonalty of the city of New York to widen Fifth avenue between One Hundred and Ninth and One Hundred and Tenth streets, and one hundred feet north of One Hundred and Tenth street . . . for a public place.*

Passed May 19, 1886.

1887, Chap. 44. Enlarging building for Museum of Natural History.

Passed February 28, 1887.

1887, Chap. 575. *An act to provide for the completion of the construction of certain public parks in the city of New York.* Passed June 15, 1887.

Section 1. "The department of public parks of the city of New York, is hereby authorized . . . to complete the construction of the Central Park, Morningside Park, Riverside Park . . . and to reconstruct the grounds around the Metropolitan Museum of Art in Central Park . . ."

1887, Chap. 579. *An act to authorize further appropriations for the maintenance of the museums in the Central Park. . . .* Passed June 15, 1887.

---

[1] Jurisdiction over this part of Fifth Avenue was transferred from the Park Department to the Borough President in 1913 (resolution of Board of Estimate and Apportionment, under Chap. 331, Laws of 1913).

1887, Chap. 580. Act authorizing public place adjacent to Central Park at 110th Street and Eighth Avenue. Passed June 15, 1887.

1887, Chap. 581. Completion of building in Central Park for Metropolitan Museum of Art. Passed June 15, 1887.

1888, Chap. 407. *An act relative to railways in the transverse roads of the Central Park in the city of New York.*
Approved by the Governor, May 26, 1888.
Authorizing railways to be built.

1888, Chap. 424. Amending Chap. 580 of 1887, establishing public place at Eighth Avenue and 110th Street.
Approved by the Governor, May 28, 1888.

1889, Chap. 89. Act to provide for completion by addition to building of American Museum of Natural History. Passed March 29, 1889.

1889, Chap. 210. *An act to provide for suitable buildings and accommodations for the Zoological collection in the Central park in the city of New York.*
(Became a law without the approval of the Governor, May 2, 1889.)

Buildings, cages, etc., to be erected "upon a site in the Central park, to be selected by the commissioners of parks, or a majority of them. . . ."

1889, Chap. 513. Completion of north extension of building, Metropolitan Museum of Art. Approved by the Governor, June 15, 1889.

1892, Chap. 142. *An act to authorize the construction of a public drive in the Central park in the city of New York.*
Approved by the Governor, March 17, 1892.

The infamous Speedway Act. The drive was to be 75 feet wide, parallel to west boundary wall, from 58th Street and Eighth Avenue, etc.

1892, Chap. 370. Repealing Chap. 142.
Approved by the Governor, April 25, 1892.

CENTRAL PARK ARSENAL DECISION

JUNE 11, 1920

229 N. Y. 248

William H. Williams, Appellant, v. Francis D. Gallatin, as Commissioner of Parks of the City of New York, et al., Respondents.

Williams v. Gallatin, 191 App. Div. 171, reversed.

(Argued June 1, 1920; decided June 11, 1920.)

Appeal from a judgment of the Appellate Division of the Supreme Court in the first judicial department, entered March 10, 1920, affirming a judgment in favor of defendants entered upon an order of the court at Special Term granting a motion for judgment on the pleadings and directing a dismissal of the complaint.

Pound, J.   The plaintiff, a taxpayer, seeks to enjoin the defendant New York city park commissioner from executing a lease of the Arsenal Building in Central Park to the other defendant, Safety Institute of America, for a term of ten years, upon the ground that the use of the premises by the tenant for the purposes expressed in the lease is contrary to the Greater New York charter in that it is foreign to park purposes.   The complaint alleges that Central Park is a public park, owned by the city of New York; that the Arsenal Building is located in Central Park, and is a part thereof, and is intended for use solely as public park property; that the defendant Francis D. Gallatin, as commissioner of parks, is the chief executive in charge of Central Park and of the Arsenal Building under the provisions of section 612 of the Greater New York charter; that under section 627 of the Greater New York charter it is unlawful for the defendants to grant, use or occupy for the purposes of a public fair or exhibition any portion of Central Park; that the defendants entered into a written lease, a copy of which is attached to the complaint, and defendants plan to proceed with the performance and execution of its terms and with the use and alteration of the said Arsenal Building; that the use of Central Park or the Arsenal Building for any of the purposes referred to will impede and materially hinder the beneficial use of Central Park by the public and the people of the city of New York as a place of resort, amusement, recreation and exercise; that it was illegal for the defendants to enter into the lease.   The lease recites it is made "in order to promote and increase the public enjoyment, use and convenience of the public park known as Central Park."   The lease further provides "that the said building, after it shall have been altered and repaired as herein provided for, shall be kept open and accessible to the public hereafter free of all charge throughout the year, five days in each week, one of which shall be Sunday afternoon, and also for two evenings in each week, within such hours and subject to such rules and regulations as may be determined by the trustees of said institute; and also that on the two days in each week during which said building may remain closed to the general public, it shall be open and accessible to students, schools and societies organized for the purpose of promoting means and methods of safety and sanitation within such hours and subject to such rules and regulations as may be determined by the trustees of said institute."

The American Museum of Safety, now the Safety Institute of America, was incorporated by chapter 152 of the Laws of 1911, which, by section 2 thereof, defines its objects as:

"Sec. 2. The objects of the corporation hereby created are to study and promote means and methods of safety and sanitation and the application thereof to any and all public or private occupations whatsoever, and of advancing knowledge of kindred subjects; and to that end to establish and maintain a museum, library and laboratories, and their branches wherein all matters, methods and means for improving the general condition of the people as to their safety and health may be studied, tested and promoted, with a view to lessening the number of casualties and avoiding the causes of physical suffering and of premature death; and to disseminate the results of such study, researches and test by lectures, exhibitions and other publications."

Chapter 466, Laws of 1914 (amending Greater New York charter), section 244-a, authorizes the board of estimate and apportionment of the city of New York to appropriate annually "such sum as it may deem proper, not exceeding fifty thousand dollars, for the keeping, preservation and exhibition of safety devices and means and methods of safety and sanitation in the building or any part thereof in the city of New York now or hereafter occupied by the American Museum of Safety." It is assumed, rather than stipulated, that the purpose of the lease is to provide a place for such exhibition, but the lease is general in its terms. The tenant occupies the building rent free, except as it agrees to expend a substantial sum on alterations of the arsenal for its purposes, for all its noncommercial purposes. The lease may, by its terms, be canceled "when said property shall be required by the party of the first part for *other* park purposes."

Defendant is one of a number of private corporations which are deemed to exercise *quasi* public functions and to be entitled to aid from the public treasury. To this end it has obtained space in Central Park and legislative authority for an annual appropriation by the city. Without reflection upon its worthiness or consideration of its constitutional right to public aid, we approach the question of the legislative authority of the park commissioner to lease to it the old Arsenal now standing in Central Park even to enable it to exhibit its safety and sanitary appliances. The park commissioner may control and manage the parks for park purposes. Are the purposes of the defendant Safety Institute of America, in any proper sense, park purposes? They are primarily utilitarian and educational in character. Its proposed exhibition is instructive. It is for a long period of years and is not a mere temporary show of things of passing interest. Incidentally it may amuse those who frequent the park for health and recreation, as any show of mechanical devices might, but so far as it fails to promote "means and methods of safety and sanitation" and to advance knowledge of such subjects, it fails to accomplish its corporate purpose.

A park is a pleasure ground set apart for recreation of the public, to promote its health and enjoyment. (Perrin v. N. Y. Cent. R.R. Co., 36 N. Y. 120, 124.)

It need not and should not be a mere field or open space, but no objects, however worthy, such as court houses and school houses, which have no connection with park purposes, should be permitted to encroach upon it without legislative authority plainly conferred, even when the dedication to park purposes is made by the public itself and the strict construction of a private grant is not insisted upon. (Brooklyn Park Commissioners v. Armstrong, 45 N. Y. 234; Higginson

v. Treasurer, etc., of Boston, 212 Mass. 583; Vil. of Riverside v. Mac Lain, 210 Ill. 308; City of Hopkinsville v. Jarrett, 156 Ky. 777.) Differences naturally arise as to the meaning of the phrase "park purposes." Under local statutes it has been held that a public library may be erected in a park without diverting it from such purposes. (Spires v. City of Los Angeles, 150 Cal. 64; Riggs v. Board of Education, 27 Mich. 262), and the city of Hartford was permitted to turn over a part of the land it had dedicated as a public park to the state for the purpose of a state capitol. (City of Hartford v. Maslen, 76 Conn. 599.) Monuments and buildings of architectural pretension which attract the eye and divert the mind of the visitor; floral and horticultural displays, zoological gardens, playing grounds, and even restaurants and rest houses and many other common incidents of a pleasure ground contribute to the use and enjoyment of the park. The end of all such embellishments and conveniences is substantially the same public good. They facilitate free public means of pleasure, recreation and amusement and thus provide for the welfare of the community. The environment must be suitable and sightly or the pleasure is abated. Art may aid or supplement nature in completing the attractions offered. The legislative will is that Central Park should be kept open as a public park ought to be and not be turned over by the commissioner of parks to other uses. It must be kept free from intrusion of every kind which would interfere in any degree with its complete use for this end.

To promote the safety of mankind and to advance the knowledge of the people in methods of lessening the number of casualties and avoiding the causes of physical suffering and premature death is the purpose of the Safety Institute of America; to provide means of innocent recreation and refreshment for the weary mind and body is the purpose of the system of public parks. The relation of the two purposes is at best remote. No reproach is cast upon the humanitarian aims of the Safety Institute when we say that it must find another place in which to bring them to the attention of the public.

The judgment should be reversed, with costs in all courts, and the motion of judgment on the pleadings denied, with ten dollar costs.

Hiscock, Ch. J., Chase, Collin, Cardozo, Crane and Andrews, JJ., concur.

APPENDIX III

THE FACTS IN THE VIELE CASE

Various misconceptions regarding the part of General Egbert L. Viele[1] in the design of Central Park, and the significance of his legal victory in 1864 in his suit against the Mayor and Aldermen of the City of New York, make it desirable to state briefly the facts involved in the case, so far as they are ascertainable with precision from the Court records, documents of the Central Park Commissioners, and the Park plans.

The Viele suit for payment for his survey and plan for Central Park was the second of two suits in which he was plaintiff, the first being a libel suit brought by him against one of the Commissioners, Mr. John A. C. Gray[2] in 1858 for having accused General Viele of being responsible for an injurious caricature of the Commissioners. This suit was apparently dropped before coming to trial.[3]

The second suit was instituted on January 21, 1860, in the Superior Court of the City and County of New York, Egbert L. Viele *agst.* The Mayor, Aldermen, and Commonalty of the City of New York. The complaint recites two causes of action:

One of these was a claim for salary as chief engineer at $2,500 a year subsequent to June, 1858, when payment of his salary had ceased upon his dismissal by the Central Park Commission created by the Act of April 17, 1857.[4] This dismissal he alleged to be invalid.

The other cause of action was expressed as follows in the complaint:

The plaintiff, after requisite surveys and examinations, prepared a map or plan for the Park so to be laid out or constructed, and in or about the month of May, 1856, submitted the same for adoption to the defendants, who did on the ninth of July, A.D., 1856,[5] adopt the same, and thereby, as the plaintiff avers,

---

[1] See biographical footnote on p. 31, *ante.*

[2] Minutes, Nov. 4, 1858.

[3] Demurrer Dec. 30, 1859, overruled, but no further record found.

[4] See p. 49.

[5] The engraving of General Viele's plan for the Park published in the First Annual Report of the original commissioners (Doc. No. 5 of the Board of Aldermen, 1857), bearing his facsimile signature and presumably prepared and inserted in the report under his orders as chief engineer, is inscribed "Adopted by the Commissioners, 3d June, 1856." In his testimony (quoted *infra*) General Viele says he has no record that this plan was adopted by the Commissioners on July 9th, but was "informed" by Mayor Wood, the chairman, that it had been adopted. Mr. Wood, under oath, denied that General Viele's plan had been adopted as alleged in the complaint. Whether the plan was formally adopted or not, it was tacitly accepted when its publication in the annual report was permitted, and the jury very properly found for General Viele though it had received no trustworthy evidence that the date of adoption stated in the complaint was correct.—ED.

became and were liable to pay him what he reasonably deserves to have therefor, which plaintiff alleges to be the sum of five thousand dollars.

That on or about the fifth day of June, 1856, the said defendants through their agents in that behalf, the Mayor and Street Commissioner of the city of New York, acting as and being Commissioners of the Central Park under an ordinance of the defendants which was passed in May, 1856, and took effect on the 21st day of that month, having then received the approval of the Mayor, appointed and employed said plaintiff as engineer-in-chief to superintend and direct the laying out and completion of said Central Park according to the aforesaid map or plan.

It will be seen from the complaint that it did not itself raise the question of the authorship of the design for Central Park which was then being carried out under the direction of Olmsted and Vaux, nor was that question touched on in the judgment in favor of General Viele rendered March 9, 1864.[1] That this was recognized by the contemporary press appears from an article in the *Independent* (March 24, 1864).

VIELE SUIT

We have been assured that our recent explanation of the point at issue between Gen. Viele and the City Corporation in regard to the Central Park, is still open to misapprehension, by which injustice may seem to be done to Messrs. Olmsted & Vaux. We therefore give the summary of the verdict in the case, from which it will be seen that the question of the authorship of the present plan of the Park was not involved at all:

"The jury, under the charge of the judge, found a verdict for the plaintiff, affirming these propositions:

"First, That the plaintiff made preliminary surveys and examinations of Central Park, and prepared a map for the laying out of the same.

"Second, That the Central Park Commissioners, Messrs. Wood & Taylor, adopted the same on the 9th June, 1856.[2]

"Third, That by its adoption the defendants became liable to pay the plaintiff therefor the sum of $5,000, on said 9th June (sic), 1856."

Nevertheless the authorship of the design of Central Park was vehemently called in question in the course of the trial.[3] The following series of statements from the record of the case unfold General Viele's contentions.

Q. You have stated that you commenced making surveys for a plan of the Park in 1853, and from that time up to 1858 you devoted a considerable portion of your time and attention, as much as you could spare from other things, to that work; now, in performing whatever work of that kind you did, before you were appointed Engineer-in-Chief of the Park, you trusted to the chance of your plan being adopted by the city authorities, and to your thus obtaining from them compensation suitable to the time and skill you had expended on the work?

A. I did, sir.

Q. There had been no contract entered into between you and any of the corporate authorities, with reference to the labor which you actually devoted to that work?

A. None whatever.

.   .   .   .

[1] The lump sum awarded was $8,625, with costs $548.94 and interest $67.00, making a total of $9,240.94.

[2] The *Independent* has this date June 9th, erroneously. It does not so appear anywhere in the court records. Cf. note as to discrepant dates, *ante*.—ED.

[3] Note that the Senate Investigation Committee report of 1861 states that "The plan adopted was that of Messrs. Olmsted & Vaux." See Part I, Chapter V, p. 62.

Q. You stated a while ago that the plan was adopted on the 9th of July, I believe; who adopted it?

A. The Board of Commissioners, Mayor Wood, and the Street Commissioner, as Commissioners of Central Park.

. . . . . .

Q. Have you any record of their adoption of it?

A. No, sir; I was informed by the Chairman of the Commission that it had been adopted—Mr. Wood.

Q. Is that the only knowledge you have on the subject?

A. I have the official report to the Common Council, in which the general features of that plan are adopted.[1]

. . . . . .

Q. Were you aware of the publication of the advertisement by the Commissioners of Central Park, inviting proposals or plans for the laying out of the Park?

A. Yes, sir; I know the advertisement very well; the principles embodied in it are all copied from my report.

. . . . . .

Q. You knew that this advertisement was published?

A. Yes, sir; and I know the object of it, too.

Q. You know, I suppose, that a number of gentlemen competed for the sums named in that advertisement?

A. I know that a certain number of copies of my plan were made and sent in.

Q. Do you know that a number of gentlemen prepared plans for the laying out of the Park, and submitted them to the Committee under that advertisement?

A. I know that the generality of those gentlemen submitted copies of my plan.

Q. How many persons submitted copies of your plan—there were thirty-three competitors?

A. I should think about half that number.

. . . . . .

Q. Did you submit a plan for the laying out of the Park under this advertisement that we have spoken of?

A. I sent my plan in to give them an opportunity to reject it, as I knew they would; it was the same, in all its essential features, as the original one; there were no material alterations in it; they rejected it; I knew they would, when I sent it.

Q. Do you know whose plans they accepted?

A. They accepted mine, copied by Olmsted & Vaux, and two others, one by——[2] and another by——[2]. I sent in another plan, too, which I knew they would adopt, if the right name went in with it, and they did. I conceived a most absurd and impracticable plan, not based upon any knowledge of the ground, which I knew they would adopt, if it had the right name to it; I did this to test the capacity of those men to judge of such things, and injure my reputation, as they tried to do.

Q. What was the name of "the right man?"

A. Miller;[3] a son-in-law of one of the Commission

---

[1] Doc. No. 5 of the Board of Aldermen, Jan., 1857, known as "First Annual Report." Cf. p. 32.—ED.

[2] These are blanks in the record of the case.—ED.

[3] There is a copy of the report accompanying the Miller plan (which received third prize) in the volume of competition reports in the New York Public Library referred to on p. 44, *ante*. Nothing in this report would seem to bear out General

MAP
of the lands included in THE CENTRAL PARK. from a
Topographical Survey, June 17ᵗʰ 1856.

PLAN
for the Improvement of THE CENTRAL PARK. Adopted by the
Commissioners, June 3ᵈ 1856.

The Viele Map and Plan

From First Annual Report, Central Park, 1857

Q. The plan that you sent in as yours was in your own name, I suppose?

A. Yes, sir; my own plan was sent in to compel them to reject it.

Q. The map or plan that Olmsted & Vaux sent in was in their own name, I suppose?

A. I suppose so; the plans were sent in sealed envelopes.

Q. You claim that Olmsted & Vaux borrowed your plan?

A. Yes, sir; and they were so sure of its adoption, that they had it already engraved, and got it into next morning's paper as the adopted plan; I have a copy of the engraving.[1]

.   .   .   .

Q. What does this paper exhibit? (Showing paper to witness.)

A. That is the original plan of mine, showing the outlines; that other is the plan called the Commissioners' plan.

Q. State what are the general features of both plans?

A. First, there is this reservoir built as decided upon by the Croton Aqueduct Board—the new reservoir or lake; the lands taken for it were a parallelogram, commencing with the Fifth avenue and running to the Seventh avenue, on the south Eighty-sixth street, and on the north, Ninety-sixth street; examining the ground topographically, I received the idea of making it a lake instead of an artificial reservoir; I submitted the idea to the Croton Board, and they discussed it and came to the conclusion that if I would procure the passage of an Act of the Legislature, authorizing the change to be made, they would consent to it; I did so, and the authority was given; this body of water being a large natural looking lake, instead of an artificial reservoir, is one of the most striking and important features of the Park, and the same idea is to be found in both these plans; then comes the general drive, entering here, at the Fifth avenue and Fifty-ninth street, following the general direction of the Fifth avenue, varying however, with the topography of the land, and coming out at the Eighth avenue; the same idea is found in this other plan; this is what is called the circular drive; the changes in the direction made in *this* plan, do not change the general features of the plan of the drive.

Q. What have you to say about those transverse roads?

A. Those were adopted on certain general principles; they are for the purpose of accommodating the traffic from one side of the city to the other; the idea was that while the Park was a pleasure ground, it ought not to interfere with the convenience of citizens, or be a hindrance to the transaction of business; this is a feature which does not exist in any other public square in the city; the same idea is to be found in this other plan; in it the roads are depressed below the surface, but that does not materially change the general feature; then the low grounds to receive water are found in both plans, only in this other one, knowing how much they could devote to that purpose, they have marked it, and the space so used is larger; then there were certain open spaces for recreation in my plan which are also in the other; here is one, they have changed the names of them; those, I believe, are the general features of the plan; and the slight internal changes of detail, are not changes of its general character, which is in contradistinction to an *artificial* plan of a park; the distinct characteristic of my plan, the main idea which pervades it is, that it is adapted to the topography of the ground.

Viele's astounding allegation or indicate that Mr. Miller's plan was other than Mr. Miller's own done in conjunction with Mr. McIntosh or that it was not submitted in good faith. The record of votes cast by the Commissioners for No. 27 (the plan by Miller and McIntosh) during the balloting for prizes shows no indication of favoritism.— ED.

[1] The engraving was undoubtedly the one used by Olmsted & Vaux as a key map on the competition sketches submitted. See illustrations, and List, pp. 232–233, *ante.*—ED.

At the time of the trial Mr. Olmsted was in California, but Mr. Vaux was called upon to testify. Pertinent extracts from the testimony of Mr. Vaux follow:

Mr. Olmsted and myself made a design in accordance with the terms of the advertisement; the Commission furnished a photograph of the survey, which we used with a personal examination of the ground in the construction of our plan. Our plan (Olmsted and Vaux's) was adopted; we knew of the plan of General Viele having been submitted when the report was made public; we received the premium for our plan; it was $2,000.

• • • • • • •

Q. In what respect does your plan differ from Viele?

A. In every respect, I think; it may be considered in regard to popular convenience outside out[1] of the Park, which Viele's plan did not provide for; our idea was to take Fifth avenue as the principal carriage entrance to the Park, and to make the drive, which would run through the middle of the Park, diagonally reach the centre of the Park as soon as possible, keeping away from the side, and thus taking people out of the city into the Park with the least possible delay; we decided to make the Ramble, which is immediately south of the old reservoir, a point of importance, and so place the water as to give a peculiar effect of distance; this is, in itself, the key of the Park; these and others were important changes.

Q. Was your design an original one; or were you indebted for that, to any other person?

A. It was entirely original in us.

Q. Was it based upon the map of any other person?

A. I had seen the map of the plaintiff's before.

CROSS EXAMINATION

At the time of preparing this plan, I resided at 136 East Eighteenth street; I knew some of the Commissioners; I had seen the plan of Gen. Viele before the making [of] ours; he presented me a copy of the report of the Commissioners containing it; Mr. Olmsted had one also; they were public property; we were somewhat familiar with the General's plans, before we undertook to make ours; we were furnished with a photograph of the map; it had the name of Egbert L. Viele on it.

• • • • • • •

Q. Did you not speak about Viele's plan, and confer with each other as to the particulars in which it could be improved?

A. We saw his plan, and spoke about it; I suppose, of course, once having seen it, we could not be in the same position as though we had not seen it.

Q. Did you not confer with each other and express opinions as to certain parts of his plan being injudicious, and capable of improvement?

A. It would be so natural to do so under the circumstances, that I have no doubt we did; the plan was public property at the time.

Q. I observe in his map, collections of water as in yours?

A. The difference is between the effect of small collections of water, and the effect of large ones.

Q. With this survey map already provided for you, how long did it take you and Olmsted to make your plan?

A. Of course, we had other work; still it occupied our minds more or less, continually, for about five months.

Q. Do you think that $2,000 for making that plan with the aid of this preliminary survey and map was more than a just compensation?

A. I do not; I would not do it again for $2,000.

_____

[1] *Sic* in the record of the case.—ED.

Mr. Andrew H. Green, Treasurer and Comptroller of the Park, having stated that photographs of the Viele survey were furnished competitors, General Viele was called in rebuttal and testified as follows:

Q. Who made the survey map that was photographed for the Board?
A. It was my original map; it was accepted by the first Commissioners of the Park; the topographical map was mine.
Q. Was anything paid you for that?
A. No, sir!

Judgment for General Viele was rendered, it thus appears, because he had furnished the city with a map of which the city had made use, both in a printed document and in the Central Park competition, and for which the maker had not been paid. Also even although the first plan made by General Viele, accompanying his survey, was not subsequently used, the services had been accepted and the plan made public property.

However justly General Viele was entitled to payment for what he had done, none of the evidence in this trial throws much light in itself upon the question of the adoption of ideas by Olmsted and Vaux from his prior design, beyond showing that General Viele was then making that accusation sweepingly and in a very embittered manner,—the more bitter because he doubtless believed that he had been thrown over for wholly political reasons. But even if his disappointment led him into making entirely untenable statements, which have been repeated by personal and political partisans, it is worth while to search, in his plan and report, for elements of value that may have been contributed by him to the design of Central Park.

General Viele seems to have claimed that this "informal" or naturalistic character of his plan was a thing so distinctive that the appearance of the same characteristic in any subsequent plan offered presumptive evidence of borrowing.[1] Of course, in the light of the history of landscape design and its fashions, there was very small chance at that date of any prevailingly formal design being offered by anyone. General Viele's plan has the merit, as he rightly claims, of being rather closely adapted to the natural topography instead of disregarding it. The mere recurrence of this admirable quality in another plan, however, is in itself no evidence of improper adoption of another man's ideas.

There are a few cases of similar features in similar places on the Viele and "Greensward" plans, dictated by good adjustment to the topography of the site in providing for things required in the program of the competition or obviously growing out of these requirements. For example: driving entrances at or very near the southeastern and southwestern corners, and one at a point on Fifty-ninth Street nearly between, where the topography was less unfavorable than elsewhere along that frontage. As to these things, it cannot be positively affirmed that there was no borrowing by the authors of the Greensward plan, since General Viele who studied the problem first, was the first to find and indicate these solutions, and since the Viele preliminary plan was published and in the hands of the competitors before they began work. It can fairly be said, however, that most of these coincident solutions were so nearly inevitable that Olmsted and Vaux, in view of

---

[1] Cf. the letter from Mr. Olmsted to Mr. Vaux, given on p. 561.

their subsequently proved skill, would probably have hit upon these even if they had not had the benefit of General Viele's preliminary work to point the way.

All of these coinciding elements are relatively unimportant, however, in view of the differences in the plans which appear on careful comparison. It is not so much a matter of specific differences as that the Viele plan shows itself as a whole to be a rather unimaginative application of some of the then usually accepted formulae for the "informal" style of landscape "improvement," whereas the "Greensward" plan if carefully studied shows itself as a creation of artistic insight, deeply purposeful in nearly all its decisions, and offering to city dwellers a refreshing illusion of Nature, interpreted in an unbroken series of blending and contrasting naturalistic effects.

A perusal of the respective reports accompanying the competition plans reinforces an understanding of these general differences. General Viele's report[1] yields the following typical sentence, along with the remarks on unity, harmony, breadth, and so on, currently accepted as appurtenant to the informal style:

> In discussing the application of these features [drives, buildings, gardens, etc.] to the ground, and in describing their localities, the fact must not be lost sight of that the shape of the park (being long and narrow) is the worst possible for a display of those lines and curves which are essential to a well-developed work of improvement.

Compare this with Olmsted and Vaux's emphasis on unity of effect in the quotation shortly to follow.

Events have proven the vital importance to the park design of the sinking of the transverse roads. In his testimony General Viele denied any essential difference between a surface or a sunken treatment. And in his competition report, we read:

> To prevent the interruption of business between the two sections of the city, certain transverse roads have been laid out across the Park, designed to be used by carts and heavily-loaded wagons. These roads have been made to conform to the general plan, and have been located so as to meet as near as possible the side streets.

This is all that is said about them. They are all treated on the plan indistinguishably from the other park drives, joining and crossing them at grade, forming in some cases integral parts of park drive circuits and in all cases but one offering very indirect routes across the park for business traffic.

Compare the above statement by General Viele with the following sentences from the three pages on the subject in the competition report of Olmsted and Vaux.

> The 700 acres allowed to the new park must, in the first instance, be subdivided definitely, although it is to be hoped to some extent invisibly, into five separate and distinct sections. . . . The problem to be solved is . . . making some plan that shall have unity of effect as a whole, and yet avoid collision in its detailed features with the intersecting lines thus suggested.
> Inevitably they [the transverse roads] will be crowded thoroughfares, having nothing in common with the park proper, but everything at variance with those agreeable sentiments which we should wish the park to inspire.

---

[1] Copy in New York Public Library in the volume of reports of competitors.

The denial of credit to Olmsted and Vaux arising from their alleged "copying" of General Viele's plan has unfortunately been perpetuated in Wilson's *Memorial History of New York* (volume four). The history of Central Park is given, and the design emphatically attributed to General Viele, no mention at all being made of Olmsted and Vaux. The biographical volume (five) refers again to General Viele's connection with Central Park in the following inaccurate manner:

> With much justice General Viele has been styled "the inventor of Central Park." He was the originator of the complete design, which, with some modifications, was carried out. His plan, submitted in a competition with a large number of European as well as home engineers and artists, was adopted in 1856 by the newly organized Park Commission of which Washington Irving was President.

Most writings on the Central Park, however, have taken a contrary view[1] of General Viele's share in the design of the park. Probably he has failed to receive the credit to which he is fairly entitled by his early work for the very reason that his partisans claimed for him the entire credit for the design[2]. While he was the initiator of a preliminary plan, Olmsted and Vaux are responsible for the constructed design and for the beautiful refinement of its conception.

The location, shape, and topography of Central Park set very definite limits to the designer's scope. The Board of Commissioners in setting the program for the competition certainly derived some points from General Viele's plan of 1856 as well as from their own undoubted knowledge of European pleasure grounds.

A discriminating examination of General Viele's plan (reproduced opposite page 556) will enable the reader to draw his own conclusions, and the Park papers of Olmsted and Vaux collected in Part Two of this Volume add incontrovertible testimony to the independence of the authors of the "Greensward" plan in solving a given problem with originality and vision.

A LETTER FROM MR. OLMSTED REGARDING THE VIELE CASE

Bear Valley [California], March 25th, 1864.

MY DEAR VAUX: .   .   .

With regard Viele I naturally don't like to see the paragraphs which I do, for instance in the *Home Journal* and in the correspondence and condensed items of the California papers but I can't think what should be done about it if anything. I should prefer, if possible, that Viele should be thrown upon his defence for making a claim to the present design of the Park before a body of gentlemen, as for instance our common peers of the Century. I think that if he has made such a claim publicly either he or we should be disgracefully dismissed from the Club or at least he should be required to retract it. I chiefly apprehend that the matter may come up again in the future in a more serious way; for instance if Viele should become candidate for an important office and the interests of a large party and its newspaper organs should become associated with his in this matter.

It appears to me that the best way to meet him with the general public would be to present the two plans side by side, or one overlying the other. A reproduc-

---

[1] See the discussion of the essential differences of the Viele and "Greensward" plans in *Scribner's Monthly*, Sept., 1873.

[2] His biographers claim also for General Viele the credit for the design of Prospect Park, Brooklyn. In 1861 he submitted a survey and a plan for improvement which was not carried out. At the close of the Civil War Olmsted and Vaux were engaged to make the plan which was carried into execution soon after under their direction.

tion of some transcript of his plans for which he is responsible would be best if such a transcript could be obtained as I think it might from Valentine's or some other official publication of Wood or the Commissioners under whom Viele first acted. I remember seeing it before our day in some public form, perhaps in the newspapers. In a popular publication it might be prudent to hint in some way that the topography of the ground was such that at certain points there could well be no choice in the lines of road to be followed and that of course at such points all plans conceived at all in the natural style must be approximately alike, also that the requirements of the Commissioners made it necessary that all the plans should contain certain common features and that the topography of the ground was such as to admit of no choice in the location of some of these. Also that if ponds were introduced they would of necessity be placed only in the low grounds of the site; it is therefore probably true that Mr. Viele knew as he stated that nine out of ten of the plans would in certain respects be similar to his, or follow his choice, his choice being, in these respects, no other than Hobson's choice. That his plan had many faults and that our design avoided these faults without sacrificing even as much as his the natural advantages of the ground could I think be easily shown by a few comparisons which would illustrate his poverty of resource and general littleness and meanness of landscape effects; this would be shown for instance, by a comparison of breadth of waters, and of the greatest extent of greensward both in area and in stretch unbroken by road or plantations. Thus, there is in our plan one stretch of unbroken view across turf from near the South drive near the Cricket ground (rock in front of the elliptical bridge) to the North end of the Green. I don't think Viele had any stretch one-quarter as long as this.

I think that such a general report to the public as you propose is quite desirable but it would be a very great undertaking to prepare it in a satisfactory manner and one in which I fear I could give you no assistance.

The great point would be that the Park has been constructed not nearly as much for the present as for the future; that no criticism could be justly made upon the effect of the planting until the result aimed at should be reached, which will not be in less than twenty years, while its perfection must not be expected in less than fifty; that it would be very easy to completely neutralize the general effect intended, in many particulars, by the introduction of what might be supposed to be unimportant objects proposed as improvements; and to indicate what real and essential additions and improvements might be made harmoniously with its design.

There need be no hurry about it and if you feel able to undertake the preparation of such a paper, taking time for it when nothing else presses upon you, I shall be very glad. If you can send it to me in whole or in detachment I shall be glad to make any suggestions or notes for additions to it that I can.

[F. L. O.]

APPENDIX IV

BIBLIOGRAPHY

The most important source of information about Central Park is, of course, the long series of official documents, first of the Commissioners of the Central Park, and after 1870, of the Department of Public Parks. In this Appendix an attempt has been made to give a complete list of those documents which relate specifically to Central Park during the period of Mr. Olmsted's connection with it. A number of the most important documents will be found to have been reprinted in part or in full in Part II, and these have been marked in this list with an *asterisk*. It is plainly impossible to attempt to make an index to the numerous references to Central Park in the Minutes of the Commissioners, or in the Annual Reports, both of which series have been extensively used in preparing our narrative account of Central Park. Although anyone studying the history of the Park deeply would wish to go over these official reports from beginning to end, for the ordinary reader the selections which have been woven into the text of Part I of this present volume give perhaps a sufficient sample of the style and content. A practically complete set of Minutes, Documents, and Reports will be found in the New York Public Library and Municipal Reference Library.

Of the descriptive books, pamphlets, guides, and magazine articles—of very unequal merit—relating to the Park, there have been too many to warrant the inclusion in this bibliography of any attempt at a complete list. It has seemed more helpful to the student to include here only a selected list, in chronological order, of the more important sources of information on Central Park hitherto published, such as Dr. Edward Hagaman Hall's account in the American Scenic and Historic Preservation Society reports and the recent *Memories of Samuel Parsons*. The history of Central Park during the critical ten-year period covered by the publication of *Garden and Forest* (begun in 1888 and edited by friends and warm defenders of the Park) is so well reflected in its pages that perhaps a disproportionate number of references—all to editorials—in this periodical have been here included. If anyone has further time to spend and wishes an entertaining hour, he should visit the Local History Room of the New York Public Library and browse through the numerous little guidebooks, mostly of the sixties and seventies, some of them even issued by mercantile houses with cover advertisements which attest the early popularity of Central Park.

The graphic record of the Park's development and use is of intense interest. In the Print Room and Stuart Collection of the New York Public Library, and in the New York Historical Society, will be found a large number of old prints and photographs which enrich and supplement the conception of the Park to be gained from the illustrations in the Annual Reports of the Park Commissioners, and in the volumes of *Valentine's Manual*.

It is to be hoped that the New York Public Library will be able to make some permanent list of at least its own treasures illuminating Central Park history, in connection with the Exhibition to be held in April, 1928.

A. LIST OF DOCUMENTS

RELATING TO CENTRAL PARK, 1857-1878

NOTE:—The period covered by each series of documents ended on April 30, and the sets are so bound up. For convenience in reference, lines have been inserted in the date column of this list to indicate where the volumes break. The wording of titles has been taken as far as possible from the Statistical Appendix prepared by Mr. Olmsted to accompany the Annual Report of 1873.

1857

Doc. 1   By-Laws, Standing Committees, and Act creating Board.

Doc. 2   May 15   Communication to the Mayor relative to the purchase by the City of New York of the Arsenal building in the Central Park.

Doc. 3   May 26   Report of the Committee on Buildings relative to the occupancy of land and buildings on the Park.

Doc. 4   June 2   Communication to the Common Council asking for appropriation of funds for the improvement of the Park. (Importance and value of Park to City stressed.)

Doc. 5   July 7   Report of Committee on Roads and Walks recommending the removal of stone walls and surface stones from the Park by contract.

Doc. 6   Sept. 1   Report of the Executive Committee defining the duties of the various officers of the Commission.

Doc. 7   Sept. 1   Ordinance of Common Council to create funds for the improvement of the Park.

Doc. 8   Sept. 11   Report of Special Committee on advertising for plans for laying out the Park.

Doc. 9   Sept. 23   Report of Chief Engineer (Viele) on present operations: enclosing the ground, drainage, manuring, removal of buildings and trees.

Doc. 10   Oct. 6   Report of Superintendent (Olmsted) on a comprehensive plan of drainage for the Park.

*Doc. 11   Oct. 20   Report of Superintendent (Olmsted) on trees, and recommending the importation and purchase of trees and plants. (*See* p. 332, *ante*.)

Doc. 12   Oct. 30   Report of Committee on Drainage, recommending immediate thorough draining; also Report of Superintendent of Drainage (Waring) on the same subject.

Doc. 13   Nov. 10   Ordinance of the Common Council to provide money for the improvement of the Park.

1858

Doc. 14   Jan. 5   Report of Chief Engineer (Viele) on the cost and character of material now being prepared for roadway construction, and on the method of construction.

Doc. 15 Mar. 16 The First Annual Report of the Commission.

Doc. 16 Mar. 16 Report of Chief Engineer (Viele) on a comprehensive system of drainage; on location, size, and depth, of drains and estimates of cost.

—————

Doc. 1 May 4 Amendments to the By-Laws.

*Doc. 2 May 10 Report of Special Committee on Plan relative to the work to be prosecuted forthwith. (*See* p. 233, *ante.*)

Doc. 3 May 17 Report of Superintendent (Olmsted) as to modifications of plan No. 33.

Doc. 4 May 13 By-Laws as amended.

*Doc. 5 May 31 Report of Architect-in-Chief (Olmsted) as to certain modifications in the plan proposed by Commissioner Dillon. (*See* p. 235, *ante.*)

Doc. 6 June 17 Report of Architect-in-Chief (Olmsted), with statement of the force employed and estimates of expenditures required for remainder of the year.

*Doc. 7 May 17 Report of Superintendent (Olmsted) on the subject of the construction of certain parts of the work on the Park by contract, recommending materials to be procured by contract, and work to be done by days' work. (*See* p. 292, *ante.*)

Doc. 8 June 17 Report of majority of the Special Committee, that it is not expedient for the work in the Park to be done by contract.

Doc. 9 June 17 Report of minority of the Special Committee, recommending that the work of construction generally be done by contract.

Doc. 10 July 15 Review of the two preceding Reports by the President (Green), recommending that the work be carried on as heretofore, and that the Board should not adopt the contract system.

*Doc. 11 Sept. 9 Communication of the Architect-in-Chief (Olmsted) with regard to details of the walks and rides laid out in the Park. (*See* p. 378, *ante.*)

Doc. 12 Sept. 16 Communication of the President (Green) to the Common Council as to the construction of the avenues adjoining the Park; their width, the projections and erections upon them, and their drainage; and recommending the extension of the Park to 110th Street.

Doc. 13 Dec. 9 Ordinance of the Common Council to provide a further sum for the improvement of the Park.

1859

Doc. 14 Jan. 14 Communication to the Common Council on the sewerage of the Park.

Doc. 15 Jan. 14 Communication to the Common Council on the subject of procuring surplus earth from Hamilton Square.

Doc. 16 Jan. 14 Memorial to the Legislature requesting amendments to the law to increase the efficiency of the Commissioners; to make the Board of Commissioners a corporation; to allow the President and Treasurer to receive compensation; to provide additional improvement fund; to provide for the appointment of a Park police force; to extend the Park to 110th Street; and to widen Seventh Avenue from 110th Street to Harlem River.

Doc. 17   Jan. 29   Draft of Annual Report to the Common Council.

Doc. 18   Feb. 3   Report on liabilities of the Board.

Doc. 19   Apr. 21   Chap. 101 of 1859.   (*See* Appendix II.)

Doc. 20   Apr. 21   Chap. 349 of 1859.   (*See* Appendix II.)

---

*Doc. 1   July 7   Report of Architect-in-Chief and Superintendent (Olmsted) upon the changes made in the original plan and their cost. (*See* p. 294, *ante.*)

Doc. 2   July 21   Report of Special Committee upon present expenditure, with estimate of amounts required to complete the present undertakings.

Doc. 3   Oct. 20   By-Laws as amended.

*Doc. 4   Dec. 31   Report of Architect-in-Chief and Superintendent (Olmsted) on his visit to European Parks.   (*See* p. 55, *ante.*)

1860

Doc. 5   Mar. 21   Chap. 85 of 1860.   (*See* Appendix II.)

Doc. 6   Apr. 26   Report of Architect-in-Chief (Olmsted) on the subject of the permanent provision of refreshments in the Park, recommending the erection of a refectory, the dairy, and other refreshment houses; and also recommending a carriage service.

Doc. 1   May 3   Report of Architect-in-Chief and Superintendent (Olmsted) on cost of transverse roads.

Doc. 2   May 24   Report of Architect-in-Chief and Superintendent (Olmsted) on the quantity of brick, sand, cement, and lumber required for the remainder of the year.

Doc. 3   June 7   Report of Architect-in-Chief (Olmsted) of the work expedient to be prosecuted during the remainder of the year.

Doc. 4   July 12   Report of Special Committee on Entrances on Fifty-ninth Street, recommending that those on Sixth and Seventh avenues be made the principal entrances architecturally.

Doc. 5   Aug. 30   Opinion of the Counsel to the Corporation on the constitutional validity of the Acts of 1857 and 1860.

1861

Doc. 6   Apr. 24   Chap. 88 of 1861.   (*See* Appendix II.)

1862

Doc. 1   Apr. 10   Chap. 46 of 1862.   (*See* Appendix II.)

*Doc. 2   Apr. 10   Report of Committee on the nomenclature of the gates of the Park.   (*See* p. 398, *ante.*)

Doc. 3   Apr. 10   By-Laws as amended.

Doc. 1 Dec. 23 Communication to Common Council requesting the appropriation of further funds for proceeding with work in the Park.

1863

Doc. 2 Jan. 26 Report of Committee recommending construction of an enclosing wall around the Park.

Doc. 1 May 14 Statement of the Comptroller (Green) concerning the finances, the force employed, and the condition and progress of the Park.

1864

Doc. 2 May 12 Chap. 319 of 1864. (*See* Appendix II.)

Doc. 3 Nov. 19 Statement from the Comptroller of the Park (Green) relative to the present condition of work, the prosecution of new work, and estimate of the cost thereof.

1865

Doc. 4 Feb. 21 Chap. 26 of 1865. (*See* Appendix II.)

Doc. 3 May 10 Report of the Committee on the subject of the appropriation of the Arsenal for the use of the New York Historical Society, recommending the appropriation under certain conditions.

1866

Doc. 5 Feb. 26 Report of the Committee on the plan for the building for the New York Historical Society on the Park.

Doc. 6 Feb. 26 Report of Comptroller of the Park (Green), relative to the persons in the employ of the Commissioners.

Doc. 4 May 3 Chap. 757 of 1866. (*See* Appendix II.)

1867

Doc. 5 Feb. 14 Report of the Committee on site for the Seventh Regiment memorial, recommending a location near the Warrior's Gate.

1869

Doc. 1 May 13 Chap. 350 of 1869. (*See* Appendix II.)

Doc. 2 May 13 Chap. 595 of 1869. (*See* Appendix II.)

1870

Doc. 6 May 24 Report of the Comptroller (Van Nort) on the cost of structures in progress on the Park.

Doc. 8 May 24 Report of the Engineer (Kellogg) on construction of enclosing walls of the Park.

Doc. 9   May 31   Report of Architect-in-Chief (Mould) on cost of completing structures in progress.

Doc. 10   May 31   Report from the Landscape Architects (Olmsted & Vaux) relative to the works in progress on their designs.

Doc. 11   May 31   Correspondence with the American Museum of Natural History relative to the collection of that society in the Arsenal building.

Doc. 12   May 31   Inventory of tools in the possession of keepers of the Park, and in the office of the Architect-in-Chief.

*Doc. 13   June 7   Report of Landscape Architects (Olmsted, Vaux & Co.) relative to works in progress on their designs. (*See* p. 477, *ante.*)

Doc. 14   June 7   Clerk's Report on unfinished engagements of the late Board.

Doc. 15   Oct. 4   Report of Engineer (Kellogg) on the adaptation of the Park to the change of grade of Eighth Avenue.

Doc. 19   Nov. 22   Report of Comptroller (Van Nort) submitting list of contributions to the zoological collection.

Doc. 20   Dec. 6   Ordinance of Common Council to create funds for the improvement of the Park.

Doc. 21   Dec. 6   Ordinances respecting the uses of streets and avenues within the distance of 350 feet from the boundary of the Park.

1871

Doc. 22   Apr. 8   Chap. 290 of 1871. (*See* Appendix II.)

Doc. 26   Sept. 12   Report of the Captain of the Park Keepers (Mills) on the number of the force.

Doc. 30   Nov. 25   Report of the Comptroller of the Department (Van Nort) on condition of accounts and liabilities of the Department, works in progress, with a list of employes.

Doc. 32   Dec. 12   Report of Surgeons of Park Keepers (Hilton and Nesmith), giving a summary of their work during the year.

Doc. 33   Dec. 12   Statement of expenditures of the Department from April 20, 1870, to November 22, 1871.

1872

Doc. 34   Mar. 6   Communication from S. B. Parsons in relation to the trees on the Park.

*Doc. 36   May 16   Communication from Landscape Architects (Olmsted & Vaux) relative to the communication between the Terrace and Reservoir; and on the deficiency of shade on the drives and walks. (*See* p. 379, *ante.*)

Doc. 39   July 17   Report of Treasurer (Olmsted) on wages.

Doc. 40   Oct. 16   Communication from the President (Olmsted) on location of a parade ground.

*Doc. 41   Oct. 24   Communication from the Treasurer (Olmsted) relative to the police and its reform. (*See* p. 442, *ante.*)

Doc. 42   Nov. 20   Report of the Director of the Menagerie (Conklin) of his European tour.

1873

*Doc. 43   Mar. 31   General Order for the organization and routine of duty of the keepers' service of the Park, and conditions of holding appointments in the force. Observations on the conduct required of the keepers; and ordinances applicable to the ordinary use of the Park. (*See* p. 444, *ante.*) Supplement containing instructions to extra keepers and night-watchmen.

Doc. 44   June 23   Report of the Landscape Architect (Olmsted), exhibiting the present standing of the principal undertakings of the Department under his supervision.

Doc. 45   June 25   Report of the Civil and Topographical Engineer (Grant) relative to the condition of all the works under his direction.

*Doc. 46   July 17   Report of the Special Committee on Statues and Monuments, recommending for adoption rules to govern the question of accepting and disposing of them. (*See* p. 488, *ante.*)

*Doc. 47   July 17   Report of the Landscape Architect (Olmsted) on the reason for the changes recently made in the management of the keeper force. (*See* p. 466, *ante.*)

*Doc. 51   Oct. 11   Report of the Landscape Architect (Olmsted) on the disposition of the zoological collection of the Department. (*See* p. 505, *ante.*)

1874

Doc. 54   Jan. 7   Report of the Landscape Architect (Olmsted) on the estimates for construction for the year 1874.

*Doc. 55   Jan. 7   Report of the Landscape Architect (Olmsted) on the boat and refreshment houses. (*See* p. 480, *ante.*)

*Doc. 57   Mar. 4   Communication of Messrs. Frederick Law Olmsted and Calvert Vaux on a proposition to place a colossal statue at the south end of the Mall in the Park. (*See* p. 494, *ante.*)

*Doc. 58   May 20   Report of the Landscape Architect (Olmsted) upon the subject of applications for appropriations of ground in the Central Park for special purposes, and recommending the adoption of certain resolutions by the Board. (*See* p. 421, *ante.*)

Doc. 59   May 20   Report of the Landscape Architect upon works proposed to be prosecuted during the remainder of the year, with a statement of the estimates therefor.

1875

Doc. 63   Jan. 29   Reports of the Landscape Architect (Olmsted) upon estimated expenditures for construction during the year 1875.

Doc. 64   Mar. 5   Communication from Commr. William R. Martin relative to the prosecution of public improvements in the City of New York. (An historical review.)

Doc. 66   Nov. 17   Report of the Landscape Architect (Olmsted) on the subject of the drainage of the Park. (Order to print this document rescinded.)

*Doc. 67 Dec. 3 Report of the Landscape Architect (Olmsted) on the subject of a promenade consisting of a drive, ride, and walks, in the Park. (*See* p. 386, *ante*.)

Doc. 68 Dec. 29 Statement of the Commissioner showing why the appropriations for the Department of Public Parks for 1876 should not be reduced below the amount appropriated for 1875.

1878

Doc. 77 Jan. 30 Agreement with the American Museum of Natural History for occupation of building in Manhattan Square, Central Park.

Doc. 79 Apr. 24 Report of Commissioner Lane upon the application of "The Trustees of the Botanical Garden in the City of New York," for permission to occupy a portion of Manhattan Square, Central Park.

Doc. 84 Dec. 18 Agreement with the Metropolitan Museum of Art for the occupation by it of the Museum of Art building in the Park.

B. LIST OF BOOKS, ARTICLES, ETC.

BOOKS, PAMPHLETS AND MONOGRAPHS

1856 COPELAND AND CLEVELAND. A Few Words on the Central Park. Boston. 7 pp. —— Sensible advice to the public at large from an early landscape firm. (*See* Vol. I, p. 124, *ante.*)

1857 RAWOLLE, CHARLES, AND IG. A. PILAT. Catalogue of Plants gathered in August and September 1857 in the ground of the Central Park. New York, M. W. Siebert. 34 pp.

1864 The Central Park, photographed by W. H. GUILD, JR. with description and a historical sketch by FRED. B. PERKINS. New York, G. W. Carleton. 78 pp. 51 pls. *Illus.*

1866 HUNT, R. M. Designs for the Gateways of the Southern Entrance to the Central Park. New York. 36 pp. *Illus.*—See review of this by Richard Grant White in *Galaxy*, Aug. 1, 1866, Vol. 1, pp. 650-656, and *Nation*, Sept. 27, Vol. 3, pp. 255-256. See also earlier comment on Central Park gates in *Nation*, 1865.

1869 [COOK, CLARENCE C.] A Description of the New York Central Park. New York, F. J. Huntington and Company. 206 pp. *Illus.*—The most comprehensive early account.

1882 More Public Parks. How New York compares. . . . The financial and sanitary aspects, etc. Published by the NEW YORK PARK ASSOCIATION. 23 pp. (Pamphlet.)—Success of Central Park as "The City's grand real estate speculation" cited. Compare the open letter referred to on pp. 173-174, *ante.*

1891 PARSONS, SAMUEL. Landscape Gardening. New York, G. P. Putnam's Sons. Pp. 271-294, City parks. *Illus.*—Relates mainly to Central Park.

1903 PARKHURST, HOWARD ELMORE. Trees, shrubs and vines of the Northeastern United States. Their characteristic landscape features. Fully described for identification by the non-botanical reader; together with an account of the principal foreign hardy trees, shrubs, and vines cultivated in our country, and found in Central Park, New York City. New York, Charles Scribner's Sons. 451 pp. *Illus.*

1903 PEET, LOUIS HARMAN. Trees and shrubs of Central Park. New York, Manhattan Press. 363 pp. 30 pls. *Illus.*

1904 PAINE, ALBERT BIGELOW. Theodore Nast, his period and his pictures. New York, Macmillan Company. 583 pp. *Illus.*—For the background of Tweed Ring administration. "Shadows of Forthcoming Events," which appeared originally in *Harper's Weekly*, is reproduced facing p. 90, *ante.*

1910   PARSONS, SAMUEL. Landscape Gardening Studies. New York, John Lane Company. Pp. 13-17, The rehabilitation and completion of Central Park, New York. *Illus.*

1911   MAYNADIER, GUSTAVUS B. Report on soils, etc., in Central Park, New York City. Submitted May 15, 1911, to Hon. Charles B. Stover, commissioner of Parks, Borough of Manhattan and Richmond. New York. 30 pp.—*See also* mention of other earlier reports on soils, p. 167, *ante.*

1911   HALL, EDWARD HAGAMAN. Central Park in the City of New York. Appendix G in 16th Annual Report, American Scenic and Historic Preservation Society, pp. 379-489.—The most authoritative and complete account to that date, giving also the early history of the region which later was included in the Park.

1912   Transactions of the AMERICAN SOCIETY OF LANDSCAPE ARCHITECTS. Vol. 1, 1899-1908, published 1912.

       Historical Notes, by Downing Vaux, pp. 81-83.

       Interesting facts in regard to the inception and development of Central Park, by Samuel Parsons, Jr., pp. 105-110.

1913   FOORD, JOHN. The Life and Public Services of Andrew Haswell Green. New York, Doubleday, Page and Company. 322 pp. *Illus.—Passim,* but especially Chapters 4 to 6.

1914   OLMSTED, FREDERICK LAW. The Beginning of Central Park, New York. A fragment of autobiography, by the late Frederick Law Olmsted, with introductory note by his son, Frederick Law Olmsted. Appendix E in 19th Annual Report, American Scenic and Historic Preservation Society, pp. 501-515.—Compare note on same fragment in *Landscape Architecture,* 1912, p. 33, *ante.*

1918   STOKES, I. N. PHELPS. The Iconography of Manhattan Island, 1498-1909. Compiled from original sources and illustrated by photo-intaglio reproductions of important maps, plans, views. . . . New York, Robert H. Dodd. Vol. III. Pp. 730-765, The Civil War: political and social development.—Note especially plates 149 (C reproducing the "Greensward" plan) 149A, 151 and 164B.

1919   PARSONS, SAMUEL. History of the development of Central Park. In Proceedings of the New York State Historical Association. XVII, 1919, pp. 164–172.

1922   NEVINS, ALLAN. The *Evening Post,* New York, Boni and Liveright. Pp. 192-201, New York becomes a metropolis; Central Park. *Illus.*

1926   PARSONS, MABEL, ED. Memories of Samuel Parsons, Landscape Architect of the Department of Public Parks, New York. New York, G. P. Putnam's Sons. 150 pp. *Illus.*

1926   CENTRAL PARK ASSOCIATION. The Central Park. New York, Thomas Seltzer. 175 pp. *Illus.*

MAGAZINE ARTICLES

1853 *Illustrated News.* (New York, Barnum and Beach.) Vol. 1.
June 11, p. 374. Are we to have a park?—Editorial.
June 25, p. 409. Central Park and Jones' Park.—With map showing proposed areas. "In common with all other intelligent journals of New York, we are strongly in favor of the selection of Central Park."

1857 *Harpers' Weekly.* Nov. 28, Vol. 1, pp. 756-757. The Central Park.— Reproduces Viele plan and gives the sketches of Park's condition included by Mr. Van Ingen in his article in *New York Times*, Dec. 24, 1922.

1858 *Frank Leslie's Illustrated Newspaper.* (New York.) May 15, Vol. 5, p. 373.—Reproduction of "Greensward" prize plan of Central Park, with brief favorable comment.

1861 *Atlantic Monthly.* Apr., Vol. 7, pp. 416-429. Cities and parks: with special reference to the New York Central Park, by H. W. Bellows.— Sympathetic interpretation of the designers' aims.

1865 *Nation.* Vol. 1.
Aug. 10, pp. 186-188. The proposed designs for the Central Park gates (ascribed to R. Sturgis).
Sept. 28, pp. 410-412. [Letter condemning gates.]

1871 *National Quarterly Review.* Mar., Vol. 22, pp. 294-315. The Central Park under ringleader rule. (Also reprinted as pamphlet, 24 pp.)—Further discussion, *Ibid.*, Sept., Vol. 23, pp. 356-372.

1873 *Scribner's Monthly.* Sept. and Oct., Vol. 6, pp. 523-539, and pp. 673-691. Central Park. *Illus.*—Discursive and critical account of Park and its artistic status. Merits of various competition plans discussed.

1879 *Harper's Magazine.* Oct., Vol. 59, p. 689. A ramble in Central Park (ascribed to H. S. Conant). *Illus.*

1888 *Garden and Forest.* (New York.) Vol. 1. (*See* p. 563, *ante.*)
Mar. 21, p. 37. The proposed speed-road in Central Park.
May 9, pp. 124-125. The meadows in Central Park. *Illus.*
July 11, p. 230. [Thinning of trees in Central Park necessary.]

1889 *Garden and Forest.* Vol. 2.
Mar. 20, p. 133. A proposed invasion of Central Park.
Apr. 3, p. 158. [Thinning the trees in Central Park.]
June 26, p. 301. Thinning plantations.
Sept. 25, p. 457. The proper use of public parks.
Oct. 2, p. 469. A crisis in the history of Central Park.
Nov. 27, p. 565. Central Park and the exposition.

1890 *Garden and Forest.* Vol. 3.
    May 21, p. 246. [Speeding track in Central Park again defeated.]
    July 9, p. 329. [Sacrifice of meadow in Central Park.]

1891 *Garden and Forest.* Jan. 21, Vol. 4, p. 25. The proposed widening of the drives in Central Park.

1891 *Munsey's Magazine.* Oct., Vol. 6, pp. 3-10. Snapshots in Central Park, by J. Crawford Hamilton. *Illus.*

1892 *Garden and Forest.* Vol. 5.
    Mar. 9, p. 109. The proposed speed-road in Central Park.
    Mar. 30, p. 145. The speed-road in Central Park.
    Apr. 21, pp. 181-182. [Speed-road in Central Park.]
    Oct. 5, p. 470. [Site recommended by Mr. Vaux for Thorwaldsen Statue.]

1893 *Garden and Forest.* Vol. 6.
    June 7, p. 241. Military parades in Central Park.
    Aug. 9, p. 331. The design of Central Park.

1894 *Garden and Forest.* Vol. 7.
    Sept. 12, p. 362. Irrigation in city parks.
    Nov. 21, p. 461. Park Boards and their professional advisers.

1895 *Garden and Forest.* Vol. 8.
    May 29, p. 211. The debt of America to A. J. Downing.
    June 12, p. 231. The defacement of city parks.

1895 *Munsey's Magazine.* Sept., Vol. 13, pp. 565-577. The playground of the metropolis, by Arthur Wakeley. *Illus.*

1897 *Atlantic Monthly.* Jan., Vol. 79, pp. 86-98. Park making as a national art, by Mary Caroline Robbins.—Includes Central Park.

1900 *Munsey's Magazine.* Feb., Vol. 22, pp. 633-641. Central Park in winter, by Raymond S. Spears. *Illus.*

1906 *Outlook.* Sept., Vol. 84, pp. 226-232. Art of landscape gardening in Central Park, by Samuel Parsons and W. R. O'Donovan. *Illus.*

1909 *Survey.* Apr. 3, Vol. 22, pp. 4-5. To preserve Central Park.—Editorial.

1910 *Landscape Architecture.* Oct., Vol. 1, pp. 9-21. The attacks on Central Park, by Robert Wheelright.

1911 *Harper's Weekly.* May 27, Vol. 55, p. 17. Central Park and its destroyers, by Samuel Parsons. *Illus.*—Plea for rehabilitation.

1912 *Landscape Architecture.* July, Vol. 2.
    Pp. 149-162. The beginning of Central Park; a fragment of autobiography by the late Frederick Law Olmsted.—Much of this will be found reprinted in Part I, Chapter III, *ante*.
    Pp. 167-176. Central Park, New York: a work of art, by Harold A. Caparn. *Illus.*—Compare p. 198, *ante*.

1912 *Outlook.* June 8, Vol. 101, pp. 285-286. New York claims its park.

1914 *Harper's Magazine.* Feb., Vol. 128, pp. 350-358. A Philosopher in Central Park, by Edward S. Martin. *Illus.*

1917 *Scribner's Magazine.* Feb., Vol. 61, pp. 253-254. Central Park. [Article in The Point of View.]

1917 *Art World.* Sept., Vol. 2, pp. 504-505. Hands off Central Park.
—Editorial.

1922 *New York Times Magazine.* Dec. 24, p. 14. Central Park—as it was in the beginning, by W. B. Van Ingen. *Illus.*

1923 *New York Times Magazine.* May 13, p. 4. Landscape illusions of Central Park, by W. B. Van Ingen. *Illus.*

1924 *Greater New York* (Merchants' Association). Jan. 7, Vol. 13, No. 1, p. 8. Against proposed desecration of Central Park.—First of several brief notices in defence of Park. The Committee on City Plan of the Merchants' Association had already opposed the war memorial in the Park (issue of Sept. 25, 1922). See further, the issues of Jan. 28, Mar. 17 and 31, 1924.

1924 *Literary Digest.* Mar. 29, Vol. 80, pp. 29-30. The art "raid" on Central Park.—Proposed music and art center, and arguments against by Park defenders.

1924 *Nation.* May 14, Vol. 118, p. 550. What is a park?—Editorial on behalf of preservation of Central Park.

1924 *Parks and Recreation.* July-Aug., Vol. 7, pp. 658-659. Defend Central Park. Letter from Harold A. Caparn.—Defending selection of site.

1924 *American City.* Aug., Vol. 31, pp. 93-94. Saving parks for their proper purposes.—Editorial, with cartoon reproduced on p. 517, *ante.*

1925 *The Avenue.* (New York, Fifth Avenue Association) June, p. 8 Association moves to preserve Central Park.

1926 *New York Times Magazine.* Sept. 5, p. 12. Central Park fathers had uphill job, by W. B. Van Ingen. *Illus.*

1927 *Fifth Avenue Association Bulletin.* Apr., No. 24, p. 2. Rehabilitation of Central Park.—Appropriation by Board of Estimate and Apportionment.